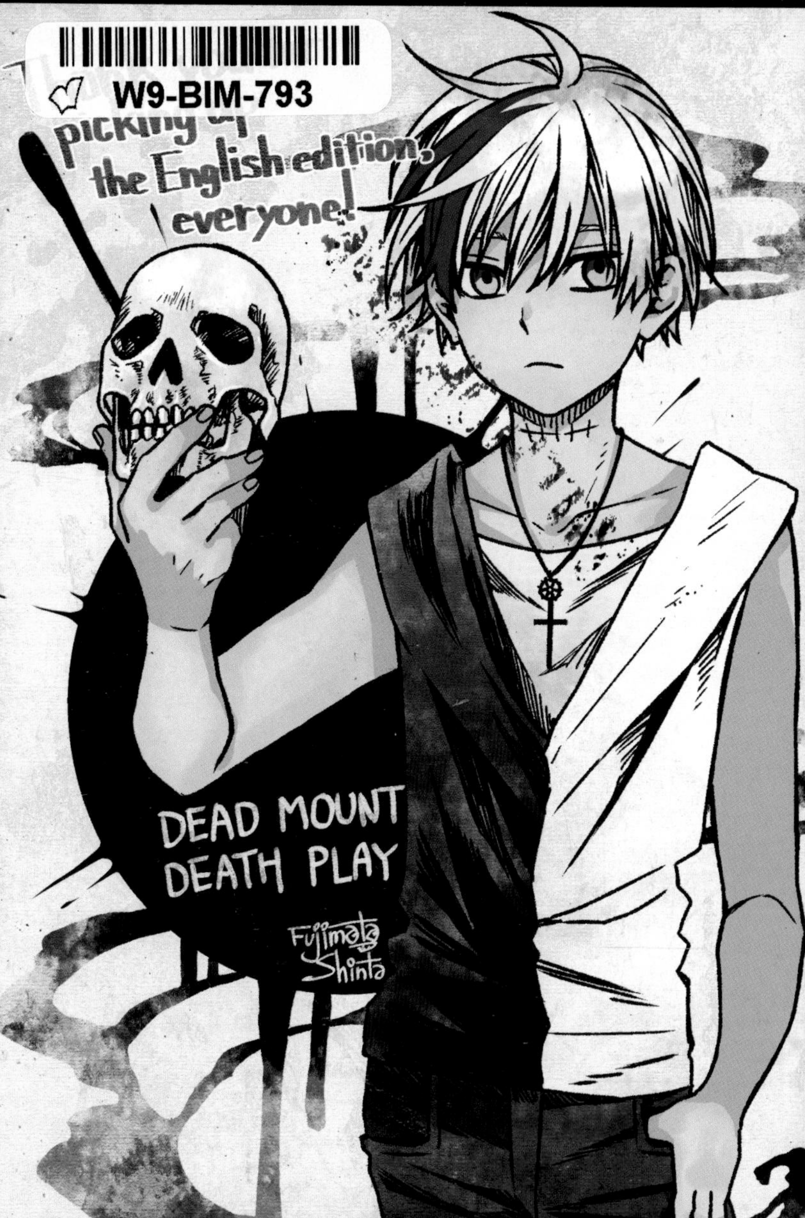
picking up the English edition, everyone!
DEAD MOUNT DEATH PLAY
Fujimoto Shinta

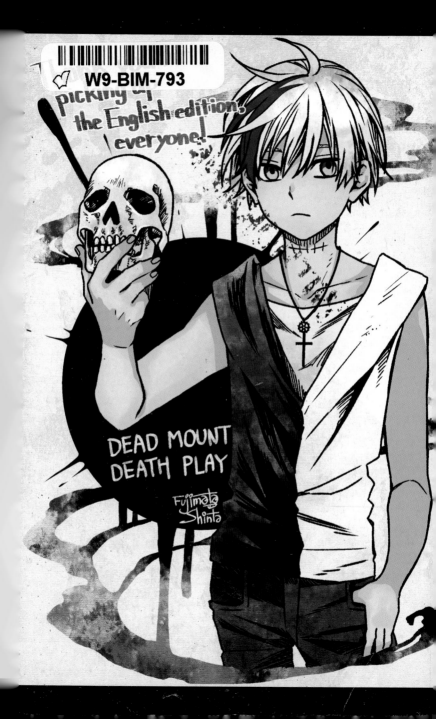

DEAD MOUNT
DEATH PLAY

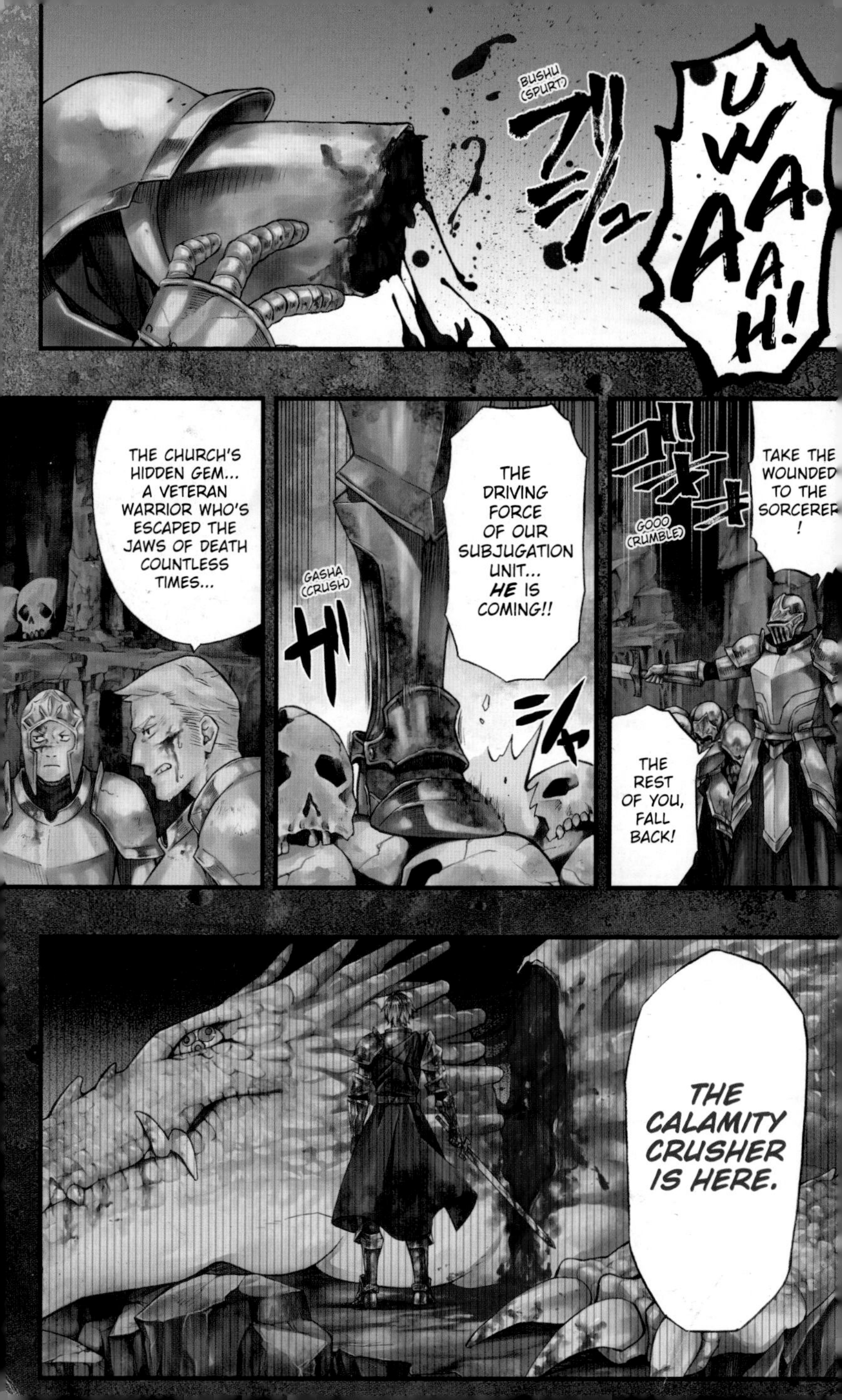
UWAAAAH!
BUSHU (SPURT)
TAKE THE WOUNDED TO THE SORCERER!
GOOO (RUMBLE)
THE REST OF YOU, FALL BACK!
THE DRIVING FORCE OF OUR SUBJUGATION UNIT... HE IS COMING!!
GASHA (CRUSH)
THE CHURCH'S HIDDEN GEM... A VETERAN WARRIOR WHO'S ESCAPED THE JAWS OF DEATH COUNTLESS TIMES...
THE CALAMITY CRUSHER IS HERE.

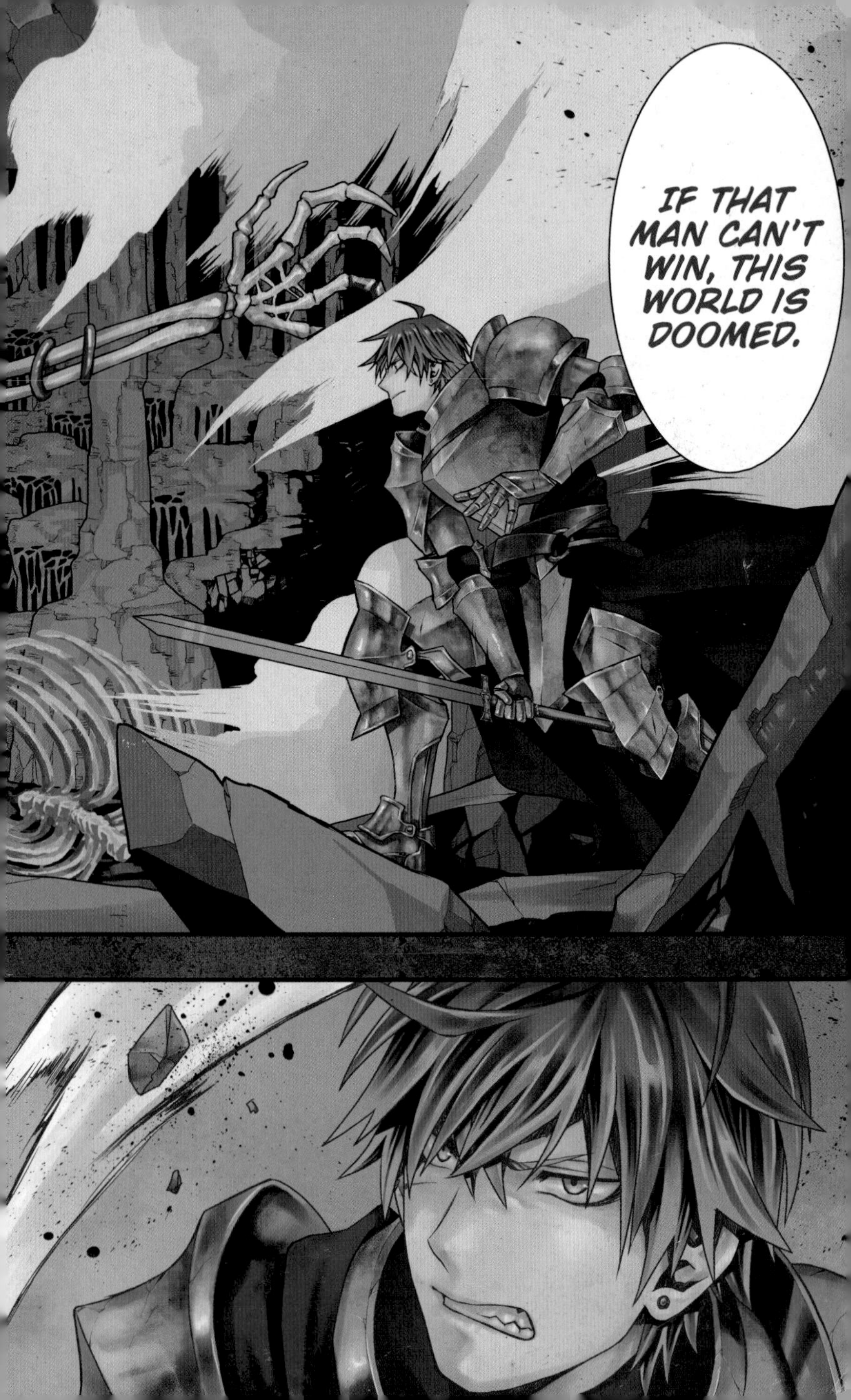
IF THAT MAN CAN'T WIN, THIS WORLD IS DOOMED.

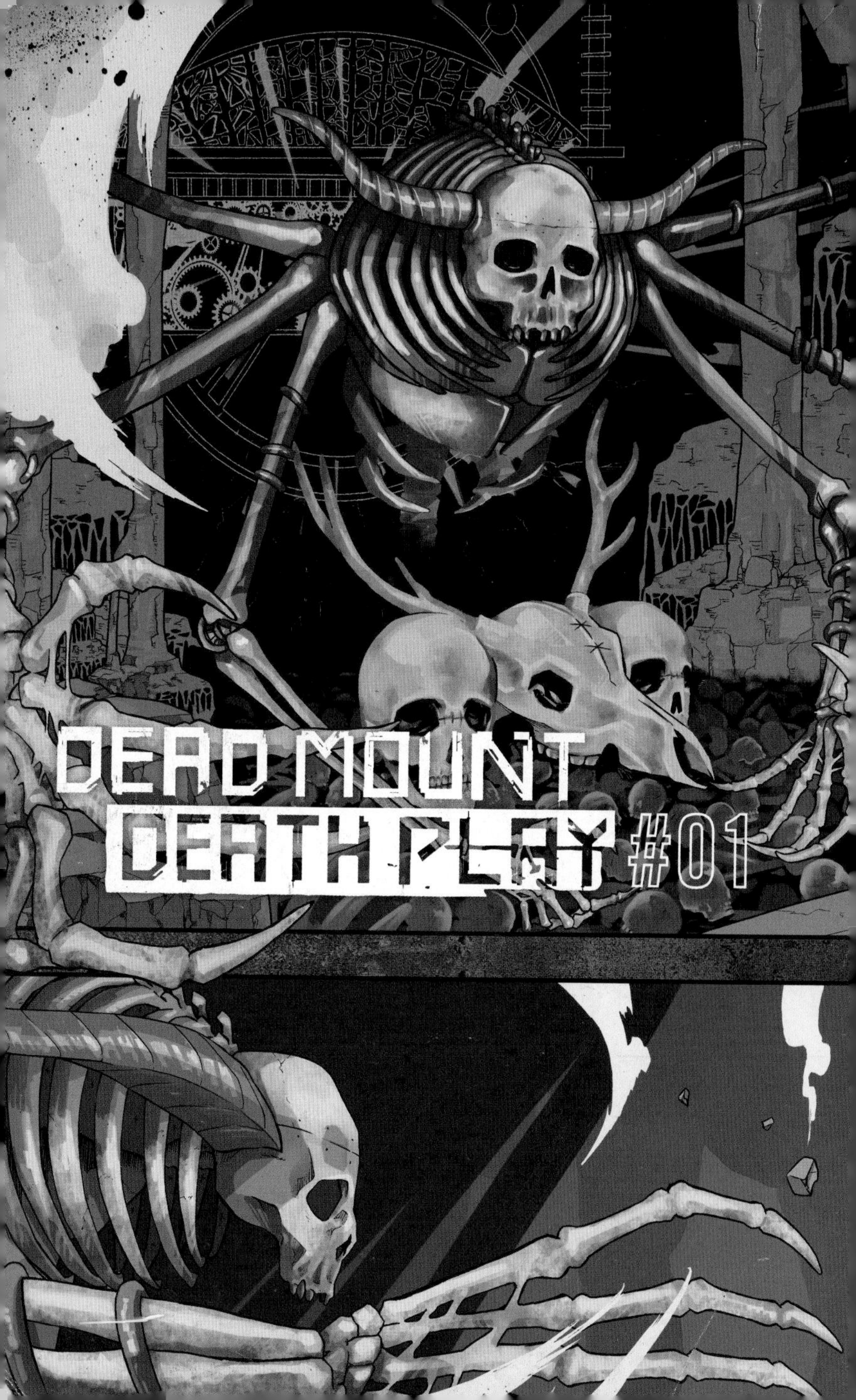
DEAD MOUNT
DEATH PLAY #01

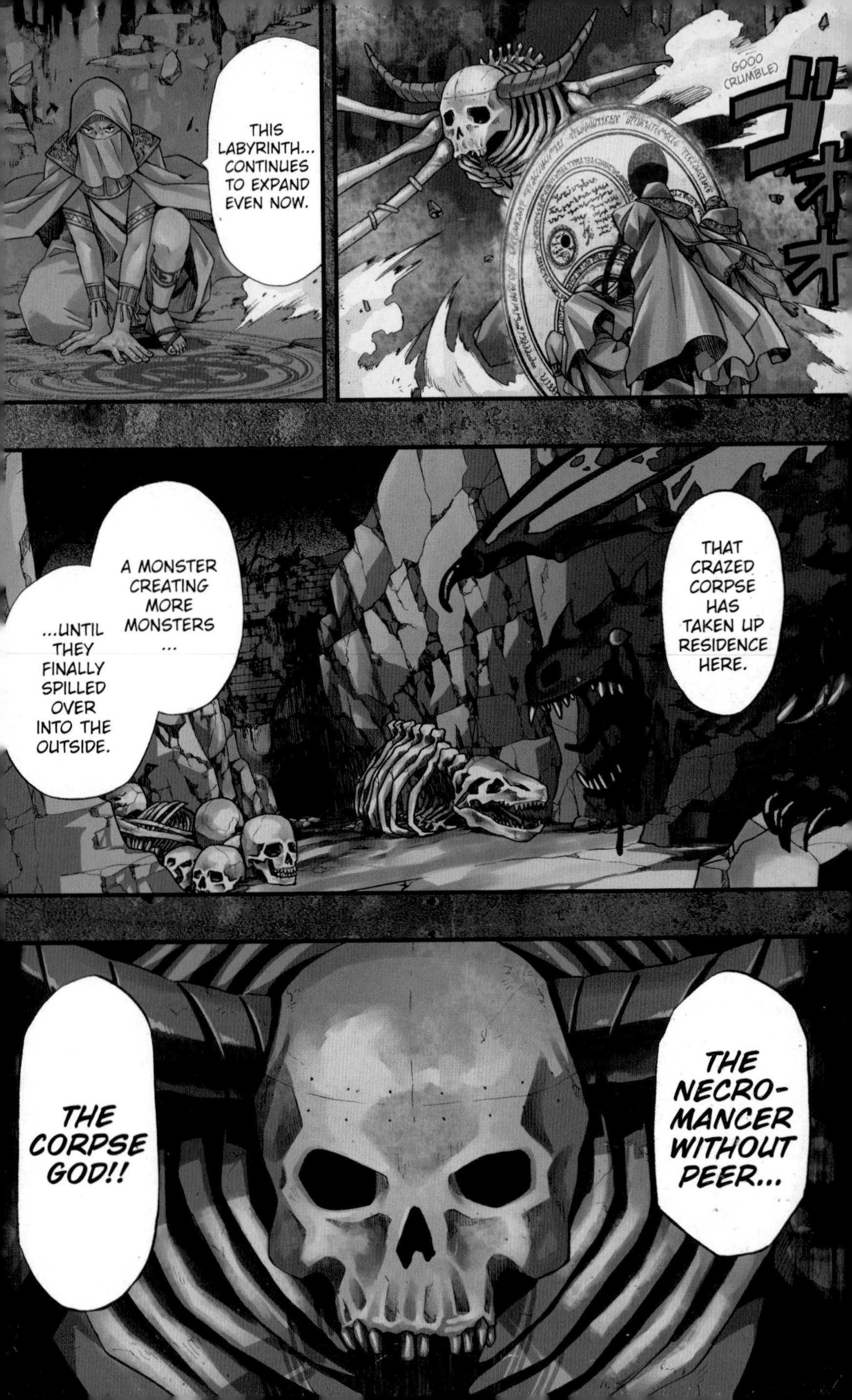
ゴオオ
GOOO (RUMBLE)
THIS LABYRINTH... CONTINUES TO EXPAND EVEN NOW.
THAT CRAZED CORPSE HAS TAKEN UP RESIDENCE HERE.
A MONSTER CREATING MORE MONSTERS ...
...UNTIL THEY FINALLY SPILLED OVER INTO THE OUTSIDE.
THE NECROMANCER WITHOUT PEER...
THE CORPSE GOD!!

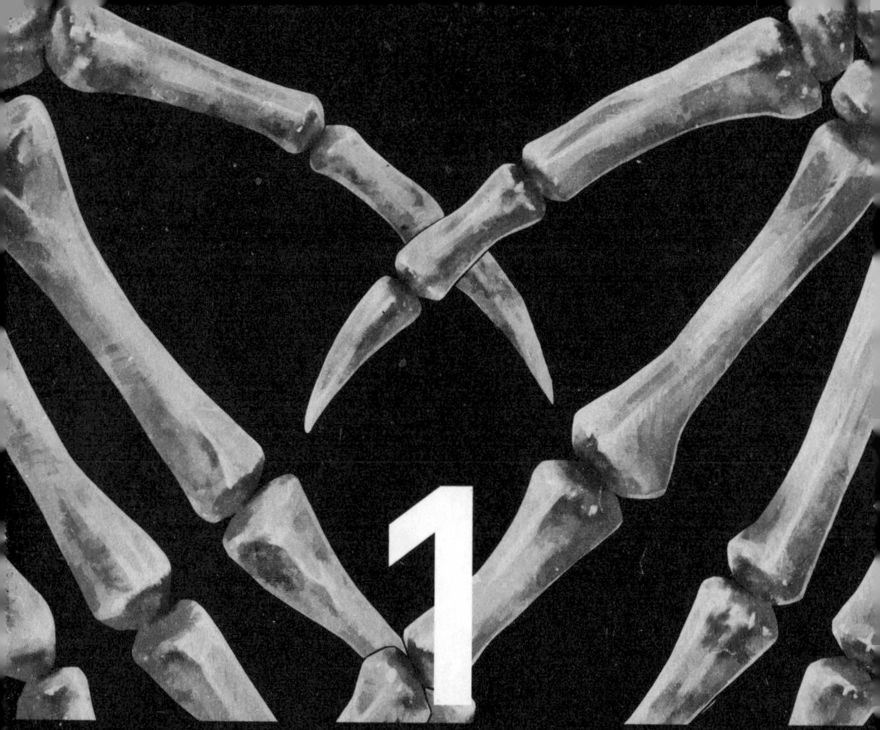

1

DEAD MOUNT DEATH PLAY

STORY RYOHGO NARITA
ART SHINTA FUJIMOTO

CONTENTS

DEAD MOUNT
DEATH PLAY

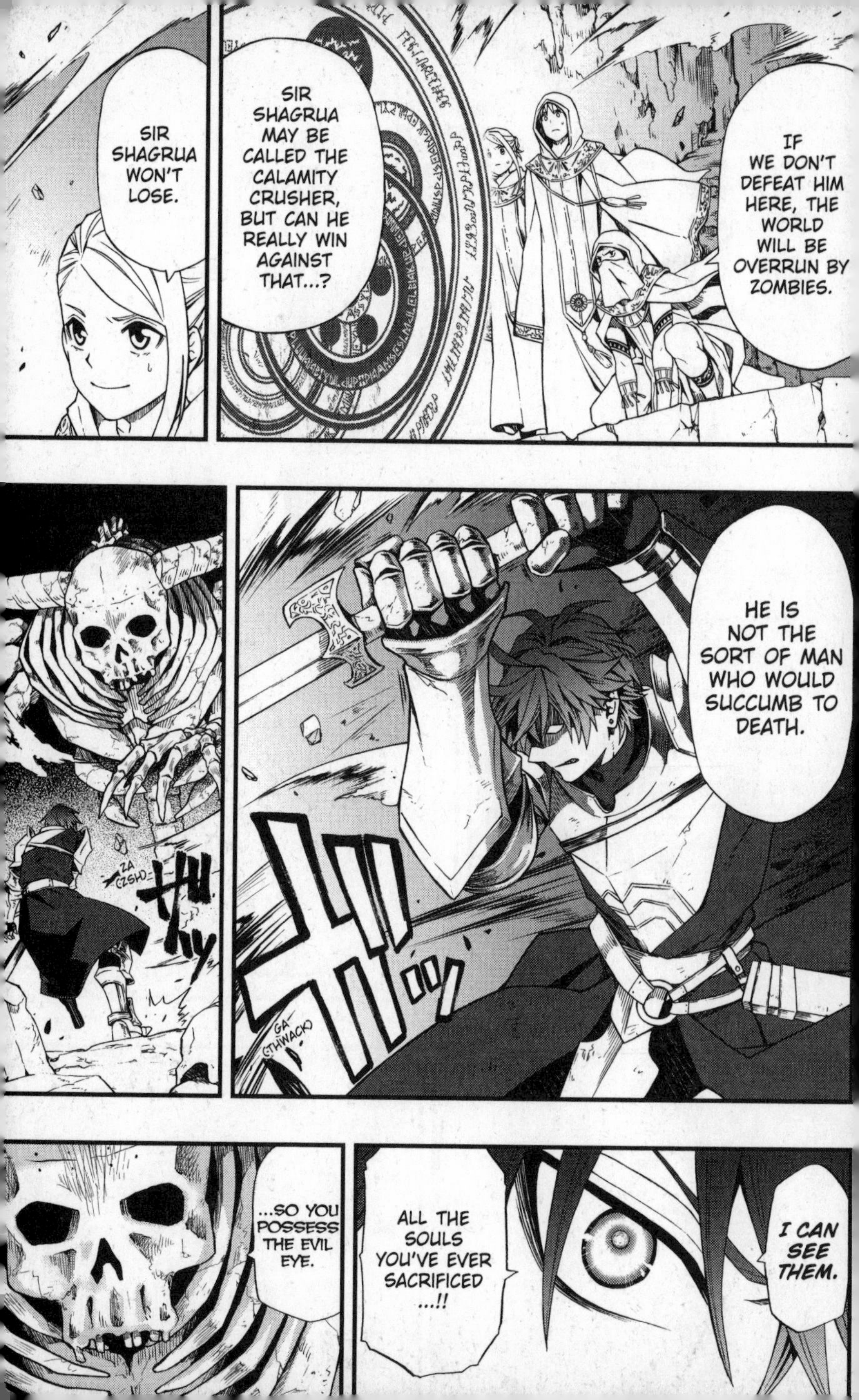

IF WE DON'T DEFEAT HIM HERE, THE WORLD WILL BE OVERRUN BY ZOMBIES.
SIR SHAGRUA MAY BE CALLED THE CALAMITY CRUSHER, BUT CAN HE REALLY WIN AGAINST THAT...?
SIR SHAGRUA WON'T LOSE.
HE IS NOT THE SORT OF MAN WHO WOULD SUCCUMB TO DEATH.
GA (THWACK)
ZA (ZSH)
I CAN SEE THEM.
ALL THE SOULS YOU'VE EVER SACRIFICED ...!!
...SO YOU POSSESS THE EVIL EYE.

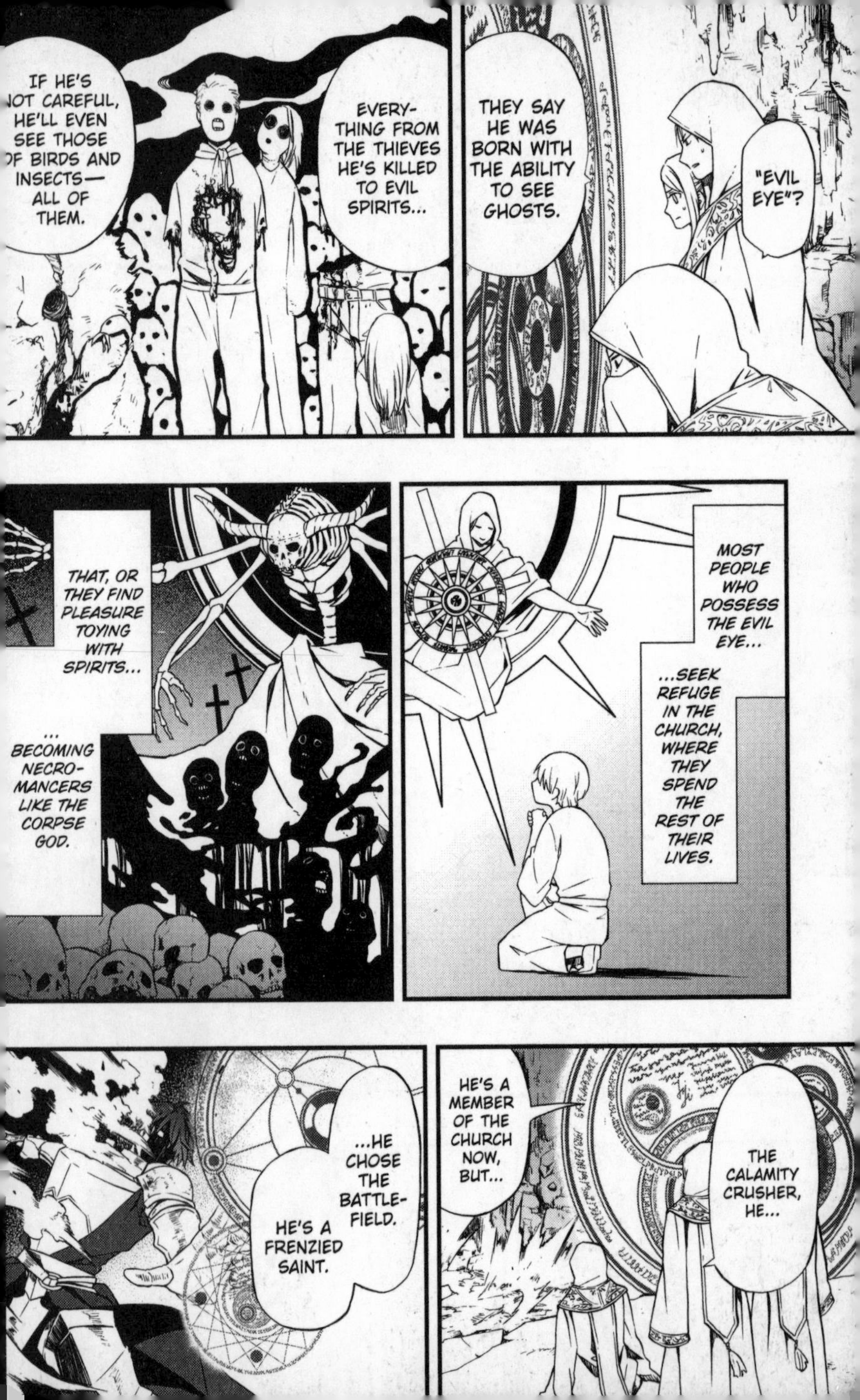
"EVIL EYE"?
THEY SAY HE WAS BORN WITH THE ABILITY TO SEE GHOSTS.
EVERYTHING FROM THE THIEVES HE'S KILLED TO EVIL SPIRITS...
IF HE'S NOT CAREFUL, HE'LL EVEN SEE THOSE OF BIRDS AND INSECTS—ALL OF THEM.
MOST PEOPLE WHO POSSESS THE EVIL EYE...
...SEEK REFUGE IN THE CHURCH, WHERE THEY SPEND THE REST OF THEIR LIVES.
THAT, OR THEY FIND PLEASURE TOYING WITH SPIRITS...
...BECOMING NECROMANCERS LIKE THE CORPSE GOD.
THE CALAMITY CRUSHER, HE...
HE'S A MEMBER OF THE CHURCH NOW, BUT...
...HE CHOSE THE BATTLEFIELD.
HE'S A FRENZIED SAINT.

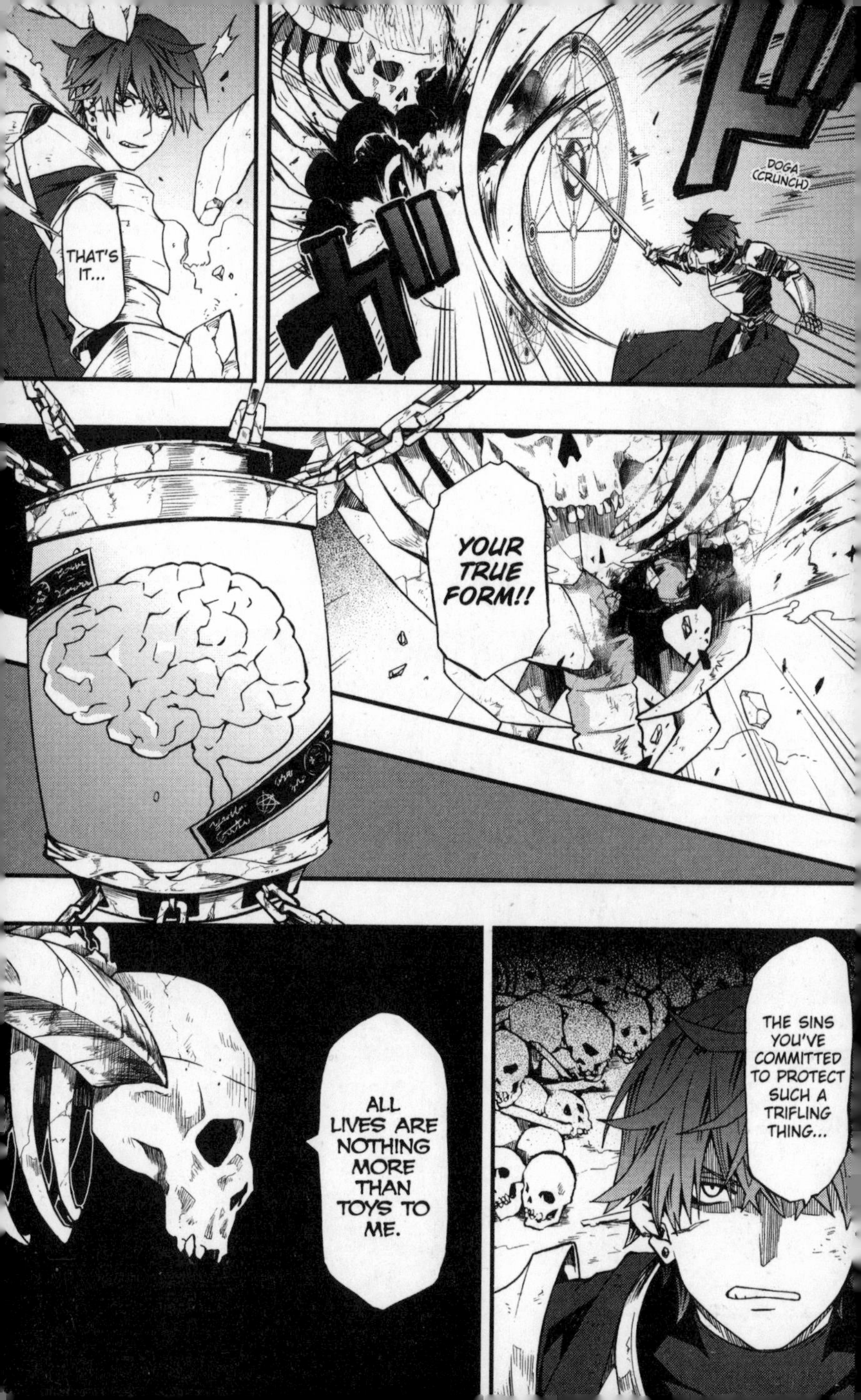

DOGA (CRUNCH)
THAT'S IT...
YOUR TRUE FORM!!
THE SINS YOU'VE COMMITTED TO PROTECT SUCH A TRIFLING THING...
ALL LIVES ARE NOTHING MORE THAN TOYS TO ME.

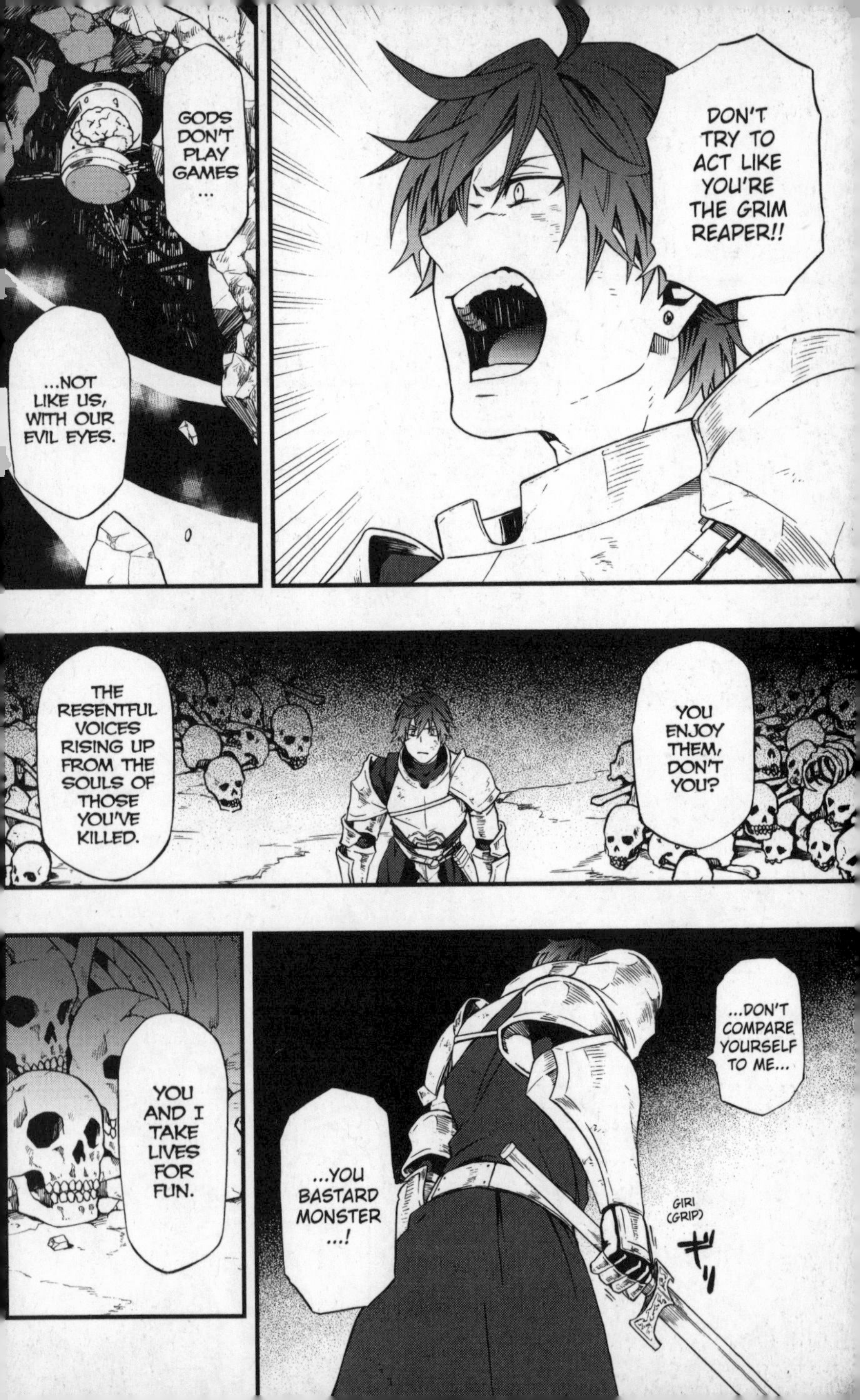
DON'T TRY TO ACT LIKE YOU'RE THE GRIM REAPER!!
GODS DON'T PLAY GAMES ...
...NOT LIKE US, WITH OUR EVIL EYES.
YOU ENJOY THEM, DON'T YOU?
THE RESENTFUL VOICES RISING UP FROM THE SOULS OF THOSE YOU'VE KILLED.
...DON'T COMPARE YOURSELF TO ME...
GIRI (GRIP)
ギリ
...YOU BASTARD MONSTER ...!
YOU AND I TAKE LIVES FOR FUN.

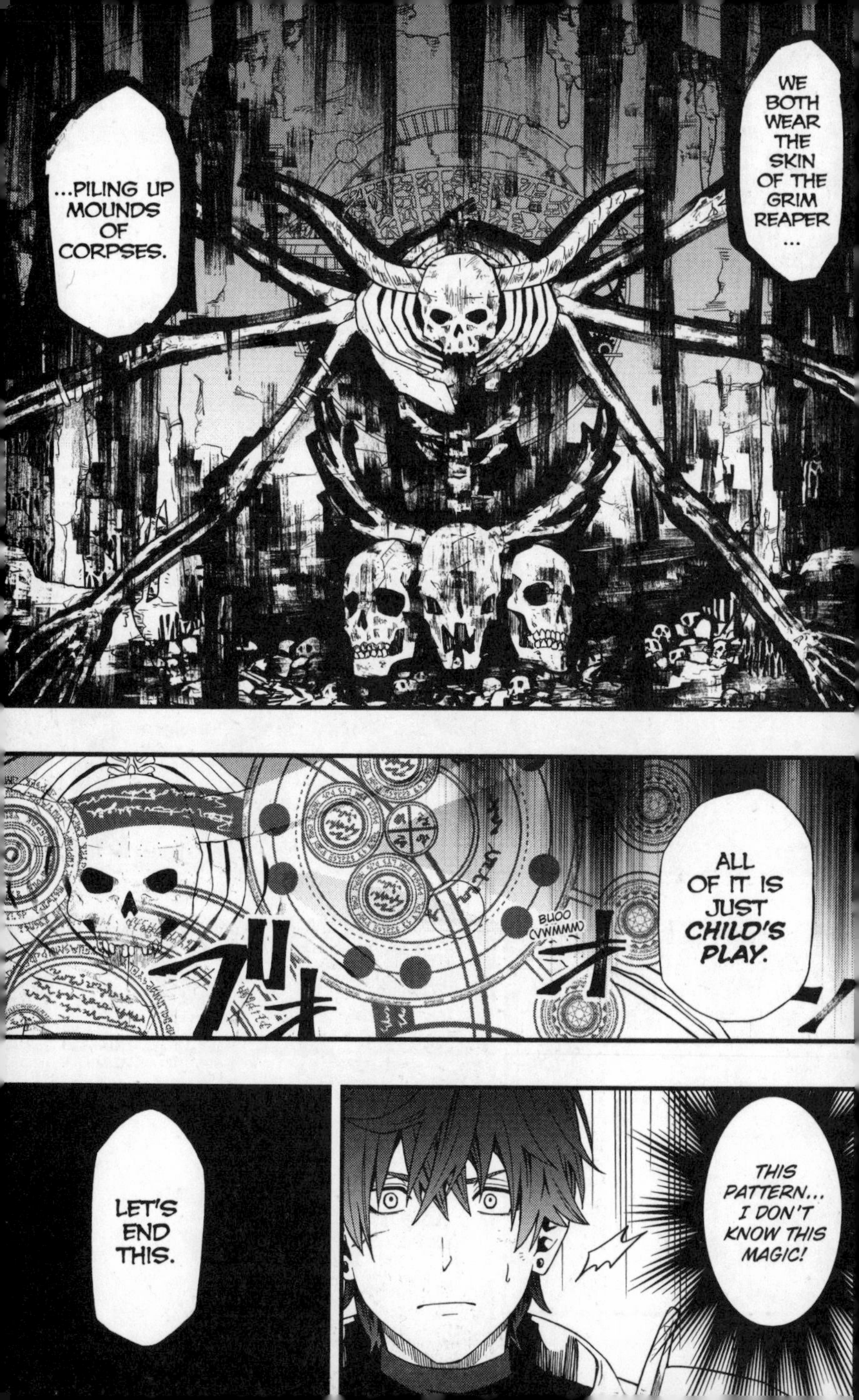
WE BOTH WEAR THE SKIN OF THE GRIM REAPER ...
...PILING UP MOUNDS OF CORPSES.
ALL OF IT IS JUST CHILD'S PLAY.
BUOO (VWMMM)
THIS PATTERN... I DON'T KNOW THIS MAGIC!
LET'S END THIS.

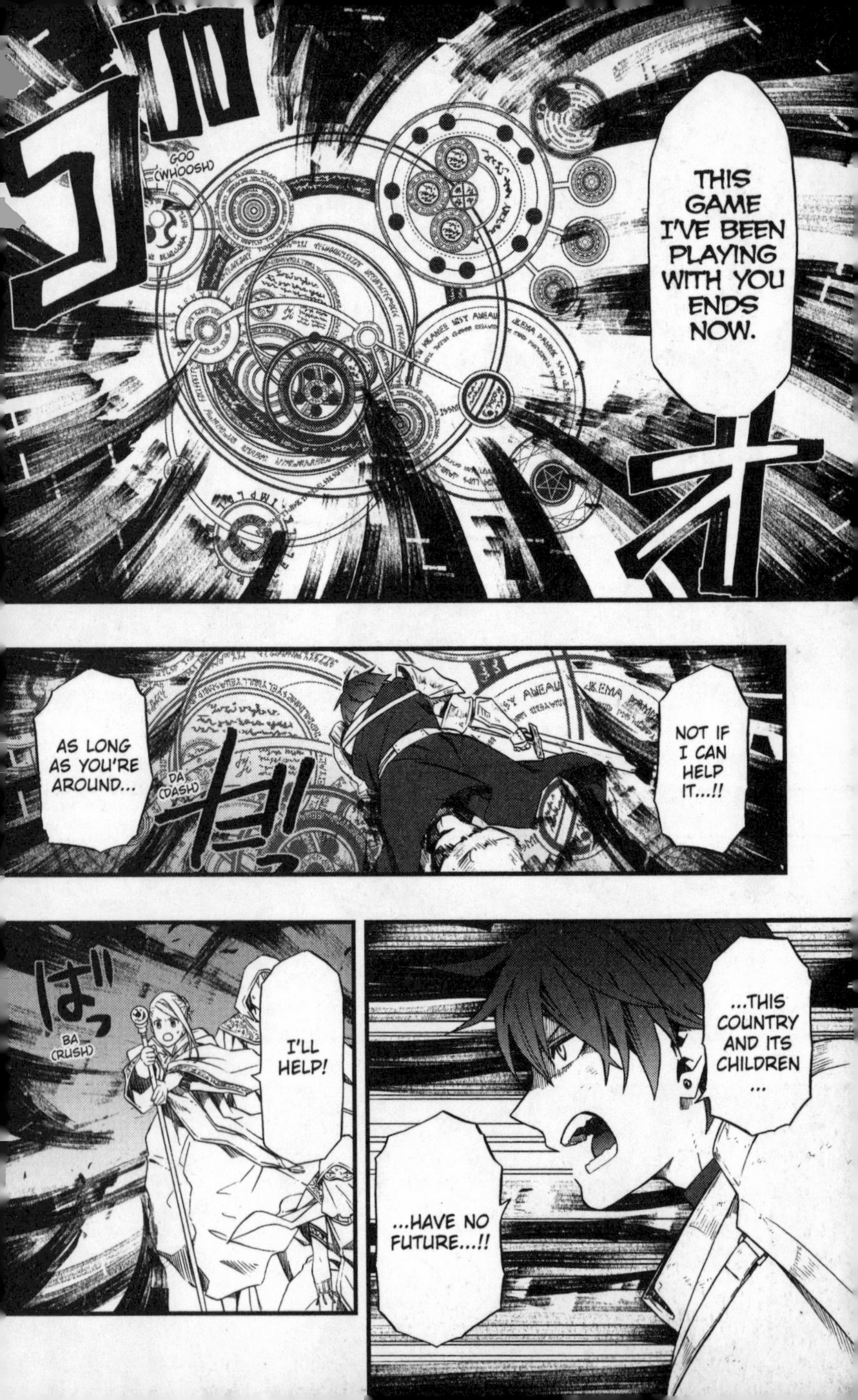
GOO (WHOOSH)
THIS GAME I'VE BEEN PLAYING WITH YOU ENDS NOW.
NOT IF I CAN HELP IT...!!
DA (DASH)
AS LONG AS YOU'RE AROUND...
...THIS COUNTRY AND ITS CHILDREN...
...HAVE NO FUTURE...!!
I'LL HELP!
ばっ
BA (RUSH)

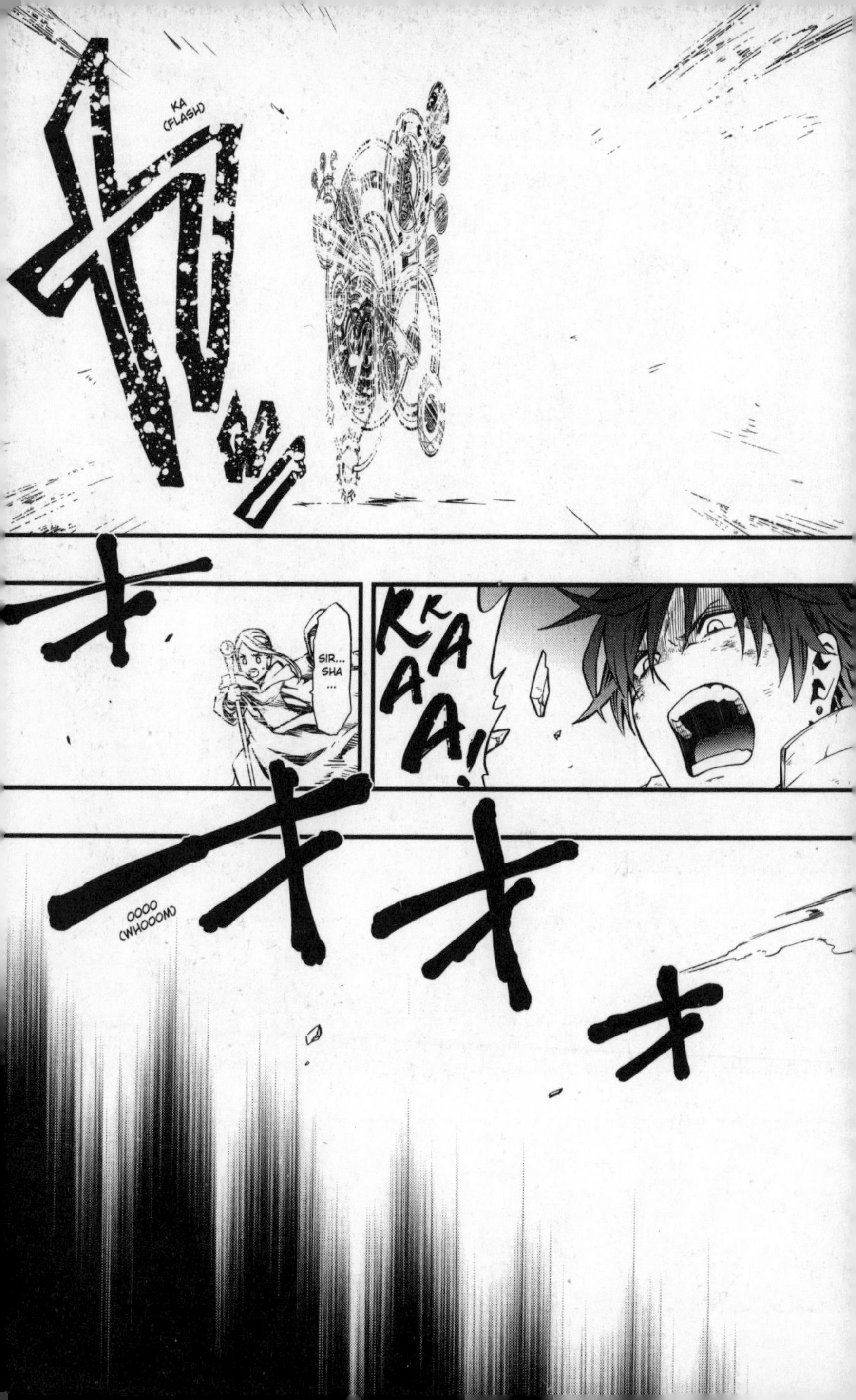
KA
(FLASH)
RKAAA!
SIR... SHA ...
OOOO
(WHOOOM)

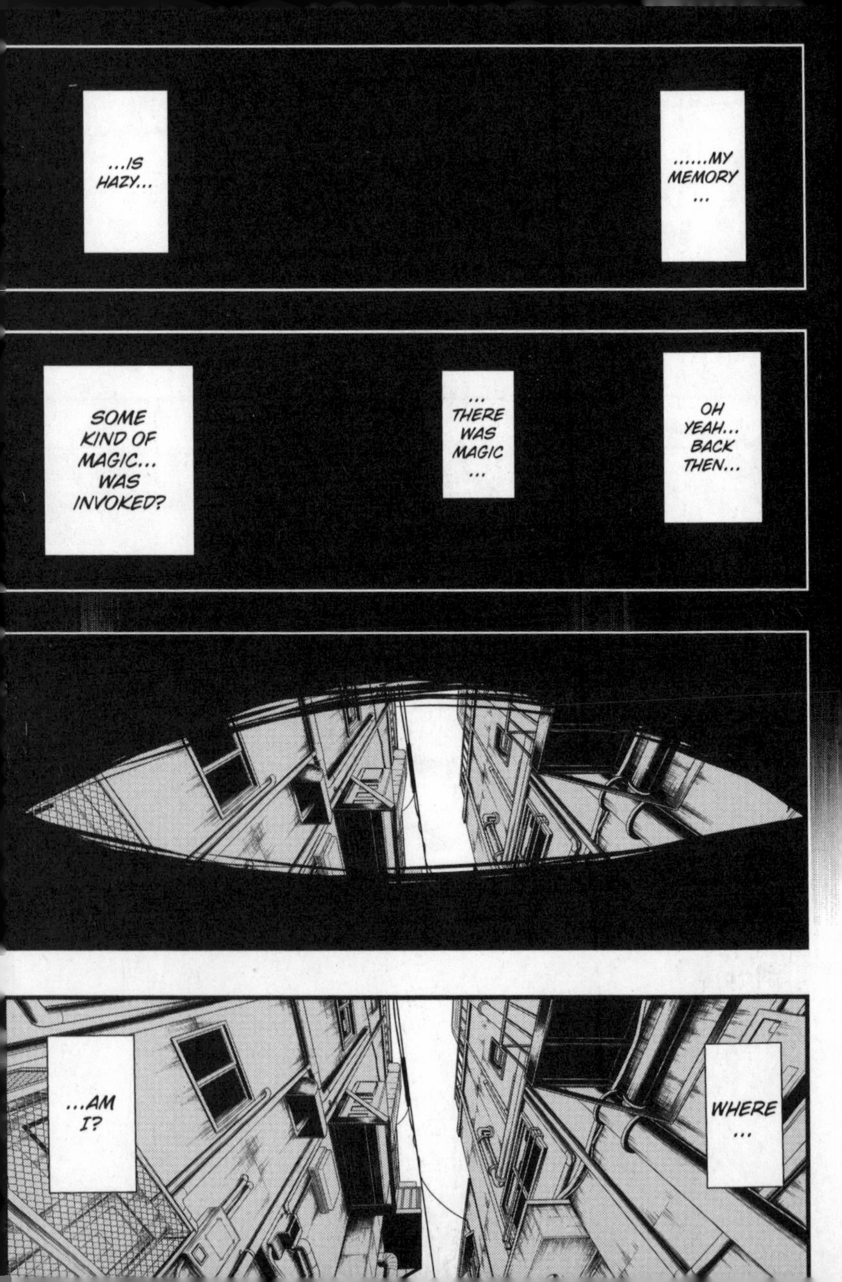
......MY MEMORY ...
...IS HAZY...
OH YEAH... BACK THEN...
... THERE WAS MAGIC ...
SOME KIND OF MAGIC... WAS INVOKED?
WHERE ...
...AM I?

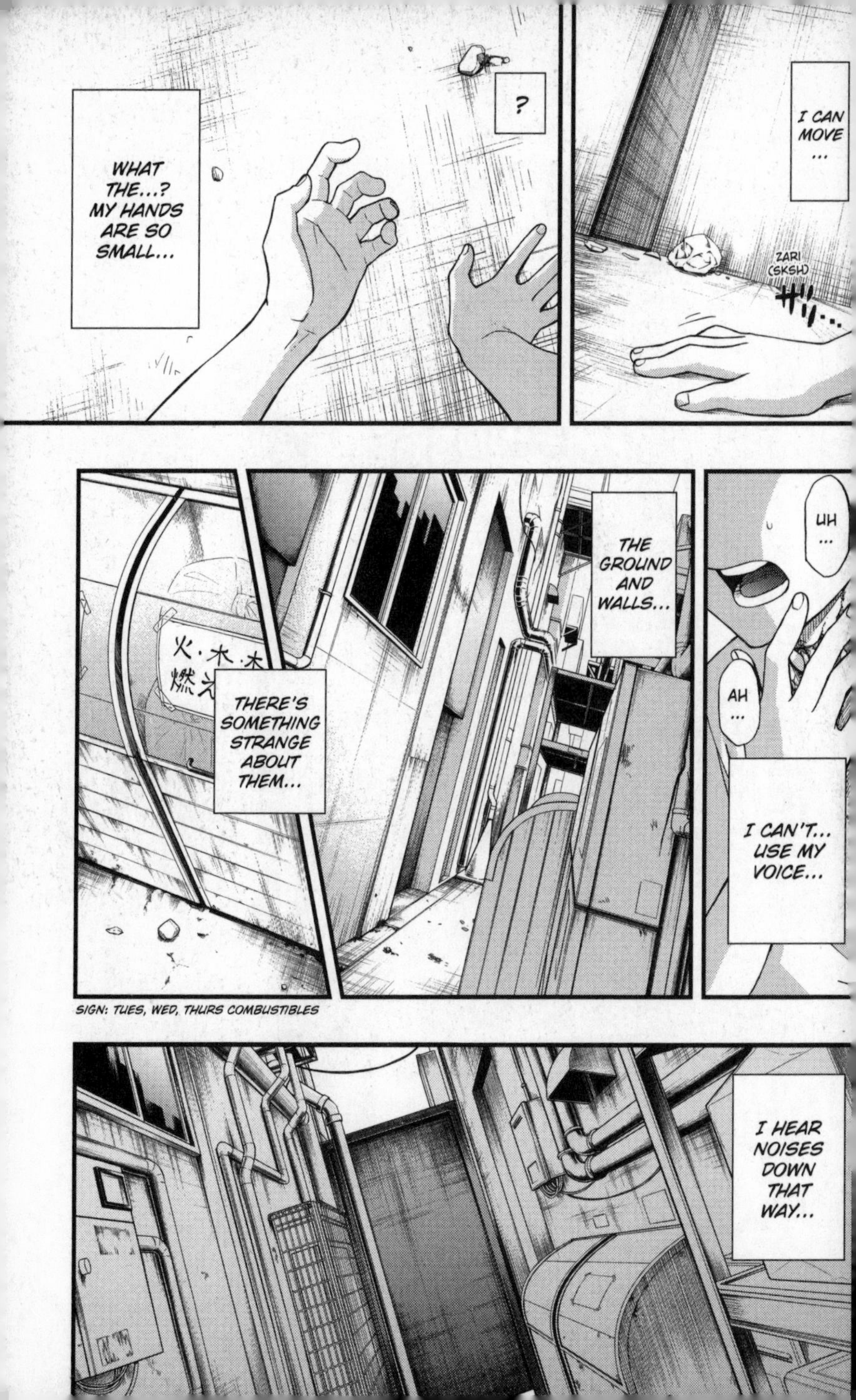

I CAN MOVE ...
ZARI (SKSH)
?
WHAT THE...? MY HANDS ARE SO SMALL...
UH ...
AH ...
I CAN'T... USE MY VOICE...
THE GROUND AND WALLS...
THERE'S SOMETHING STRANGE ABOUT THEM...
SIGN: TUES, WED, THURS COMBUSTIBLES
I HEAR NOISES DOWN THAT WAY...

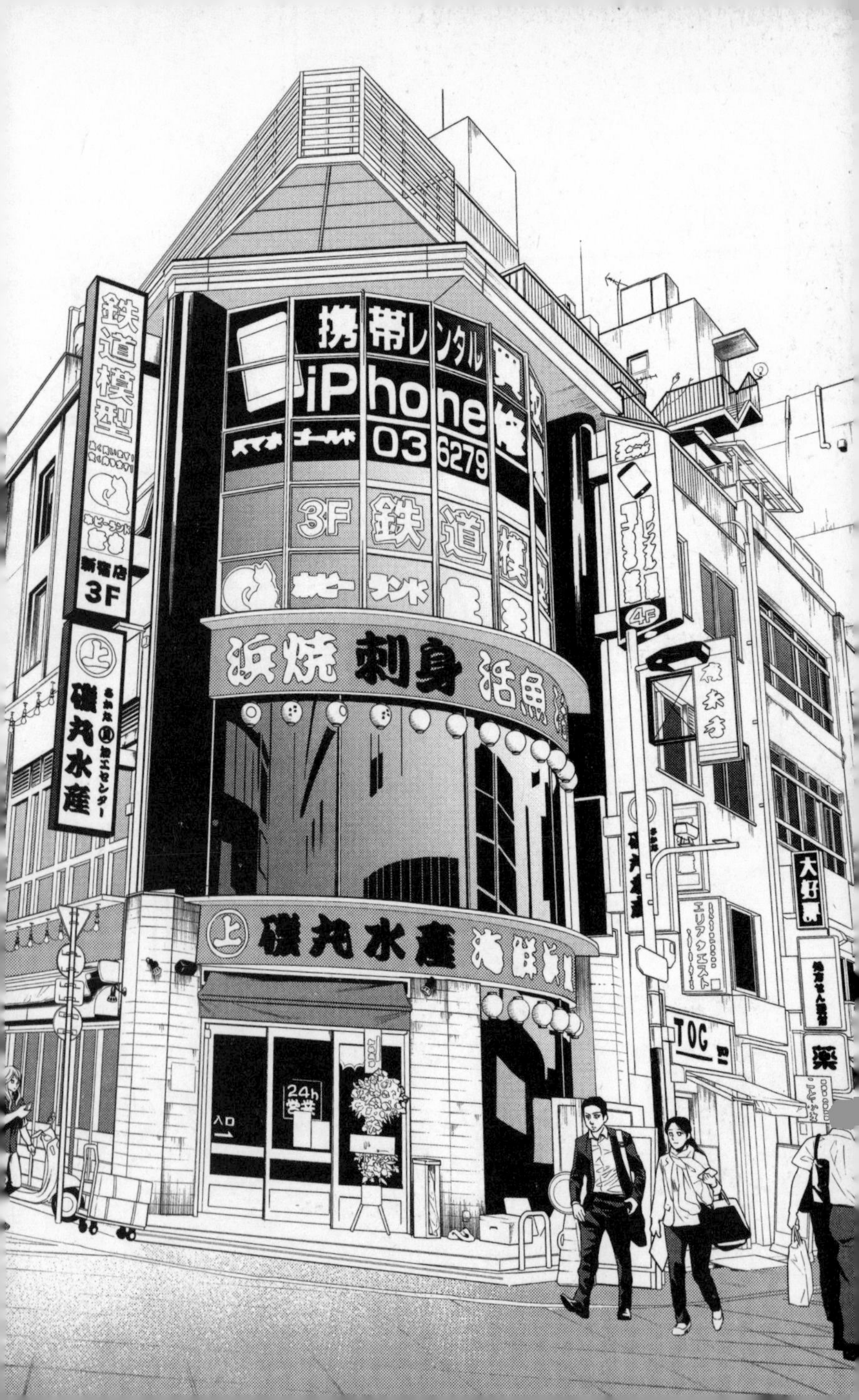
鉄道模型
新宿店 3F
携帯レンタル
iPhone
03 6279
3F 鉄道模
浜焼 刺身 活魚
磯丸水産
24h 営業
入口
4F
大好
エリアクエスト
TOG
薬

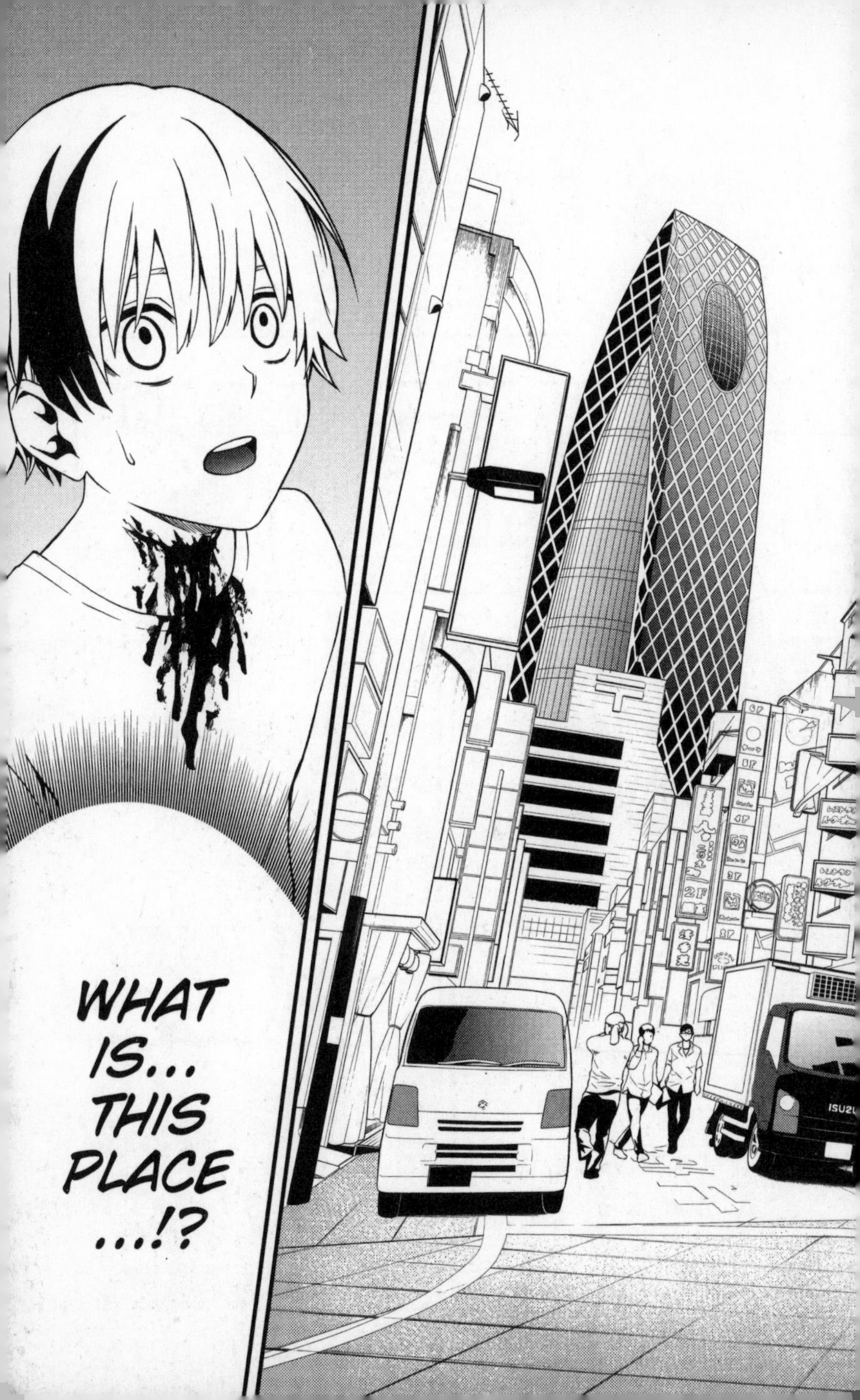
WHAT IS... THIS PLACE ...!?
ISUZU

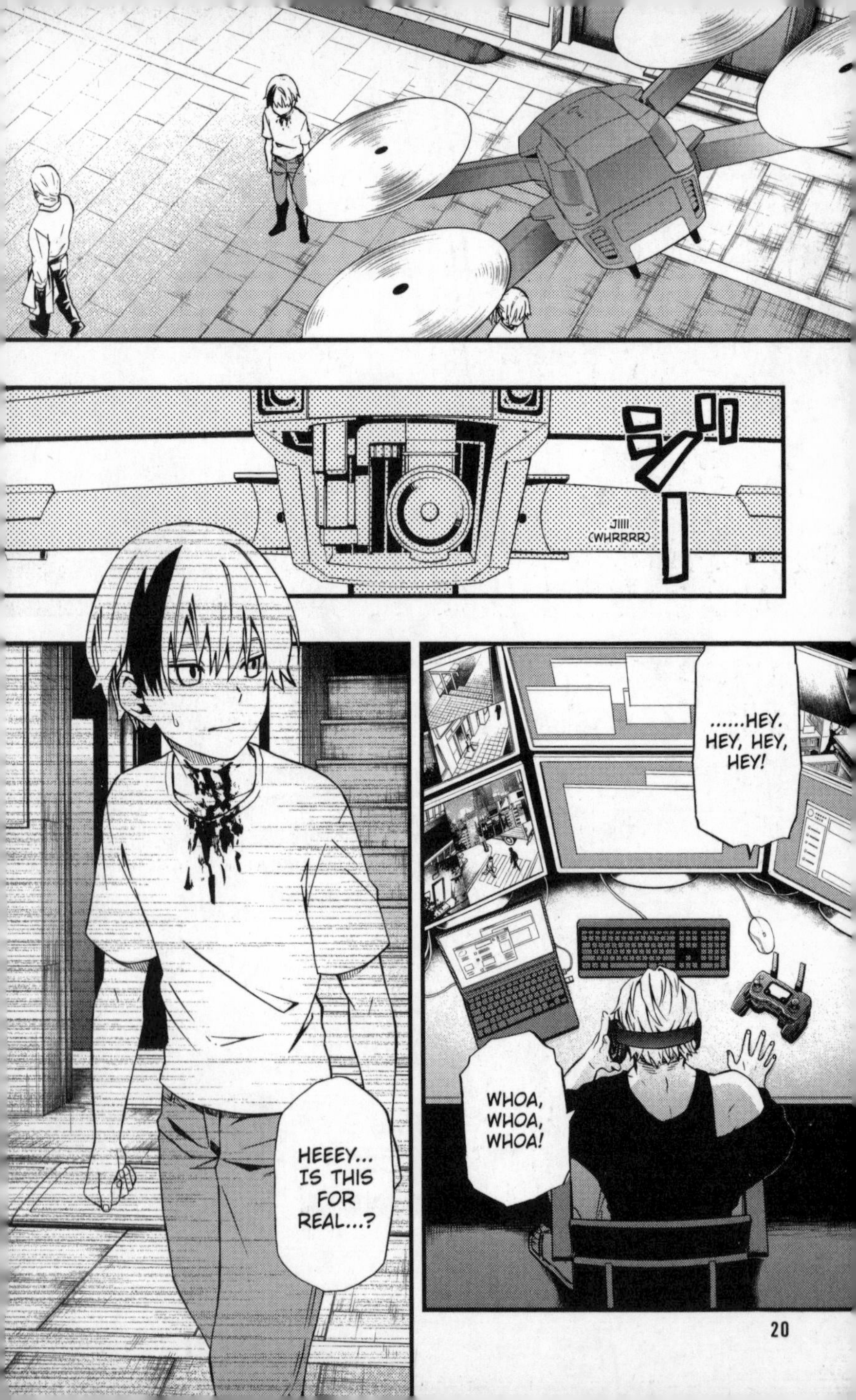
JIIII
(WHRRRR)
......HEY. HEY, HEY, HEY!
WHOA, WHOA, WHOA!
HEEEY... IS THIS FOR REAL...?

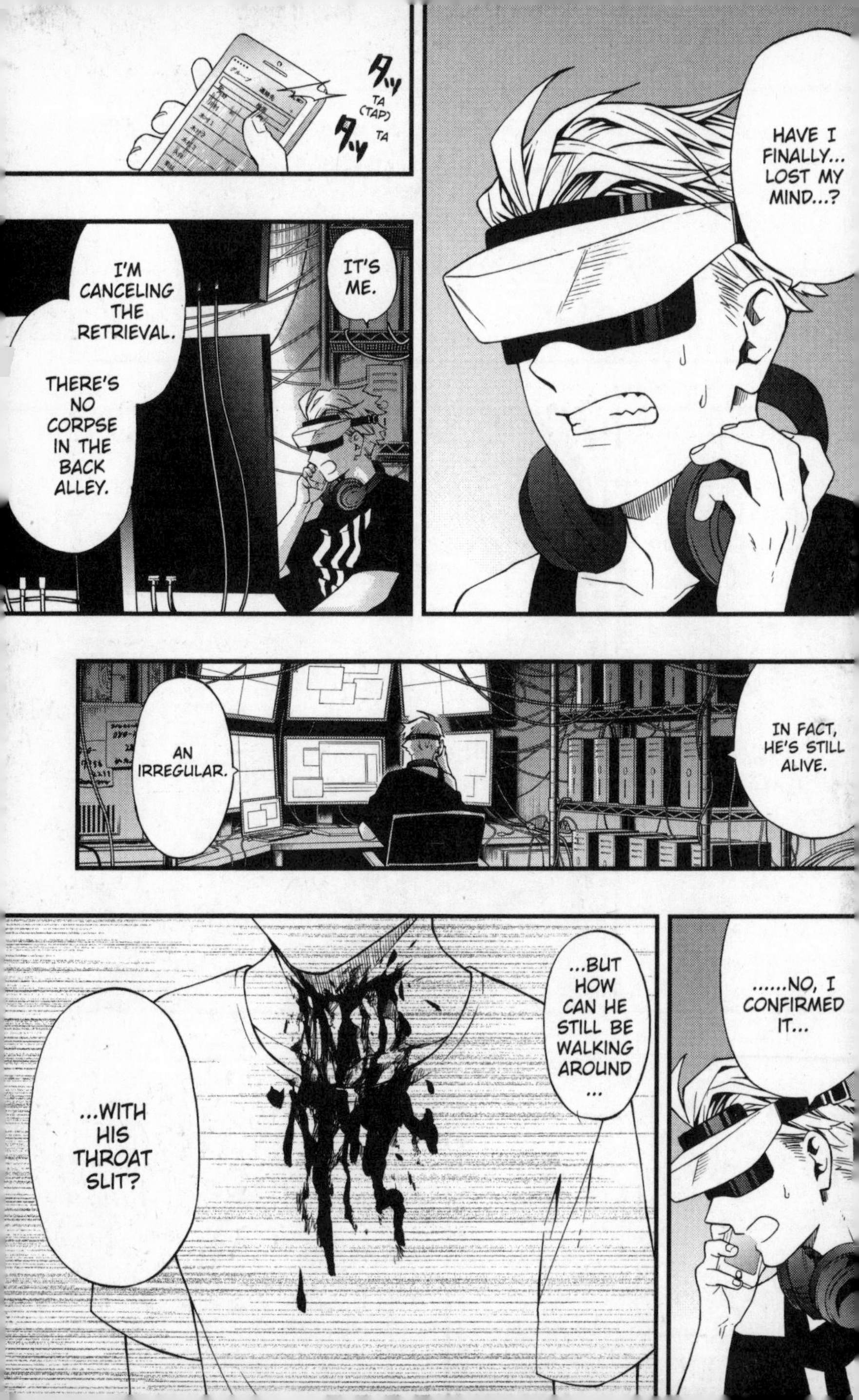
HAVE I FINALLY... LOST MY MIND...?
タッ TA (TAP)
タッ TA
IT'S ME.
I'M CANCELING THE RETRIEVAL.
THERE'S NO CORPSE IN THE BACK ALLEY.
IN FACT, HE'S STILL ALIVE.
AN IRREGULAR.
......NO, I CONFIRMED IT...
...BUT HOW CAN HE STILL BE WALKING AROUND ...
...WITH HIS THROAT SLIT?

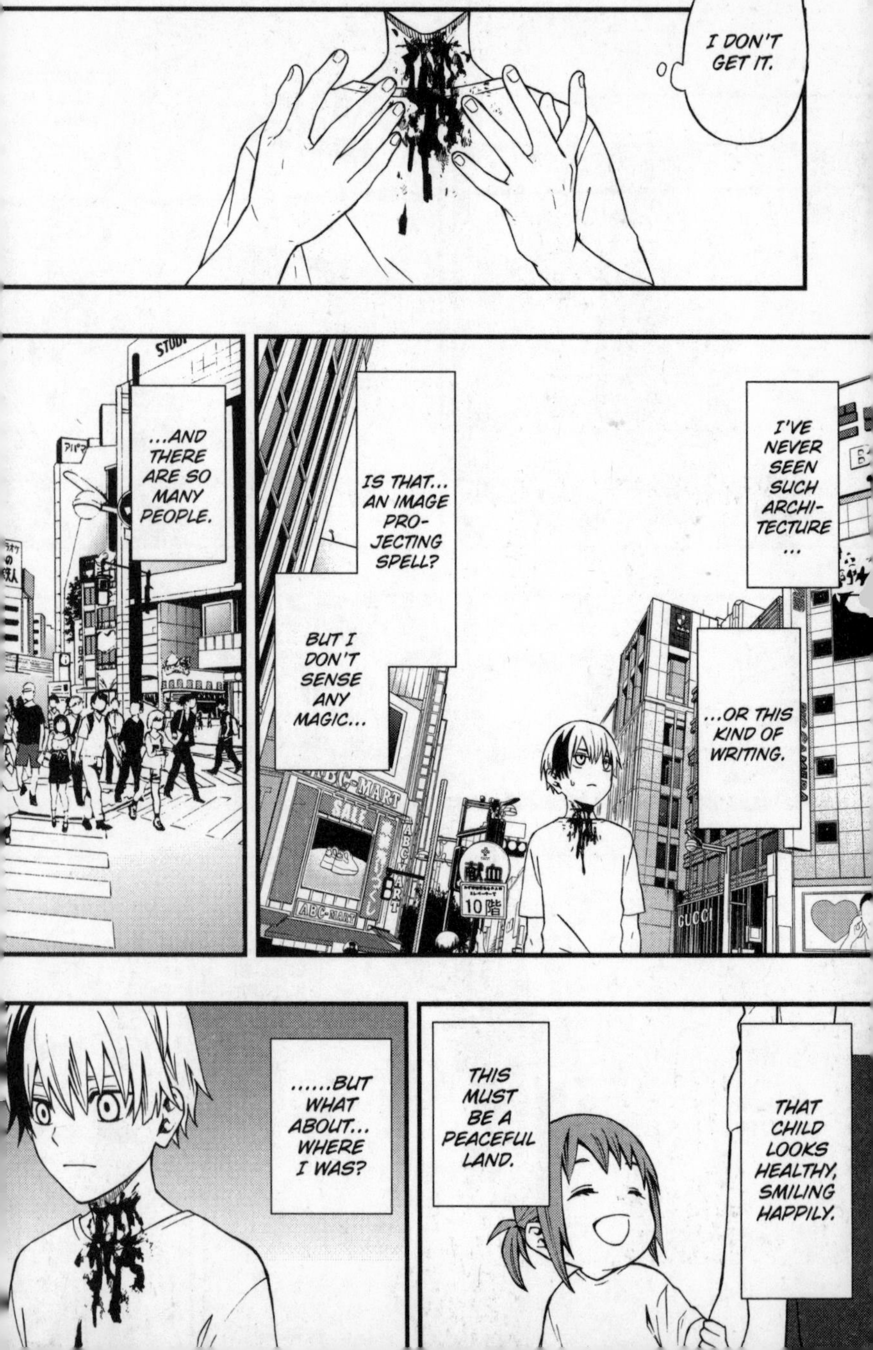
I DON'T GET IT.
I'VE NEVER SEEN SUCH ARCHITECTURE...
...OR THIS KIND OF WRITING.
IS THAT... AN IMAGE PROJECTING SPELL?
BUT I DON'T SENSE ANY MAGIC...
ABC-MART
SALE
献血
10階
GUCCI
...AND THERE ARE SO MANY PEOPLE.
THAT CHILD LOOKS HEALTHY, SMILING HAPPILY.
THIS MUST BE A PEACEFUL LAND.
......BUT WHAT ABOUT... WHERE I WAS?

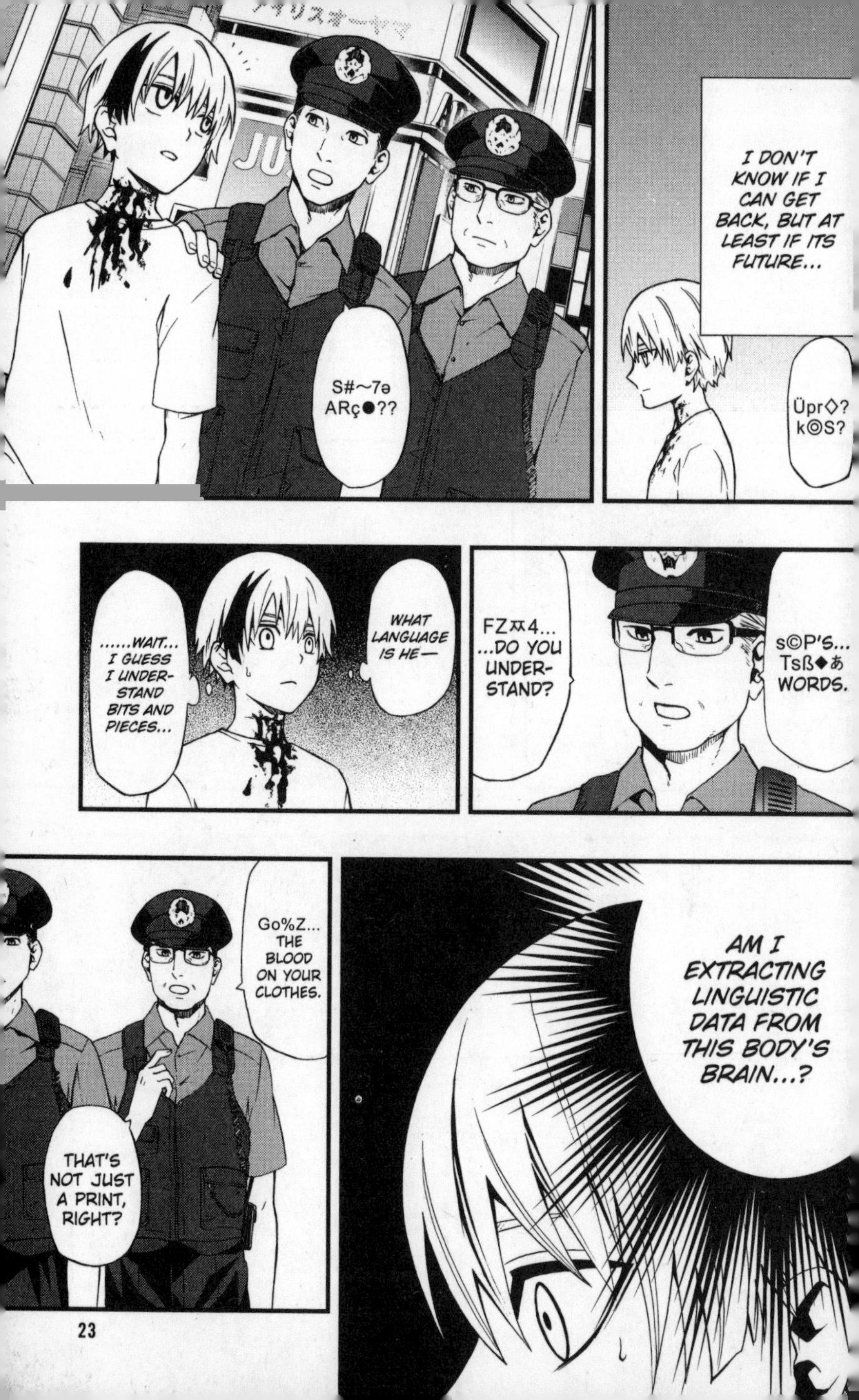
I DON'T KNOW IF I CAN GET BACK, BUT AT LEAST IF ITS FUTURE...
Üpr◇? k◎S?
S#~7ə ARç●??
s©P'S... Tsß◆あ WORDS.
FZㅉ4... ...DO YOU UNDER-STAND?
WHAT LANGUAGE IS HE—
......WAIT... I GUESS I UNDER-STAND BITS AND PIECES...
AM I EXTRACTING LINGUISTIC DATA FROM THIS BODY'S BRAIN...?
Go%Z... THE BLOOD ON YOUR CLOTHES.
THAT'S NOT JUST A PRINT, RIGHT?

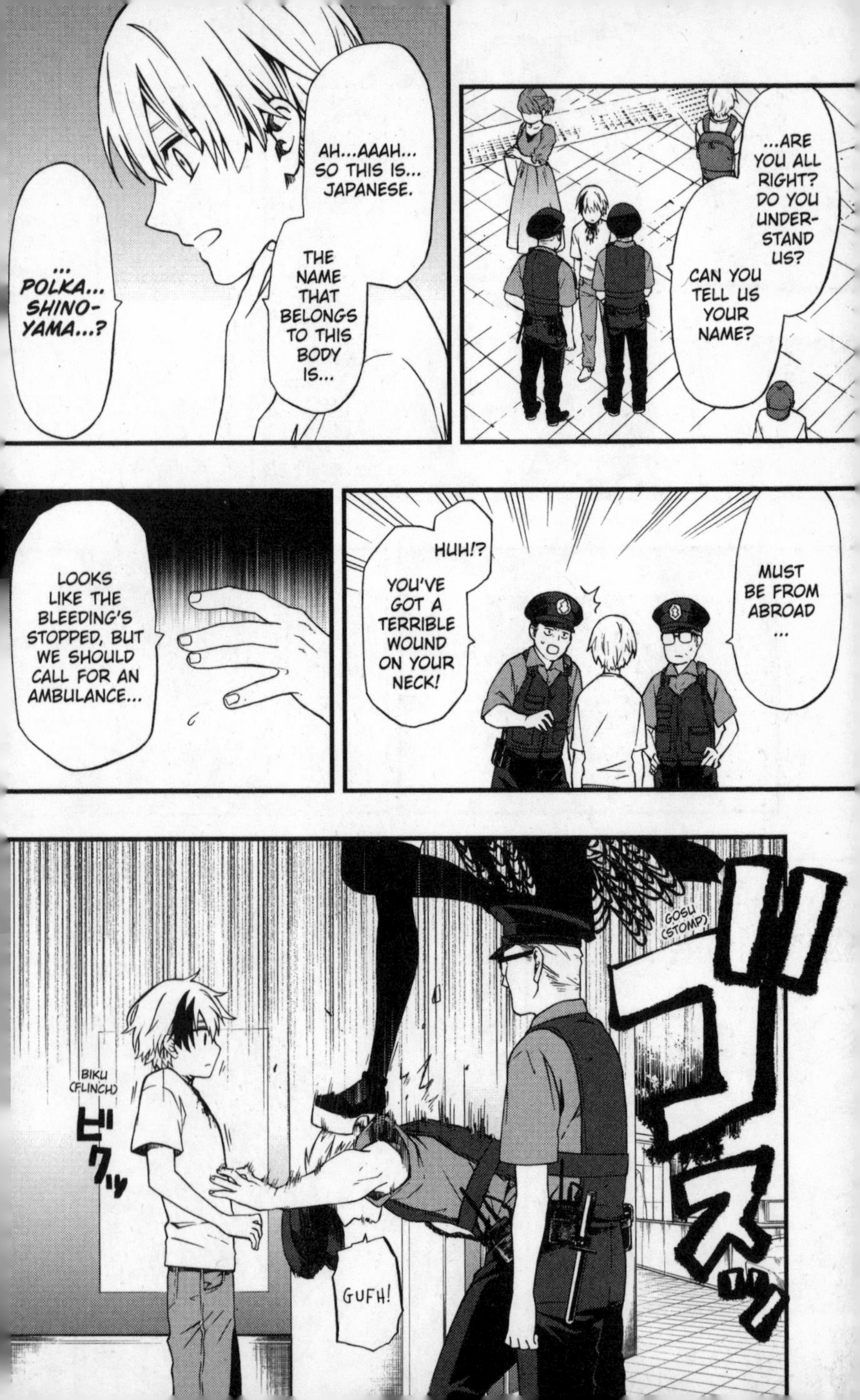
...ARE YOU ALL RIGHT? DO YOU UNDERSTAND US?
CAN YOU TELL US YOUR NAME?
AH...AAAH... SO THIS IS... JAPANESE.
THE NAME THAT BELONGS TO THIS BODY IS...
...POLKA... SHINOYAMA...?
MUST BE FROM ABROAD...
HUH!?
YOU'VE GOT A TERRIBLE WOUND ON YOUR NECK!
LOOKS LIKE THE BLEEDING'S STOPPED, BUT WE SHOULD CALL FOR AN AMBULANCE...
GOSU (STOMP)
ゴスッ
BIKU (FLINCH)
ビクッ
GUFH!

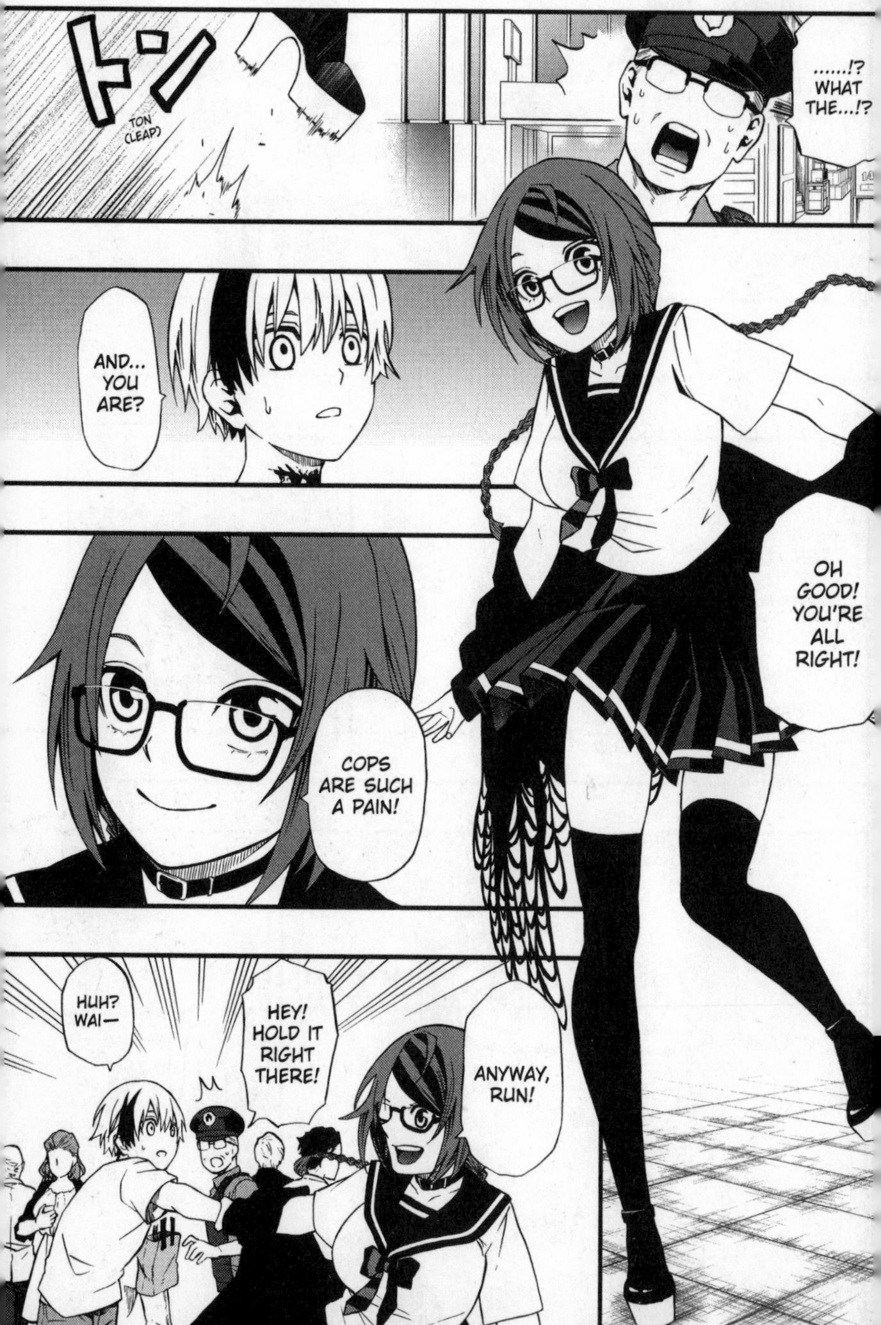
......!? WHAT THE...!?
トーン
TON (LEAP)
OH GOOD! YOU'RE ALL RIGHT!
AND... YOU ARE?
COPS ARE SUCH A PAIN!
ANYWAY, RUN!
HEY! HOLD IT RIGHT THERE!
HUH? WAI—

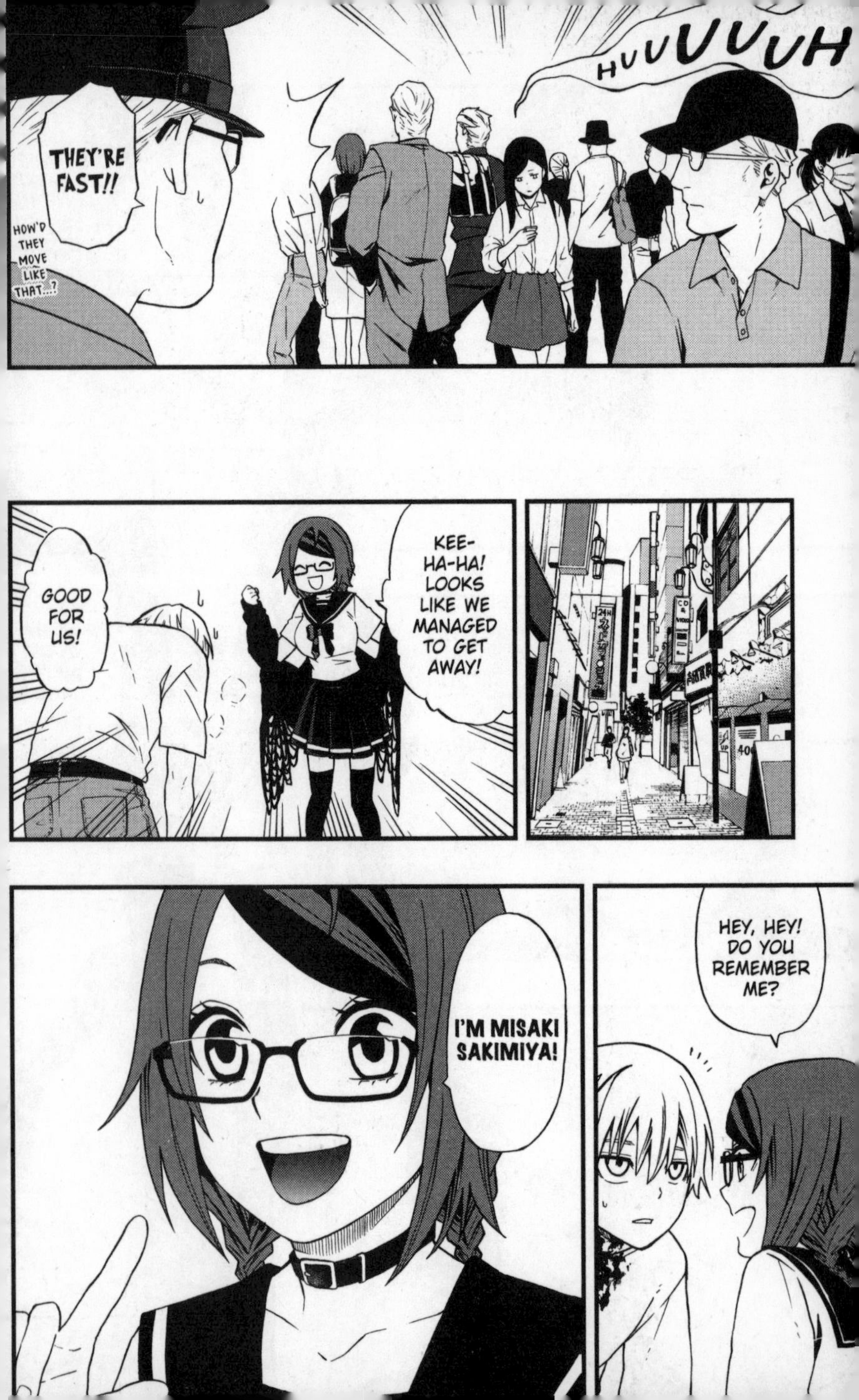
HUUUUUUH
THEY'RE FAST!!
HOW'D THEY MOVE LIKE THAT...?
KEE-HA-HA! LOOKS LIKE WE MANAGED TO GET AWAY!
GOOD FOR US!
HEY, HEY! DO YOU REMEMBER ME?
I'M MISAKI SAKIMIYA!

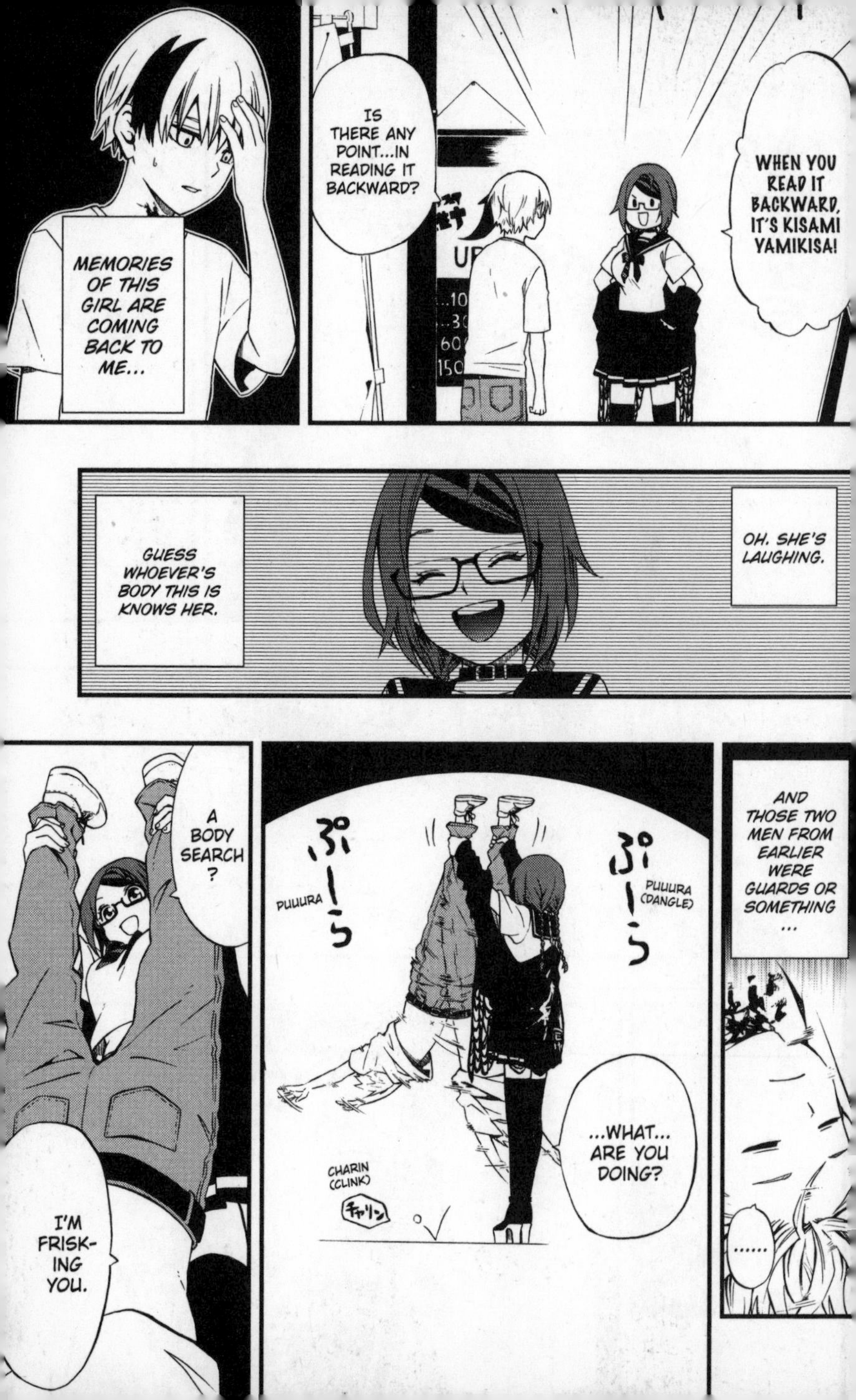
WHEN YOU READ IT BACKWARD, IT'S KISAMI YAMIKISA!
IS THERE ANY POINT...IN READING IT BACKWARD?
MEMORIES OF THIS GIRL ARE COMING BACK TO ME...
OH. SHE'S LAUGHING.
GUESS WHOEVER'S BODY THIS IS KNOWS HER.
AND THOSE TWO MEN FROM EARLIER WERE GUARDS OR SOMETHING...
......
ぷーら
PUUURA (DANGLE)
ぷーら
PUUURA
...WHAT... ARE YOU DOING?
チャリン
CHARIN (CLINK)
A BODY SEARCH?
I'M FRISK-ING YOU.

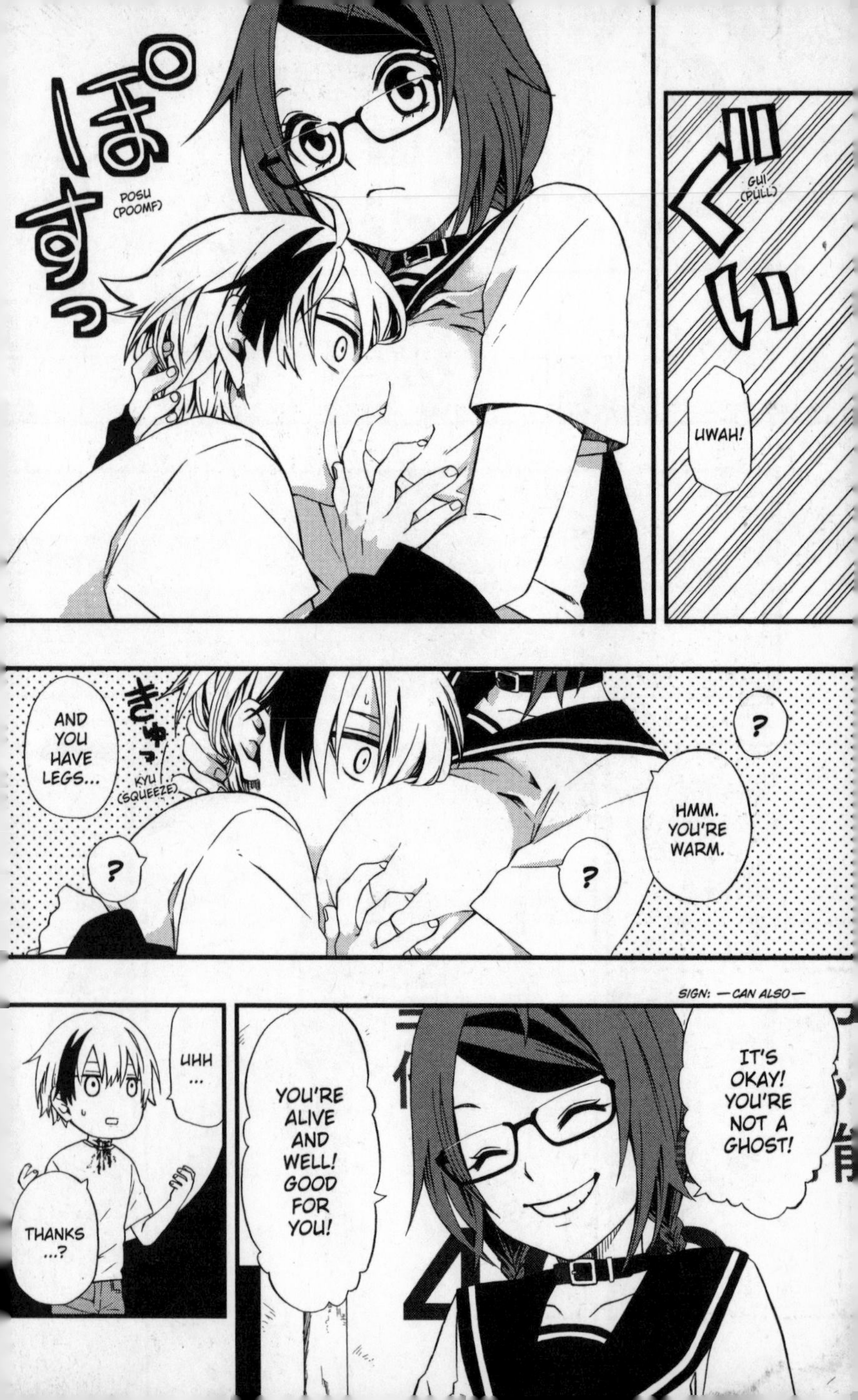

ぐい
GUI (PULL)
UWAH!
ぽすっ
POSU (POOMF)
?
HMM. YOU'RE WARM.
?
きゅっ
KYU (SQUEEZE)
AND YOU HAVE LEGS...
?
SIGN: —CAN ALSO—
IT'S OKAY! YOU'RE NOT A GHOST!
YOU'RE ALIVE AND WELL! GOOD FOR YOU!
UHH ...
THANKS ...?

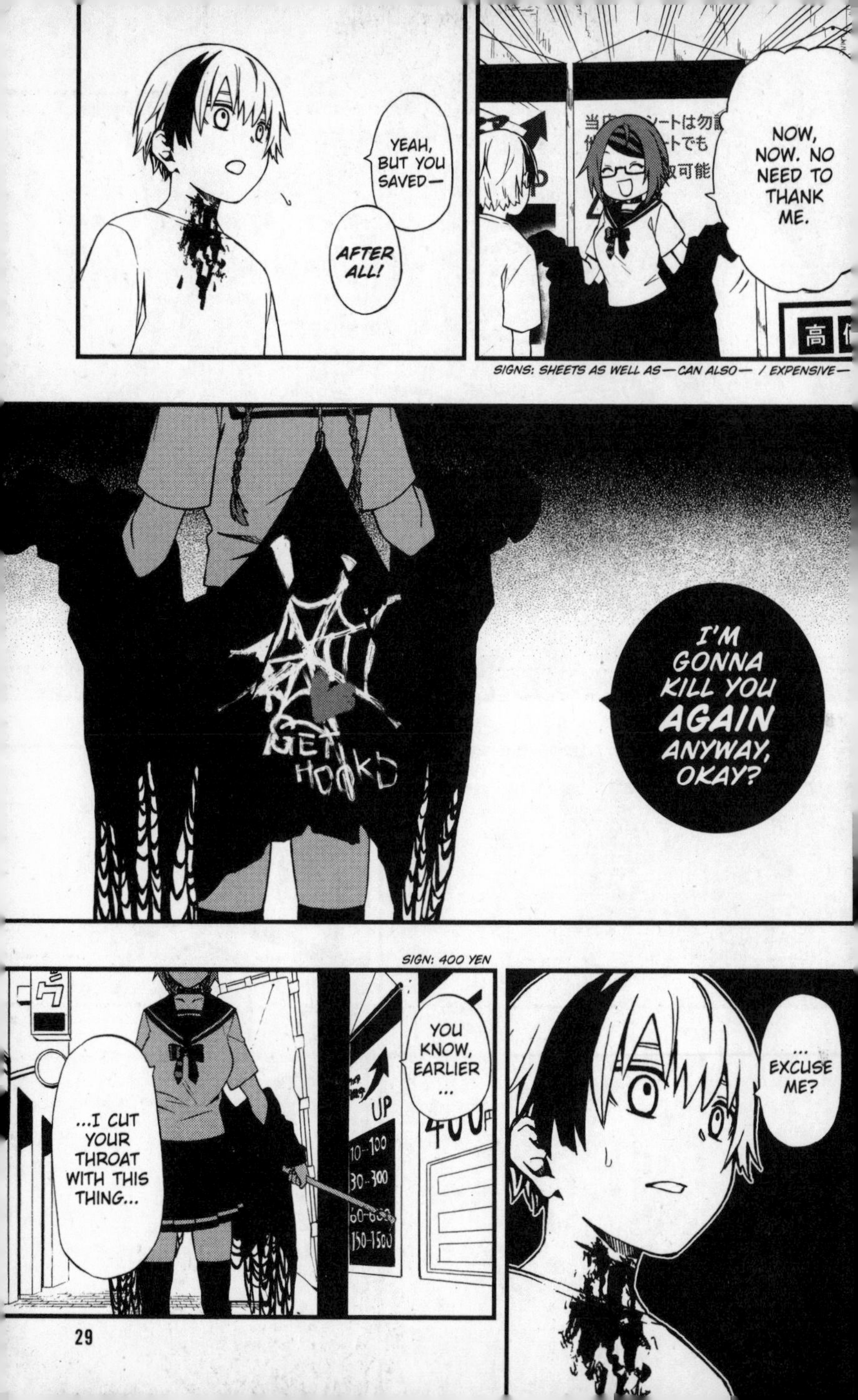
NOW, NOW. NO NEED TO THANK ME.
YEAH, BUT YOU SAVED—
AFTER ALL!
SIGNS: SHEETS AS WELL AS—CAN ALSO— / EXPENSIVE—
I'M GONNA KILL YOU AGAIN ANYWAY, OKAY?
SIGN: 400 YEN
YOU KNOW, EARLIER...
...I CUT YOUR THROAT WITH THIS THING...
...EXCUSE ME?

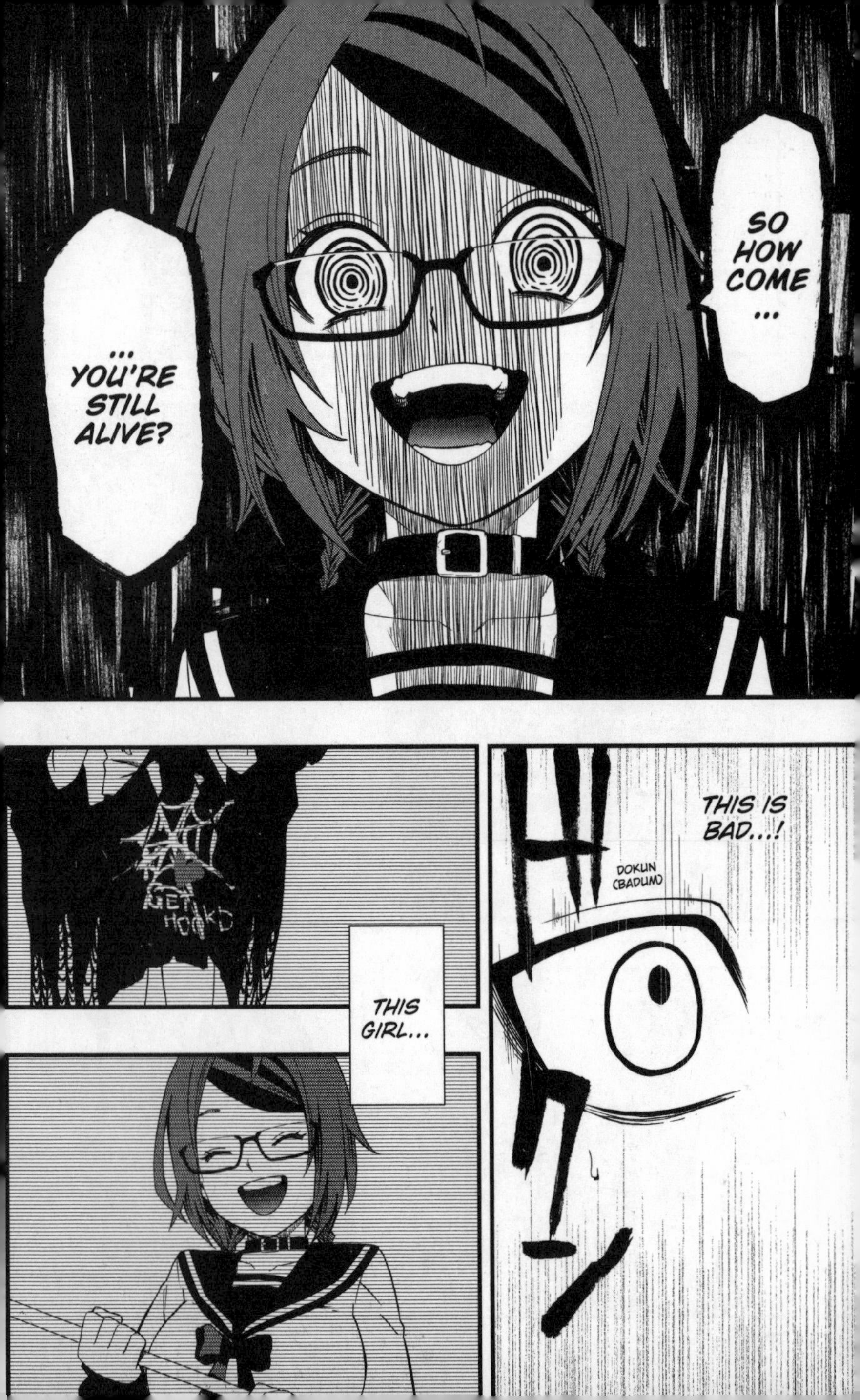
SO HOW COME ...
... YOU'RE STILL ALIVE?
THIS IS BAD...!
DOKUN (BADUM)
THIS GIRL...

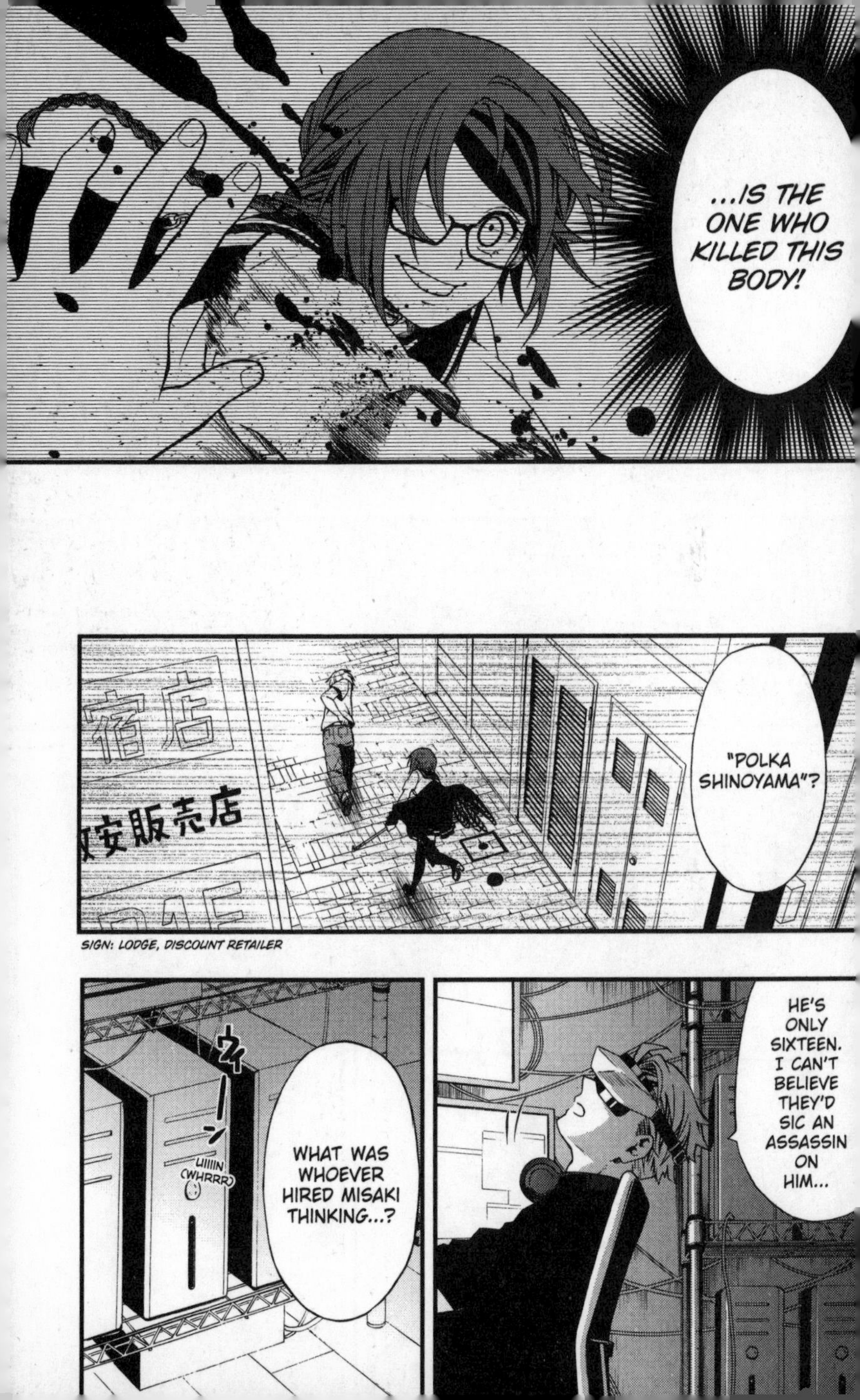
...IS THE ONE WHO KILLED THIS BODY!
"POLKA SHINOYAMA"?
SIGN: LODGE, DISCOUNT RETAILER
HE'S ONLY SIXTEEN. I CAN'T BELIEVE THEY'D SIC AN ASSASSIN ON HIM...
WHAT WAS WHOEVER HIRED MISAKI THINKING...?
UIIIIN (WHRRR)

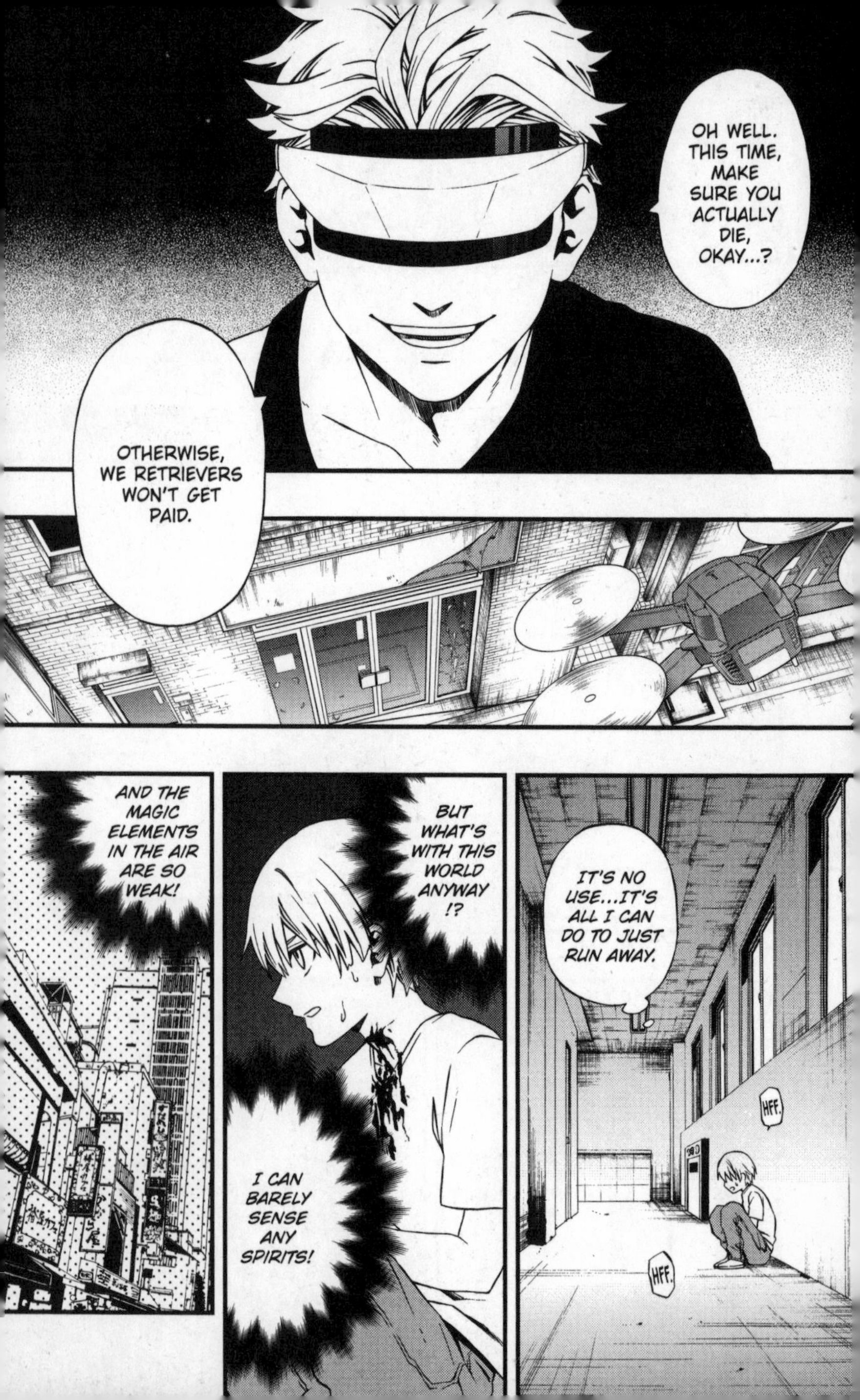
OH WELL. THIS TIME, MAKE SURE YOU ACTUALLY DIE, OKAY...?
OTHERWISE, WE RETRIEVERS WON'T GET PAID.
IT'S NO USE...IT'S ALL I CAN DO TO JUST RUN AWAY.
HFF.
HFF.
BUT WHAT'S WITH THIS WORLD ANYWAY!?
I CAN BARELY SENSE ANY SPIRITS!
AND THE MAGIC ELEMENTS IN THE AIR ARE SO WEAK!

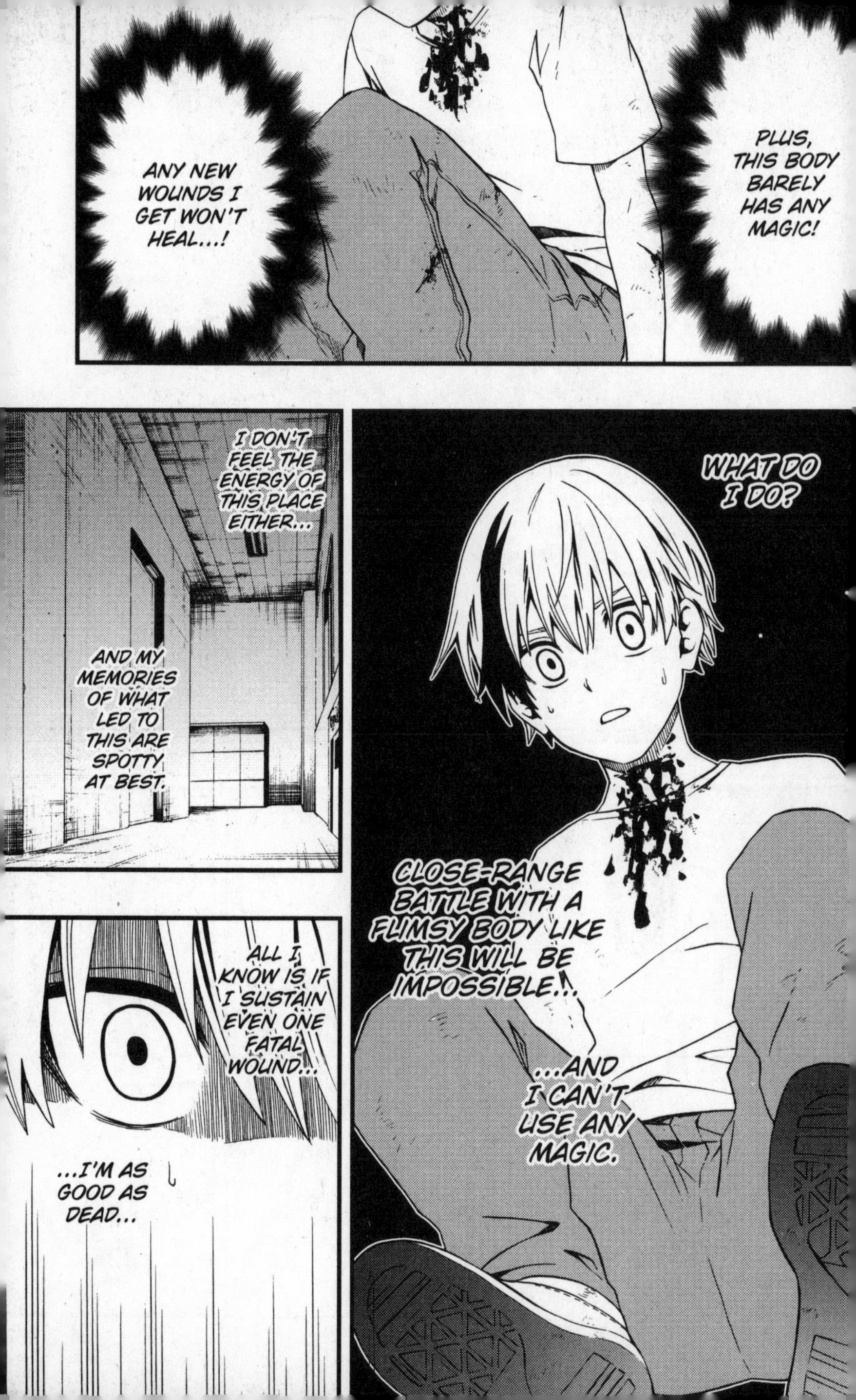
PLUS, THIS BODY BARELY HAS ANY MAGIC!
ANY NEW WOUNDS I GET WON'T HEAL...!
WHAT DO I DO?
CLOSE-RANGE BATTLE WITH A FLIMSY BODY LIKE THIS WILL BE IMPOSSIBLE...
...AND I CAN'T USE ANY MAGIC.
I DON'T FEEL THE ENERGY OF THIS PLACE EITHER...
AND MY MEMORIES OF WHAT LED TO THIS ARE SPOTTY AT BEST.
ALL I KNOW IS IF I SUSTAIN EVEN ONE FATAL WOUND...
...I'M AS GOOD AS DEAD...

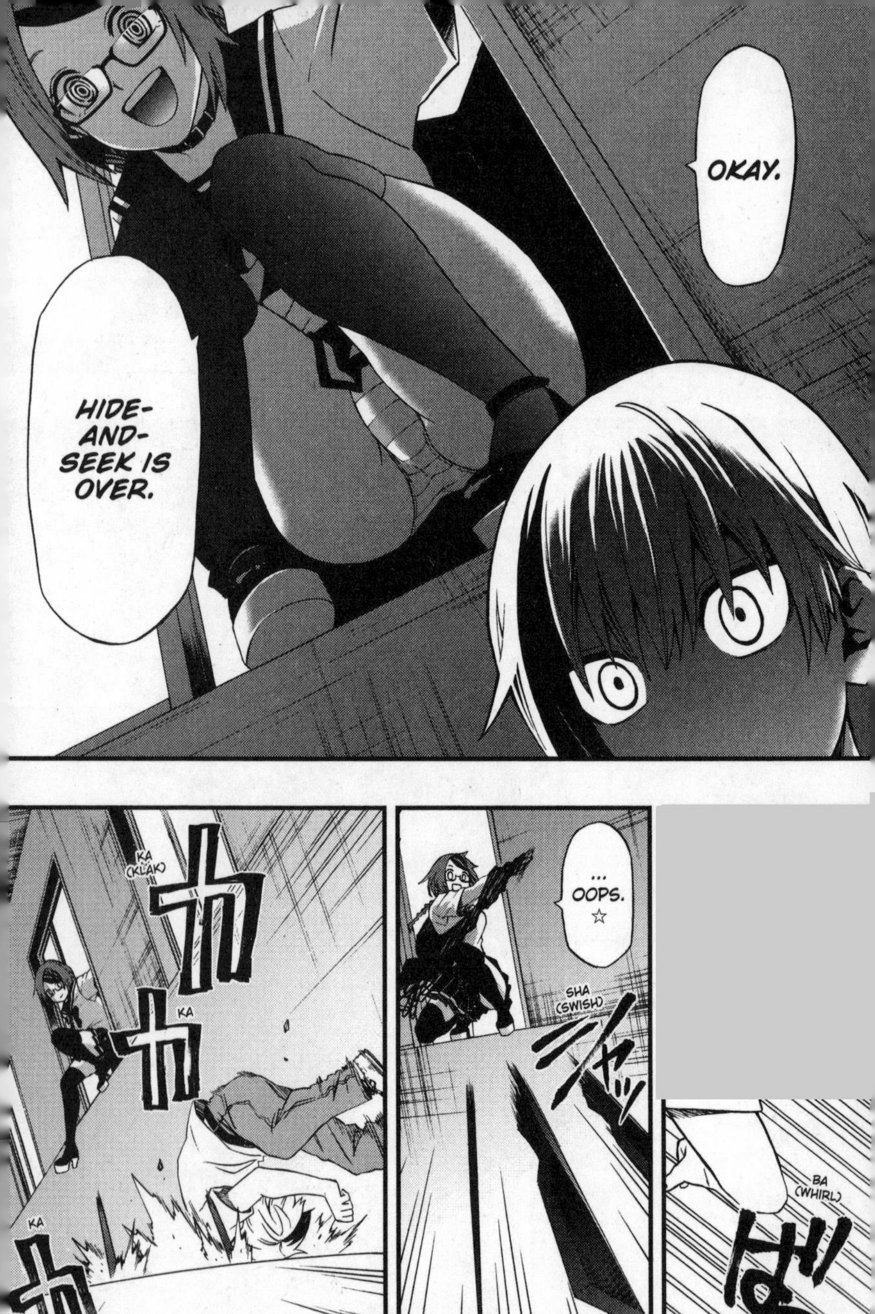
OKAY.
HIDE-AND-SEEK IS OVER.
... OOPS. ☆
SHA (SWISH)
KA (KLAK)
KA
KA
BA (WHIRL)

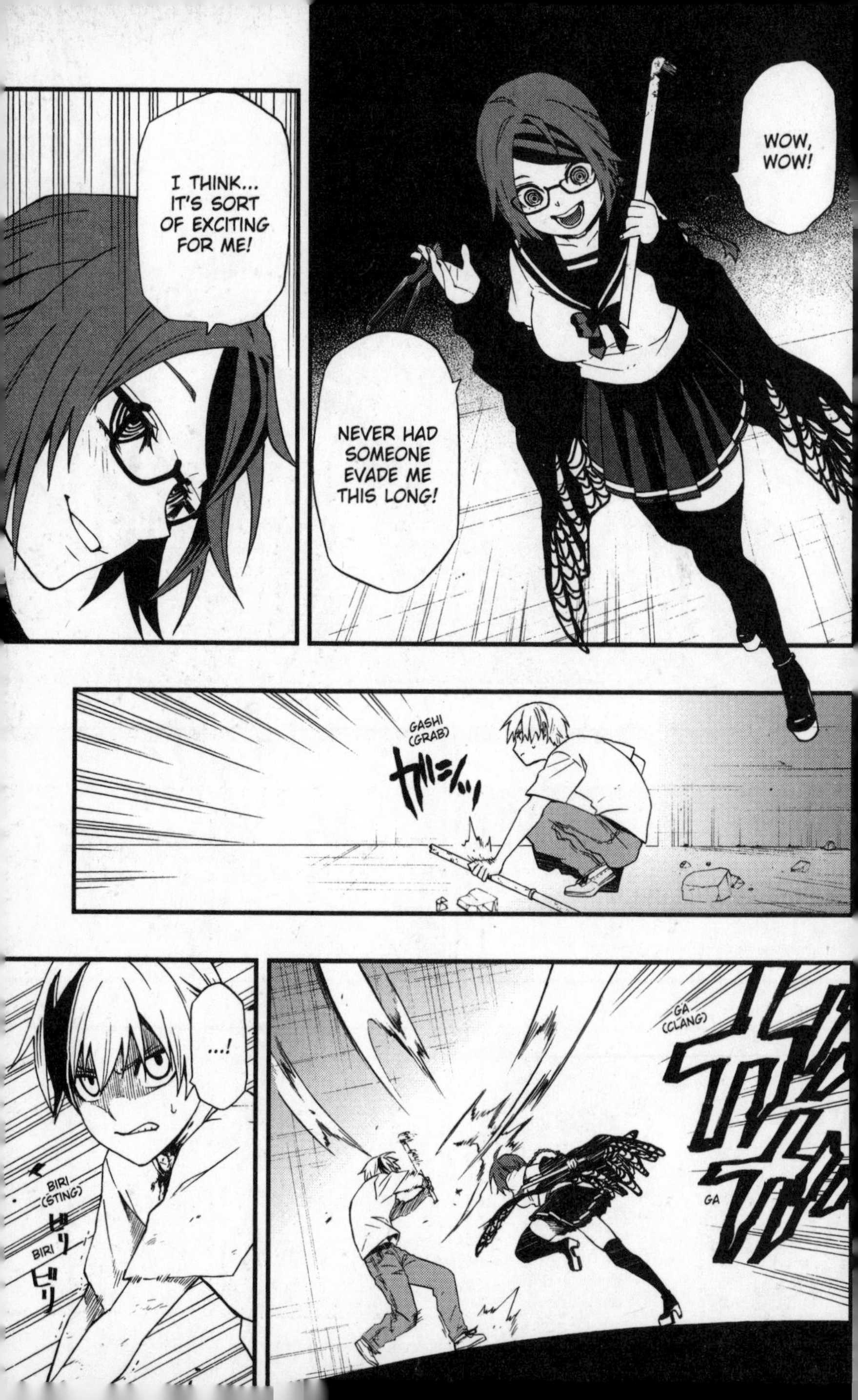
WOW, WOW!
NEVER HAD SOMEONE EVADE ME THIS LONG!
I THINK... IT'S SORT OF EXCITING FOR ME!
GASHI (GRAB)
GA (CLANG)
GA
...!
BIRI (STING)
BIRI

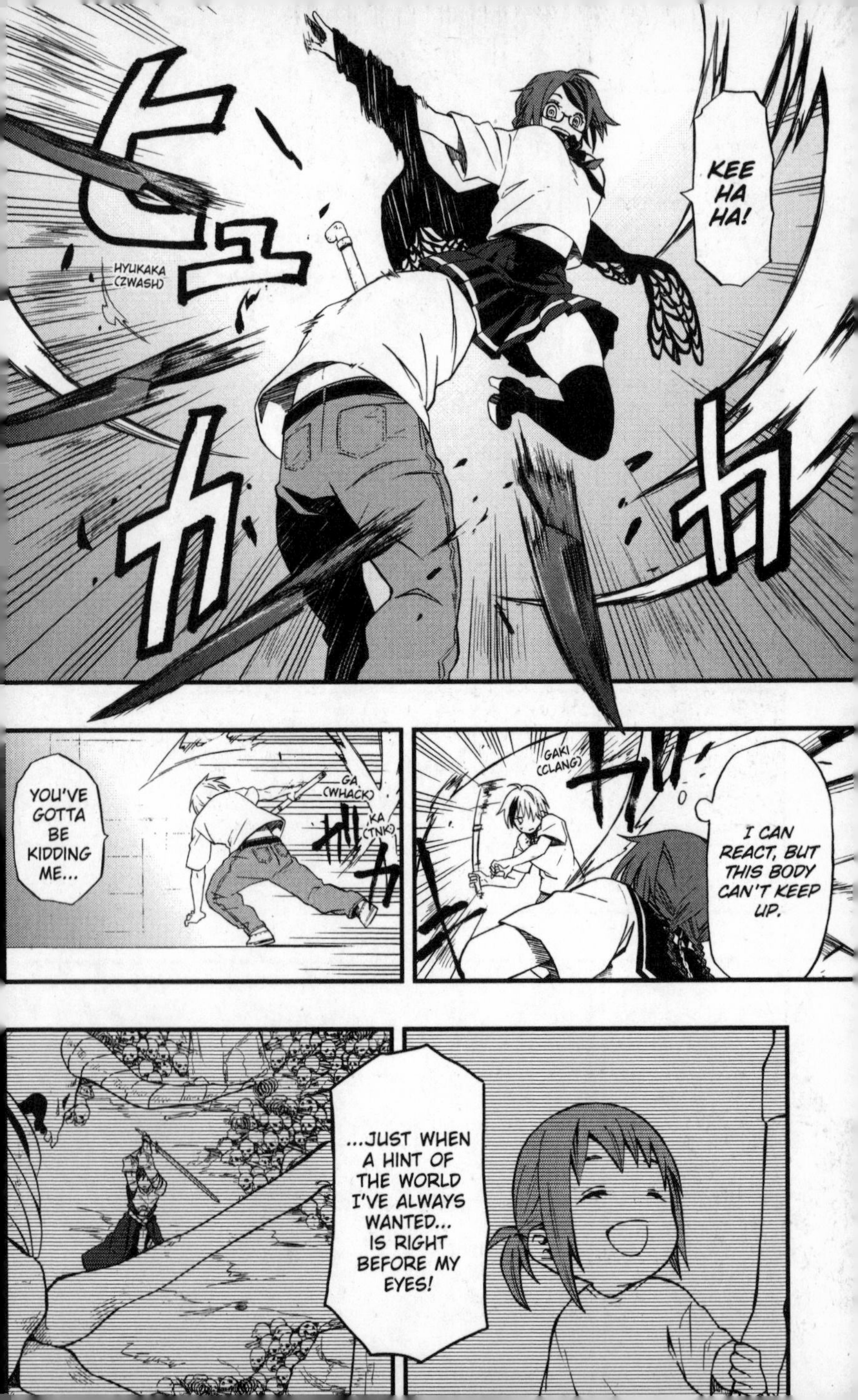
KEE HA HA!
HYUKAKA (ZWASH)
GAKI (CLANG)
I CAN REACT, BUT THIS BODY CAN'T KEEP UP.
GA (WHACK)
KA (TNK)
YOU'VE GOTTA BE KIDDING ME...
...JUST WHEN A HINT OF THE WORLD I'VE ALWAYS WANTED... IS RIGHT BEFORE MY EYES!

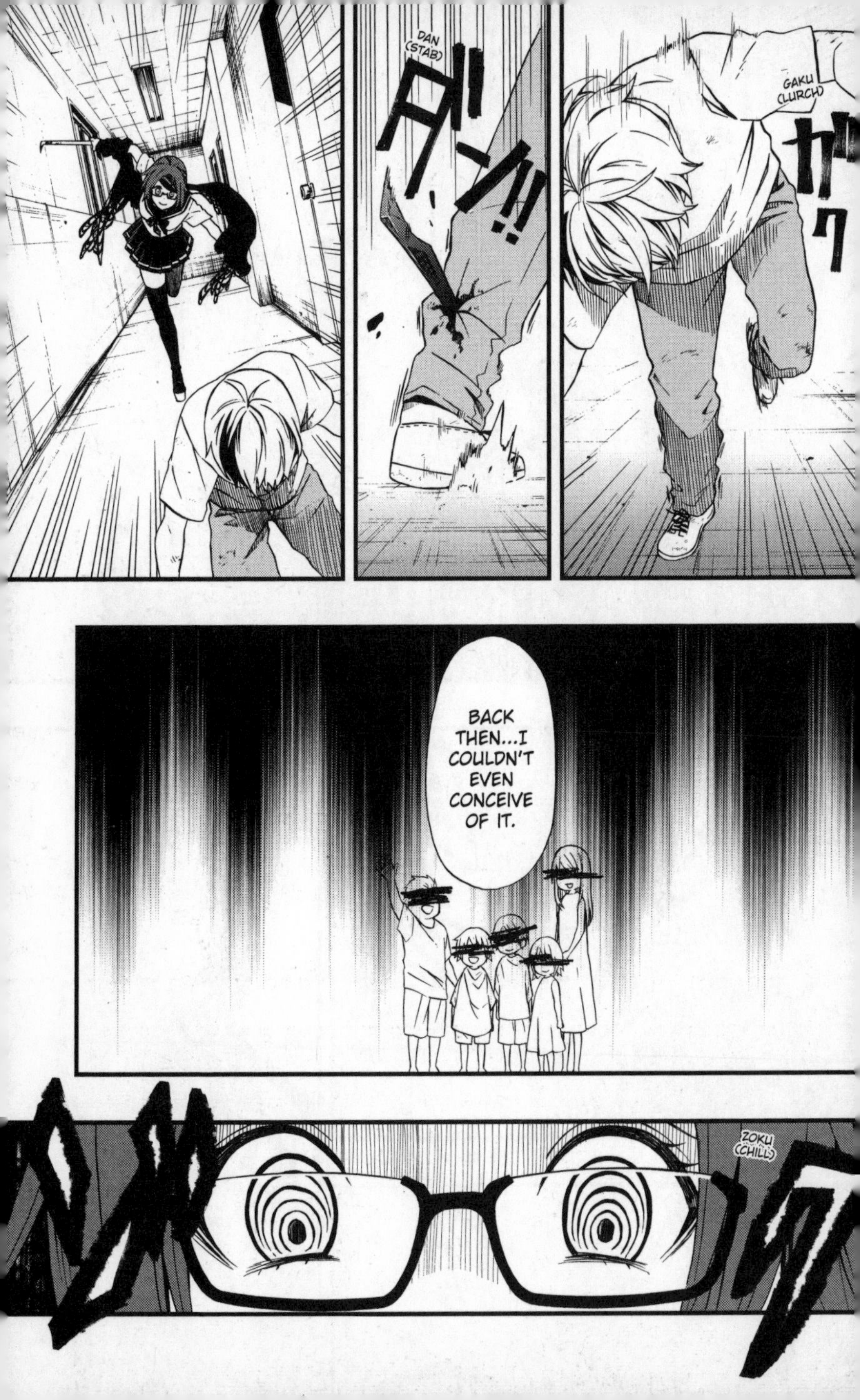
GAKU (LURCH)
DAN (STAB)
BACK THEN...I COULDN'T EVEN CONCEIVE OF IT.
ZOKU (CHILL)

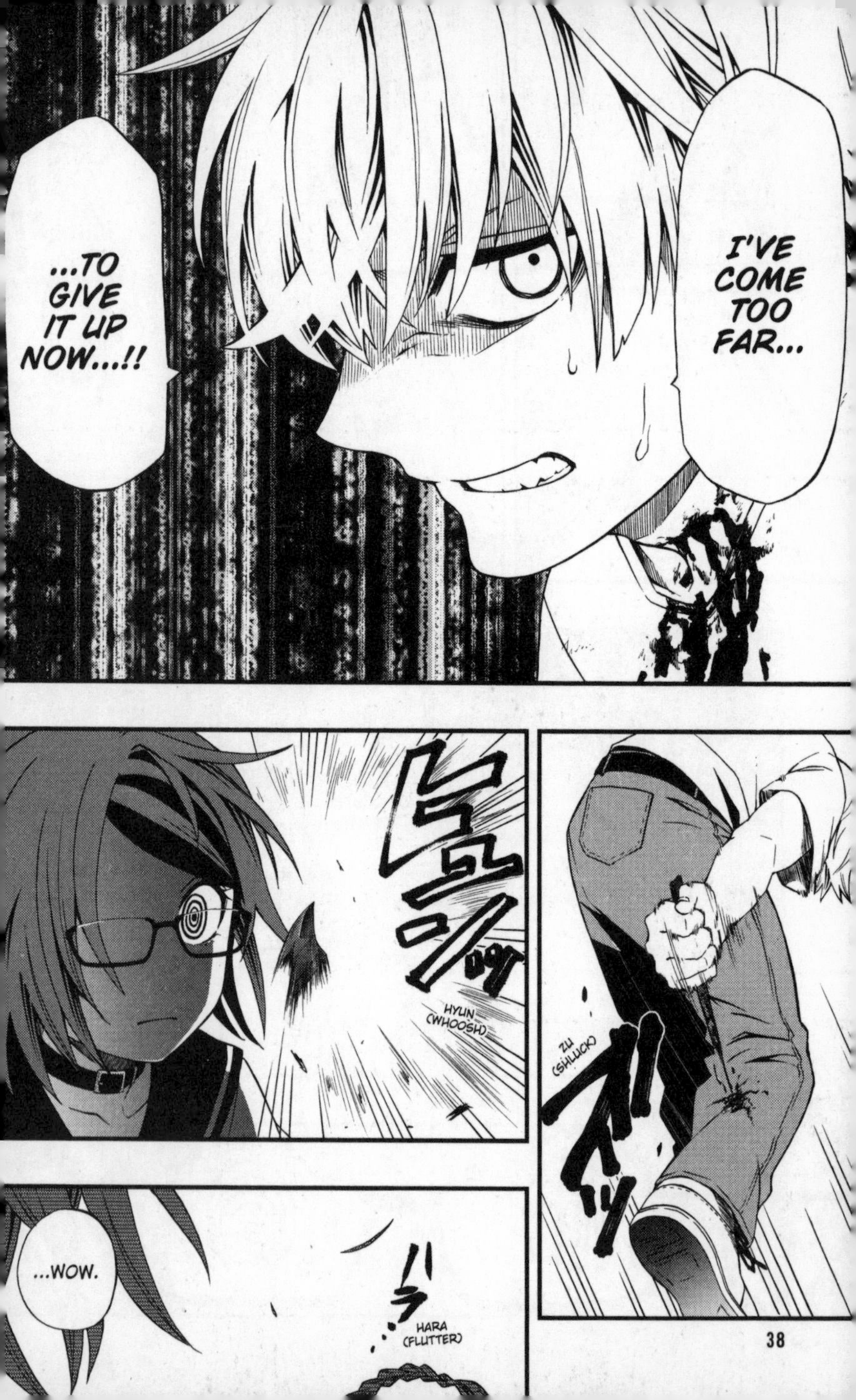
I'VE COME TOO FAR...
...TO GIVE IT UP NOW...!!
ZU (SHLUCK)
HYUN (WHOOSH)
...WOW.
HARA (FLUTTER)

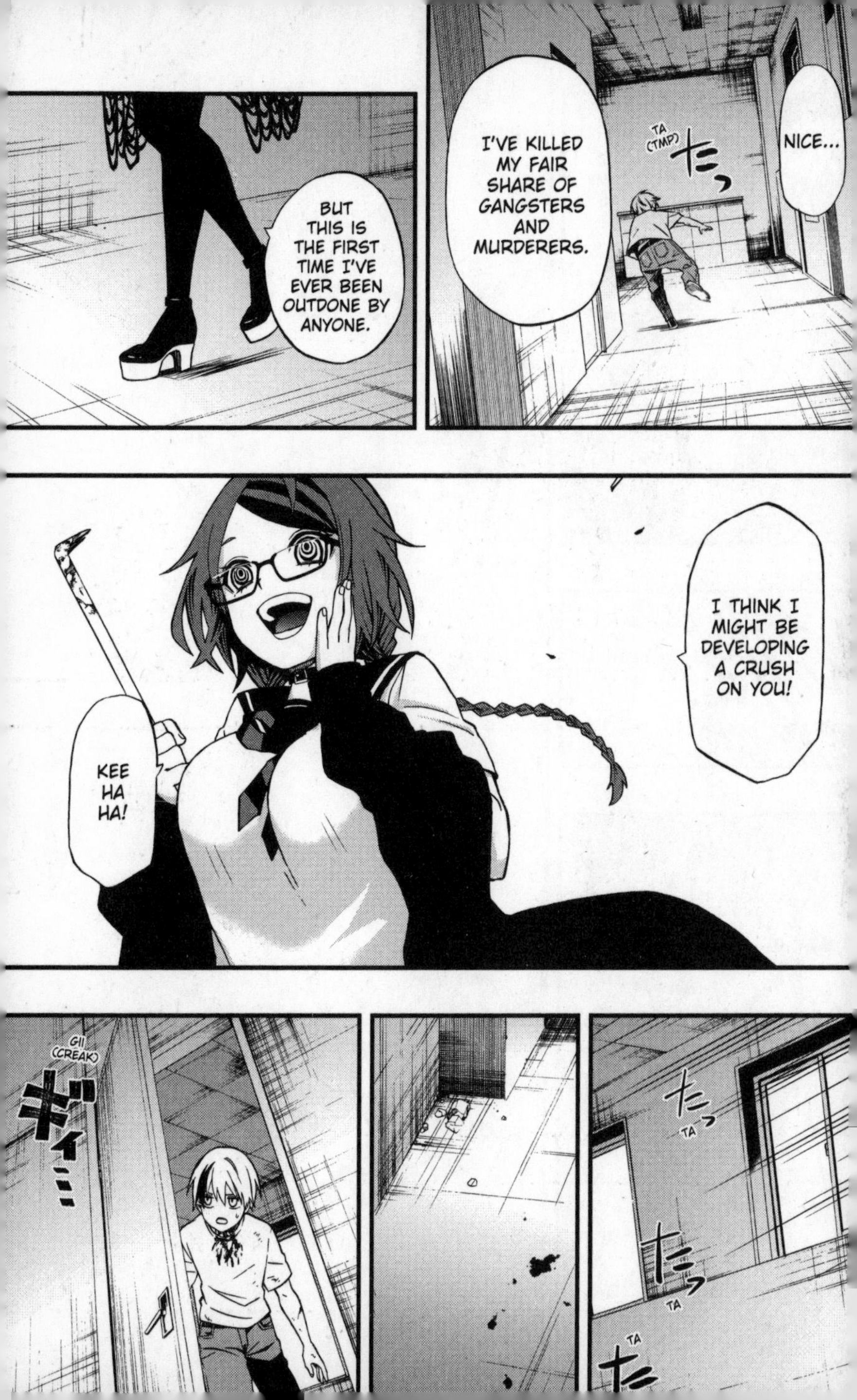
NICE...
TA (TMP)
I'VE KILLED MY FAIR SHARE OF GANGSTERS AND MURDERERS.
BUT THIS IS THE FIRST TIME I'VE EVER BEEN OUTDONE BY ANYONE.
I THINK I MIGHT BE DEVELOPING A CRUSH ON YOU!
KEE HA HA!
TA
TA
TA
GII (CREAK)

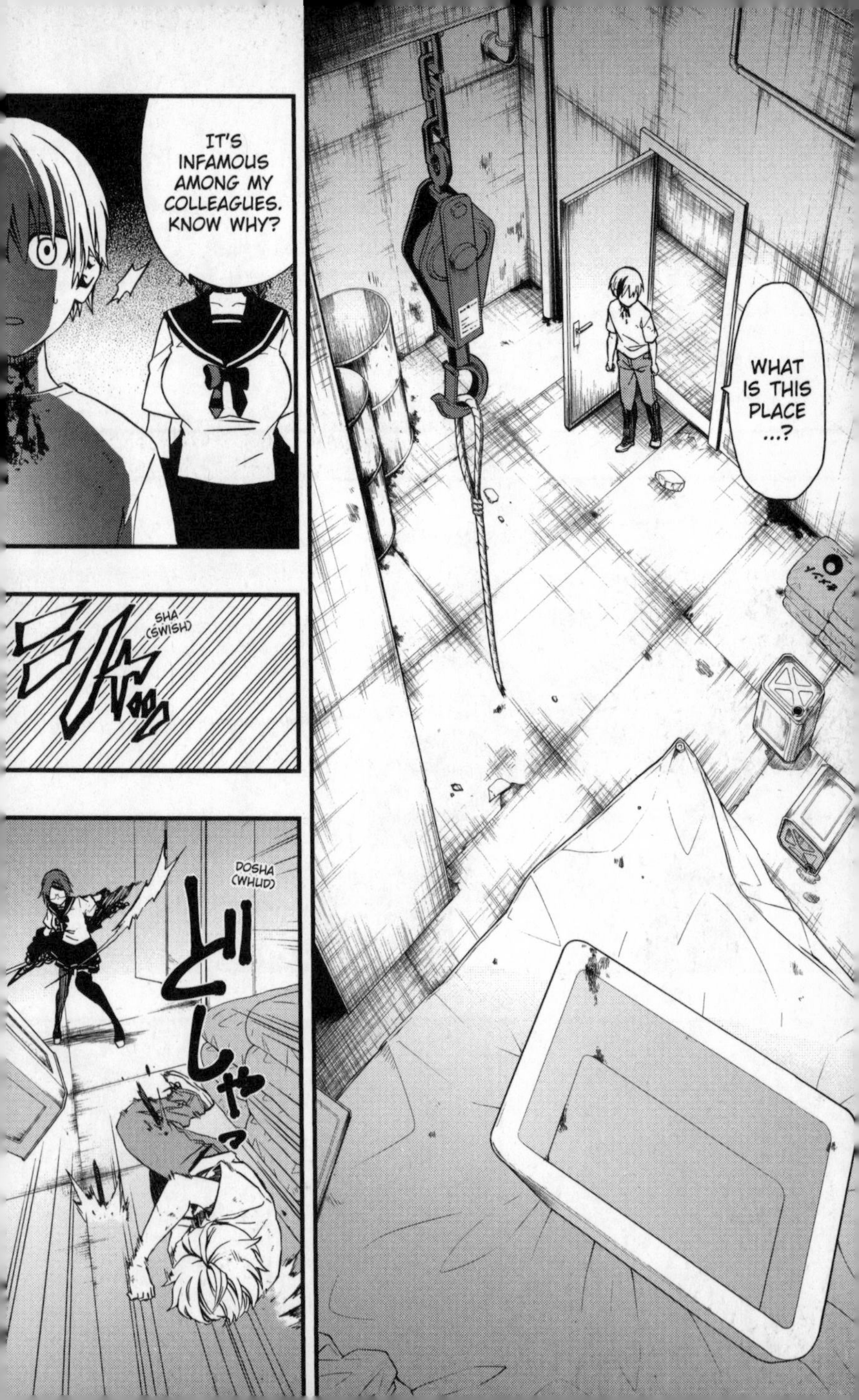
WHAT IS THIS PLACE ...?
IT'S INFAMOUS AMONG MY COLLEAGUES. KNOW WHY?
SHA (SWISH)
DOSHA (WHUD)
どしゃっ

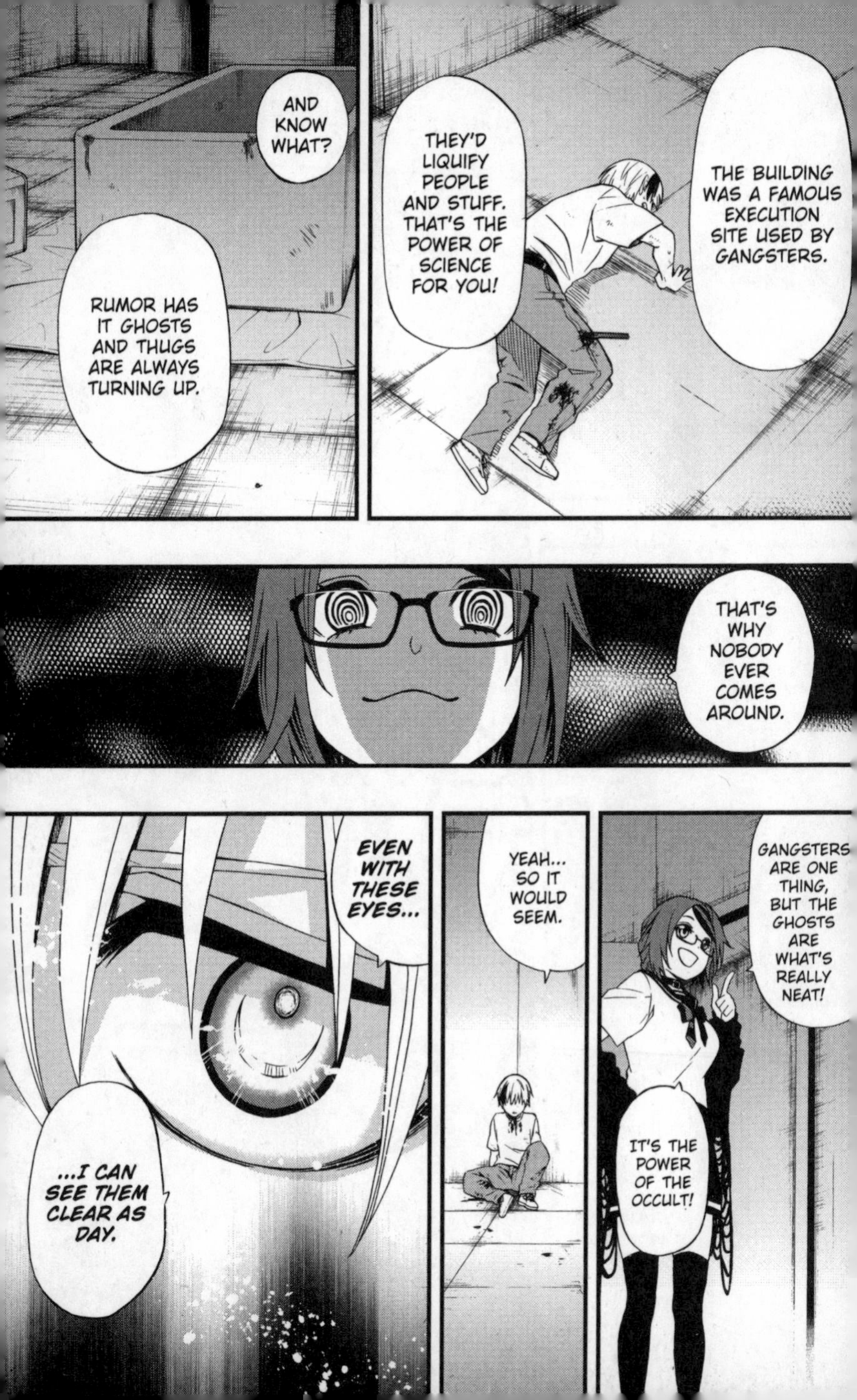
THE BUILDING WAS A FAMOUS EXECUTION SITE USED BY GANGSTERS.
THEY'D LIQUIFY PEOPLE AND STUFF. THAT'S THE POWER OF SCIENCE FOR YOU!
AND KNOW WHAT?
RUMOR HAS IT GHOSTS AND THUGS ARE ALWAYS TURNING UP.
THAT'S WHY NOBODY EVER COMES AROUND.
GANGSTERS ARE ONE THING, BUT THE GHOSTS ARE WHAT'S REALLY NEAT!
IT'S THE POWER OF THE OCCULT!
YEAH... SO IT WOULD SEEM.
EVEN WITH THESE EYES...
...I CAN SEE THEM CLEAR AS DAY.

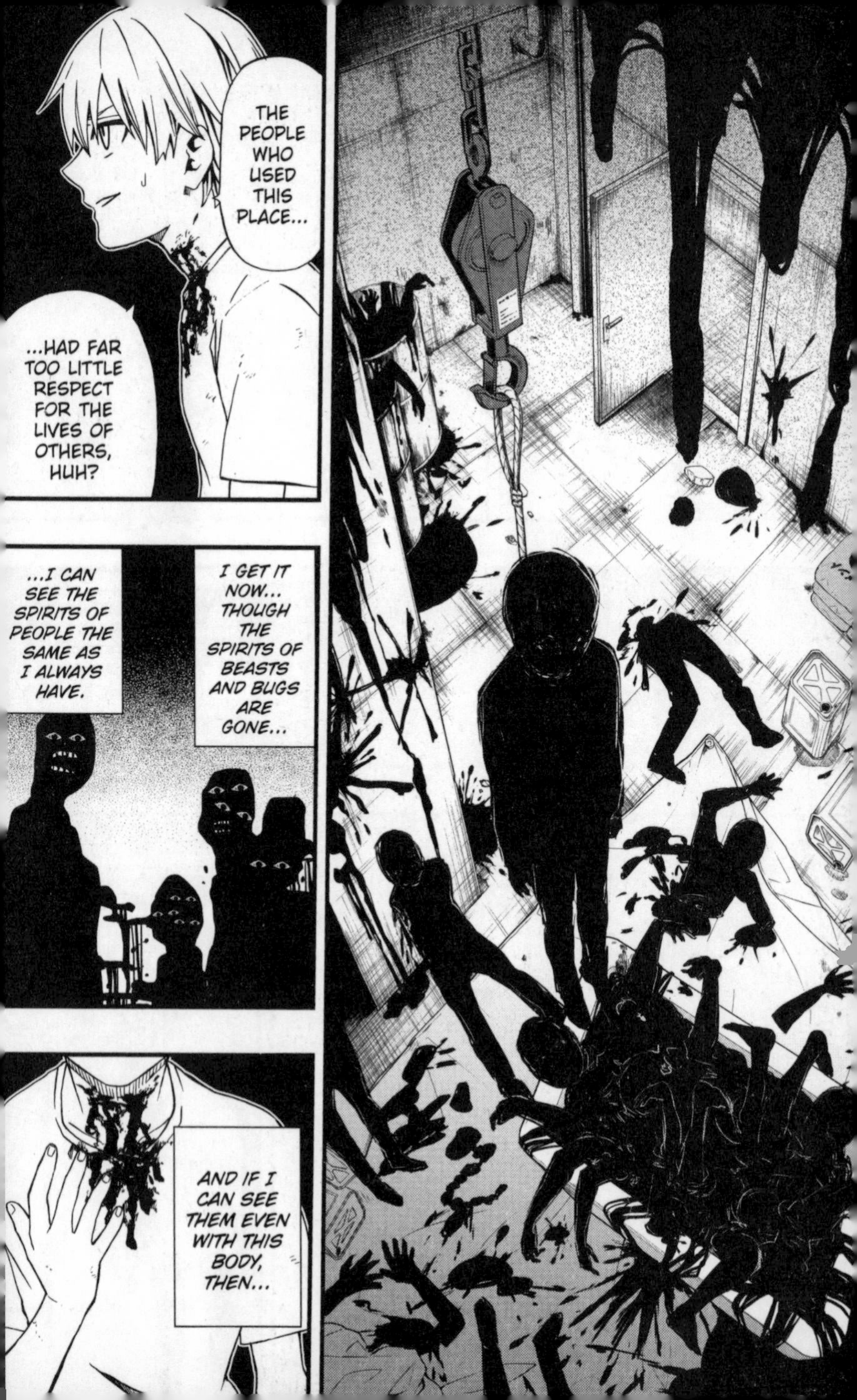
THE PEOPLE WHO USED THIS PLACE...
...HAD FAR TOO LITTLE RESPECT FOR THE LIVES OF OTHERS, HUH?
I GET IT NOW... THOUGH THE SPIRITS OF BEASTS AND BUGS ARE GONE...
...I CAN SEE THE SPIRITS OF PEOPLE THE SAME AS I ALWAYS HAVE.
AND IF I CAN SEE THEM EVEN WITH THIS BODY, THEN...

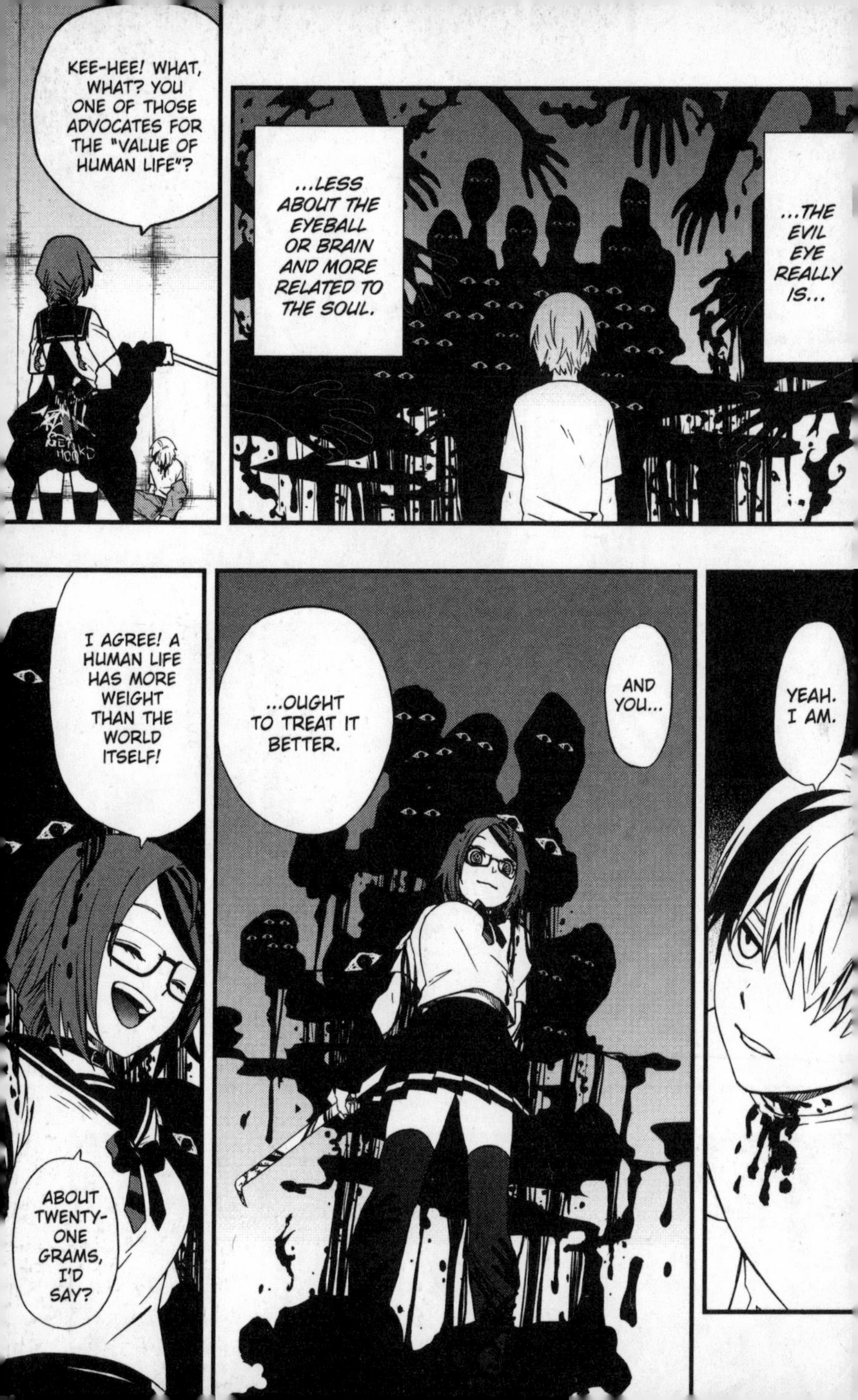
...THE EVIL EYE REALLY IS...
...LESS ABOUT THE EYEBALL OR BRAIN AND MORE RELATED TO THE SOUL.
KEE-HEE! WHAT, WHAT? YOU ONE OF THOSE ADVOCATES FOR THE "VALUE OF HUMAN LIFE"?
YEAH. I AM.
AND YOU...
...OUGHT TO TREAT IT BETTER.
I AGREE! A HUMAN LIFE HAS MORE WEIGHT THAN THE WORLD ITSELF!
ABOUT TWENTY-ONE GRAMS, I'D SAY?

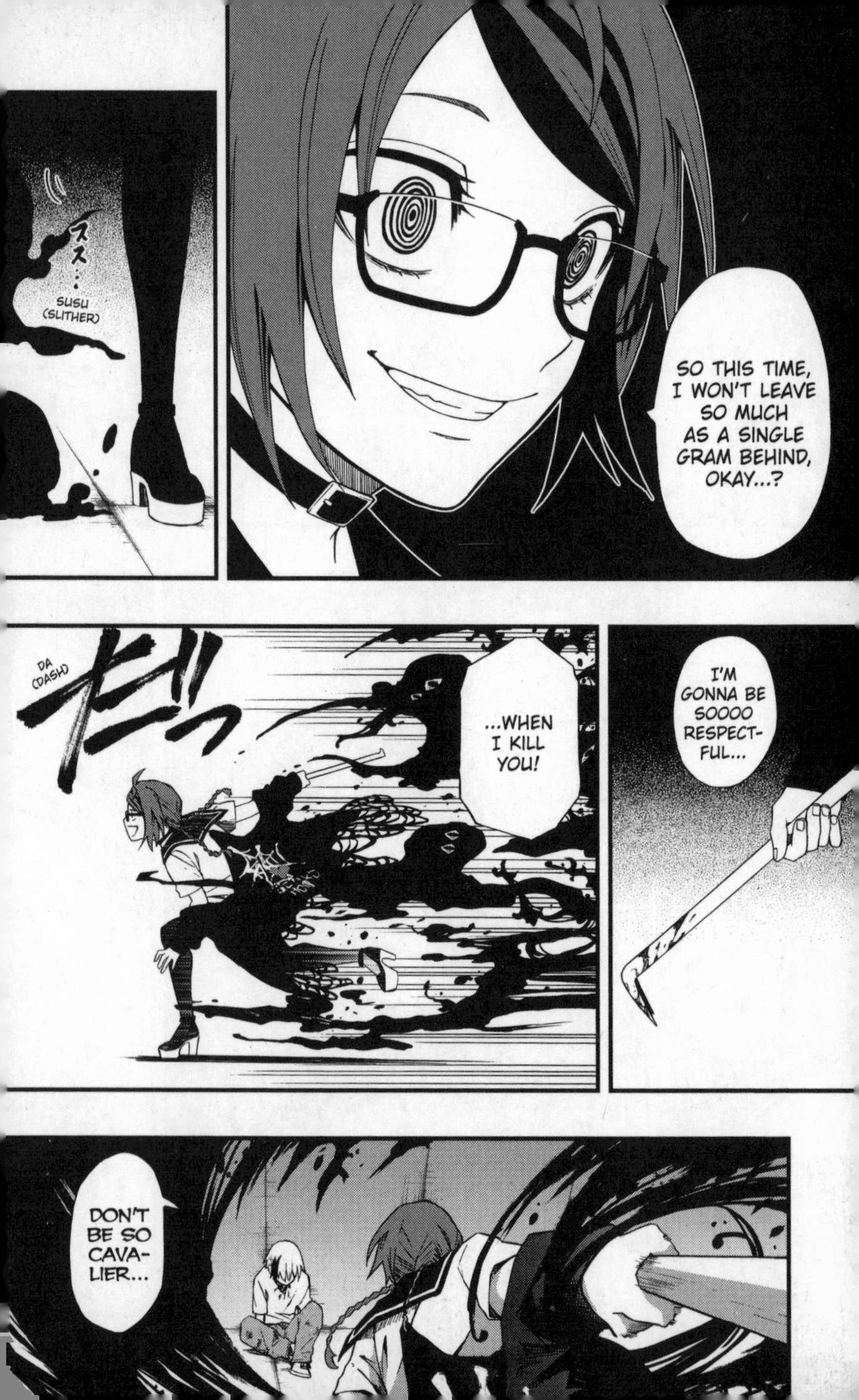
SO THIS TIME, I WON'T LEAVE SO MUCH AS A SINGLE GRAM BEHIND, OKAY...?
ススッ…
SUSU (SLITHER)
I'M GONNA BE SOOOO RESPECT-FUL...
...WHEN I KILL YOU!
DA (DASH)
DON'T BE SO CAVA-LIER...

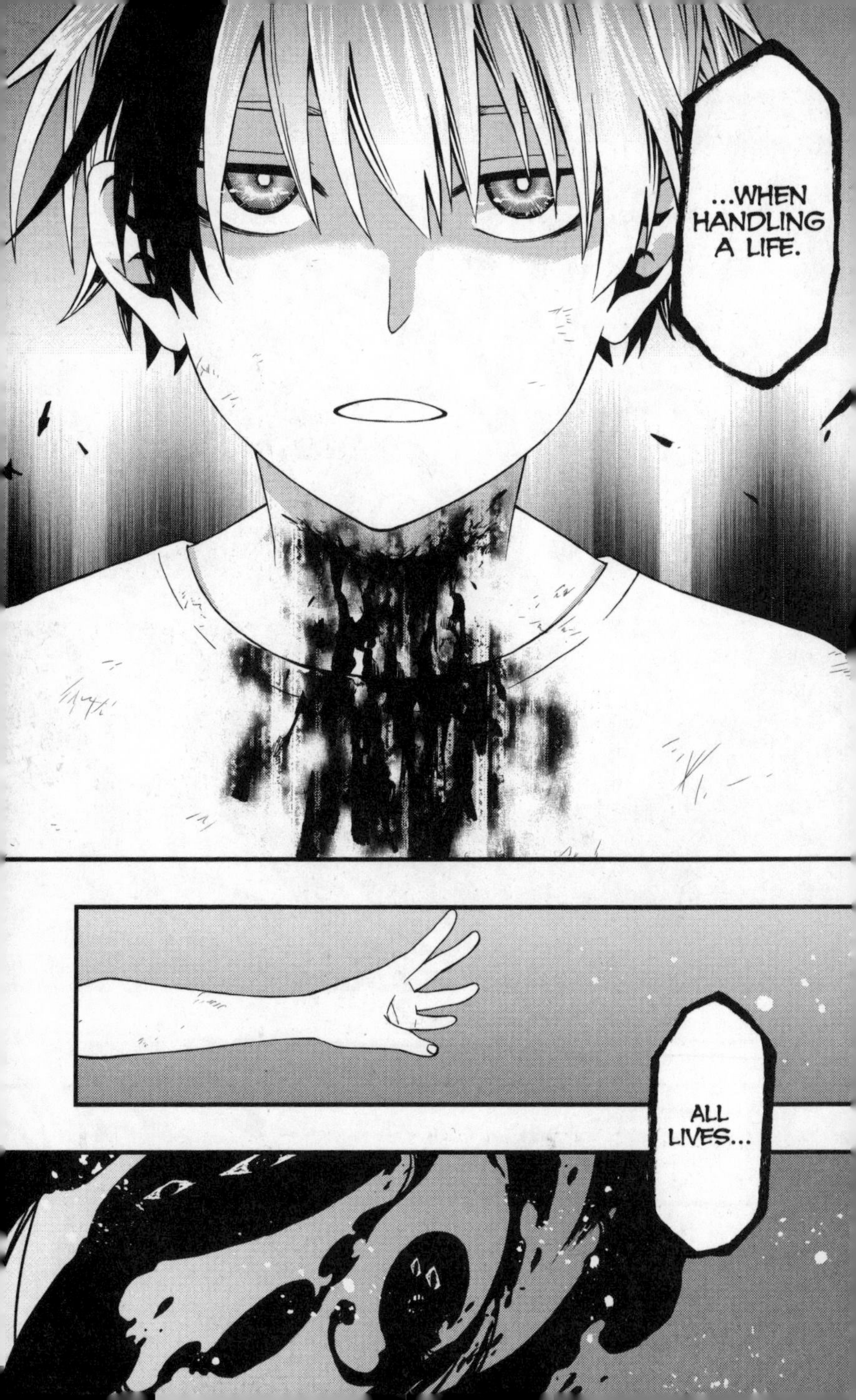
...WHEN HANDLING A LIFE.
ALL LIVES...

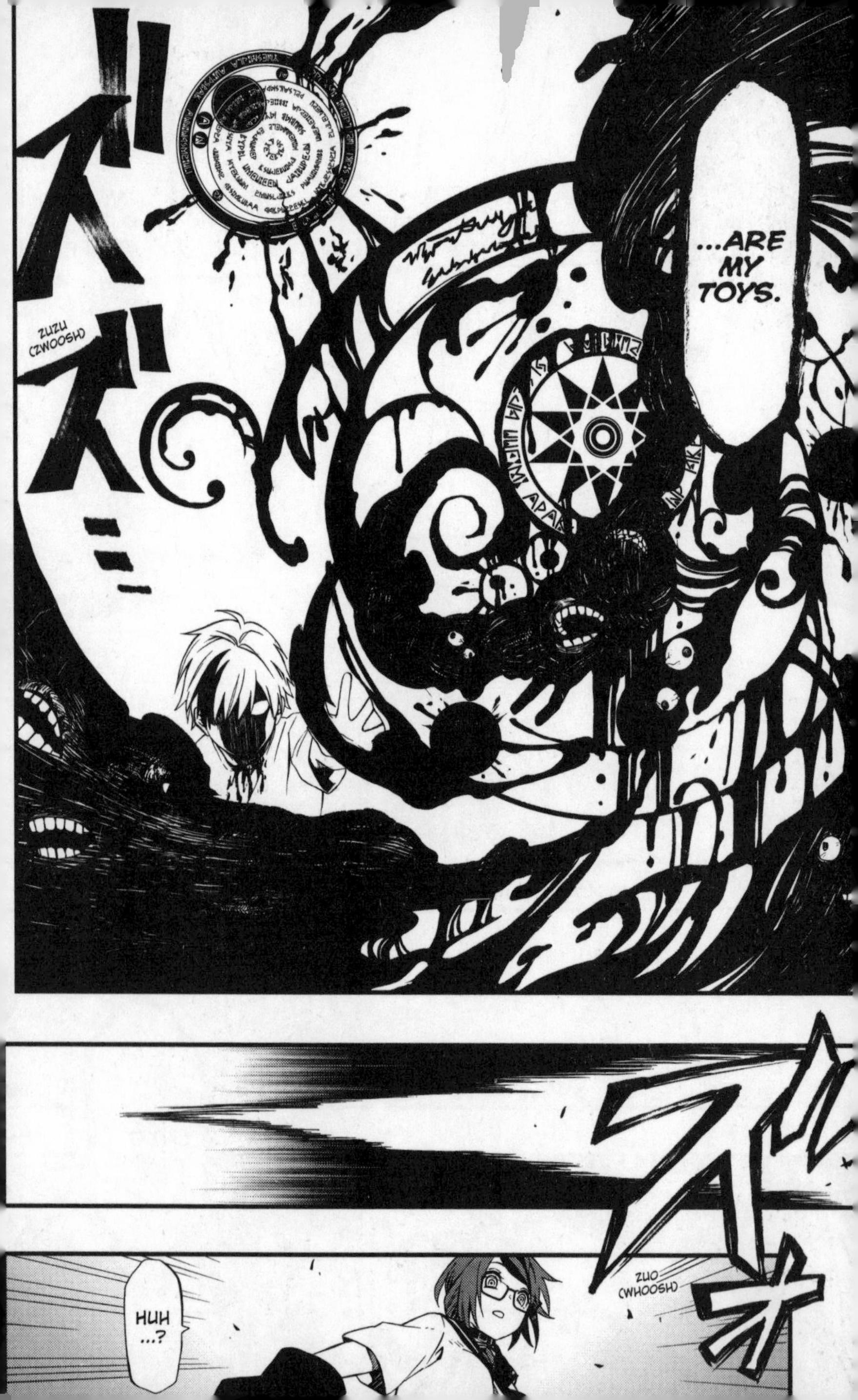
...ARE MY TOYS.
ZUZU (ZWOOSH)
ZUO (WHOOSH)
HUH ...?

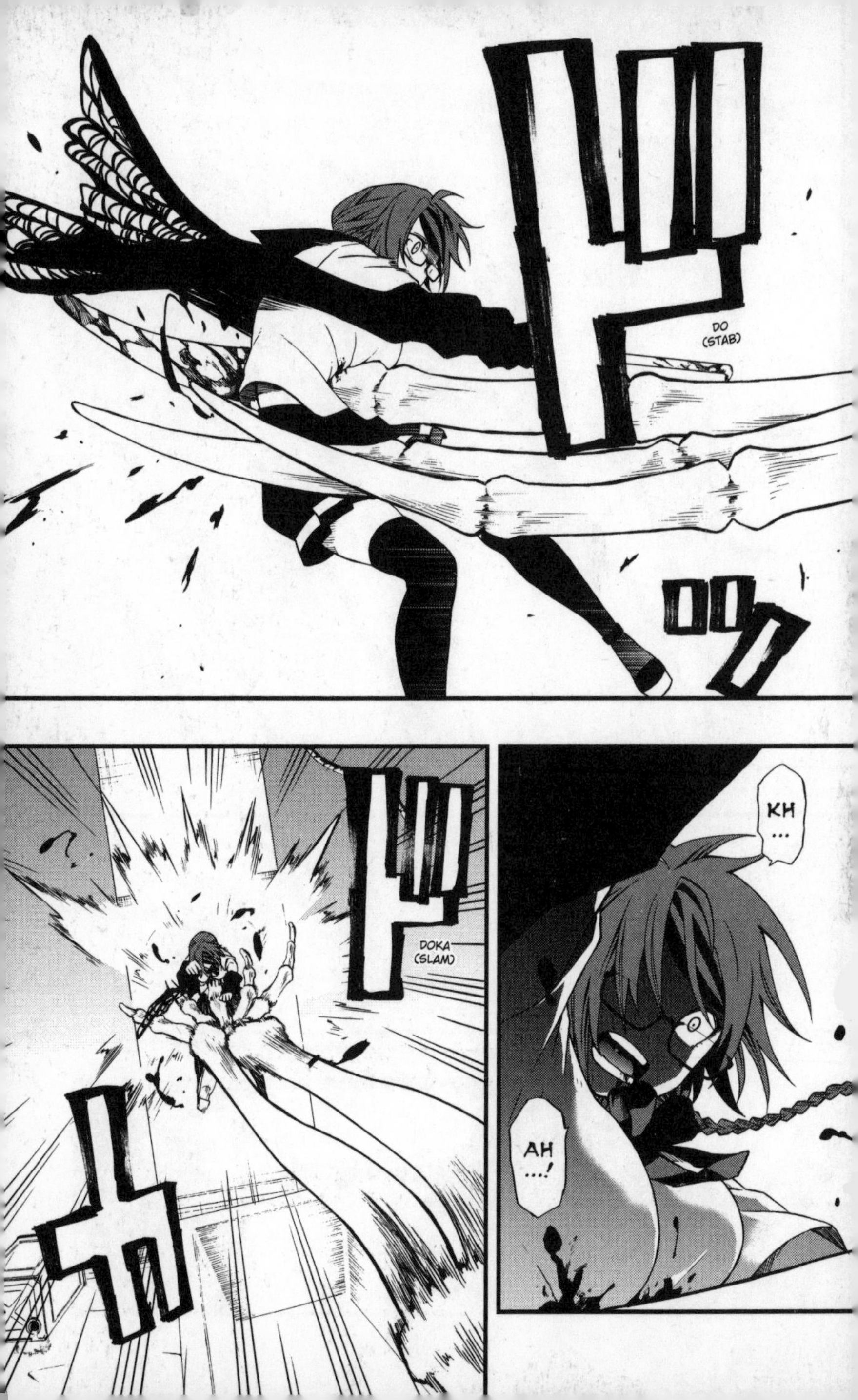
DO
(STAB)
KH ...
AH ...!
DOKA
(SLAM)

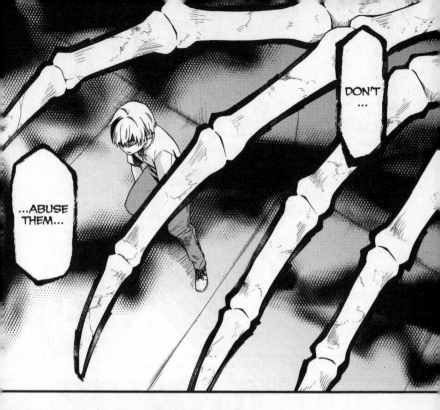

DON'T
...

...ABUSE
THEM...

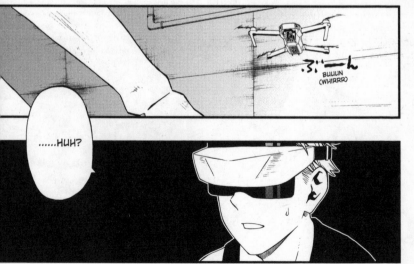

BUUUN
(WHIRRR)

......HUH?

48

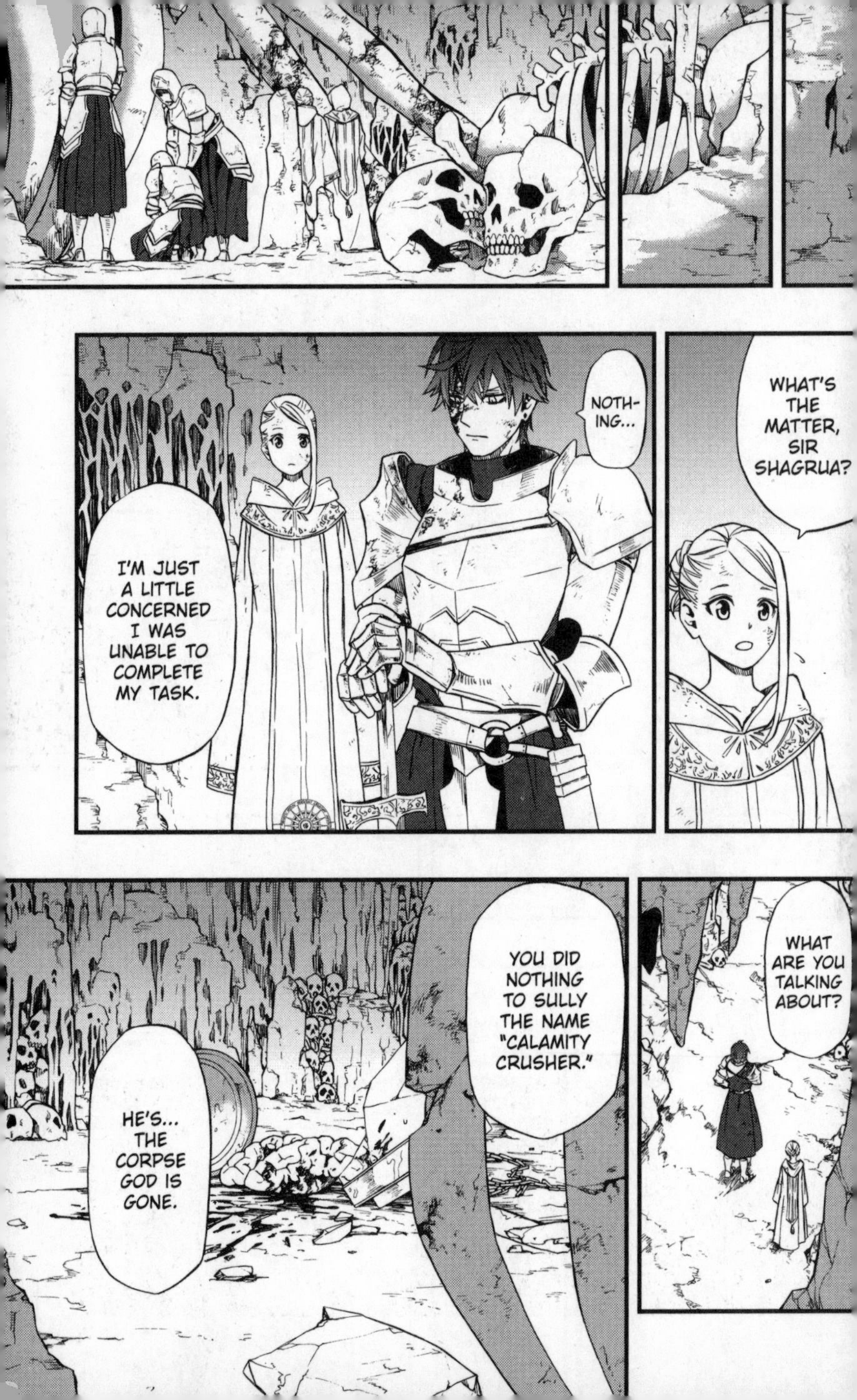
WHAT'S THE MATTER, SIR SHAGRUA?
NOTH-ING...
I'M JUST A LITTLE CONCERNED I WAS UNABLE TO COMPLETE MY TASK.
WHAT ARE YOU TALKING ABOUT?
YOU DID NOTHING TO SULLY THE NAME "CALAMITY CRUSHER."
HE'S... THE CORPSE GOD IS GONE.

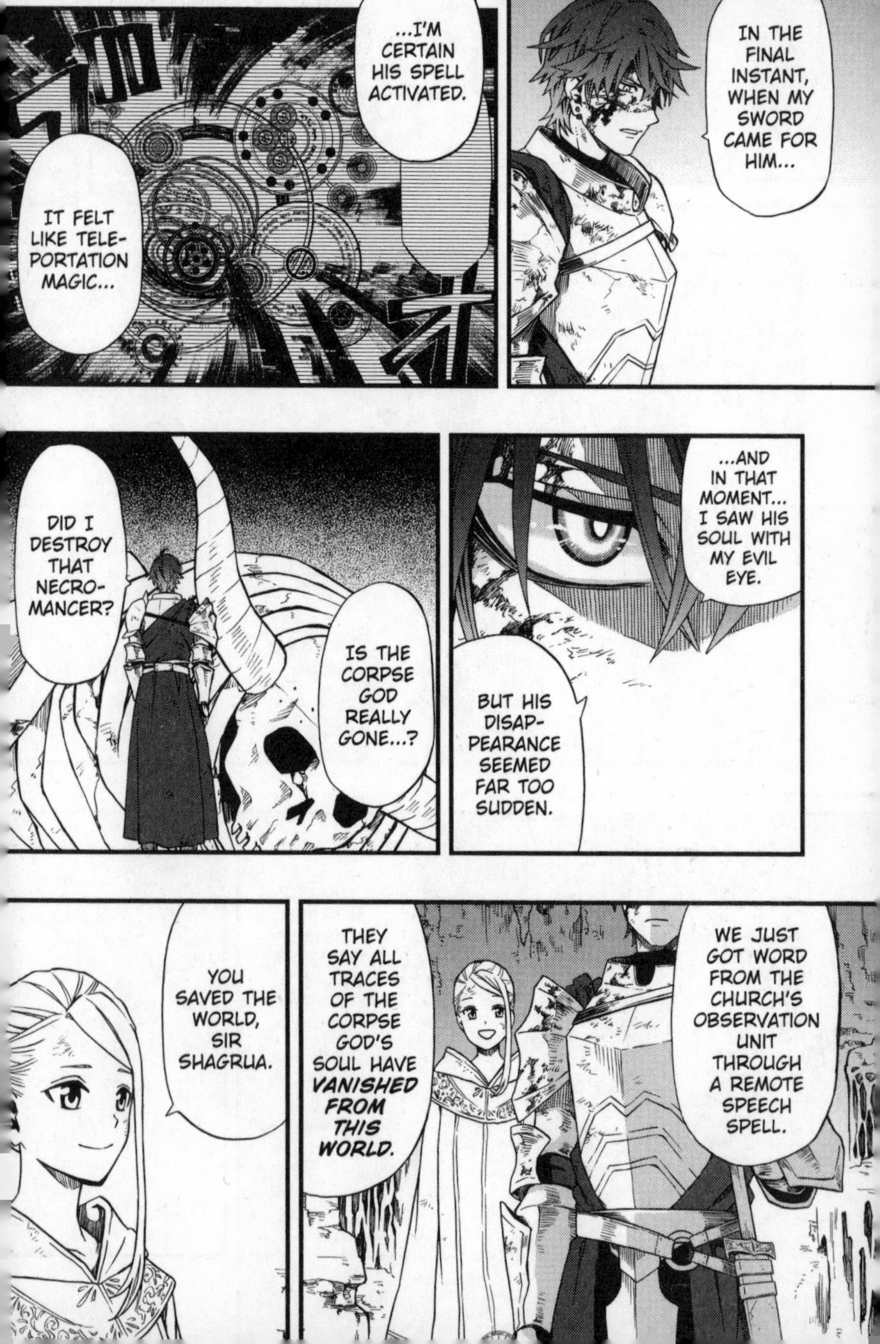
IN THE FINAL INSTANT, WHEN MY SWORD CAME FOR HIM...
...I'M CERTAIN HIS SPELL ACTIVATED.
IT FELT LIKE TELE-PORTATION MAGIC...
...AND IN THAT MOMENT... I SAW HIS SOUL WITH MY EVIL EYE.
BUT HIS DISAP-PEARANCE SEEMED FAR TOO SUDDEN.
DID I DESTROY THAT NECRO-MANCER?
IS THE CORPSE GOD REALLY GONE...?
WE JUST GOT WORD FROM THE CHURCH'S OBSERVATION UNIT THROUGH A REMOTE SPEECH SPELL.
THEY SAY ALL TRACES OF THE CORPSE GOD'S SOUL HAVE *VANISHED FROM THIS WORLD.*
YOU SAVED THE WORLD, SIR SHAGRUA.

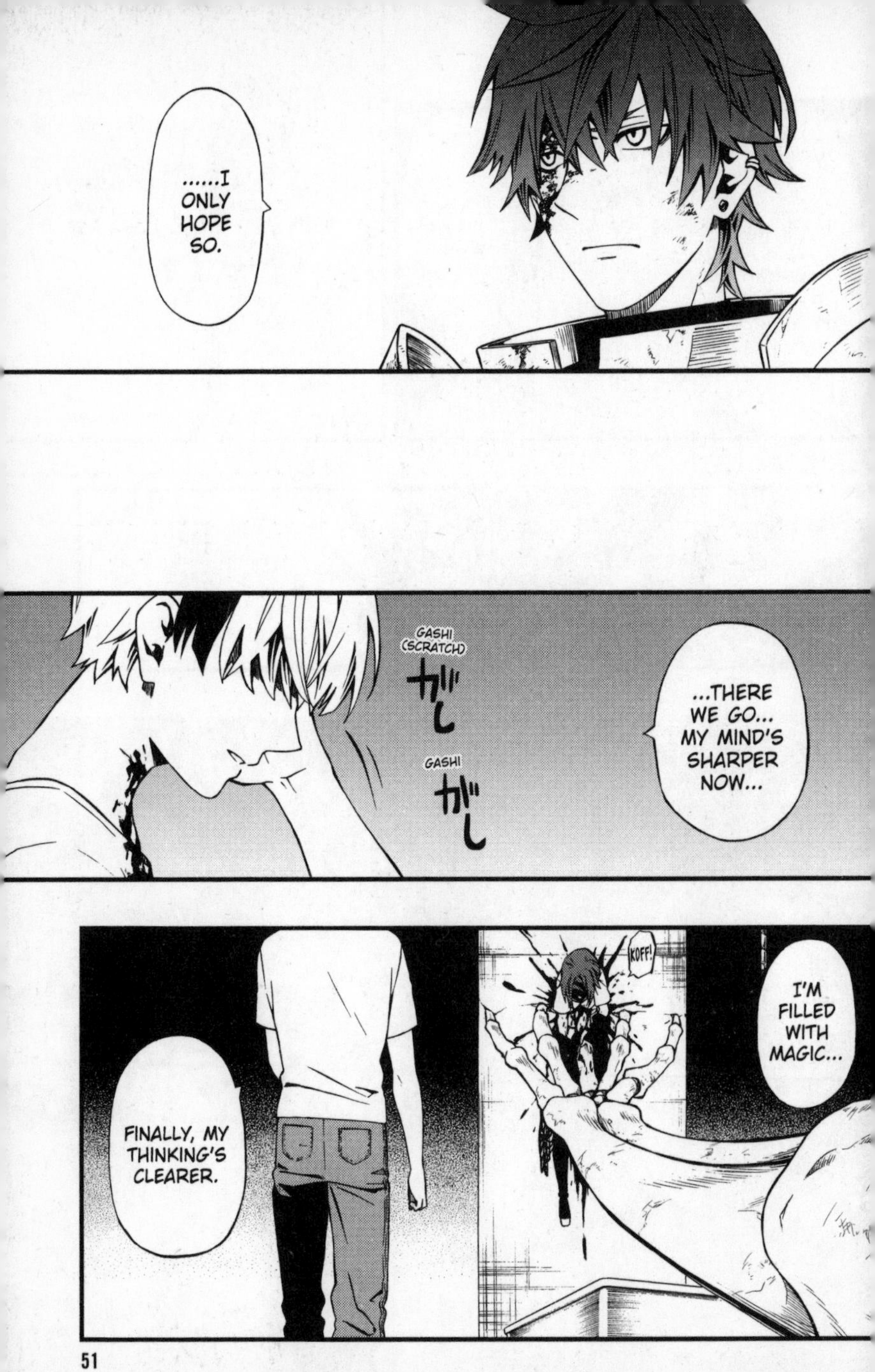
......I ONLY HOPE SO.
...THERE WE GO... MY MIND'S SHARPER NOW...
GASHI (SCRATCH)
がし
GASHI
がし
KOFF!
I'M FILLED WITH MAGIC...
FINALLY, MY THINKING'S CLEARER.

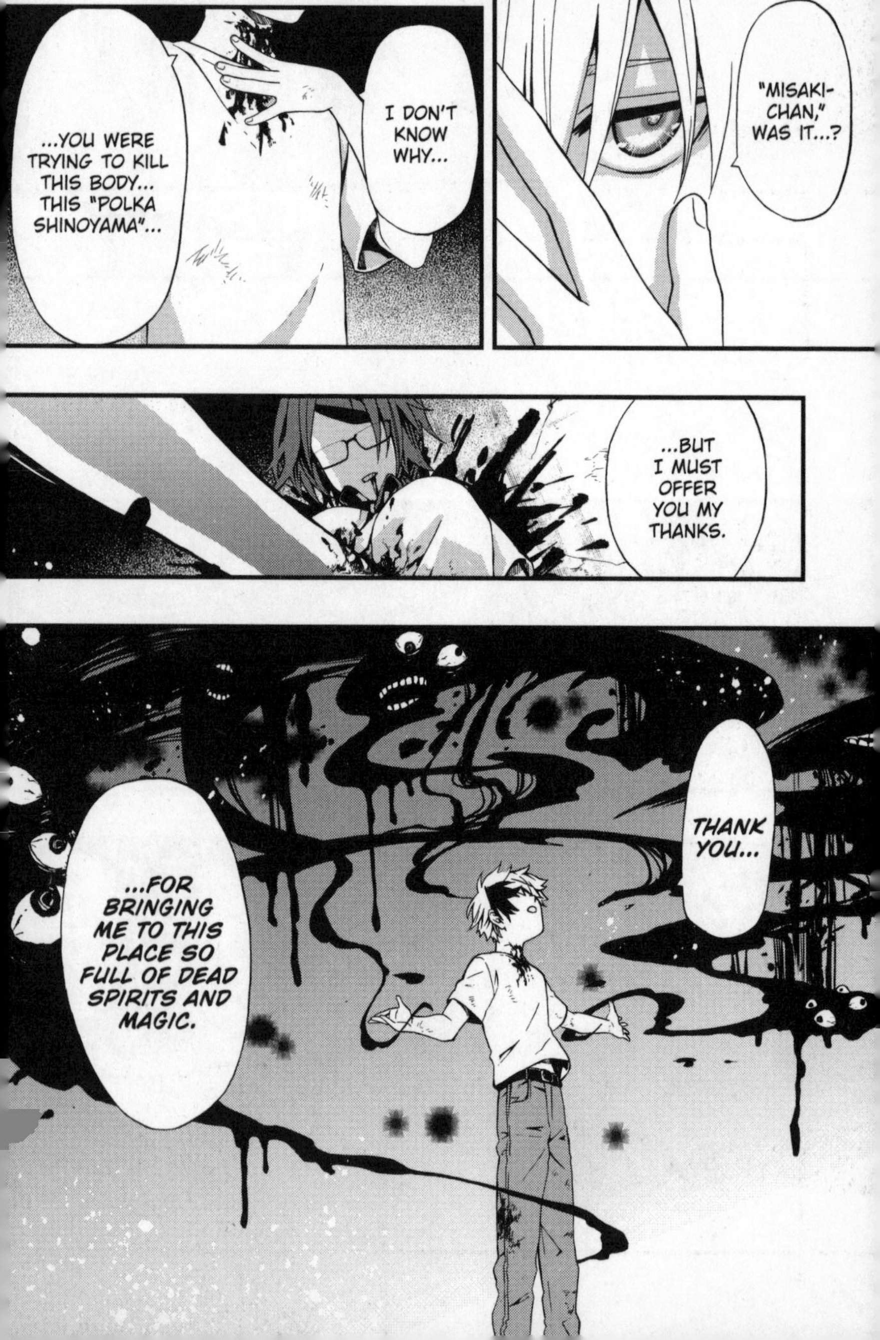
"MISAKI-CHAN," WAS IT...?
I DON'T KNOW WHY...
...YOU WERE TRYING TO KILL THIS BODY... THIS "POLKA SHINOYAMA"...
...BUT I MUST OFFER YOU MY THANKS.
THANK YOU...
...FOR BRINGING ME TO THIS PLACE SO FULL OF DEAD SPIRITS AND MAGIC.

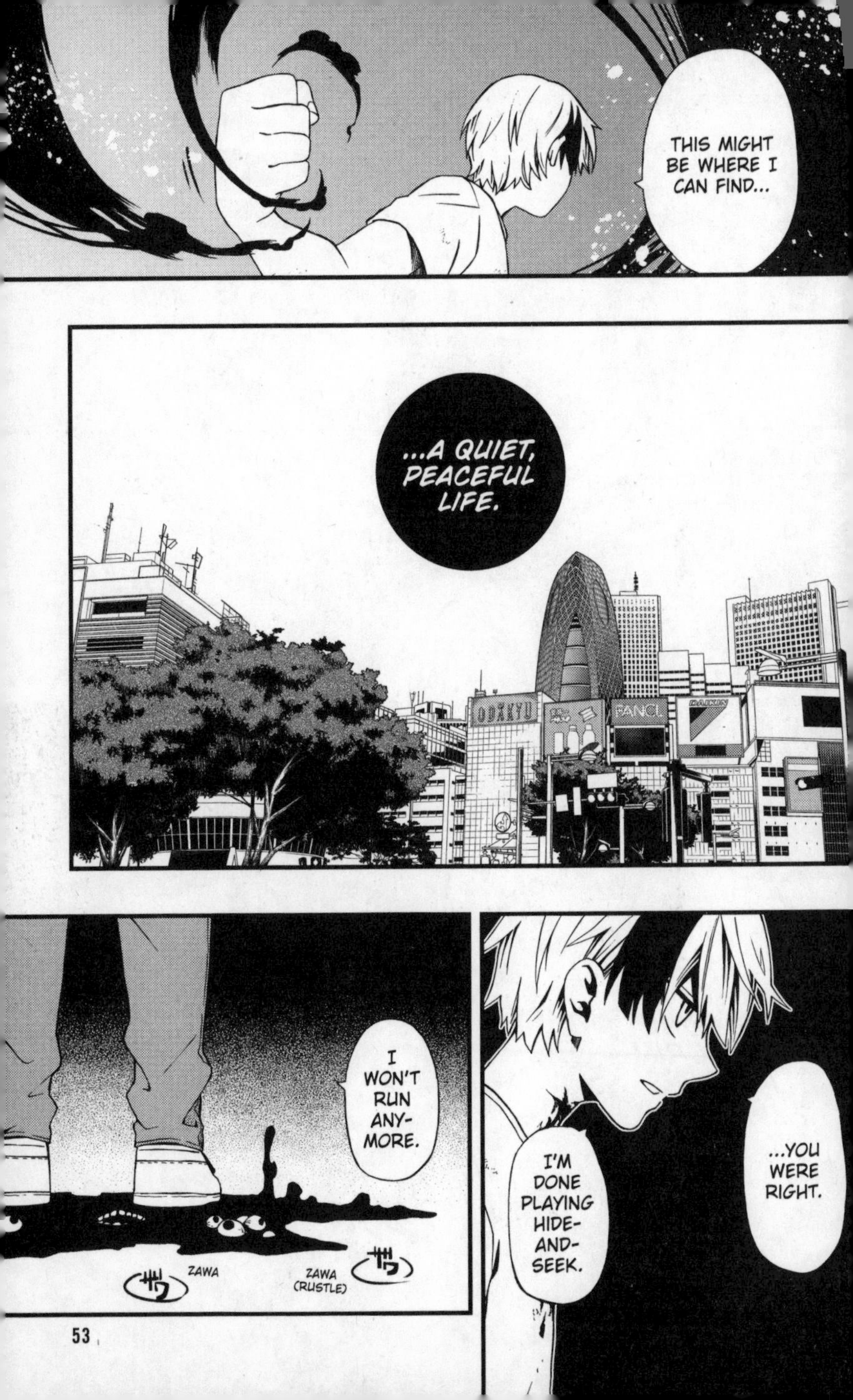

THIS MIGHT BE WHERE I CAN FIND...
...A QUIET, PEACEFUL LIFE.
ODAKYU
FANCL
DAIKIN
...YOU WERE RIGHT.
I'M DONE PLAYING HIDE-AND-SEEK.
I WON'T RUN ANY-MORE.
ZAWA (RUSTLE)
ZAWA

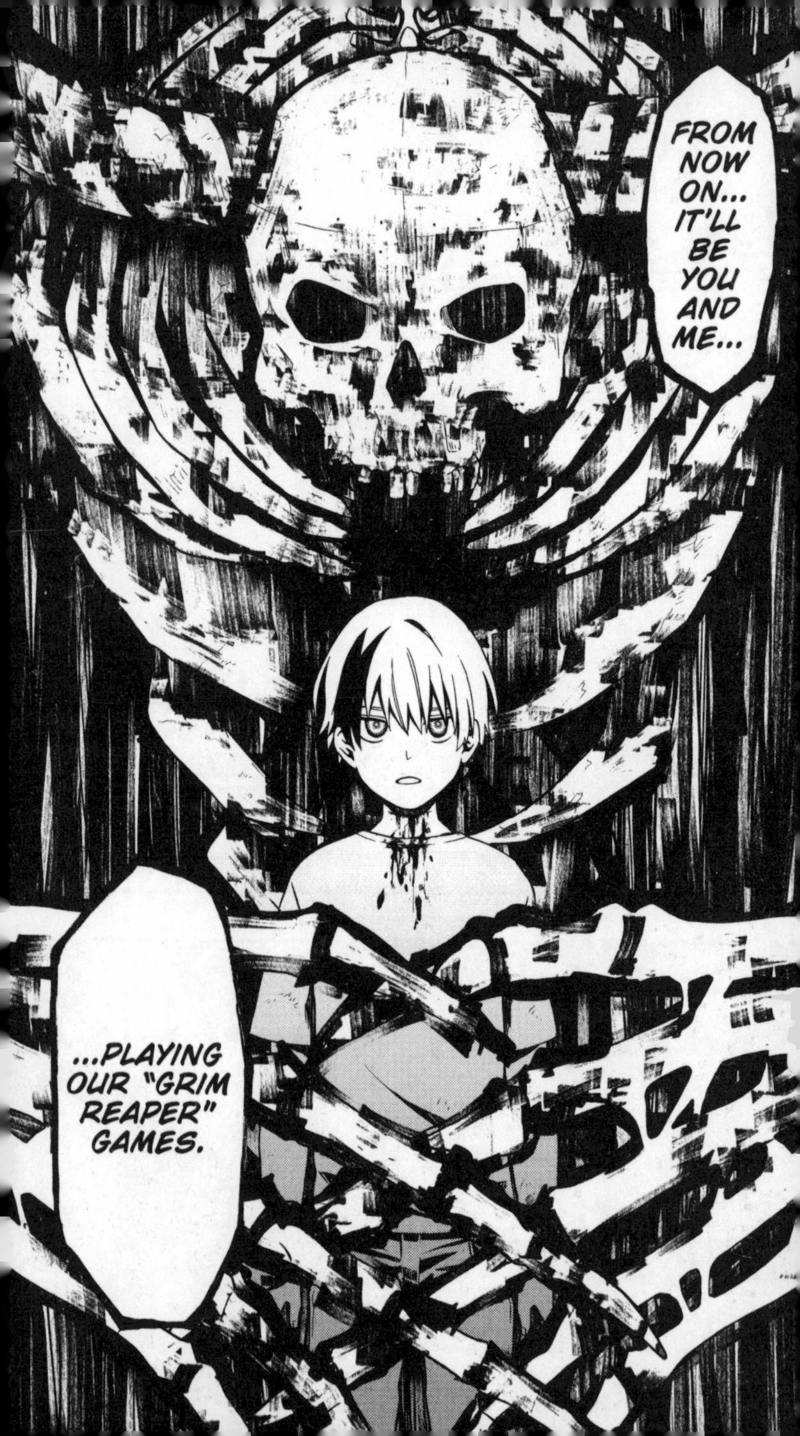
FROM NOW ON... IT'LL BE YOU AND ME...
...PLAYING OUR "GRIM REAPER" GAMES.

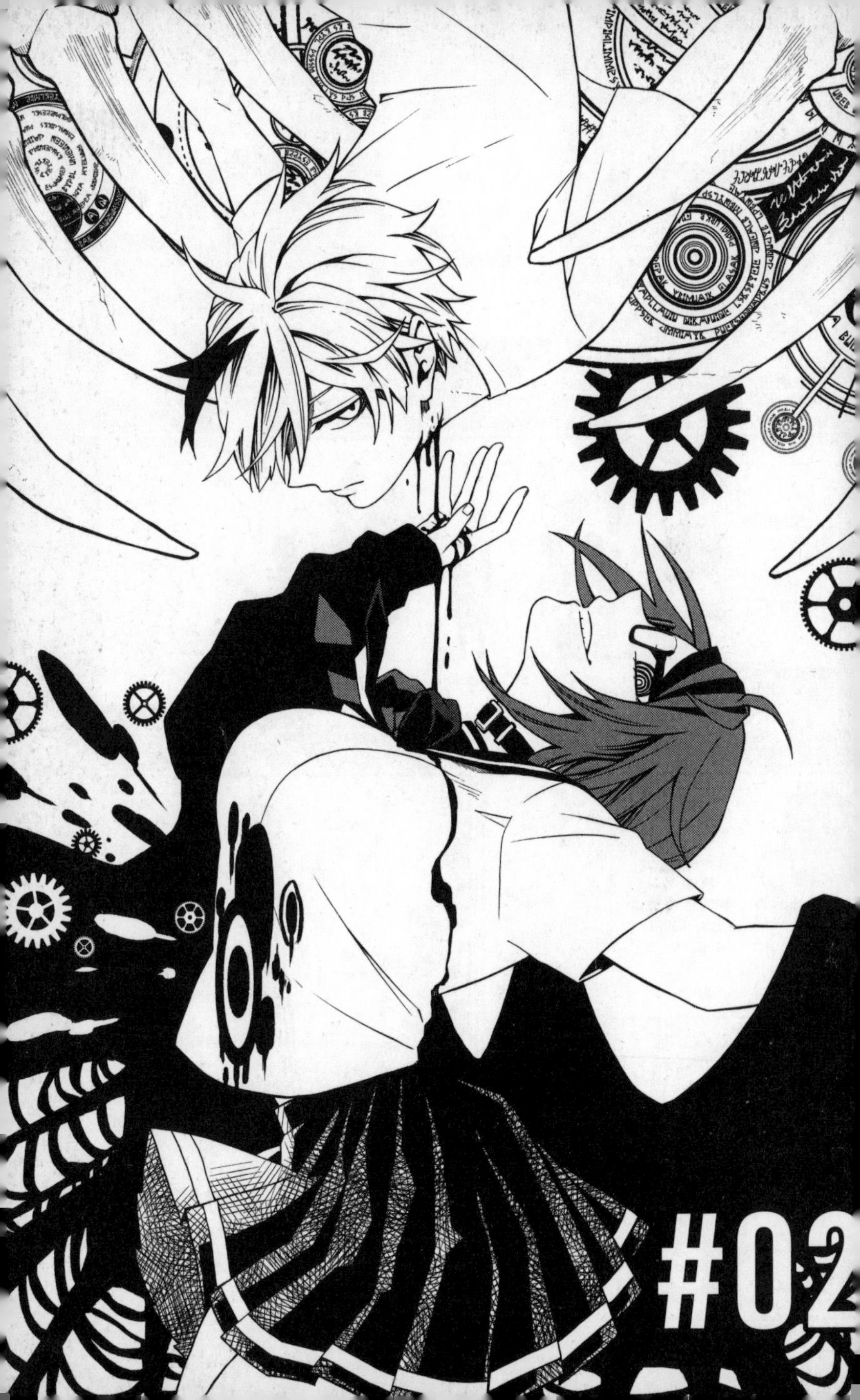
#02

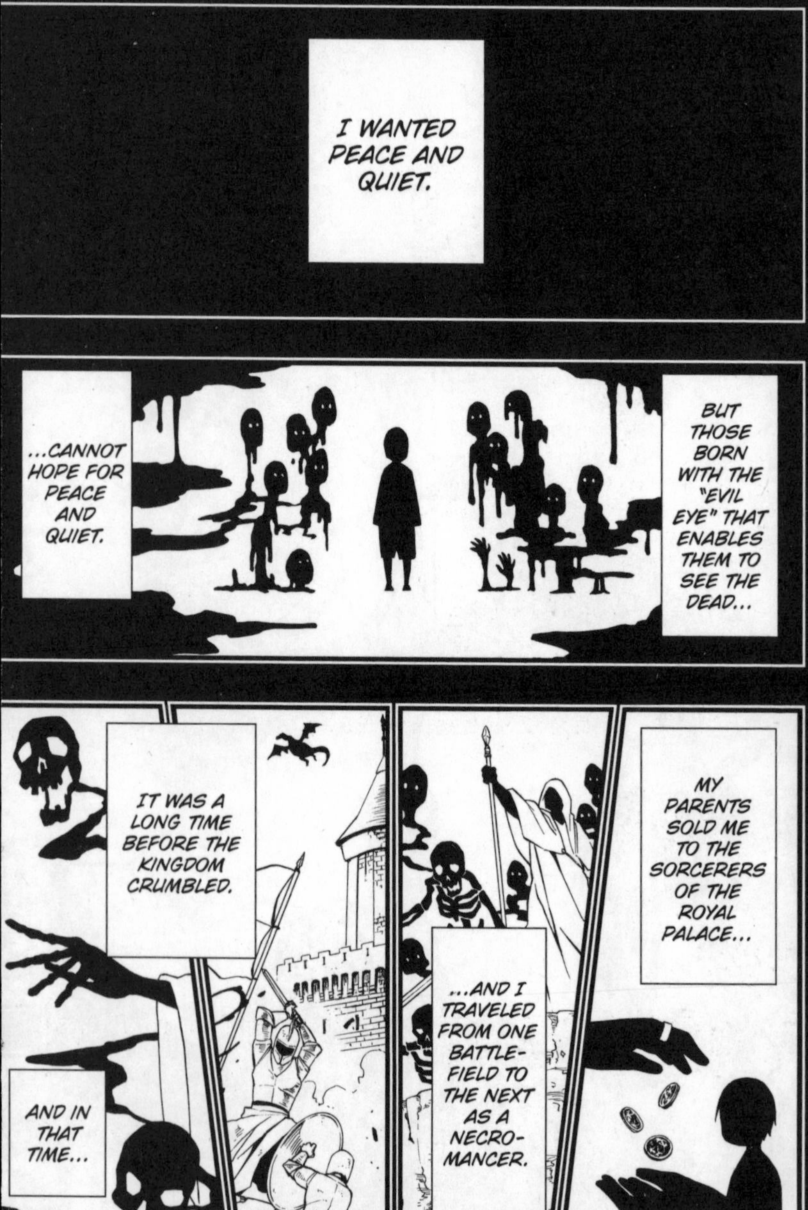
I WANTED PEACE AND QUIET.
BUT THOSE BORN WITH THE "EVIL EYE" THAT ENABLES THEM TO SEE THE DEAD...
...CANNOT HOPE FOR PEACE AND QUIET.
MY PARENTS SOLD ME TO THE SORCERERS OF THE ROYAL PALACE...
...AND I TRAVELED FROM ONE BATTLE-FIELD TO THE NEXT AS A NECRO-MANCER.
IT WAS A LONG TIME BEFORE THE KINGDOM CRUMBLED.
AND IN THAT TIME...

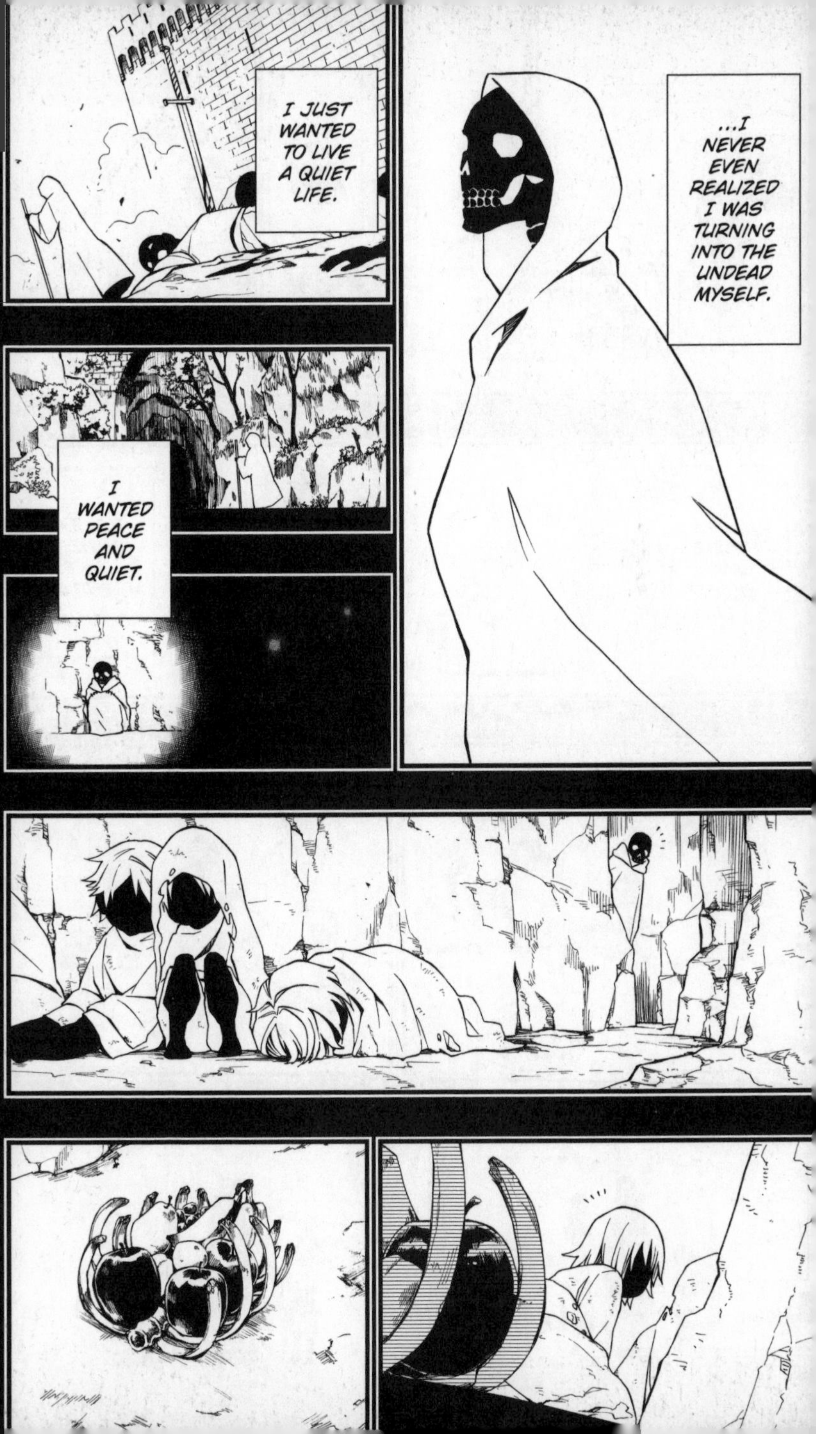
...I NEVER EVEN REALIZED I WAS TURNING INTO THE UNDEAD MYSELF.
I JUST WANTED TO LIVE A QUIET LIFE.
I WANTED PEACE AND QUIET.

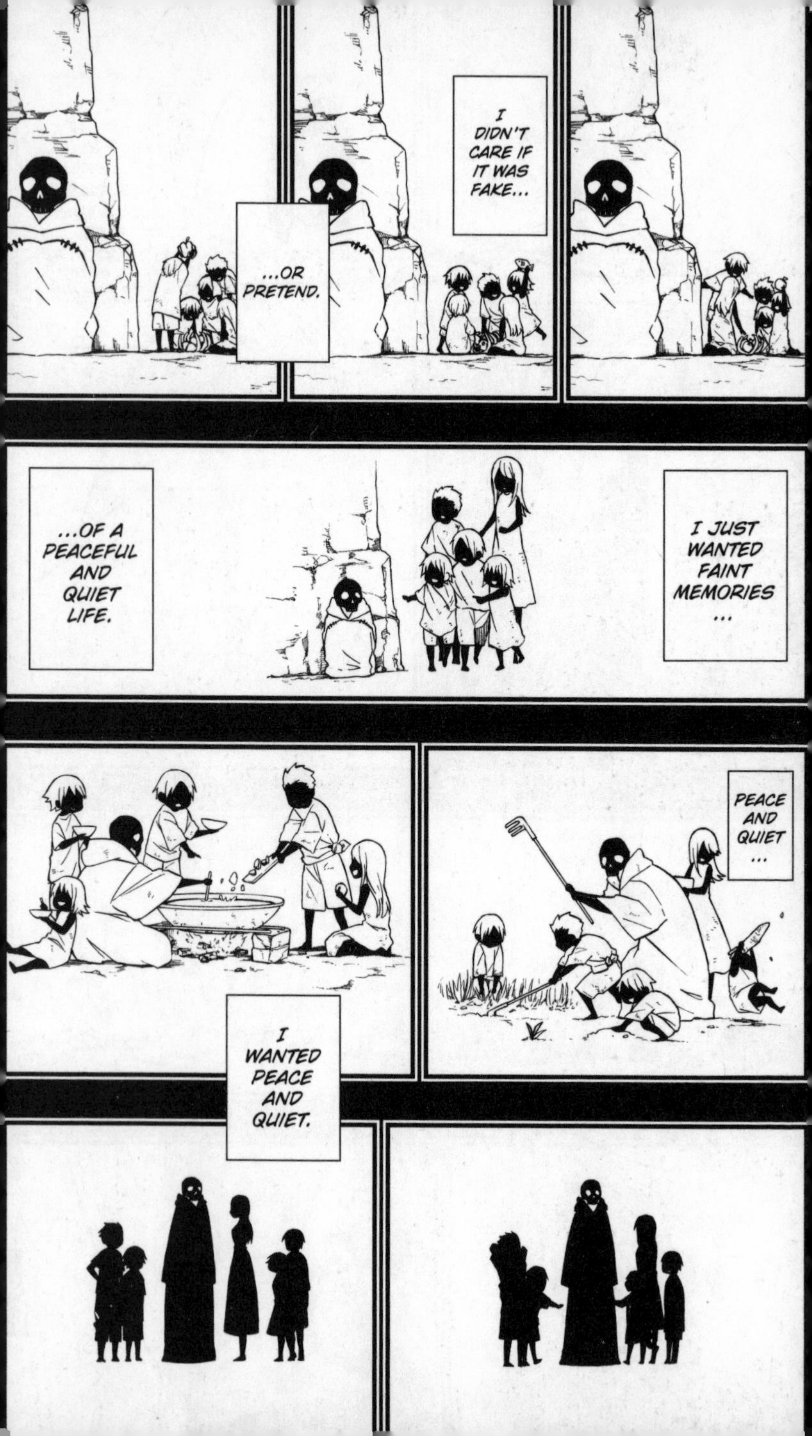
I DIDN'T CARE IF IT WAS FAKE...
...OR PRETEND.
I JUST WANTED FAINT MEMORIES...
...OF A PEACEFUL AND QUIET LIFE.
PEACE AND QUIET...
I WANTED PEACE AND QUIET.

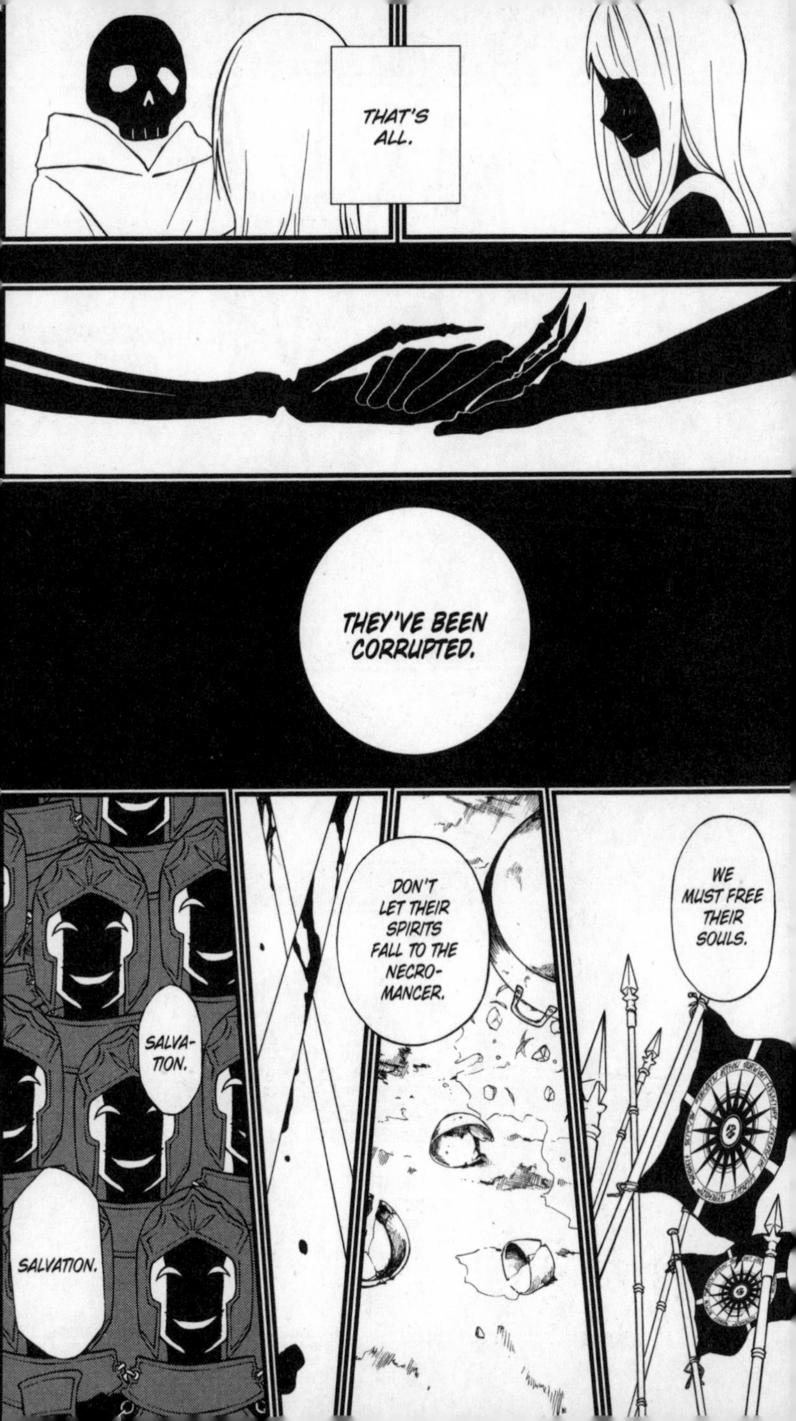
THAT'S ALL.
THEY'VE BEEN CORRUPTED.
WE MUST FREE THEIR SOULS.
DON'T LET THEIR SPIRITS FALL TO THE NECRO-MANCER.
SALVA-TION.
SALVATION.

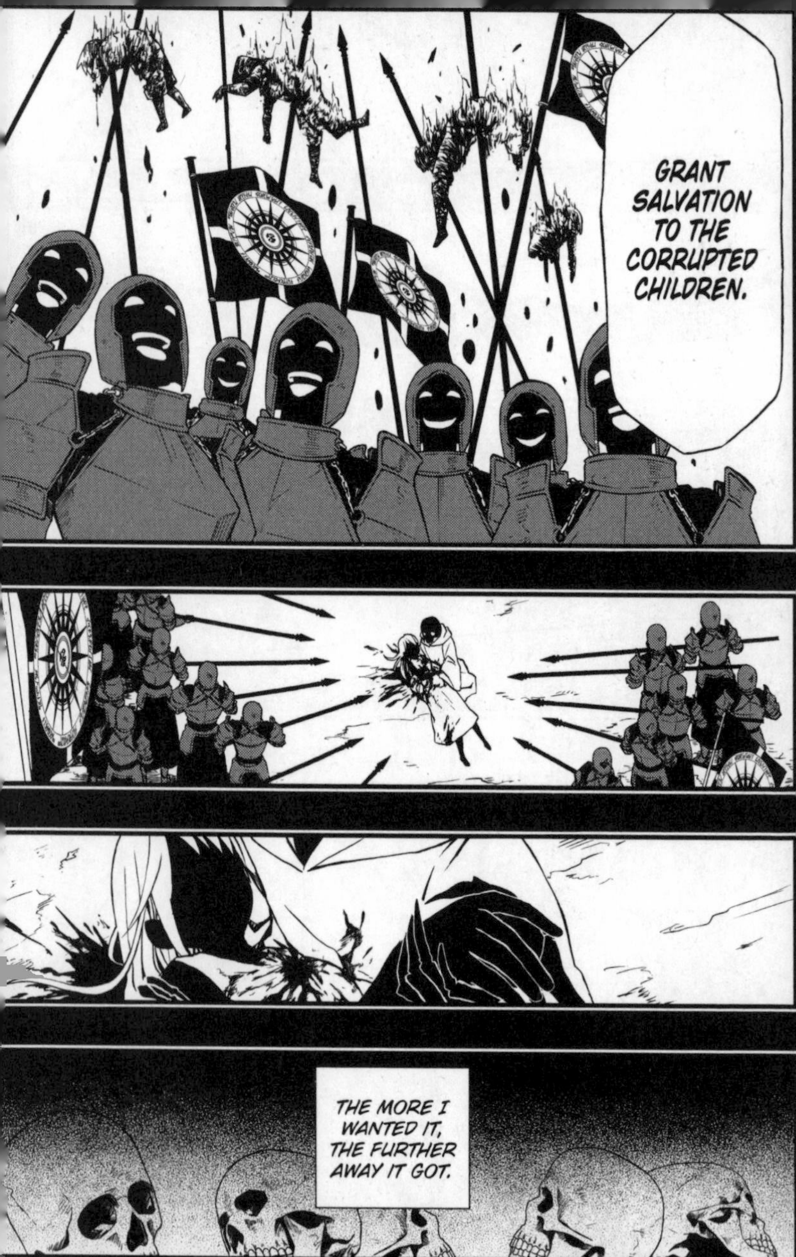
GRANT SALVATION TO THE CORRUPTED CHILDREN.
THE MORE I WANTED IT, THE FURTHER AWAY IT GOT.

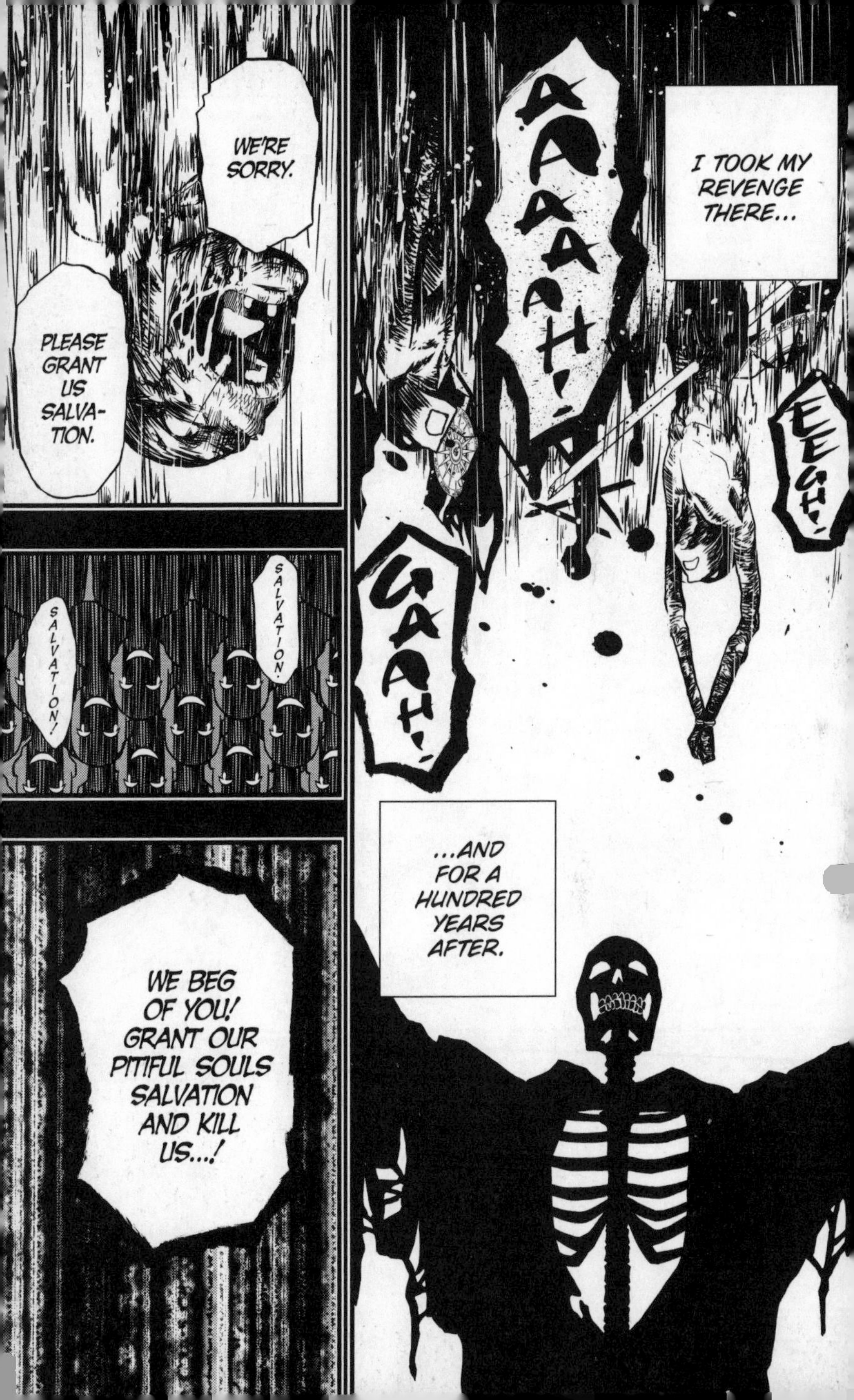
I TOOK MY REVENGE THERE...
AAAAAH!
EEGH!
UAAAH!
...AND FOR A HUNDRED YEARS AFTER.
WE'RE SORRY.
PLEASE GRANT US SALVATION.
SALVATION.
SALVATION!
WE BEG OF YOU! GRANT OUR PITIFUL SOULS SALVATION AND KILL US...!

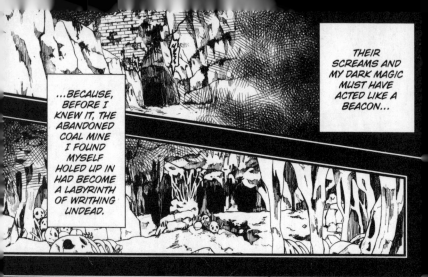

THEIR SCREAMS AND MY DARK MAGIC MUST HAVE ACTED LIKE A BEACON...
...BECAUSE, BEFORE I KNEW IT, THE ABANDONED COAL MINE I FOUND MYSELF HOLED UP IN HAD BECOME A LABYRINTH OF WRITHING UNDEAD.
EVEN SO, I STILL CRAVED PEACE AND QUIET.
AND SO I WAITED DECADES... CENTURIES...
...FOR SOMEONE WHO COULD KILL ME TO ARRIVE...
...AS I WAS NO LONGER CAPABLE OF SUICIDE.
AND THEN...
...I SUCCEEDED IN THE SECRET ART OF REINCARNATION.

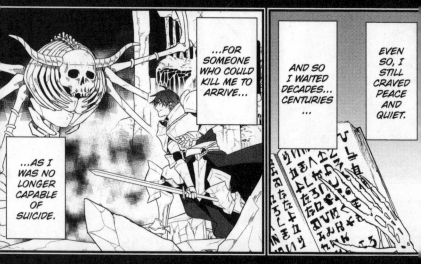

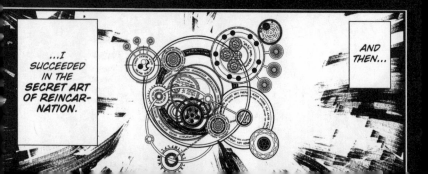

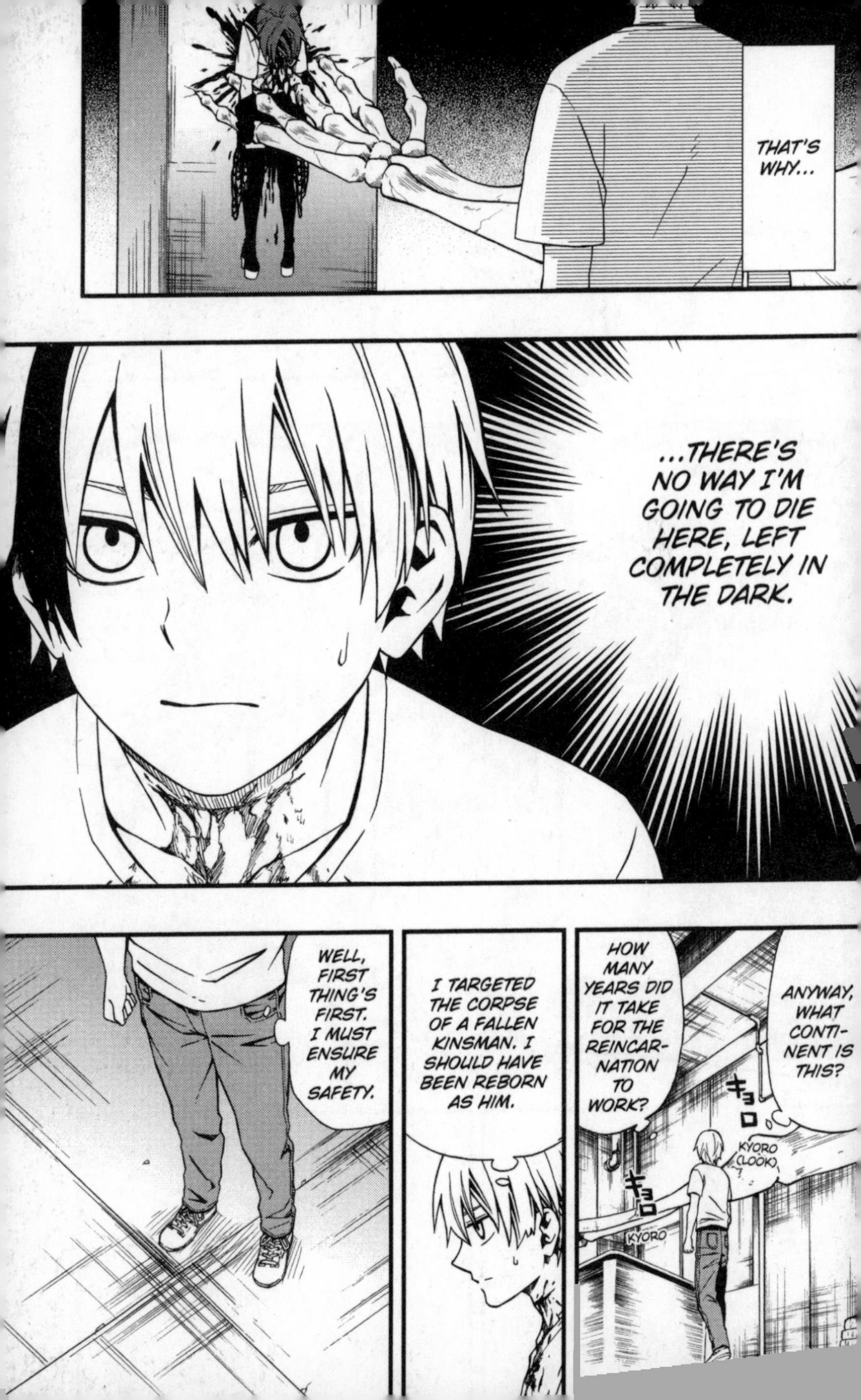
THAT'S WHY...
...THERE'S NO WAY I'M GOING TO DIE HERE, LEFT COMPLETELY IN THE DARK.
ANYWAY, WHAT CONTI-NENT IS THIS?
キョロ
KYORO (LOOK)
キョロ
KYORO
HOW MANY YEARS DID IT TAKE FOR THE REINCAR-NATION TO WORK?
I TARGETED THE CORPSE OF A FALLEN KINSMAN. I SHOULD HAVE BEEN REBORN AS HIM.
WELL, FIRST THING'S FIRST. I MUST ENSURE MY SAFETY.

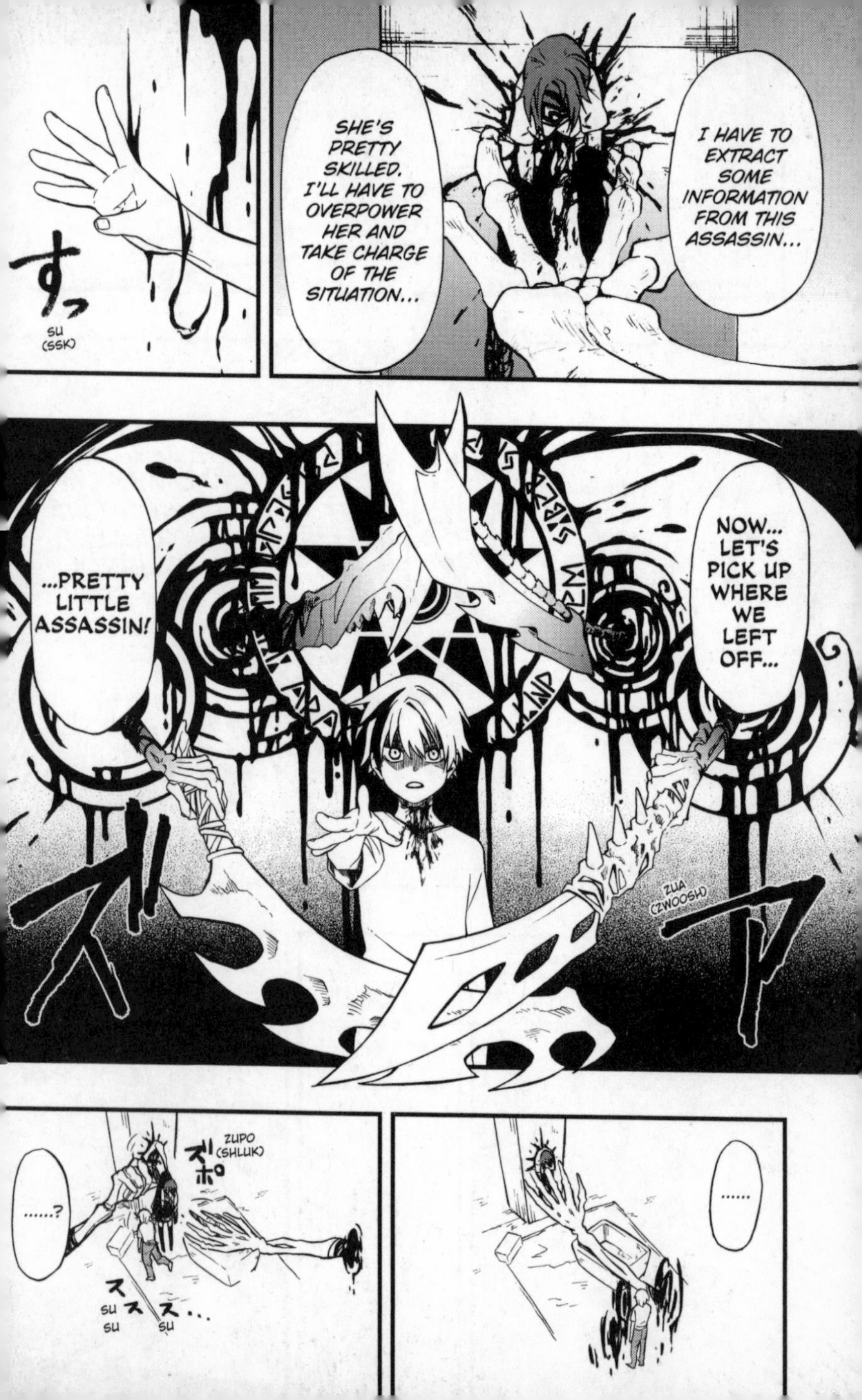
I HAVE TO EXTRACT SOME INFORMATION FROM THIS ASSASSIN...
SHE'S PRETTY SKILLED. I'LL HAVE TO OVERPOWER HER AND TAKE CHARGE OF THE SITUATION...
SU (SSK)
NOW... LET'S PICK UP WHERE WE LEFT OFF...
...PRETTY LITTLE ASSASSIN!
ZUA (ZWOOSH)
......
ZUPO (SHLUK)
......?
SU SU SU...

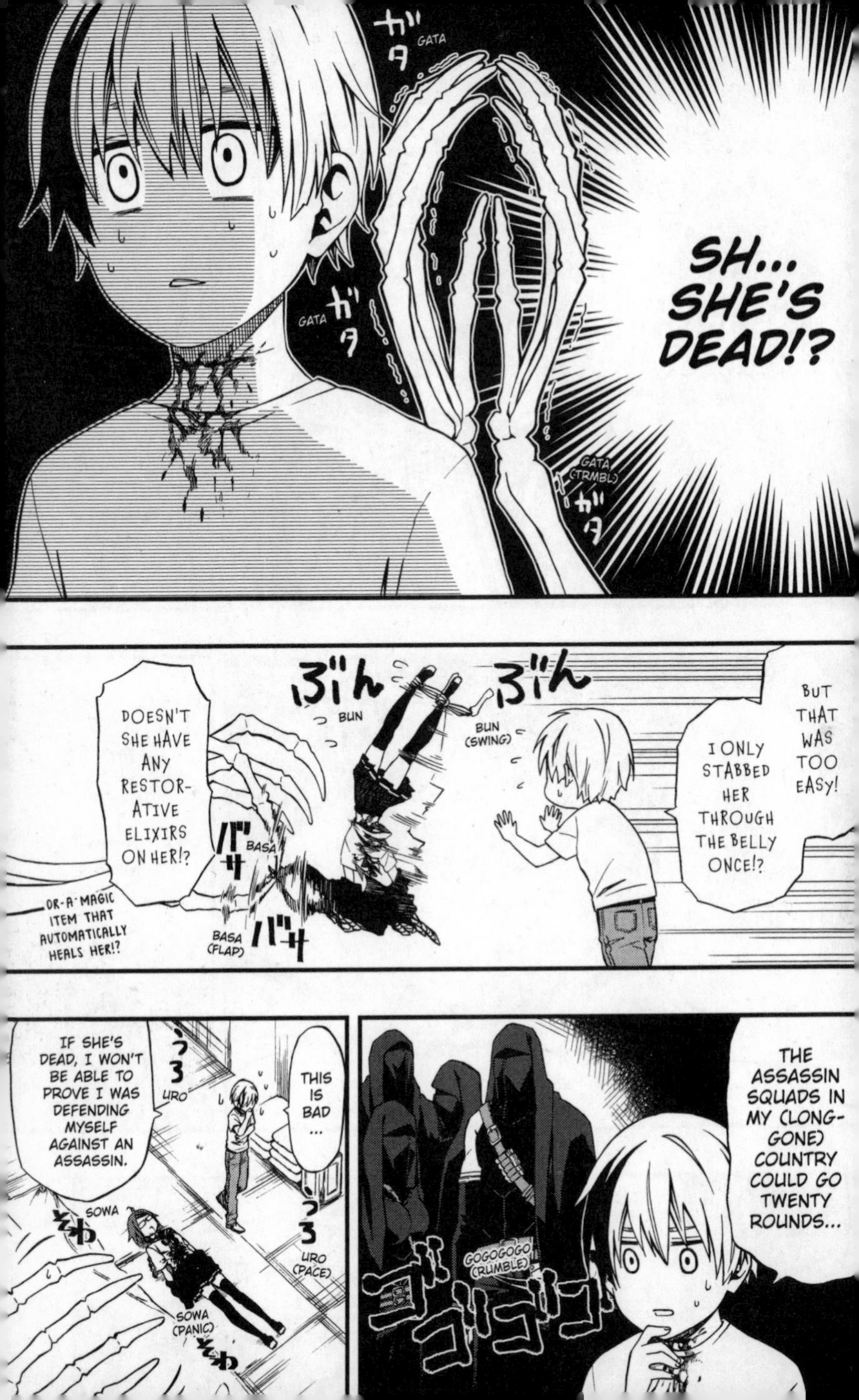
ガタ
GATA
ガタ
GATA
SH... SHE'S DEAD!?
GATA (TRMBL)
ガタ
BUT THAT WAS TOO EASY!
I ONLY STABBED HER THROUGH THE BELLY ONCE!?
ぶん
BUN (SWING)
ぶん
BUN
DOESN'T SHE HAVE ANY RESTOR-ATIVE ELIXIRS ON HER!?
OR A MAGIC ITEM THAT AUTOMATICALLY HEALS HER!?
バサ
BASA
バサ
BASA (FLAP)
THE ASSASSIN SQUADS IN MY (LONG-GONE) COUNTRY COULD GO TWENTY ROUNDS...
GOGOGOGO (RUMBLE)
THIS IS BAD...
うろ
URO
うろ
URO (PACE)
IF SHE'S DEAD, I WON'T BE ABLE TO PROVE I WAS DEFENDING MYSELF AGAINST AN ASSASSIN.
そわ
SOWA
SOWA (PANIC)
そわ

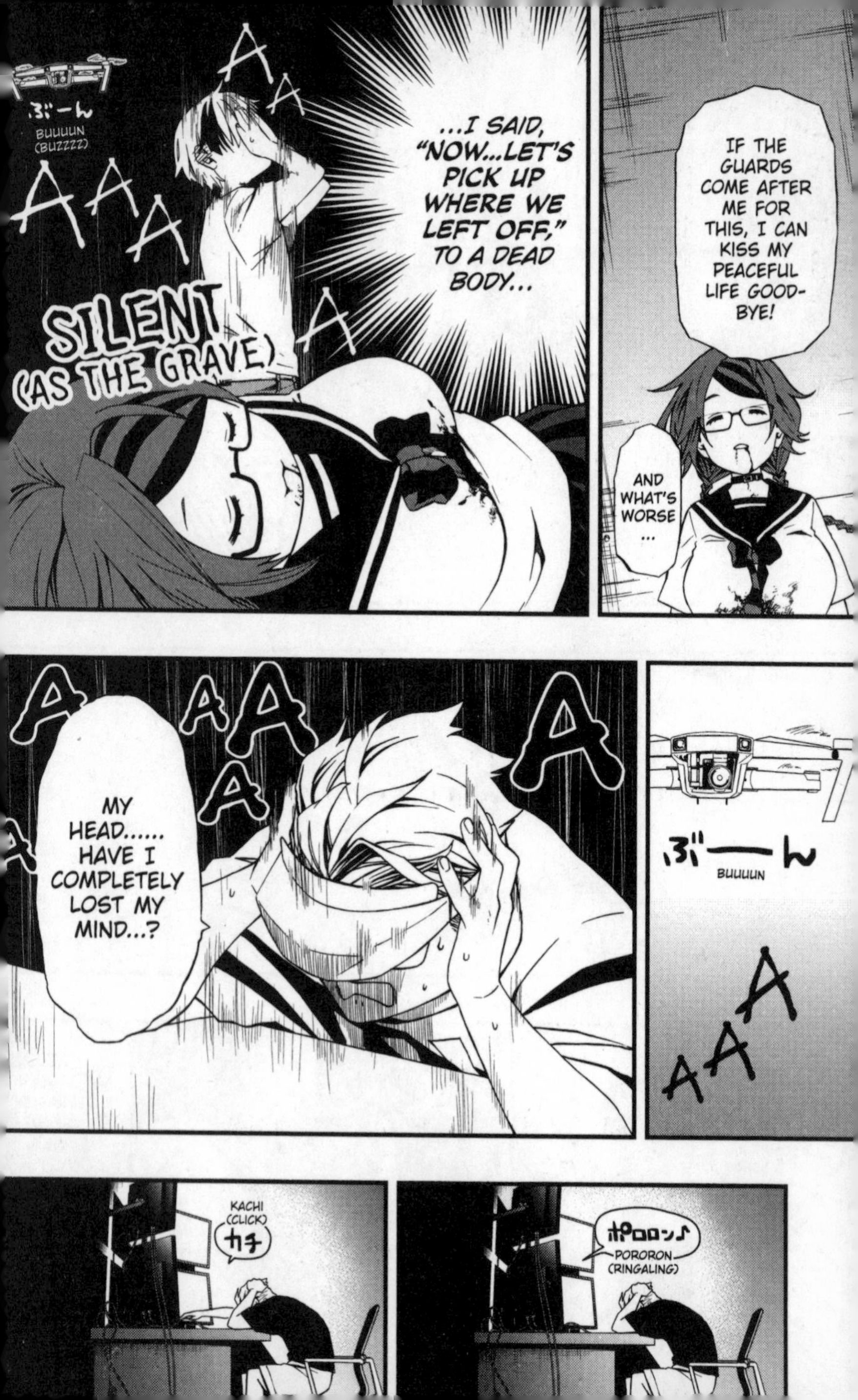
IF THE GUARDS COME AFTER ME FOR THIS, I CAN KISS MY PEACEFUL LIFE GOOD-BYE!
AND WHAT'S WORSE ...
...I SAID, "NOW...LET'S PICK UP WHERE WE LEFT OFF," TO A DEAD BODY...
ぶーん
BUUUUN (BUZZZZ)
AAAAAAAA
SILENT (AS THE GRAVE)
ぶーん
BUUUUN
AAA
AAAAAA
MY HEAD...... HAVE I COMPLETELY LOST MY MIND...?
ポロロン♪
PORORON (RINGALING)
カチ
KACHI (CLICK)

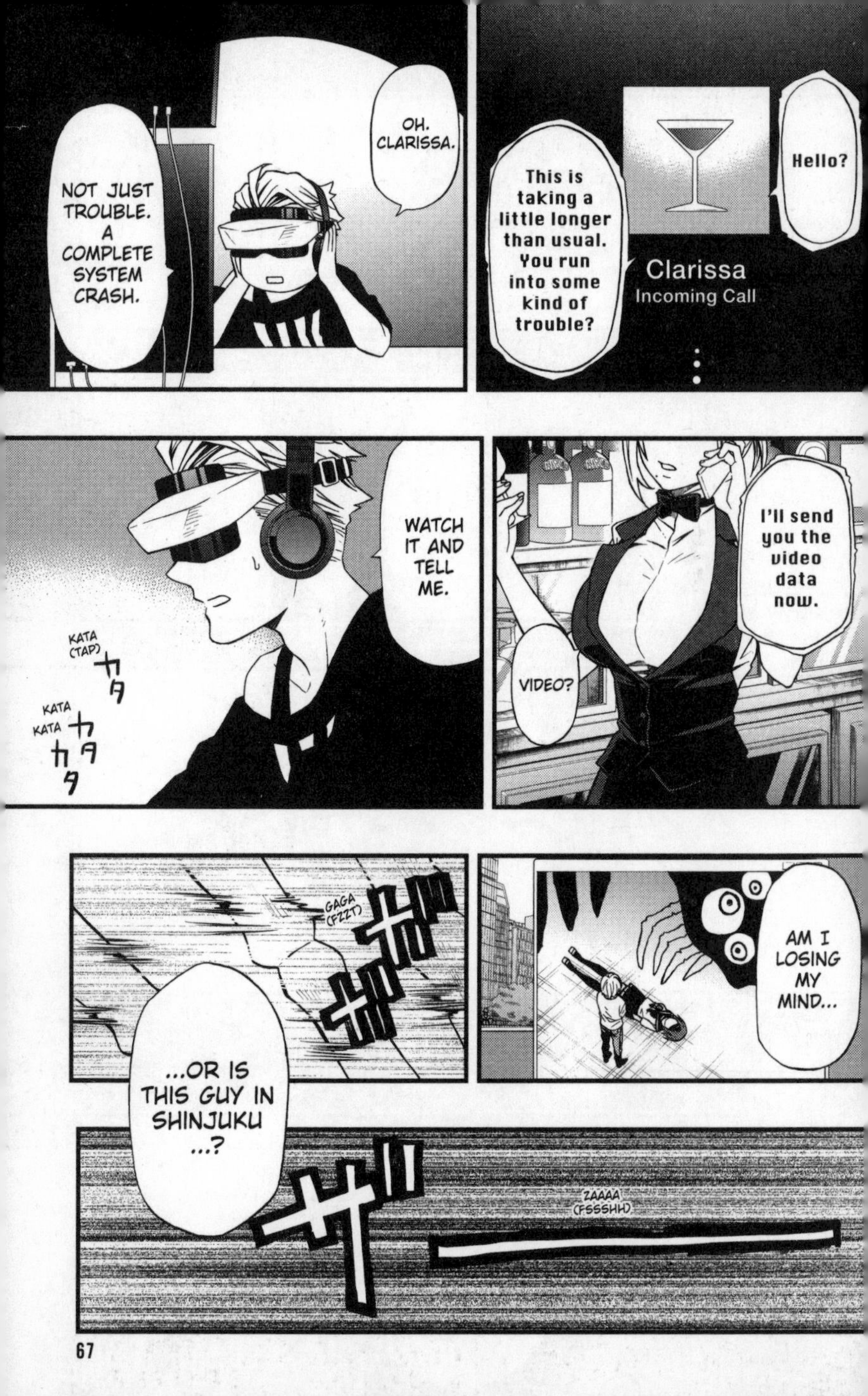
Clarissa
Incoming Call
Hello?
This is taking a little longer than usual. You run into some kind of trouble?
OH. CLARISSA.
NOT JUST TROUBLE. A COMPLETE SYSTEM CRASH.
I'll send you the video data now.
VIDEO?
WATCH IT AND TELL ME.
KATA (TAP)
KATA KATA
AM I LOSING MY MIND...
GAGA (FZZT)
...OR IS THIS GUY IN SHINJUKU ...?
ZAAAA (FSSSHH)

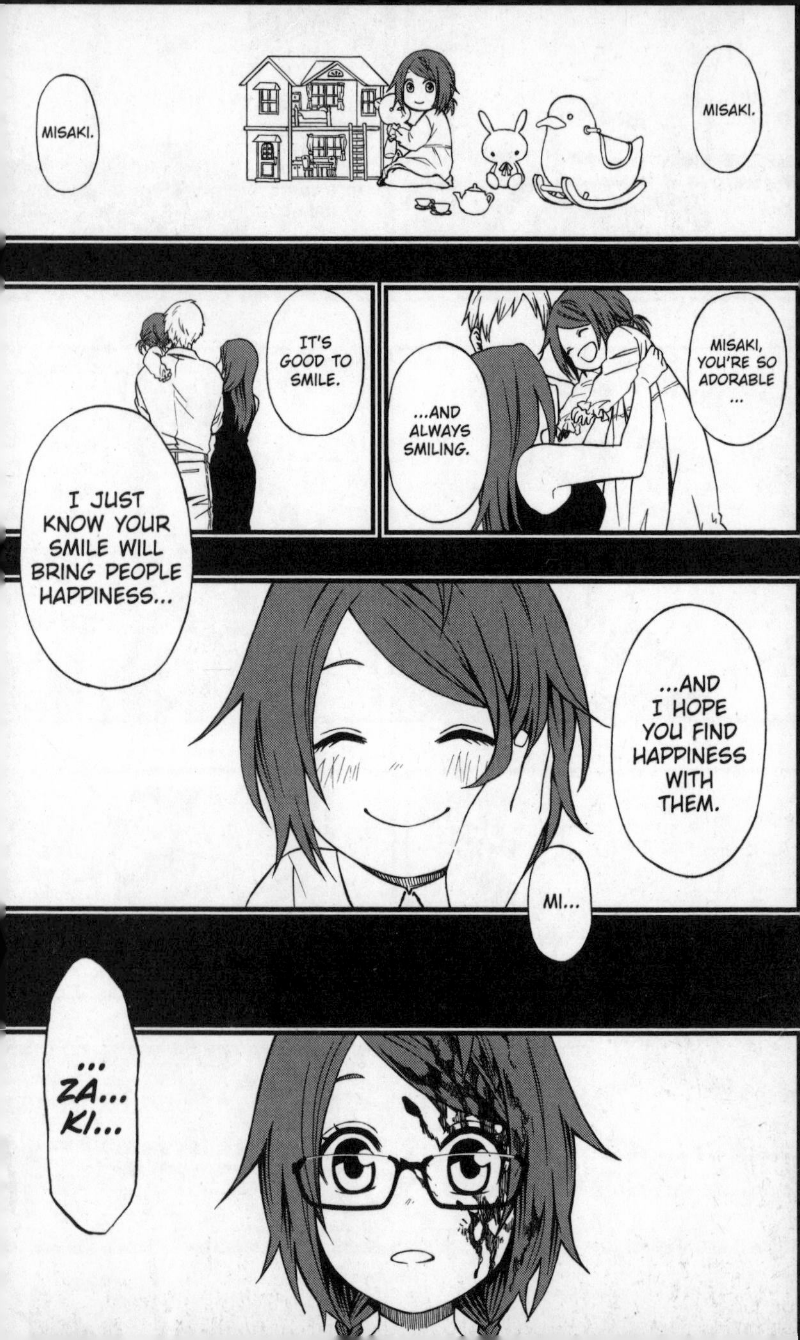
MISAKI.
MISAKI.
MISAKI, YOU'RE SO ADORABLE ...
...AND ALWAYS SMILING.
IT'S GOOD TO SMILE.
I JUST KNOW YOUR SMILE WILL BRING PEOPLE HAPPINESS...
...AND I HOPE YOU FIND HAPPINESS WITH THEM.
MI...
... ZÄ... KI...

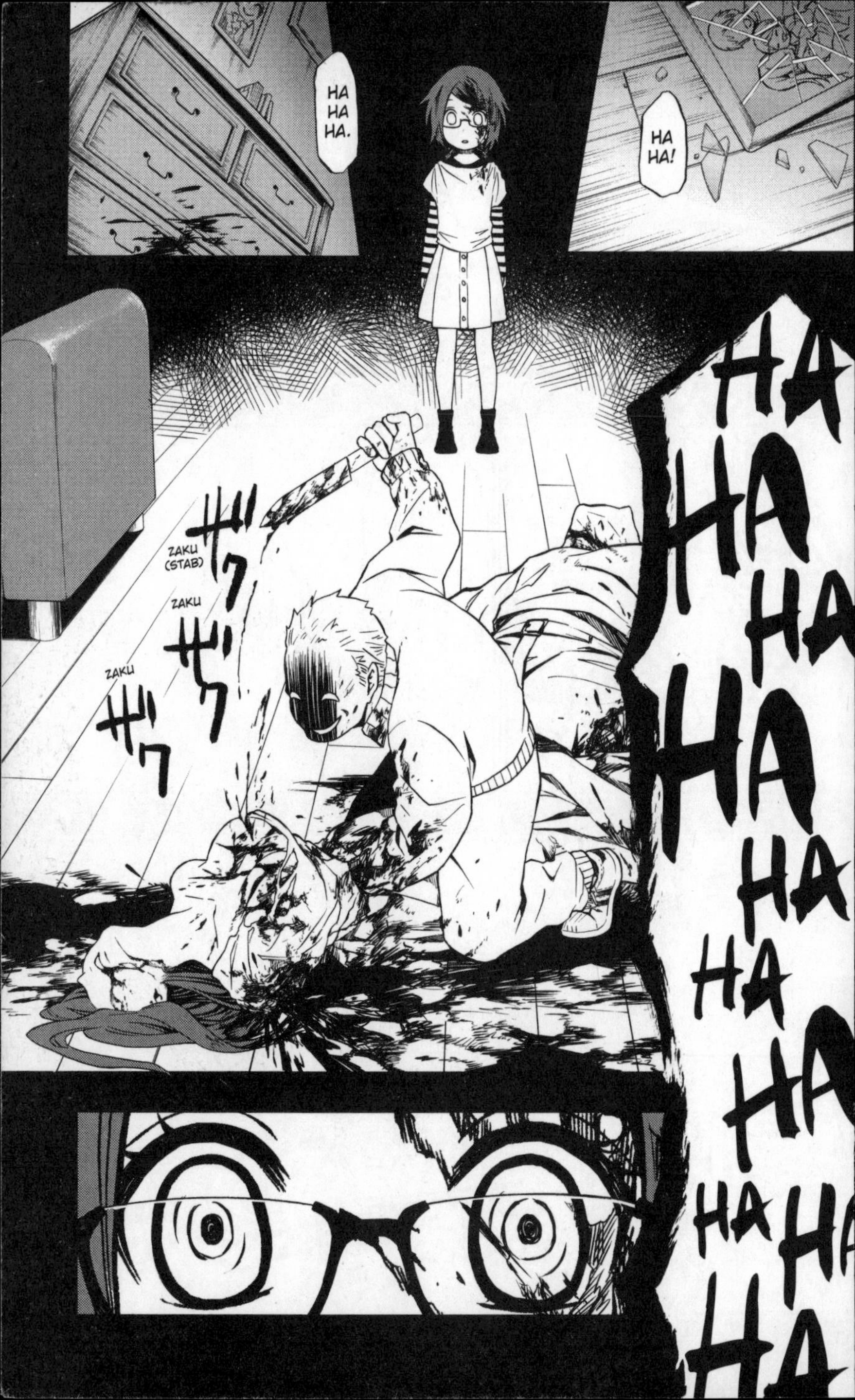
HA HA!
HA HA HA.
ザク
ZAKU (STAB)
ザク
ZAKU
ザク
ZAKU
HA HA HA HA HA HA HA HA HA HA

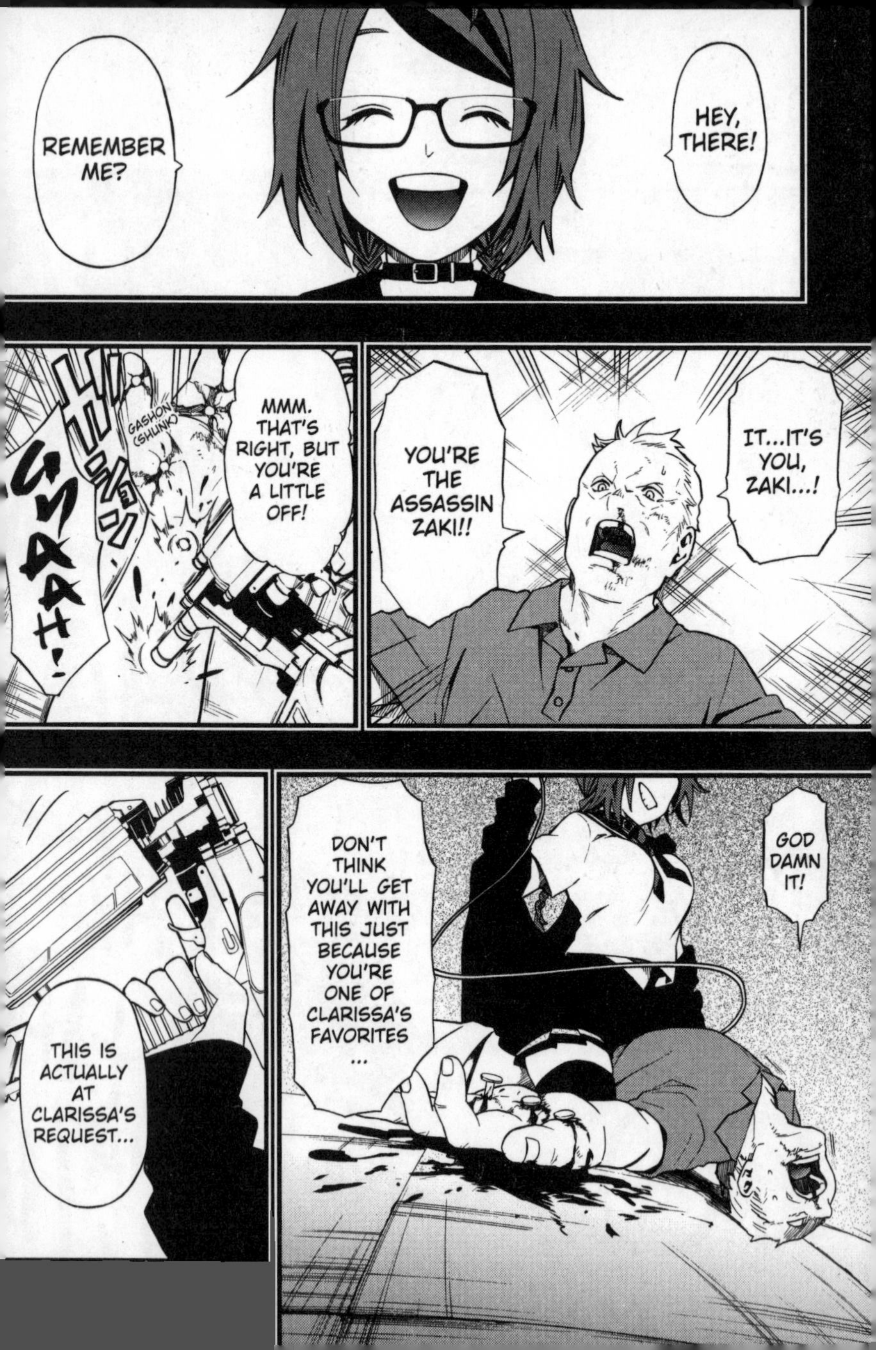
HEY, THERE!
REMEMBER ME?
IT...IT'S YOU, ZAKI...!
YOU'RE THE ASSASSIN ZAKI!!
MMM. THAT'S RIGHT, BUT YOU'RE A LITTLE OFF!
GASHON (SHUNK)
UWAAH!
GOD DAMN IT!
DON'T THINK YOU'LL GET AWAY WITH THIS JUST BECAUSE YOU'RE ONE OF CLARISSA'S FAVORITES ...
THIS IS ACTUALLY AT CLARISSA'S REQUEST...

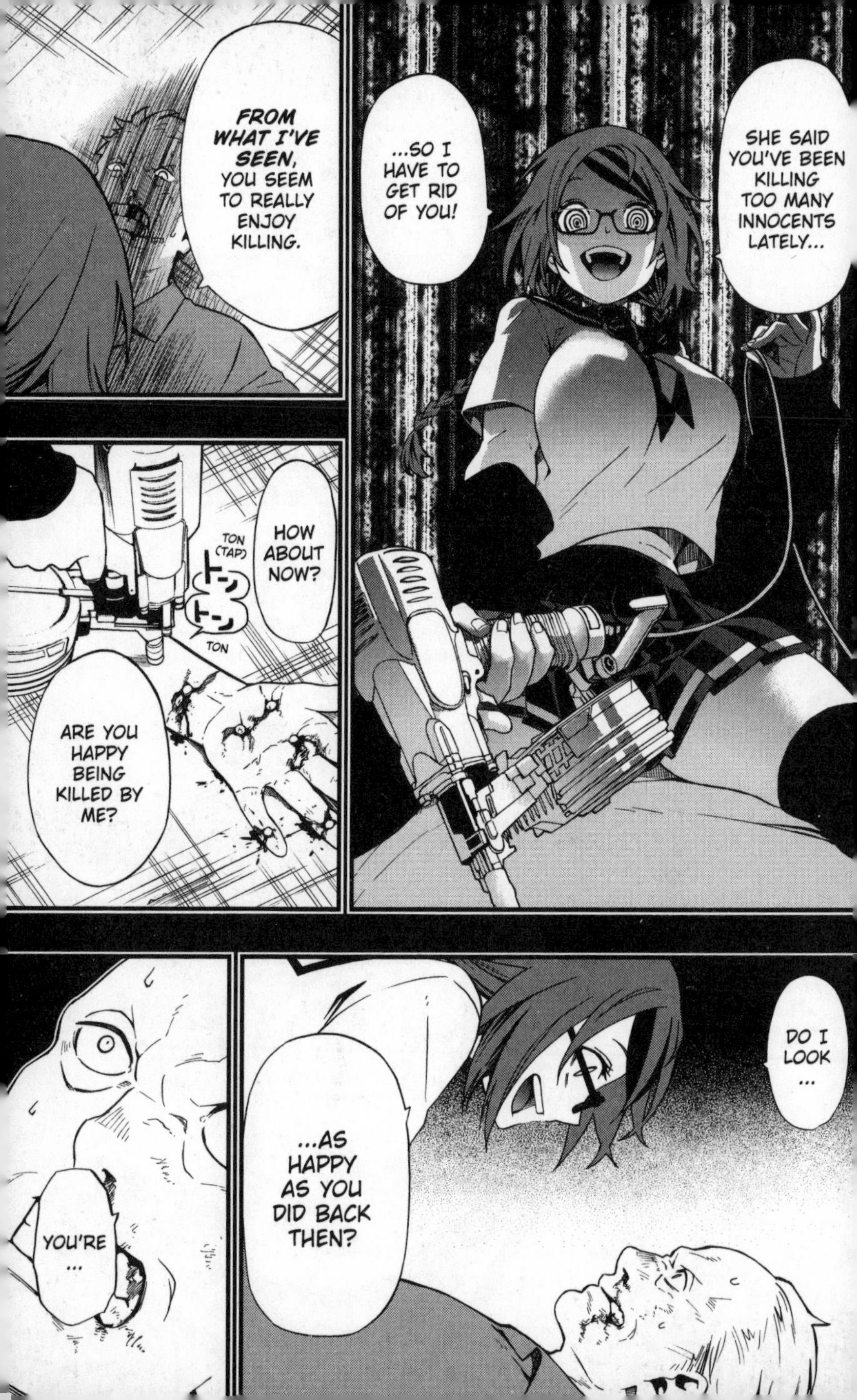
SHE SAID YOU'VE BEEN KILLING TOO MANY INNOCENTS LATELY...
...SO I HAVE TO GET RID OF YOU!
FROM WHAT I'VE SEEN, YOU SEEM TO REALLY ENJOY KILLING.
HOW ABOUT NOW?
TON (TAP)
トーン
トーン
TON
ARE YOU HAPPY BEING KILLED BY ME?
DO I LOOK ...
...AS HAPPY AS YOU DID BACK THEN?
YOU'RE ...

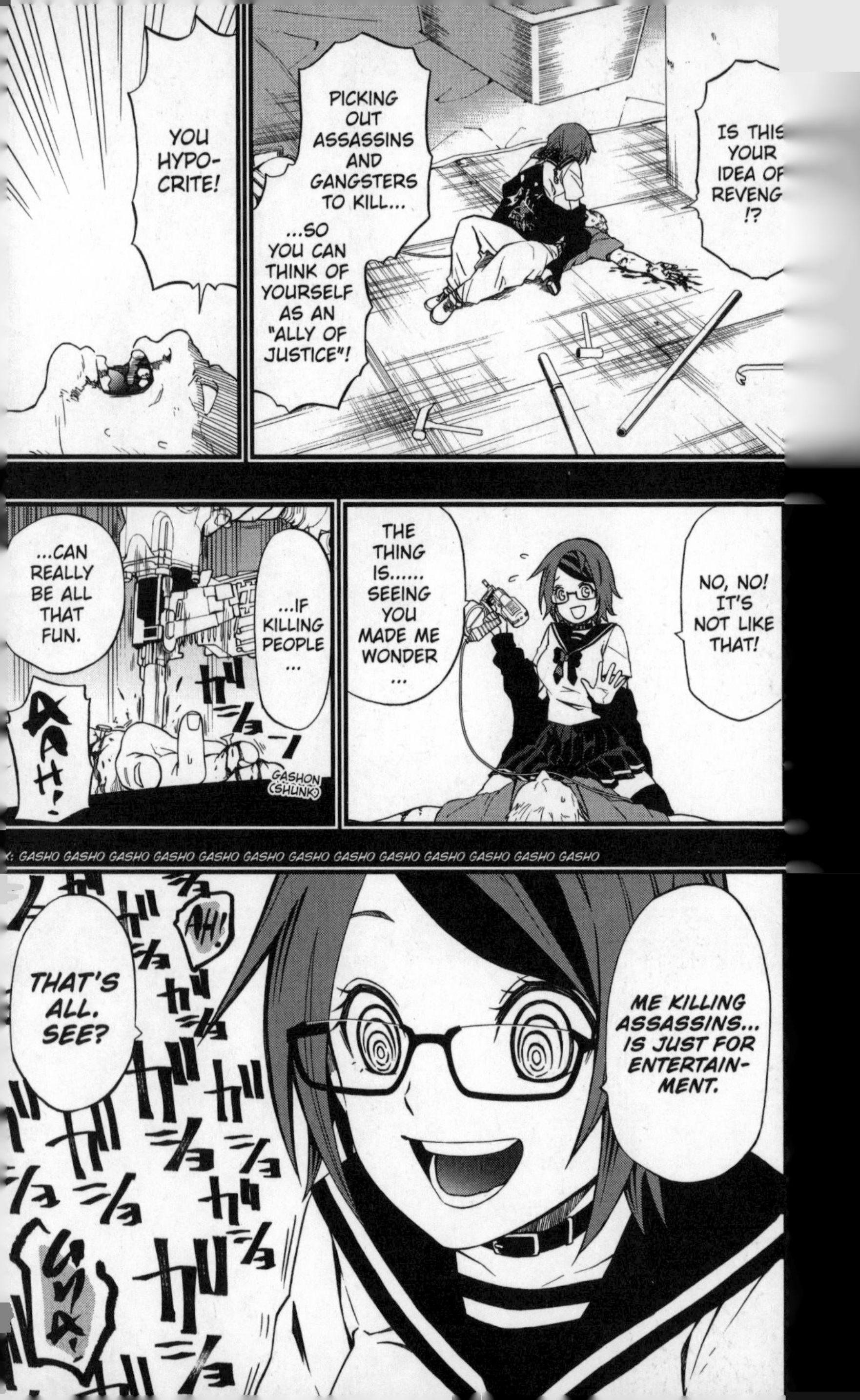
IS THIS YOUR IDEA OF REVENG !?
PICKING OUT ASSASSINS AND GANGSTERS TO KILL...
...SO YOU CAN THINK OF YOURSELF AS AN "ALLY OF JUSTICE"!
YOU HYPO-CRITE!
NO, NO! IT'S NOT LIKE THAT!
THE THING IS...... SEEING YOU MADE ME WONDER ...
...IF KILLING PEOPLE ...
...CAN REALLY BE ALL THAT FUN.
AAH!
GASHON (SHUNK)
GASHO GASHO GASHO GASHO GASHO GASHO GASHO GASHO GASHO GASHO GASHO GASHO GASHO
ME KILLING ASSASSINS... IS JUST FOR ENTERTAIN-MENT.
AH!
THAT'S ALL. SEE?

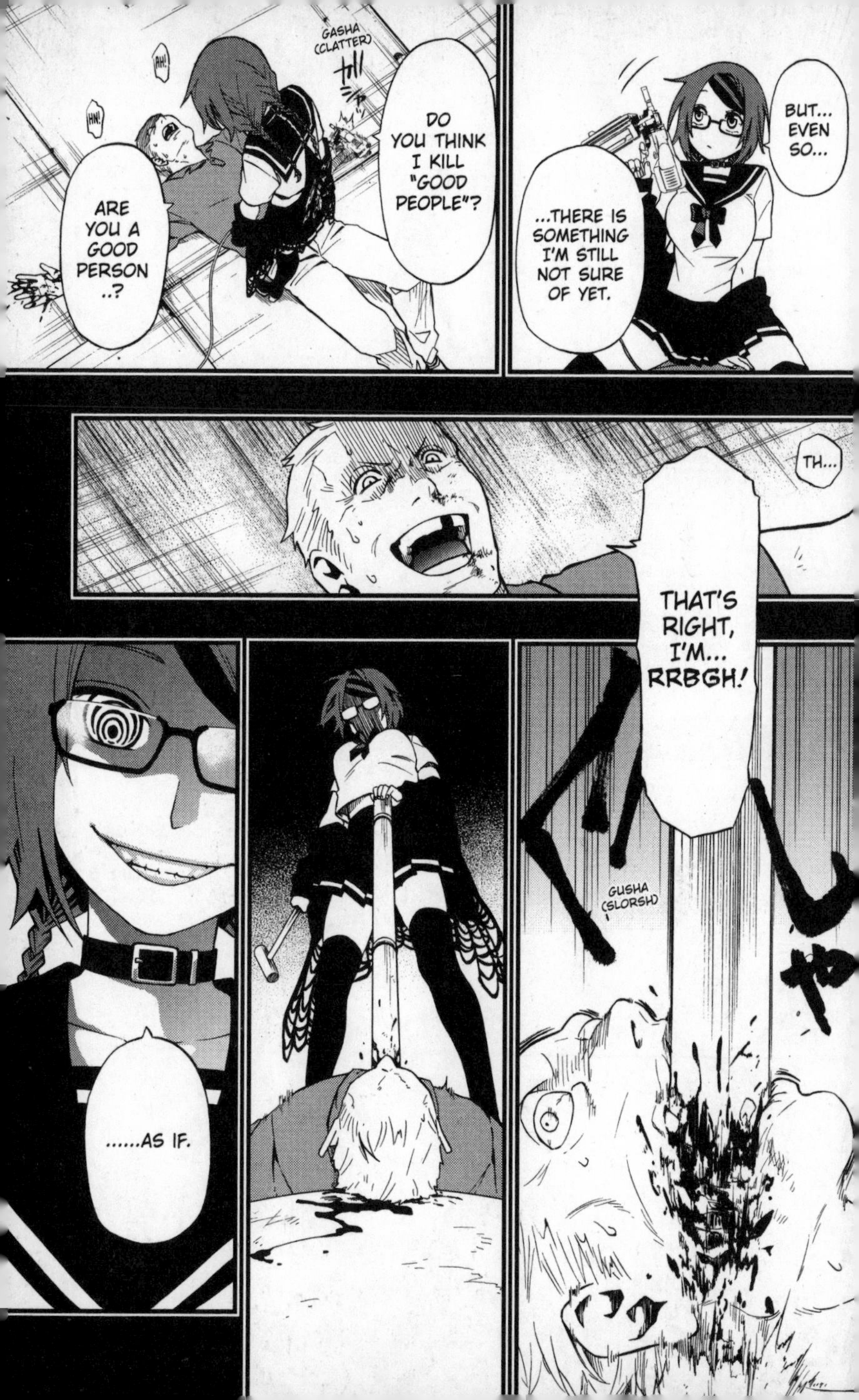

BUT... EVEN SO...
...THERE IS SOMETHING I'M STILL NOT SURE OF YET.
GASHA (CLATTER)
DO YOU THINK I KILL "GOOD PEOPLE"?
AH!
HN!
ARE YOU A GOOD PERSON ..?
TH...
THAT'S RIGHT, I'M... RRBGH!
GUSHA (SLORSH)
......AS IF.

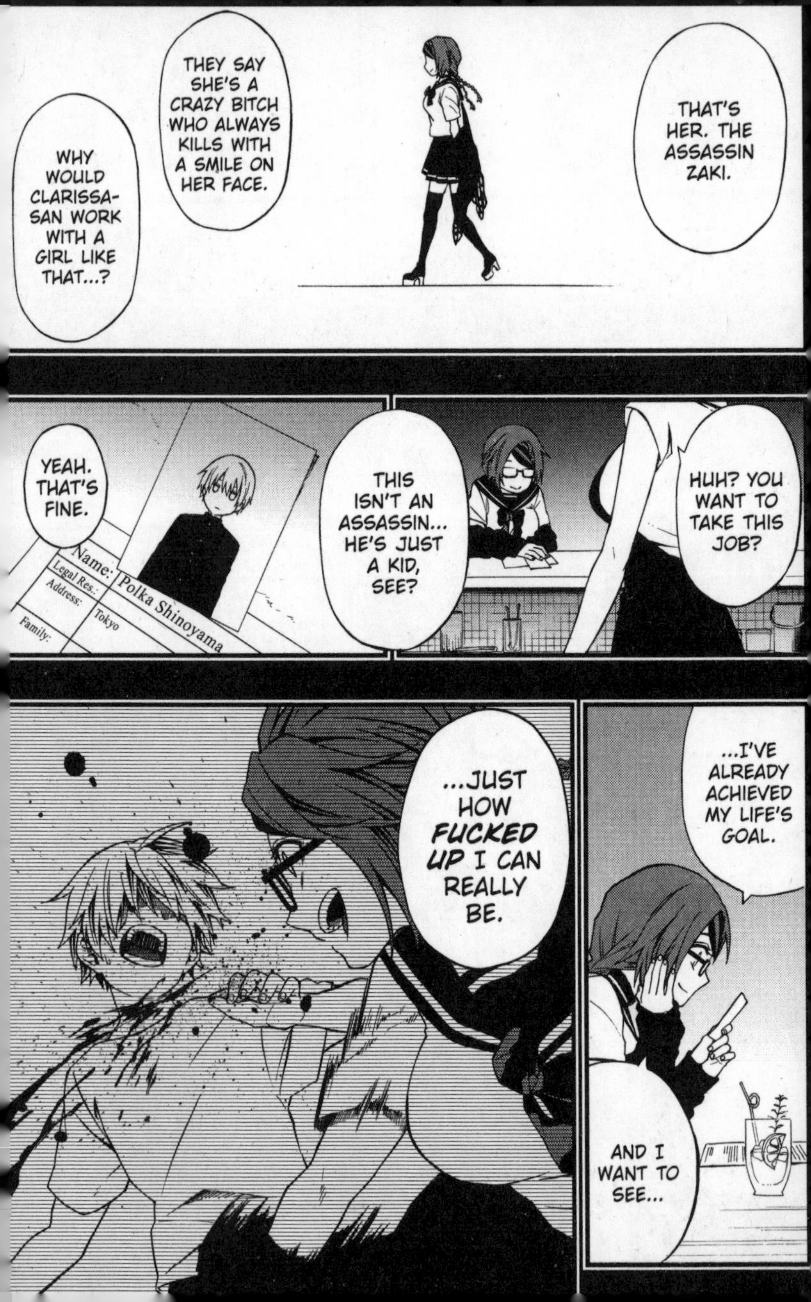
THAT'S HER. THE ASSASSIN ZAKI.
THEY SAY SHE'S A CRAZY BITCH WHO ALWAYS KILLS WITH A SMILE ON HER FACE.
WHY WOULD CLARISSA-SAN WORK WITH A GIRL LIKE THAT...?
HUH? YOU WANT TO TAKE THIS JOB?
THIS ISN'T AN ASSASSIN... HE'S JUST A KID, SEE?
YEAH. THAT'S FINE.
Name: Polka Shinoyama
Legal Res.:
Address: Tokyo
Family:
...I'VE ALREADY ACHIEVED MY LIFE'S GOAL.
AND I WANT TO SEE...
...JUST HOW *FUCKED UP* I CAN REALLY BE.

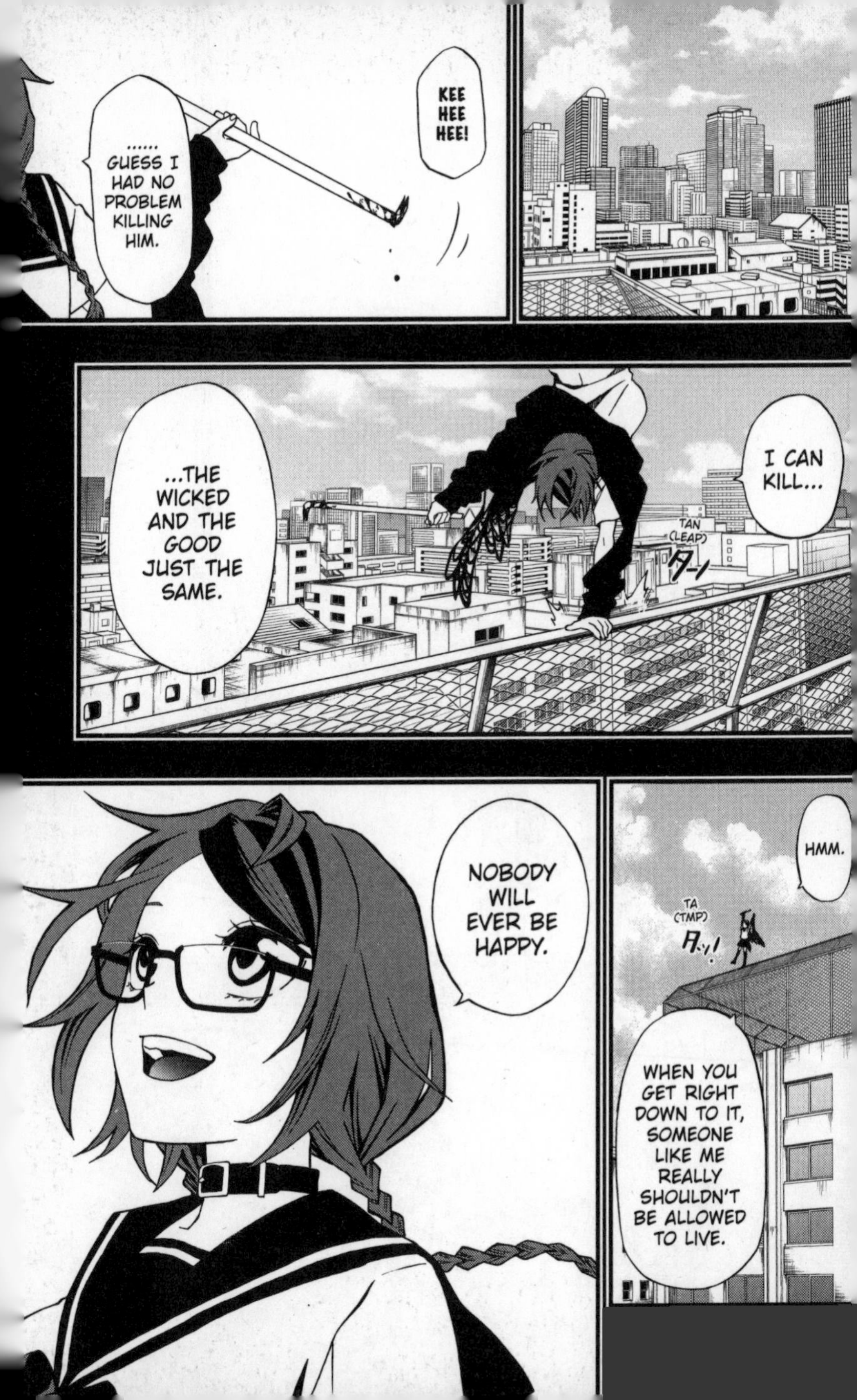
KEE HEE HEE!
...... GUESS I HAD NO PROBLEM KILLING HIM.
I CAN KILL...
TAN (LEAP)
...THE WICKED AND THE GOOD JUST THE SAME.
HMM.
TA (TMP)
WHEN YOU GET RIGHT DOWN TO IT, SOMEONE LIKE ME REALLY SHOULDN'T BE ALLOWED TO LIVE.
NOBODY WILL EVER BE HAPPY.

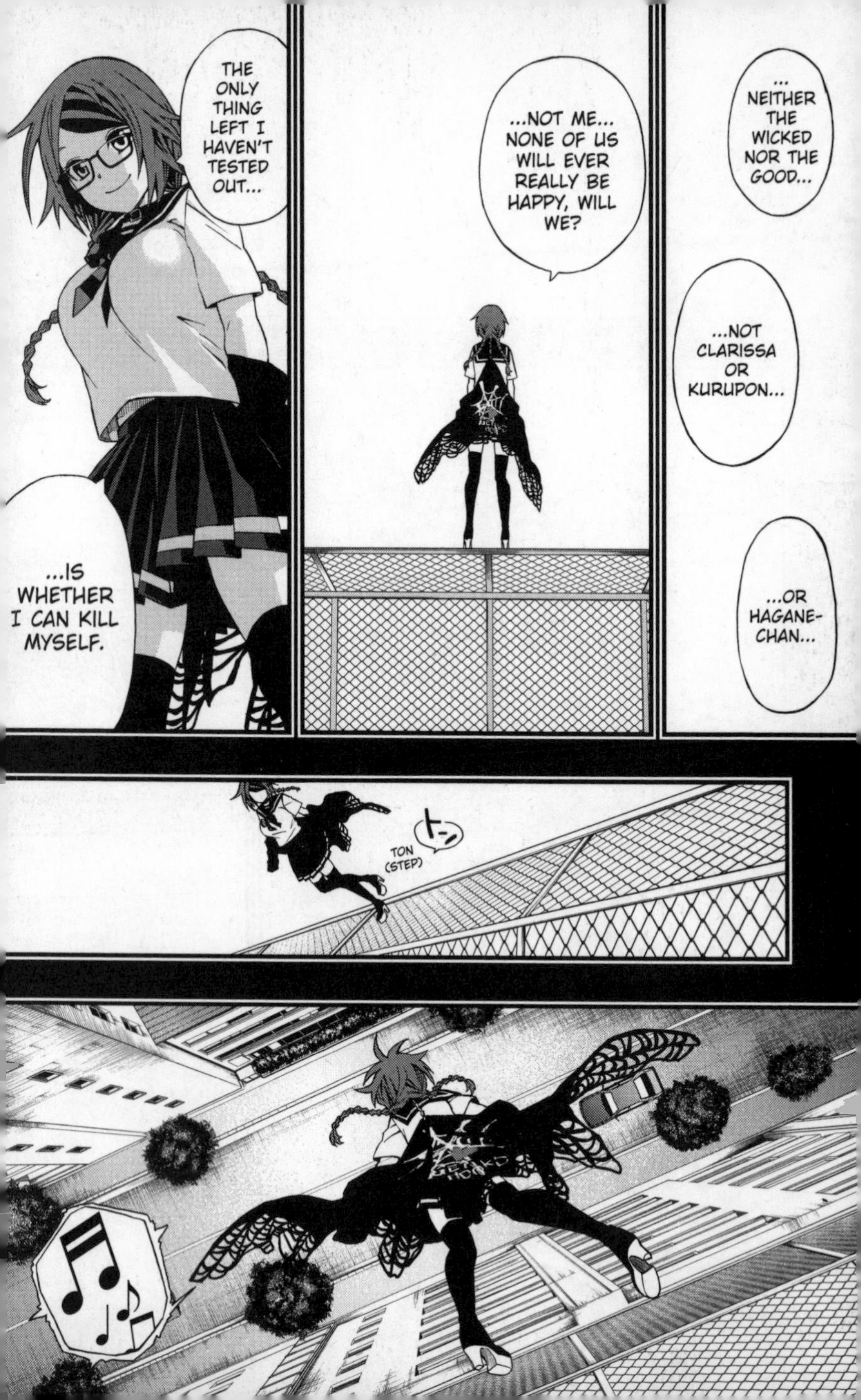
...NEITHER THE WICKED NOR THE GOOD...
...NOT CLARISSA OR KURUPON...
...OR HAGANE-CHAN...
...NOT ME... NONE OF US WILL EVER REALLY BE HAPPY, WILL WE?
THE ONLY THING LEFT I HAVEN'T TESTED OUT...
...IS WHETHER I CAN KILL MYSELF.
トン
TON (STEP)

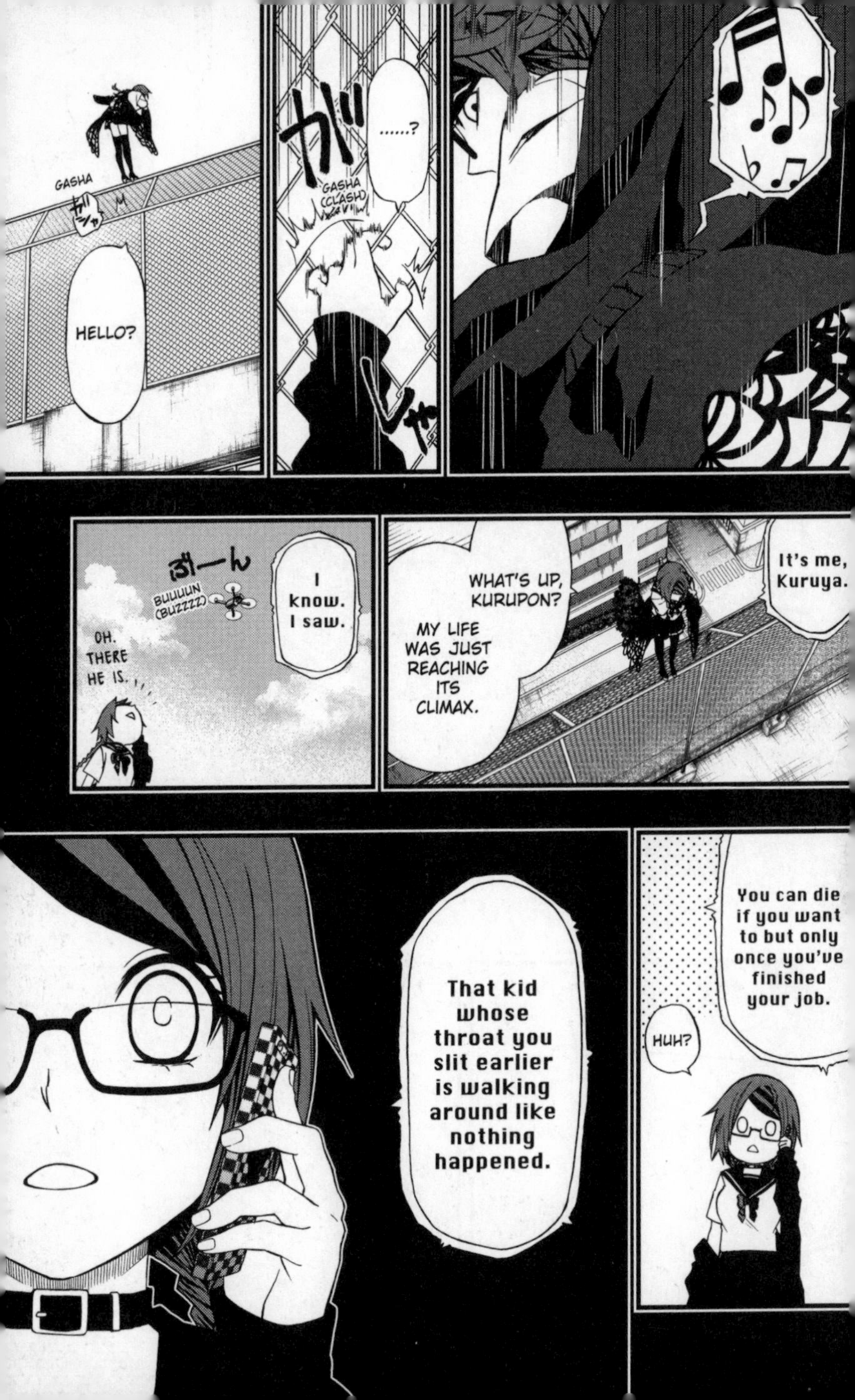
......?
GASHA (CLASH)
GASHA
HELLO?
It's me, Kuruya.
WHAT'S UP, KURUPON?
MY LIFE WAS JUST REACHING ITS CLIMAX.
I know. I saw.
ぶーん
BUUUUN (BUZZZZ)
OH. THERE HE IS.
You can die if you want to but only once you've finished your job.
HUH?
That kid whose throat you slit earlier is walking around like nothing happened.

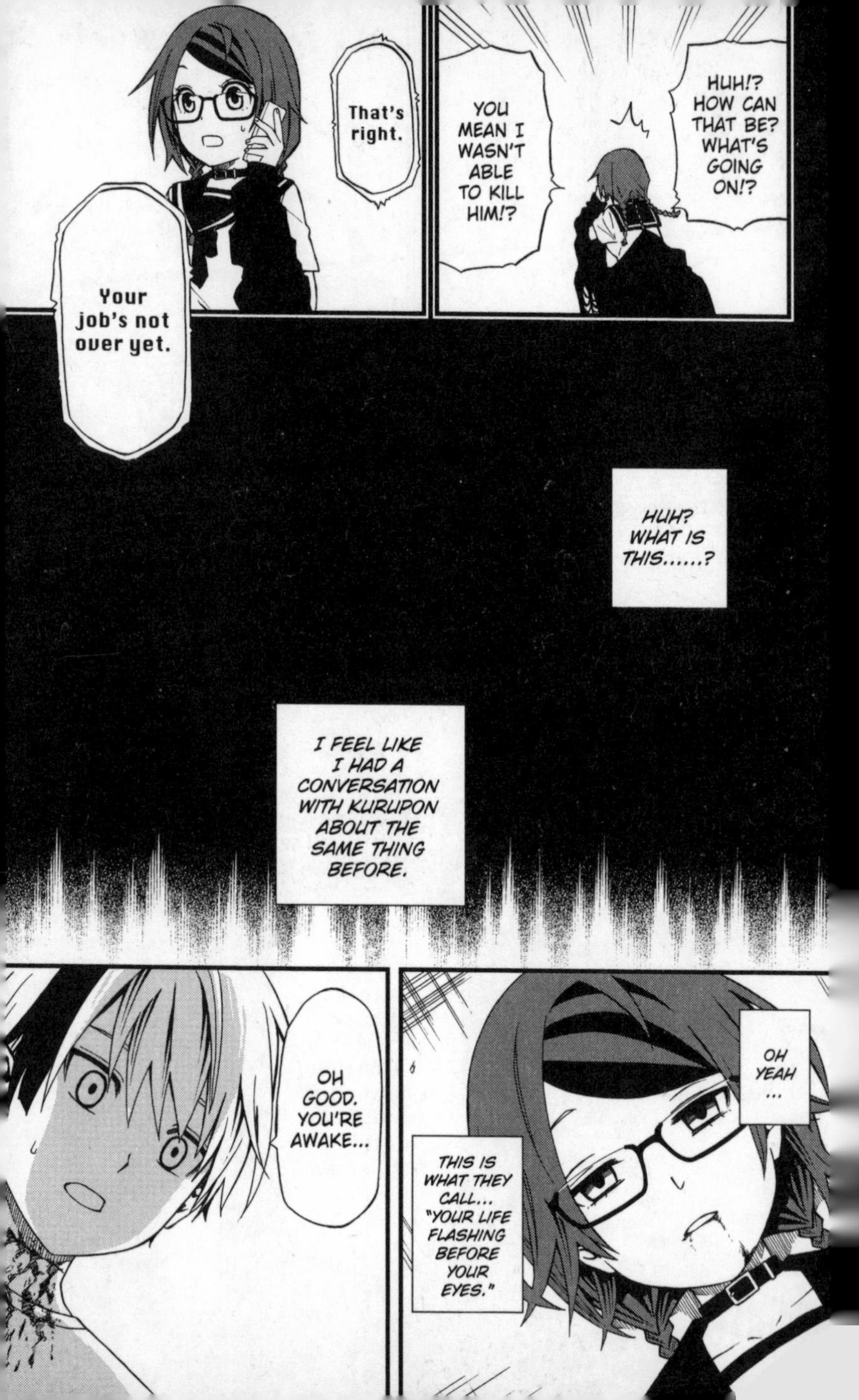
HUH!? HOW CAN THAT BE? WHAT'S GOING ON!?
YOU MEAN I WASN'T ABLE TO KILL HIM!?
That's right.
Your job's not over yet.
HUH? WHAT IS THIS......?
I FEEL LIKE I HAD A CONVERSATION WITH KURUPON ABOUT THE SAME THING BEFORE.
OH YEAH ...
THIS IS WHAT THEY CALL... "YOUR LIFE FLASHING BEFORE YOUR EYES."
OH GOOD. YOU'RE AWAKE...

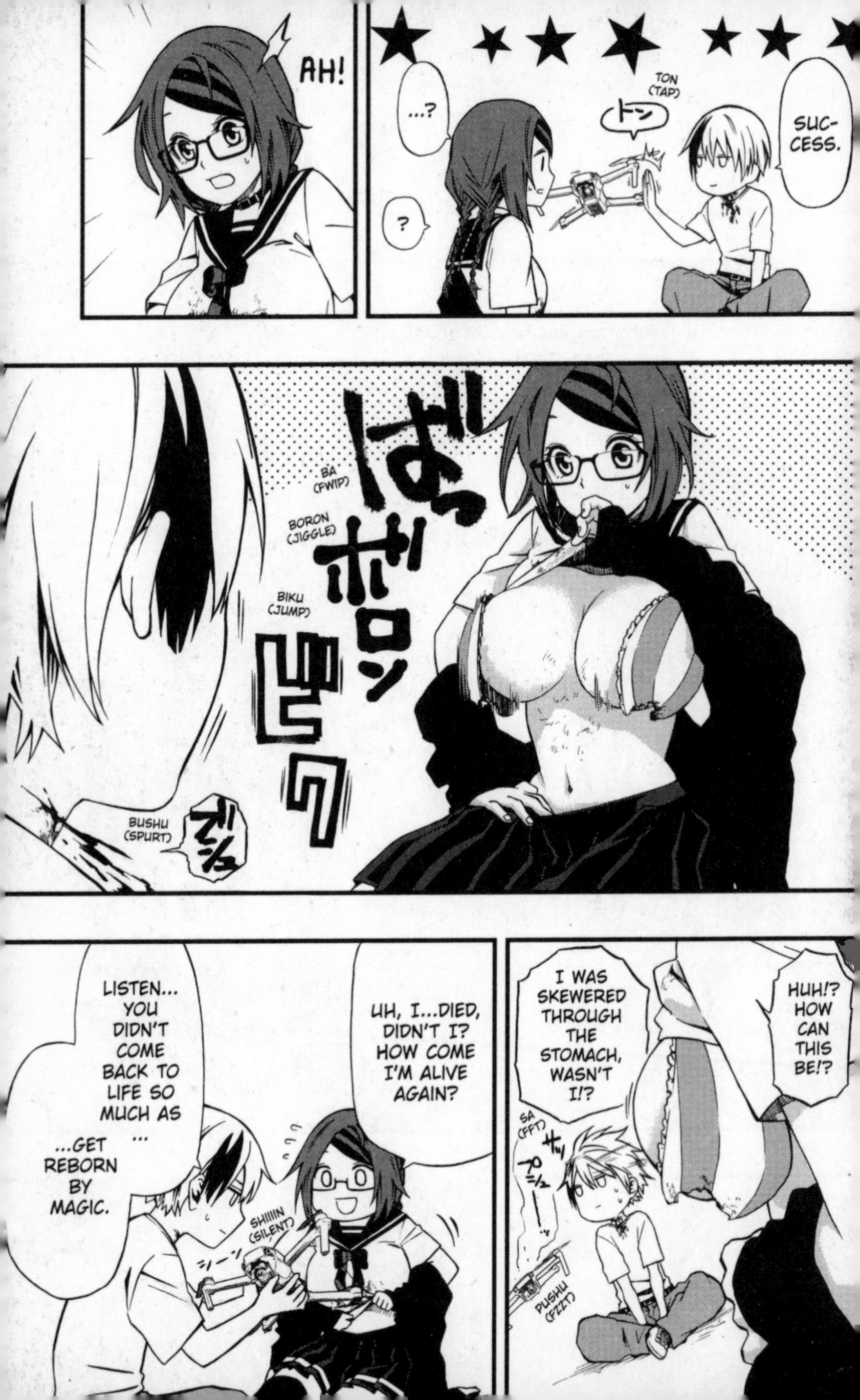

SUC-CESS.
TON (TAP)
トン
...?
?
AH!
BA (FWIP)
BORON (JIGGLE)
BIKU (JUMP)
BUSHU (SPURT)
HUH!? HOW CAN THIS BE!?
I WAS SKEWERED THROUGH THE STOMACH, WASN'T I!?
SA (FFT)
PUSHU (FZZT)
UH, I...DIED, DIDN'T I? HOW COME I'M ALIVE AGAIN?
LISTEN... YOU DIDN'T COME BACK TO LIFE SO MUCH AS ...
...GET REBORN BY MAGIC.
SHIIIIN (SILENT)

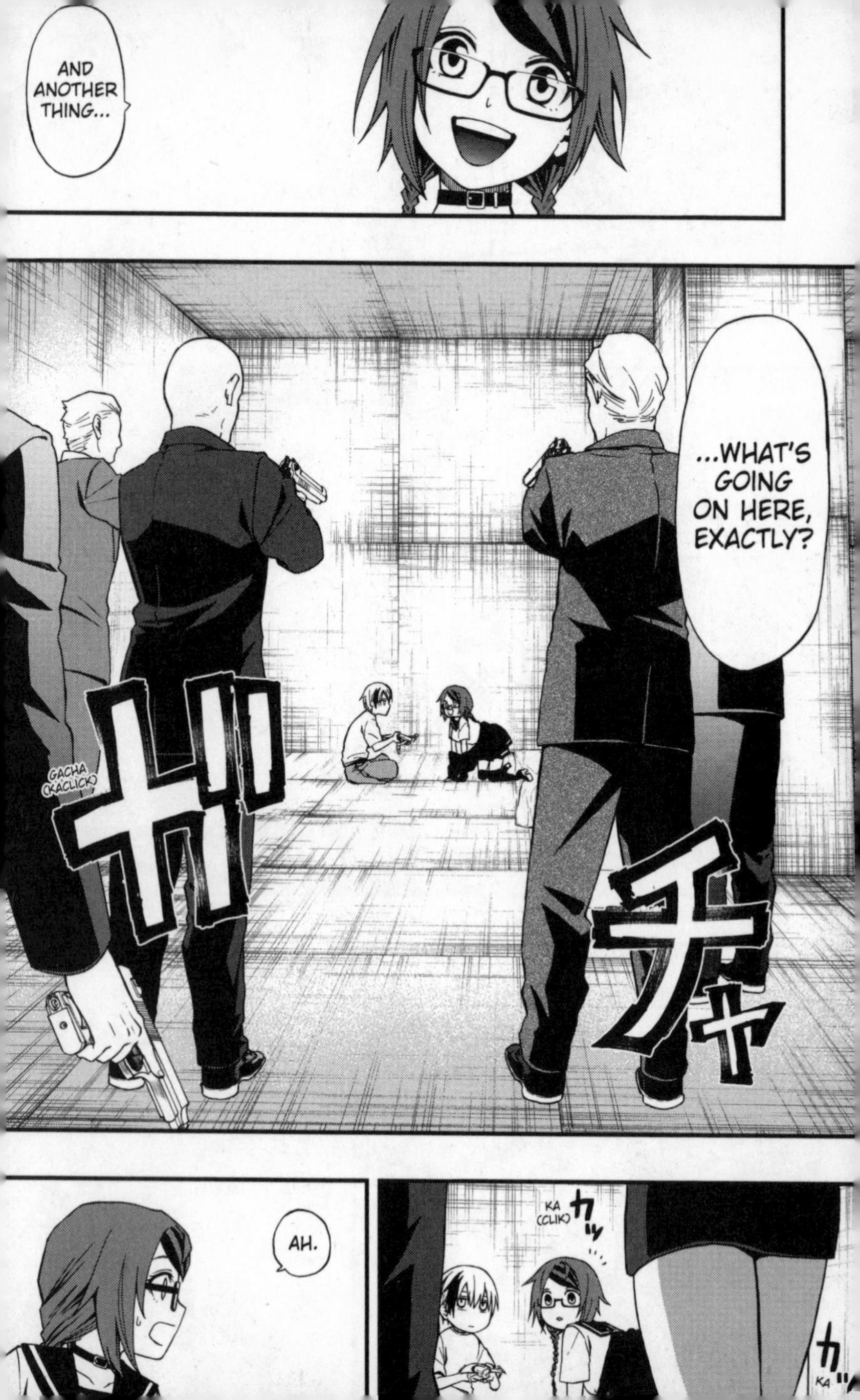
AND ANOTHER THING...
...WHAT'S GOING ON HERE, EXACTLY?
ガチャ
GACHA (KACLICK)
カッ
KA (CLIK)
カッ
KA
AH.

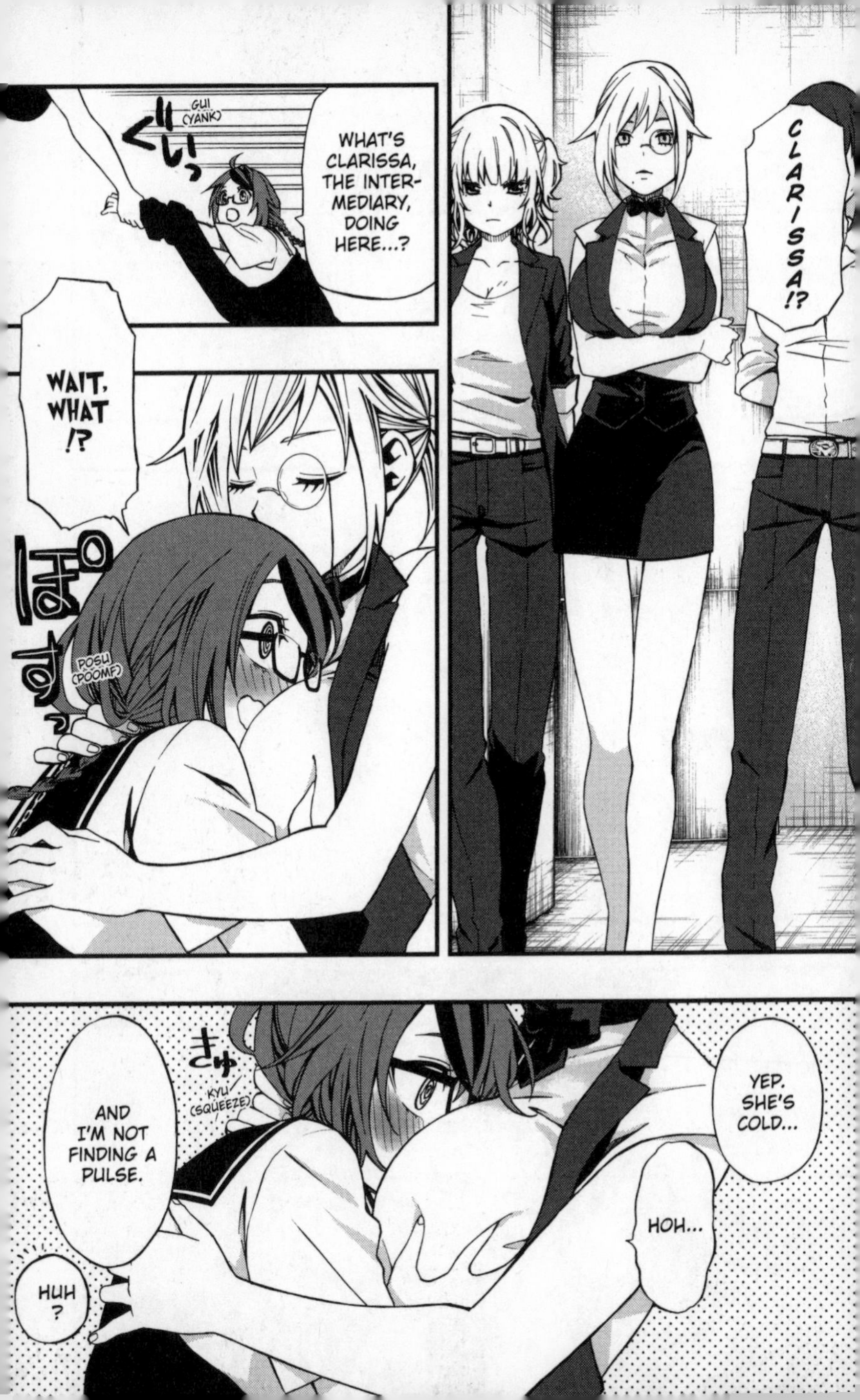
CLARISSA!?
ぐいっ
GUI (YANK)
WHAT'S CLARISSA, THE INTER-MEDIARY, DOING HERE...?
WAIT, WHAT!?
ぽすっ
POSU (POOMF)
YEP. SHE'S COLD...
HOH...
きゅ
KYU (SQUEEZE)
AND I'M NOT FINDING A PULSE.
HUH?

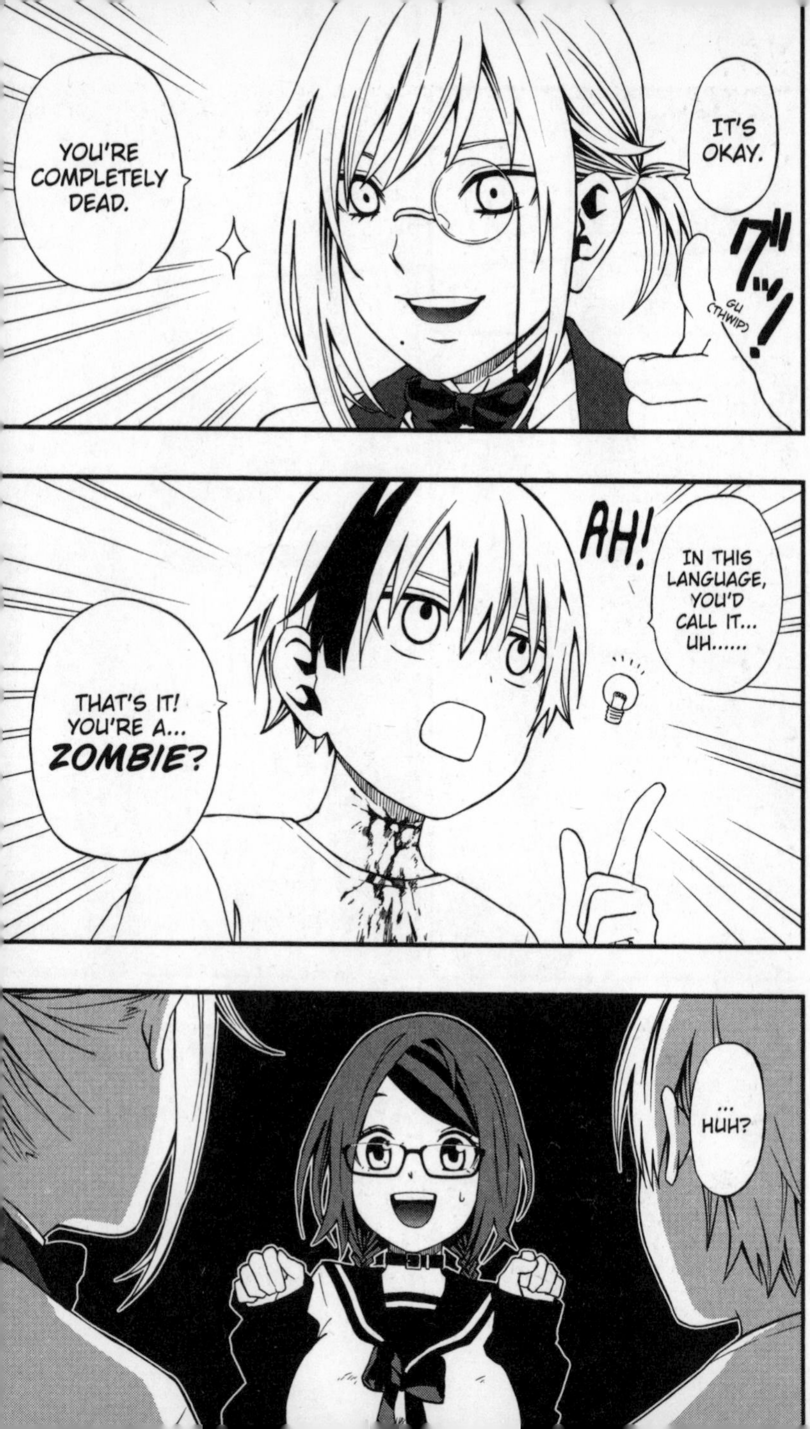
IT'S OKAY.
グッ!
GU (THWIP)
YOU'RE COMPLETELY DEAD.
AH!
IN THIS LANGUAGE, YOU'D CALL IT... UH......
THAT'S IT! YOU'RE A... **ZOMBIE?**
... HUH?

#03

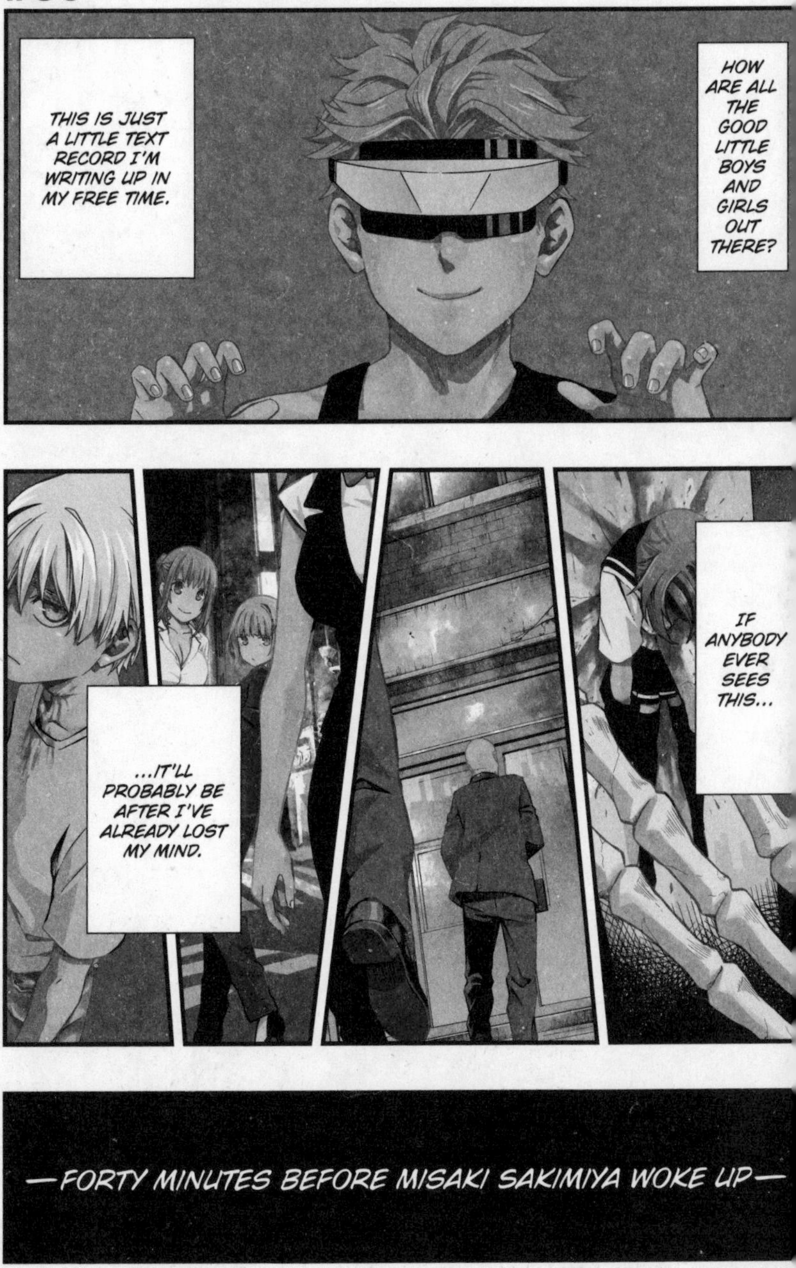
HOW ARE ALL THE GOOD LITTLE BOYS AND GIRLS OUT THERE?
THIS IS JUST A LITTLE TEXT RECORD I'M WRITING UP IN MY FREE TIME.
IF ANYBODY EVER SEES THIS...
...IT'LL PROBABLY BE AFTER I'VE ALREADY LOST MY MIND.
—FORTY MINUTES BEFORE MISAKI SAKIMIYA WOKE UP—

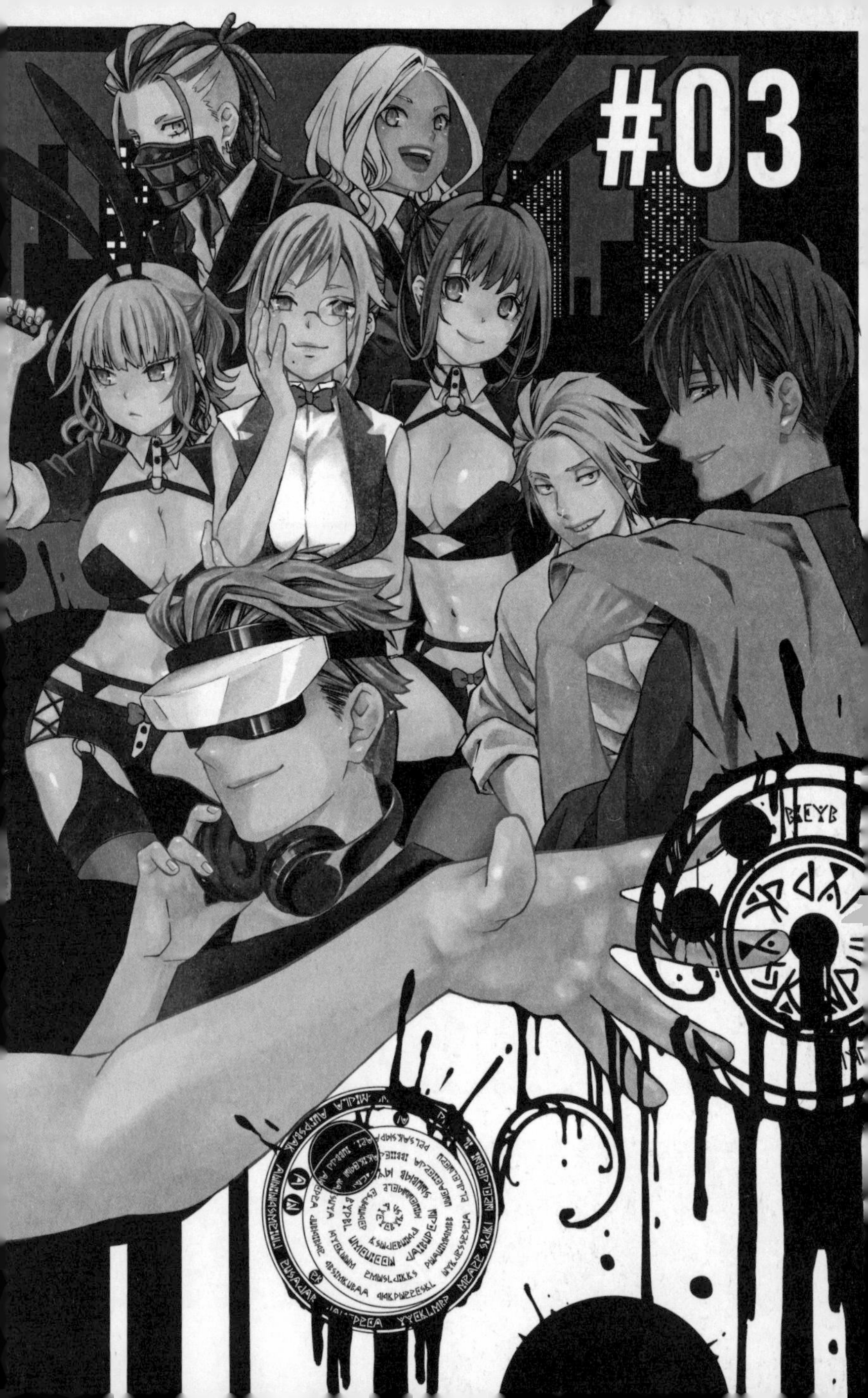
#03

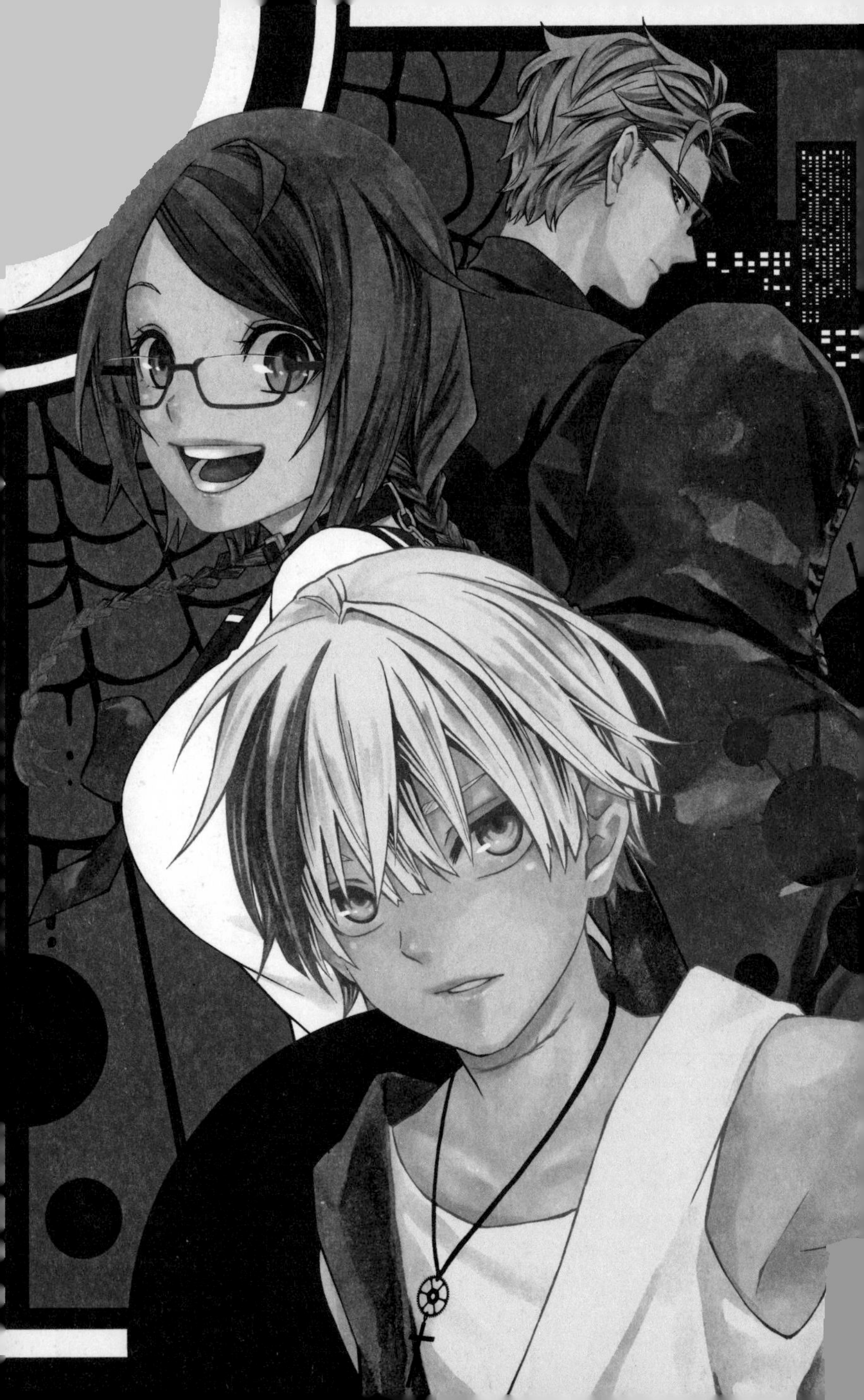

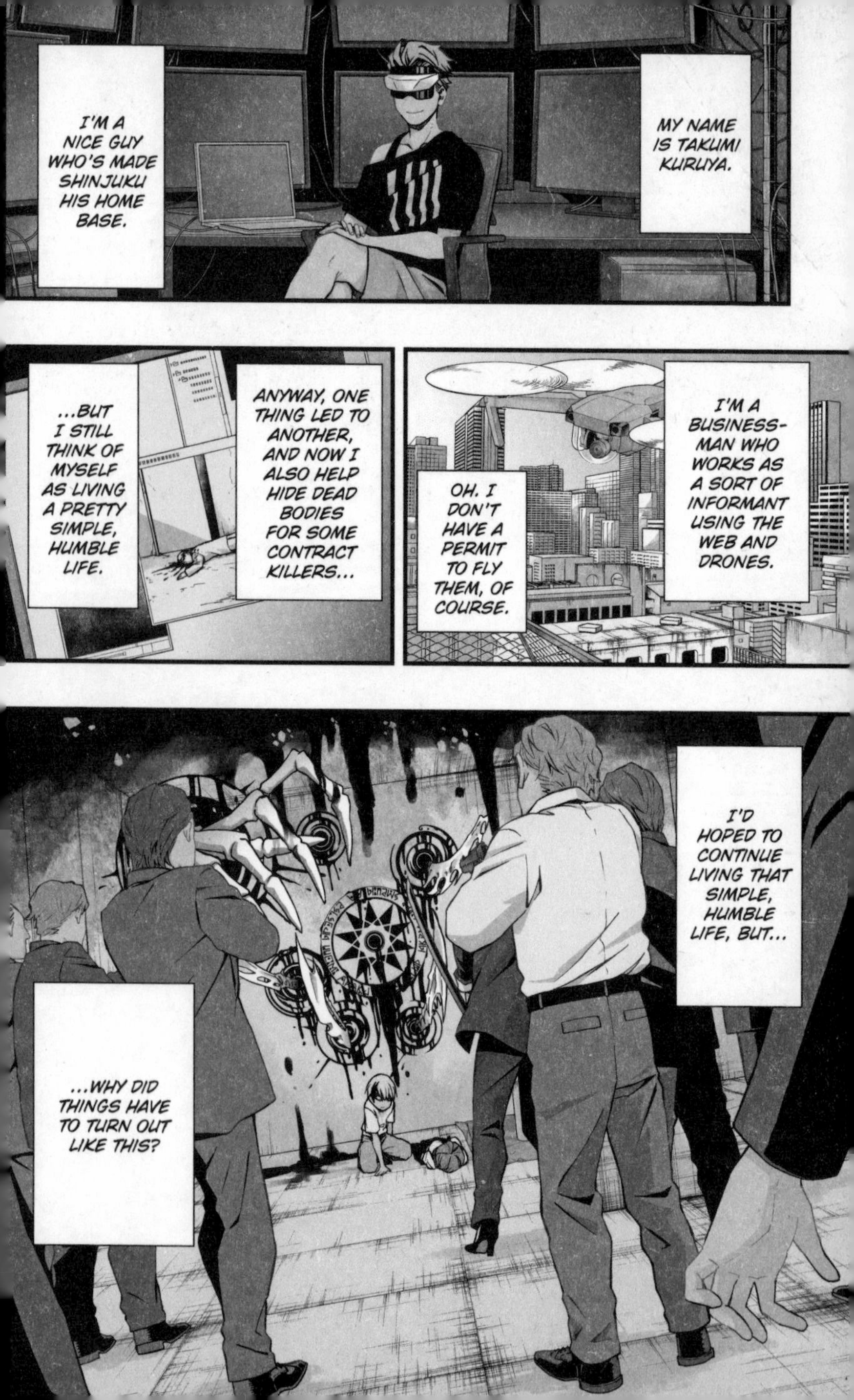
MY NAME IS TAKUMI KURUYA.
I'M A NICE GUY WHO'S MADE SHINJUKU HIS HOME BASE.
I'M A BUSINESS-MAN WHO WORKS AS A SORT OF INFORMANT USING THE WEB AND DRONES.
OH. I DON'T HAVE A PERMIT TO FLY THEM, OF COURSE.
ANYWAY, ONE THING LED TO ANOTHER, AND NOW I ALSO HELP HIDE DEAD BODIES FOR SOME CONTRACT KILLERS...
...BUT I STILL THINK OF MYSELF AS LIVING A PRETTY SIMPLE, HUMBLE LIFE.
I'D HOPED TO CONTINUE LIVING THAT SIMPLE, HUMBLE LIFE, BUT...
...WHY DID THINGS HAVE TO TURN OUT LIKE THIS?

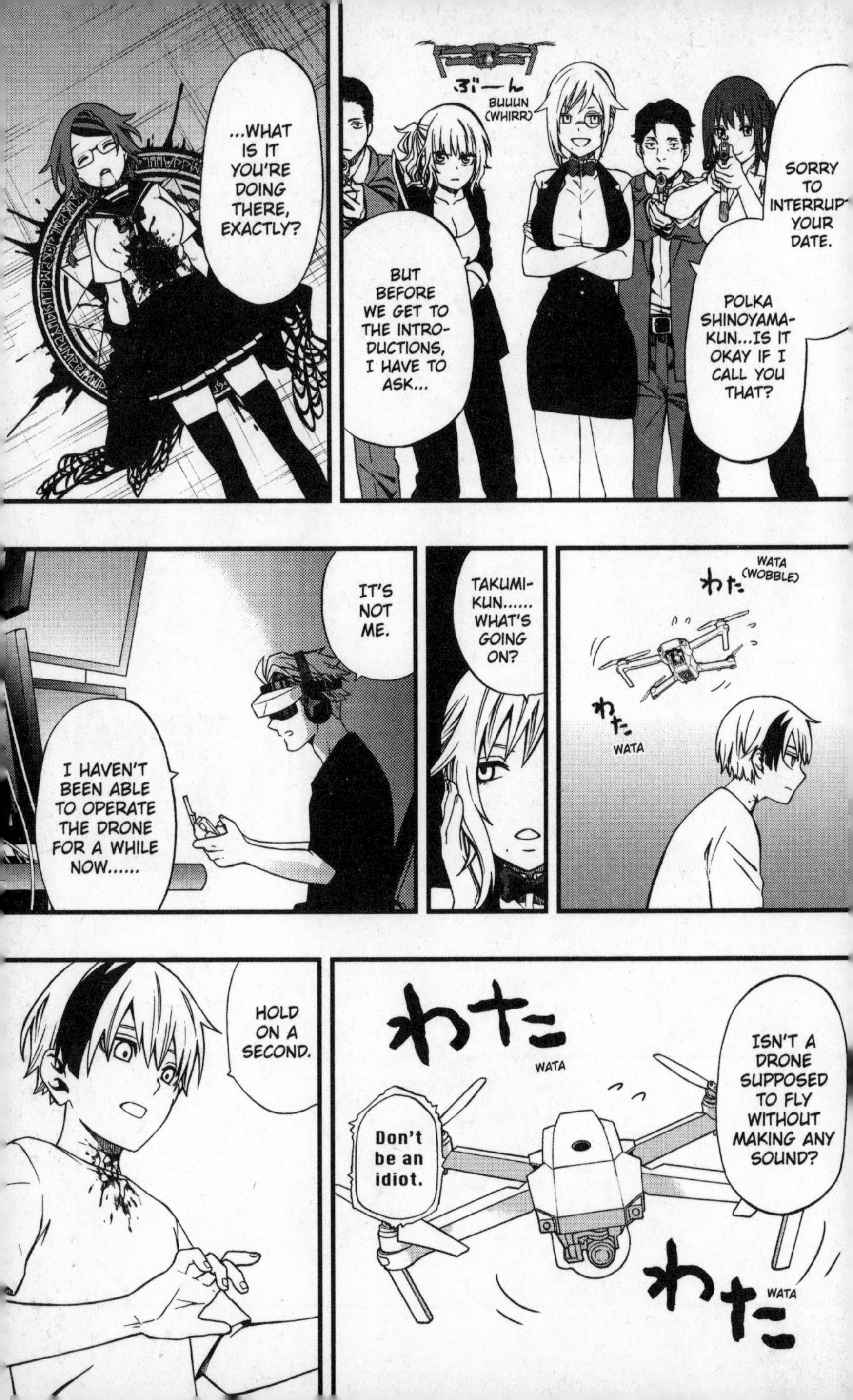
SORRY TO INTERRUP YOUR DATE.
POLKA SHINOYAMA-KUN...IS IT OKAY IF I CALL YOU THAT?
ぶーん
BUUUN (WHIRR)
BUT BEFORE WE GET TO THE INTRO-DUCTIONS, I HAVE TO ASK...
...WHAT IS IT YOU'RE DOING THERE, EXACTLY?
わた
WATA (WOBBLE)
わた
WATA
TAKUMI-KUN...... WHAT'S GOING ON?
IT'S NOT ME.
I HAVEN'T BEEN ABLE TO OPERATE THE DRONE FOR A WHILE NOW......
わた
WATA
ISN'T A DRONE SUPPOSED TO FLY WITHOUT MAKING ANY SOUND?
Don't be an idiot.
わた
WATA
HOLD ON A SECOND.

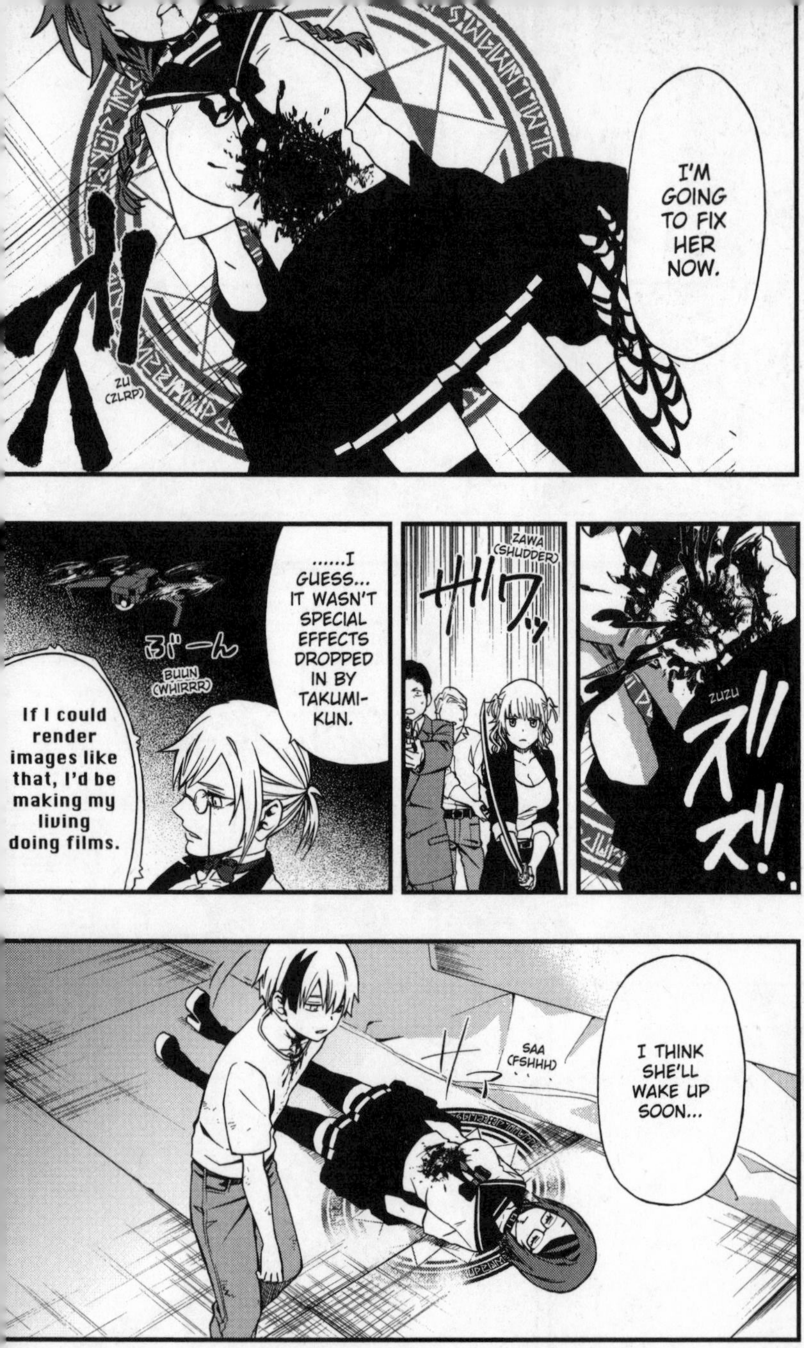
I'M GOING TO FIX HER NOW.
ZU (ZLRP)
ZUZU
ZAWA (SHUDDER)
......I GUESS... IT WASN'T SPECIAL EFFECTS DROPPED IN BY TAKUMI-KUN.
ぶーん
BUUN (WHIRRR)
If I could render images like that, I'd be making my living doing films.
SAA (FSHHH)
I THINK SHE'LL WAKE UP SOON...

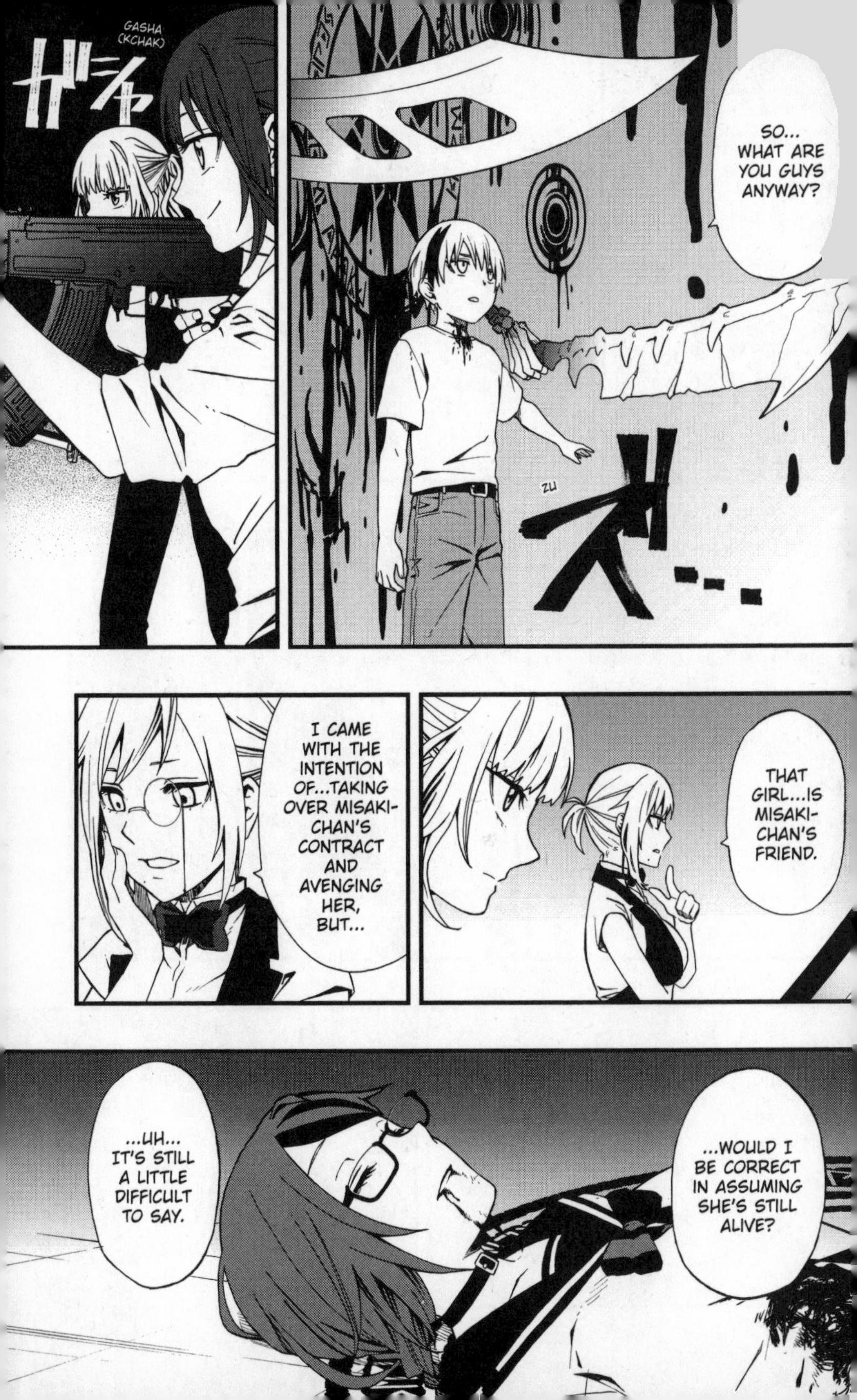
SO... WHAT ARE YOU GUYS ANYWAY?
ZU
GASHA (KCHAK)
THAT GIRL...IS MISAKI-CHAN'S FRIEND.
I CAME WITH THE INTENTION OF...TAKING OVER MISAKI-CHAN'S CONTRACT AND AVENGING HER, BUT...
...WOULD I BE CORRECT IN ASSUMING SHE'S STILL ALIVE?
...UH... IT'S STILL A LITTLE DIFFICULT TO SAY.

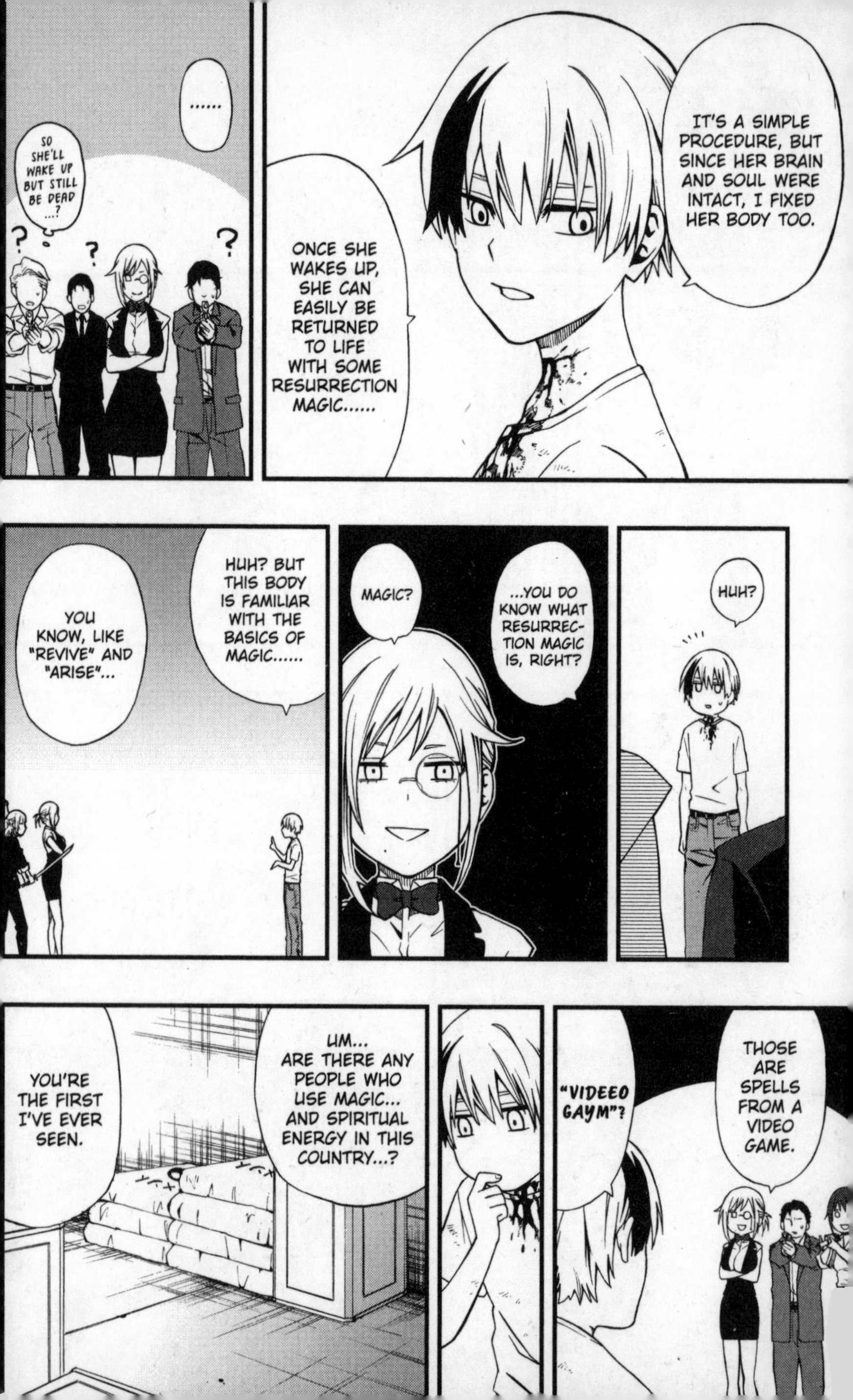
IT'S A SIMPLE PROCEDURE, BUT SINCE HER BRAIN AND SOUL WERE INTACT, I FIXED HER BODY TOO.
ONCE SHE WAKES UP, SHE CAN EASILY BE RETURNED TO LIFE WITH SOME RESURRECTION MAGIC......
......
SO SHE'LL WAKE UP BUT STILL BE DEAD ...?
HUH?
...YOU DO KNOW WHAT RESURREC-TION MAGIC IS, RIGHT?
MAGIC?
HUH? BUT THIS BODY IS FAMILIAR WITH THE BASICS OF MAGIC......
YOU KNOW, LIKE "REVIVE" AND "ARISE"...
THOSE ARE SPELLS FROM A VIDEO GAME.
"VIDEEO GAYM"?
UM... ARE THERE ANY PEOPLE WHO USE MAGIC... AND SPIRITUAL ENERGY IN THIS COUNTRY...?
YOU'RE THE FIRST I'VE EVER SEEN.

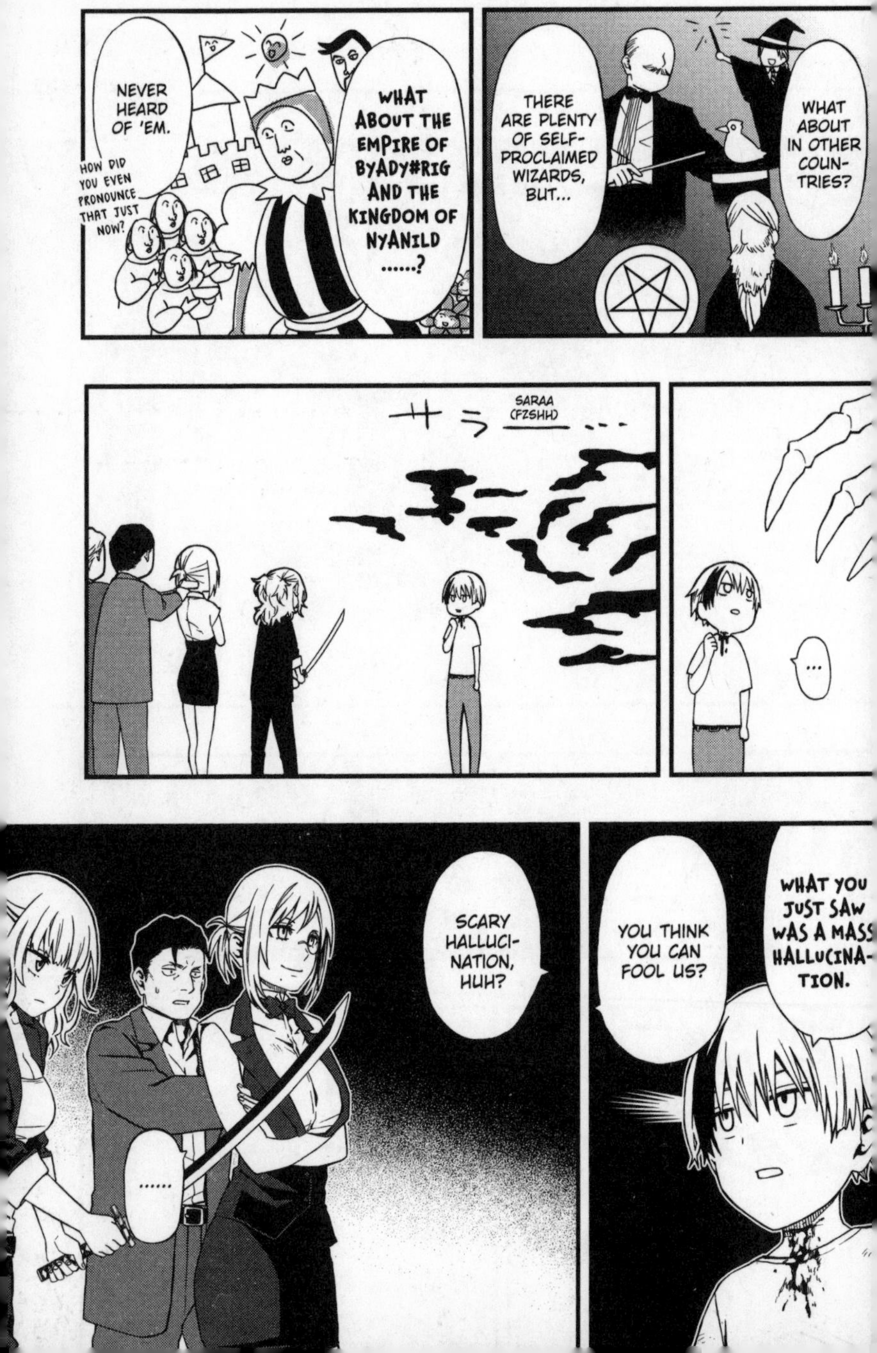
WHAT ABOUT IN OTHER COUN-TRIES?
THERE ARE PLENTY OF SELF-PROCLAIMED WIZARDS, BUT...
WHAT ABOUT THE EMPIRE OF BYADY#RIG AND THE KINGDOM OF NYANILD ......?
NEVER HEARD OF 'EM.
HOW DID YOU EVEN PRONOUNCE THAT JUST NOW?
...
SARAA (FZSHH)
WHAT YOU JUST SAW WAS A MASS HALLUCINA-TION.
YOU THINK YOU CAN FOOL US?
SCARY HALLUCI-NATION, HUH?
......

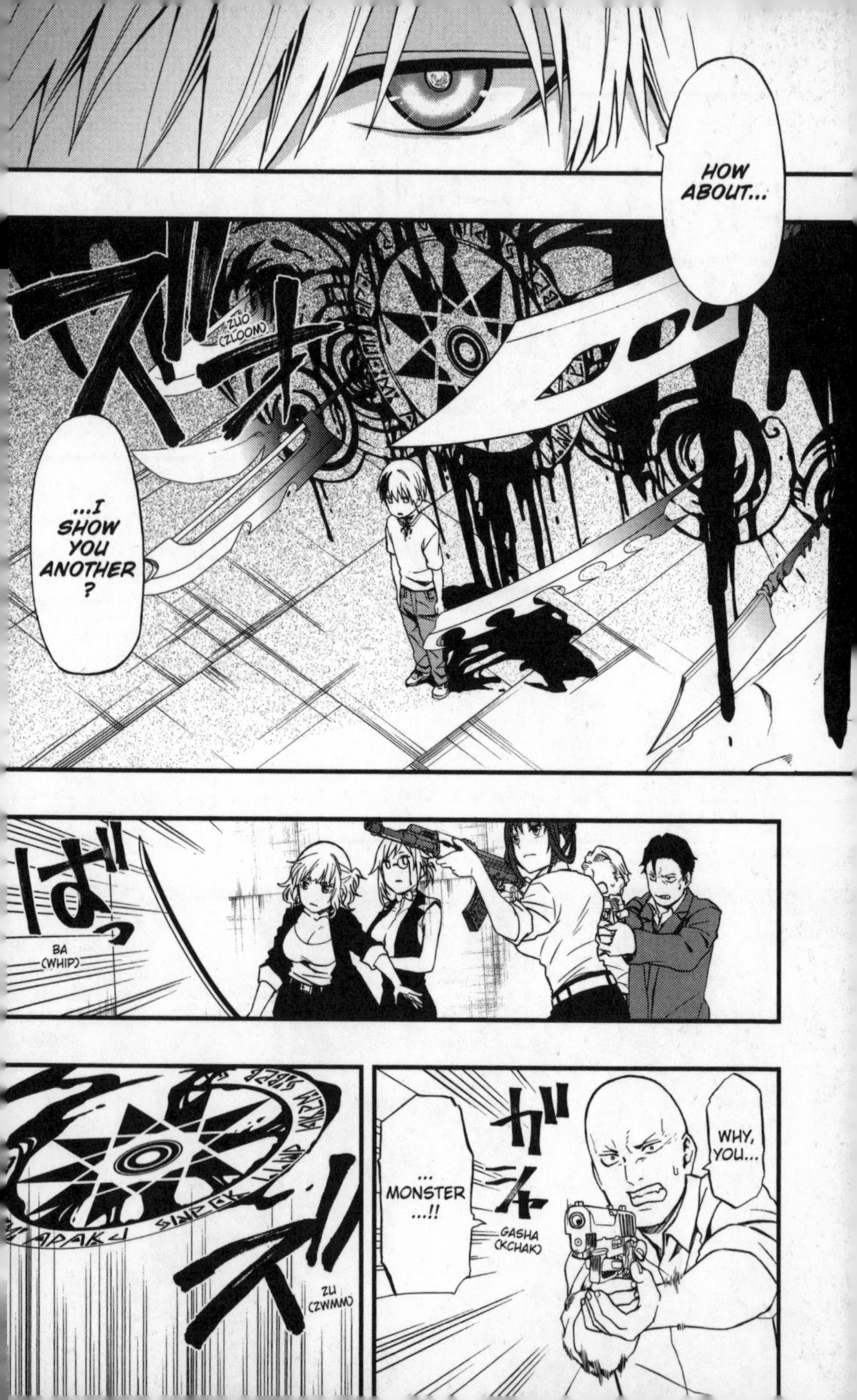
HOW ABOUT...
...I SHOW YOU ANOTHER ?
ZUO (ZLOOM)
BA (WHIP)
WHY, YOU...
GASHA (KCHAK)
... MONSTER ...!!
ZU (ZWMM)

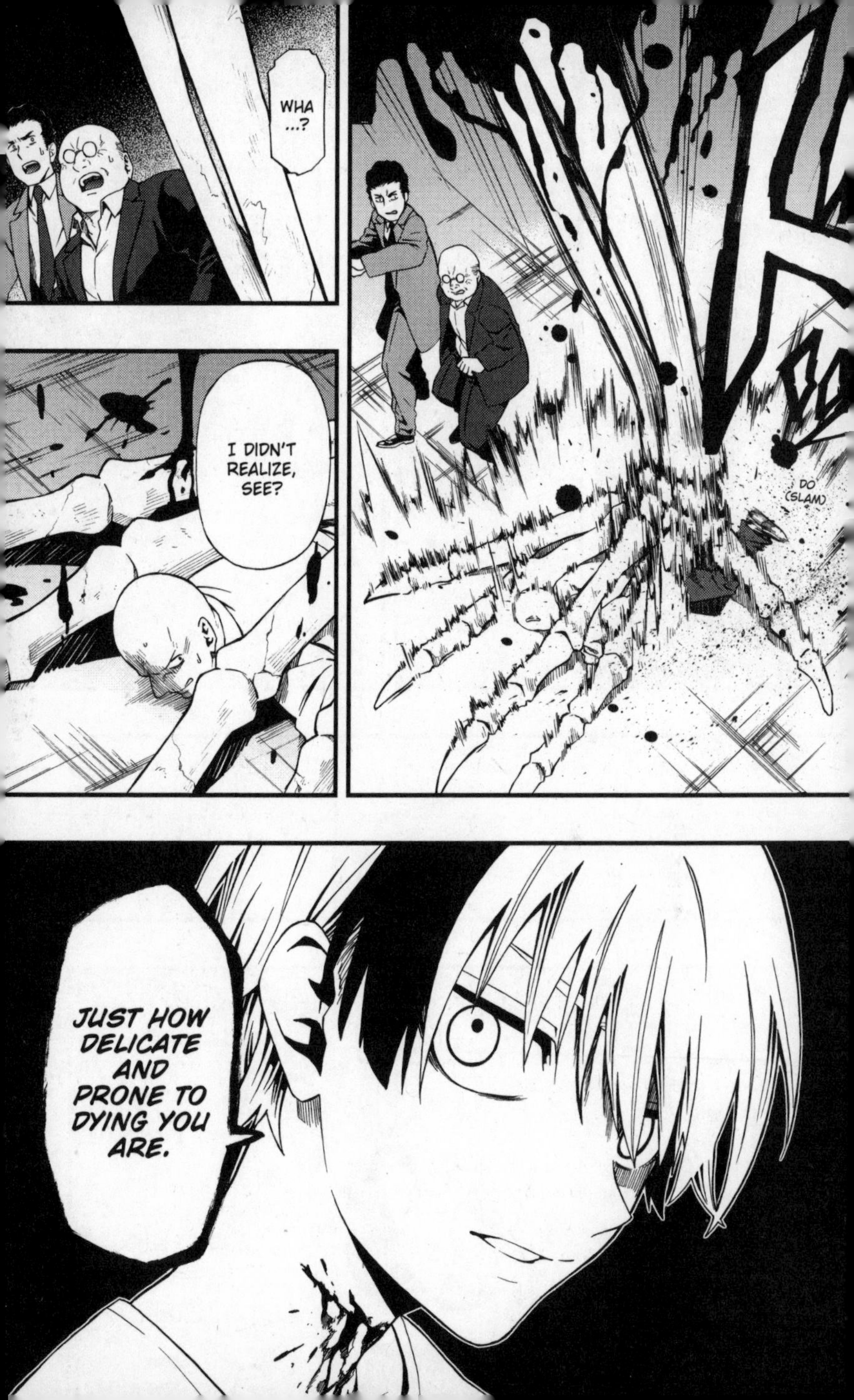
DO
(SLAM)
WHA
...?
I DIDN'T REALIZE, SEE?
JUST HOW DELICATE AND PRONE TO DYING YOU ARE.

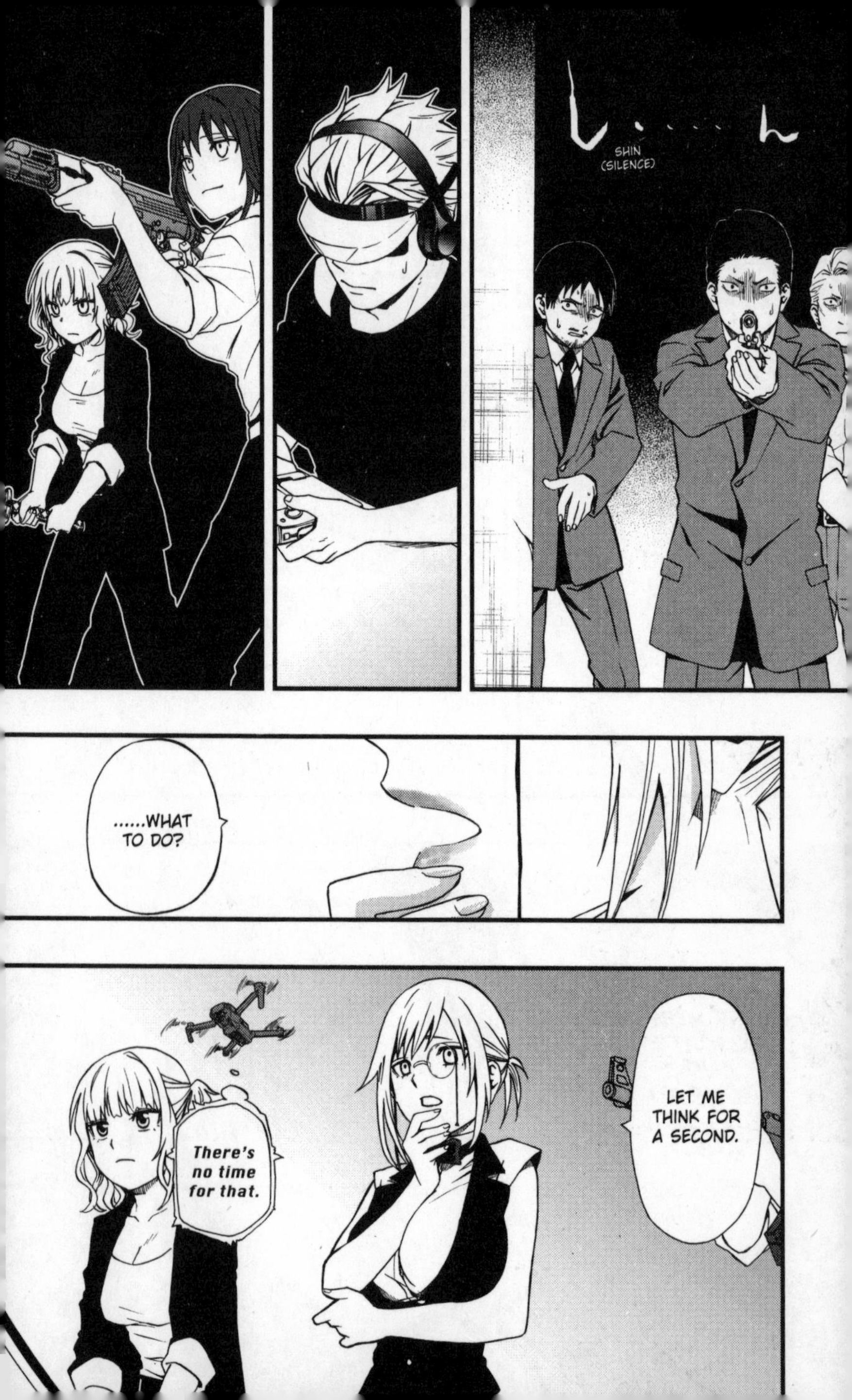

し・・・ん
SHIN (SILENCE)
......WHAT TO DO?
LET ME THINK FOR A SECOND.
There's no time for that.

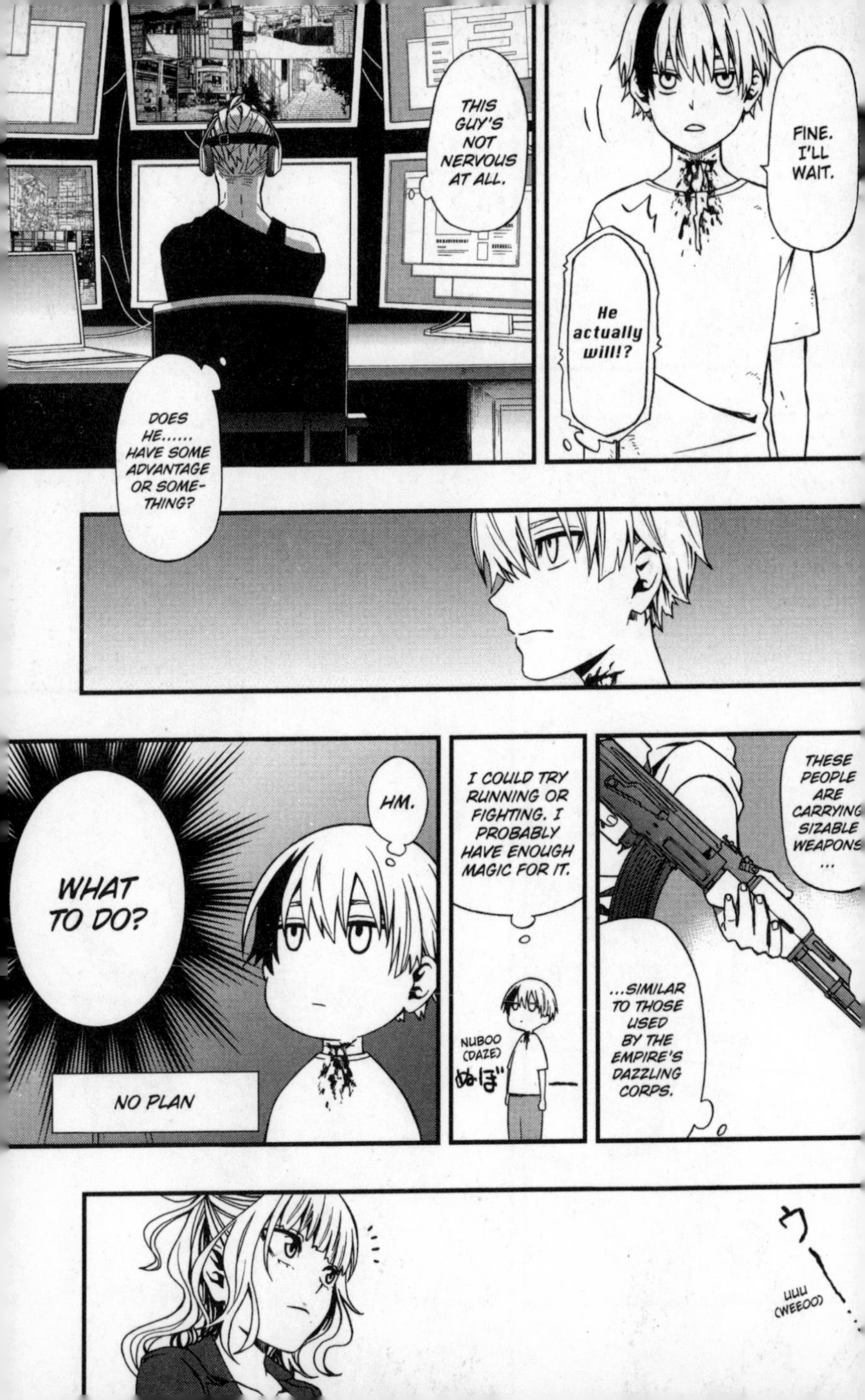
FINE. I'LL WAIT.
He actually will!?
THIS GUY'S NOT NERVOUS AT ALL.
DOES HE...... HAVE SOME ADVANTAGE OR SOME-THING?
THESE PEOPLE ARE CARRYING SIZABLE WEAPONS ...
...SIMILAR TO THOSE USED BY THE EMPIRE'S DAZZLING CORPS.
I COULD TRY RUNNING OR FIGHTING. I PROBABLY HAVE ENOUGH MAGIC FOR IT.
ぬぼ
NUBOO (DAZE)
HM.
WHAT TO DO?
NO PLAN
ウー
UUU (WEEOO)

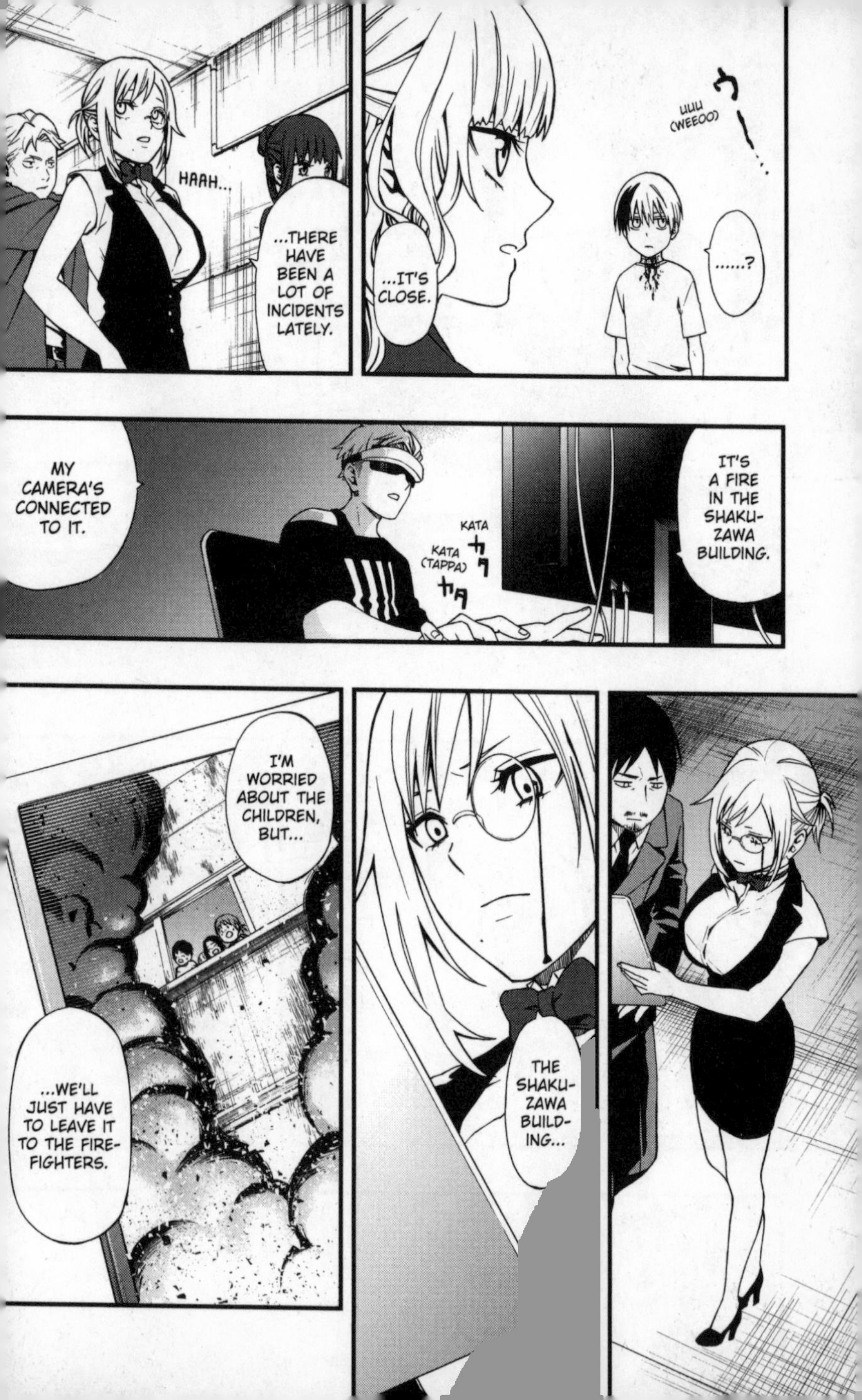
UUU (WEEOO)
......?
...IT'S CLOSE.
HAAH...
...THERE HAVE BEEN A LOT OF INCIDENTS LATELY.
IT'S A FIRE IN THE SHAKU-ZAWA BUILDING.
KATA KATA (TAPPA)
MY CAMERA'S CONNECTED TO IT.
THE SHAKU-ZAWA BUILD-ING...
I'M WORRIED ABOUT THE CHILDREN, BUT...
...WE'LL JUST HAVE TO LEAVE IT TO THE FIRE-FIGHTERS.

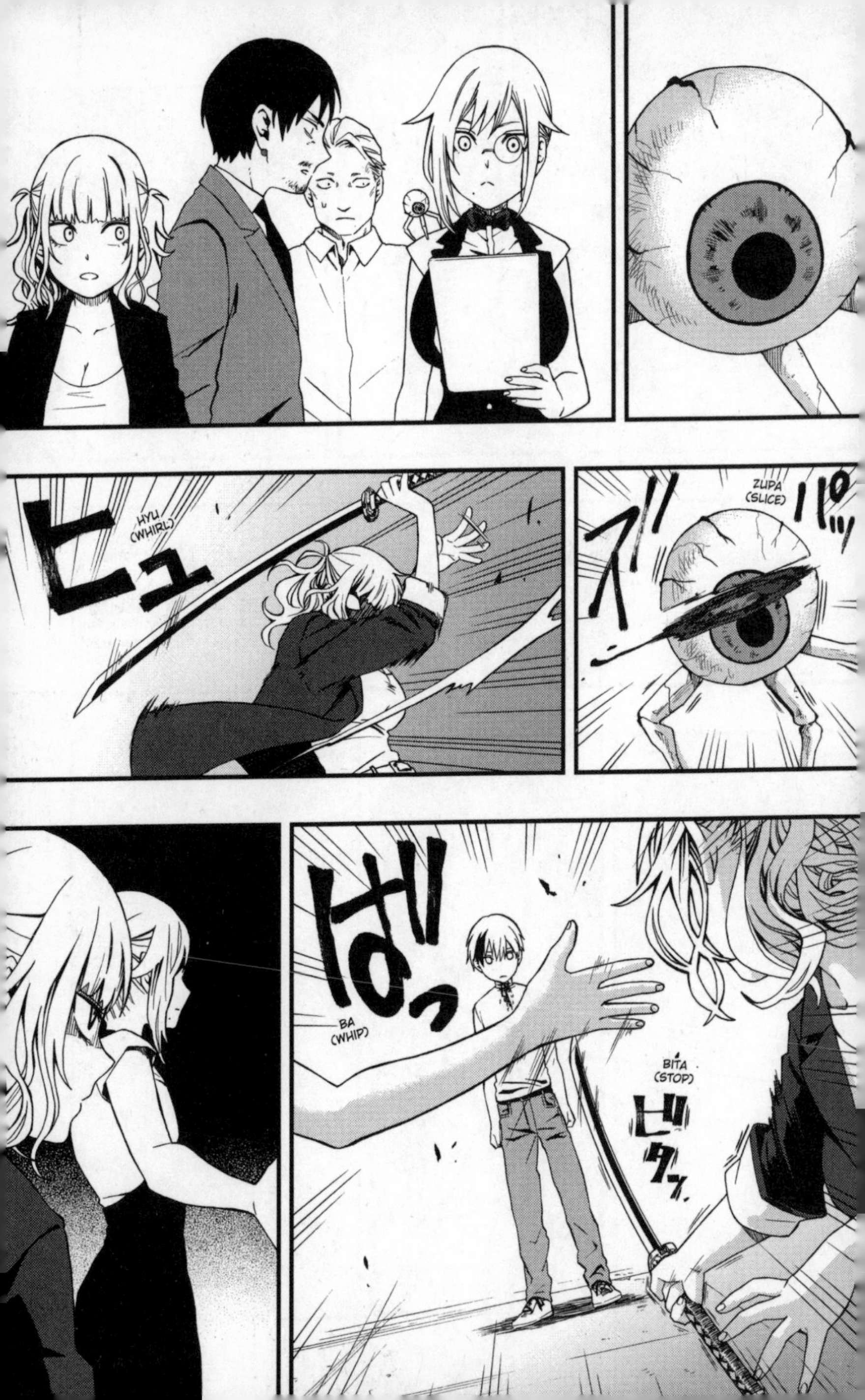
ZUPA
(SLICE)
ズパッ
HYU
(WHIRL)
ヒュ
BITA
(STOP)
ビタッ
BA
(WHIP)
ばっ

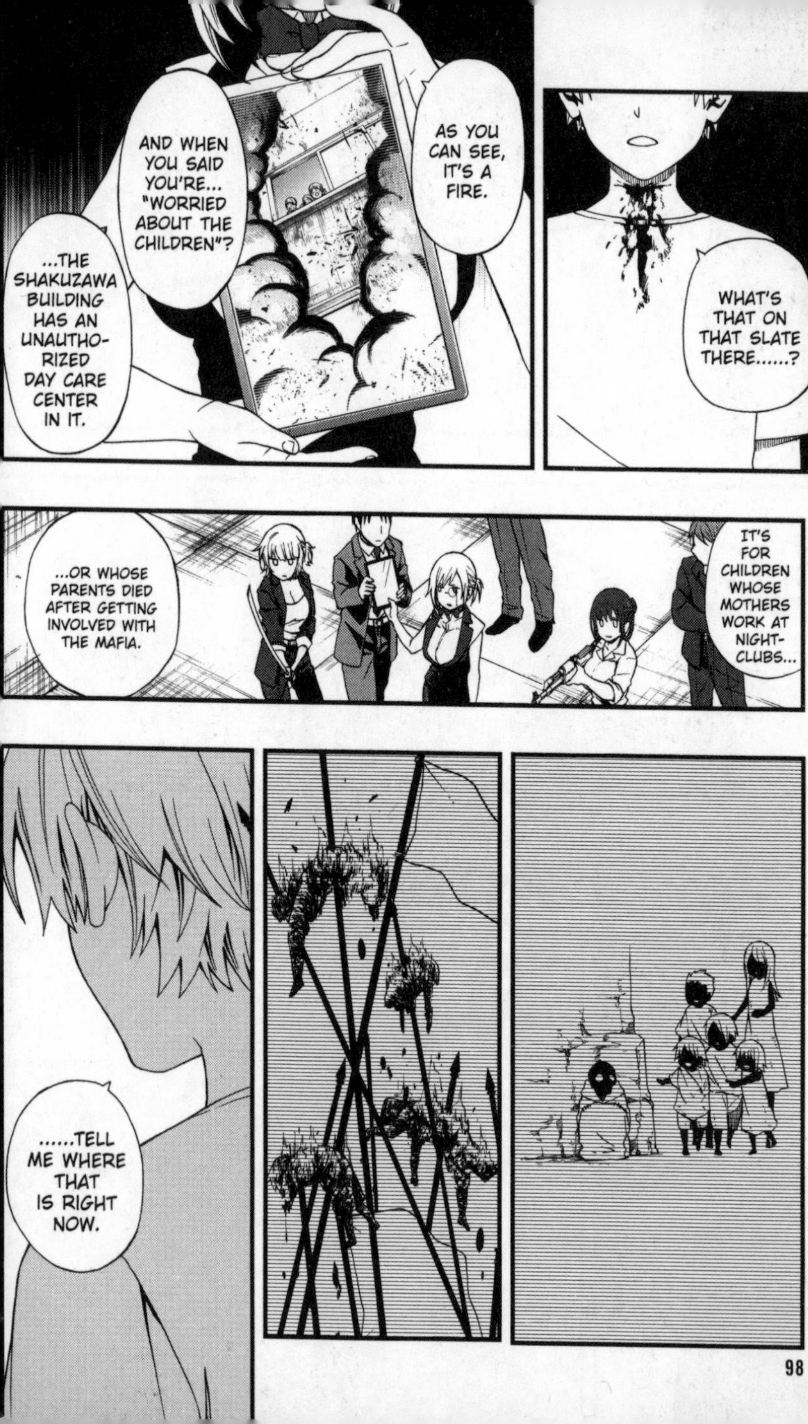
WHAT'S THAT ON THAT SLATE THERE......?
AS YOU CAN SEE, IT'S A FIRE.
...THE SHAKUZAWA BUILDING HAS AN UNAUTHO-RIZED DAY CARE CENTER IN IT.
AND WHEN YOU SAID YOU'RE... "WORRIED ABOUT THE CHILDREN"?
IT'S FOR CHILDREN WHOSE MOTHERS WORK AT NIGHT-CLUBS...
...OR WHOSE PARENTS DIED AFTER GETTING INVOLVED WITH THE MAFIA.
......TELL ME WHERE THAT IS RIGHT NOW.

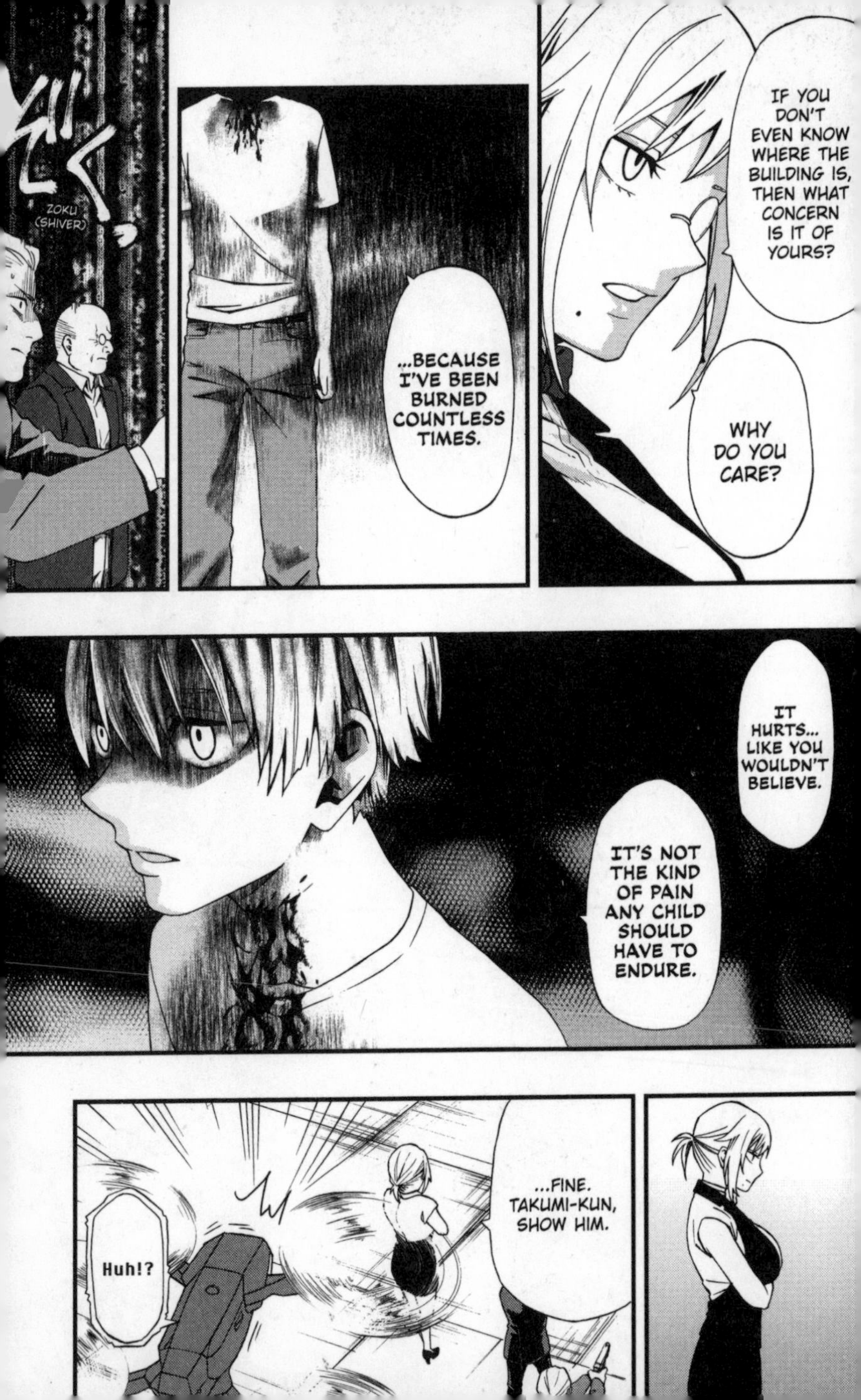
IF YOU DON'T EVEN KNOW WHERE THE BUILDING IS, THEN WHAT CONCERN IS IT OF YOURS?
WHY DO YOU CARE?
...BECAUSE I'VE BEEN BURNED COUNTLESS TIMES.
ZOKU (SHIVER)
IT HURTS... LIKE YOU WOULDN'T BELIEVE.
IT'S NOT THE KIND OF PAIN ANY CHILD SHOULD HAVE TO ENDURE.
...FINE. TAKUMI-KUN, SHOW HIM.
Huh!?

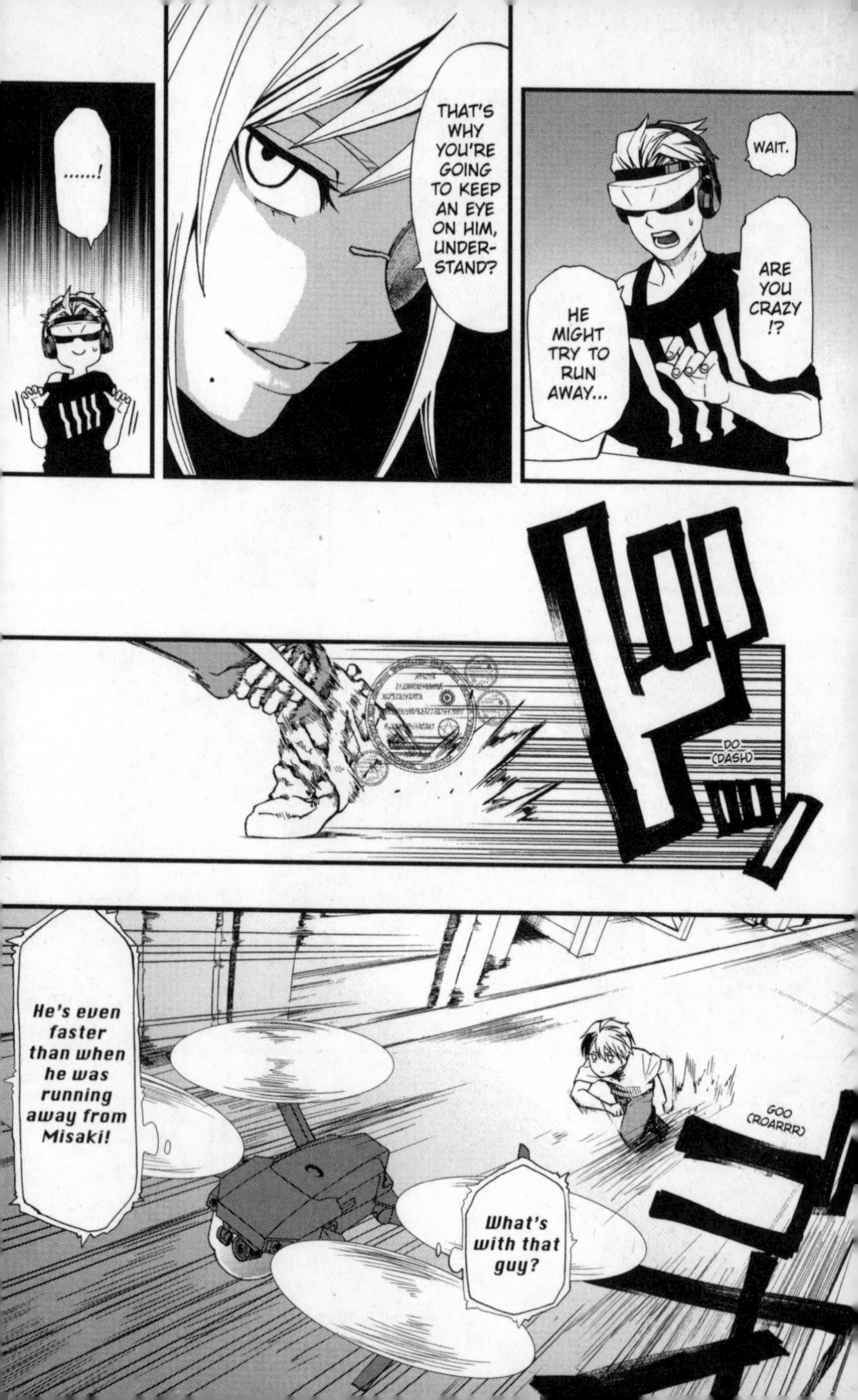
WAIT.
ARE YOU CRAZY!?
HE MIGHT TRY TO RUN AWAY...
THAT'S WHY YOU'RE GOING TO KEEP AN EYE ON HIM, UNDERSTAND?
......!
DO (DASH)
GOO (ROARRR)
What's with that guy?
He's even faster than when he was running away from Misaki!

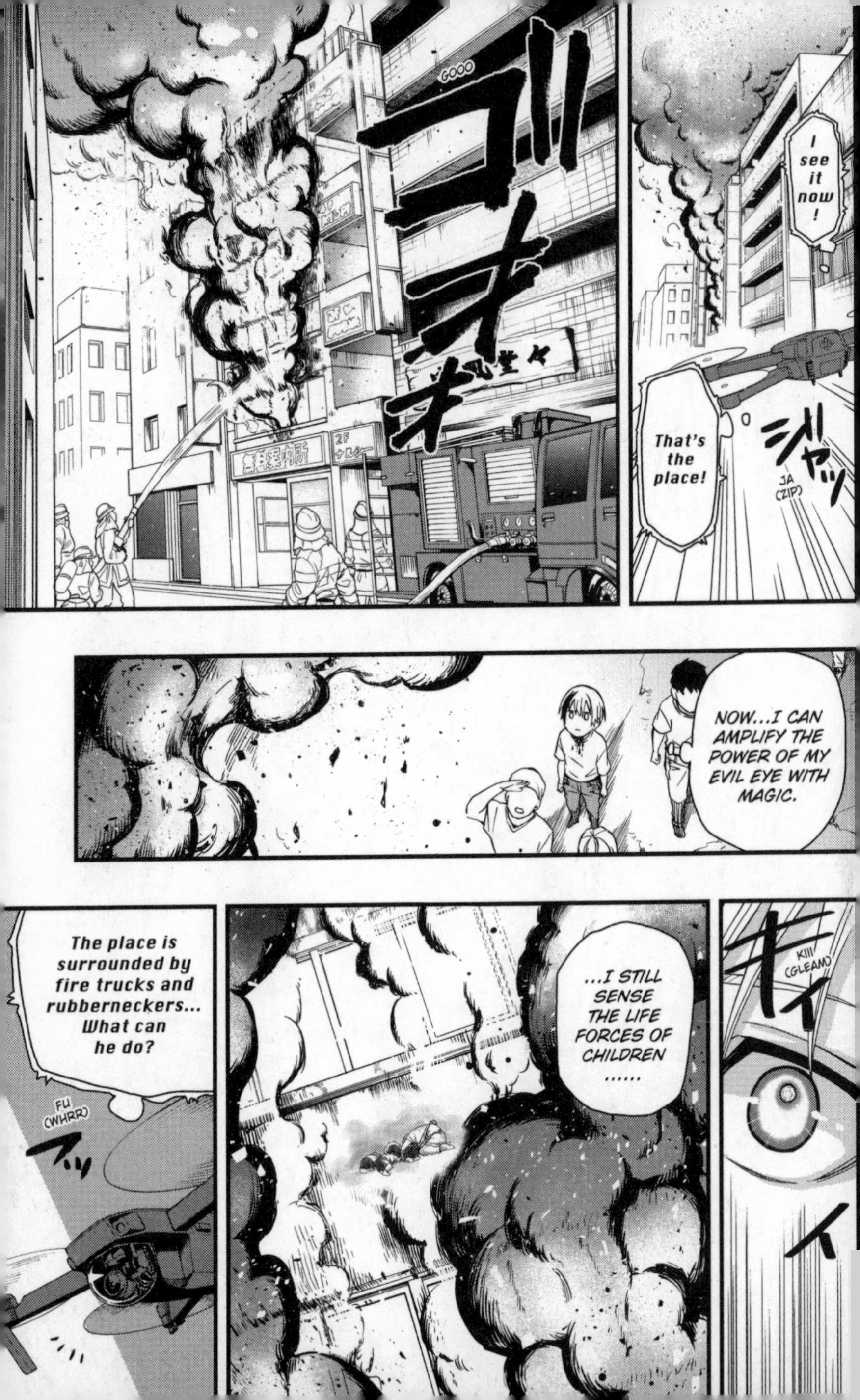
I see it now!
That's the place!
JA (ZIP)
GOOO
NOW...I CAN AMPLIFY THE POWER OF MY EVIL EYE WITH MAGIC.
KIII (GLEAM)
...I STILL SENSE THE LIFE FORCES OF CHILDREN ......
The place is surrounded by fire trucks and rubberneckers... What can he do?
FU (WHRR)

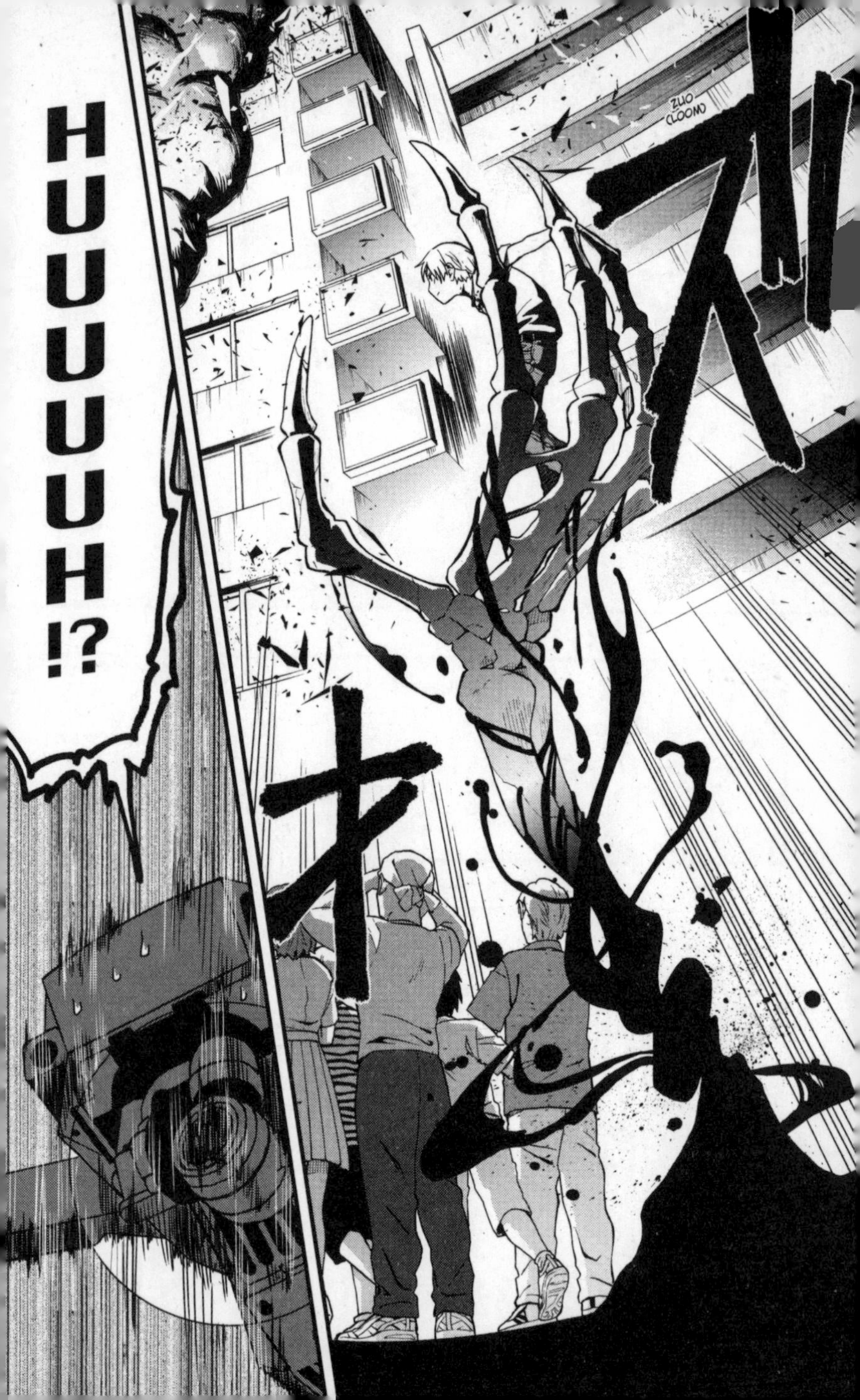
ZUO
(LOOM)
HUUUUUH!?

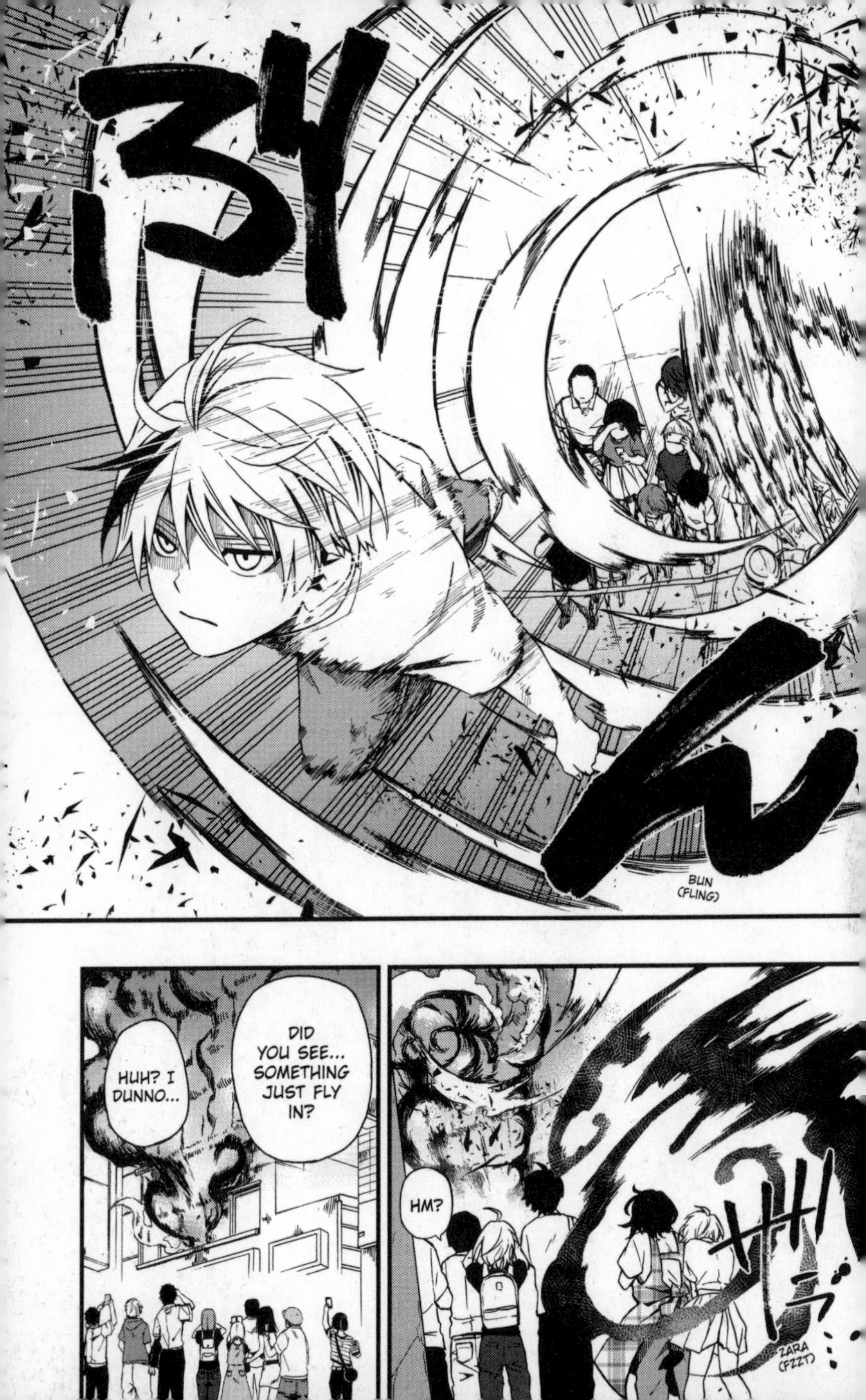
BUN
(FLING)
HM?
ZARA
(FZZT)
DID YOU SEE... SOMETHING JUST FLY IN?
HUH? I DUNNO...

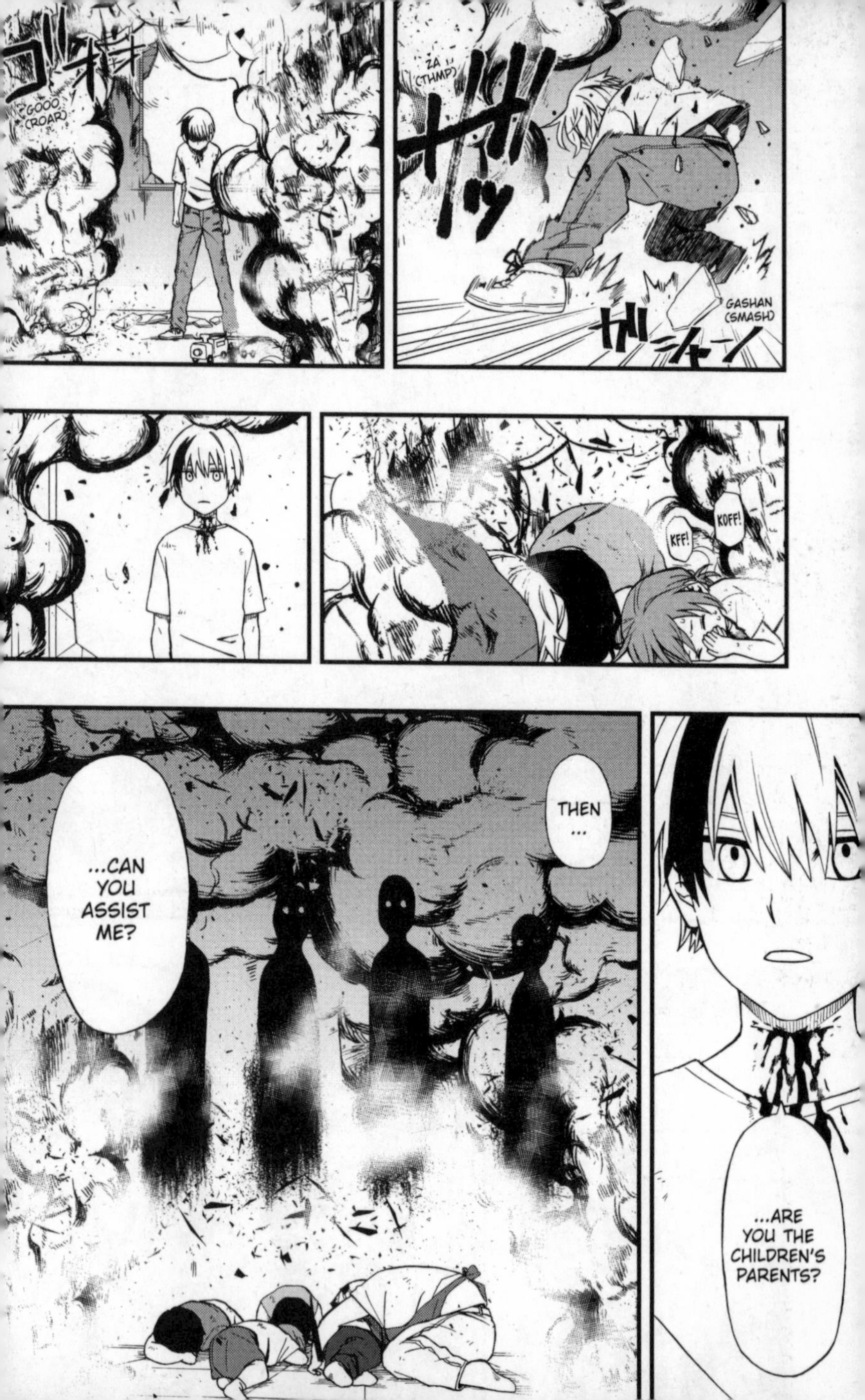
ZA (THMP)
GASHAN (SMASH)
GOOO (ROAR)
KOFF!
KFF!
THEN ...
...ARE YOU THE CHILDREN'S PARENTS?
...CAN YOU ASSIST ME?

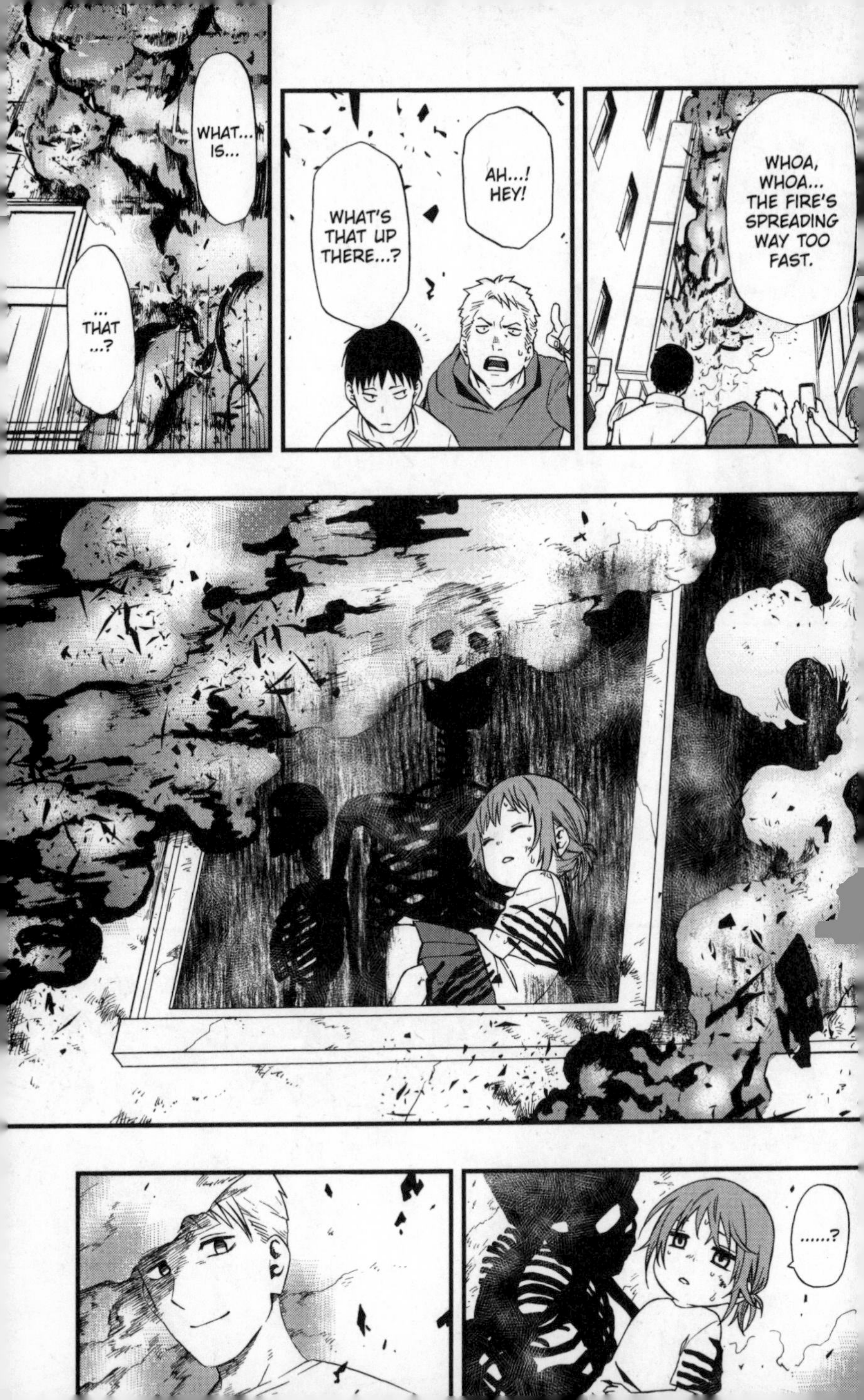
WHOA, WHOA... THE FIRE'S SPREADING WAY TOO FAST.
AH...! HEY!
WHAT'S THAT UP THERE...?
WHAT... IS...
... THAT ...?
......?

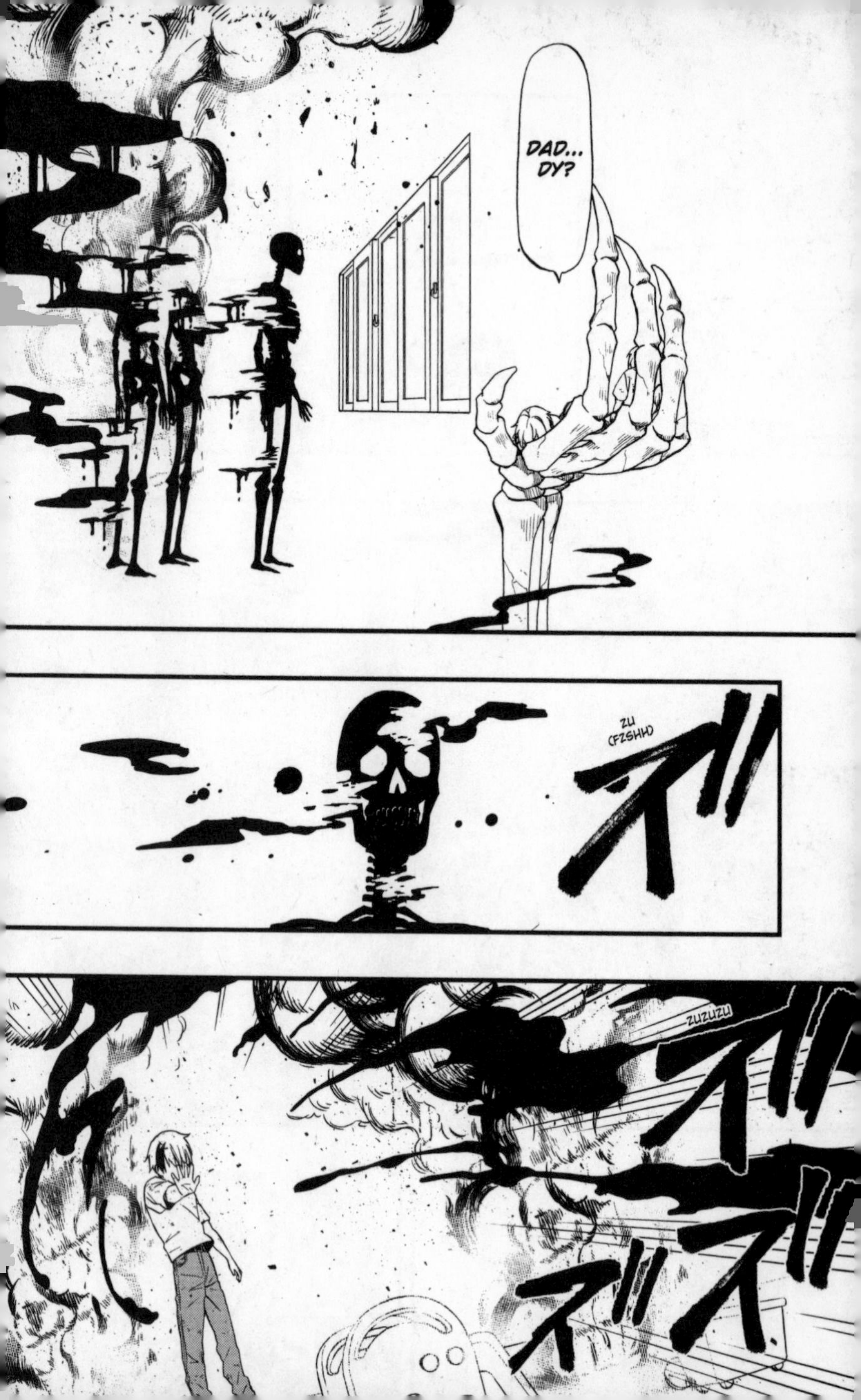
DAD... DY?
ZU (FZSHH)
ZUZUZU

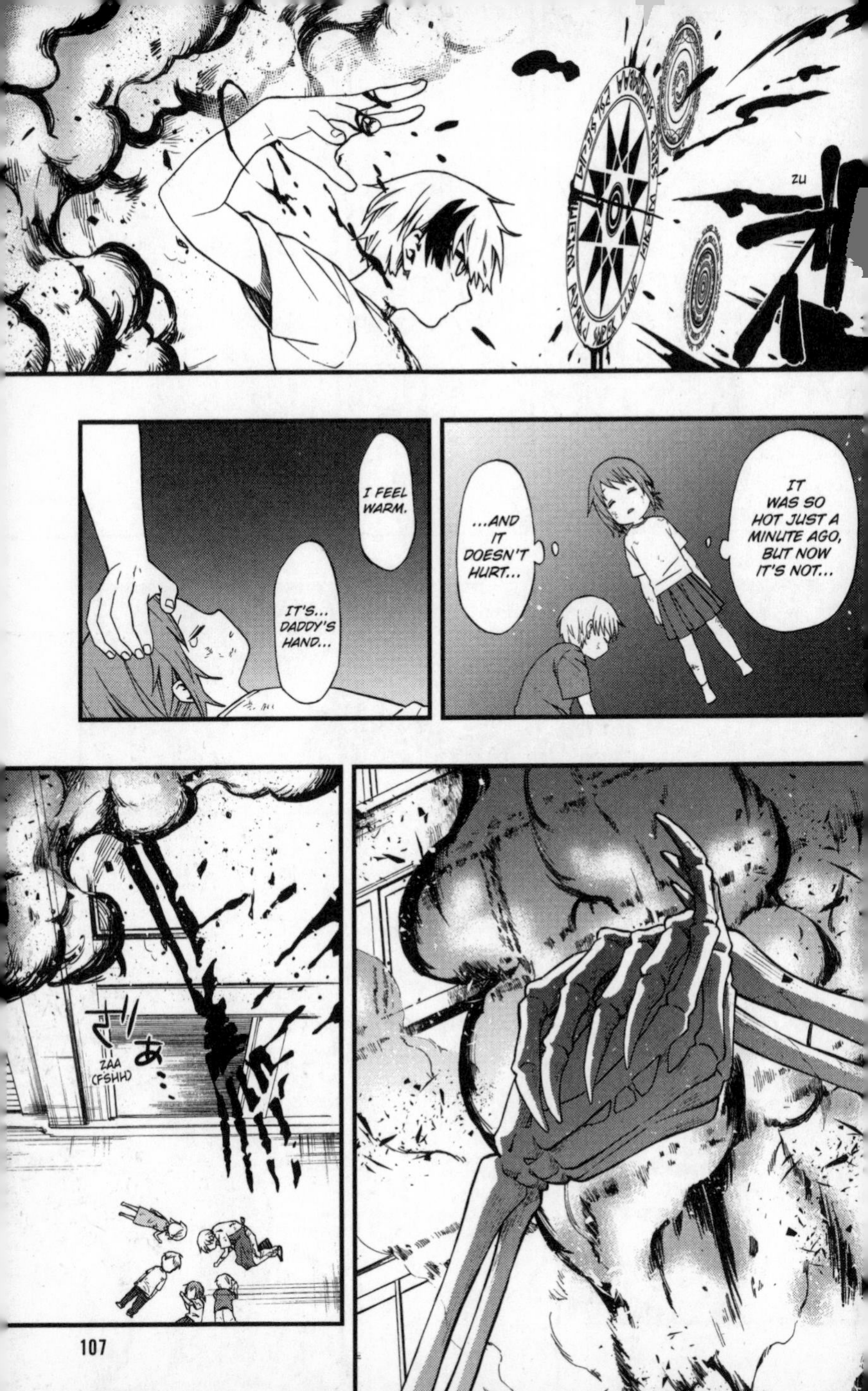
ZU
IT WAS SO HOT JUST A MINUTE AGO, BUT NOW IT'S NOT...
...AND IT DOESN'T HURT...
I FEEL WARM.
IT'S... DADDY'S HAND...
ZAA (FSHH)

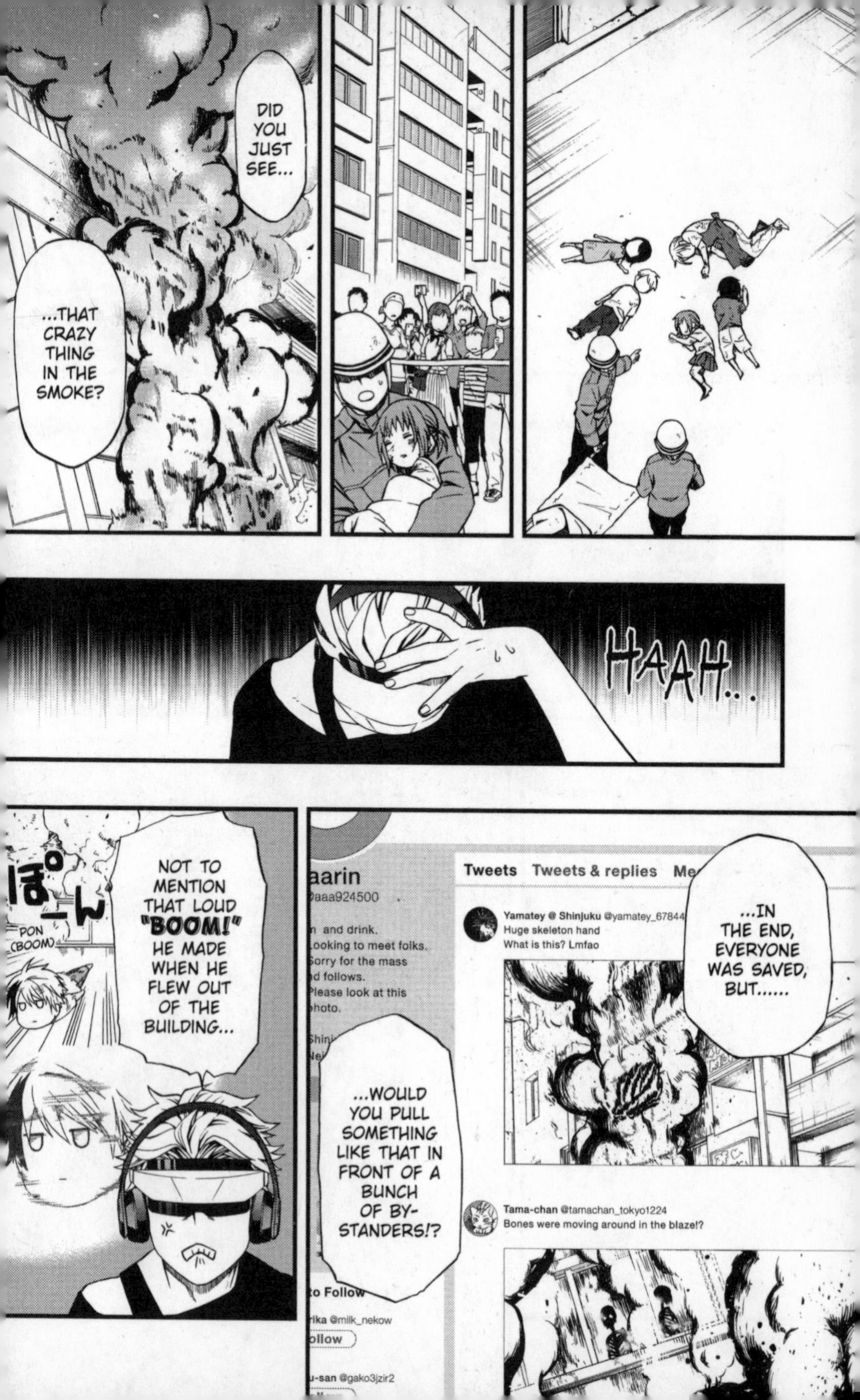

DID YOU JUST SEE...
...THAT CRAZY THING IN THE SMOKE?
HAAH...
...IN THE END, EVERYONE WAS SAVED, BUT......
Tweets
Tweets & replies
aarin
and drink.
Looking to meet folks.
Sorry for the mass
Please look at this
Yamatey @ Shinjuku @yamatey_67844
Huge skeleton hand
What is this? Lmfao
Tama-chan @tamachan_tokyo1224
Bones were moving around in the blaze!?
rika @milk_nekow
...WOULD YOU PULL SOMETHING LIKE THAT IN FRONT OF A BUNCH OF BY-STANDERS!?
NOT TO MENTION THAT LOUD "BOOM!" HE MADE WHEN HE FLEW OUT OF THE BUILDING...
ぽーん
PON (BOOM)

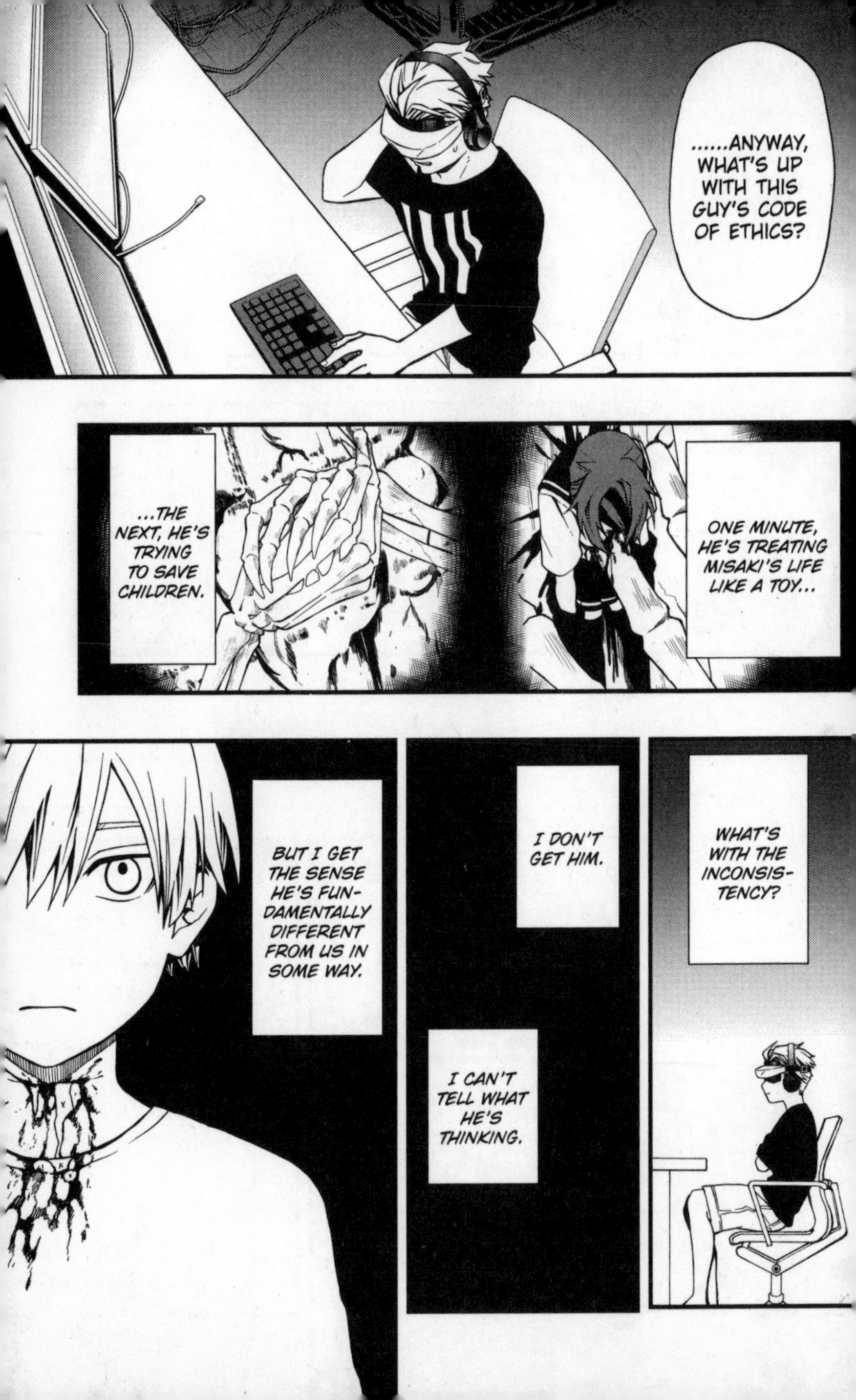
......ANYWAY, WHAT'S UP WITH THIS GUY'S CODE OF ETHICS?
ONE MINUTE, HE'S TREATING MISAKI'S LIFE LIKE A TOY...
...THE NEXT, HE'S TRYING TO SAVE CHILDREN.
WHAT'S WITH THE INCONSISTENCY?
I DON'T GET HIM.
I CAN'T TELL WHAT HE'S THINKING.
BUT I GET THE SENSE HE'S FUNDAMENTALLY DIFFERENT FROM US IN SOME WAY.

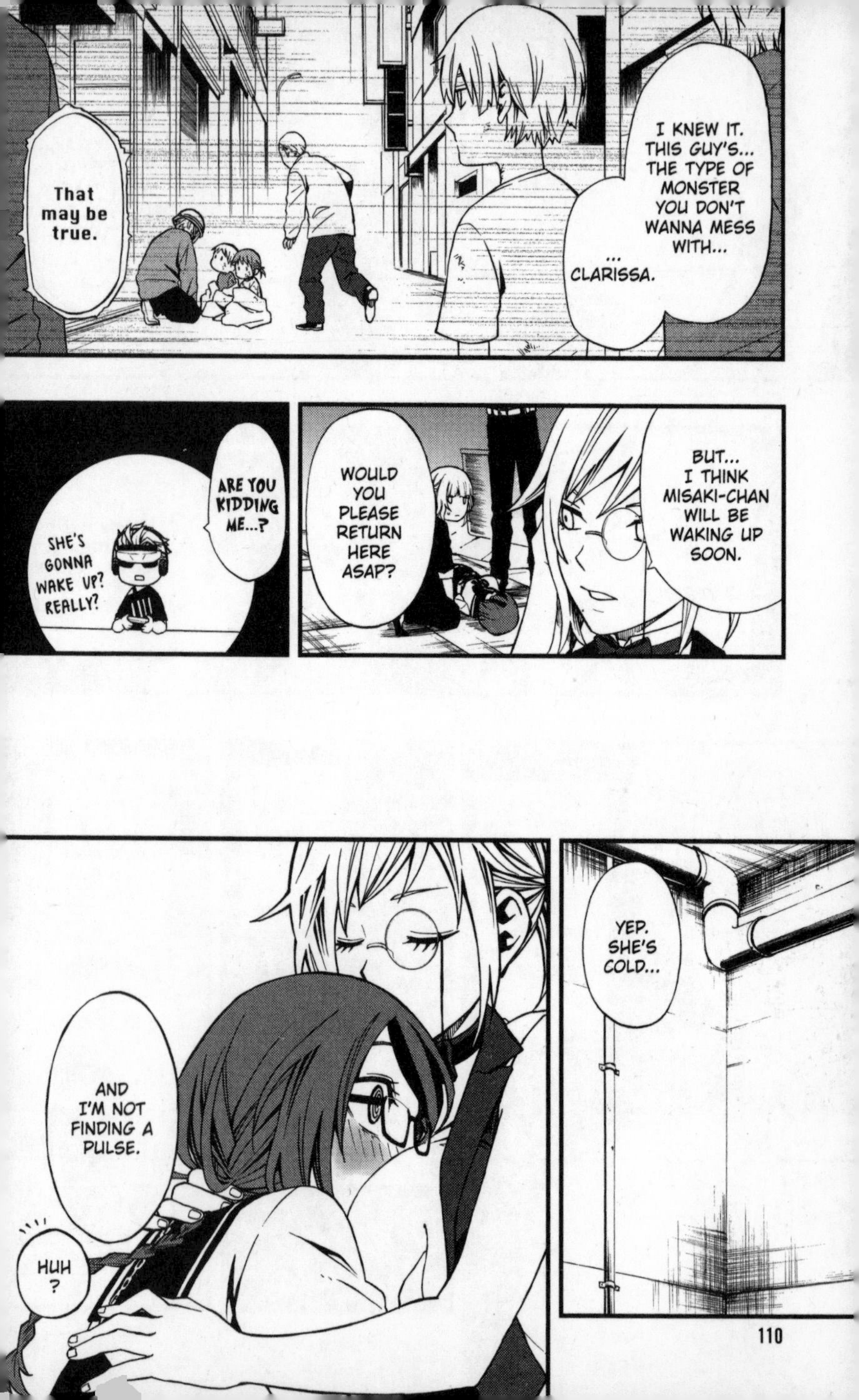
I KNEW IT. THIS GUY'S... THE TYPE OF MONSTER YOU DON'T WANNA MESS WITH... ... CLARISSA.
That may be true.
BUT... I THINK MISAKI-CHAN WILL BE WAKING UP SOON.
WOULD YOU PLEASE RETURN HERE ASAP?
ARE YOU KIDDING ME...?
SHE'S GONNA WAKE UP? REALLY?
YEP. SHE'S COLD...
AND I'M NOT FINDING A PULSE.
HUH?

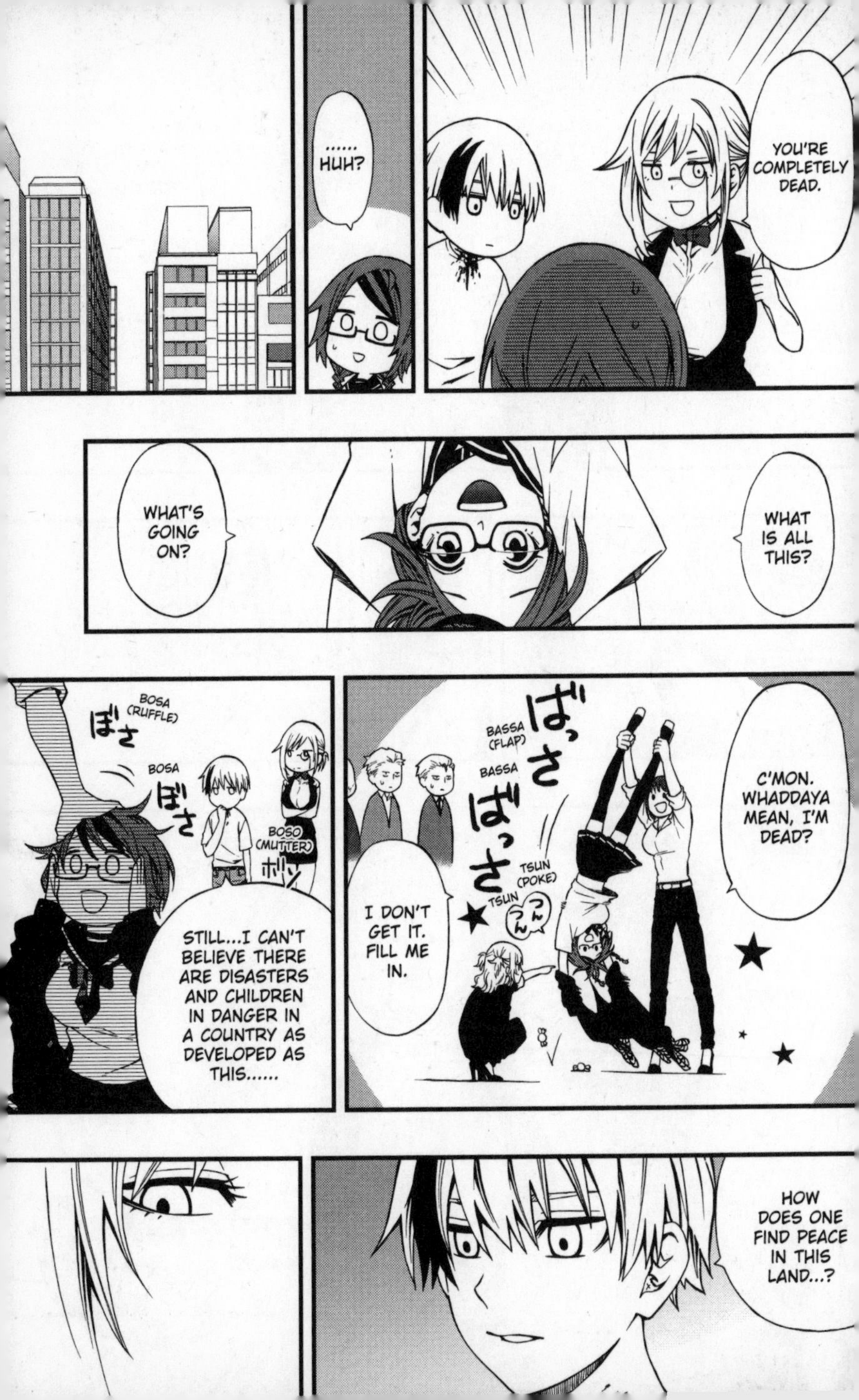
YOU'RE COMPLETELY DEAD.
......HUH?
WHAT IS ALL THIS?
WHAT'S GOING ON?
C'MON. WHADDAYA MEAN, I'M DEAD?
ばっさ
BASSA (FLAP)
ばっさ
BASSA
つん
TSUN (POKE)
つん
TSUN
I DON'T GET IT. FILL ME IN.
ぼさ
BOSA (RUFFLE)
ぼさ
BOSA
ボソ
BOSO (MUTTER)
STILL...I CAN'T BELIEVE THERE ARE DISASTERS AND CHILDREN IN DANGER IN A COUNTRY AS DEVELOPED AS THIS......
HOW DOES ONE FIND PEACE IN THIS LAND...?

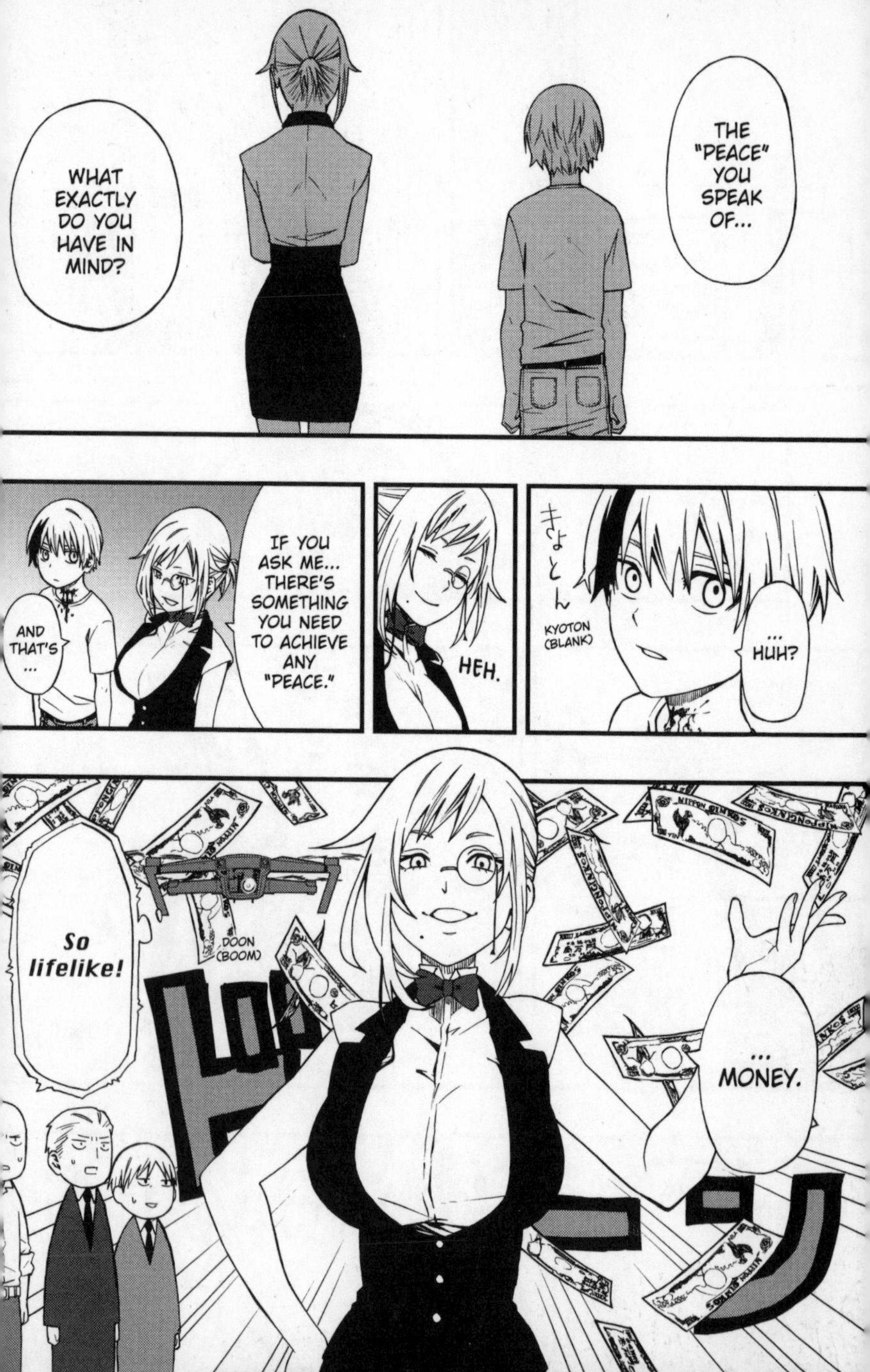
THE "PEACE" YOU SPEAK OF...
WHAT EXACTLY DO YOU HAVE IN MIND?
きょとん
KYOTON (BLANK)
... HUH?
HEH.
IF YOU ASK ME... THERE'S SOMETHING YOU NEED TO ACHIEVE ANY "PEACE."
AND THAT'S ...
... MONEY.
DOON (BOOM)
So lifelike!

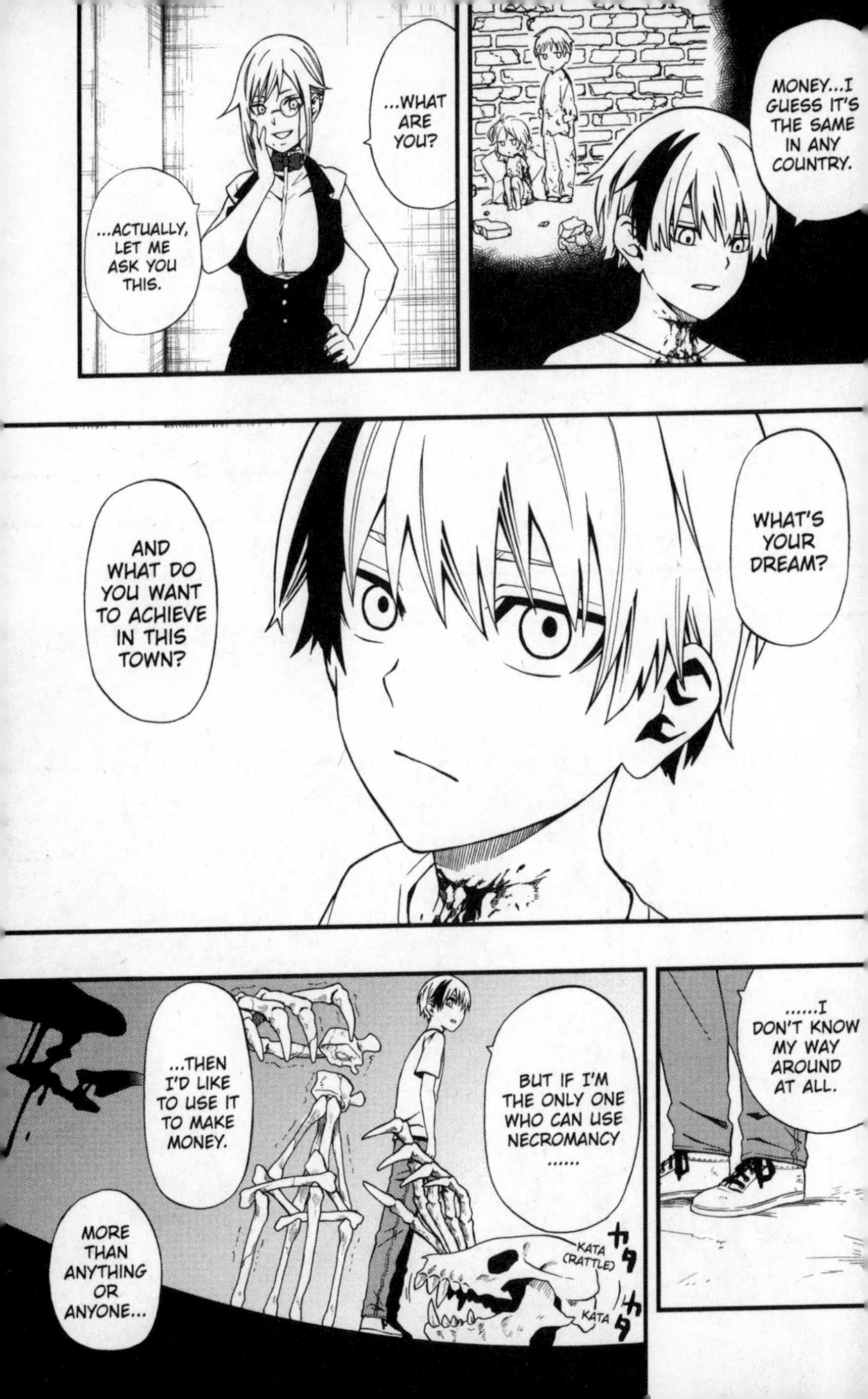
MONEY...I GUESS IT'S THE SAME IN ANY COUNTRY.
...WHAT ARE YOU?
...ACTUALLY, LET ME ASK YOU THIS.
WHAT'S YOUR DREAM?
AND WHAT DO YOU WANT TO ACHIEVE IN THIS TOWN?
......I DON'T KNOW MY WAY AROUND AT ALL.
BUT IF I'M THE ONLY ONE WHO CAN USE NECROMANCY ......
...THEN I'D LIKE TO USE IT TO MAKE MONEY.
MORE THAN ANYTHING OR ANYONE...
カタ KATA (RATTLE)
カタ KATA

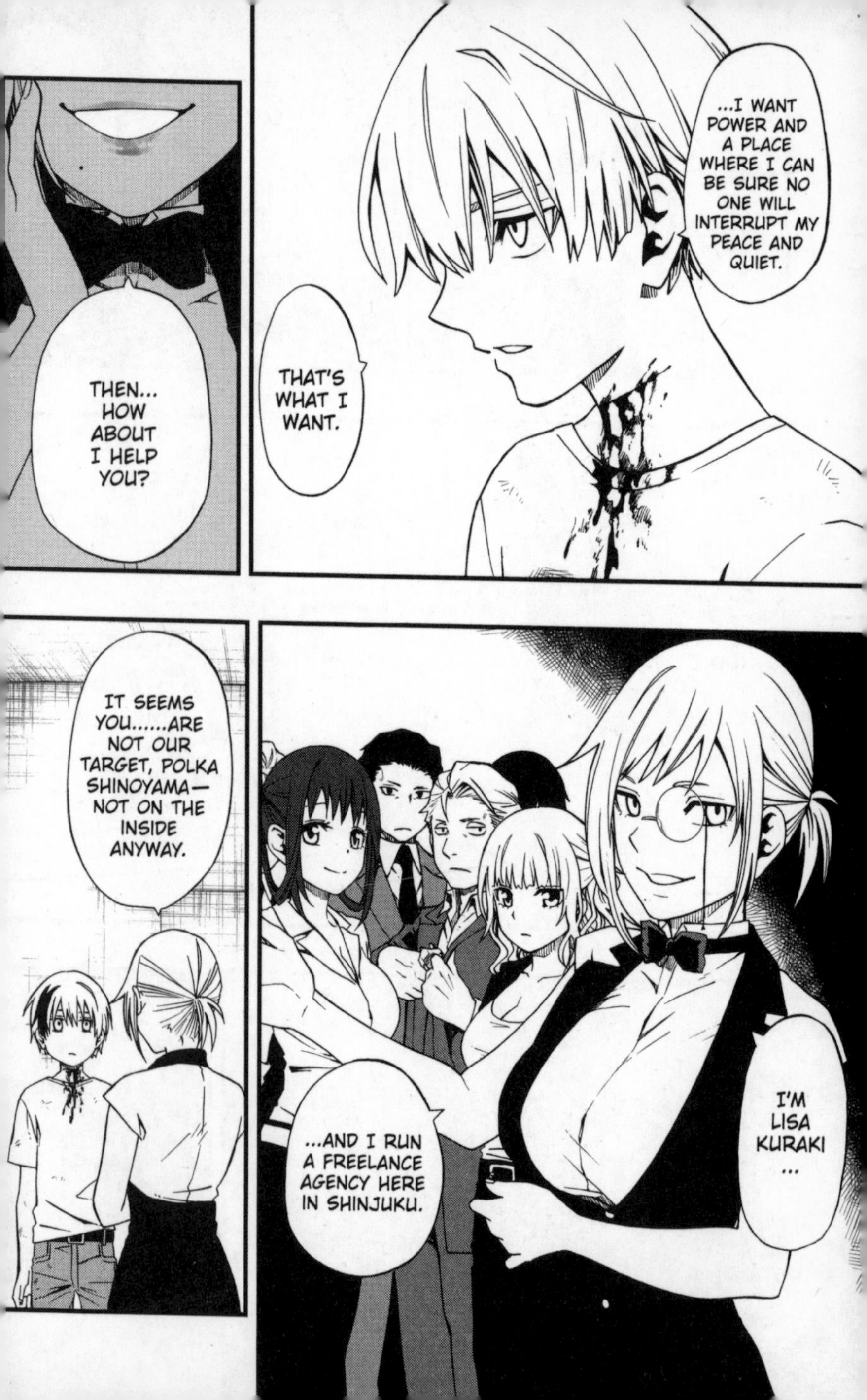
...I WANT POWER AND A PLACE WHERE I CAN BE SURE NO ONE WILL INTERRUPT MY PEACE AND QUIET.
THAT'S WHAT I WANT.
THEN... HOW ABOUT I HELP YOU?
I'M LISA KURAKI ...
...AND I RUN A FREELANCE AGENCY HERE IN SHINJUKU.
IT SEEMS YOU......ARE NOT OUR TARGET, POLKA SHINOYAMA—NOT ON THE INSIDE ANYWAY.

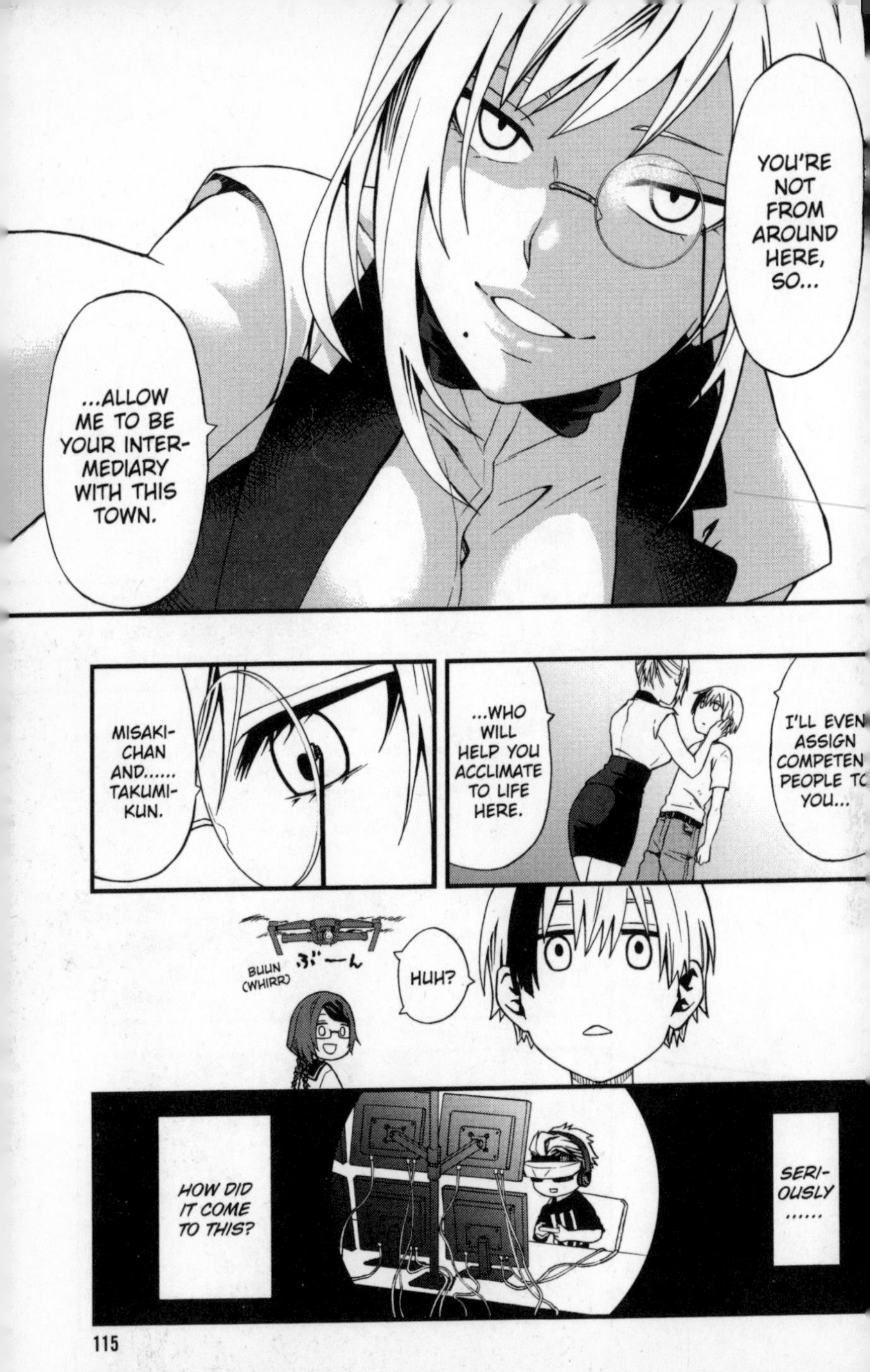

YOU'RE NOT FROM AROUND HERE, SO...
...ALLOW ME TO BE YOUR INTER-MEDIARY WITH THIS TOWN.
I'LL EVEN ASSIGN COMPETEN PEOPLE T YOU...
...WHO WILL HELP YOU ACCLIMATE TO LIFE HERE.
MISAKI-CHAN AND...... TAKUMI-KUN.
HUH?
ぶーん
BUUN (WHIRR)
SERI-OUSLY ......
HOW DID IT COME TO THIS?

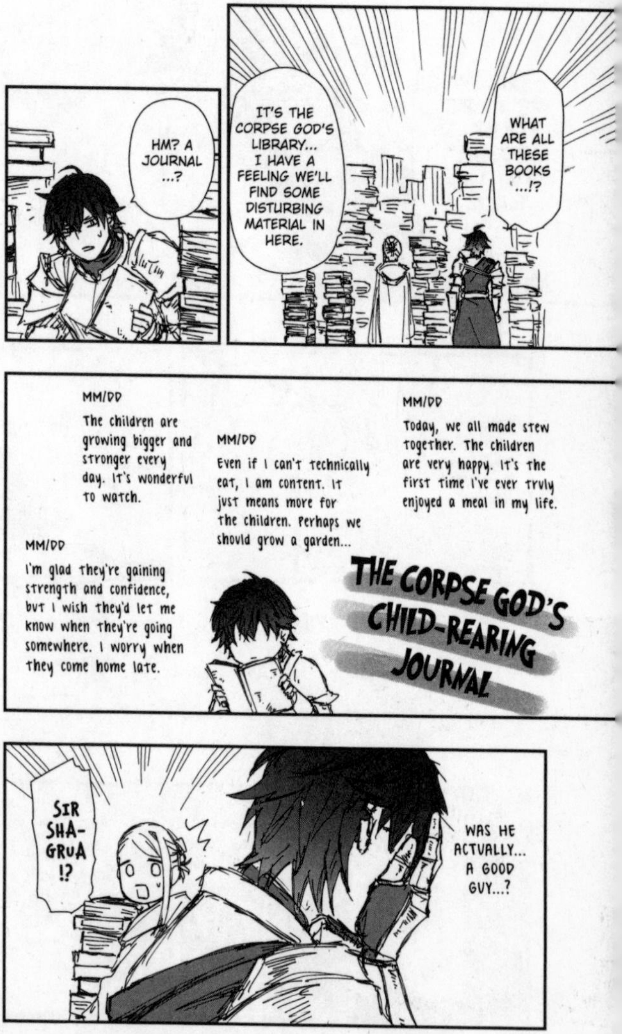
WHAT ARE ALL THESE BOOKS ...!?
IT'S THE CORPSE GOD'S LIBRARY... I HAVE A FEELING WE'LL FIND SOME DISTURBING MATERIAL IN HERE.
HM? A JOURNAL ...?
MM/DD Today, we all made stew together. The children are very happy. It's the first time I've ever truly enjoyed a meal in my life.
MM/DD Even if I can't technically eat, I am content. It just means more for the children. Perhaps we should grow a garden...
MM/DD The children are growing bigger and stronger every day. It's wonderful to watch.
MM/DD I'm glad they're gaining strength and confidence, but I wish they'd let me know when they're going somewhere. I worry when they come home late.
THE CORPSE GOD'S CHILD-REARING JOURNAL
WAS HE ACTUALLY... A GOOD GUY...?
SIR SHA-GRUA !?

#04

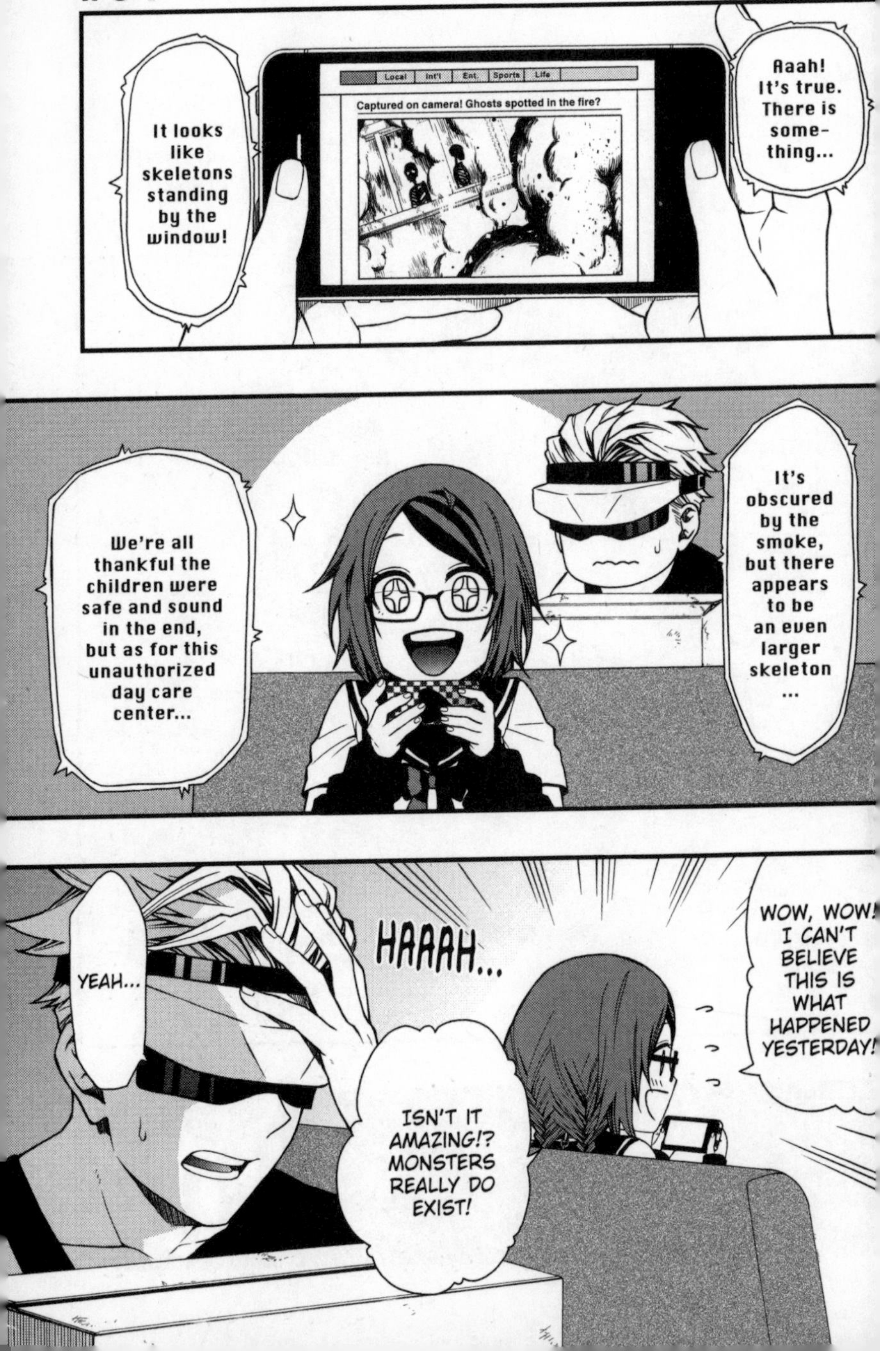
Local
Int'l
Ent.
Sports
Life
Captured on camera! Ghosts spotted in the fire?
Aaah! It's true. There is some-thing...
It looks like skeletons standing by the window!
It's obscured by the smoke, but there appears to be an even larger skeleton...
We're all thankful the children were safe and sound in the end, but as for this unauthorized day care center...
WOW, WOW! I CAN'T BELIEVE THIS IS WHAT HAPPENED YESTERDAY!
ISN'T IT AMAZING!? MONSTERS REALLY DO EXIST!
HAAAH...
YEAH...

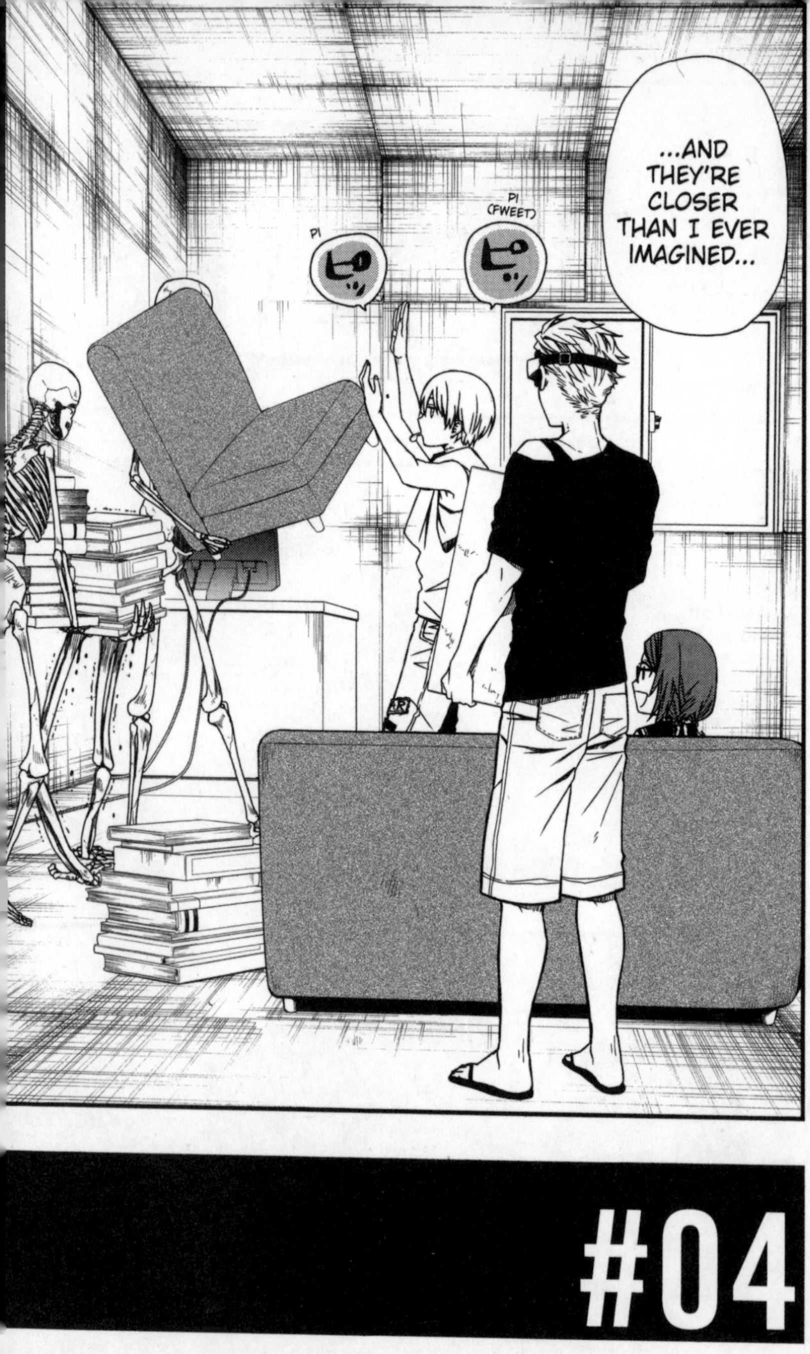
...AND THEY'RE CLOSER THAN I EVER IMAGINED...
ピッ
PI (FWEET)
ピッ
PI

#04

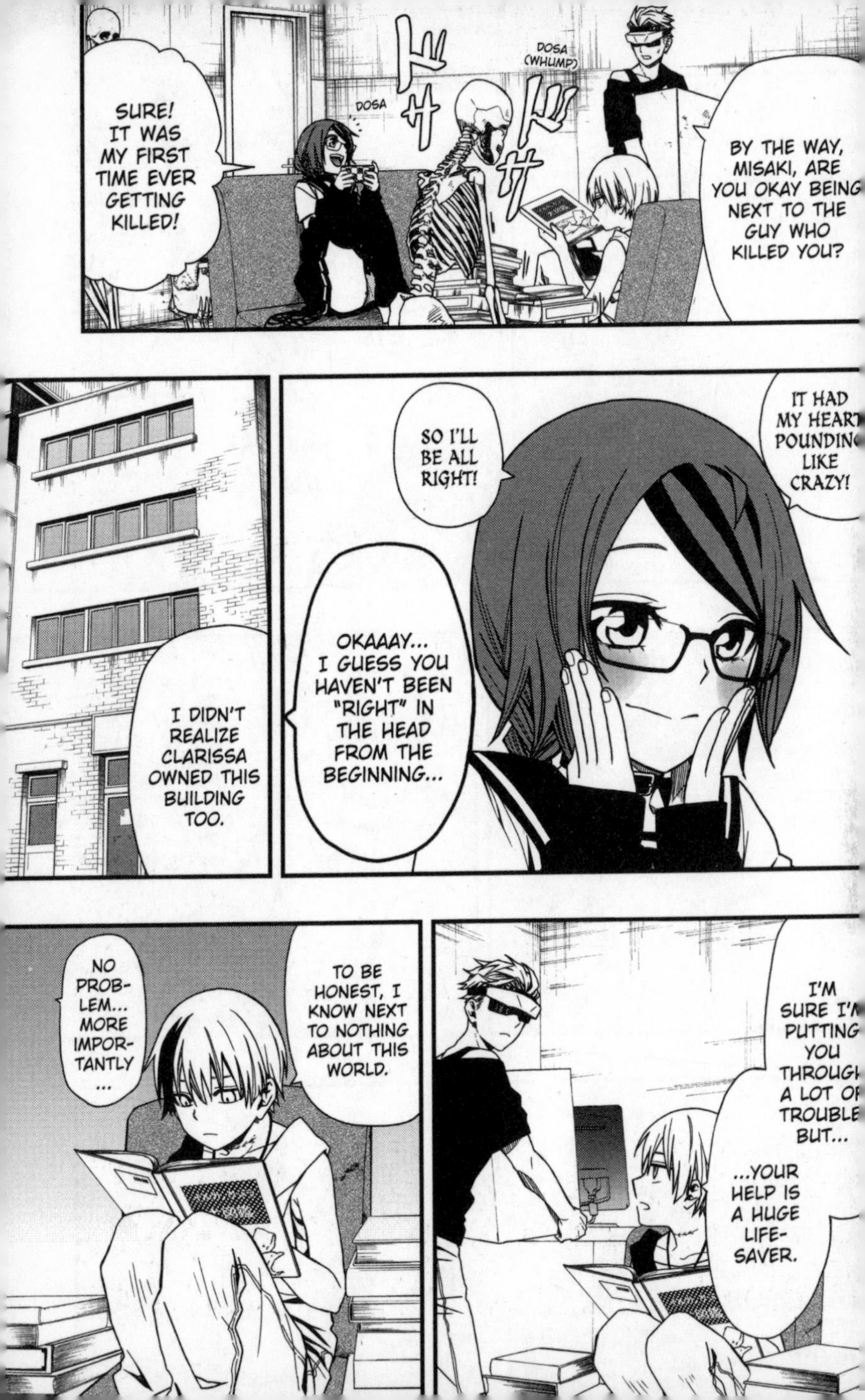
BY THE WAY, MISAKI, ARE YOU OKAY BEING NEXT TO THE GUY WHO KILLED YOU?
DOSA (WHUMP)
ドサ
DOSA
ドサ
SURE! IT WAS MY FIRST TIME EVER GETTING KILLED!
IT HAD MY HEART POUNDING LIKE CRAZY!
SO I'LL BE ALL RIGHT!
OKAAAY... I GUESS YOU HAVEN'T BEEN "RIGHT" IN THE HEAD FROM THE BEGINNING...
I DIDN'T REALIZE CLARISSA OWNED THIS BUILDING TOO.
I'M SURE I'M PUTTING YOU THROUGH A LOT OF TROUBLE BUT...
...YOUR HELP IS A HUGE LIFE-SAVER.
TO BE HONEST, I KNOW NEXT TO NOTHING ABOUT THIS WORLD.
NO PROB-LEM... MORE IMPOR-TANTLY ...

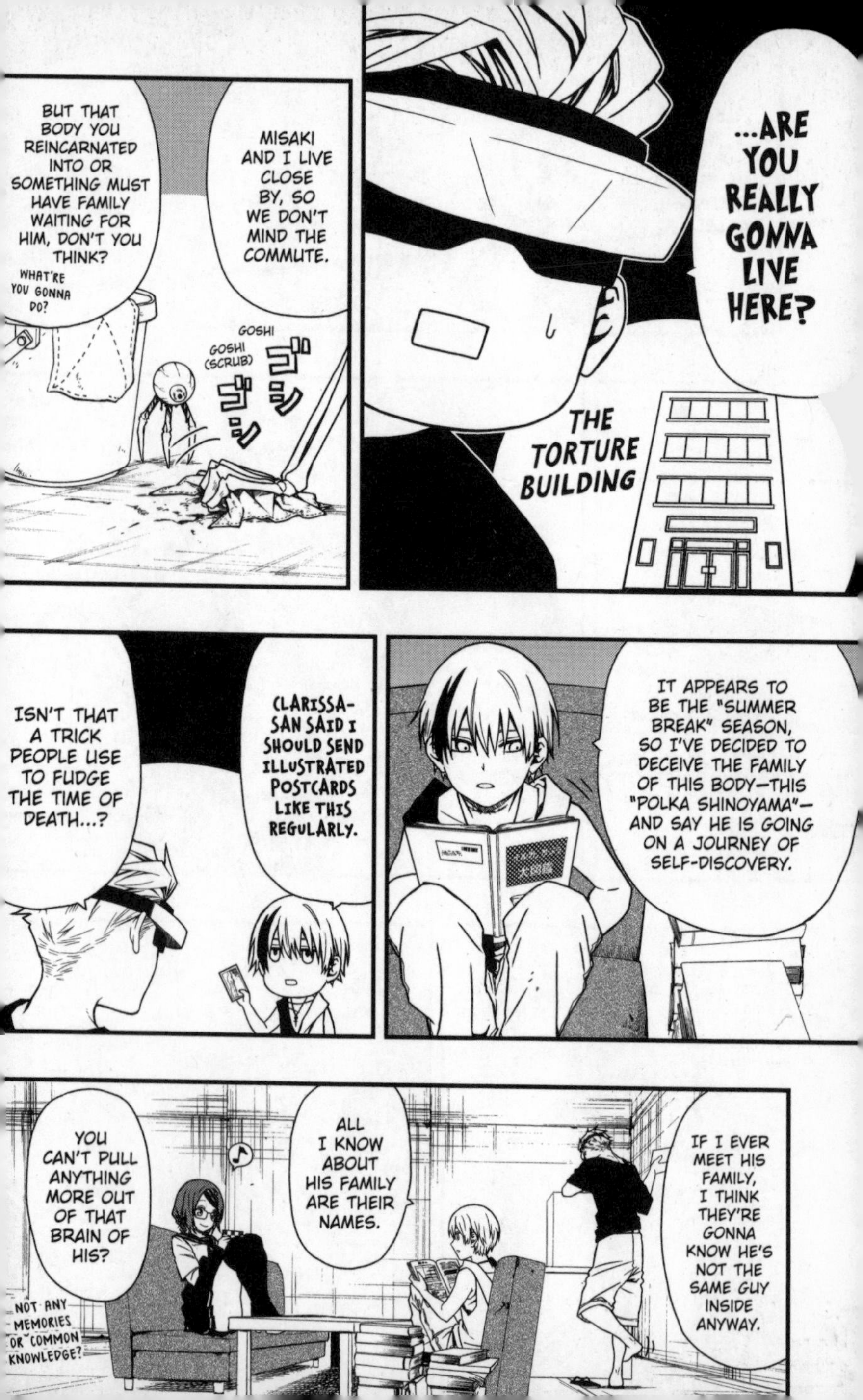
...ARE YOU REALLY GONNA LIVE HERE?
THE TORTURE BUILDING
MISAKI AND I LIVE CLOSE BY, SO WE DON'T MIND THE COMMUTE.
BUT THAT BODY YOU REINCARNATED INTO OR SOMETHING MUST HAVE FAMILY WAITING FOR HIM, DON'T YOU THINK?
WHAT'RE YOU GONNA DO?
ゴシゴシ
GOSHI GOSHI (SCRUB)
IT APPEARS TO BE THE "SUMMER BREAK" SEASON, SO I'VE DECIDED TO DECEIVE THE FAMILY OF THIS BODY—THIS "POLKA SHINOYAMA"—AND SAY HE IS GOING ON A JOURNEY OF SELF-DISCOVERY.
CLARISSA-SAN SAID I SHOULD SEND ILLUSTRATED POSTCARDS LIKE THIS REGULARLY.
ISN'T THAT A TRICK PEOPLE USE TO FUDGE THE TIME OF DEATH...?
IF I EVER MEET HIS FAMILY, I THINK THEY'RE GONNA KNOW HE'S NOT THE SAME GUY INSIDE ANYWAY.
ALL I KNOW ABOUT HIS FAMILY ARE THEIR NAMES.
YOU CAN'T PULL ANYTHING MORE OUT OF THAT BRAIN OF HIS?
NOT ANY MEMORIES OR COMMON KNOWLEDGE?

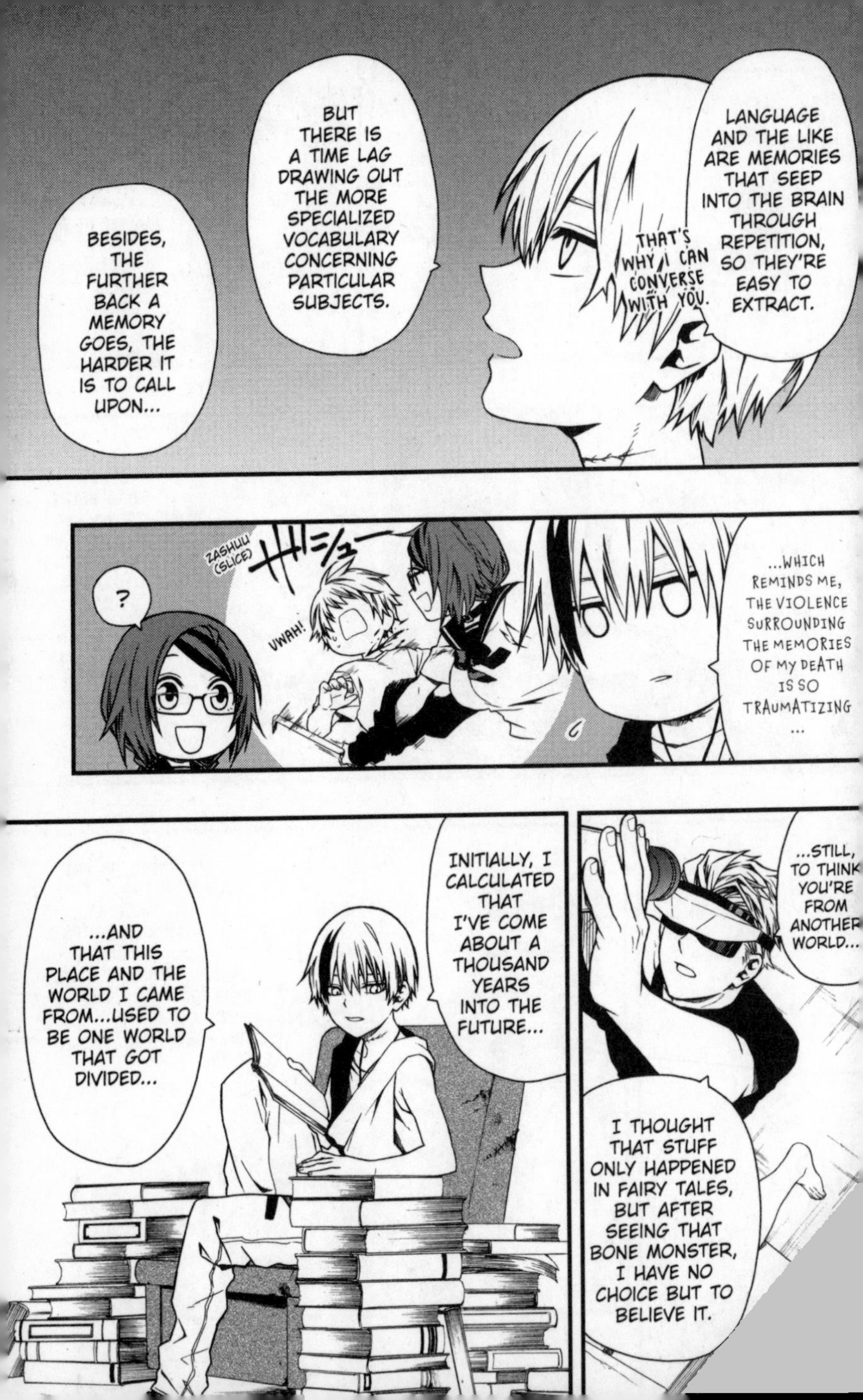
LANGUAGE AND THE LIKE ARE MEMORIES THAT SEEP INTO THE BRAIN THROUGH REPETITION, SO THEY'RE EASY TO EXTRACT.
THAT'S WHY I CAN CONVERSE WITH YOU.
BUT THERE IS A TIME LAG DRAWING OUT THE MORE SPECIALIZED VOCABULARY CONCERNING PARTICULAR SUBJECTS.
BESIDES, THE FURTHER BACK A MEMORY GOES, THE HARDER IT IS TO CALL UPON...
...WHICH REMINDS ME, THE VIOLENCE SURROUNDING THE MEMORIES OF MY DEATH IS SO TRAUMATIZING...
ザシュー
ZASHUU (SLICE)
UWAH!
?
...STILL, TO THINK YOU'RE FROM ANOTHER WORLD...
I THOUGHT THAT STUFF ONLY HAPPENED IN FAIRY TALES, BUT AFTER SEEING THAT BONE MONSTER, I HAVE NO CHOICE BUT TO BELIEVE IT.
INITIALLY, I CALCULATED THAT I'VE COME ABOUT A THOUSAND YEARS INTO THE FUTURE...
...AND THAT THIS PLACE AND THE WORLD I CAME FROM...USED TO BE ONE WORLD THAT GOT DIVIDED...

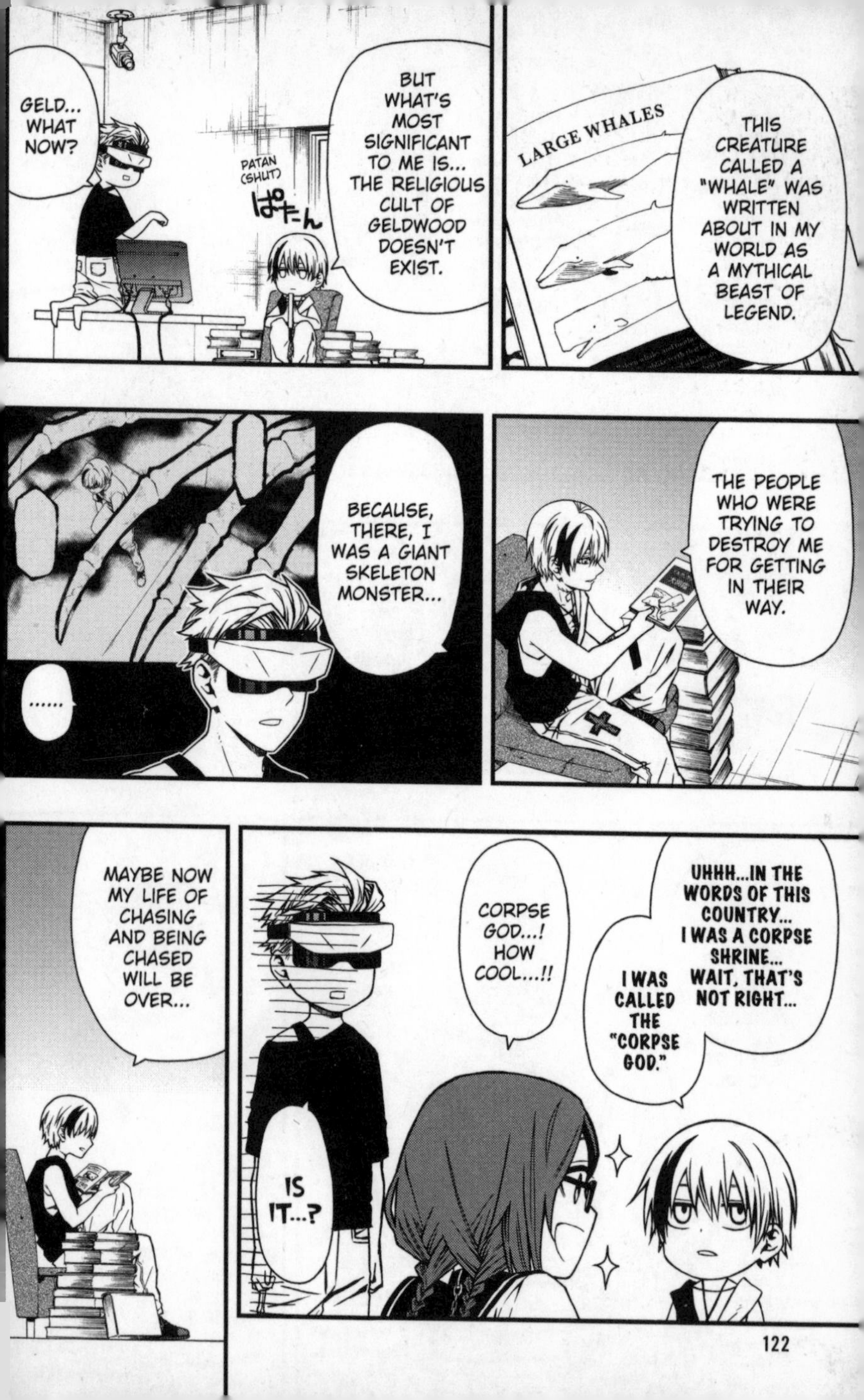
LARGE WHALES
THIS CREATURE CALLED A "WHALE" WAS WRITTEN ABOUT IN MY WORLD AS A MYTHICAL BEAST OF LEGEND.
BUT WHAT'S MOST SIGNIFICANT TO ME IS... THE RELIGIOUS CULT OF GELDWOOD DOESN'T EXIST.
PATAN (SHUT)
ぱたん
GELD... WHAT NOW?
THE PEOPLE WHO WERE TRYING TO DESTROY ME FOR GETTING IN THEIR WAY.
BECAUSE, THERE, I WAS A GIANT SKELETON MONSTER...
......
UHHH...IN THE WORDS OF THIS COUNTRY... I WAS A CORPSE SHRINE... WAIT, THAT'S NOT RIGHT...
I WAS CALLED THE "CORPSE GOD."
CORPSE GOD...! HOW COOL...!!
IS IT...?
MAYBE NOW MY LIFE OF CHASING AND BEING CHASED WILL BE OVER...

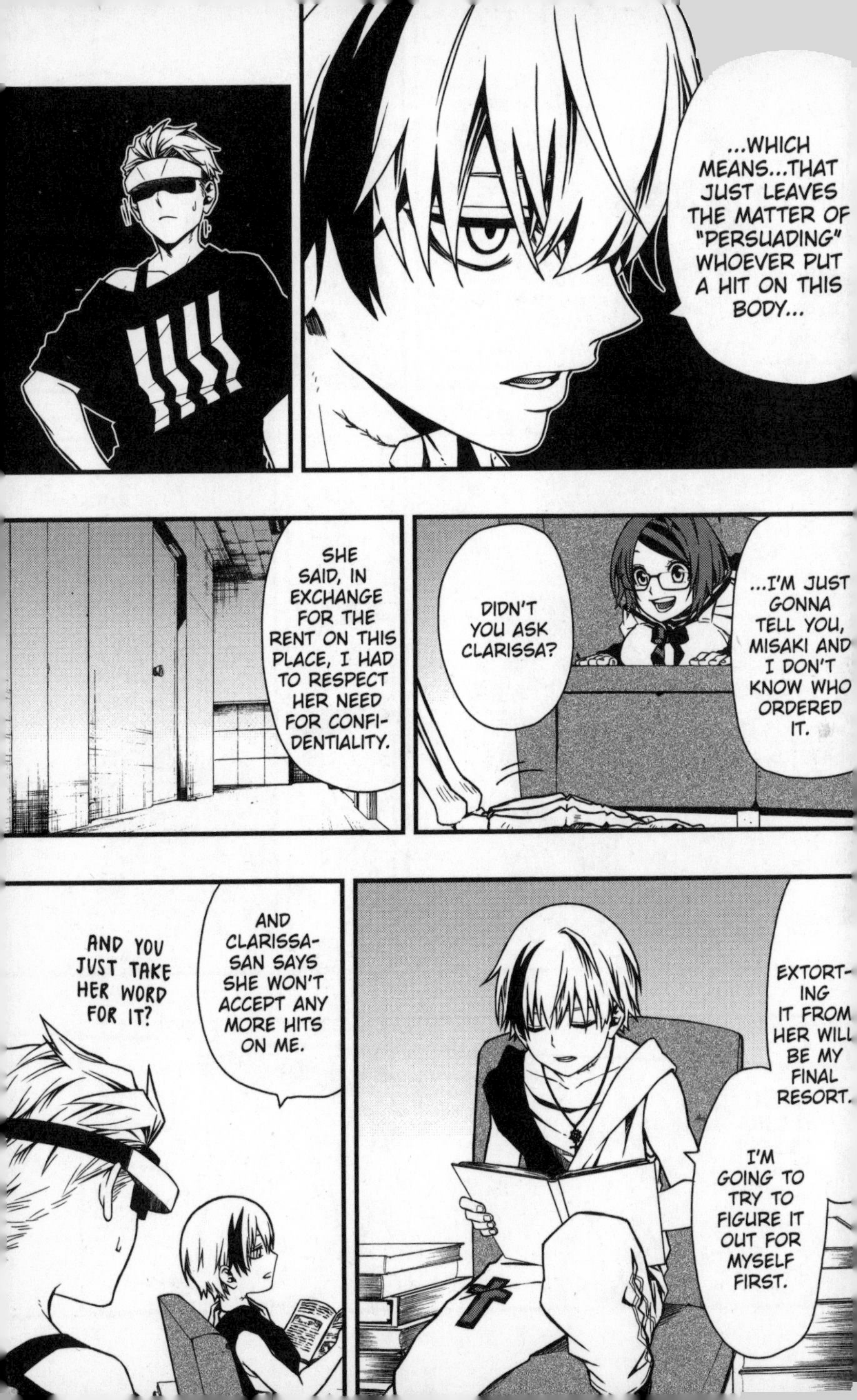
...WHICH MEANS...THAT JUST LEAVES THE MATTER OF "PERSUADING" WHOEVER PUT A HIT ON THIS BODY...
...I'M JUST GONNA TELL YOU, MISAKI AND I DON'T KNOW WHO ORDERED IT.
DIDN'T YOU ASK CLARISSA?
SHE SAID, IN EXCHANGE FOR THE RENT ON THIS PLACE, I HAD TO RESPECT HER NEED FOR CONFI-DENTIALITY.
AND CLARISSA-SAN SAYS SHE WON'T ACCEPT ANY MORE HITS ON ME.
AND YOU JUST TAKE HER WORD FOR IT?
EXTORT-ING IT FROM HER WILL BE MY FINAL RESORT.
I'M GOING TO TRY TO FIGURE IT OUT FOR MYSELF FIRST.

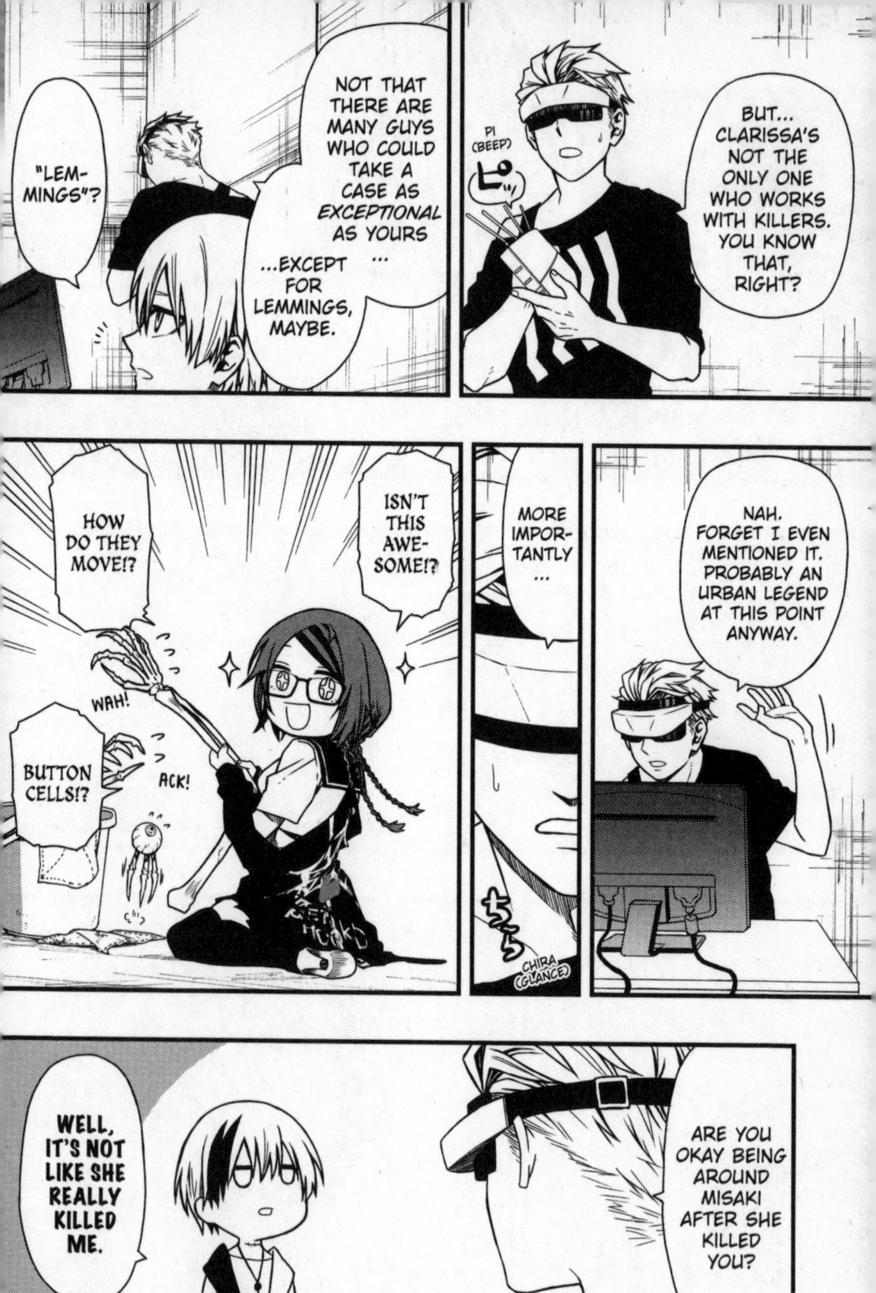
BUT... CLARISSA'S NOT THE ONLY ONE WHO WORKS WITH KILLERS. YOU KNOW THAT, RIGHT?
PI (BEEP)
NOT THAT THERE ARE MANY GUYS WHO COULD TAKE A CASE AS *EXCEPTIONAL* AS YOURS ...
...EXCEPT FOR LEMMINGS, MAYBE.
"LEM-MINGS"?
NAH. FORGET I EVEN MENTIONED IT. PROBABLY AN URBAN LEGEND AT THIS POINT ANYWAY.
MORE IMPOR-TANTLY ...
CHIRA (GLANCE)
ISN'T THIS AWE-SOME!?
HOW DO THEY MOVE!?
WAH!
BUTTON CELLS!?
ACK!
ARE YOU OKAY BEING AROUND MISAKI AFTER SHE KILLED YOU?
WELL, IT'S NOT LIKE SHE REALLY KILLED ME.

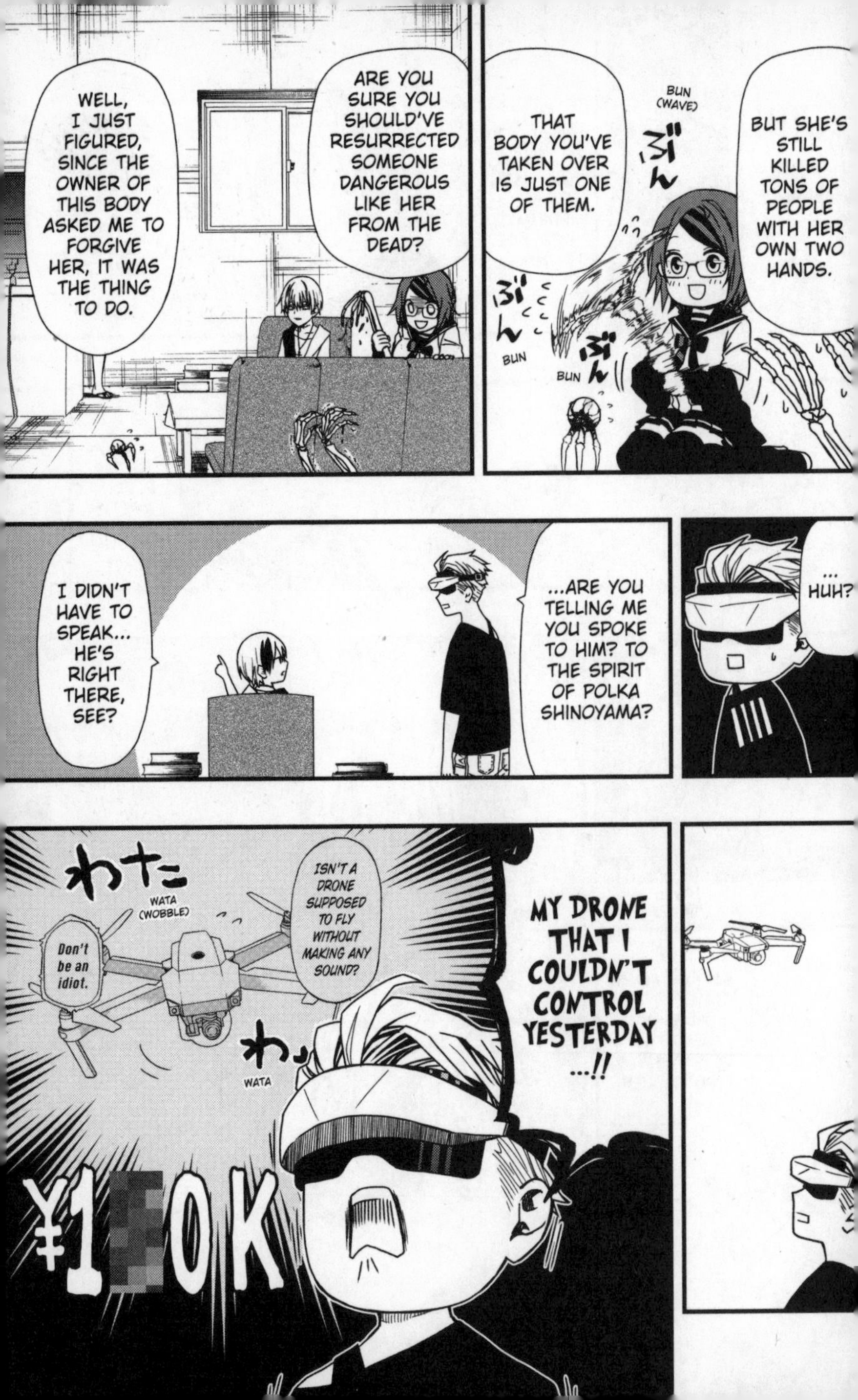
BUT SHE'S STILL KILLED TONS OF PEOPLE WITH HER OWN TWO HANDS.
ぶん
BUN (WAVE)
THAT BODY YOU'VE TAKEN OVER IS JUST ONE OF THEM.
ぶん
BUN
ぶん
BUN
ARE YOU SURE YOU SHOULD'VE RESURRECTED SOMEONE DANGEROUS LIKE HER FROM THE DEAD?
WELL, I JUST FIGURED, SINCE THE OWNER OF THIS BODY ASKED ME TO FORGIVE HER, IT WAS THE THING TO DO.
... HUH?
...ARE YOU TELLING ME YOU SPOKE TO HIM? TO THE SPIRIT OF POLKA SHINOYAMA?
I DIDN'T HAVE TO SPEAK... HE'S RIGHT THERE, SEE?
MY DRONE THAT I COULDN'T CONTROL YESTERDAY ...!!
ISN'T A DRONE SUPPOSED TO FLY WITHOUT MAKING ANY SOUND?
わた
WATA (WOBBLE)
Don't be an idiot.
わ
WATA
¥1[redacted]0K

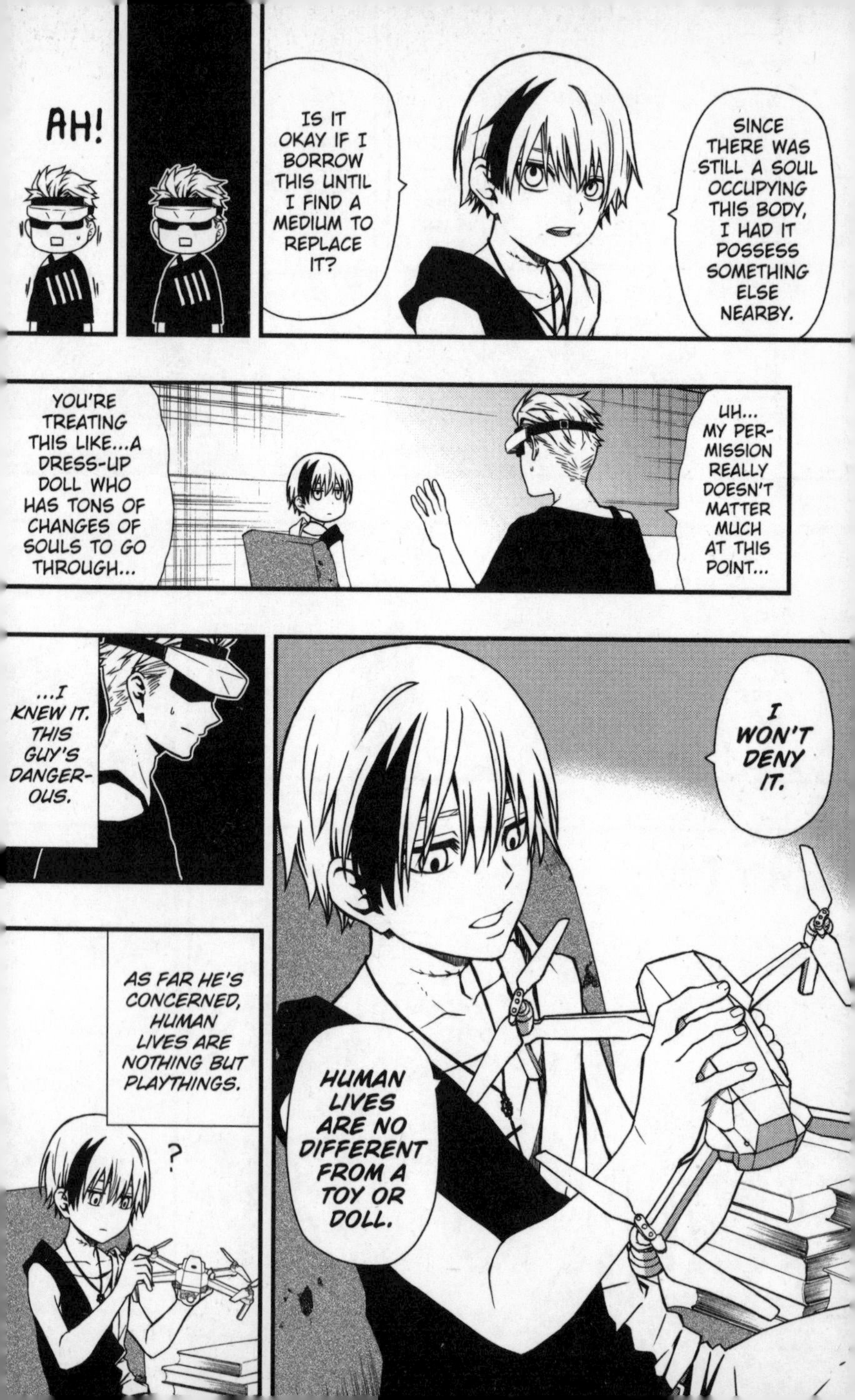
SINCE THERE WAS STILL A SOUL OCCUPYING THIS BODY, I HAD IT POSSESS SOMETHING ELSE NEARBY.
IS IT OKAY IF I BORROW THIS UNTIL I FIND A MEDIUM TO REPLACE IT?
AH!
UH... MY PER-MISSION REALLY DOESN'T MATTER MUCH AT THIS POINT...
YOU'RE TREATING THIS LIKE...A DRESS-UP DOLL WHO HAS TONS OF CHANGES OF SOULS TO GO THROUGH...
I WON'T DENY IT.
...I KNEW IT. THIS GUY'S DANGER-OUS.
HUMAN LIVES ARE NO DIFFERENT FROM A TOY OR DOLL.
AS FAR HE'S CONCERNED, HUMAN LIVES ARE NOTHING BUT PLAYTHINGS.
?

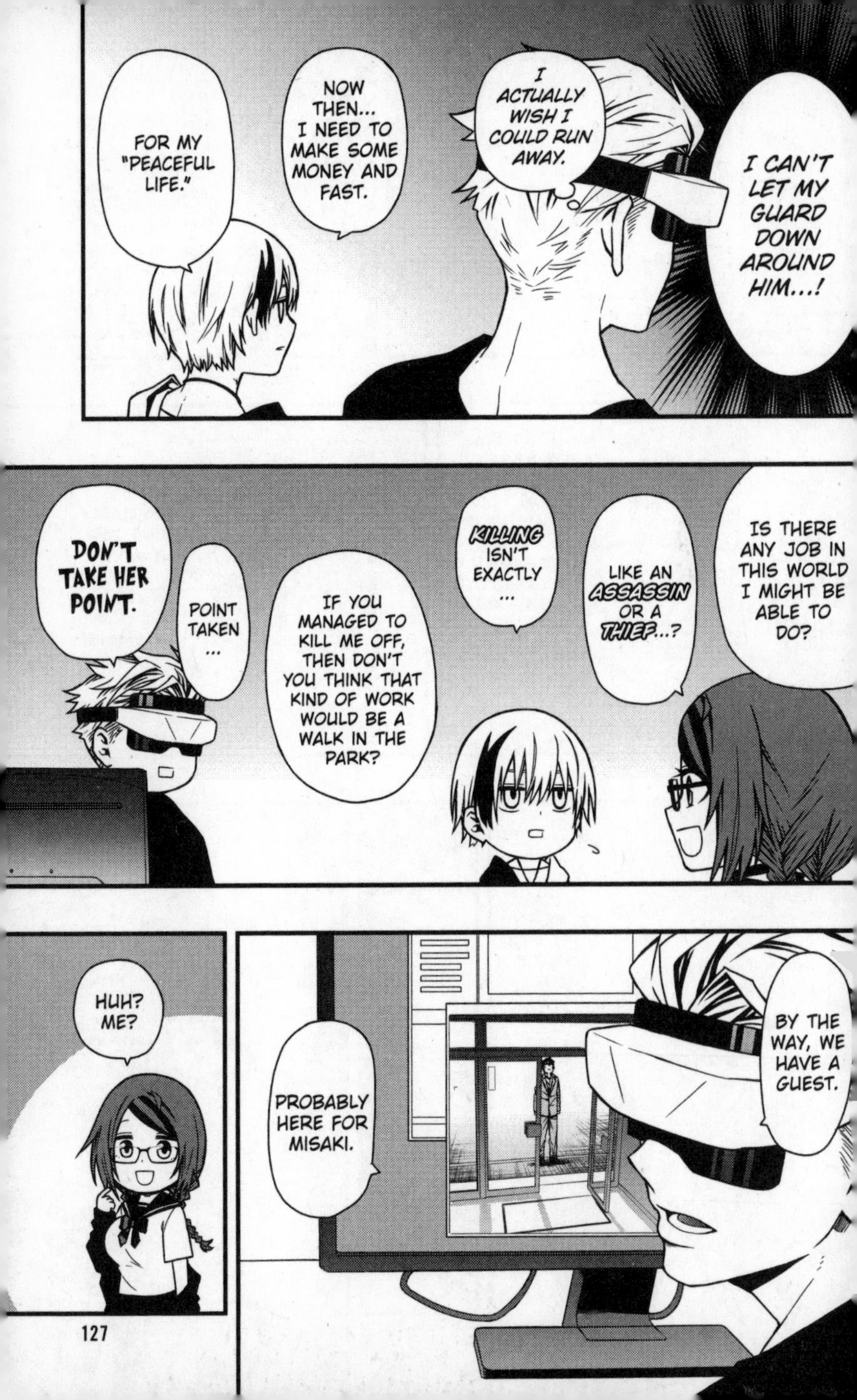
I CAN'T LET MY GUARD DOWN AROUND HIM...!
I ACTUALLY WISH I COULD RUN AWAY.
NOW THEN... I NEED TO MAKE SOME MONEY AND FAST.
FOR MY "PEACEFUL LIFE."
IS THERE ANY JOB IN THIS WORLD I MIGHT BE ABLE TO DO?
LIKE AN ASSASSIN OR A THIEF...?
KILLING ISN'T EXACTLY ...
IF YOU MANAGED TO KILL ME OFF, THEN DON'T YOU THINK THAT KIND OF WORK WOULD BE A WALK IN THE PARK?
POINT TAKEN ...
DON'T TAKE HER POINT.
BY THE WAY, WE HAVE A GUEST.
PROBABLY HERE FOR MISAKI.
HUH? ME?

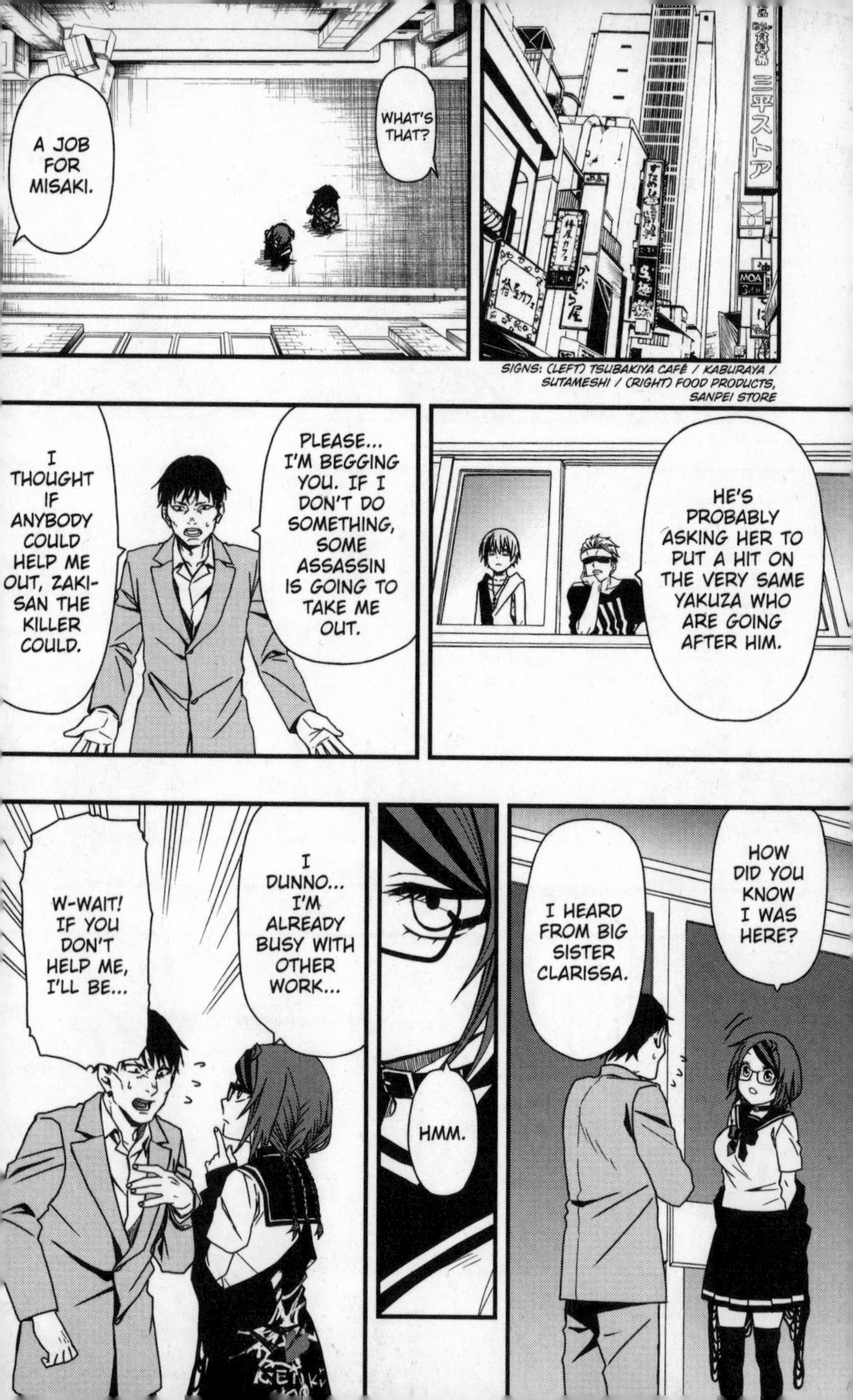
SIGNS: (LEFT) TSUBAKIYA CAFÉ / KABURAYA / SUTAMESHI / (RIGHT) FOOD PRODUCTS, SANPEI STORE
WHAT'S THAT?
A JOB FOR MISAKI.
HE'S PROBABLY ASKING HER TO PUT A HIT ON THE VERY SAME YAKUZA WHO ARE GOING AFTER HIM.
PLEASE... I'M BEGGING YOU. IF I DON'T DO SOMETHING, SOME ASSASSIN IS GOING TO TAKE ME OUT.
I THOUGHT IF ANYBODY COULD HELP ME OUT, ZAKI-SAN THE KILLER COULD.
HOW DID YOU KNOW I WAS HERE?
I HEARD FROM BIG SISTER CLARISSA.
HMM.
I DUNNO... I'M ALREADY BUSY WITH OTHER WORK...
W-WAIT! IF YOU DON'T HELP ME, I'LL BE...

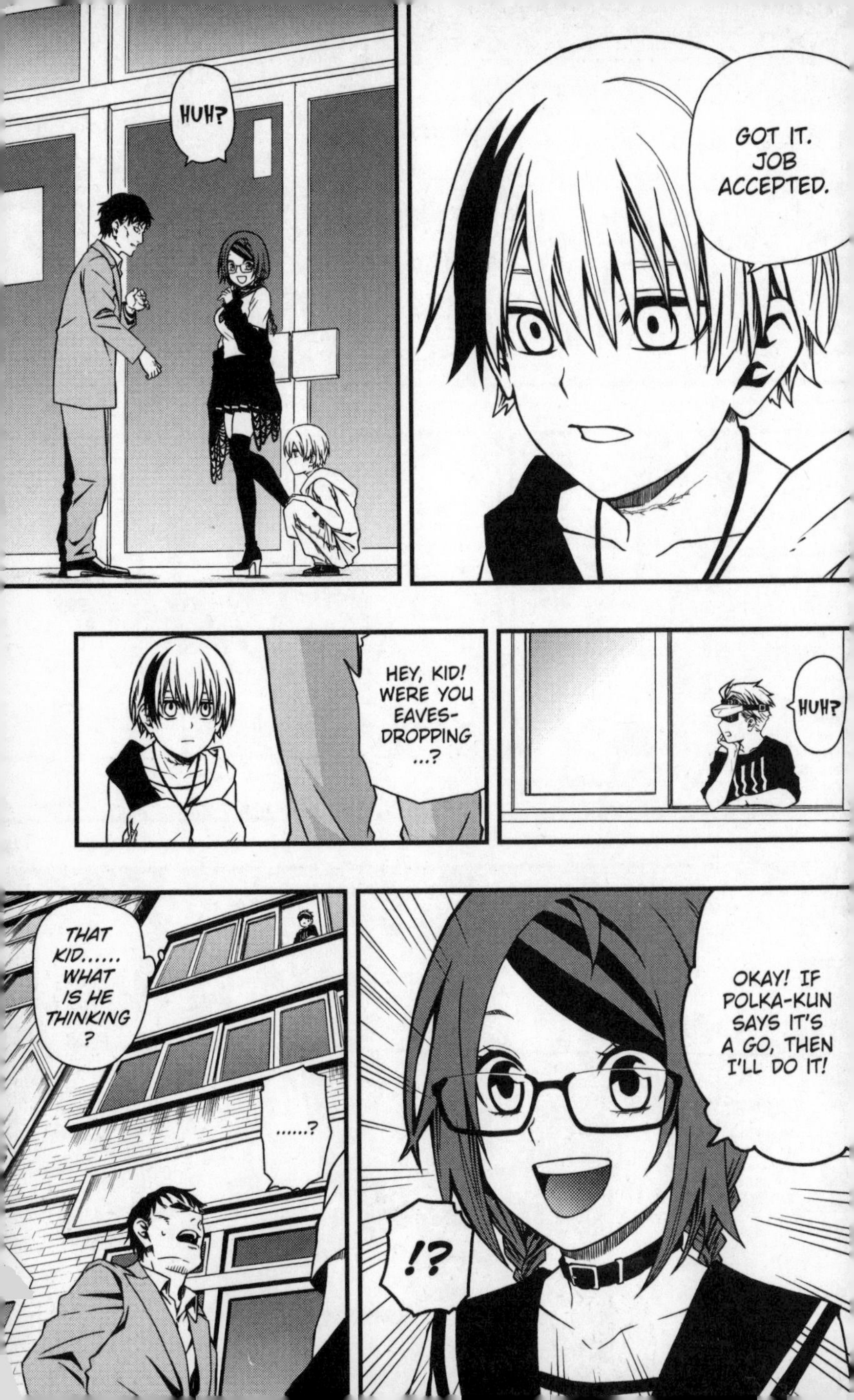
GOT IT. JOB ACCEPTED.
HUH?
HUH?
HEY, KID! WERE YOU EAVES-DROPPING ...?
OKAY! IF POLKA-KUN SAYS IT'S A GO, THEN I'LL DO IT!
!?
THAT KID...... WHAT IS HE THINKING ?
......?

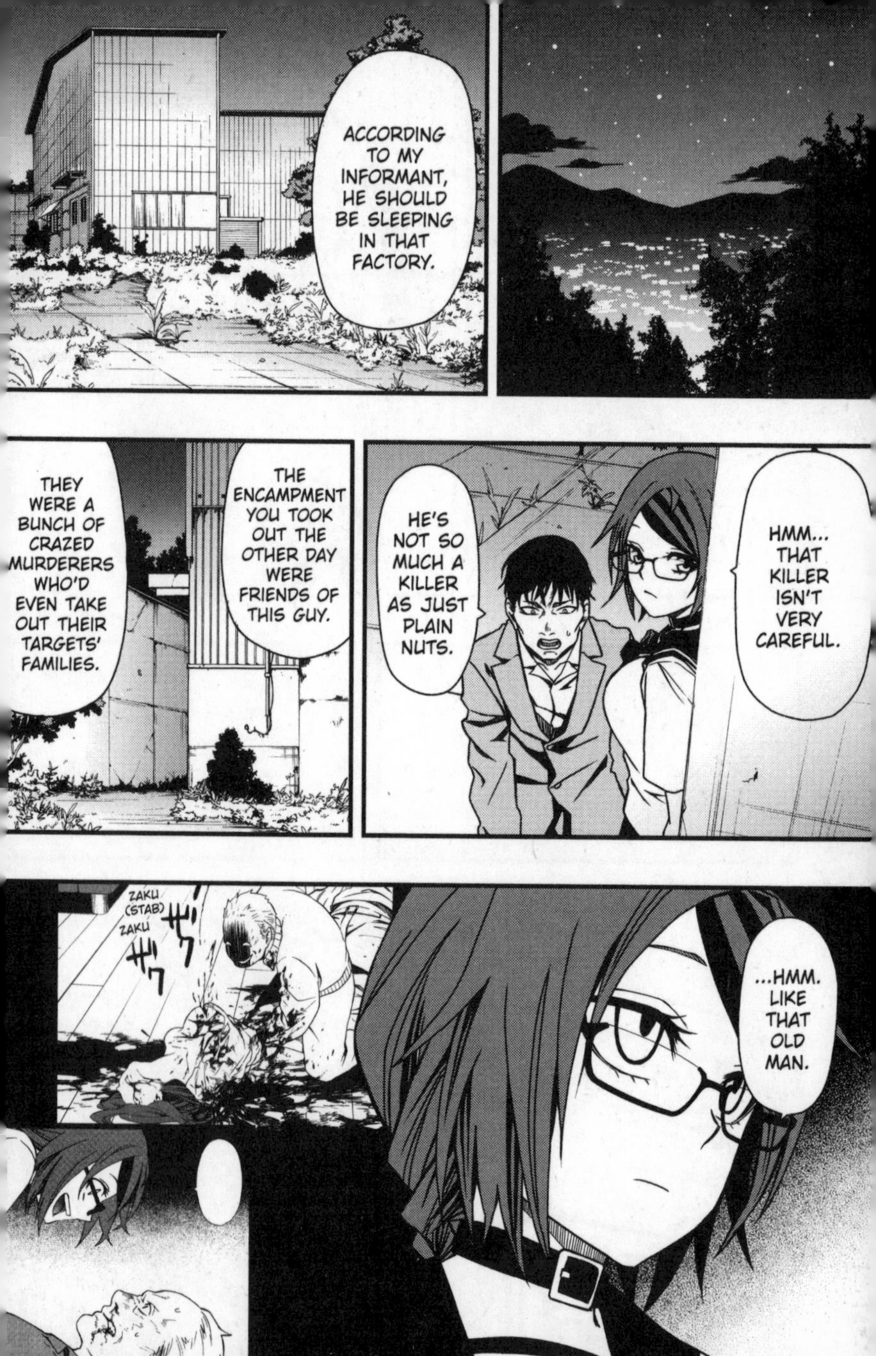
ACCORDING TO MY INFORMANT, HE SHOULD BE SLEEPING IN THAT FACTORY.
HMM... THAT KILLER ISN'T VERY CAREFUL.
HE'S NOT SO MUCH A KILLER AS JUST PLAIN NUTS.
THE ENCAMPMENT YOU TOOK OUT THE OTHER DAY WERE FRIENDS OF THIS GUY.
THEY WERE A BUNCH OF CRAZED MURDERERS WHO'D EVEN TAKE OUT THEIR TARGETS' FAMILIES.
...HMM. LIKE THAT OLD MAN.
ZAKU (STAB)
ZAKU

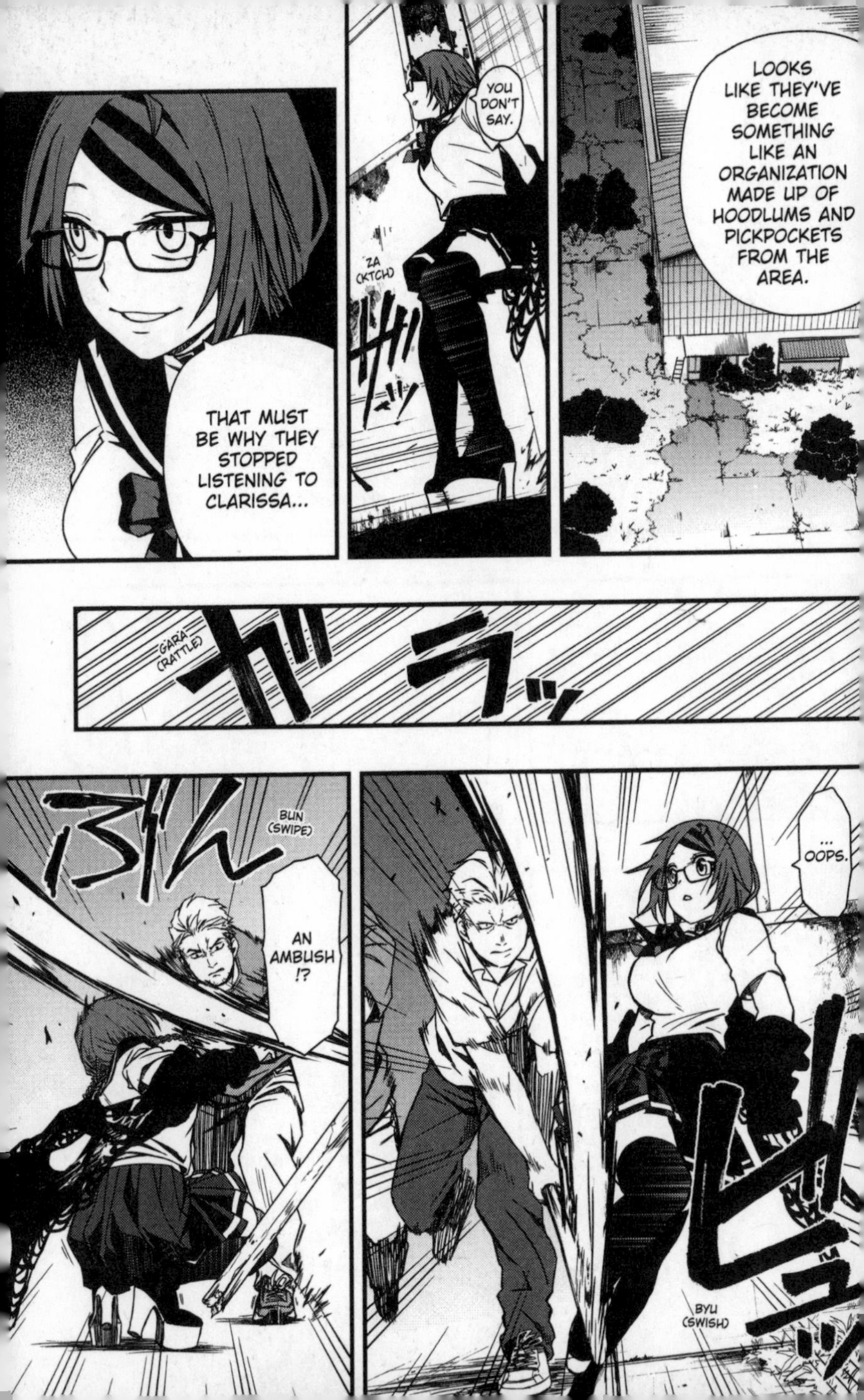

LOOKS LIKE THEY'VE BECOME SOMETHING LIKE AN ORGANIZATION MADE UP OF HOODLUMS AND PICKPOCKETS FROM THE AREA.
YOU DON'T SAY.
ZA (KTCH)
THAT MUST BE WHY THEY STOPPED LISTENING TO CLARISSA...
GARA (RATTLE)
... OOPS.
BYU (SWISH)
BUN (SWIPE)
AN AMBUSH !?

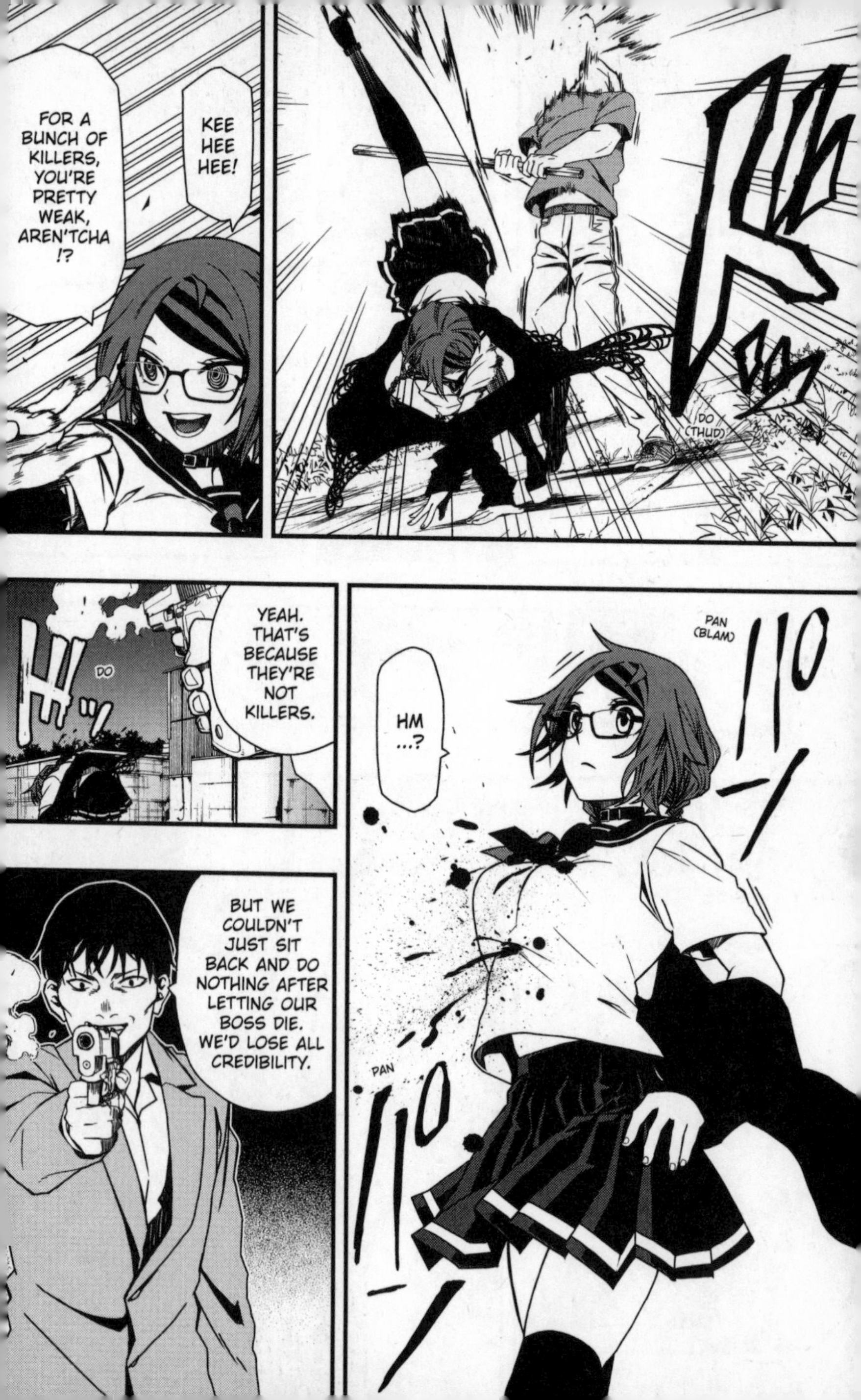
DO (THUD)
KEE HEE HEE!
FOR A BUNCH OF KILLERS, YOU'RE PRETTY WEAK, AREN'TCHA !?
PAN (BLAM)
HM ...?
PAN
DO
YEAH. THAT'S BECAUSE THEY'RE NOT KILLERS.
BUT WE COULDN'T JUST SIT BACK AND DO NOTHING AFTER LETTING OUR BOSS DIE. WE'D LOSE ALL CREDIBILITY.

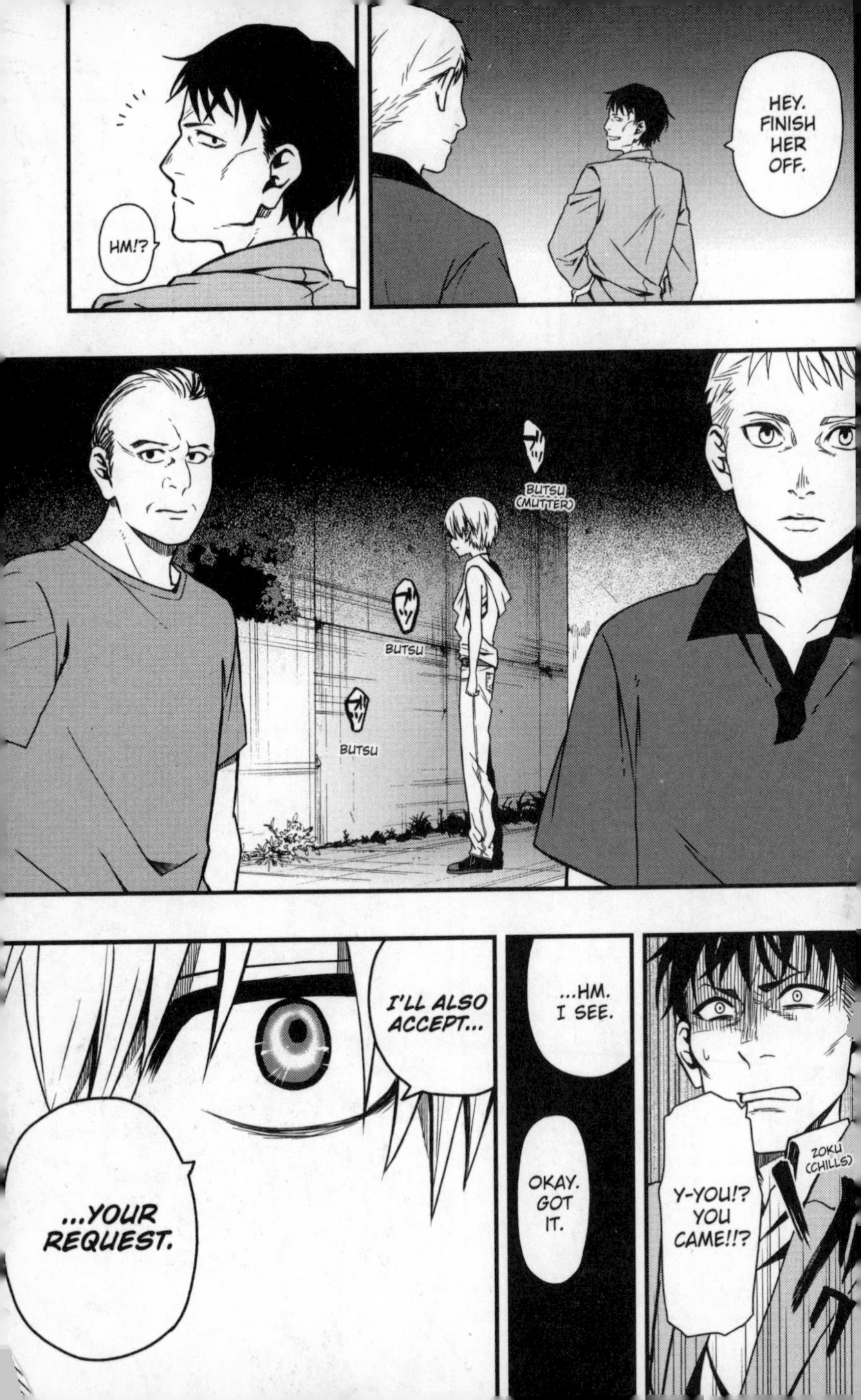
HEY. FINISH HER OFF.
HM!?
BUTSU (MUTTER)
BUTSU
BUTSU
Y-YOU!? YOU CAME!!?
ZOKU (CHILLS)
...HM. I SEE.
OKAY. GOT IT.
I'LL ALSO ACCEPT...
...YOUR REQUEST.

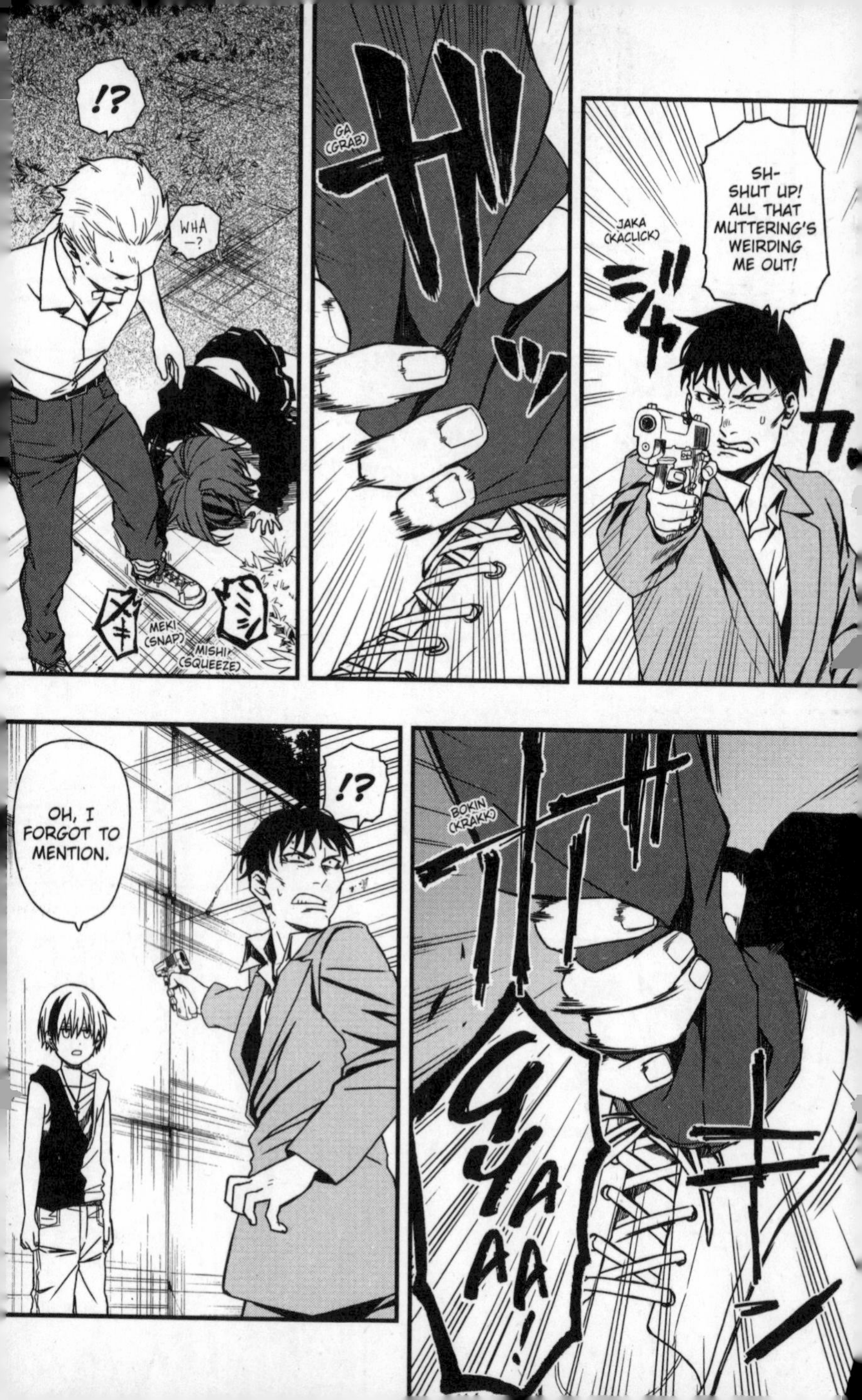
JAKA (KACLICK)
SH-SHUT UP! ALL THAT MUTTERING'S WEIRDING ME OUT!
GA (GRAB)
!?
WHA—?
MEKI (SNAP)
MISHI (SQUEEZE)
BOKIN (KRAKK)
GYAAAA!
!?
OH, I FORGOT TO MENTION.

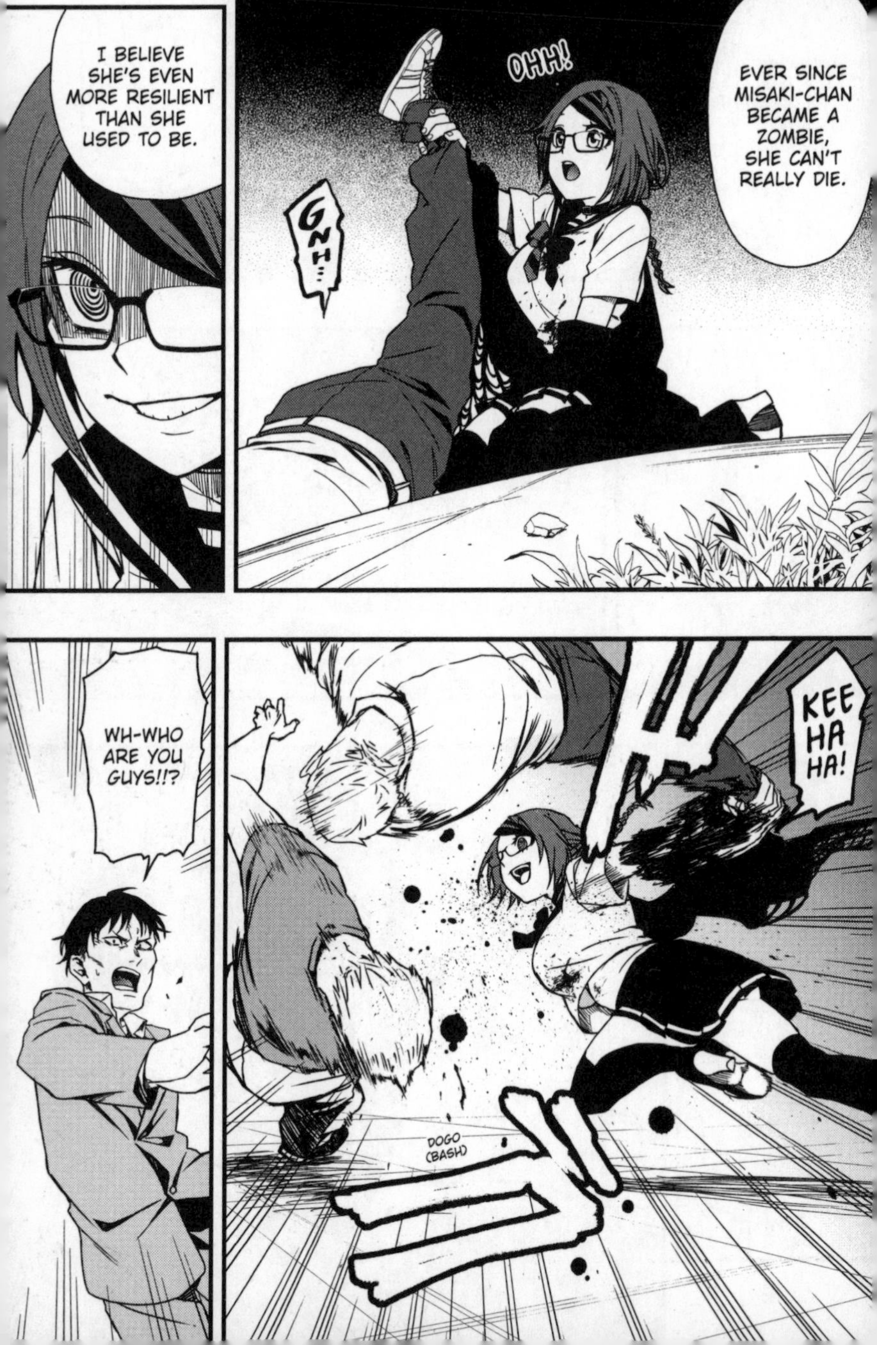
EVER SINCE MISAKI-CHAN BECAME A ZOMBIE, SHE CAN'T REALLY DIE.
OHH!
GNH...
I BELIEVE SHE'S EVEN MORE RESILIENT THAN SHE USED TO BE.
KEE HA HA!
DOGO (BASH)
WH-WHO ARE YOU GUYS!!?

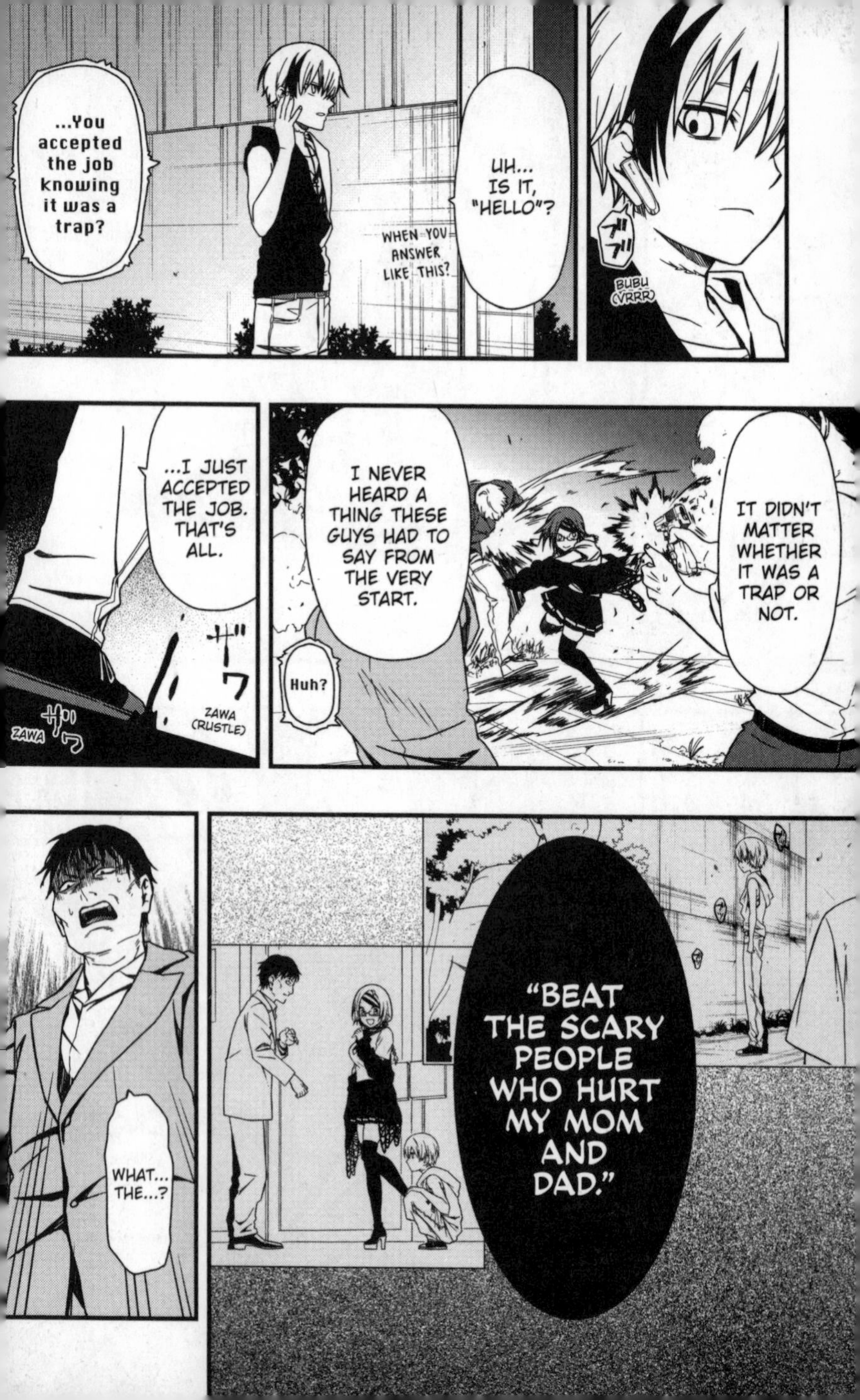
BUBU (VRRR)
UH... IS IT, "HELLO"?
WHEN YOU ANSWER LIKE THIS?
...You accepted the job knowing it was a trap?
IT DIDN'T MATTER WHETHER IT WAS A TRAP OR NOT.
I NEVER HEARD A THING THESE GUYS HAD TO SAY FROM THE VERY START.
Huh?
...I JUST ACCEPTED THE JOB. THAT'S ALL.
ZAWA (RUSTLE)
ZAWA
"BEAT THE SCARY PEOPLE WHO HURT MY MOM AND DAD."
WHAT... THE...?

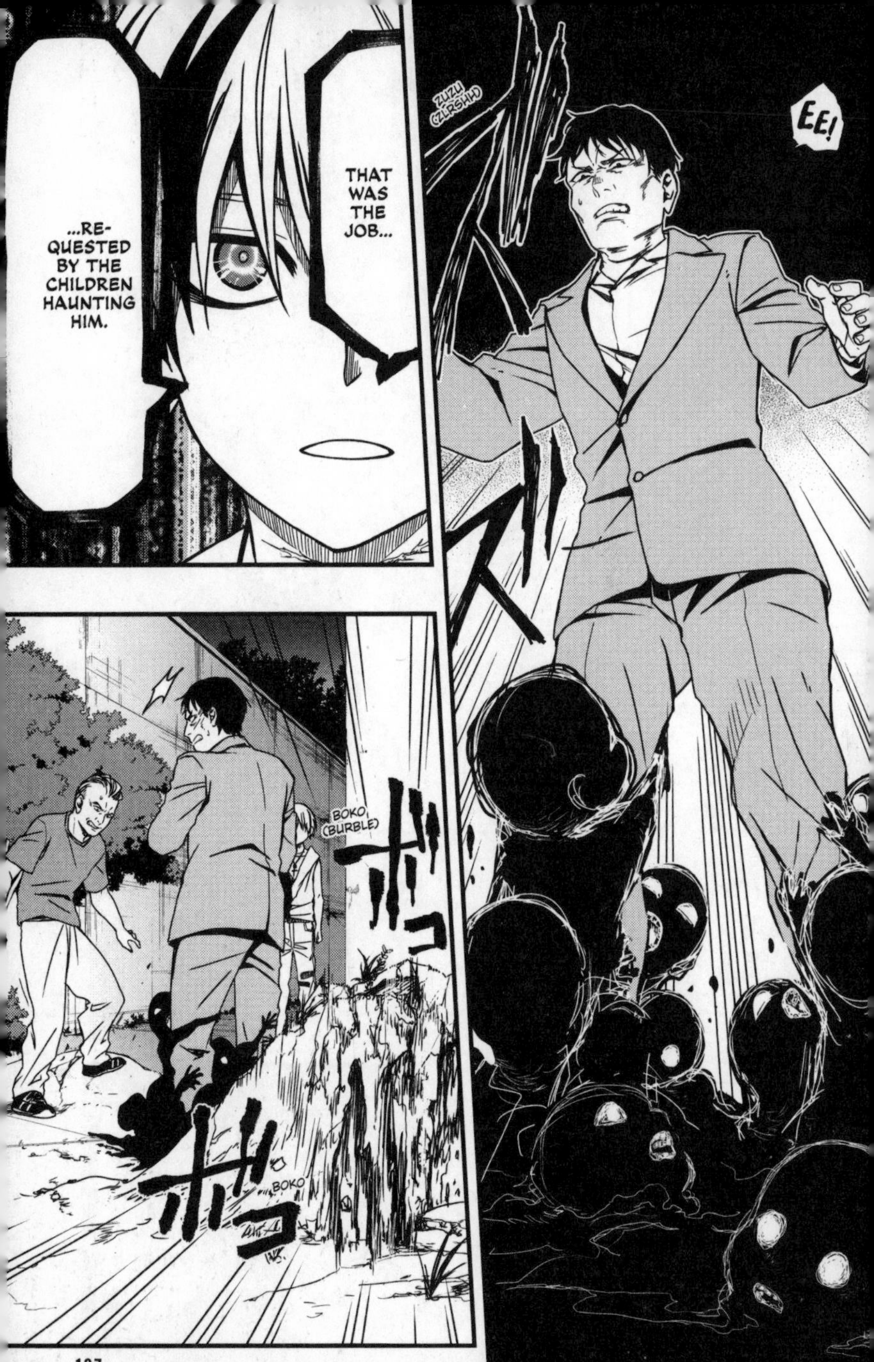
ZUZU (ZLRSHH)
EE!
THAT WAS THE JOB...
...RE-QUESTED BY THE CHILDREN HAUNTING HIM.
BOKO (BURBLE)
BOKO

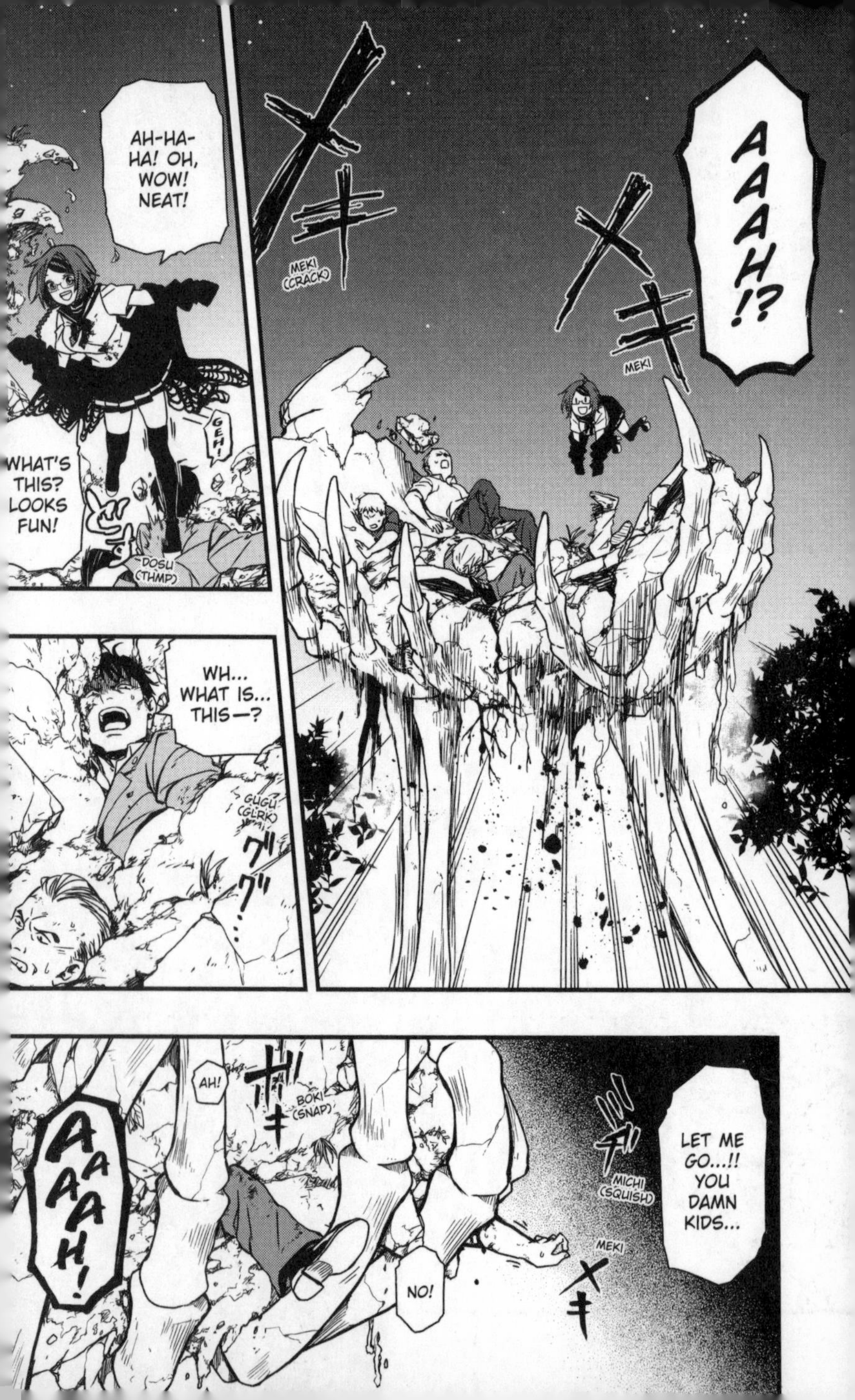
AAAAH!?
MEKI
MEKI (CRACK)
AH-HA-HA! OH, WOW! NEAT!
GEH!
WHAT'S THIS? LOOKS FUN!
DOSU (THMP)
WH... WHAT IS... THIS—?
GUGU (GLRK)
LET ME GO...!! YOU DAMN KIDS...
MICHI (SQUISH)
MEKI
BOKI (SNAP)
AH!
NO!
AAAAH!

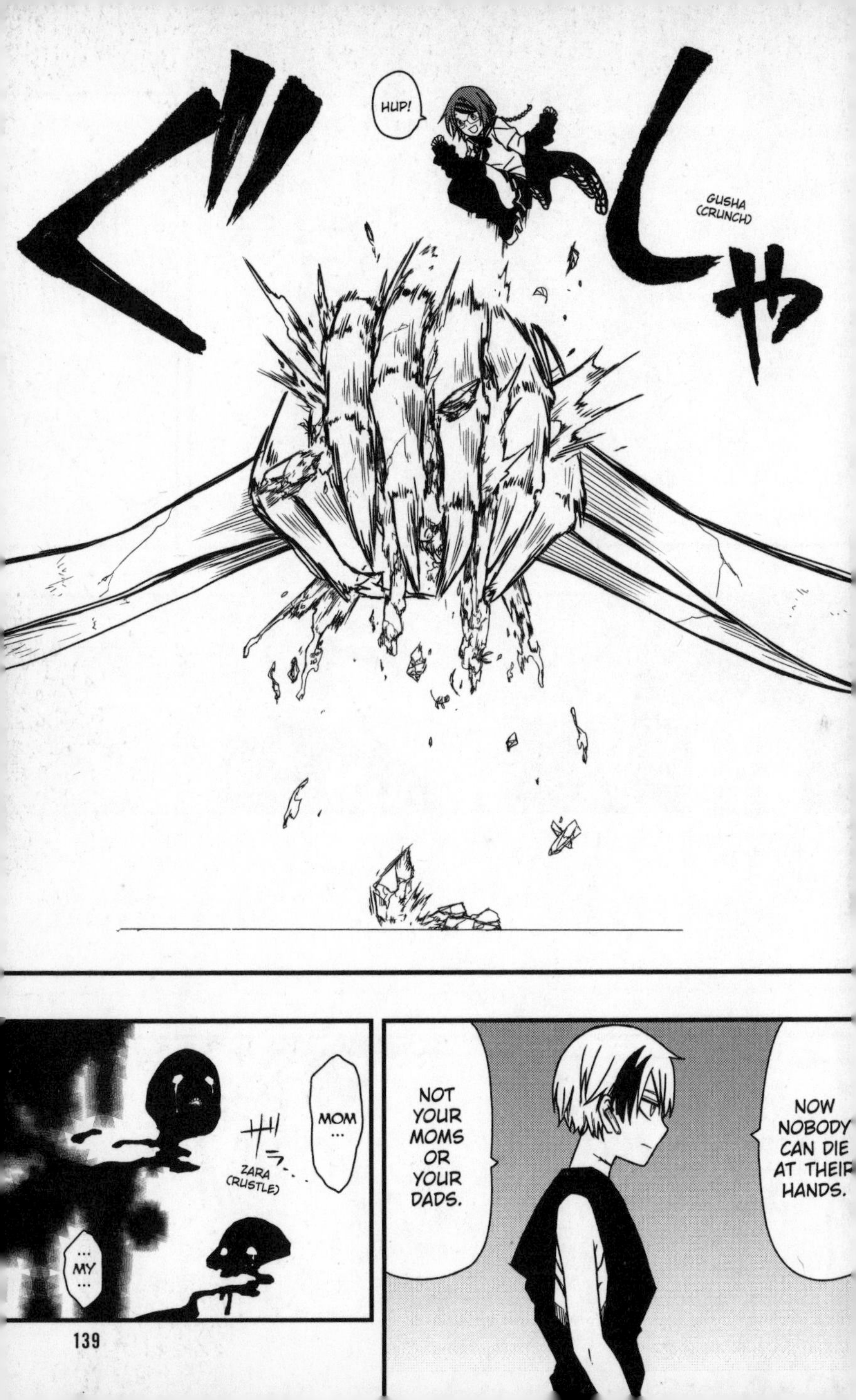
ぐしゃ
HUP!
GUSHA (CRUNCH)
NOW NOBODY CAN DIE AT THEIR HANDS.
NOT YOUR MOMS OR YOUR DADS.
MOM ...
ZARA (RUSTLE)
... MY ...

THIS ISN'T SALVA-TION.

...IT'S HALF JUST MY VENTING MY ANGER.

help ...

help ...

...I'M SORRY.

So you don't have to compen-sate me.

......

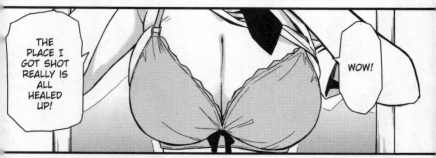

THE PLACE I GOT SHOT REALLY IS ALL HEALED UP!

WOW!

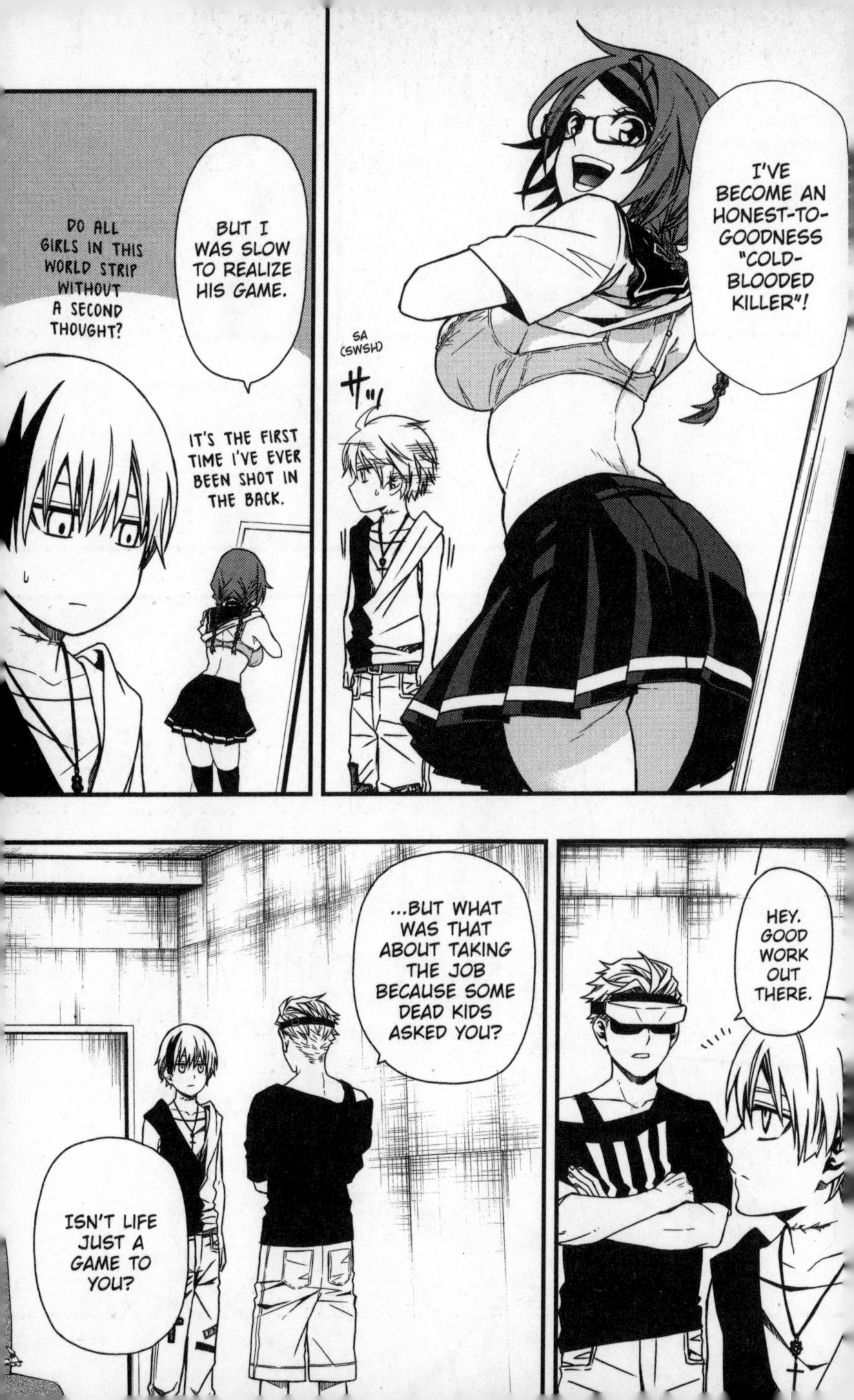
I'VE BECOME AN HONEST-TO-GOODNESS "COLD-BLOODED KILLER"!
SA (SWSH)
BUT I WAS SLOW TO REALIZE HIS GAME.
DO ALL GIRLS IN THIS WORLD STRIP WITHOUT A SECOND THOUGHT?
IT'S THE FIRST TIME I'VE EVER BEEN SHOT IN THE BACK.
HEY. GOOD WORK OUT THERE.
...BUT WHAT WAS THAT ABOUT TAKING THE JOB BECAUSE SOME DEAD KIDS ASKED YOU?
ISN'T LIFE JUST A GAME TO YOU?

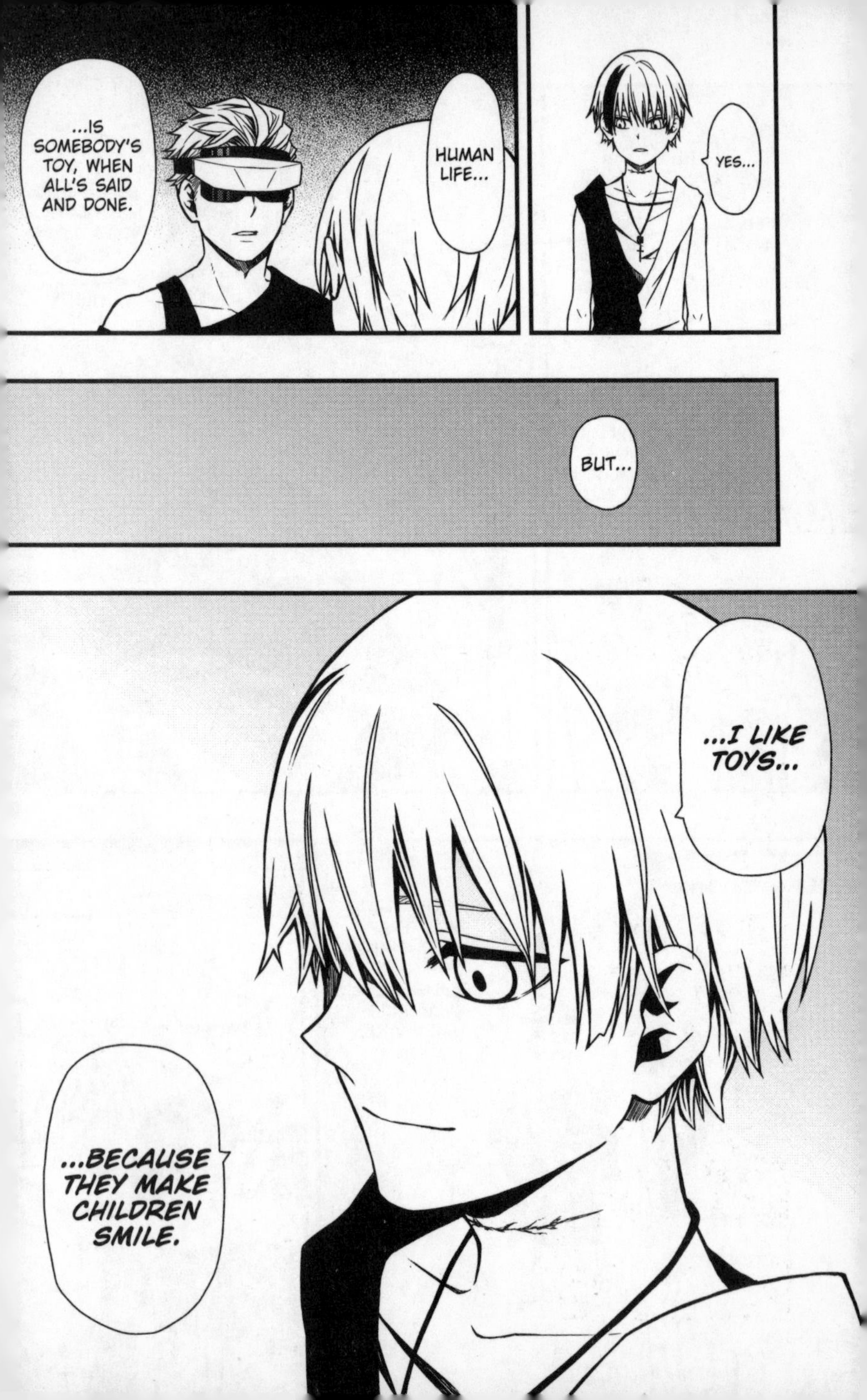
YES...
HUMAN LIFE...
...IS SOMEBODY'S TOY, WHEN ALL'S SAID AND DONE.
BUT...
...I LIKE TOYS...
...BECAUSE THEY MAKE CHILDREN SMILE.

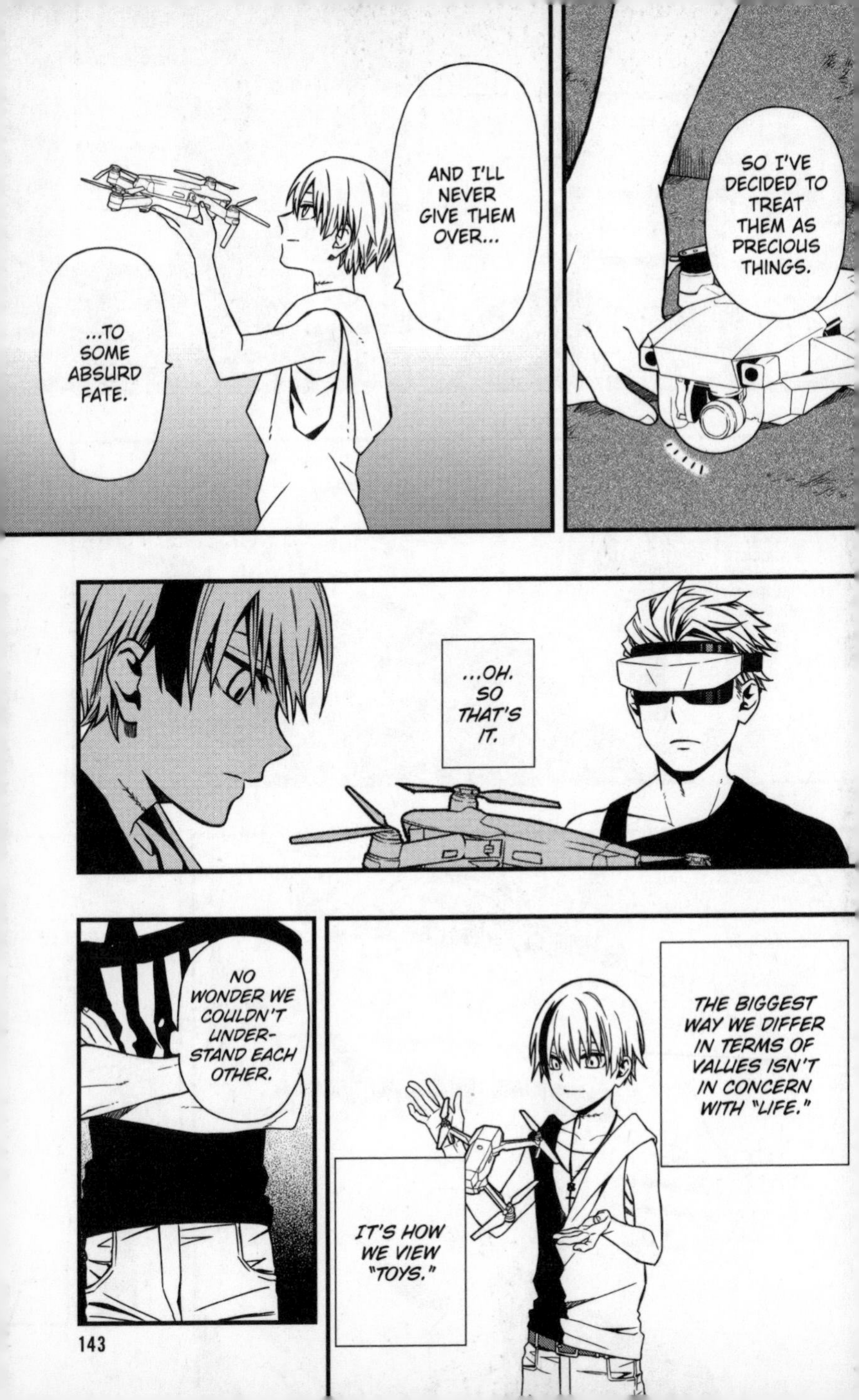

SO I'VE DECIDED TO TREAT THEM AS PRECIOUS THINGS.
AND I'LL NEVER GIVE THEM OVER...
...TO SOME ABSURD FATE.
...OH. SO THAT'S IT.
THE BIGGEST WAY WE DIFFER IN TERMS OF VALUES ISN'T IN CONCERN WITH "LIFE."
IT'S HOW WE VIEW "TOYS."
NO WONDER WE COULDN'T UNDER-STAND EACH OTHER.

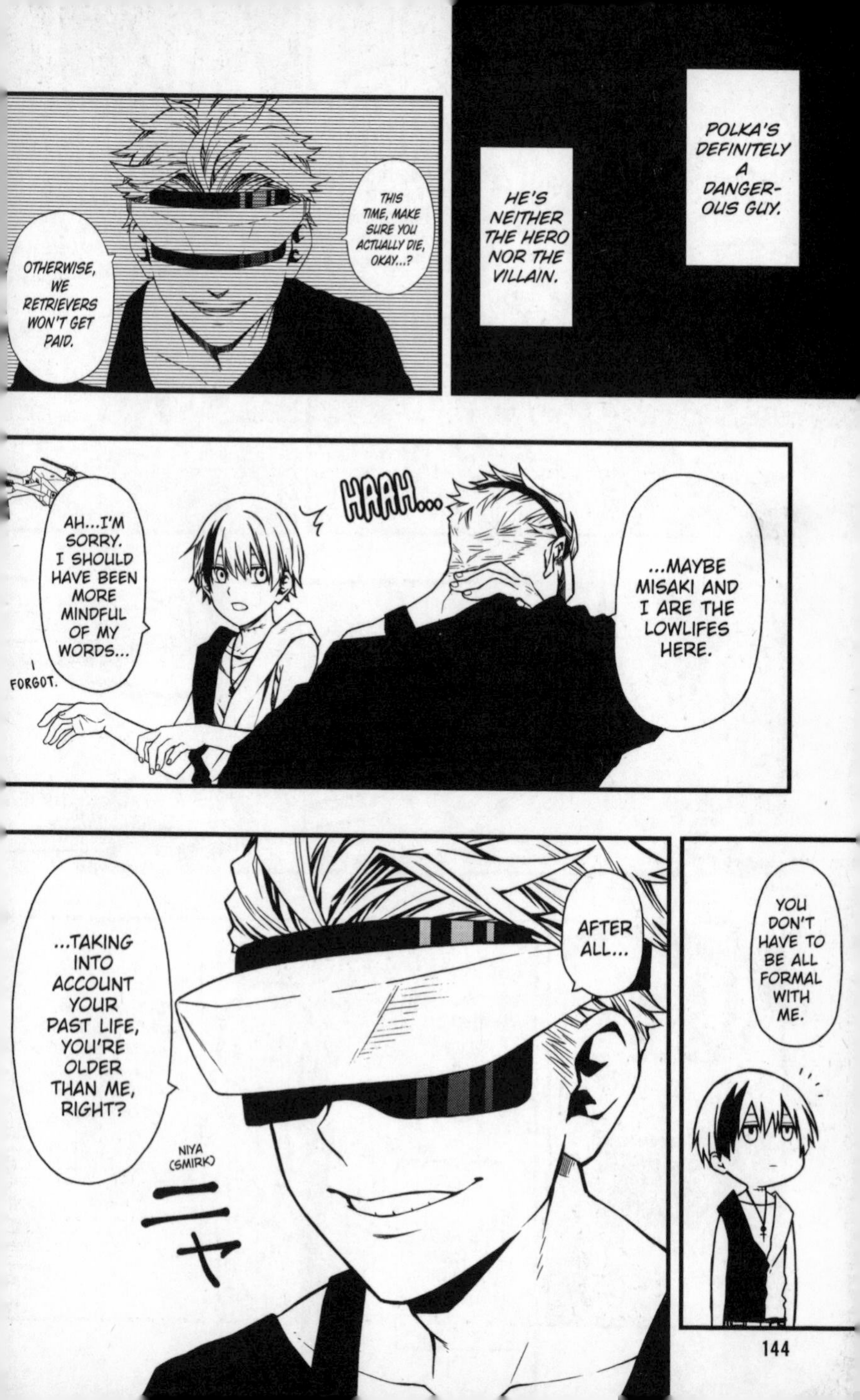
POLKA'S DEFINITELY A DANGER-OUS GUY.
HE'S NEITHER THE HERO NOR THE VILLAIN.
THIS TIME, MAKE SURE YOU ACTUALLY DIE, OKAY...?
OTHERWISE, WE RETRIEVERS WON'T GET PAID.
...MAYBE MISAKI AND I ARE THE LOWLIFES HERE.
HAAH...
AH...I'M SORRY. I SHOULD HAVE BEEN MORE MINDFUL OF MY WORDS...
I FORGOT.
YOU DON'T HAVE TO BE ALL FORMAL WITH ME.
AFTER ALL...
...TAKING INTO ACCOUNT YOUR PAST LIFE, YOU'RE OLDER THAN ME, RIGHT?
NIYA (SMIRK)

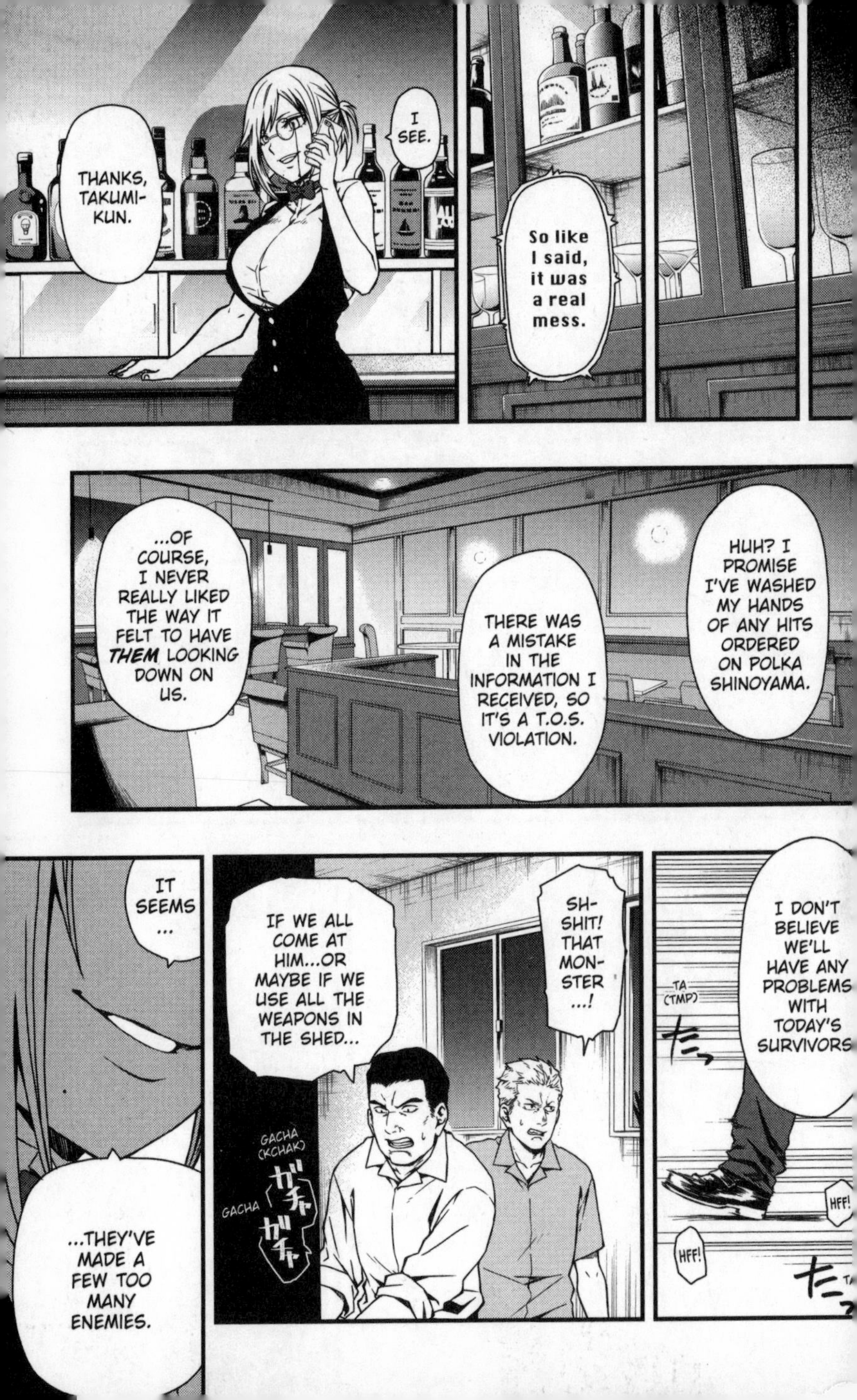
So like I said, it was a real mess.
I SEE.
THANKS, TAKUMI-KUN.
HUH? I PROMISE I'VE WASHED MY HANDS OF ANY HITS ORDERED ON POLKA SHINOYAMA.
THERE WAS A MISTAKE IN THE INFORMATION I RECEIVED, SO IT'S A T.O.S. VIOLATION.
...OF COURSE, I NEVER REALLY LIKED THE WAY IT FELT TO HAVE THEM LOOKING DOWN ON US.
I DON'T BELIEVE WE'LL HAVE ANY PROBLEMS WITH TODAY'S SURVIVORS.
TA (TMP)
HFF!
HFF!
SH-SHIT! THAT MON-STER...!
IF WE ALL COME AT HIM...OR MAYBE IF WE USE ALL THE WEAPONS IN THE SHED...
GACHA (KCHAK)
ガチャ
GACHA
ガチャ
IT SEEMS...
...THEY'VE MADE A FEW TOO MANY ENEMIES.

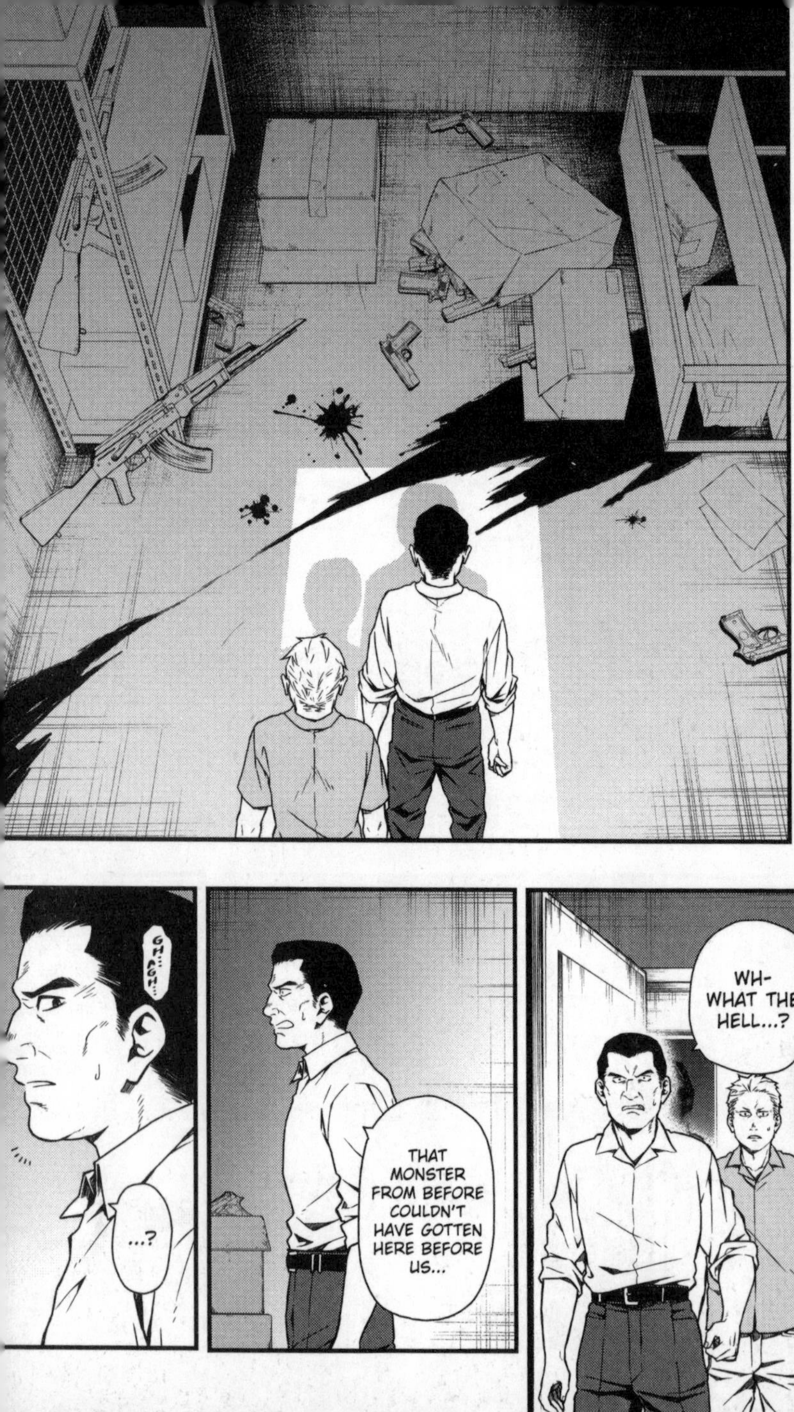
WH- WHAT THE HELL...?
THAT MONSTER FROM BEFORE COULDN'T HAVE GOTTEN HERE BEFORE US...
GH... AGH...
...?

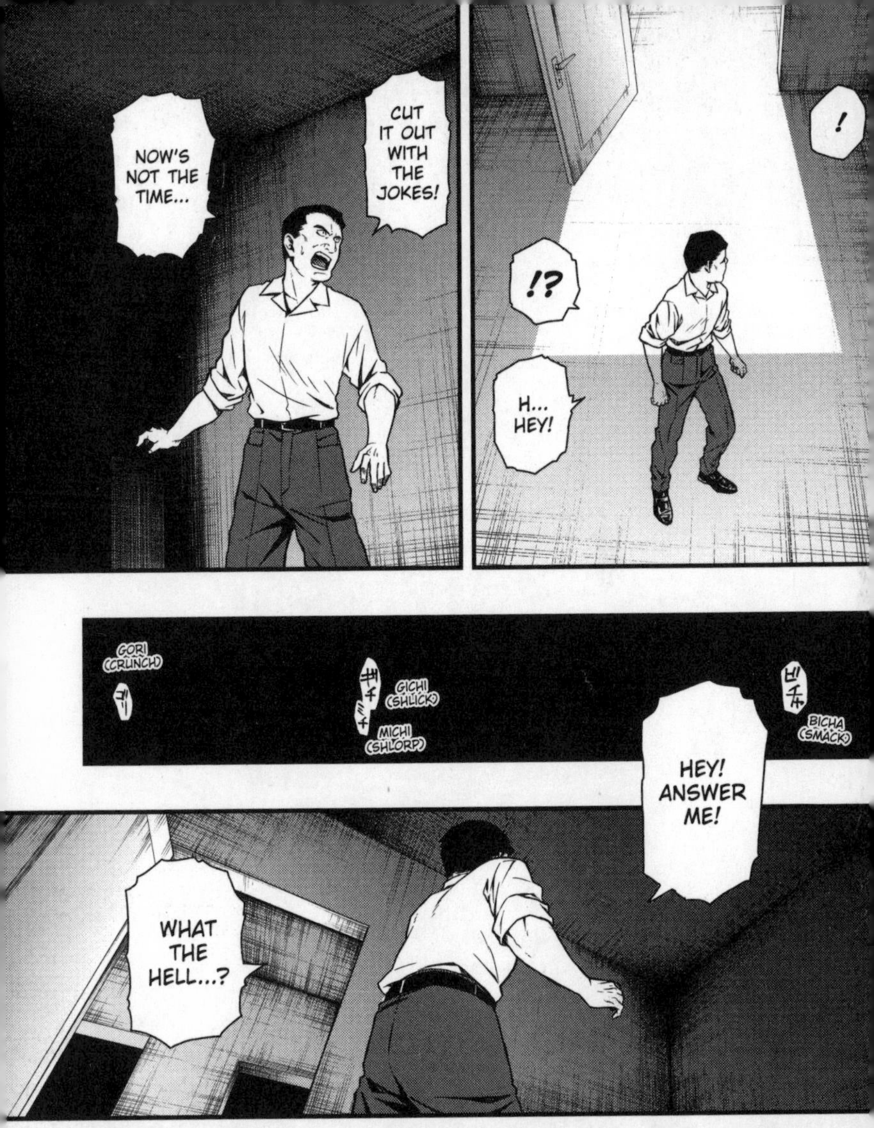
!
!?
H... HEY!
CUT IT OUT WITH THE JOKES!
NOW'S NOT THE TIME...
BICHA (SMACK)
GICHI (SHLICK)
MICHI (SHLORP)
GORI (CRUNCH)
HEY! ANSWER ME!
WHAT THE HELL...?

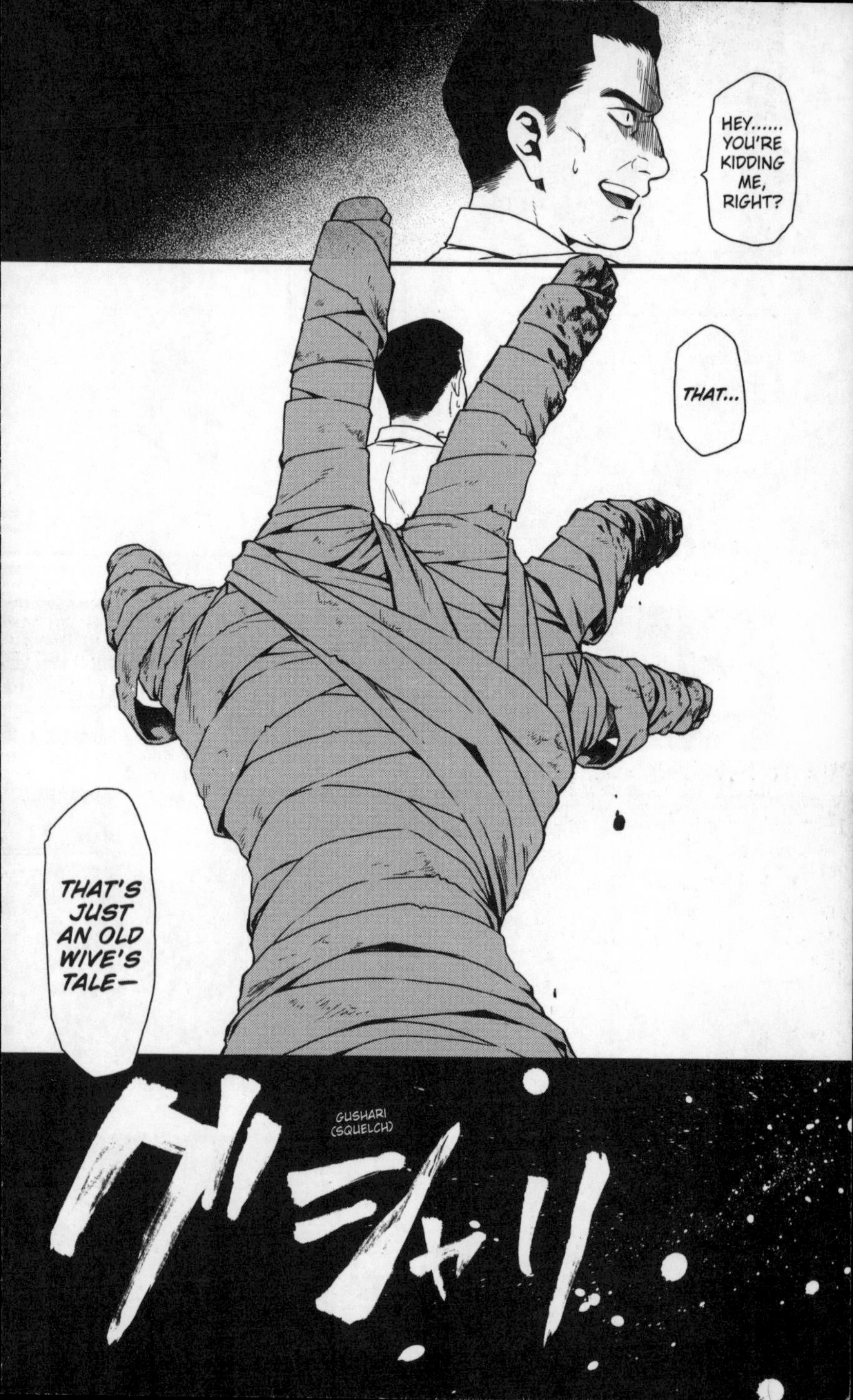
HEY...... YOU'RE KIDDING ME, RIGHT?
THAT...
THAT'S JUST AN OLD WIVE'S TALE—
GUSHARI (SQUELCH)
グシャリ

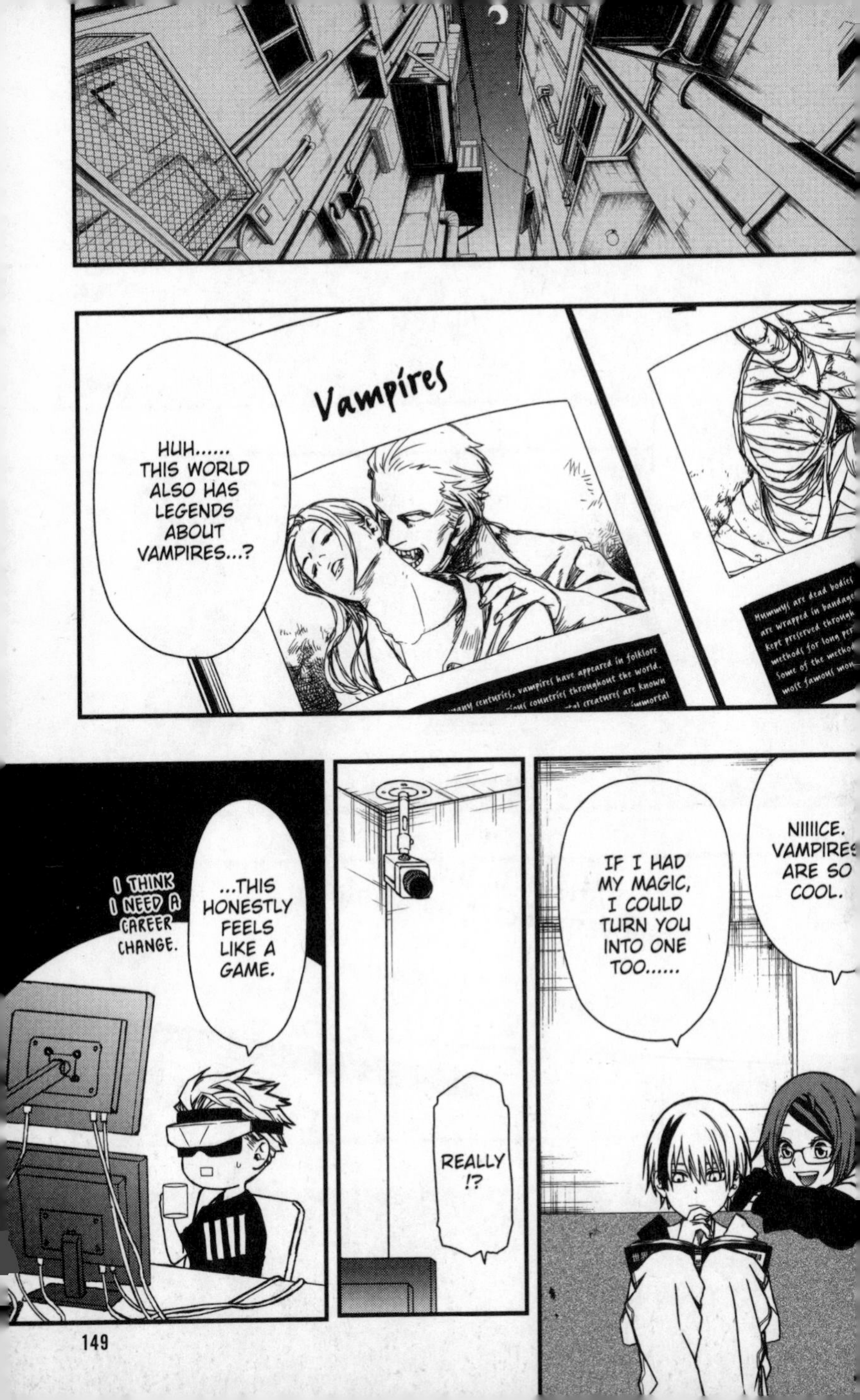
Vampires
HUH...... THIS WORLD ALSO HAS LEGENDS ABOUT VAMPIRES...?
NIIIICE. VAMPIRES ARE SO COOL.
IF I HAD MY MAGIC, I COULD TURN YOU INTO ONE TOO......
REALLY!?
...THIS HONESTLY FEELS LIKE A GAME.
I THINK I NEED A CAREER CHANGE.

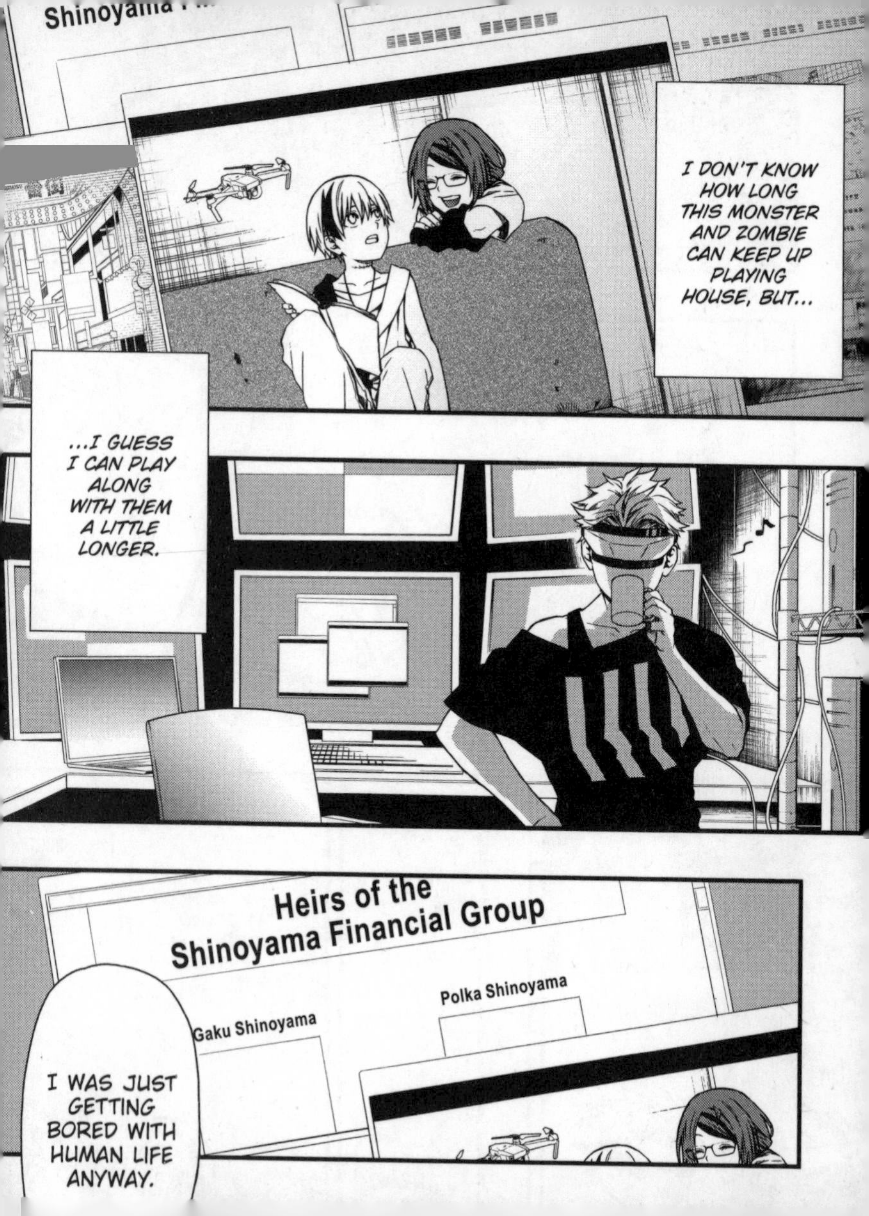
I DON'T KNOW HOW LONG THIS MONSTER AND ZOMBIE CAN KEEP UP PLAYING HOUSE, BUT...
...I GUESS I CAN PLAY ALONG WITH THEM A LITTLE LONGER.
Heirs of the Shinoyama Financial Group
Polka Shinoyama
Gaku Shinoyama
I WAS JUST GETTING BORED WITH HUMAN LIFE ANYWAY.

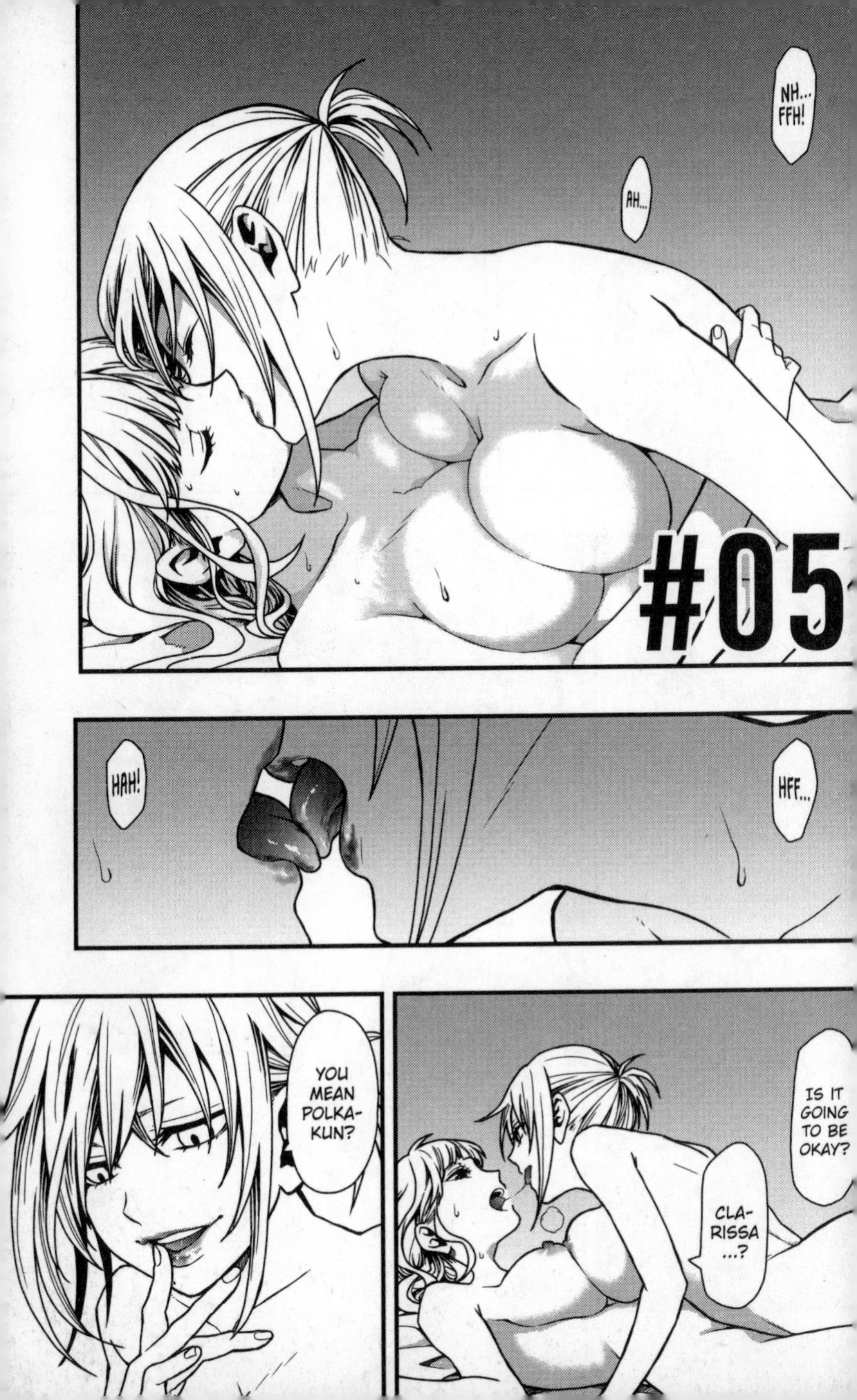
NH... FFH!
AH...
#05
HFF...
HAH!
IS IT GOING TO BE OKAY?
CLARISSA ...?
YOU MEAN POLKA-KUN?

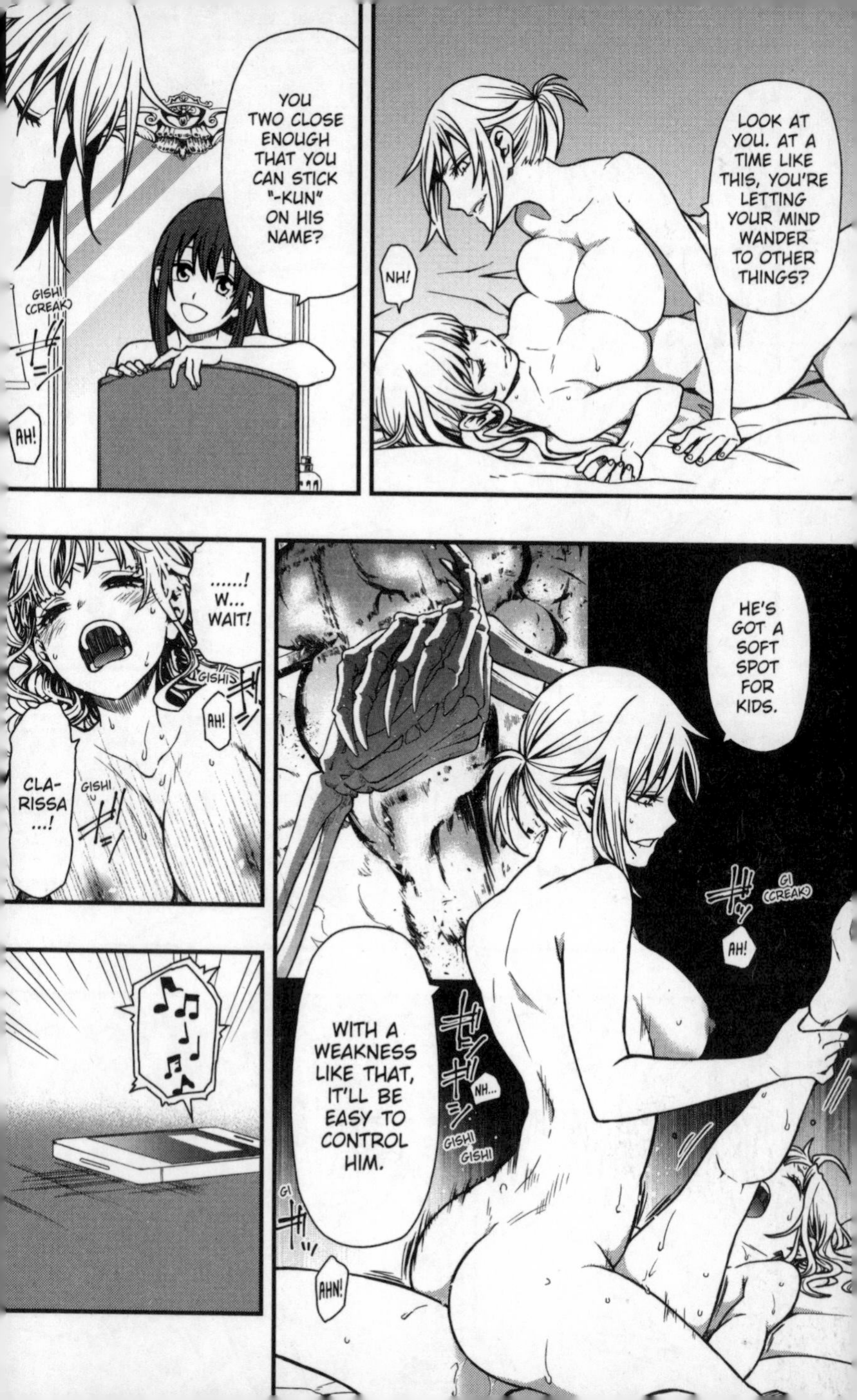
LOOK AT YOU. AT A TIME LIKE THIS, YOU'RE LETTING YOUR MIND WANDER TO OTHER THINGS?
NH!
YOU TWO CLOSE ENOUGH THAT YOU CAN STICK "-KUN" ON HIS NAME?
GISHI (CREAK)
AH!
HE'S GOT A SOFT SPOT FOR KIDS.
GI (CREAK)
AH!
WITH A WEAKNESS LIKE THAT, IT'LL BE EASY TO CONTROL HIM.
NH...
GISHI GISHI
GI
AHN!
......! W... WAIT!
GISHI
AH!
CLA-RISSA ...!
GISHI

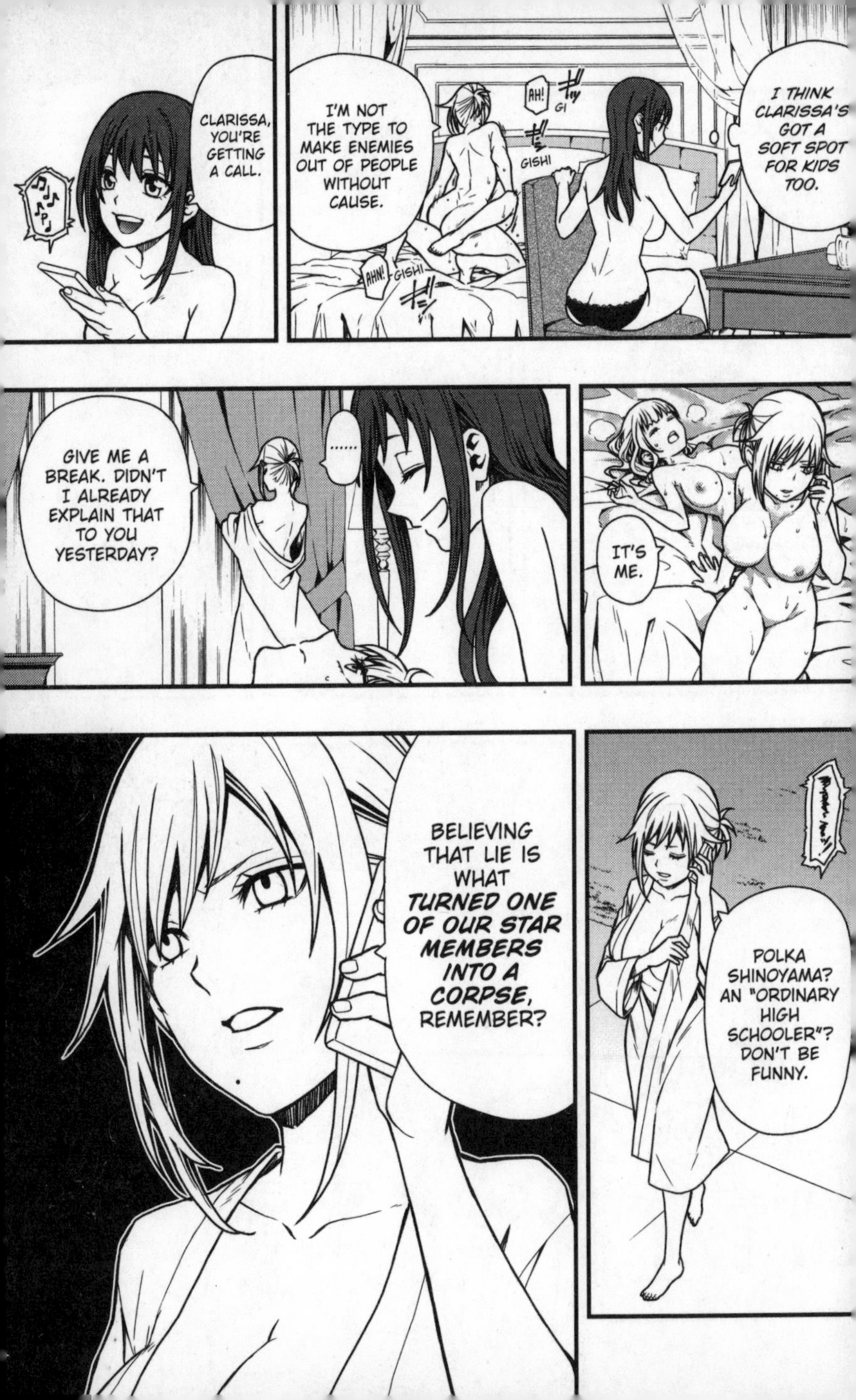
I THINK CLARISSA'S GOT A SOFT SPOT FOR KIDS TOO.
GI
GISHI
AH!
I'M NOT THE TYPE TO MAKE ENEMIES OUT OF PEOPLE WITHOUT CAUSE.
AHN!
GISHI
CLARISSA, YOU'RE GETTING A CALL.
IT'S ME.
......
GIVE ME A BREAK. DIDN'T I ALREADY EXPLAIN THAT TO YOU YESTERDAY?
POLKA SHINOYAMA? AN "ORDINARY HIGH SCHOOLER"? DON'T BE FUNNY.
BELIEVING THAT LIE IS WHAT *TURNED ONE OF OUR STAR MEMBERS INTO A CORPSE*, REMEMBER?

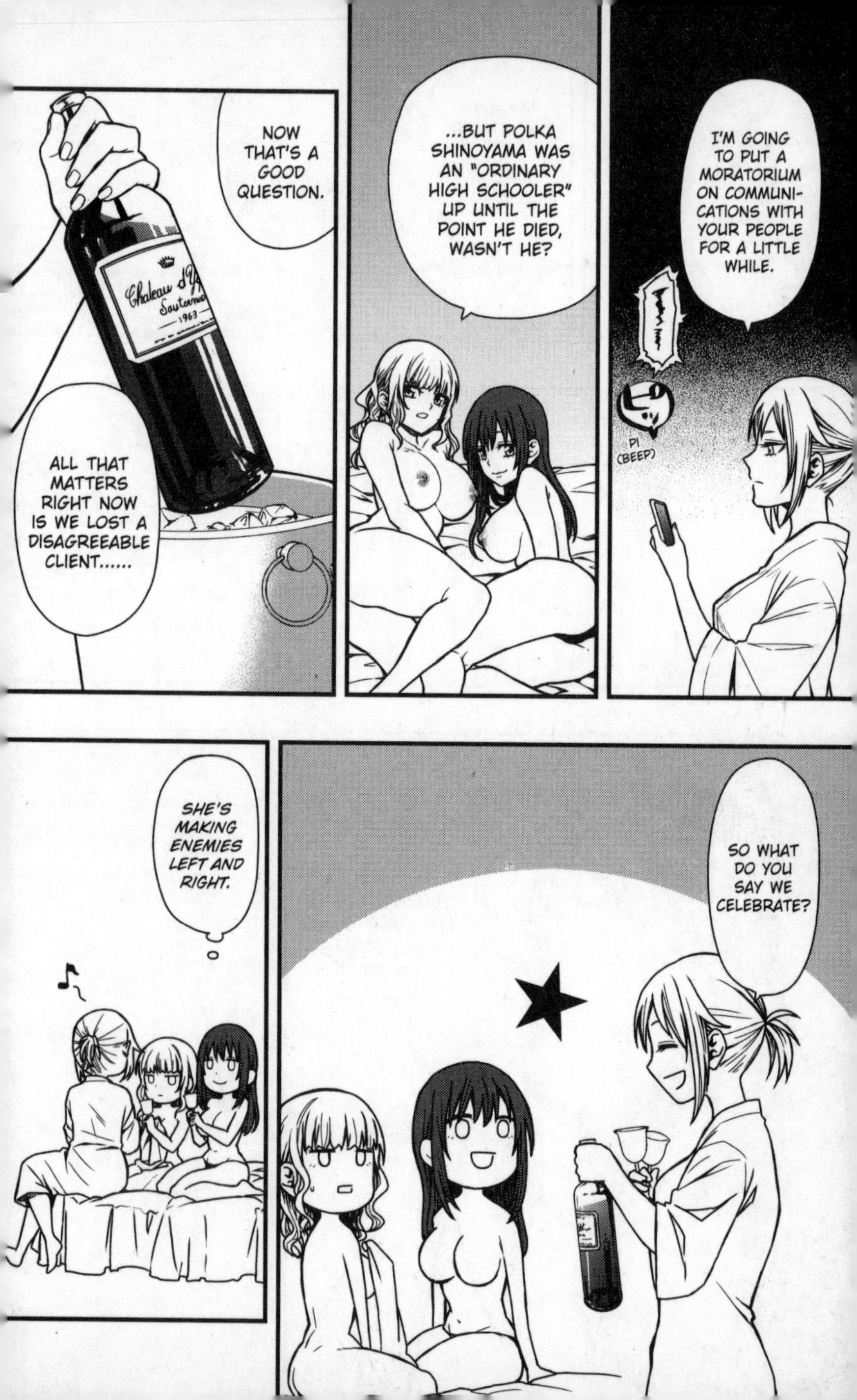
I'M GOING TO PUT A MORATORIUM ON COMMUNICATIONS WITH YOUR PEOPLE FOR A LITTLE WHILE.
PI (BEEP)
...BUT POLKA SHINOYAMA WAS AN "ORDINARY HIGH SCHOOLER" UP UNTIL THE POINT HE DIED, WASN'T HE?
NOW THAT'S A GOOD QUESTION.
ALL THAT MATTERS RIGHT NOW IS WE LOST A DISAGREEABLE CLIENT......
SO WHAT DO YOU SAY WE CELEBRATE?
SHE'S MAKING ENEMIES LEFT AND RIGHT.

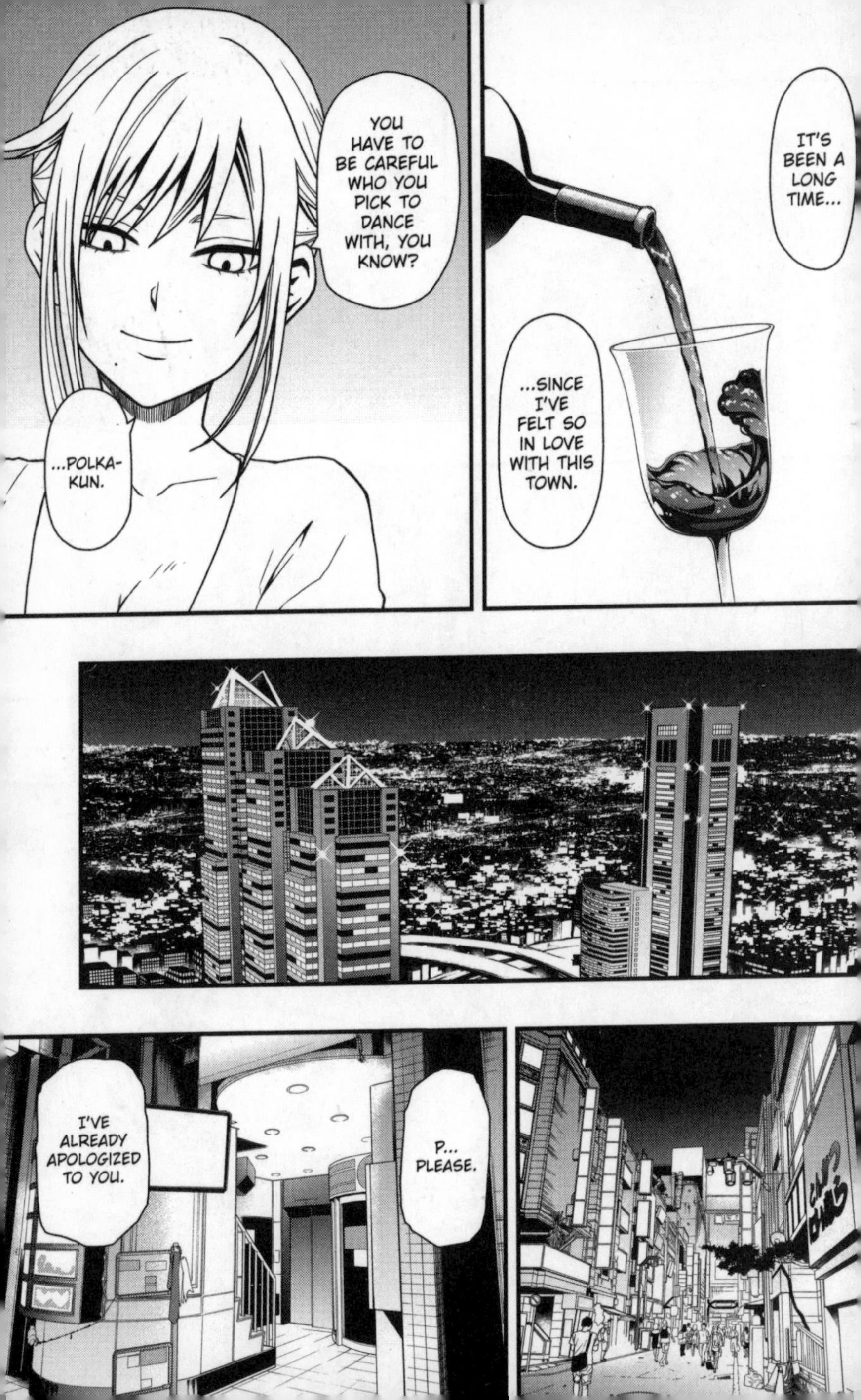
IT'S BEEN A LONG TIME...
...SINCE I'VE FELT SO IN LOVE WITH THIS TOWN.
YOU HAVE TO BE CAREFUL WHO YOU PICK TO DANCE WITH, YOU KNOW?
...POLKA-KUN.
P... PLEASE.
I'VE ALREADY APOLOGIZED TO YOU.

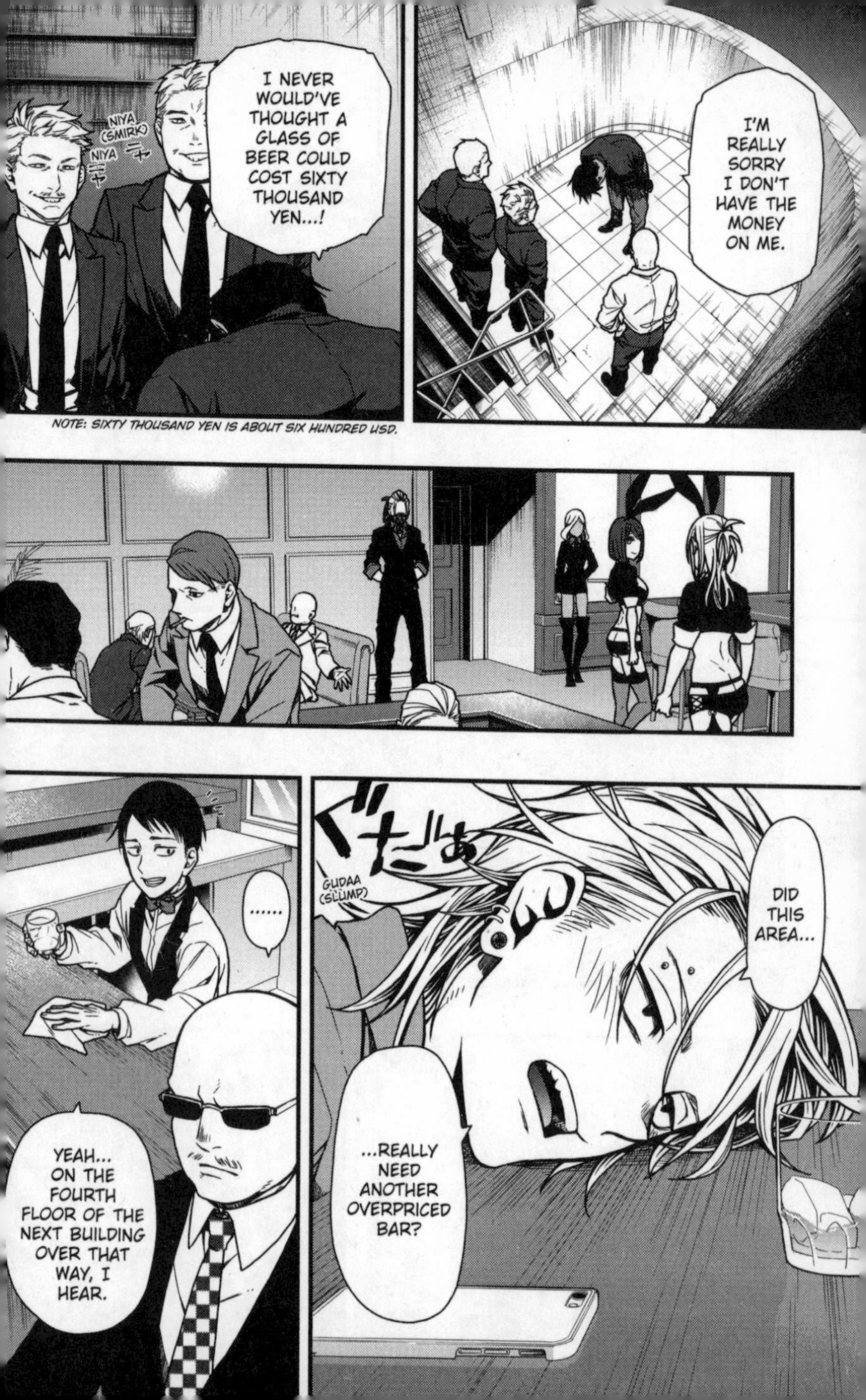
I'M REALLY SORRY I DON'T HAVE THE MONEY ON ME.
NIYA (SMIRK)
NIYA
I NEVER WOULD'VE THOUGHT A GLASS OF BEER COULD COST SIXTY THOUSAND YEN...!
NOTE: SIXTY THOUSAND YEN IS ABOUT SIX HUNDRED USD.
GUDAA (SLUMP)
DID THIS AREA...
...REALLY NEED ANOTHER OVERPRICED BAR?
......
YEAH... ON THE FOURTH FLOOR OF THE NEXT BUILDING OVER THAT WAY, I HEAR.

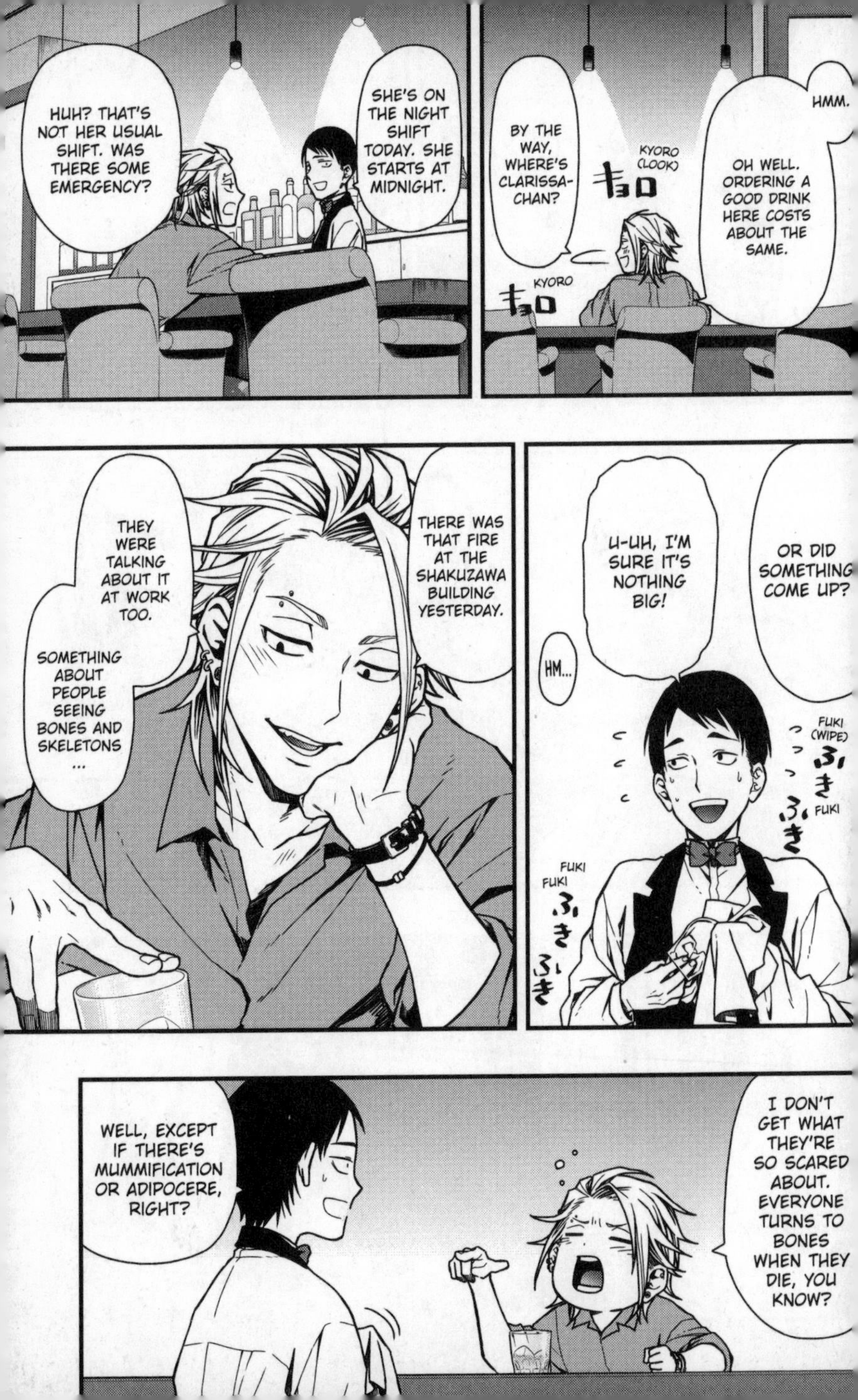
HMM.
OH WELL. ORDERING A GOOD DRINK HERE COSTS ABOUT THE SAME.
KYORO (LOOK)
BY THE WAY, WHERE'S CLARISSA-CHAN?
KYORO
SHE'S ON THE NIGHT SHIFT TODAY. SHE STARTS AT MIDNIGHT.
HUH? THAT'S NOT HER USUAL SHIFT. WAS THERE SOME EMERGENCY?
OR DID SOMETHING COME UP?
U-UH, I'M SURE IT'S NOTHING BIG!
HM...
FUKI (WIPE)
FUKI
FUKI FUKI
THERE WAS THAT FIRE AT THE SHAKUZAWA BUILDING YESTERDAY.
THEY WERE TALKING ABOUT IT AT WORK TOO.
SOMETHING ABOUT PEOPLE SEEING BONES AND SKELETONS...
I DON'T GET WHAT THEY'RE SO SCARED ABOUT. EVERYONE TURNS TO BONES WHEN THEY DIE, YOU KNOW?
WELL, EXCEPT IF THERE'S MUMMIFICATION OR ADIPOCERE, RIGHT?

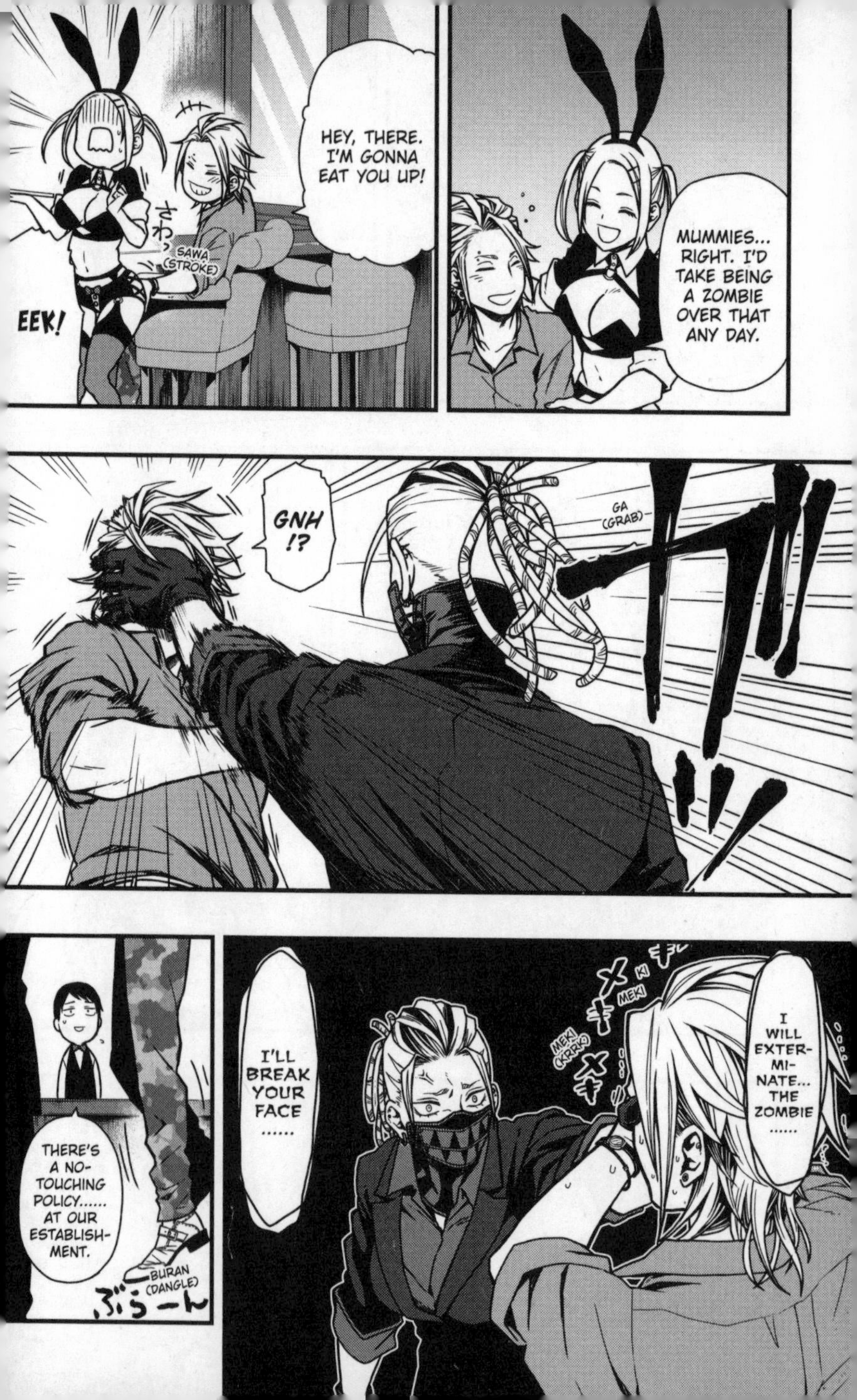
MUMMIES... RIGHT. I'D TAKE BEING A ZOMBIE OVER THAT ANY DAY.
HEY, THERE. I'M GONNA EAT YOU UP!
さわっ
SAWA (STROKE)
EEK!
ガッ
GA (GRAB)
GNH !?
I WILL EXTER-MI-NATE... THE ZOMBIE ......
メキメキ
MEKI MEKI (KRRK)
I'LL BREAK YOUR FACE ......
THERE'S A NO-TOUCHING POLICY...... AT OUR ESTABLISH-MENT.
BURAN (DANGLE)
ぶらーん

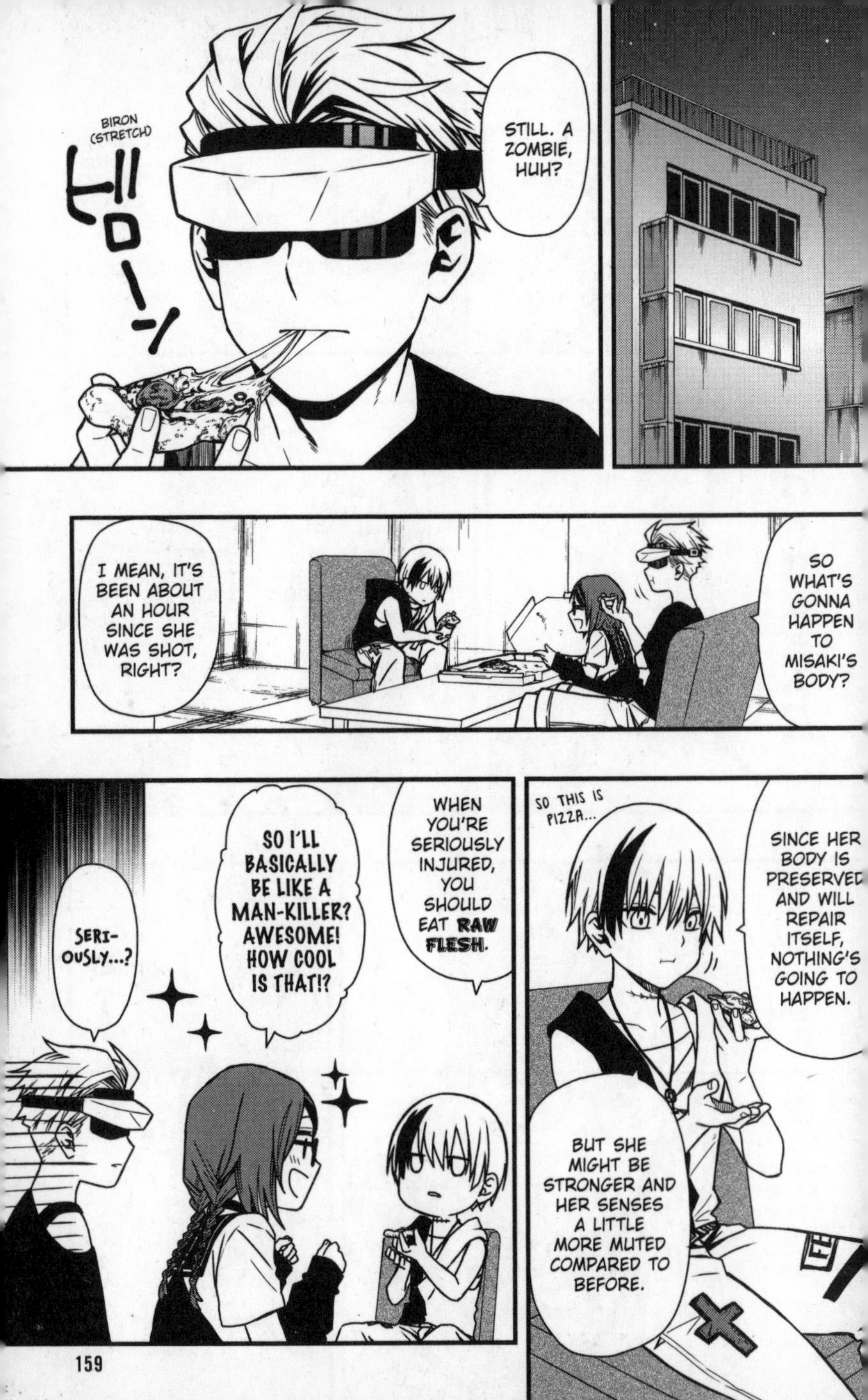
STILL. A ZOMBIE, HUH?
BIRON (STRETCH)
ビローン
SO WHAT'S GONNA HAPPEN TO MISAKI'S BODY?
I MEAN, IT'S BEEN ABOUT AN HOUR SINCE SHE WAS SHOT, RIGHT?
SINCE HER BODY IS PRESERVED AND WILL REPAIR ITSELF, NOTHING'S GOING TO HAPPEN.
SO THIS IS PIZZA...
BUT SHE MIGHT BE STRONGER AND HER SENSES A LITTLE MORE MUTED COMPARED TO BEFORE.
WHEN YOU'RE SERIOUSLY INJURED, YOU SHOULD EAT RAW FLESH.
SO I'LL BASICALLY BE LIKE A MAN-KILLER? AWESOME! HOW COOL IS THAT!?
SERI-OUSLY...?

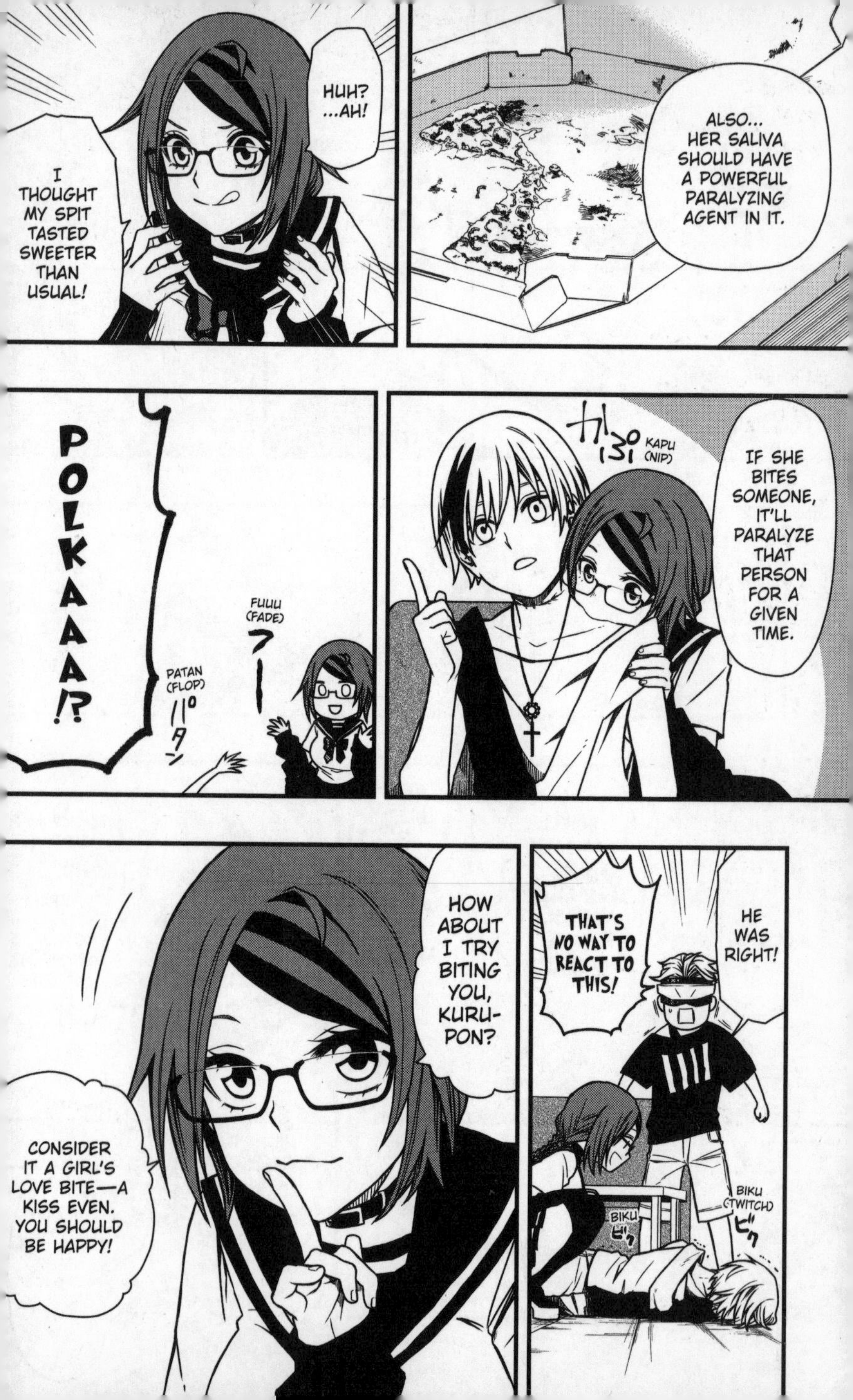

ALSO... HER SALIVA SHOULD HAVE A POWERFUL PARALYZING AGENT IN IT.
HUH? ...AH!
I THOUGHT MY SPIT TASTED SWEETER THAN USUAL!
KAPU (NIP)
IF SHE BITES SOMEONE, IT'LL PARALYZE THAT PERSON FOR A GIVEN TIME.
FUUU (FADE)
PATAN (FLOP)
POLKAAAA!?
HE WAS RIGHT!
THAT'S NO WAY TO REACT TO THIS!
BIKU (TWITCH)
BIKU
HOW ABOUT I TRY BITING YOU, KURU-PON?
CONSIDER IT A GIRL'S LOVE BITE—A KISS EVEN. YOU SHOULD BE HAPPY!

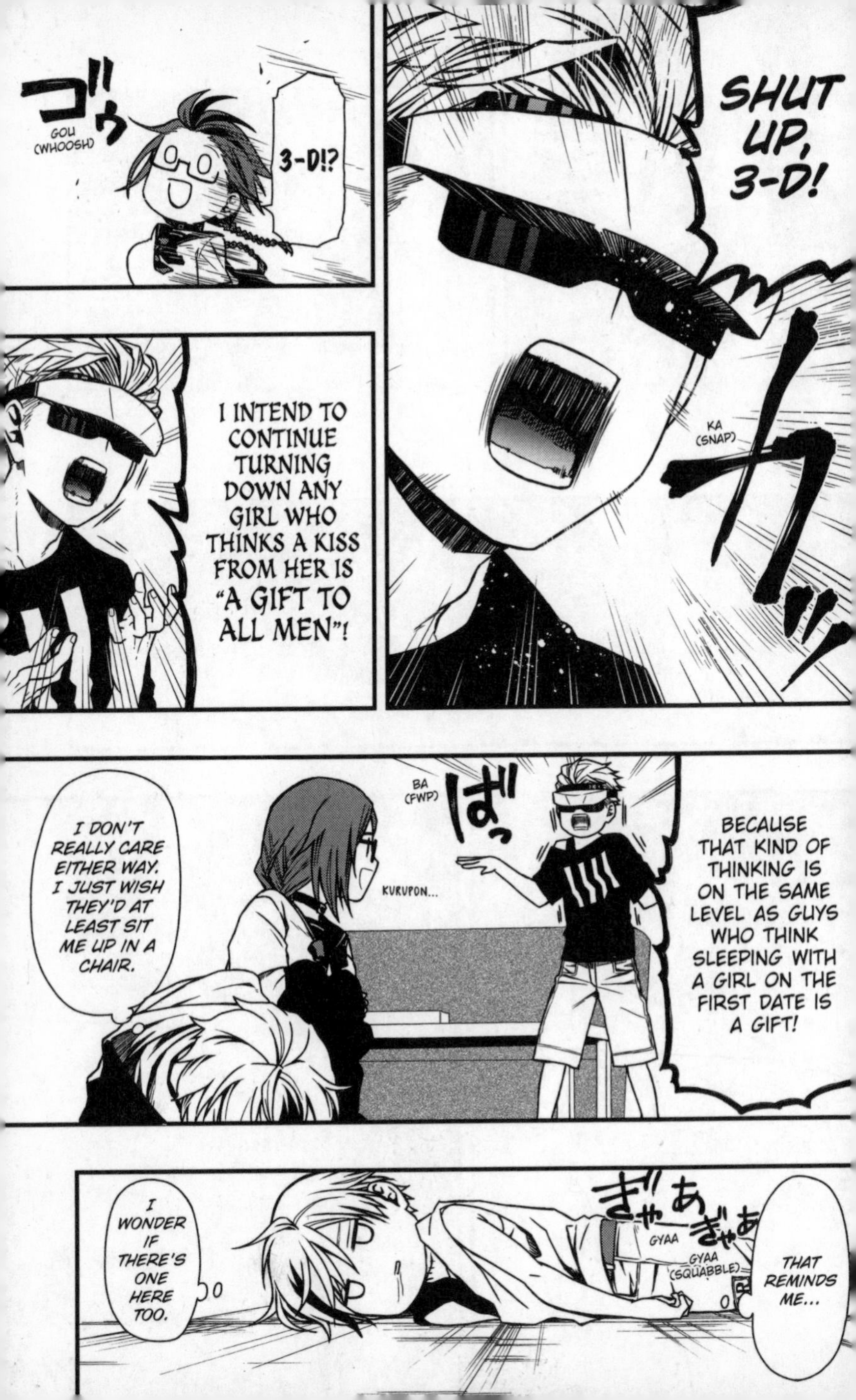
SHUT UP, 3-D!
カッ
KA (SNAP)
ゴウ
GOU (WHOOSH)
3-D!?
I INTEND TO CONTINUE TURNING DOWN ANY GIRL WHO THINKS A KISS FROM HER IS "A GIFT TO ALL MEN"!
BECAUSE THAT KIND OF THINKING IS ON THE SAME LEVEL AS GUYS WHO THINK SLEEPING WITH A GIRL ON THE FIRST DATE IS A GIFT!
ばっ
BA (FWP)
KURUPON...
I DON'T REALLY CARE EITHER WAY. I JUST WISH THEY'D AT LEAST SIT ME UP IN A CHAIR.
THAT REMINDS ME...
ぎゃあぎゃあ
GYAA GYAA (SQUABBLE)
I WONDER IF THERE'S ONE HERE TOO.

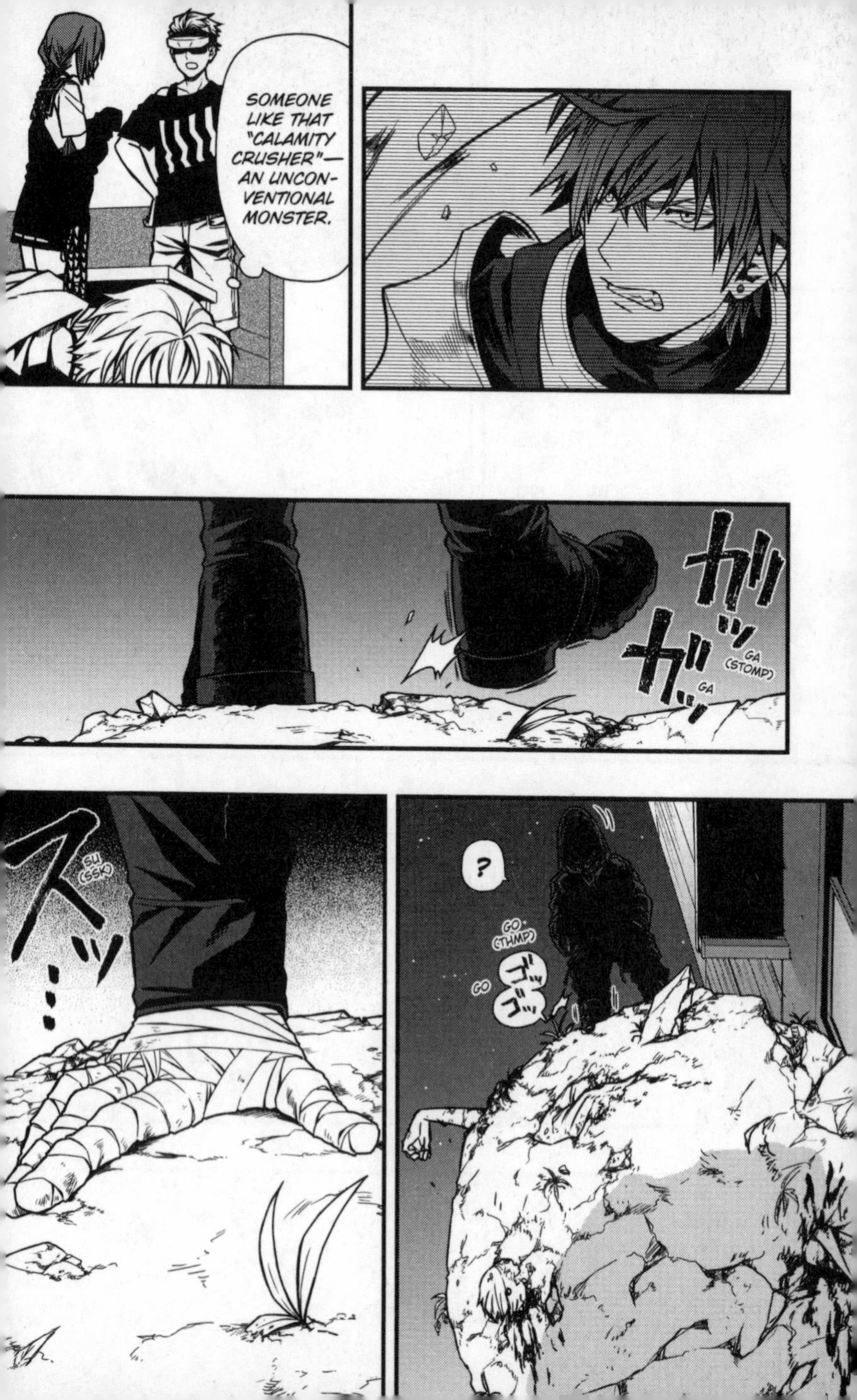
SOMEONE LIKE THAT "CALAMITY CRUSHER"—AN UNCONVENTIONAL MONSTER.
カッ GA (STOMP)
ガッ GA
スッ… SU (SSK)
?
ゴッ GO (THMP)
ゴッ GO

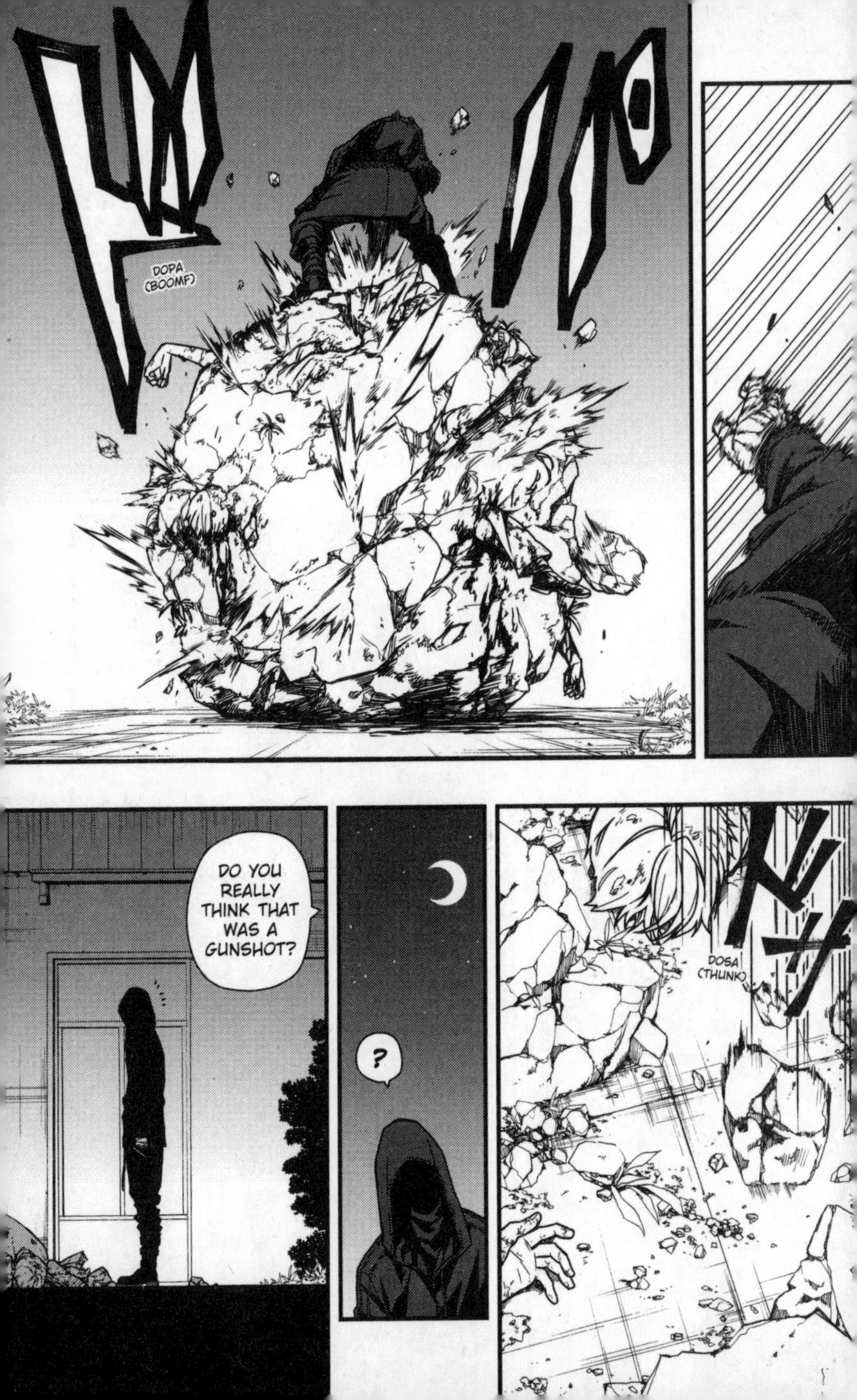
DOPA
(BOOMF)
DOSA
(THUNK)
?
DO YOU REALLY THINK THAT WAS A GUNSHOT?

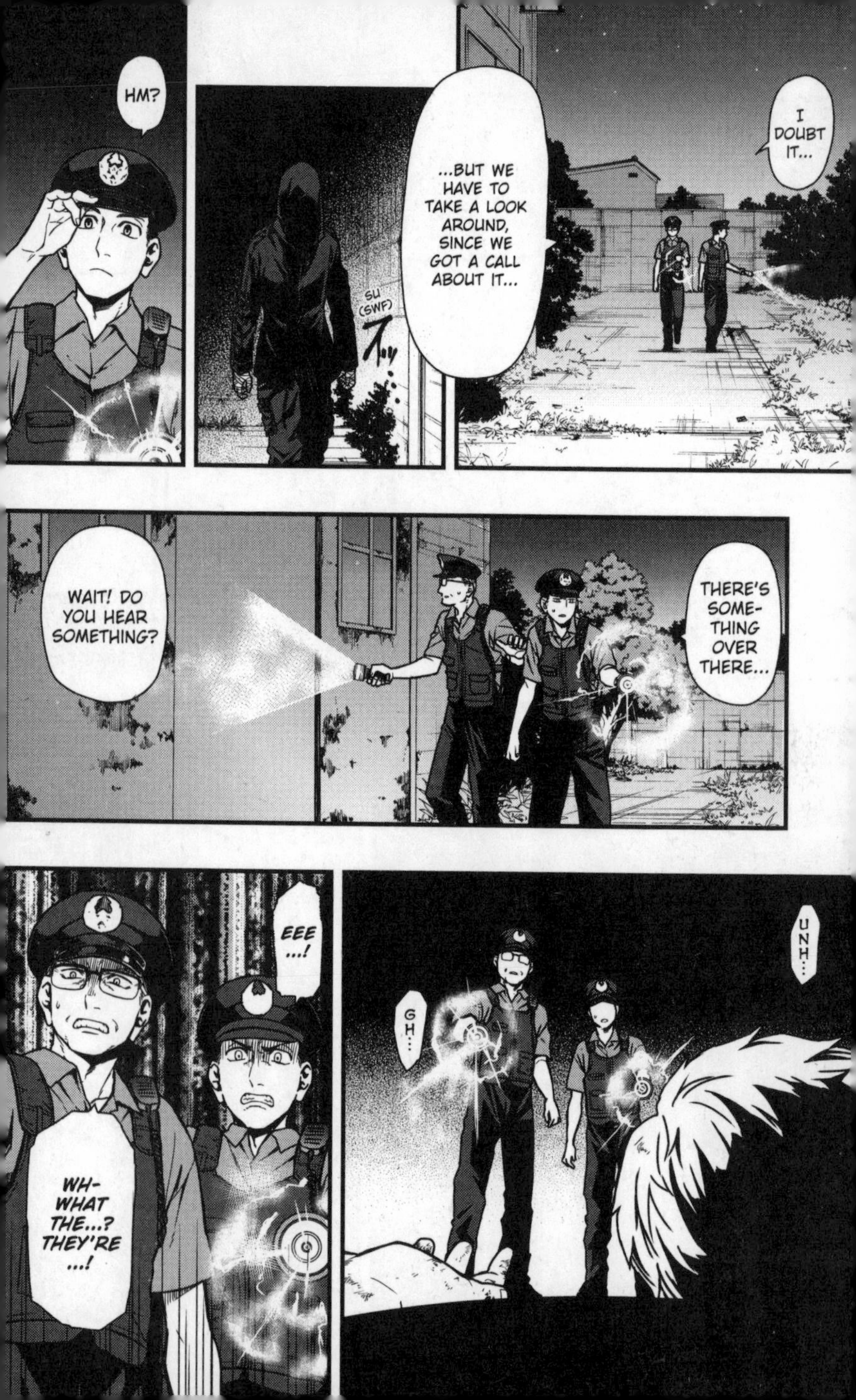
I DOUBT IT...
...BUT WE HAVE TO TAKE A LOOK AROUND, SINCE WE GOT A CALL ABOUT IT...
SU (SWF)
HM?
THERE'S SOMETHING OVER THERE...
WAIT! DO YOU HEAR SOMETHING?
UNH...
GH...
EEE...!
WH-WHAT THE...? THEY'RE...!

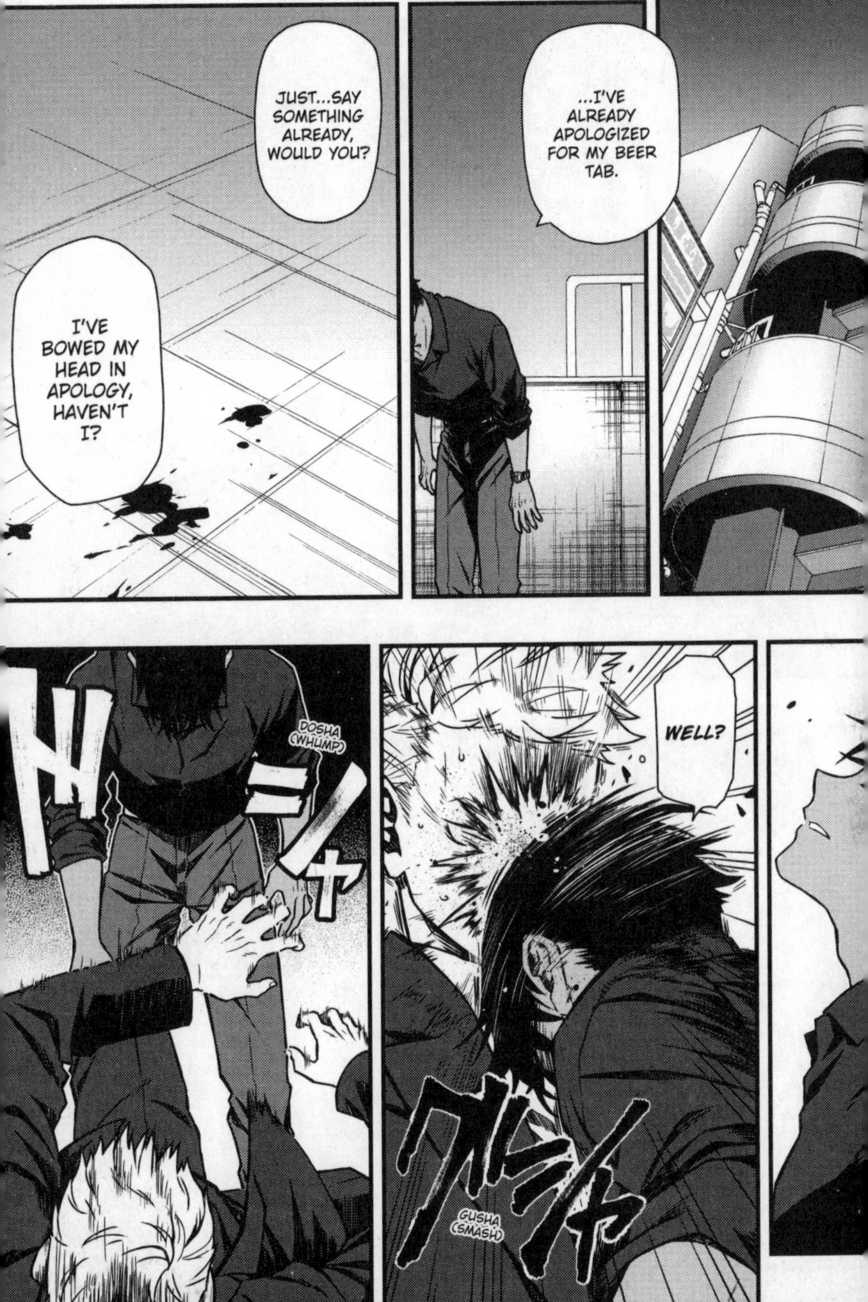
...I'VE ALREADY APOLOGIZED FOR MY BEER TAB.
JUST...SAY SOMETHING ALREADY, WOULD YOU?
I'VE BOWED MY HEAD IN APOLOGY, HAVEN'T I?
WELL?
GUSHA (SMASH)
DOSHA (WHUMP)

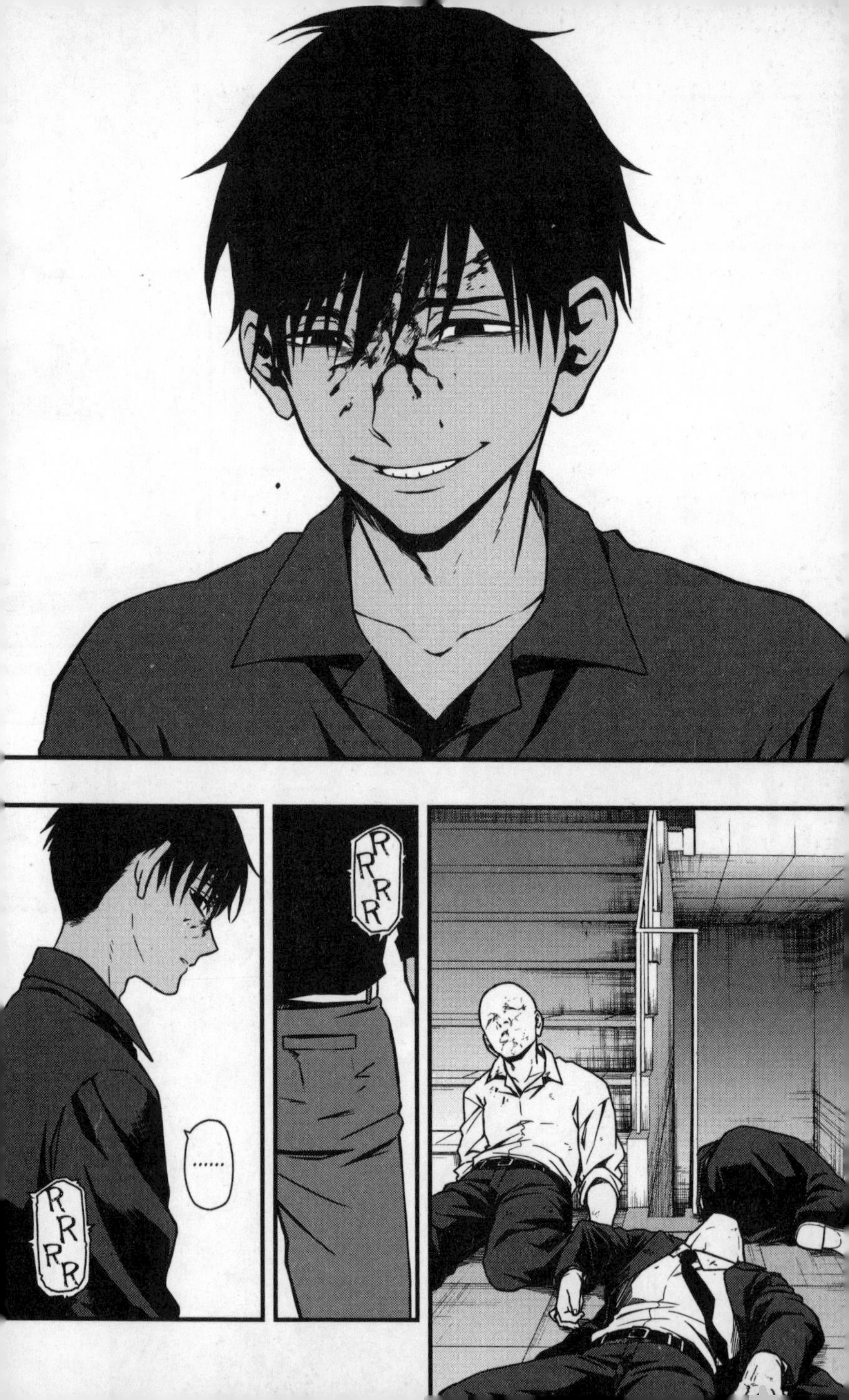
RRRR
RRRR
......

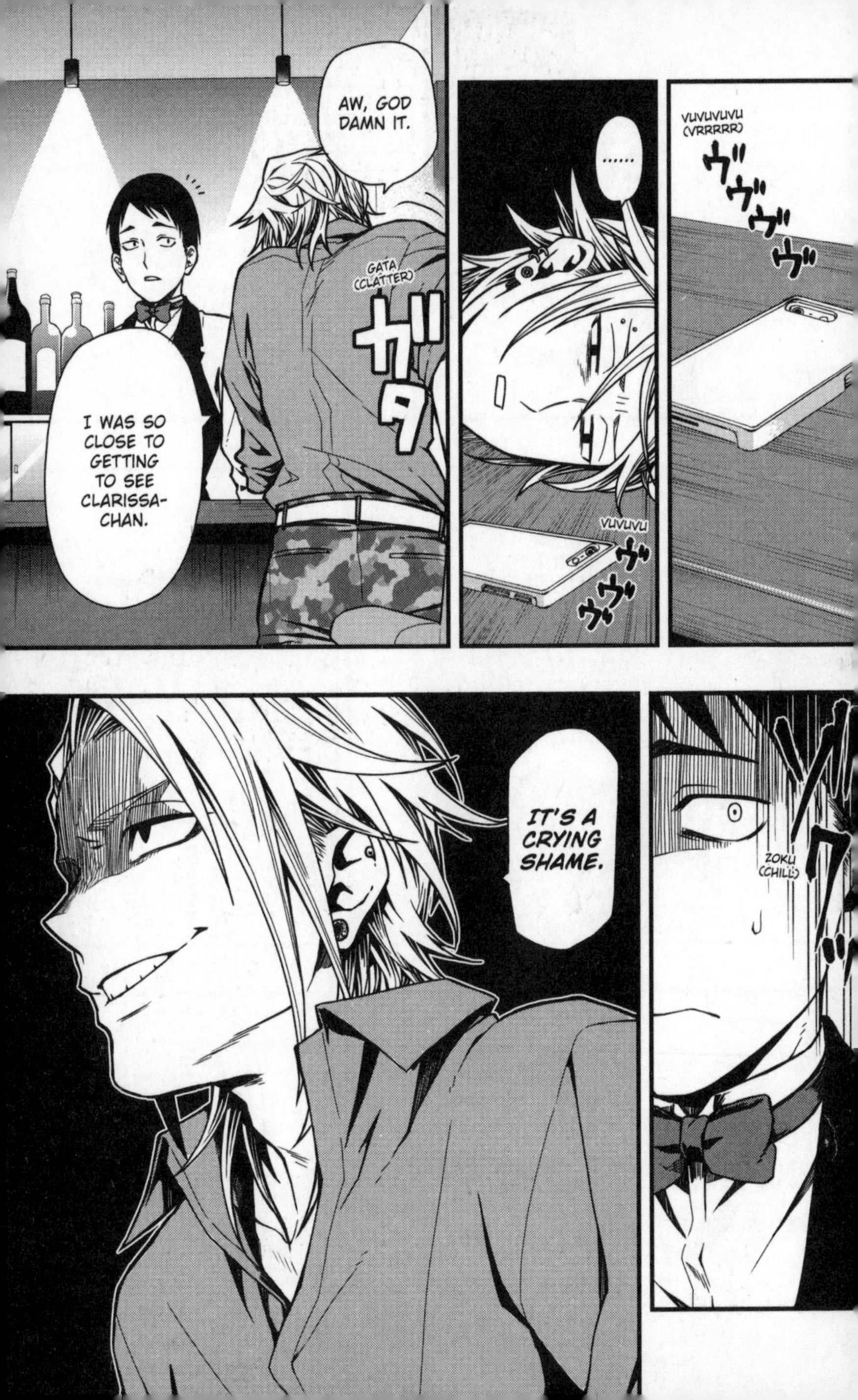
VUVUVUVU (VRRRRR)
ヴヴヴヴ
VUVUVU
ヴヴヴ
......
AW, GOD DAMN IT.
GATA (CLATTER)
ガタ
I WAS SO CLOSE TO GETTING TO SEE CLARISSA-CHAN.
ZOKU (CHILL)
IT'S A CRYING SHAME.

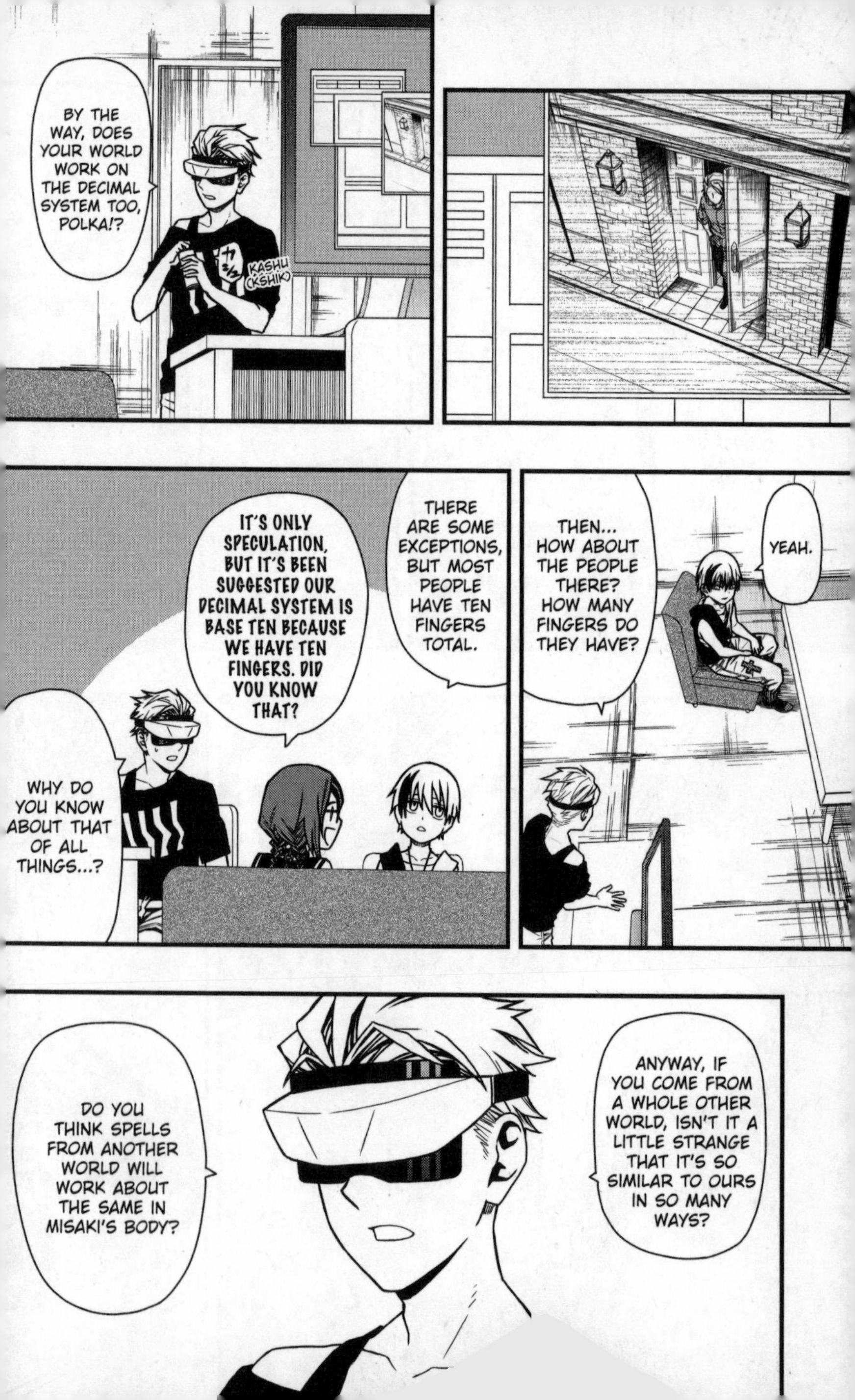
BY THE WAY, DOES YOUR WORLD WORK ON THE DECIMAL SYSTEM TOO, POLKA!?
KASHU (KSHIK)
YEAH.
THEN... HOW ABOUT THE PEOPLE THERE? HOW MANY FINGERS DO THEY HAVE?
THERE ARE SOME EXCEPTIONS, BUT MOST PEOPLE HAVE TEN FINGERS TOTAL.
IT'S ONLY SPECULATION, BUT IT'S BEEN SUGGESTED OUR DECIMAL SYSTEM IS BASE TEN BECAUSE WE HAVE TEN FINGERS. DID YOU KNOW THAT?
WHY DO YOU KNOW ABOUT THAT OF ALL THINGS...?
ANYWAY, IF YOU COME FROM A WHOLE OTHER WORLD, ISN'T IT A LITTLE STRANGE THAT IT'S SO SIMILAR TO OURS IN SO MANY WAYS?
DO YOU THINK SPELLS FROM ANOTHER WORLD WILL WORK ABOUT THE SAME IN MISAKI'S BODY?

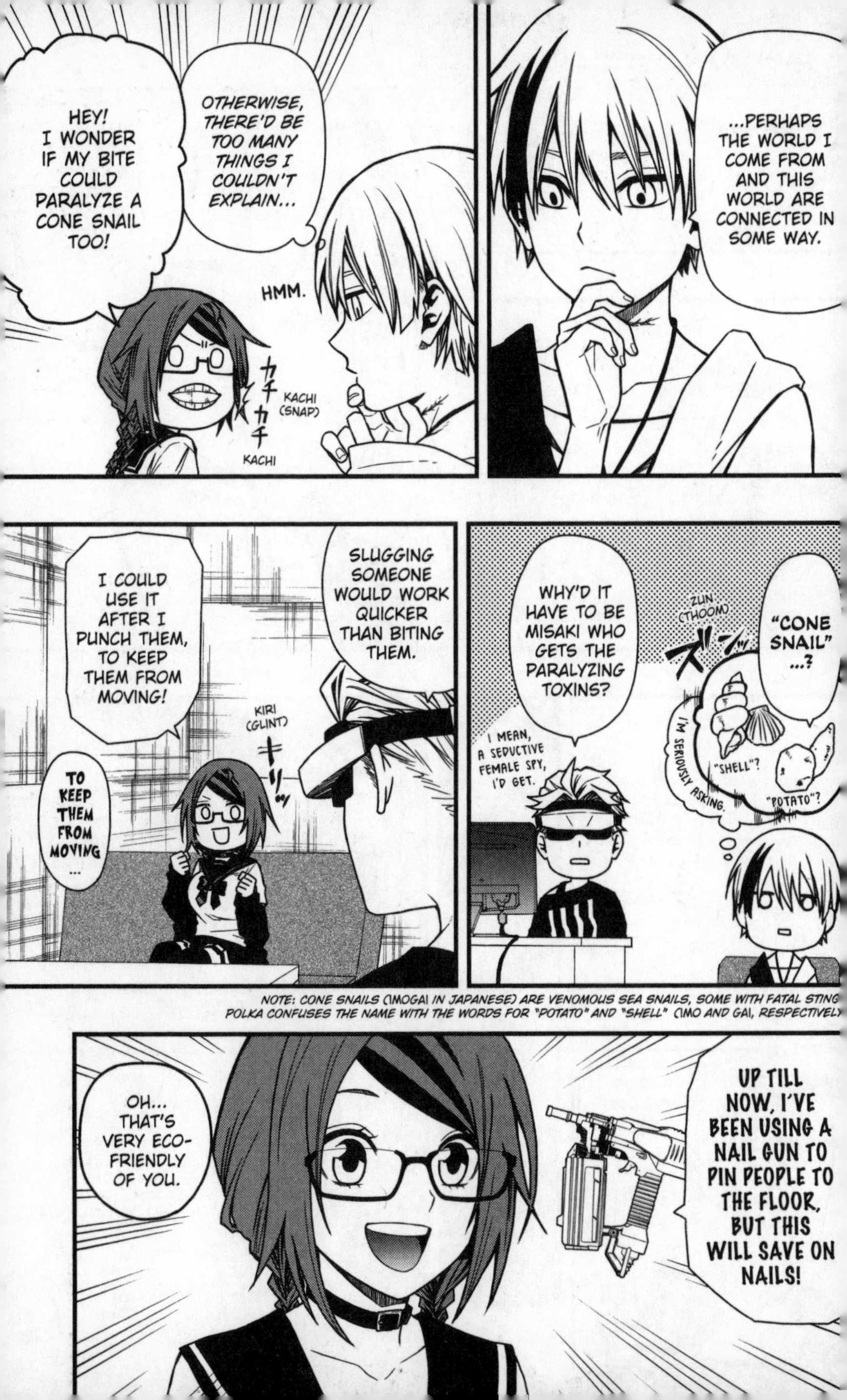
...PERHAPS THE WORLD I COME FROM AND THIS WORLD ARE CONNECTED IN SOME WAY.
OTHERWISE, THERE'D BE TOO MANY THINGS I COULDN'T EXPLAIN...
HMM.
HEY! I WONDER IF MY BITE COULD PARALYZE A CONE SNAIL TOO!
カチ カチ
KACHI (SNAP)
KACHI
"CONE SNAIL"...?
"SHELL"?
"POTATO"?
I'M SERIOUSLY ASKING.
ZUN (THOOM)
WHY'D IT HAVE TO BE MISAKI WHO GETS THE PARALYZING TOXINS?
I MEAN, A SEDUCTIVE FEMALE SPY, I'D GET.
SLUGGING SOMEONE WOULD WORK QUICKER THAN BITING THEM.
I COULD USE IT AFTER I PUNCH THEM, TO KEEP THEM FROM MOVING!
KIRI (GLINT)
TO KEEP THEM FROM MOVING...
UP TILL NOW, I'VE BEEN USING A NAIL GUN TO PIN PEOPLE TO THE FLOOR, BUT THIS WILL SAVE ON NAILS!
OH... THAT'S VERY ECO-FRIENDLY OF YOU.

NOTE: CONE SNAILS (IMOGAI IN JAPANESE) ARE VENOMOUS SEA SNAILS, SOME WITH FATAL STING
POLKA CONFUSES THE NAME WITH THE WORDS FOR "POTATO" AND "SHELL" (IMO AND GAI, RESPECTIVELY

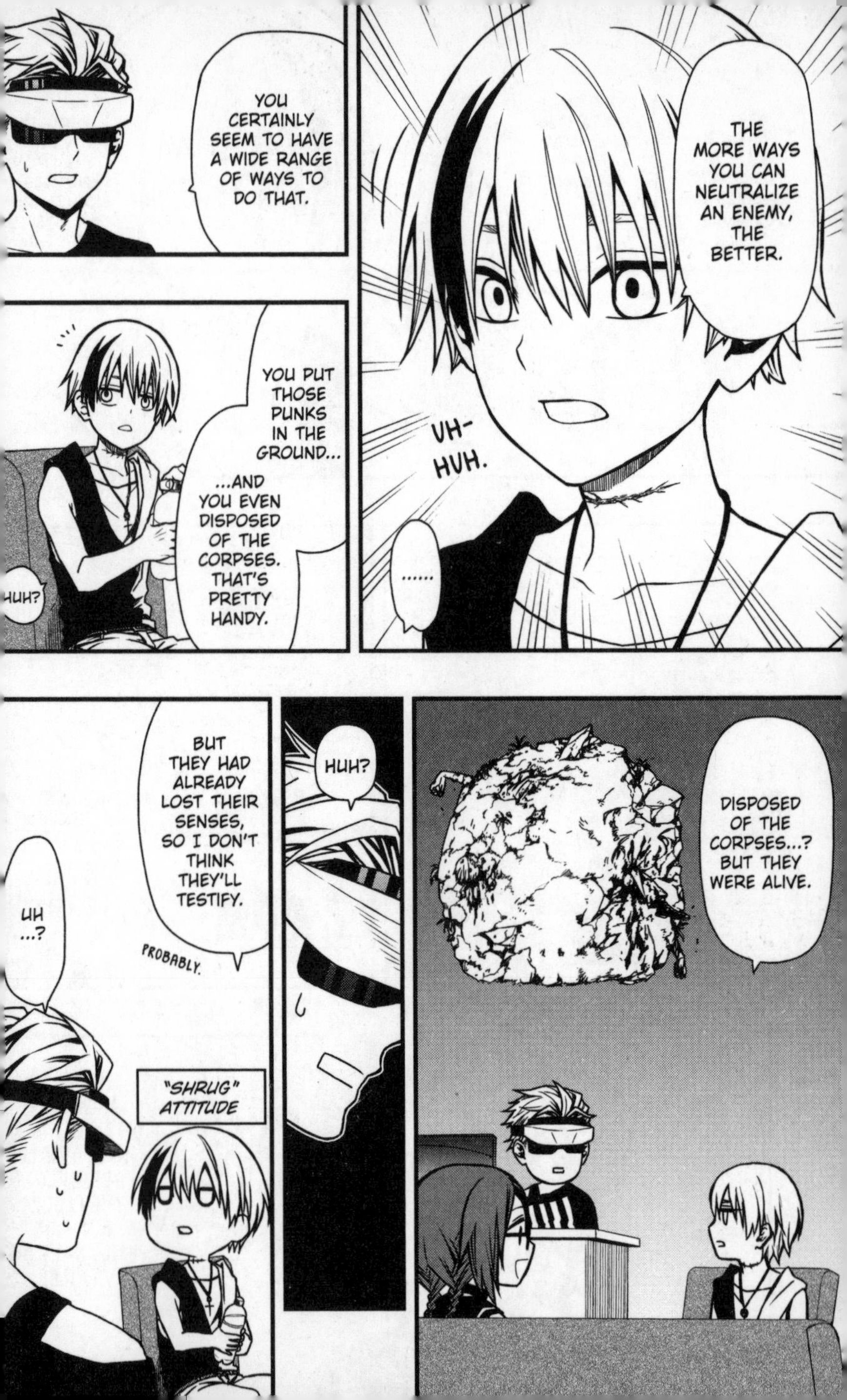
YOU CERTAINLY SEEM TO HAVE A WIDE RANGE OF WAYS TO DO THAT.
THE MORE WAYS YOU CAN NEUTRALIZE AN ENEMY, THE BETTER.
UH-HUH.
YOU PUT THOSE PUNKS IN THE GROUND...
...AND YOU EVEN DISPOSED OF THE CORPSES. THAT'S PRETTY HANDY.
......
HUH?
DISPOSED OF THE CORPSES...? BUT THEY WERE ALIVE.
HUH?
BUT THEY HAD ALREADY LOST THEIR SENSES, SO I DON'T THINK THEY'LL TESTIFY.
PROBABLY.
UH ...?
"SHRUG" ATTITUDE

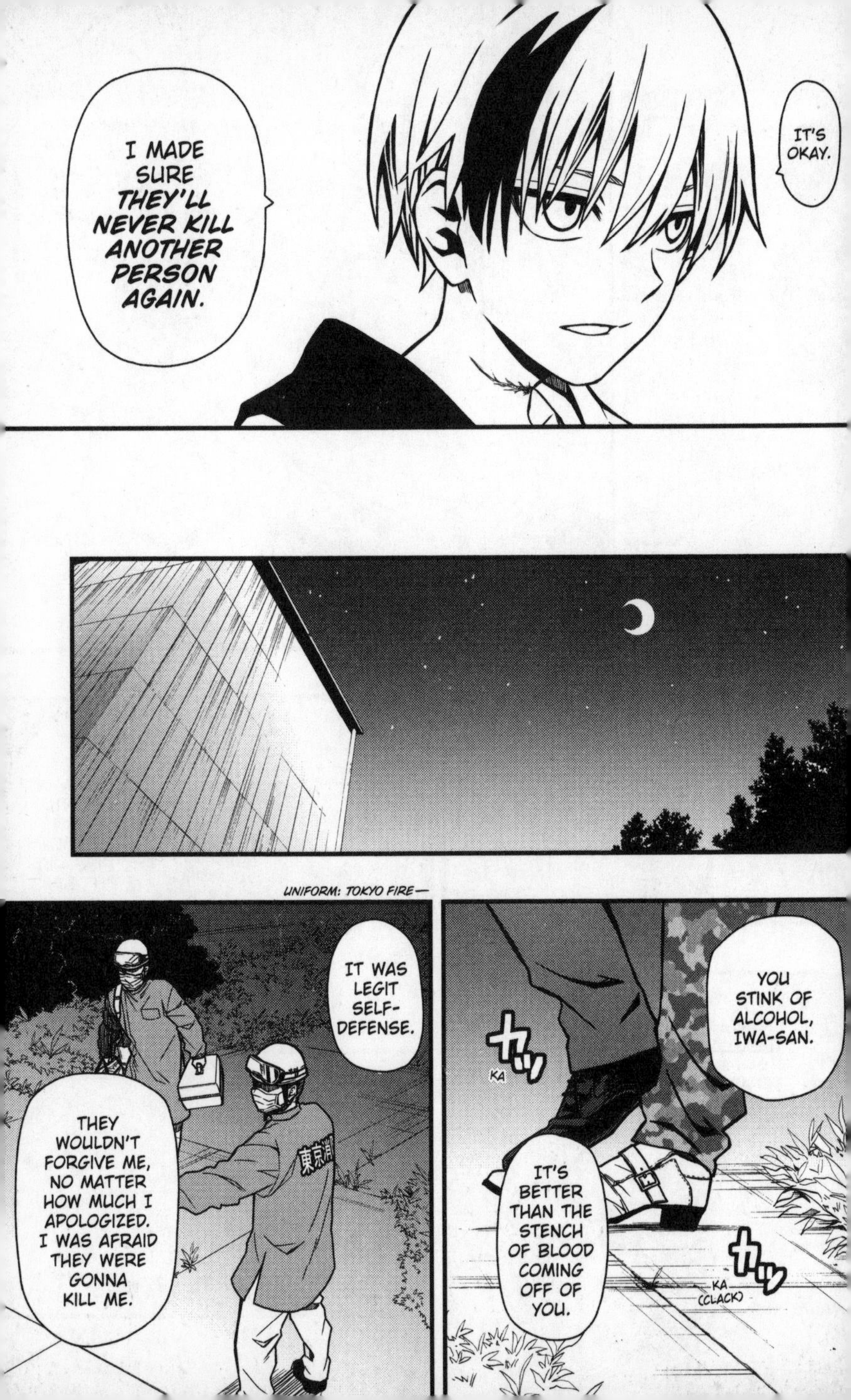
IT'S OKAY.
I MADE SURE *THEY'LL NEVER KILL ANOTHER PERSON AGAIN.*
UNIFORM: TOKYO FIRE—
YOU STINK OF ALCOHOL, IWA-SAN.
カッ
KA
IT'S BETTER THAN THE STENCH OF BLOOD COMING OFF OF YOU.
カッ
KA (CLACK)
IT WAS LEGIT SELF-DEFENSE.
東京消
THEY WOULDN'T FORGIVE ME, NO MATTER HOW MUCH I APOLOGIZED. I WAS AFRAID THEY WERE GONNA KILL ME.

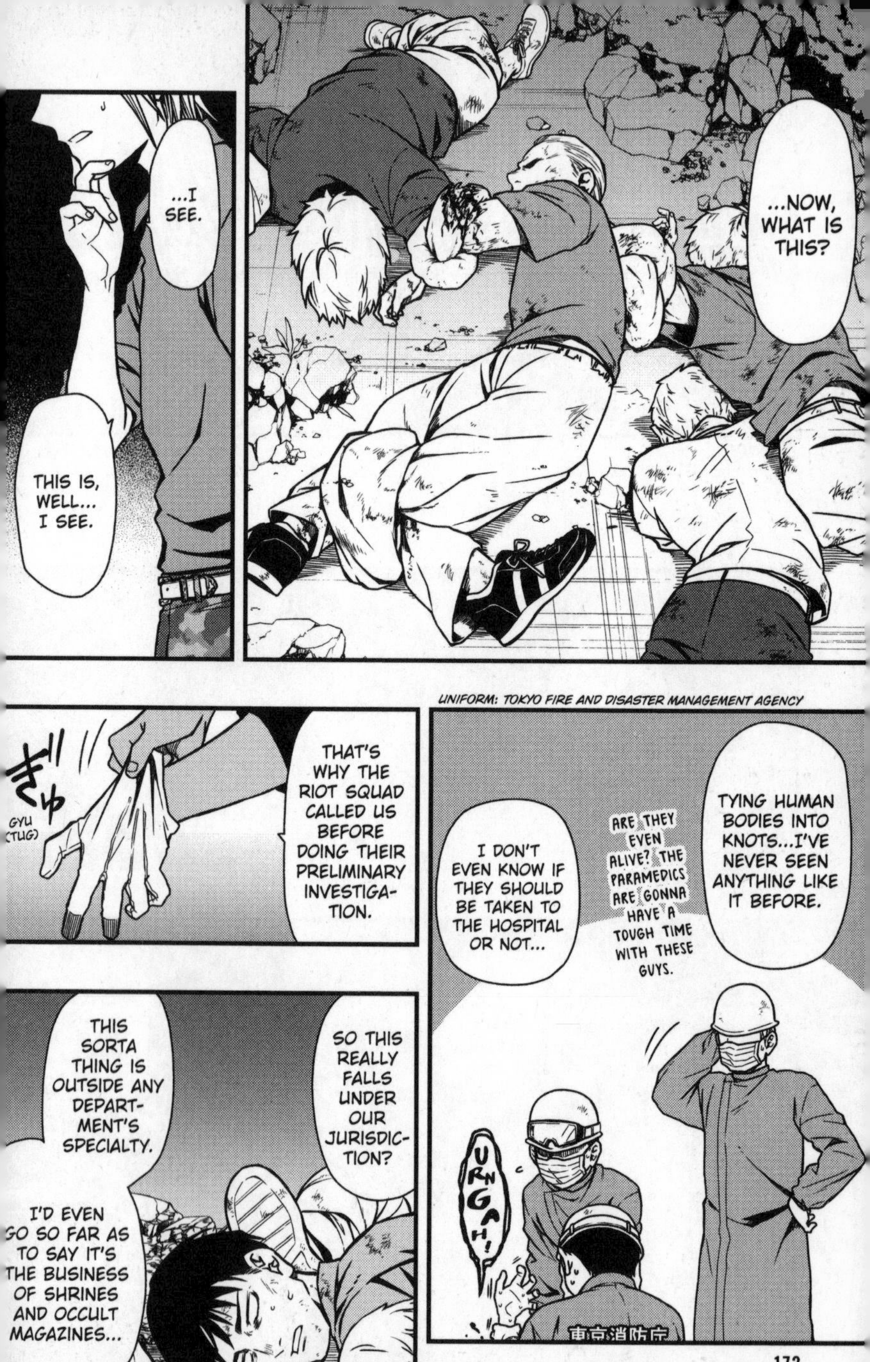
...NOW, WHAT IS THIS?
...I SEE.
THIS IS, WELL... I SEE.
UNIFORM: TOKYO FIRE AND DISASTER MANAGEMENT AGENCY
TYING HUMAN BODIES INTO KNOTS...I'VE NEVER SEEN ANYTHING LIKE IT BEFORE.
ARE THEY EVEN ALIVE? THE PARAMEDICS ARE GONNA HAVE A TOUGH TIME WITH THESE GUYS.
I DON'T EVEN KNOW IF THEY SHOULD BE TAKEN TO THE HOSPITAL OR NOT...
URNGAH!
東京消防庁
THAT'S WHY THE RIOT SQUAD CALLED US BEFORE DOING THEIR PRELIMINARY INVESTIGA-TION.
ぎゅ
GYU (TUG)
SO THIS REALLY FALLS UNDER OUR JURISDIC-TION?
THIS SORTA THING IS OUTSIDE ANY DEPART-MENT'S SPECIALTY.
I'D EVEN GO SO FAR AS TO SAY IT'S THE BUSINESS OF SHRINES AND OCCULT MAGAZINES...

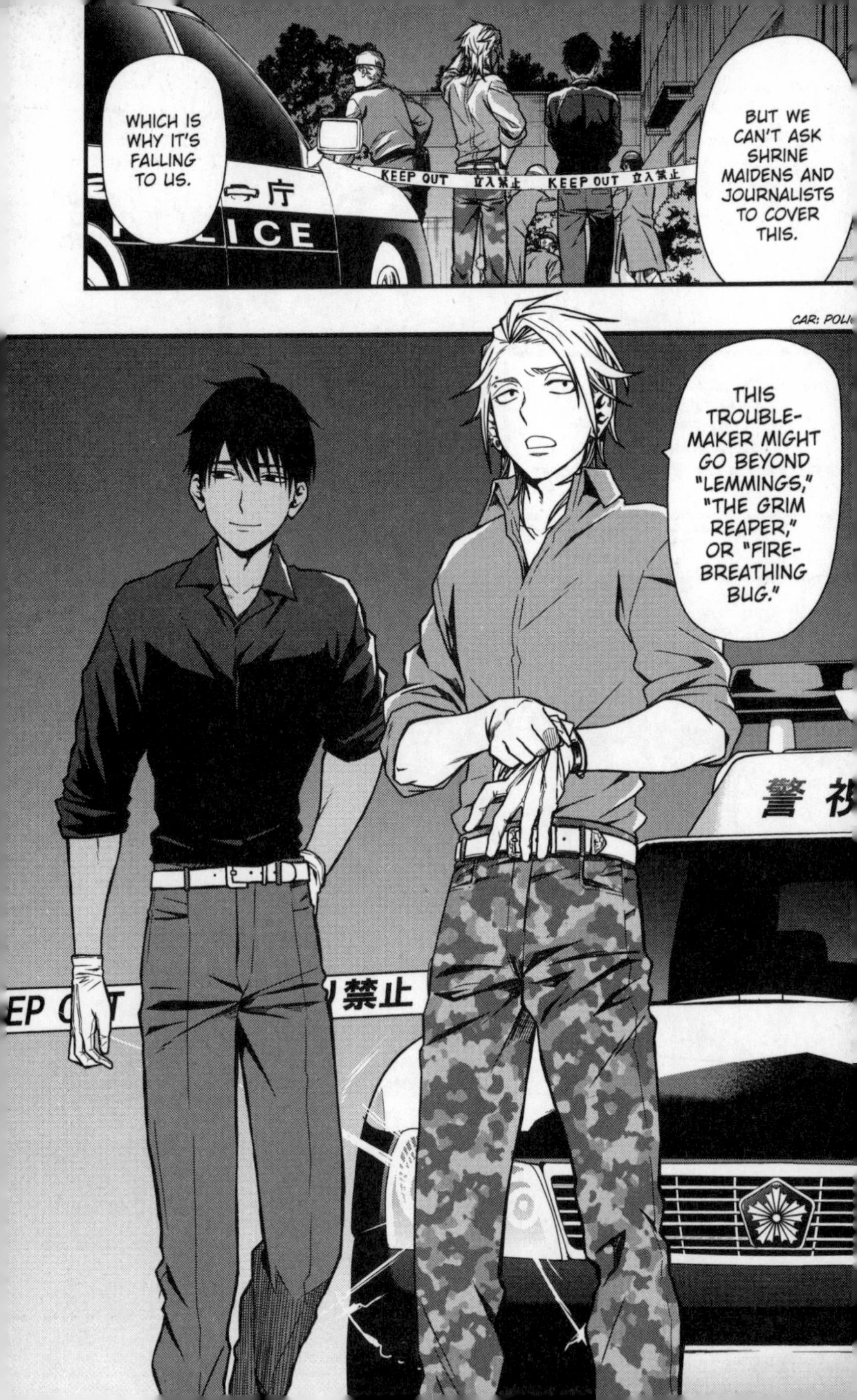
BUT WE CAN'T ASK SHRINE MAIDENS AND JOURNALISTS TO COVER THIS.
WHICH IS WHY IT'S FALLING TO US.
KEEP OUT 立入禁止 KEEP OUT 立入禁止
POLICE
CAR: POLI
THIS TROUBLE-MAKER MIGHT GO BEYOND "LEMMINGS," "THE GRIM REAPER," OR "FIRE-BREATHING BUG."
禁止

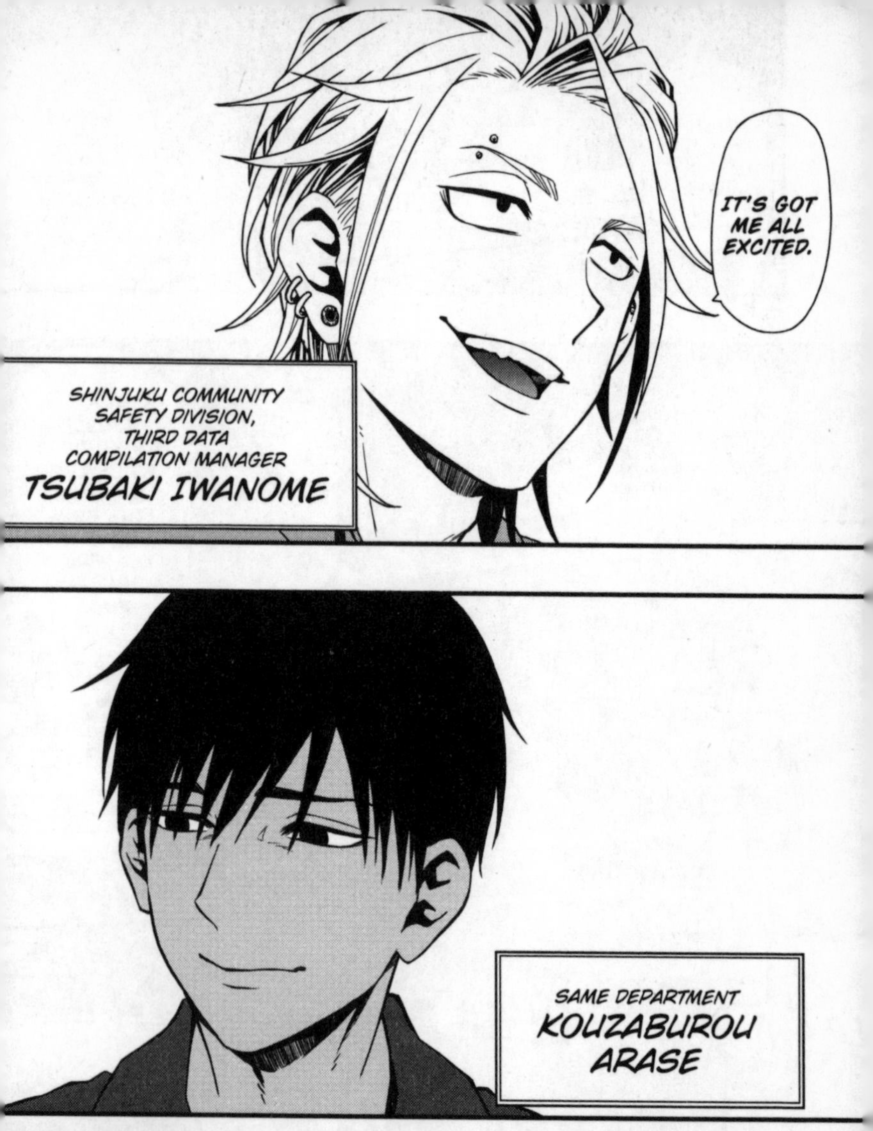
IT'S GOT ME ALL EXCITED.
SHINJUKU COMMUNITY SAFETY DIVISION, THIRD DATA COMPILATION MANAGER TSUBAKI IWANOME
SAME DEPARTMENT KOUZABUROU ARASE

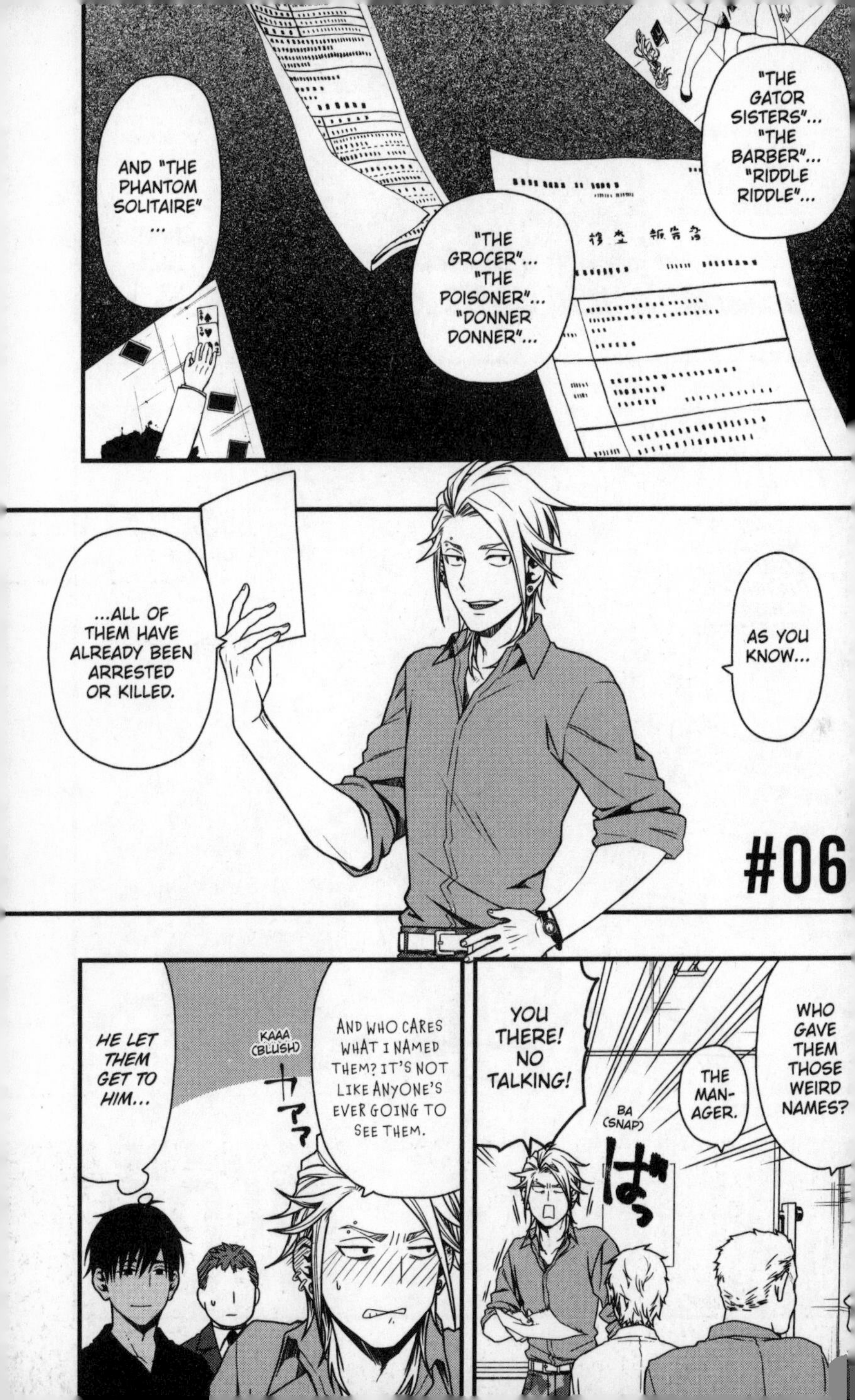
"THE GATOR SISTERS"... "THE BARBER"... "RIDDLE RIDDLE"...
"THE GROCER"... "THE POISONER"... "DONNER DONNER"...
AND "THE PHANTOM SOLITAIRE" ...
AS YOU KNOW...
...ALL OF THEM HAVE ALREADY BEEN ARRESTED OR KILLED.
#06
WHO GAVE THEM THOSE WEIRD NAMES?
THE MAN-AGER.
YOU THERE! NO TALKING!
BA (SNAP)
ばっ
AND WHO CARES WHAT I NAMED THEM? IT'S NOT LIKE ANYONE'S EVER GOING TO SEE THEM.
KAAA (BLUSH)
カァァ
HE LET THEM GET TO HIM...

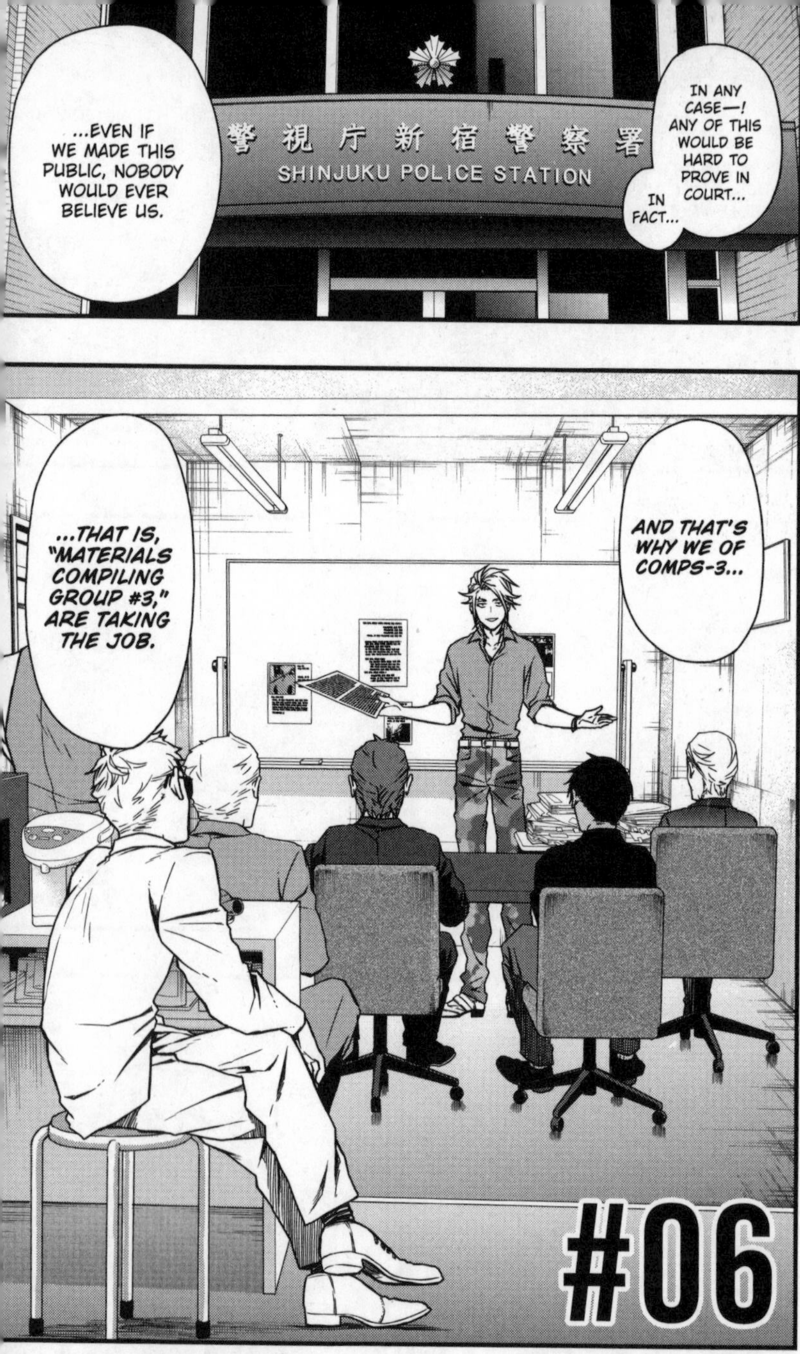

IN ANY CASE—! ANY OF THIS WOULD BE HARD TO PROVE IN COURT...
IN FACT...
警視庁新宿警察署
SHINJUKU POLICE STATION
...EVEN IF WE MADE THIS PUBLIC, NOBODY WOULD EVER BELIEVE US.
AND THAT'S WHY WE OF COMPS-3...
...THAT IS, "MATERIALS COMPILING GROUP #3," ARE TAKING THE JOB.
#06

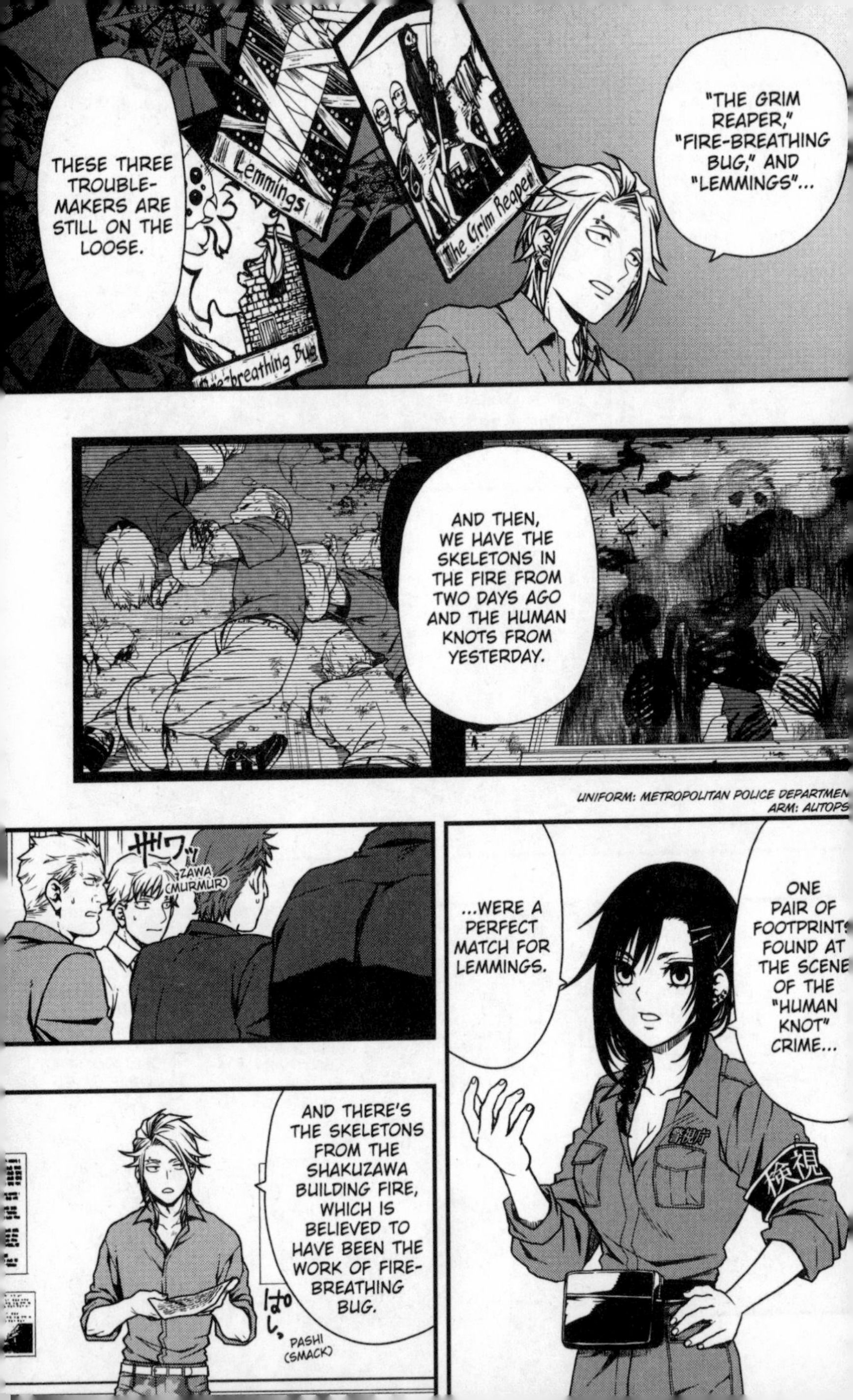
"THE GRIM REAPER," "FIRE-BREATHING BUG," AND "LEMMINGS"...
THESE THREE TROUBLE-MAKERS ARE STILL ON THE LOOSE.
The Grim Reaper
Lemmings
breathing Bug
AND THEN, WE HAVE THE SKELETONS IN THE FIRE FROM TWO DAYS AGO AND THE HUMAN KNOTS FROM YESTERDAY.
UNIFORM: METROPOLITAN POLICE DEPARTMEN
ARM: AUTOPS
ONE PAIR OF FOOTPRINTS FOUND AT THE SCENE OF THE "HUMAN KNOT" CRIME...
...WERE A PERFECT MATCH FOR LEMMINGS.
ZAWA (MURMUR)
AND THERE'S THE SKELETONS FROM THE SHAKUZAWA BUILDING FIRE, WHICH IS BELIEVED TO HAVE BEEN THE WORK OF FIRE-BREATHING BUG.
PASHI (SMACK)

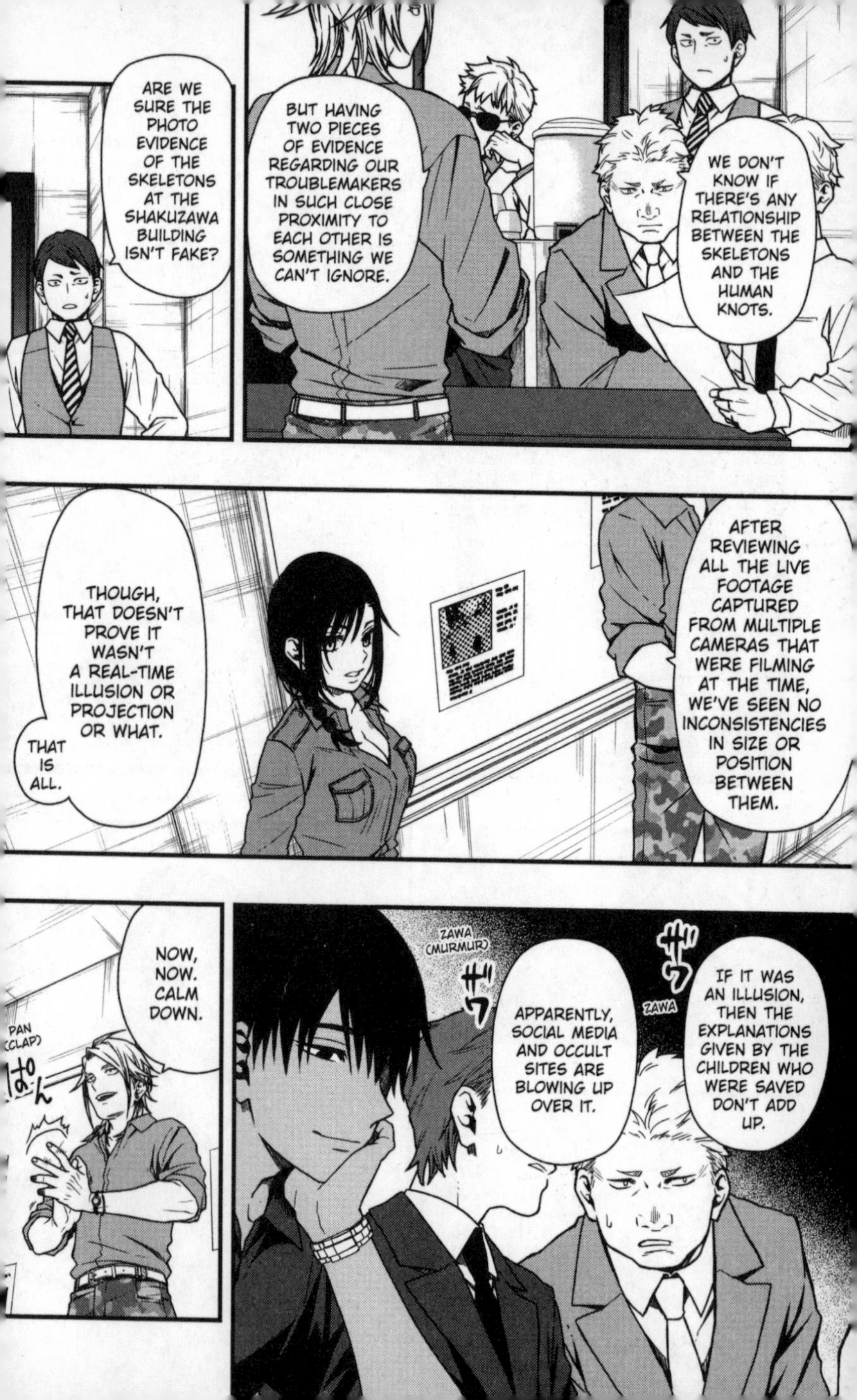
WE DON'T KNOW IF THERE'S ANY RELATIONSHIP BETWEEN THE SKELETONS AND THE HUMAN KNOTS.
BUT HAVING TWO PIECES OF EVIDENCE REGARDING OUR TROUBLEMAKERS IN SUCH CLOSE PROXIMITY TO EACH OTHER IS SOMETHING WE CAN'T IGNORE.
ARE WE SURE THE PHOTO EVIDENCE OF THE SKELETONS AT THE SHAKUZAWA BUILDING ISN'T FAKE?
AFTER REVIEWING ALL THE LIVE FOOTAGE CAPTURED FROM MULTIPLE CAMERAS THAT WERE FILMING AT THE TIME, WE'VE SEEN NO INCONSISTENCIES IN SIZE OR POSITION BETWEEN THEM.
THOUGH, THAT DOESN'T PROVE IT WASN'T A REAL-TIME ILLUSION OR PROJECTION OR WHAT.
THAT IS ALL.
ZAWA
IF IT WAS AN ILLUSION, THEN THE EXPLANATIONS GIVEN BY THE CHILDREN WHO WERE SAVED DON'T ADD UP.
APPARENTLY, SOCIAL MEDIA AND OCCULT SITES ARE BLOWING UP OVER IT.
ZAWA (MURMUR)
NOW, NOW. CALM DOWN.
PAN (CLAP)

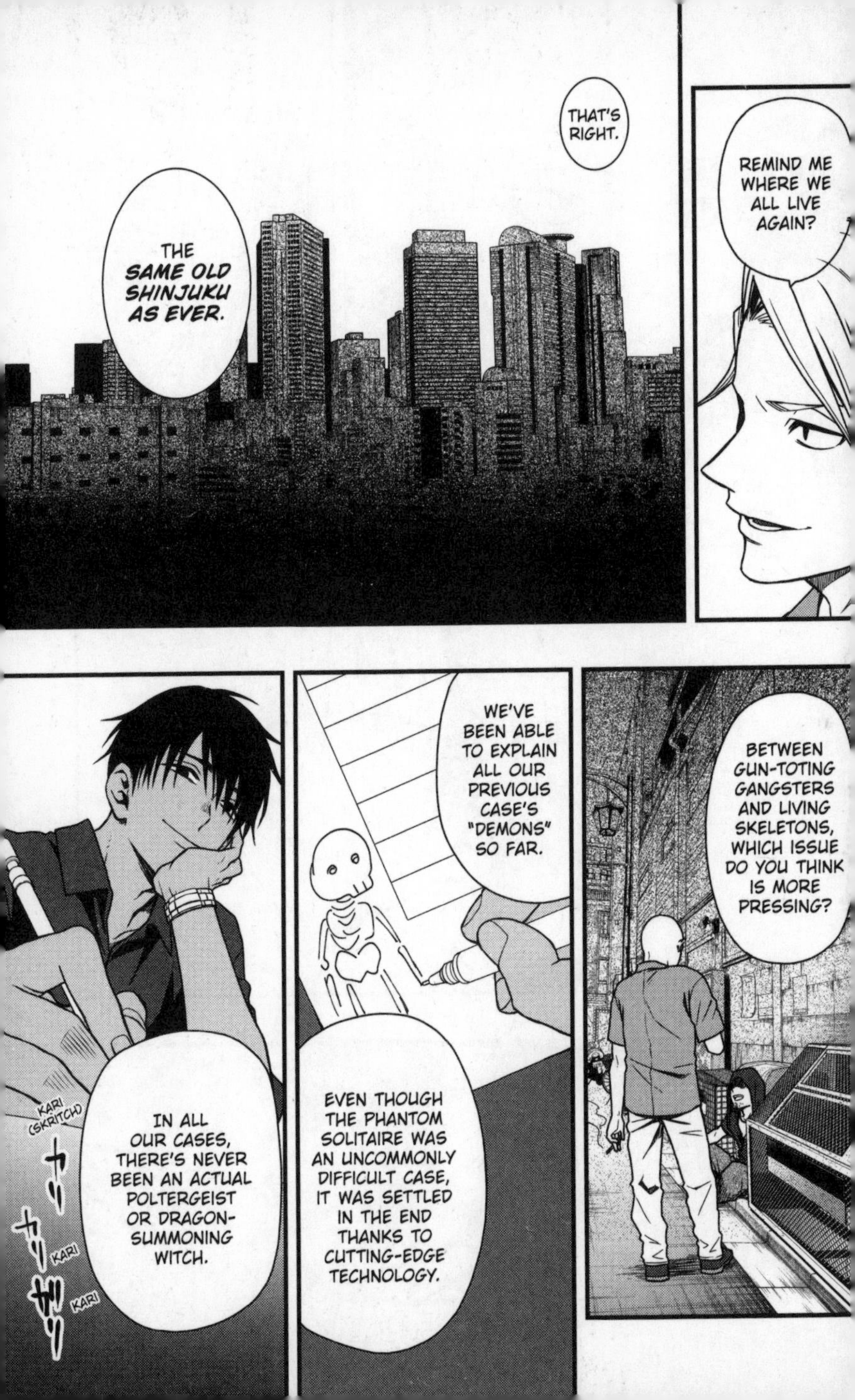
REMIND ME WHERE WE ALL LIVE AGAIN?
THAT'S RIGHT.
THE SAME OLD SHINJUKU AS EVER.
BETWEEN GUN-TOTING GANGSTERS AND LIVING SKELETONS, WHICH ISSUE DO YOU THINK IS MORE PRESSING?
WE'VE BEEN ABLE TO EXPLAIN ALL OUR PREVIOUS CASE'S "DEMONS" SO FAR.
EVEN THOUGH THE PHANTOM SOLITAIRE WAS AN UNCOMMONLY DIFFICULT CASE, IT WAS SETTLED IN THE END THANKS TO CUTTING-EDGE TECHNOLOGY.
IN ALL OUR CASES, THERE'S NEVER BEEN AN ACTUAL POLTERGEIST OR DRAGON-SUMMONING WITCH.
KARI (SKRITCH)
KARI
KARI

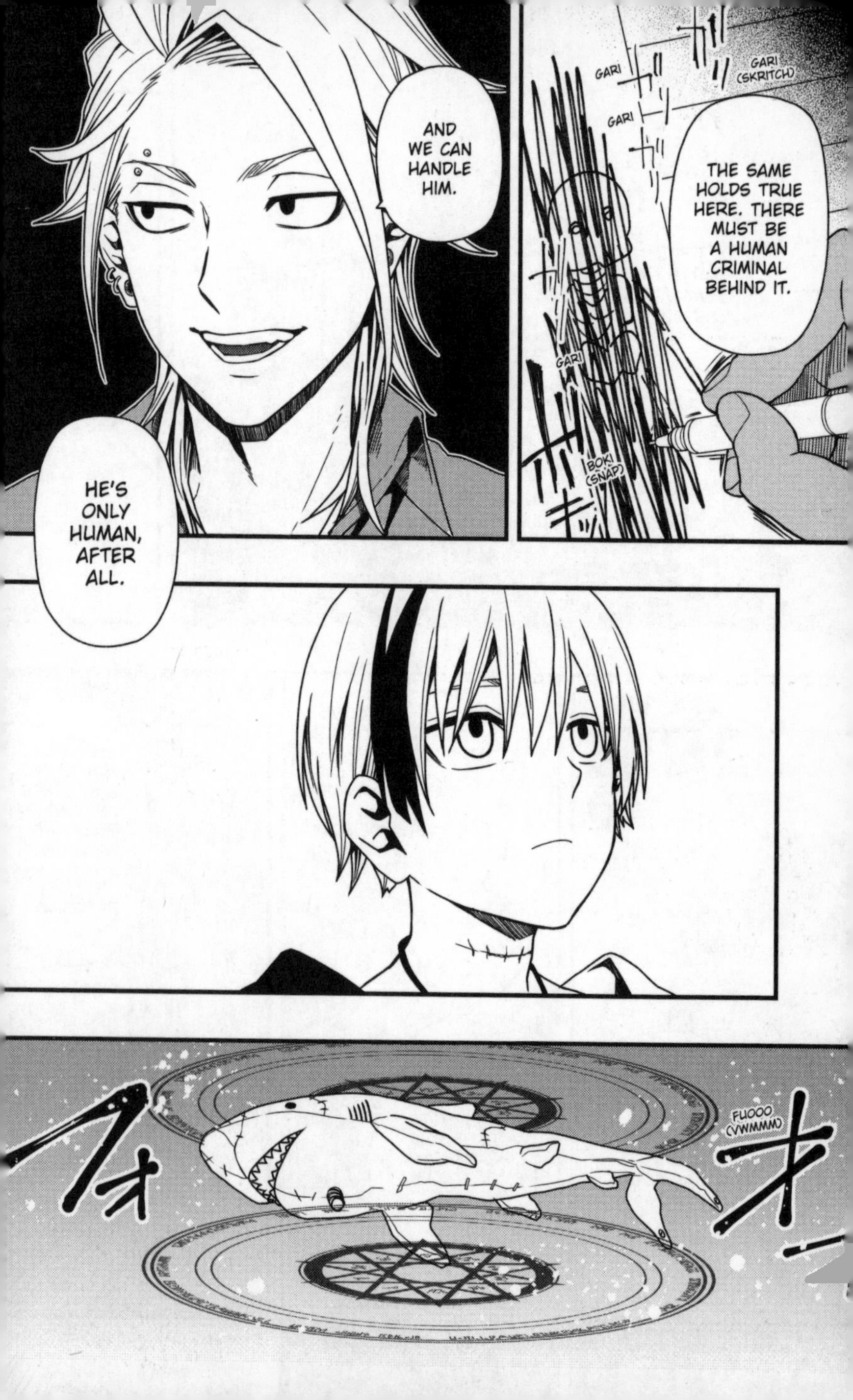
GARI
GARI (SKRITCH)
GARI
THE SAME HOLDS TRUE HERE. THERE MUST BE A HUMAN CRIMINAL BEHIND IT.
GARI
BOKI (SNAP)
AND WE CAN HANDLE HIM.
HE'S ONLY HUMAN, AFTER ALL.
FUOOO (VWMMM)

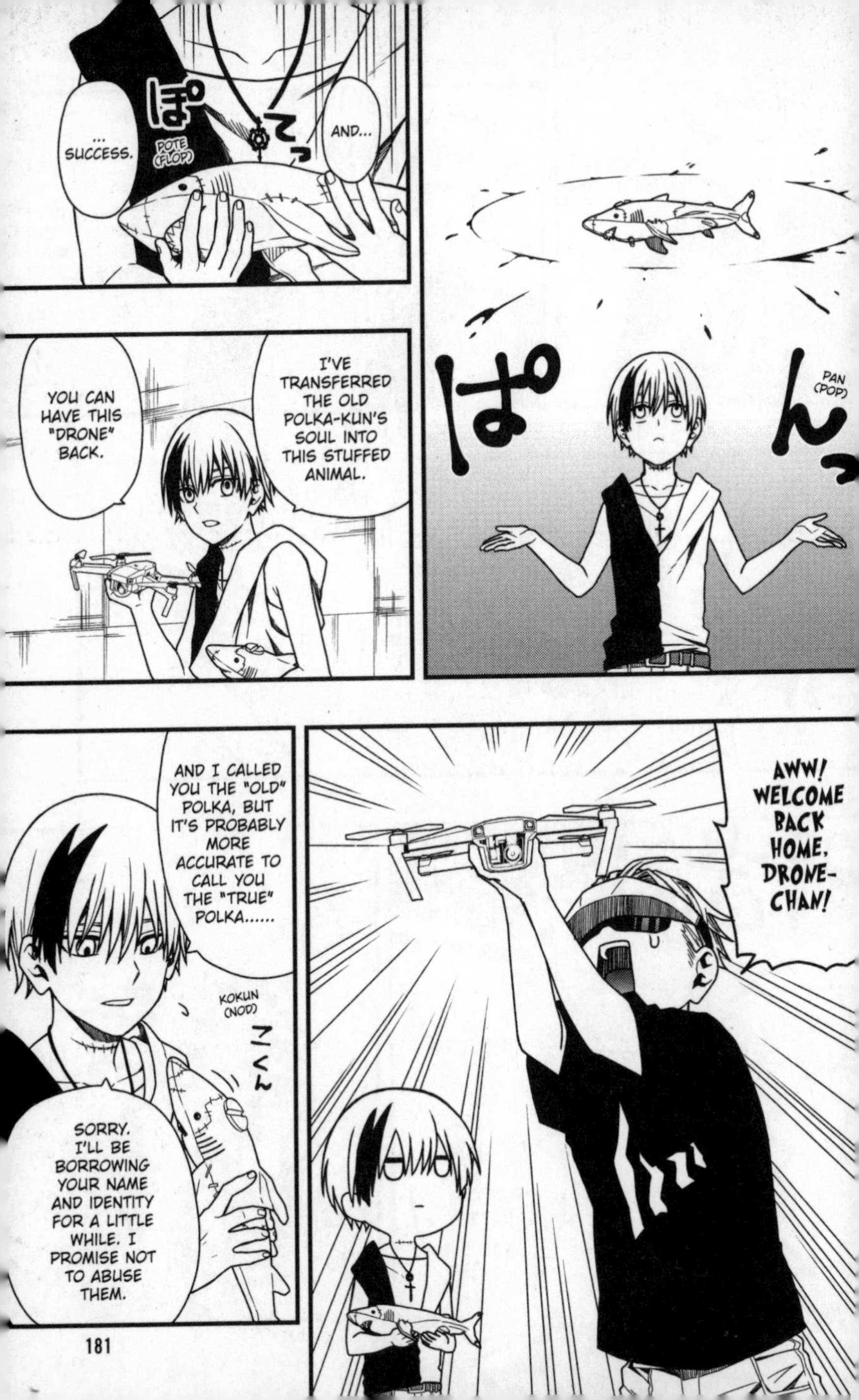
ぱんっ
PAN (POP)
ぽてっ
POTE (FLOP)
AND...
... SUCCESS.
I'VE TRANSFERRED THE OLD POLKA-KUN'S SOUL INTO THIS STUFFED ANIMAL.
YOU CAN HAVE THIS "DRONE" BACK.
AWW! WELCOME BACK HOME, DRONE-CHAN!
AND I CALLED YOU THE "OLD" POLKA, BUT IT'S PROBABLY MORE ACCURATE TO CALL YOU THE "TRUE" POLKA......
こくん
KOKUN (NOD)
SORRY. I'LL BE BORROWING YOUR NAME AND IDENTITY FOR A LITTLE WHILE. I PROMISE NOT TO ABUSE THEM.

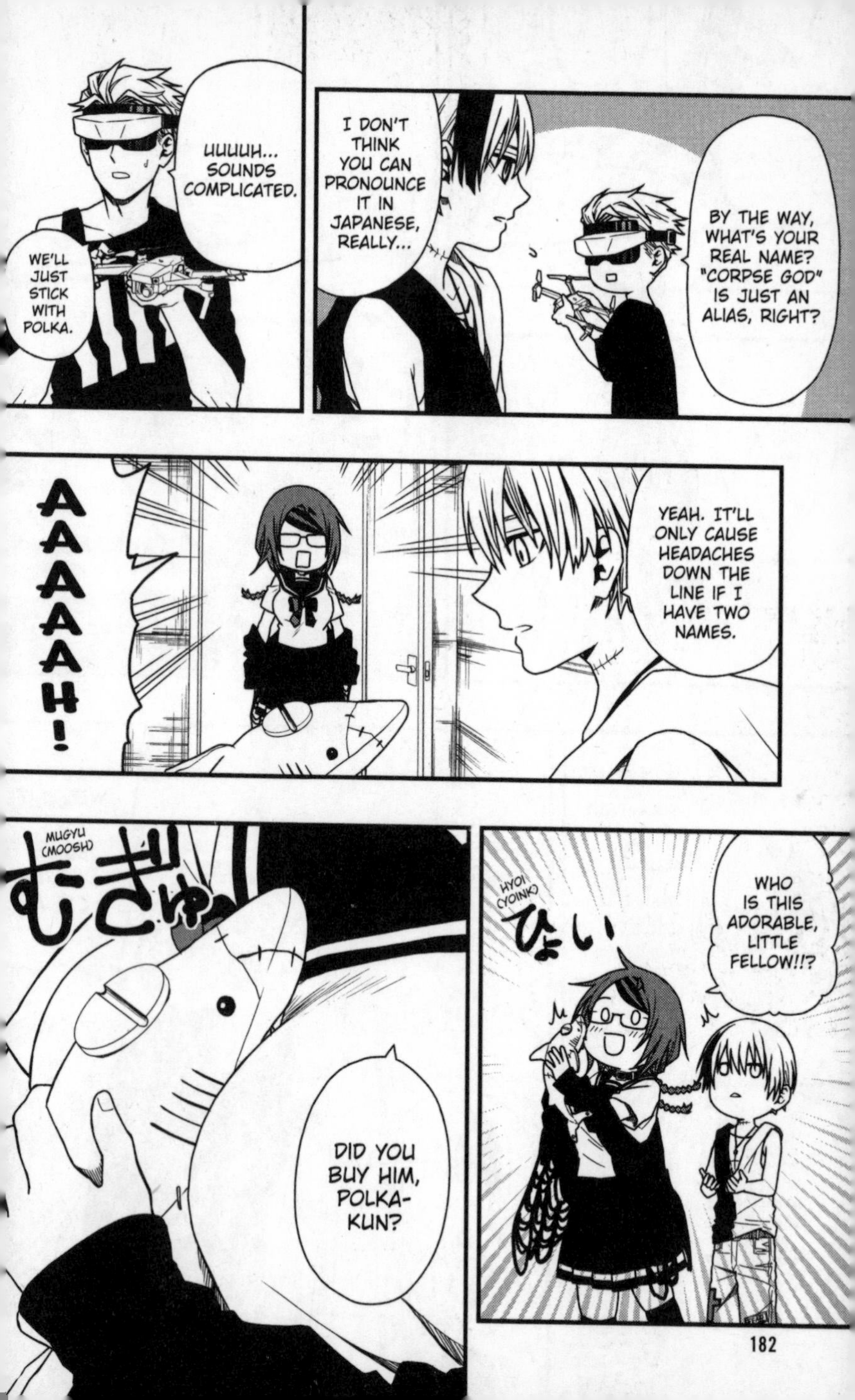
BY THE WAY, WHAT'S YOUR REAL NAME? "CORPSE GOD" IS JUST AN ALIAS, RIGHT?
I DON'T THINK YOU CAN PRONOUNCE IT IN JAPANESE, REALLY...
UUUUH... SOUNDS COMPLICATED.
WE'LL JUST STICK WITH POLKA.
YEAH. IT'LL ONLY CAUSE HEADACHES DOWN THE LINE IF I HAVE TWO NAMES.
AAAAAAH!
WHO IS THIS ADORABLE, LITTLE FELLOW!!?
HYOI (YOINK)
ひょい
MUGYU (MOOSH)
むぎゅ
DID YOU BUY HIM, POLKA-KUN?

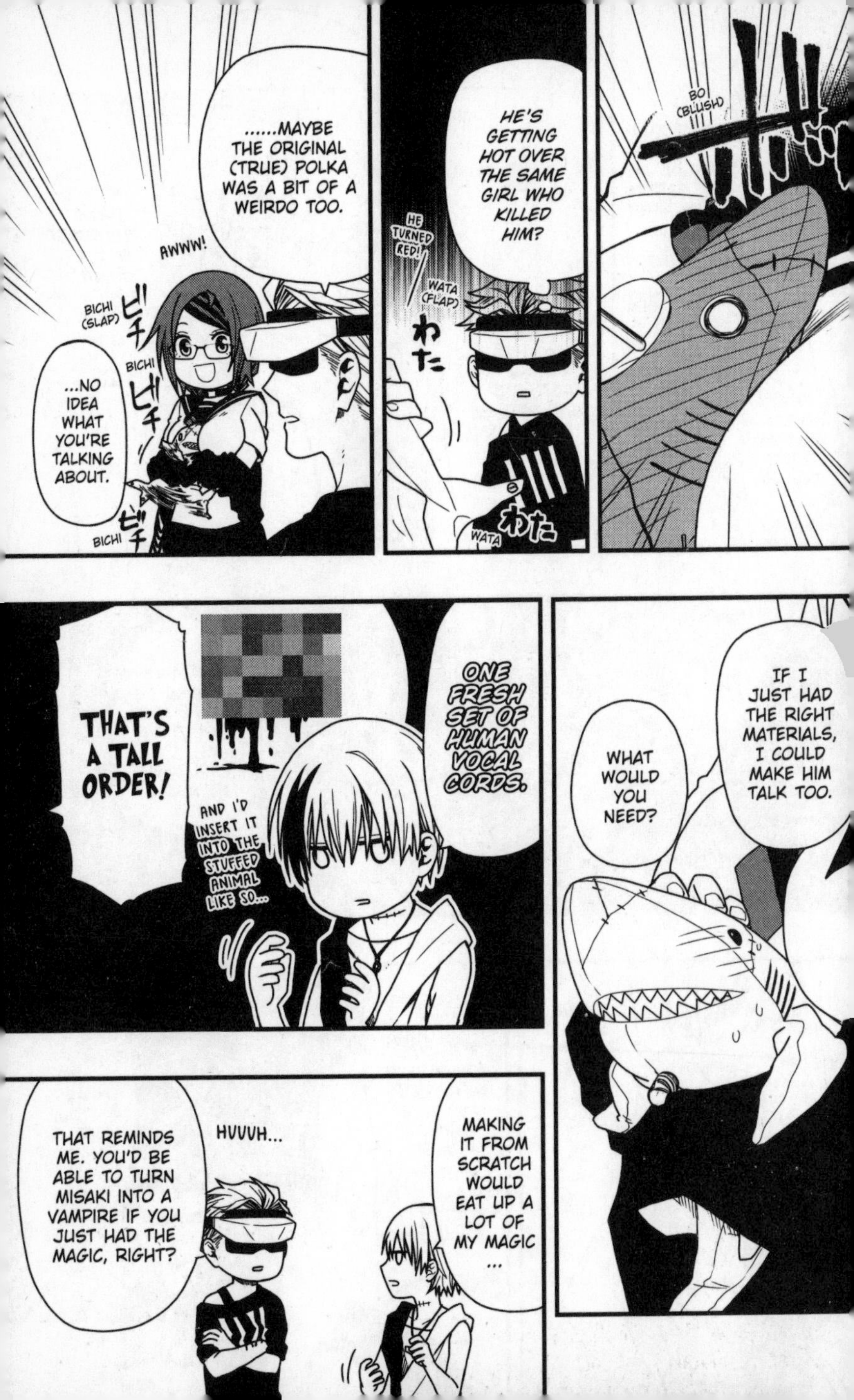
BO (BLUSH)
HE'S GETTING HOT OVER THE SAME GIRL WHO KILLED HIM?
HE TURNED RED!
WATA (FLAP) わた
わた WATA
......MAYBE THE ORIGINAL (TRUE) POLKA WAS A BIT OF A WEIRDO TOO.
AWWW!
BICHI (SLAP) ビチ
BICHI ビチ
...NO IDEA WHAT YOU'RE TALKING ABOUT.
BICHI ビチ
IF I JUST HAD THE RIGHT MATERIALS, I COULD MAKE HIM TALK TOO.
WHAT WOULD YOU NEED?
ONE FRESH SET OF HUMAN VOCAL CORDS.
AND I'D INSERT IT INTO THE STUFFED ANIMAL LIKE SO...
THAT'S A TALL ORDER!
MAKING IT FROM SCRATCH WOULD EAT UP A LOT OF MY MAGIC ...
HUUUH...
THAT REMINDS ME. YOU'D BE ABLE TO TURN MISAKI INTO A VAMPIRE IF YOU JUST HAD THE MAGIC, RIGHT?

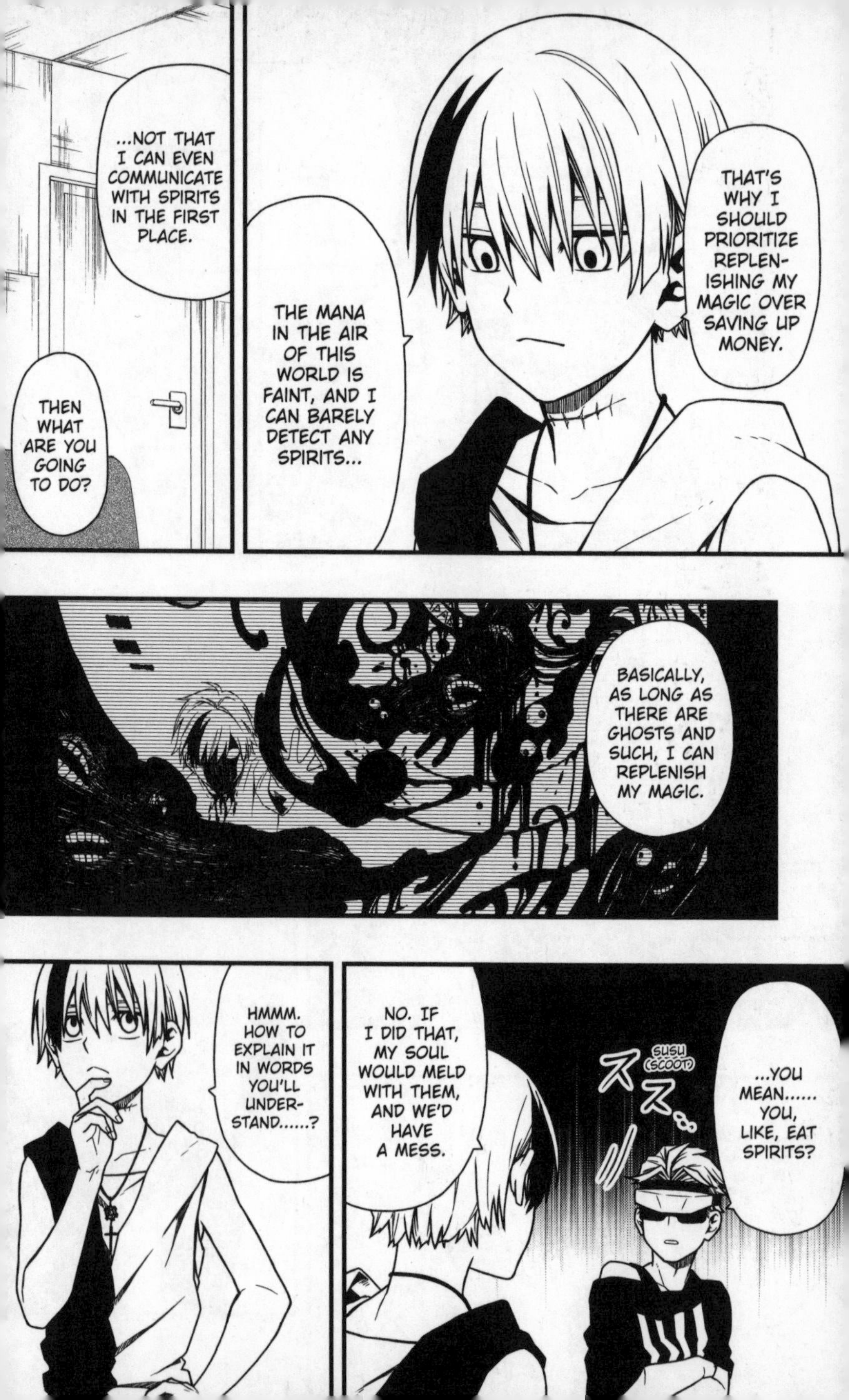
THAT'S WHY I SHOULD PRIORITIZE REPLEN-ISHING MY MAGIC OVER SAVING UP MONEY.
THE MANA IN THE AIR OF THIS WORLD IS FAINT, AND I CAN BARELY DETECT ANY SPIRITS...
...NOT THAT I CAN EVEN COMMUNICATE WITH SPIRITS IN THE FIRST PLACE.
THEN WHAT ARE YOU GOING TO DO?
BASICALLY, AS LONG AS THERE ARE GHOSTS AND SUCH, I CAN REPLENISH MY MAGIC.
...YOU MEAN...... YOU, LIKE, EAT SPIRITS?
SUSU (SCOOT)
NO. IF I DID THAT, MY SOUL WOULD MELD WITH THEM, AND WE'D HAVE A MESS.
HMMM. HOW TO EXPLAIN IT IN WORDS YOU'LL UNDER-STAND......?

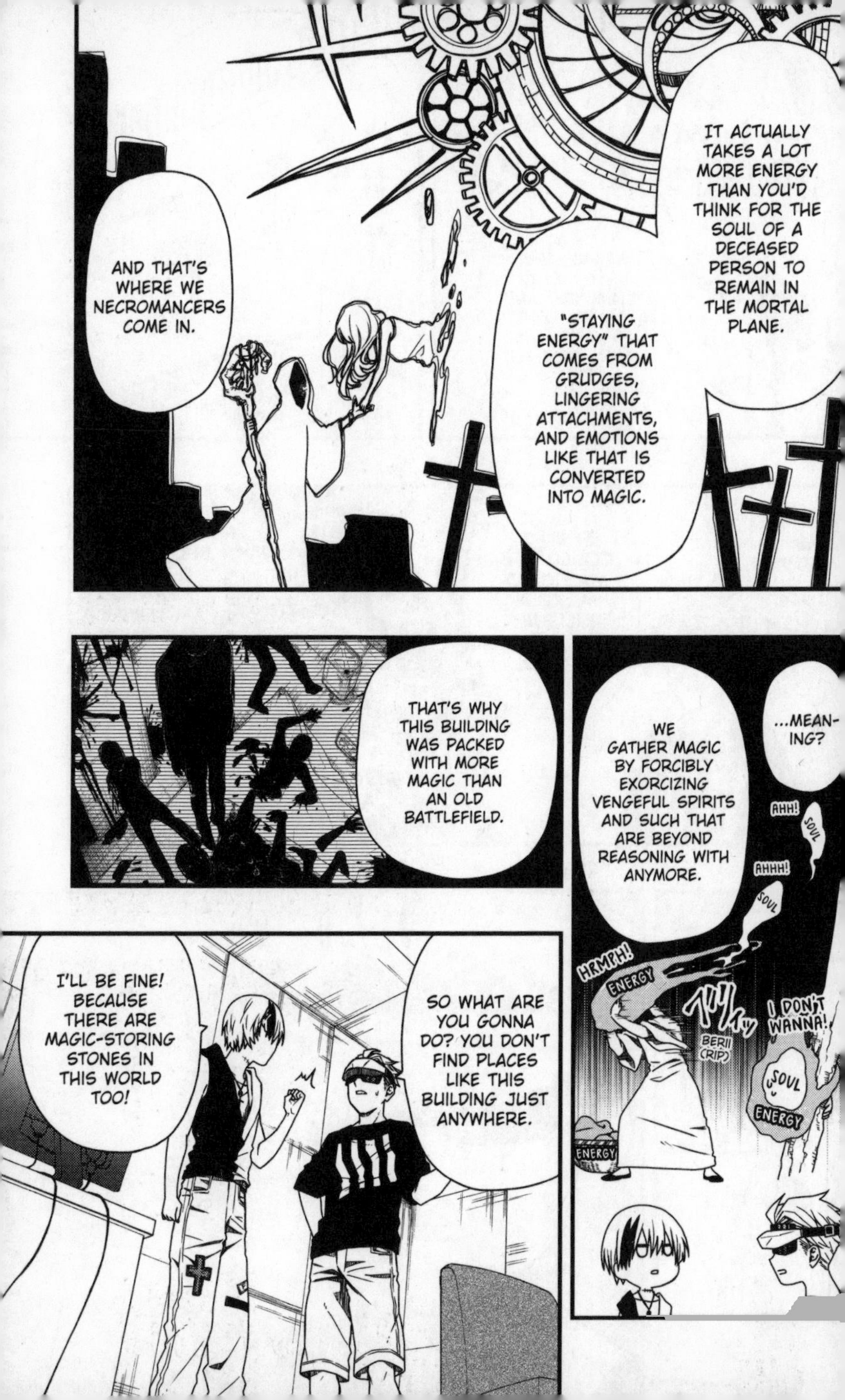

IT ACTUALLY TAKES A LOT MORE ENERGY THAN YOU'D THINK FOR THE SOUL OF A DECEASED PERSON TO REMAIN IN THE MORTAL PLANE.
"STAYING ENERGY" THAT COMES FROM GRUDGES, LINGERING ATTACHMENTS, AND EMOTIONS LIKE THAT IS CONVERTED INTO MAGIC.
AND THAT'S WHERE WE NECROMANCERS COME IN.
...MEAN-ING?
WE GATHER MAGIC BY FORCIBLY EXORCIZING VENGEFUL SPIRITS AND SUCH THAT ARE BEYOND REASONING WITH ANYMORE.
AHH!
SOUL
AHHH!
SOUL
HRMPH!
ENERGY
BERII (RIP)
I DON'T WANNA!
SOUL
ENERGY
ENERGY
THAT'S WHY THIS BUILDING WAS PACKED WITH MORE MAGIC THAN AN OLD BATTLEFIELD.
SO WHAT ARE YOU GONNA DO? YOU DON'T FIND PLACES LIKE THIS BUILDING JUST ANYWHERE.
I'LL BE FINE! BECAUSE THERE ARE MAGIC-STORING STONES IN THIS WORLD TOO!

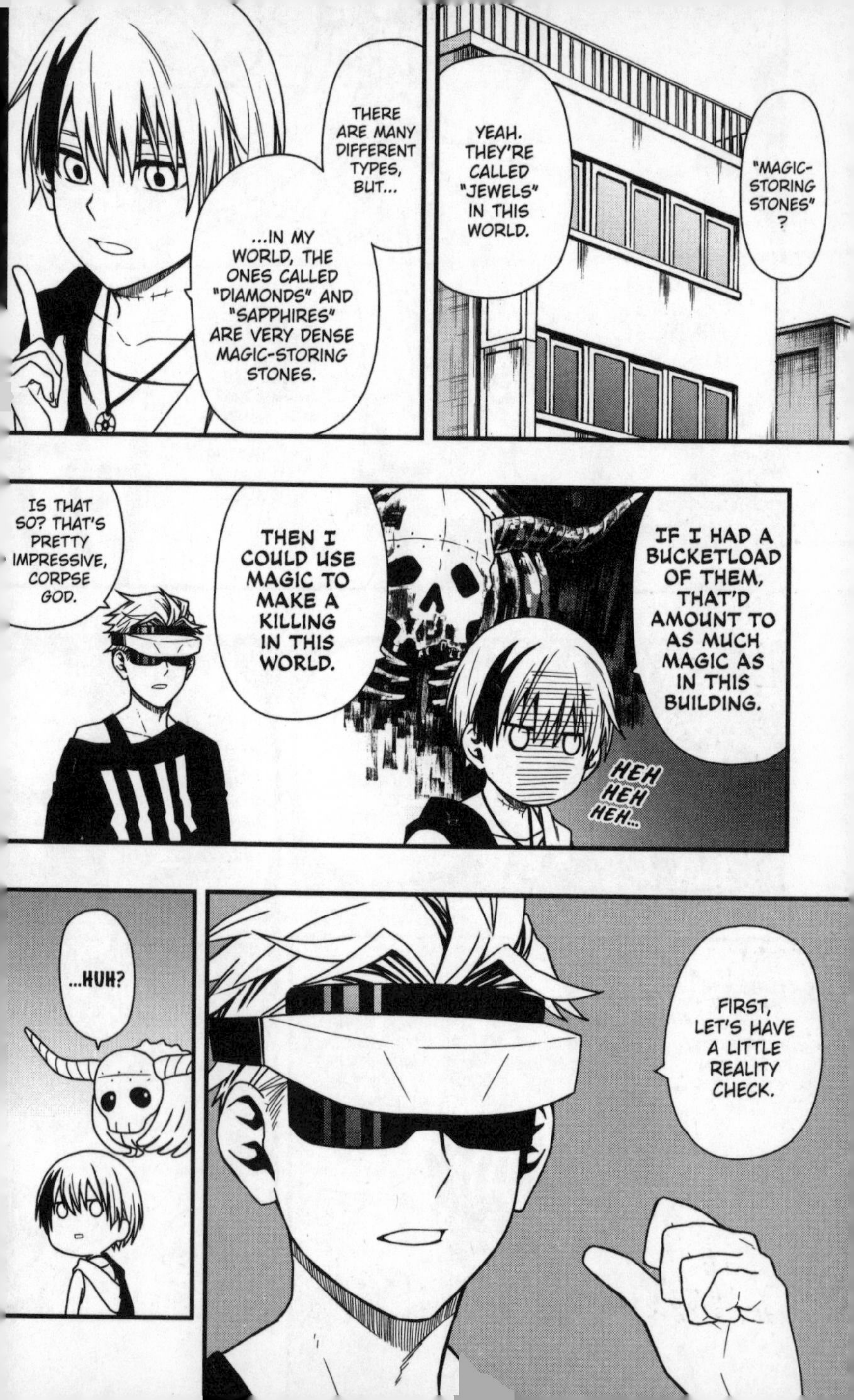
"MAGIC-STORING STONES"?
YEAH. THEY'RE CALLED "JEWELS" IN THIS WORLD.
THERE ARE MANY DIFFERENT TYPES, BUT...
...IN MY WORLD, THE ONES CALLED "DIAMONDS" AND "SAPPHIRES" ARE VERY DENSE MAGIC-STORING STONES.
IF I HAD A BUCKETLOAD OF THEM, THAT'D AMOUNT TO AS MUCH MAGIC AS IN THIS BUILDING.
HEH HEH HEH...
THEN I COULD USE MAGIC TO MAKE A KILLING IN THIS WORLD.
IS THAT SO? THAT'S PRETTY IMPRESSIVE, CORPSE GOD.
FIRST, LET'S HAVE A LITTLE REALITY CHECK.
...HUH?

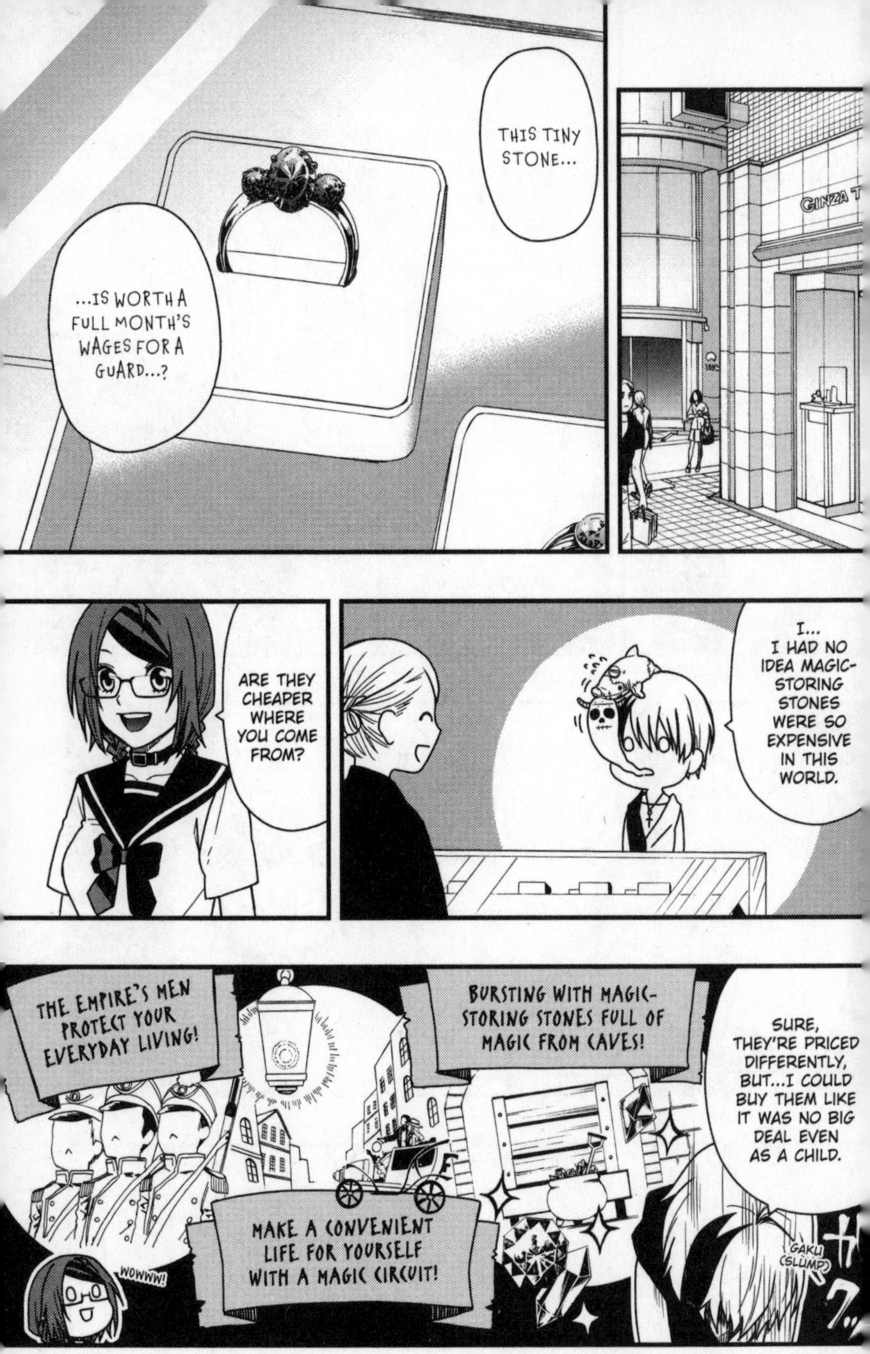
GINZA T
THIS TINY STONE...
...IS WORTH A FULL MONTH'S WAGES FOR A GUARD...?
I... I HAD NO IDEA MAGIC-STORING STONES WERE SO EXPENSIVE IN THIS WORLD.
ARE THEY CHEAPER WHERE YOU COME FROM?
SURE, THEY'RE PRICED DIFFERENTLY, BUT...I COULD BUY THEM LIKE IT WAS NO BIG DEAL EVEN AS A CHILD.
GAKU (SLUMP)
BURSTING WITH MAGIC-STORING STONES FULL OF MAGIC FROM CAVES!
THE EMPIRE'S MEN PROTECT YOUR EVERYDAY LIVING!
MAKE A CONVENIENT LIFE FOR YOURSELF WITH A MAGIC CIRCUIT!
WOWWW!

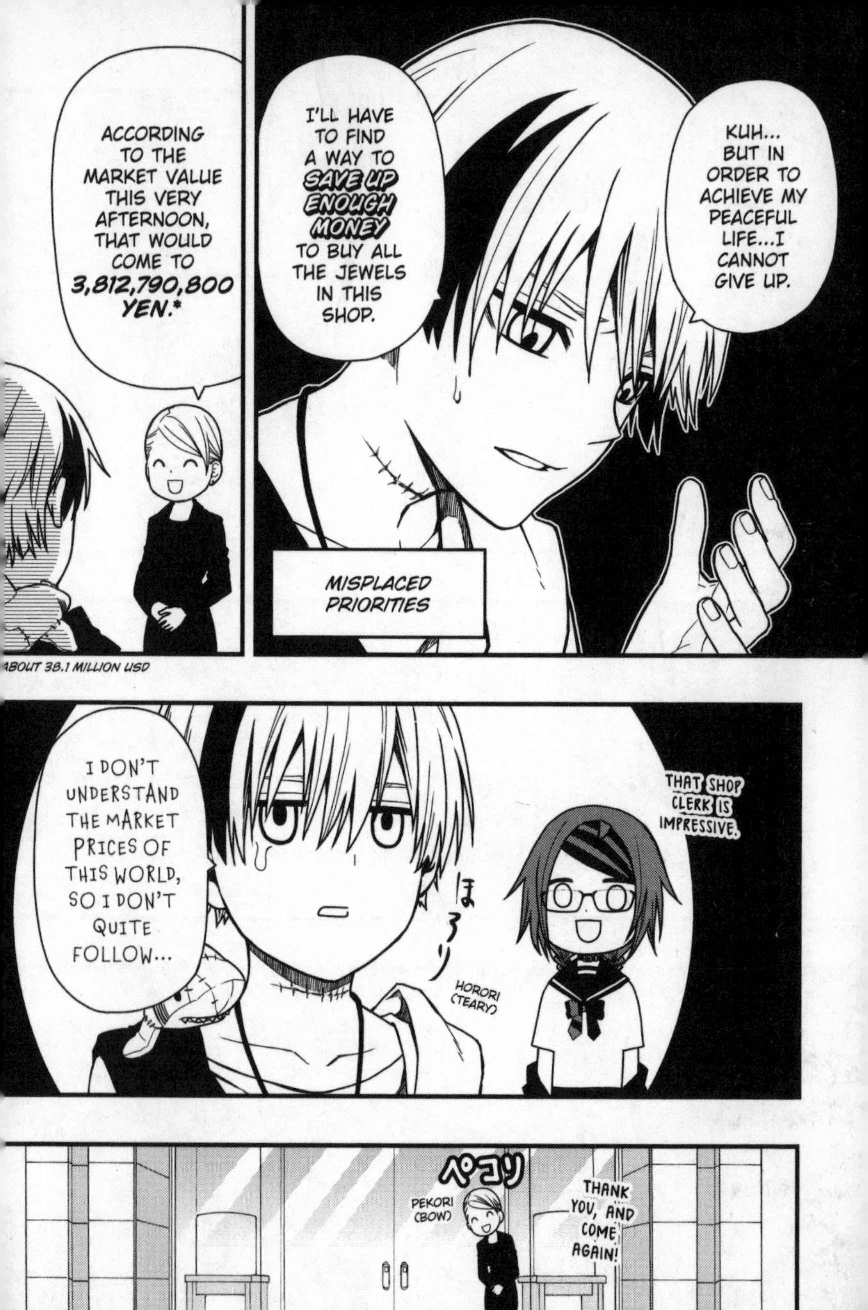
KUH... BUT IN ORDER TO ACHIEVE MY PEACEFUL LIFE...I CANNOT GIVE UP.
I'LL HAVE TO FIND A WAY TO SAVE UP ENOUGH MONEY TO BUY ALL THE JEWELS IN THIS SHOP.
MISPLACED PRIORITIES
ACCORDING TO THE MARKET VALUE THIS VERY AFTERNOON, THAT WOULD COME TO 3,812,790,800 YEN.*
THAT SHOP CLERK IS IMPRESSIVE.
ほろり
HORORI (TEARY)
I DON'T UNDERSTAND THE MARKET PRICES OF THIS WORLD, SO I DON'T QUITE FOLLOW...
THANK YOU, AND COME AGAIN!
ペコリ
PEKORI (BOW)

*ABOUT 38.1 MILLION USD

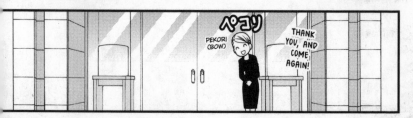

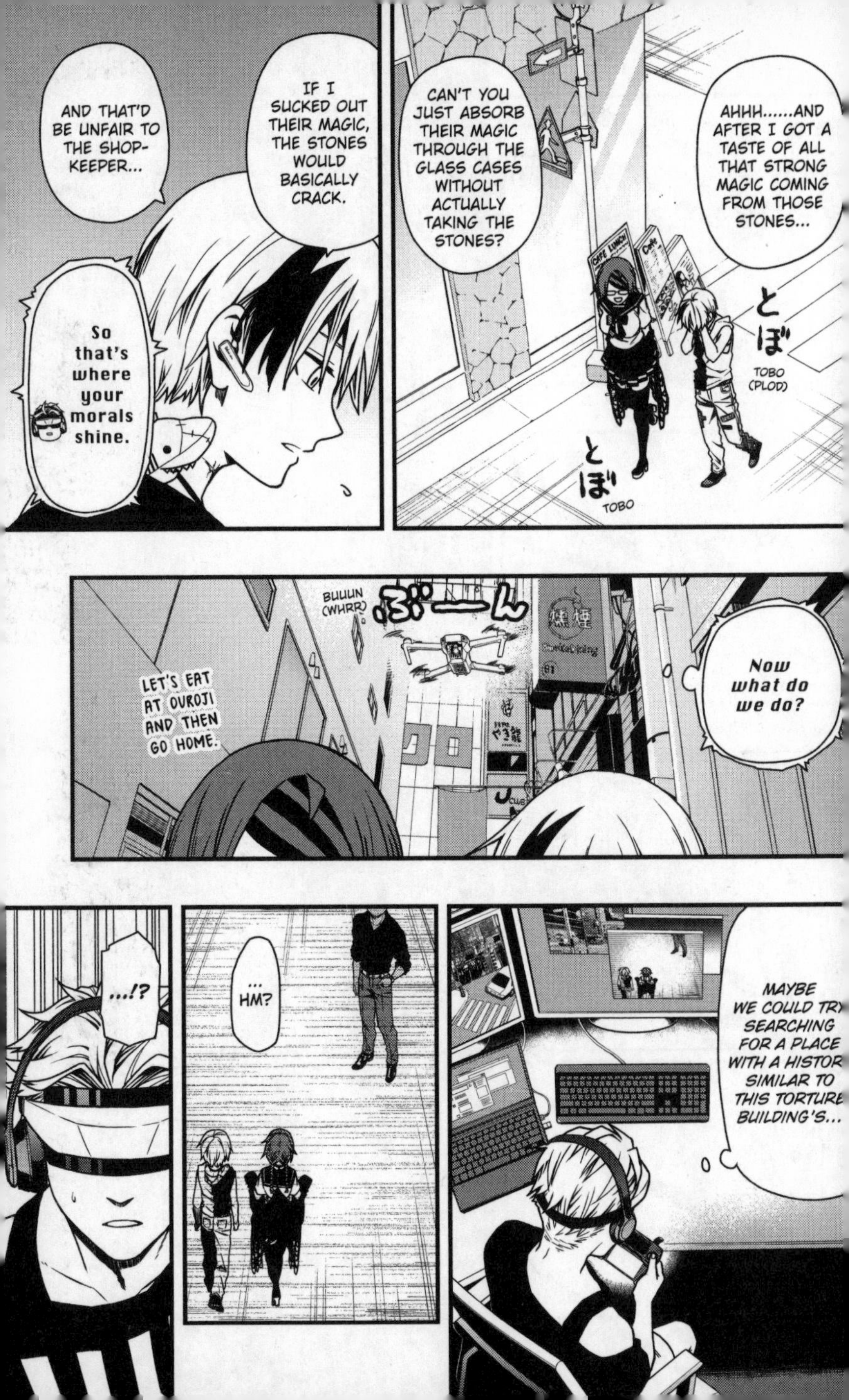
AHHH......AND AFTER I GOT A TASTE OF ALL THAT STRONG MAGIC COMING FROM THOSE STONES...
CAN'T YOU JUST ABSORB THEIR MAGIC THROUGH THE GLASS CASES WITHOUT ACTUALLY TAKING THE STONES?
とぼ
TOBO (PLOD)
とぼ
TOBO
IF I SUCKED OUT THEIR MAGIC, THE STONES WOULD BASICALLY CRACK.
AND THAT'D BE UNFAIR TO THE SHOP-KEEPER...
So that's where your morals shine.
Now what do we do?
ぶーーん
BUUUN (WHRR)
LET'S EAT AT OUROJI AND THEN GO HOME.
MAYBE WE COULD TRY SEARCHING FOR A PLACE WITH A HISTOR SIMILAR TO THIS TORTURE BUILDING'S...
... HM?
...!?

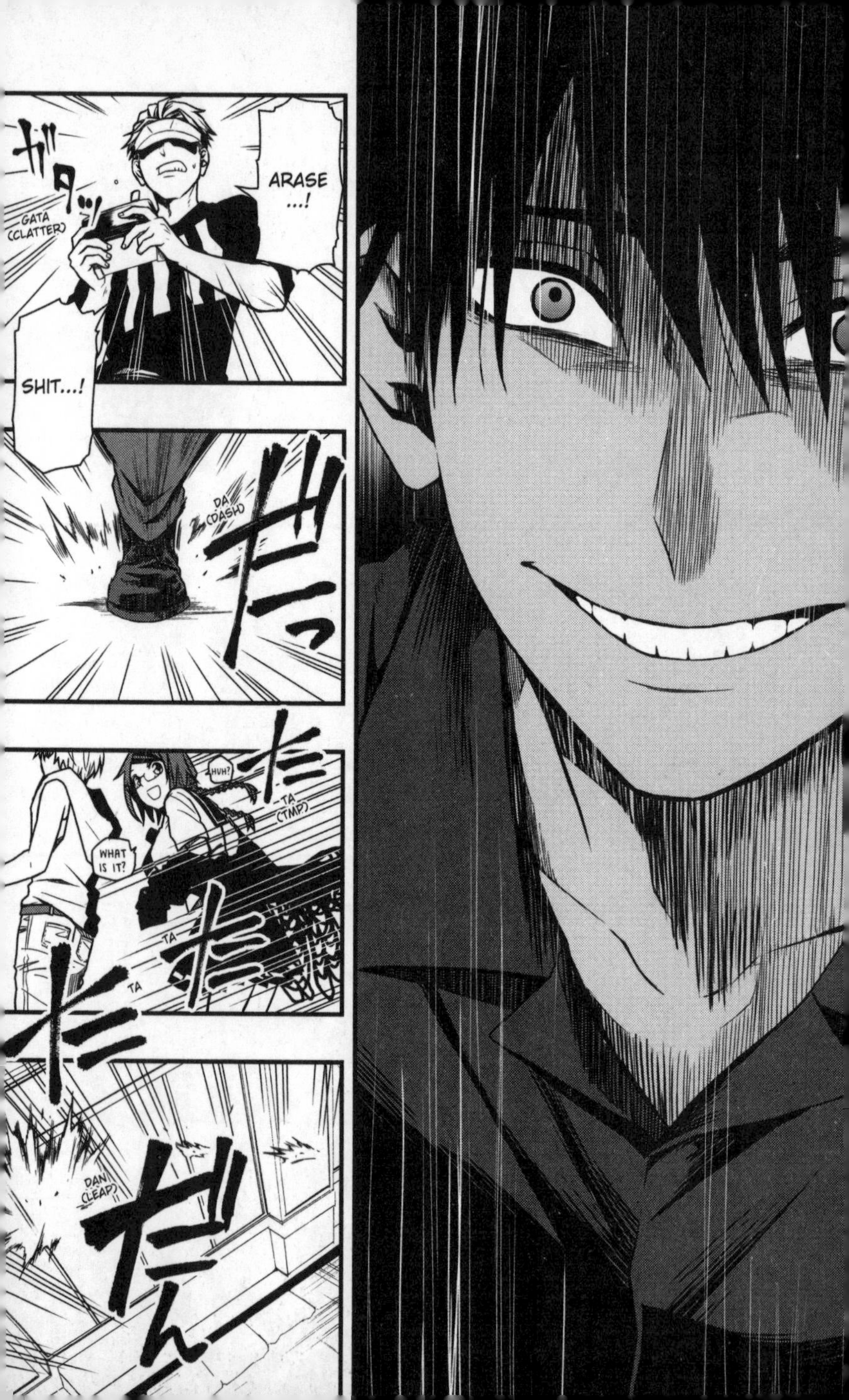
ARASE ...!
GATA (CLATTER)
SHIT...!
DA (DASH)
HUH?
TA (TMP)
WHAT IS IT?
TA
TA
DAN (LEAP)

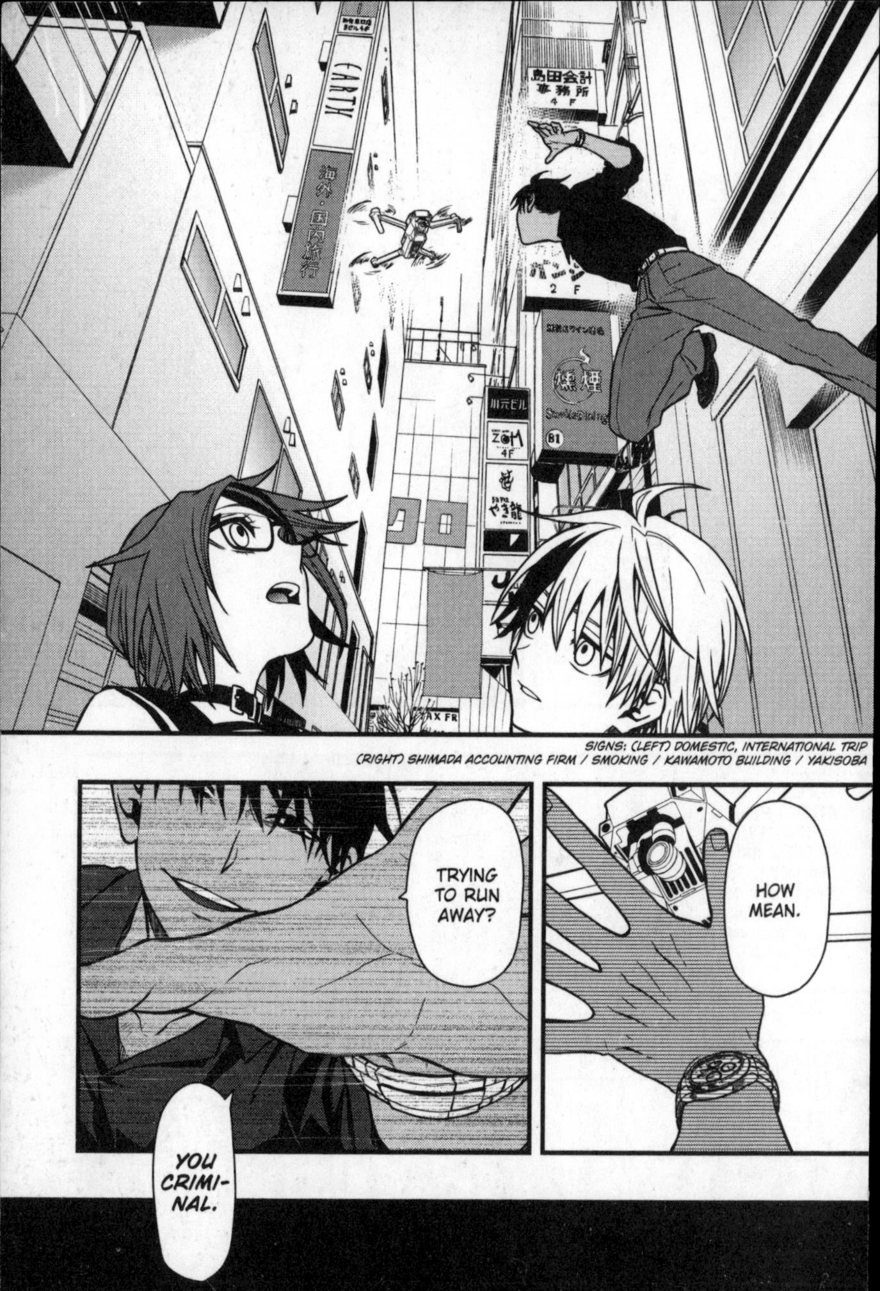
SIGNS: (LEFT) DOMESTIC, INTERNATIONAL TRIP
(RIGHT) SHIMADA ACCOUNTING FIRM / SMOKING / KAWAMOTO BUILDING / YAKISOBA
HOW MEAN.
TRYING TO RUN AWAY?
YOU CRIMINAL.

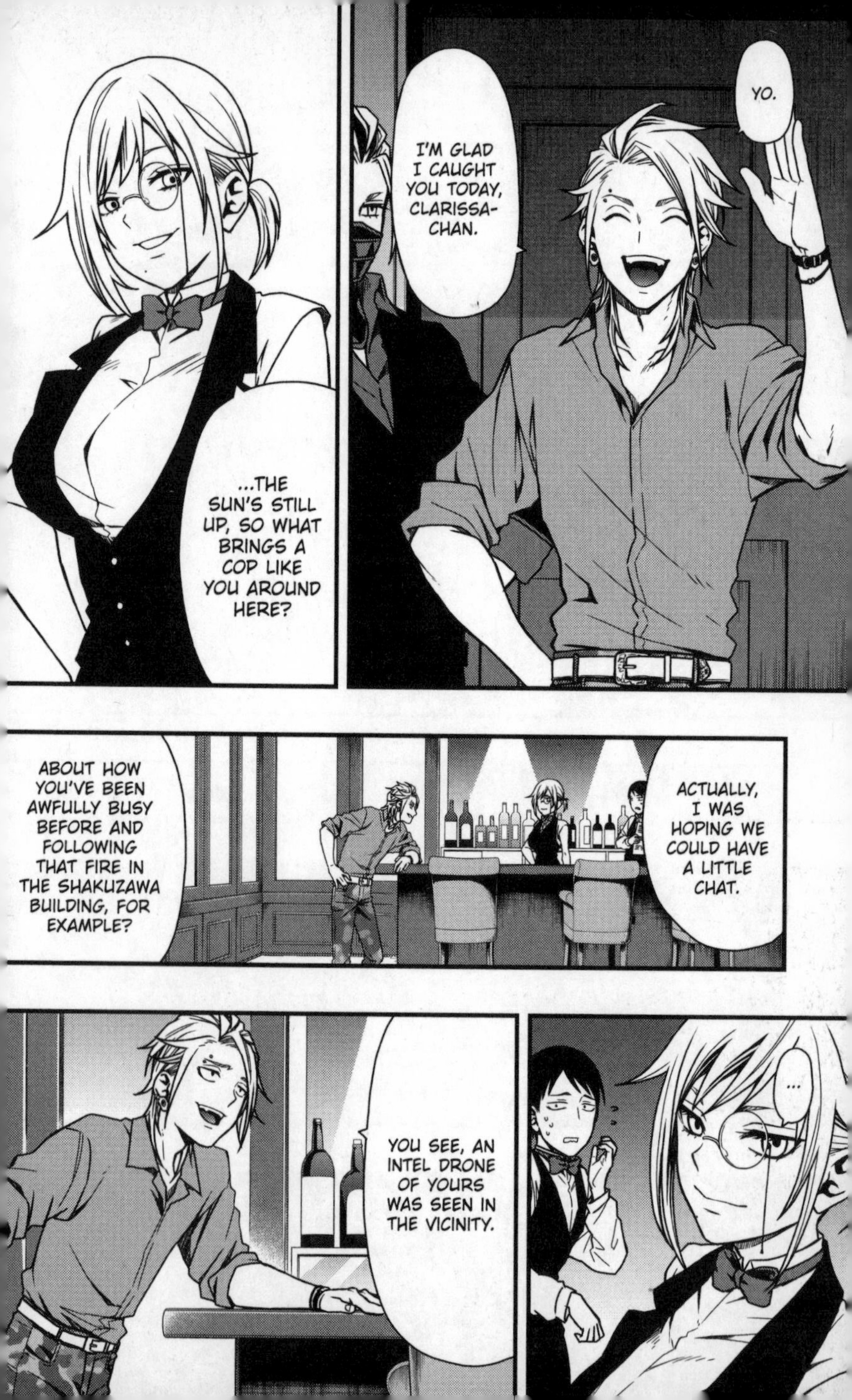
YO.
I'M GLAD I CAUGHT YOU TODAY, CLARISSA-CHAN.
...THE SUN'S STILL UP, SO WHAT BRINGS A COP LIKE YOU AROUND HERE?
ACTUALLY, I WAS HOPING WE COULD HAVE A LITTLE CHAT.
ABOUT HOW YOU'VE BEEN AWFULLY BUSY BEFORE AND FOLLOWING THAT FIRE IN THE SHAKUZAWA BUILDING, FOR EXAMPLE?
...
YOU SEE, AN INTEL DRONE OF YOURS WAS SEEN IN THE VICINITY.

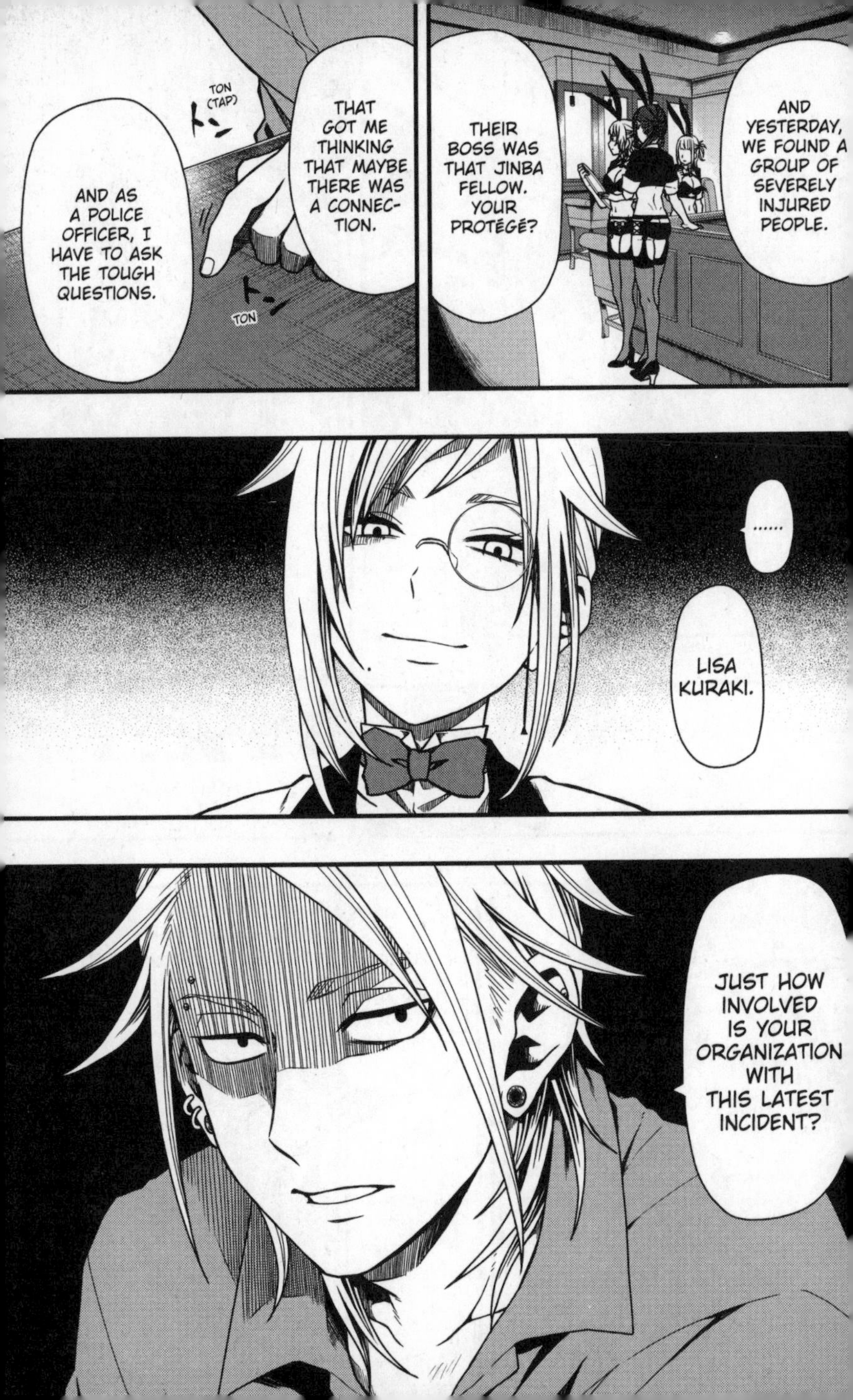
AND YESTERDAY, WE FOUND A GROUP OF SEVERELY INJURED PEOPLE.
THEIR BOSS WAS THAT JINBA FELLOW. YOUR PROTÉGÉ?
THAT GOT ME THINKING THAT MAYBE THERE WAS A CONNECTION.
TON (TAP)
TON
AND AS A POLICE OFFICER, I HAVE TO ASK THE TOUGH QUESTIONS.
......
LISA KURAKI.
JUST HOW INVOLVED IS YOUR ORGANIZATION WITH THIS LATEST INCIDENT?

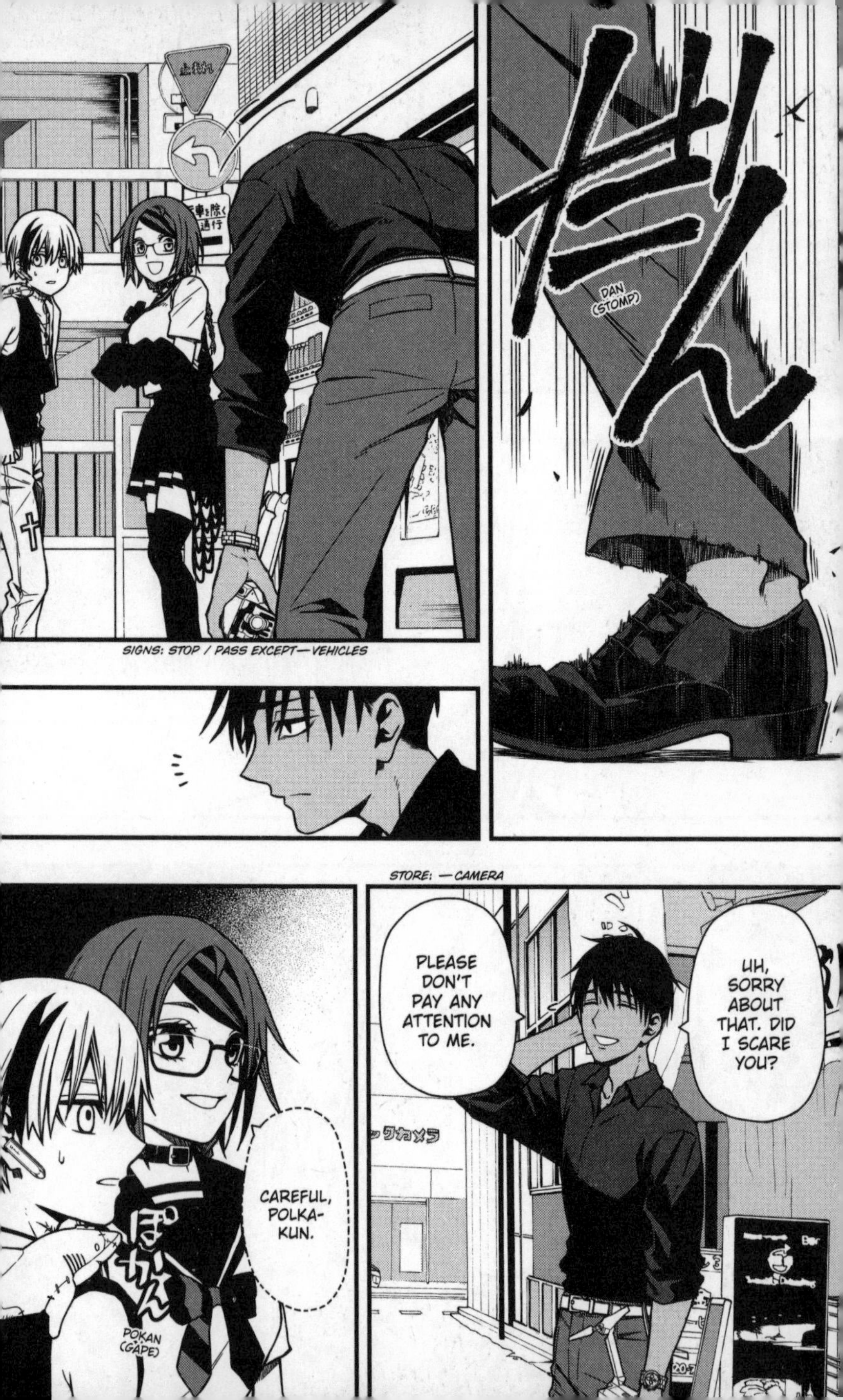
DAN (STOMP)
SIGNS: STOP / PASS EXCEPT—VEHICLES
STORE: —CAMERA
UH, SORRY ABOUT THAT. DID I SCARE YOU?
PLEASE DON'T PAY ANY ATTENTION TO ME.
CAREFUL, POLKA-KUN.
POKAN (GAPE)

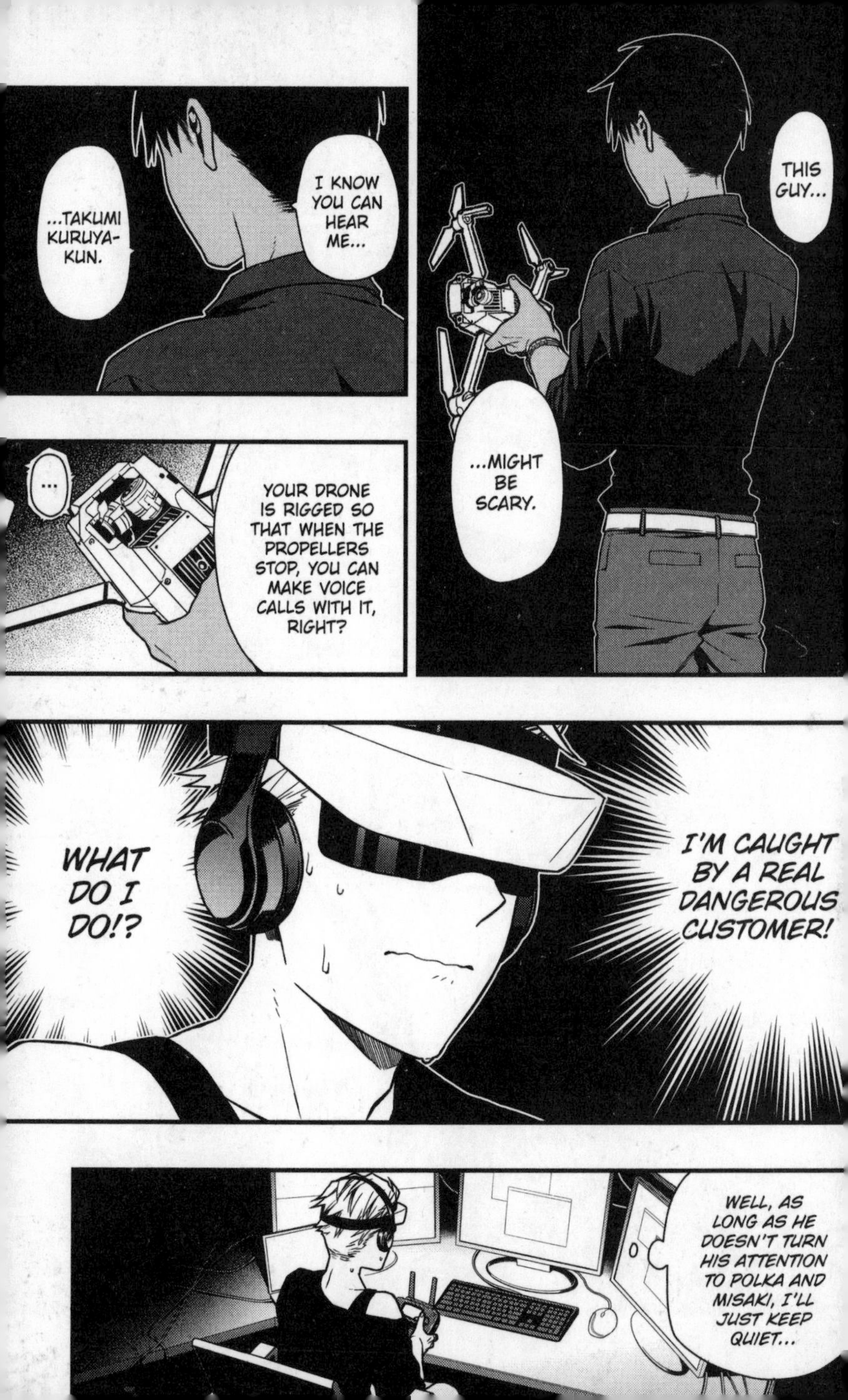
THIS GUY...
...MIGHT BE SCARY.
I KNOW YOU CAN HEAR ME...
...TAKUMI KURUYA-KUN.
YOUR DRONE IS RIGGED SO THAT WHEN THE PROPELLERS STOP, YOU CAN MAKE VOICE CALLS WITH IT, RIGHT?
...
I'M CAUGHT BY A REAL DANGEROUS CUSTOMER!
WHAT DO I DO!?
WELL, AS LONG AS HE DOESN'T TURN HIS ATTENTION TO POLKA AND MISAKI, I'LL JUST KEEP QUIET...

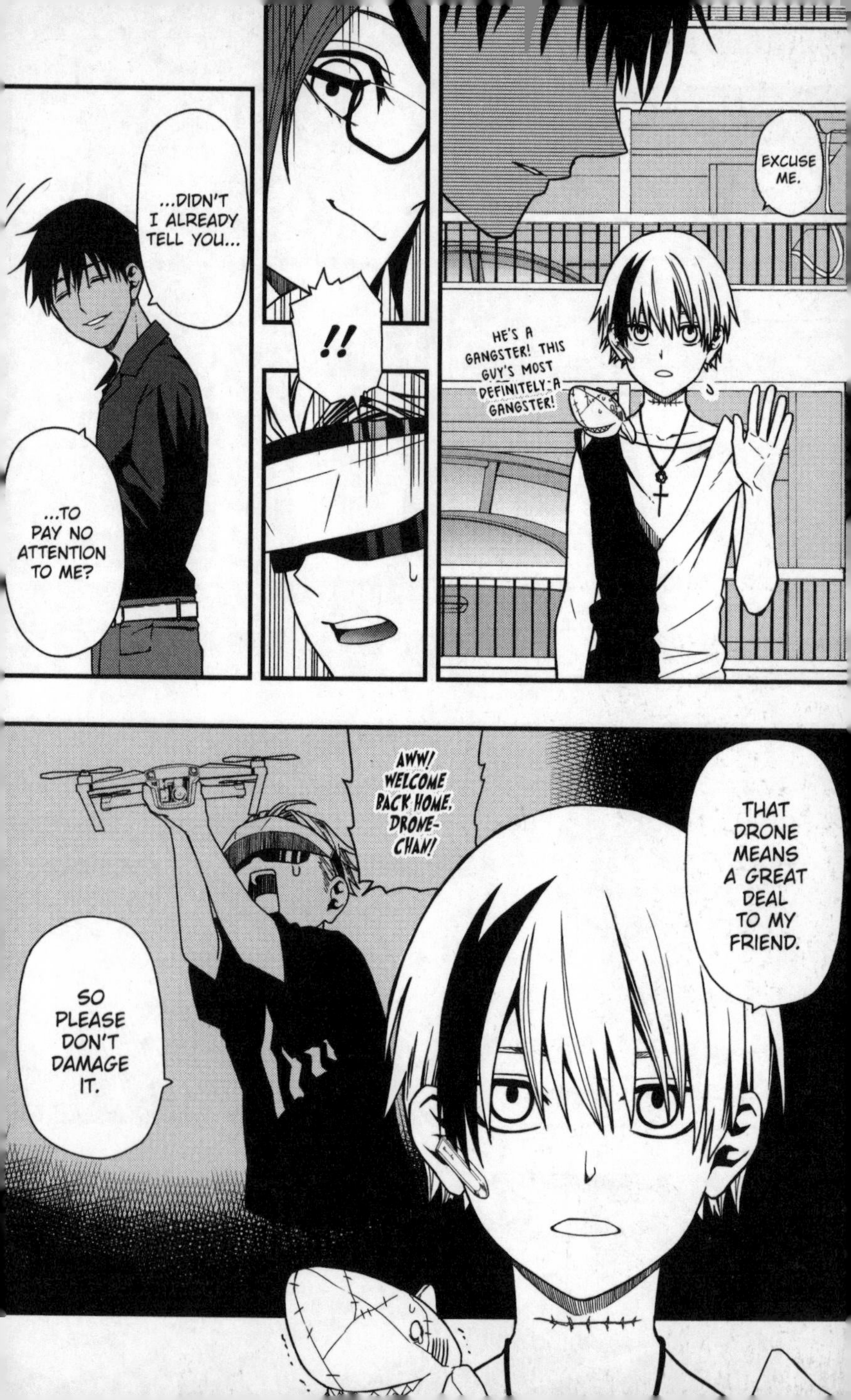
EXCUSE ME.
HE'S A GANGSTER! THIS GUY'S MOST DEFINITELY A GANGSTER!
!!
...DIDN'T I ALREADY TELL YOU...
...TO PAY NO ATTENTION TO ME?
THAT DRONE MEANS A GREAT DEAL TO MY FRIEND.
AWW! WELCOME BACK HOME, DRONE-CHAN!
SO PLEASE DON'T DAMAGE IT.

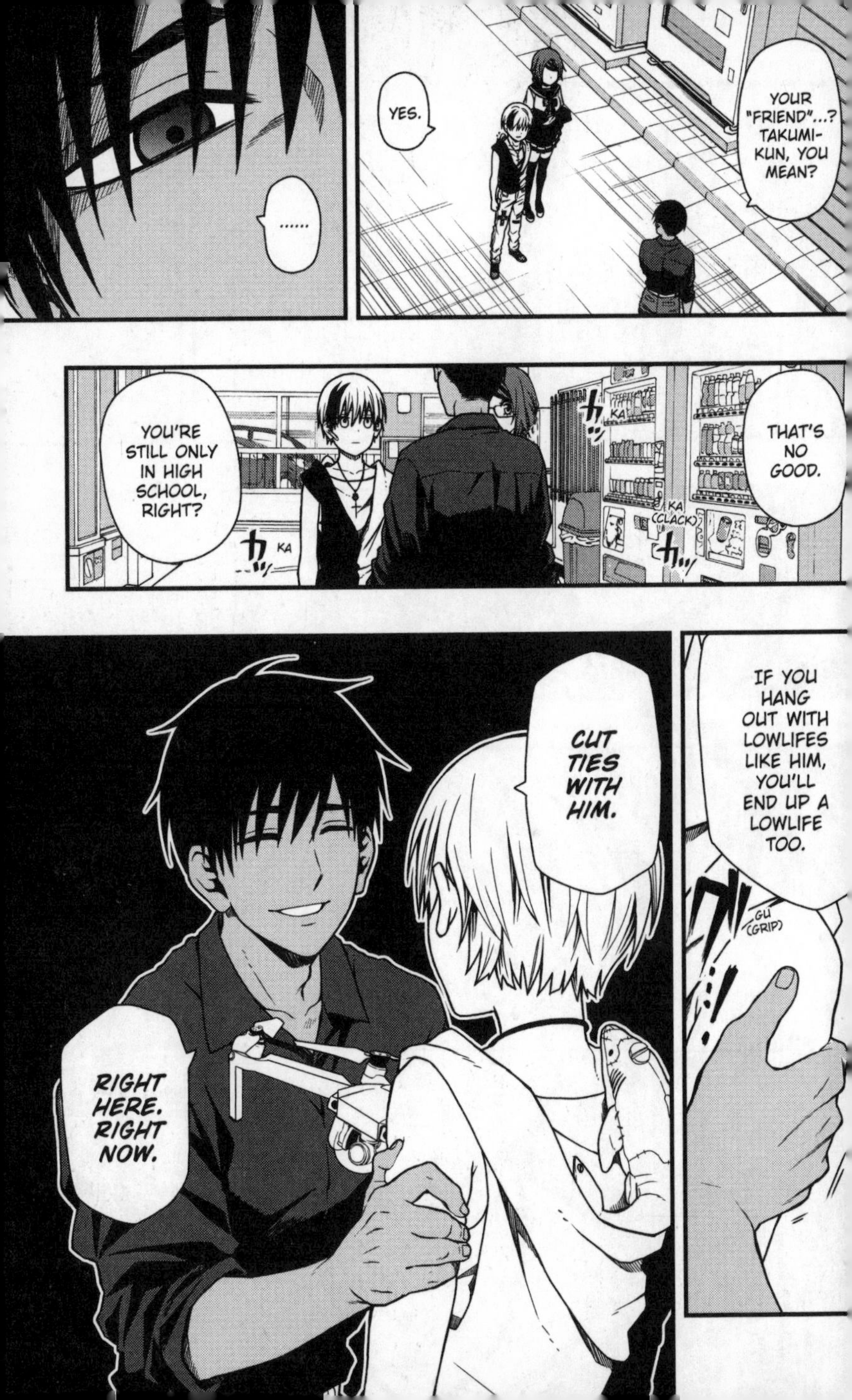
YOUR "FRIEND"...? TAKUMI-KUN, YOU MEAN?
YES.
......
THAT'S NO GOOD.
KA
KA (CLACK)
YOU'RE STILL ONLY IN HIGH SCHOOL, RIGHT?
KA
IF YOU HANG OUT WITH LOWLIFES LIKE HIM, YOU'LL END UP A LOWLIFE TOO.
GU (GRIP)
CUT TIES WITH HIM.
RIGHT HERE. RIGHT NOW.

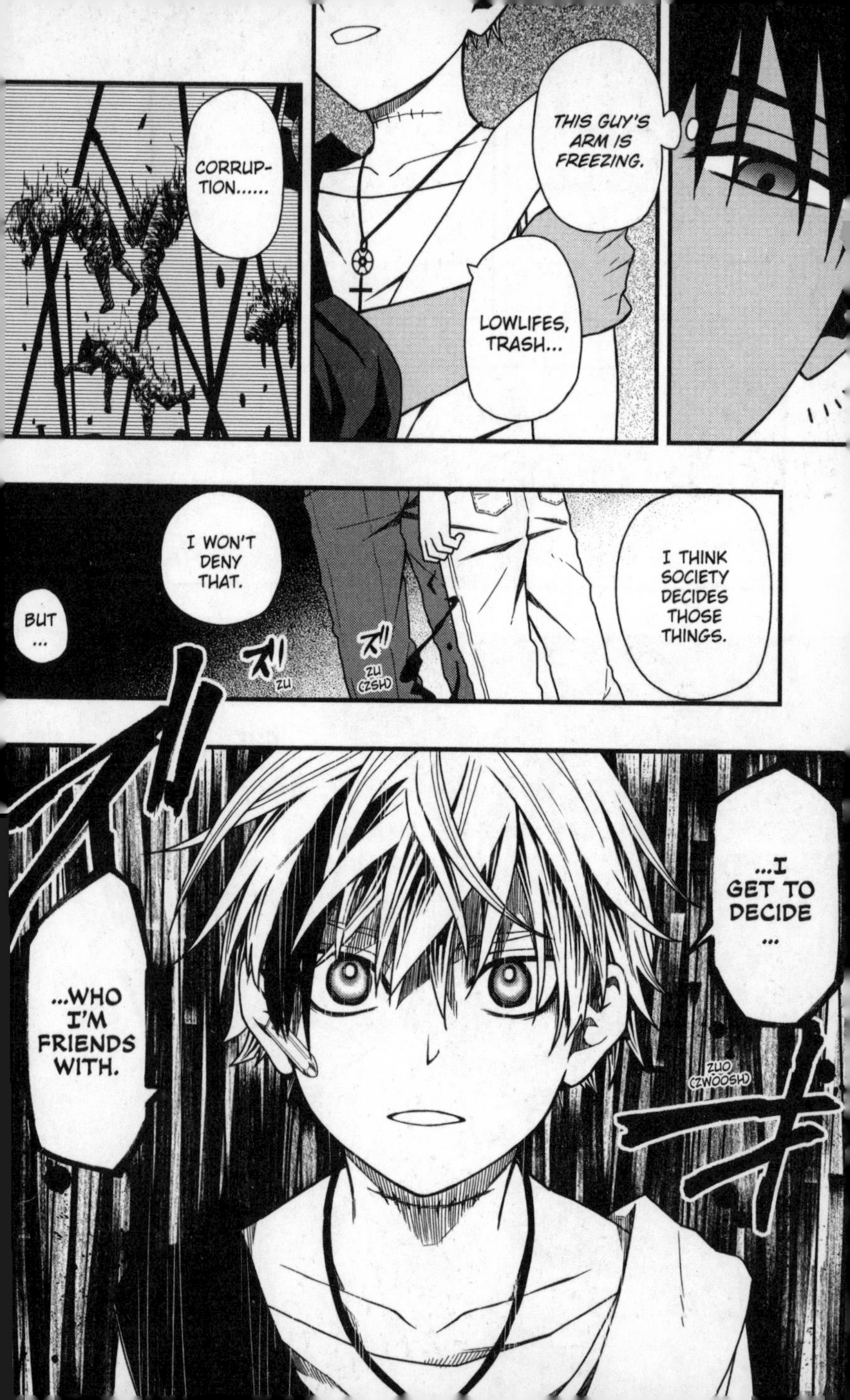
THIS GUY'S ARM IS FREEZING.
LOWLIFES, TRASH...
CORRUP-TION......
I THINK SOCIETY DECIDES THOSE THINGS.
ズ
ZU (ZSH)
ズ
ZU
I WON'T DENY THAT.
BUT ...
...I GET TO DECIDE ...
ZUO (ZWOOSH)
...WHO I'M FRIENDS WITH.

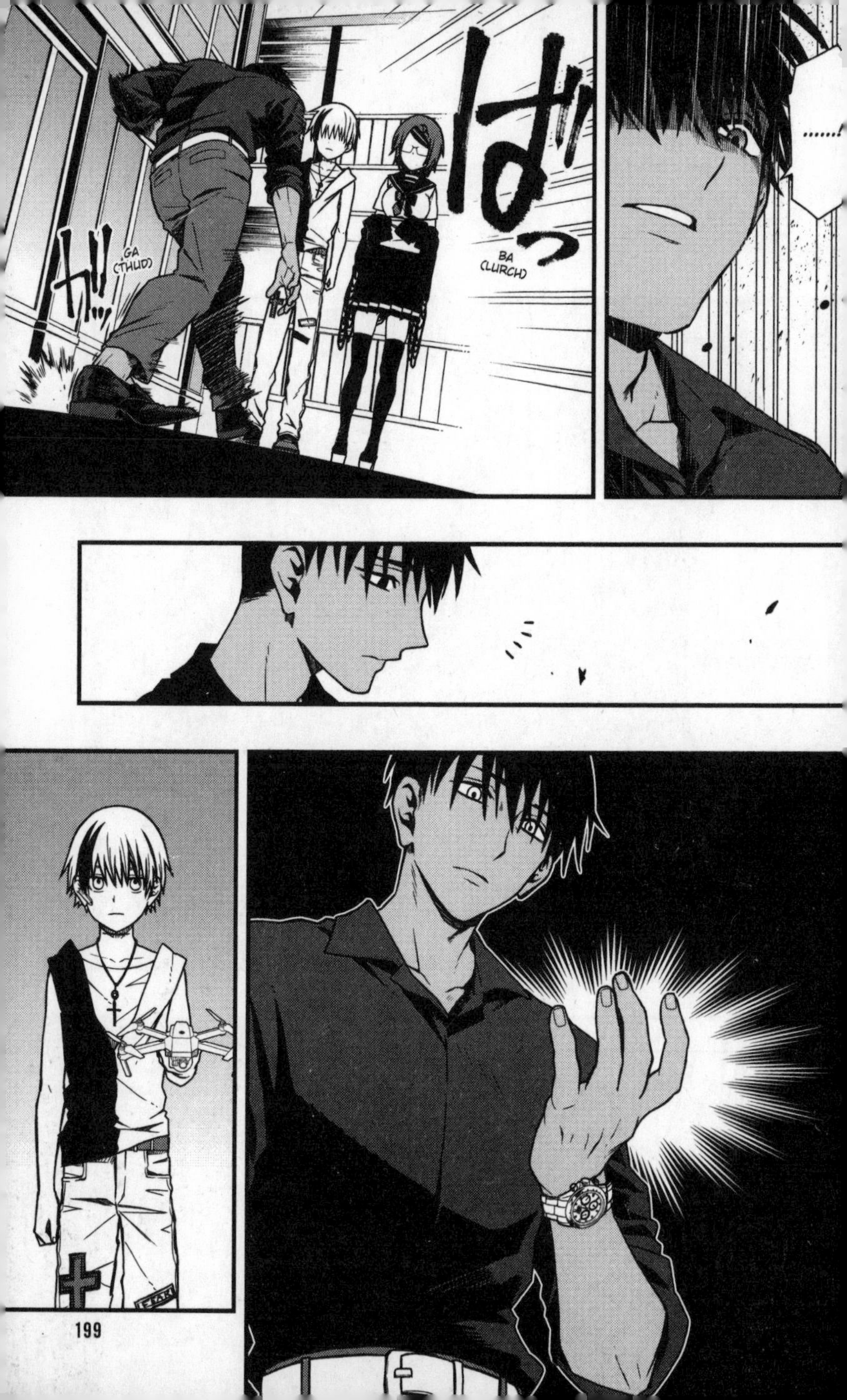

ばっ
BA (LURCH)
ガ
GA (THUD)
……!

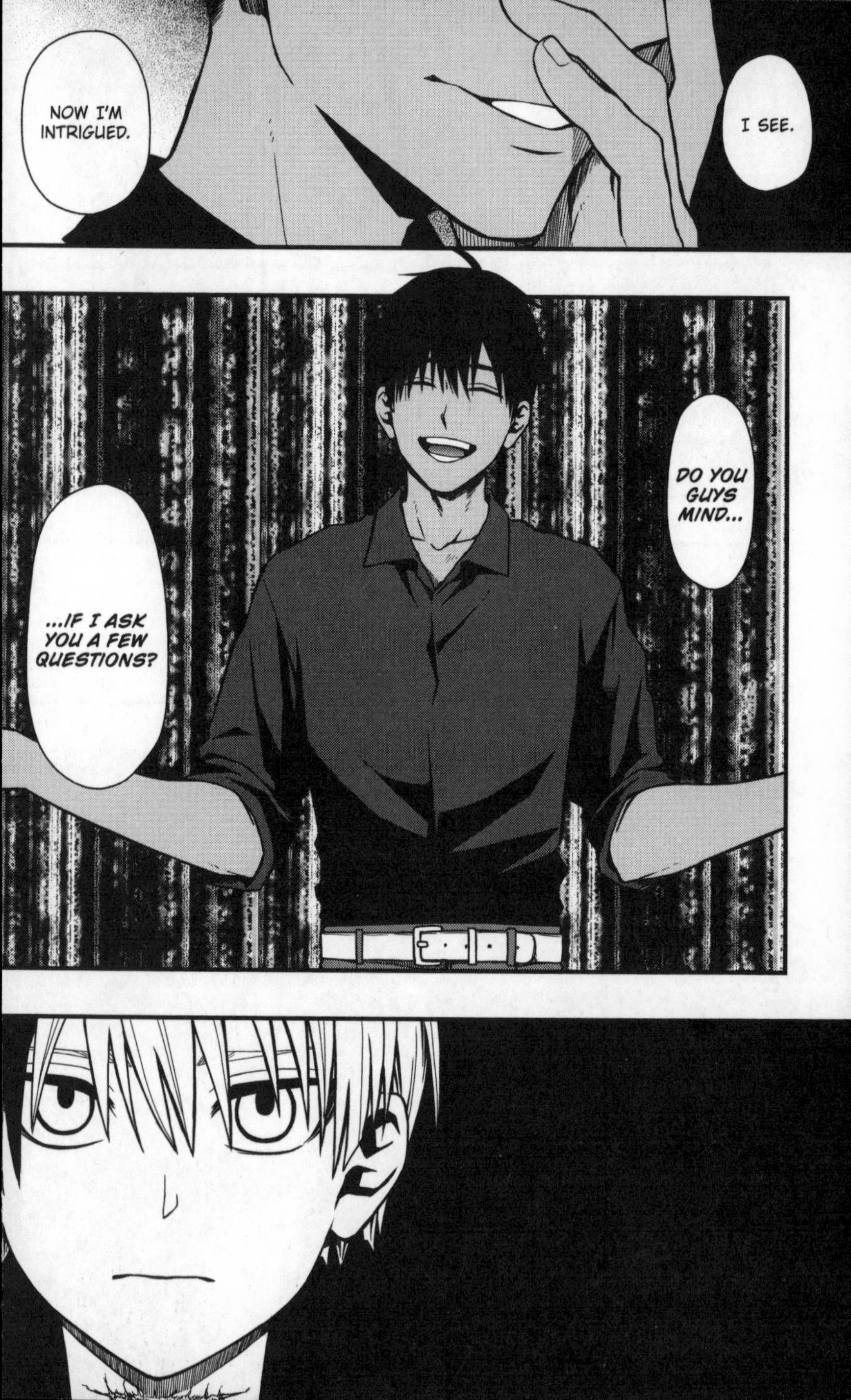
I SEE.
NOW I'M INTRIGUED.
DO YOU GUYS MIND...
...IF I ASK YOU A FEW QUESTIONS?

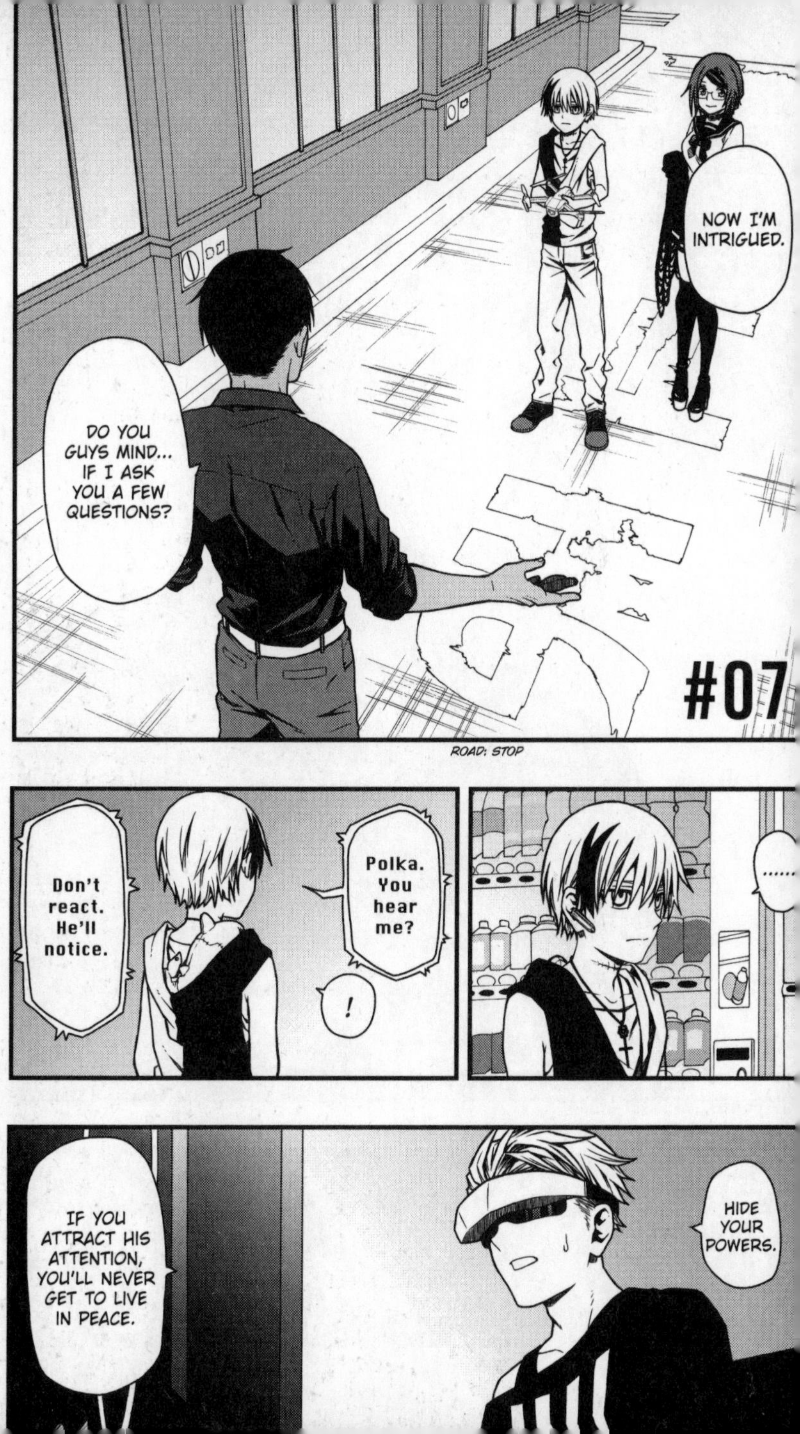
NOW I'M INTRIGUED.
DO YOU GUYS MIND... IF I ASK YOU A FEW QUESTIONS?
#07
ROAD: STOP
......
Polka. You hear me?
!
Don't react. He'll notice.
HIDE YOUR POWERS.
IF YOU ATTRACT HIS ATTENTION, YOU'LL NEVER GET TO LIVE IN PEACE.

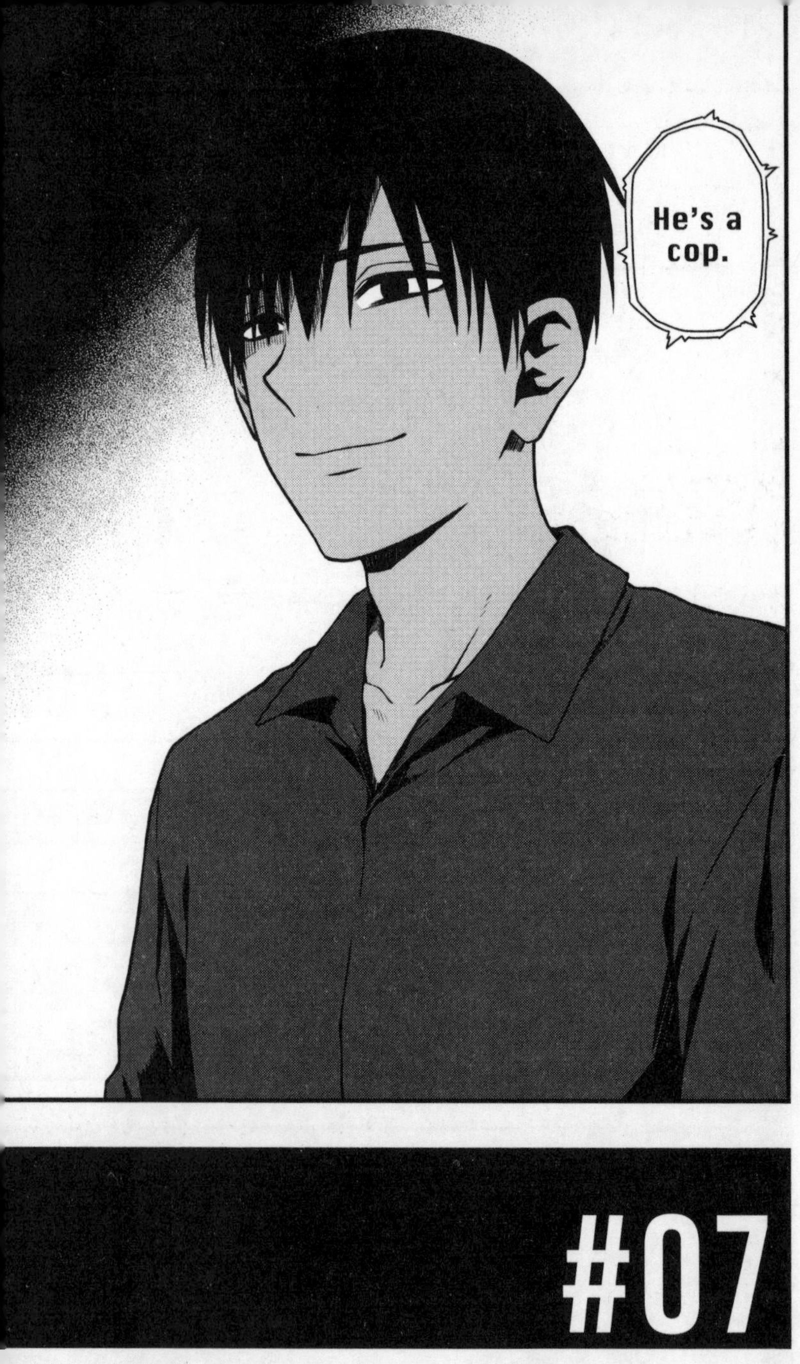
He's a cop.

#07

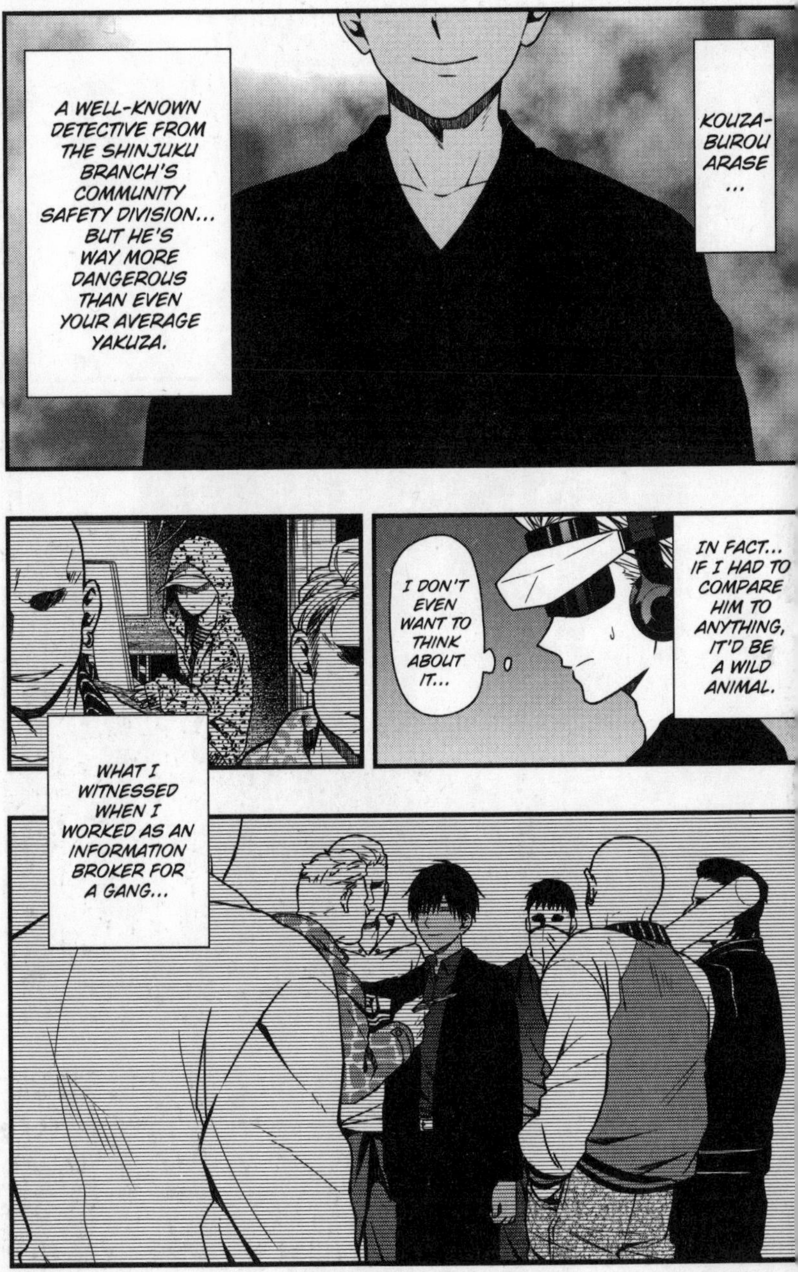
KOUZA-BUROU ARASE...
A WELL-KNOWN DETECTIVE FROM THE SHINJUKU BRANCH'S COMMUNITY SAFETY DIVISION... BUT HE'S WAY MORE DANGEROUS THAN EVEN YOUR AVERAGE YAKUZA.
IN FACT... IF I HAD TO COMPARE HIM TO ANYTHING, IT'D BE A WILD ANIMAL.
I DON'T EVEN WANT TO THINK ABOUT IT...
WHAT I WITNESSED WHEN I WORKED AS AN INFORMATION BROKER FOR A GANG...

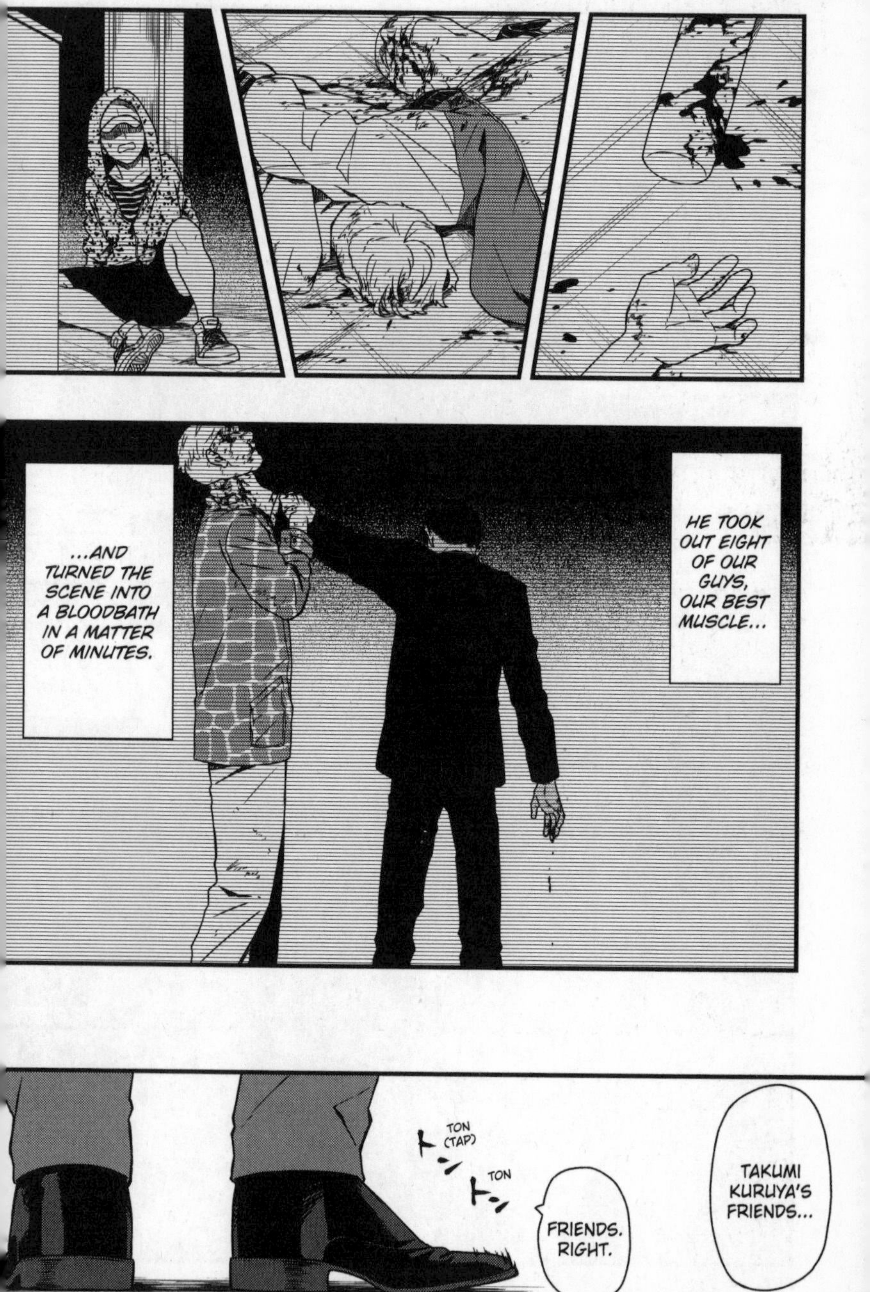
HE TOOK OUT EIGHT OF OUR GUYS, OUR BEST MUSCLE...
...AND TURNED THE SCENE INTO A BLOODBATH IN A MATTER OF MINUTES.
TAKUMI KURUYA'S FRIENDS...
TON (TAP)
TON
FRIENDS. RIGHT.

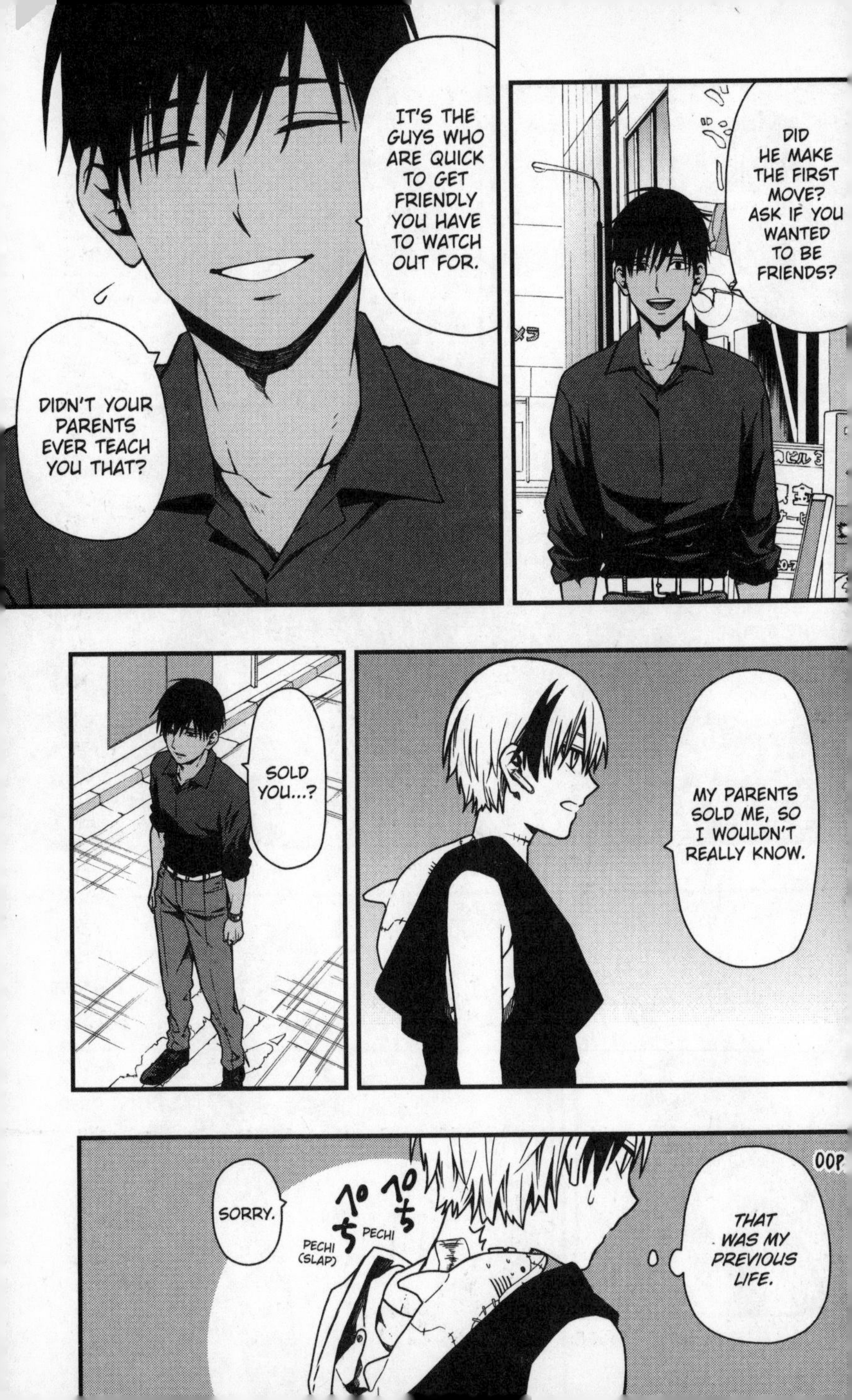
DID HE MAKE THE FIRST MOVE? ASK IF YOU WANTED TO BE FRIENDS?
IT'S THE GUYS WHO ARE QUICK TO GET FRIENDLY YOU HAVE TO WATCH OUT FOR.
DIDN'T YOUR PARENTS EVER TEACH YOU THAT?
MY PARENTS SOLD ME, SO I WOULDN'T REALLY KNOW.
SOLD YOU...?
OOP
THAT WAS MY PREVIOUS LIFE.
PECHI
PECHI (SLAP)
SORRY.

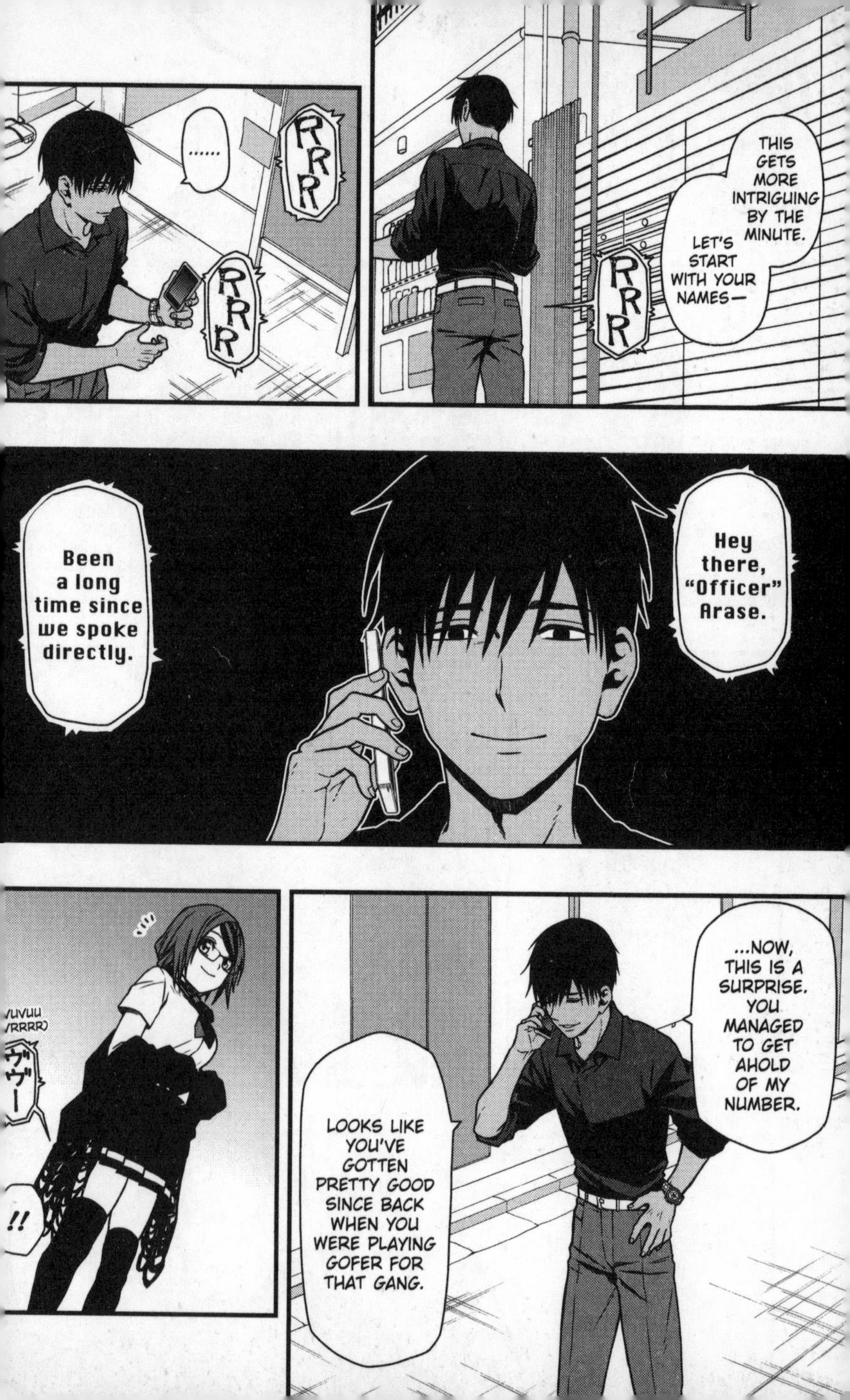
THIS GETS MORE INTRIGUING BY THE MINUTE.
LET'S START WITH YOUR NAMES—
RRR
......
RRR
RRR
Hey there, "Officer" Arase.
Been a long time since we spoke directly.
...NOW, THIS IS A SURPRISE. YOU MANAGED TO GET AHOLD OF MY NUMBER.
LOOKS LIKE YOU'VE GOTTEN PRETTY GOOD SINCE BACK WHEN YOU WERE PLAYING GOFER FOR THAT GANG.
!!
VUVUU (VRRRR)
ヴヴー
!!

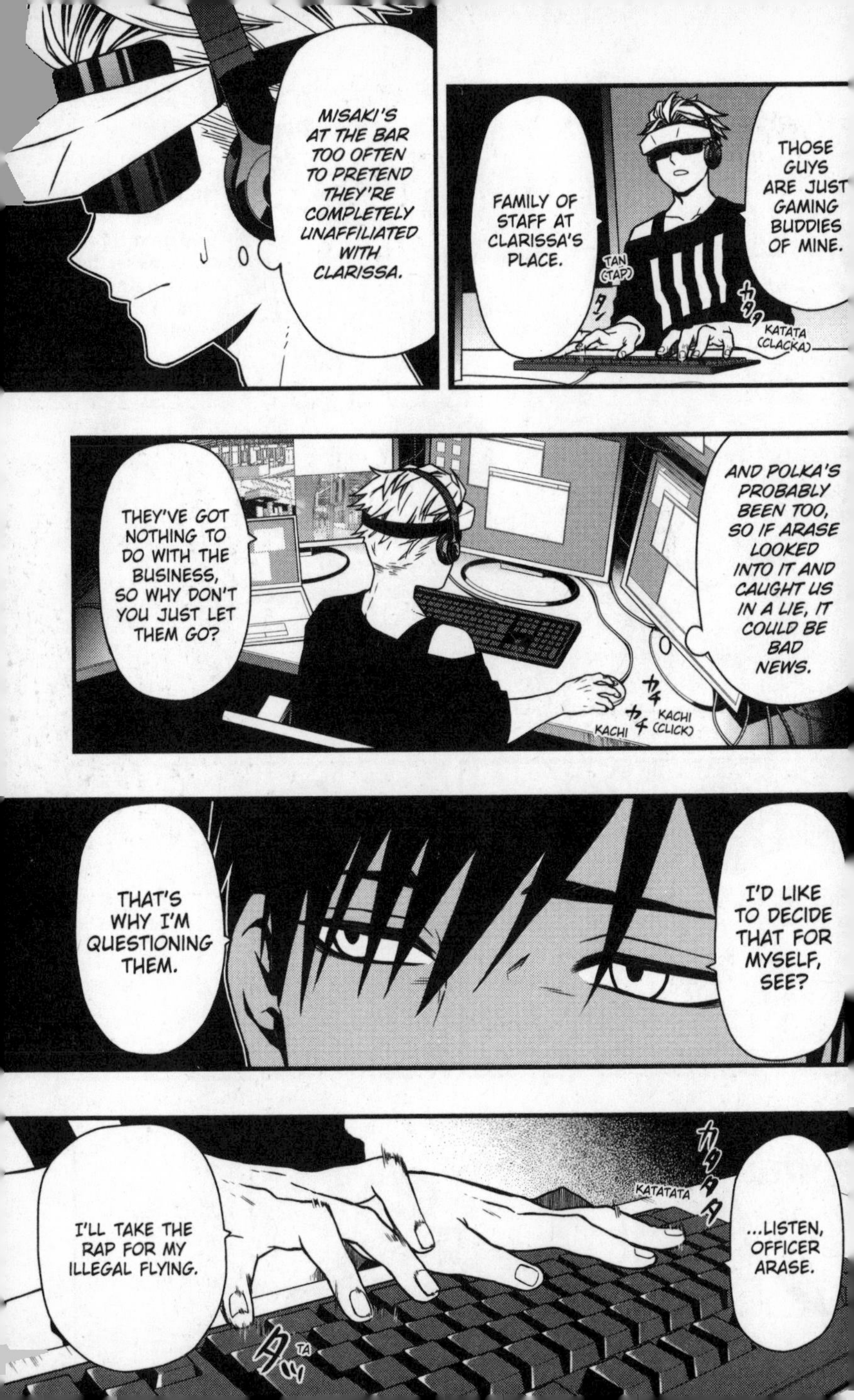

THOSE GUYS ARE JUST GAMING BUDDIES OF MINE.
KATATA (CLACKA)
TAN (TAP)
FAMILY OF STAFF AT CLARISSA'S PLACE.
MISAKI'S AT THE BAR TOO OFTEN TO PRETEND THEY'RE COMPLETELY UNAFFILIATED WITH CLARISSA.
AND POLKA'S PROBABLY BEEN TOO, SO IF ARASE LOOKED INTO IT AND CAUGHT US IN A LIE, IT COULD BE BAD NEWS.
KACHI (CLICK)
KACHI
THEY'VE GOT NOTHING TO DO WITH THE BUSINESS, SO WHY DON'T YOU JUST LET THEM GO?
I'D LIKE TO DECIDE THAT FOR MYSELF, SEE?
THAT'S WHY I'M QUESTIONING THEM.
KATATATA
...LISTEN, OFFICER ARASE.
I'LL TAKE THE RAP FOR MY ILLEGAL FLYING.
TA

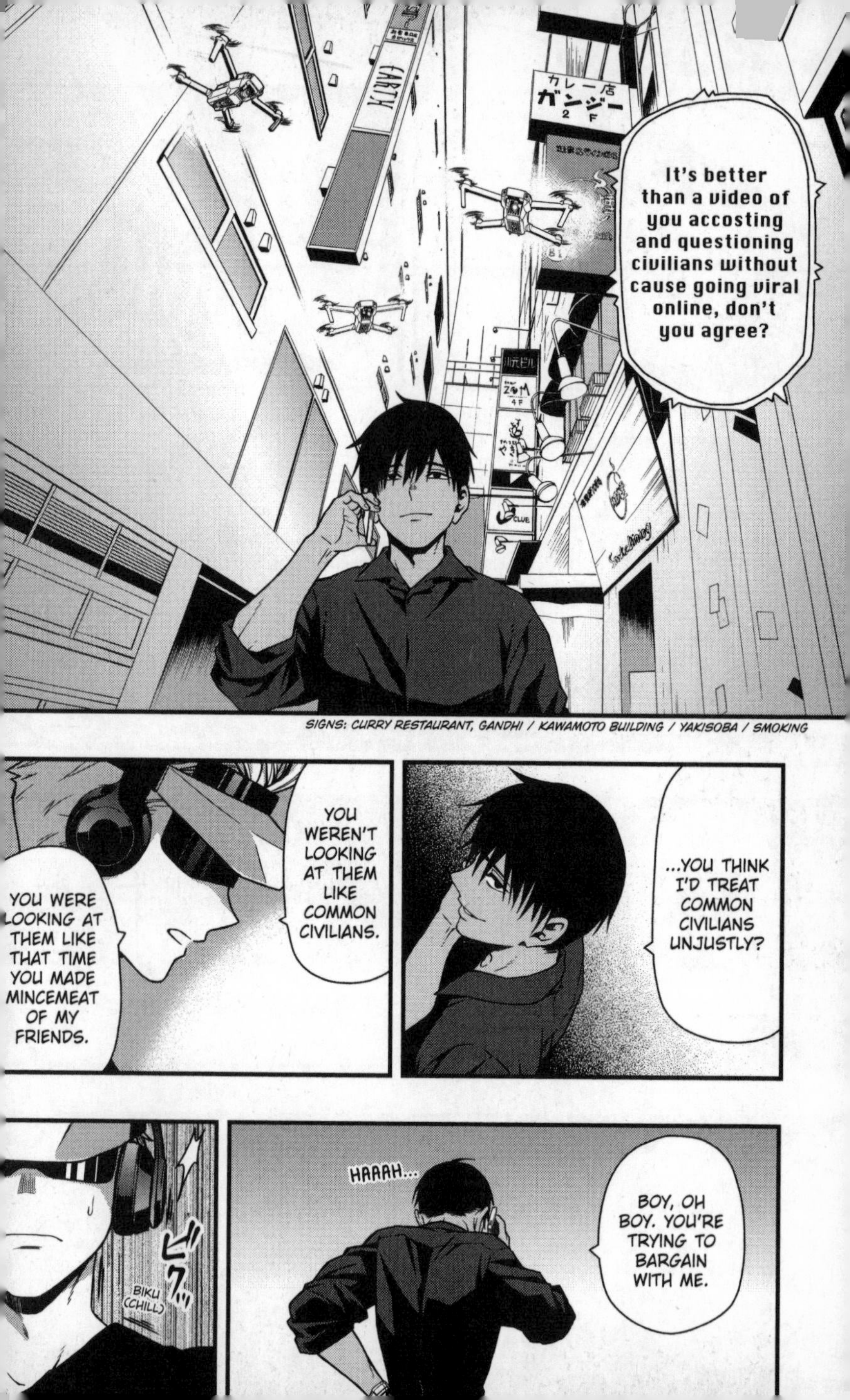
カレー店
ガンジー
2F
It's better than a video of you accosting and questioning civilians without cause going viral online, don't you agree?
SIGNS: CURRY RESTAURANT, GANDHI / KAWAMOTO BUILDING / YAKISOBA / SMOKING
...YOU THINK I'D TREAT COMMON CIVILIANS UNJUSTLY?
YOU WEREN'T LOOKING AT THEM LIKE COMMON CIVILIANS.
YOU WERE LOOKING AT THEM LIKE THAT TIME YOU MADE MINCEMEAT OF MY FRIENDS.
HAAAH...
BOY, OH BOY. YOU'RE TRYING TO BARGAIN WITH ME.
BIKU (CHILL)

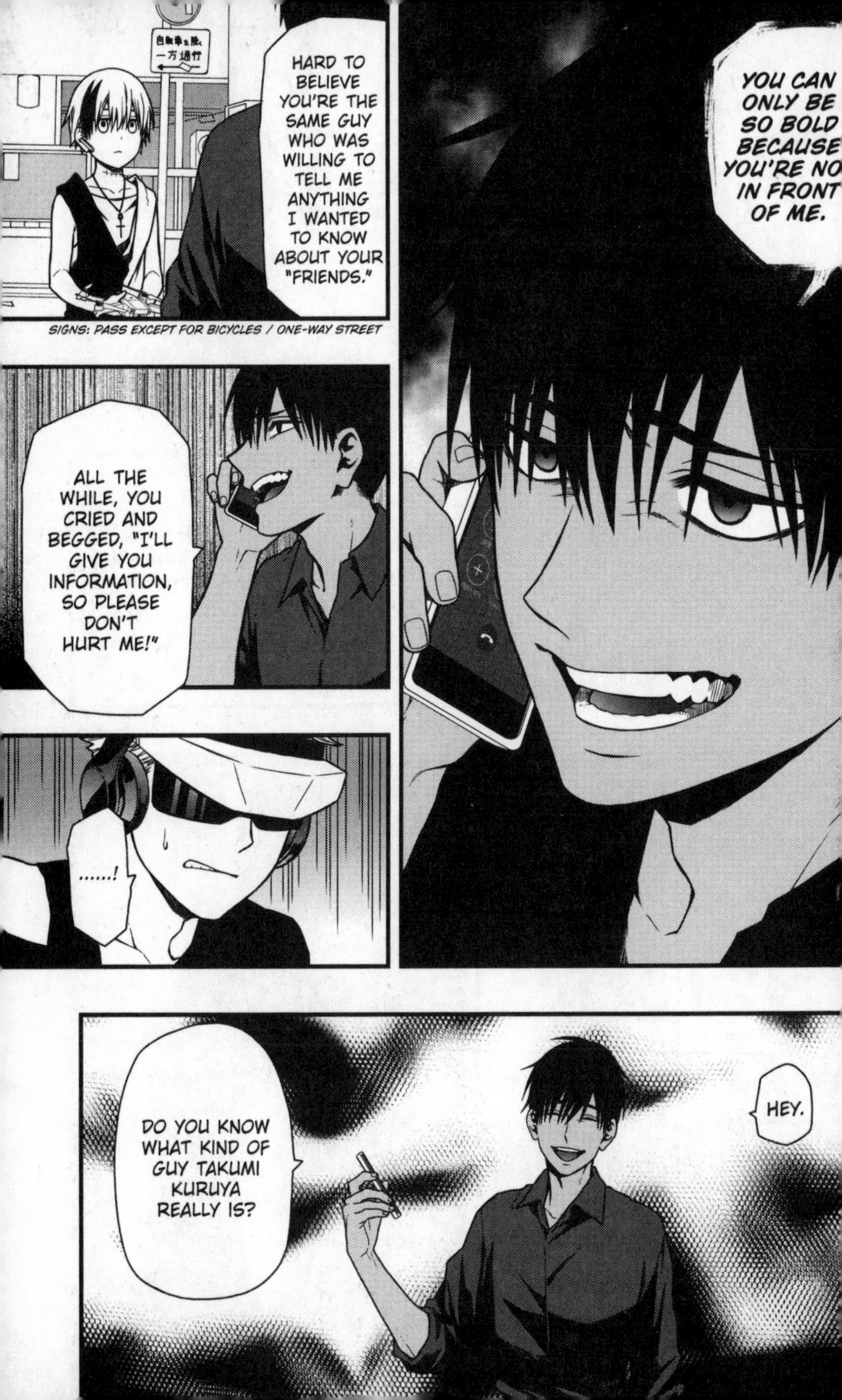
YOU CAN ONLY BE SO BOLD BECAUSE YOU'RE NO IN FRONT OF ME.
HARD TO BELIEVE YOU'RE THE SAME GUY WHO WAS WILLING TO TELL ME ANYTHING I WANTED TO KNOW ABOUT YOUR "FRIENDS."
SIGNS: PASS EXCEPT FOR BICYCLES / ONE-WAY STREET
ALL THE WHILE, YOU CRIED AND BEGGED, "I'LL GIVE YOU INFORMATION, SO PLEASE DON'T HURT ME!"
......!
HEY.
DO YOU KNOW WHAT KIND OF GUY TAKUMI KURUYA REALLY IS?

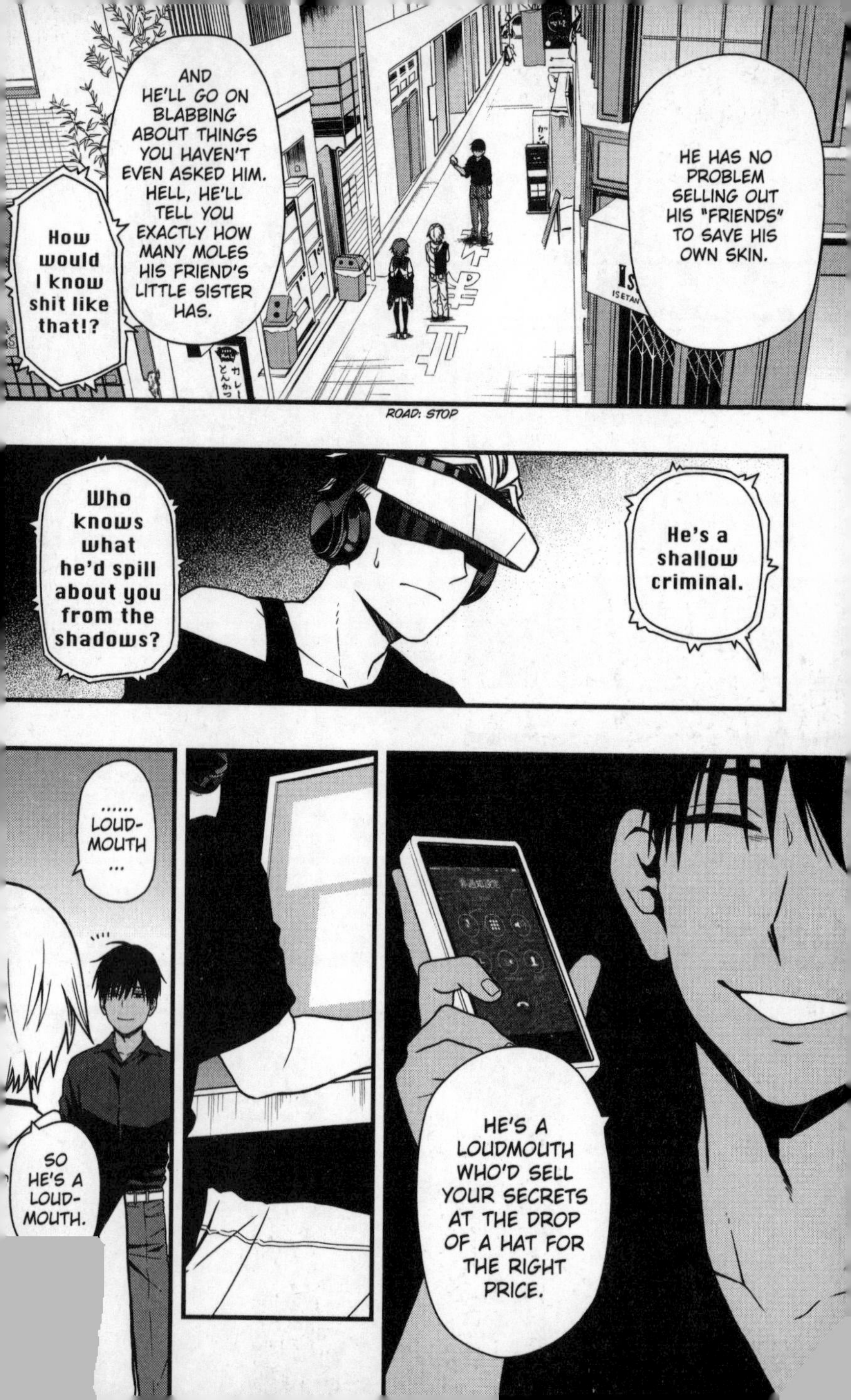
HE HAS NO PROBLEM SELLING OUT HIS "FRIENDS" TO SAVE HIS OWN SKIN.
AND HE'LL GO ON BLABBING ABOUT THINGS YOU HAVEN'T EVEN ASKED HIM. HELL, HE'LL TELL YOU EXACTLY HOW MANY MOLES HIS FRIEND'S LITTLE SISTER HAS.
How would I know shit like that!?
ROAD: STOP
He's a shallow criminal.
Who knows what he'd spill about you from the shadows?
HE'S A LOUDMOUTH WHO'D SELL YOUR SECRETS AT THE DROP OF A HAT FOR THE RIGHT PRICE.
...... LOUD-MOUTH ...
SO HE'S A LOUD-MOUTH.

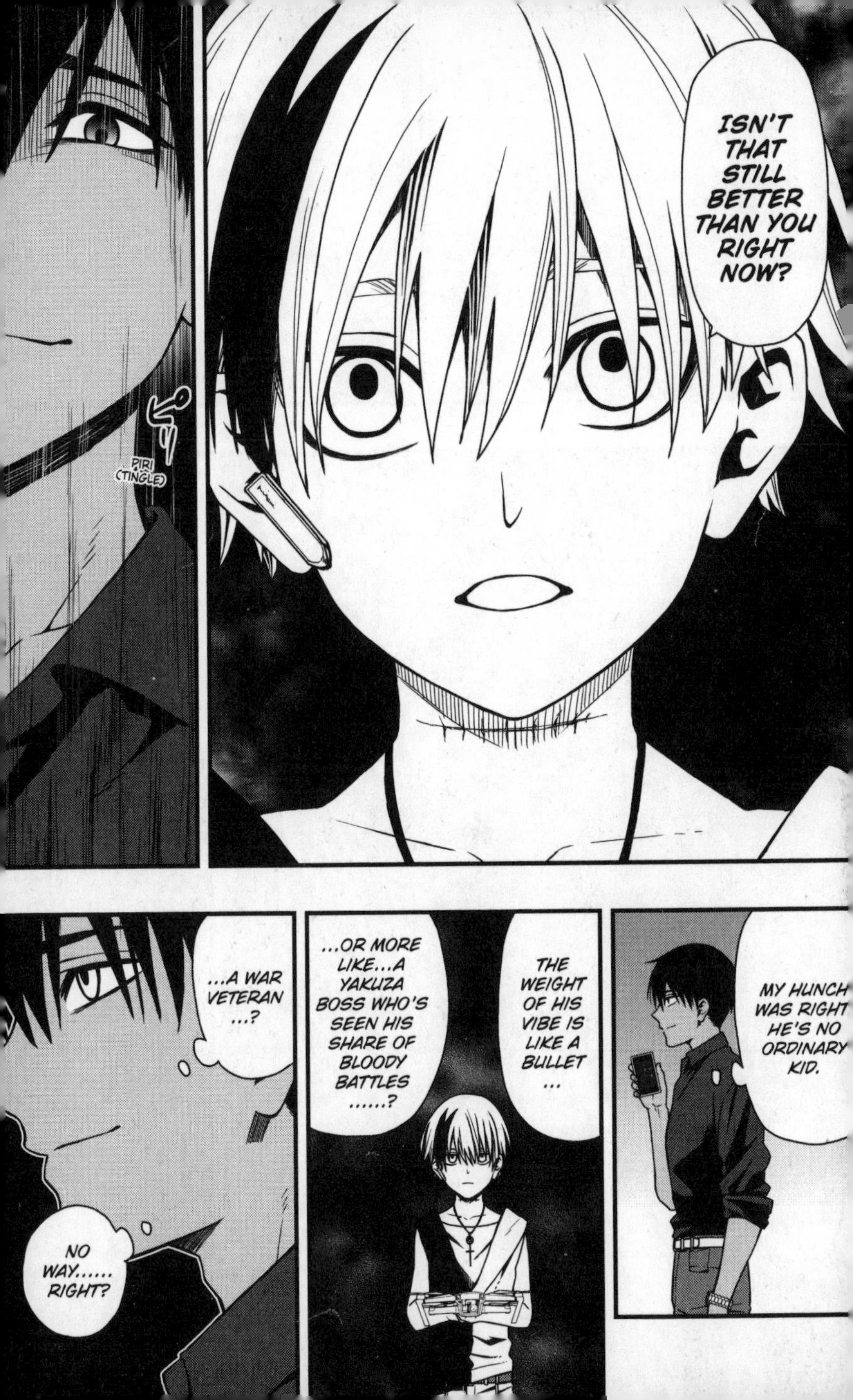
ISN'T THAT STILL BETTER THAN YOU RIGHT NOW?
PIRI (TINGLE)
MY HUNCH WAS RIGHT HE'S NO ORDINARY KID.
THE WEIGHT OF HIS VIBE IS LIKE A BULLET ...
...OR MORE LIKE...A YAKUZA BOSS WHO'S SEEN HIS SHARE OF BLOODY BATTLES ......?
...A WAR VETERAN ...?
NO WAY...... RIGHT?

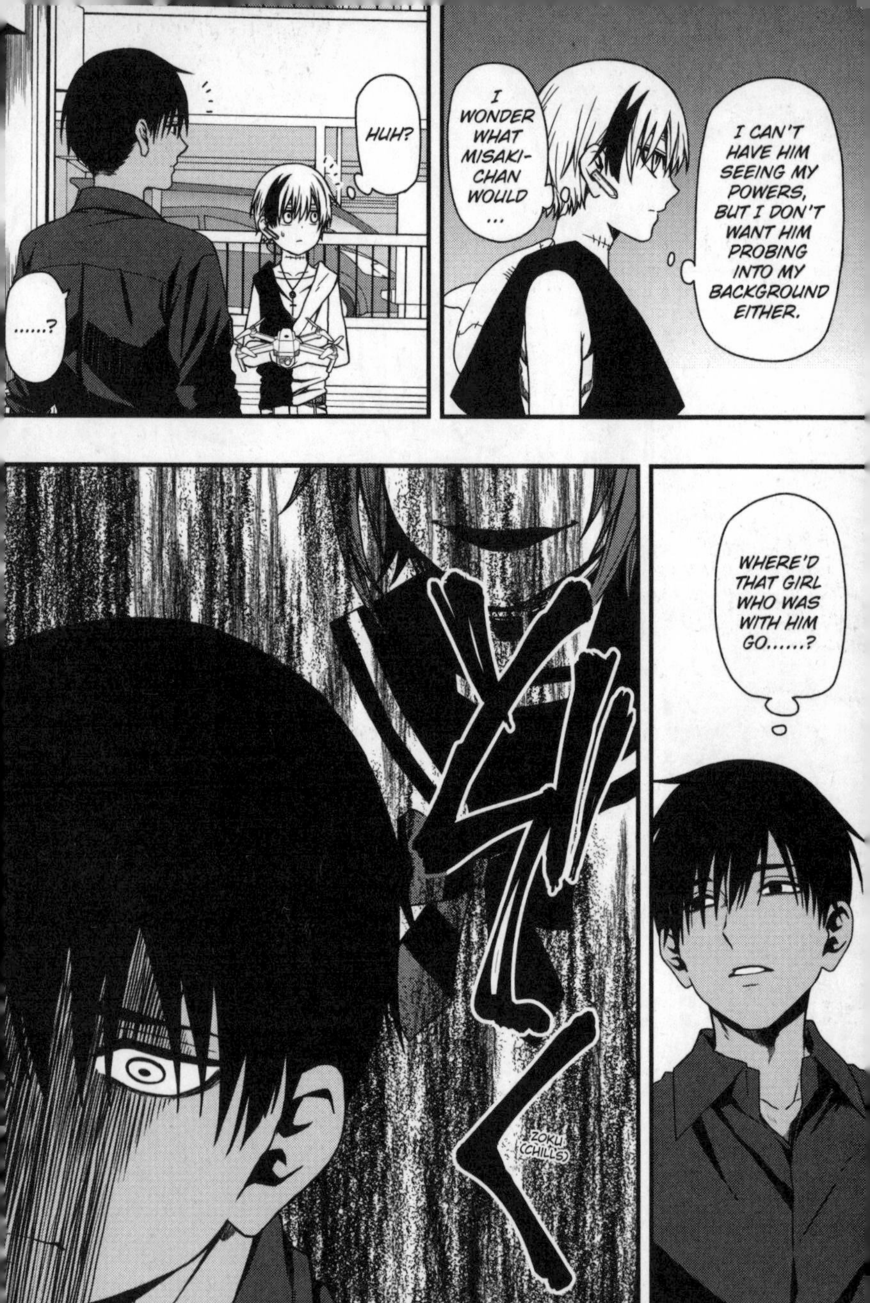
I CAN'T HAVE HIM SEEING MY POWERS, BUT I DON'T WANT HIM PROBING INTO MY BACKGROUND EITHER.
I WONDER WHAT MISAKI-CHAN WOULD ...
HUH?
......?
WHERE'D THAT GIRL WHO WAS WITH HIM GO......?
ZOKU (CHILLS)

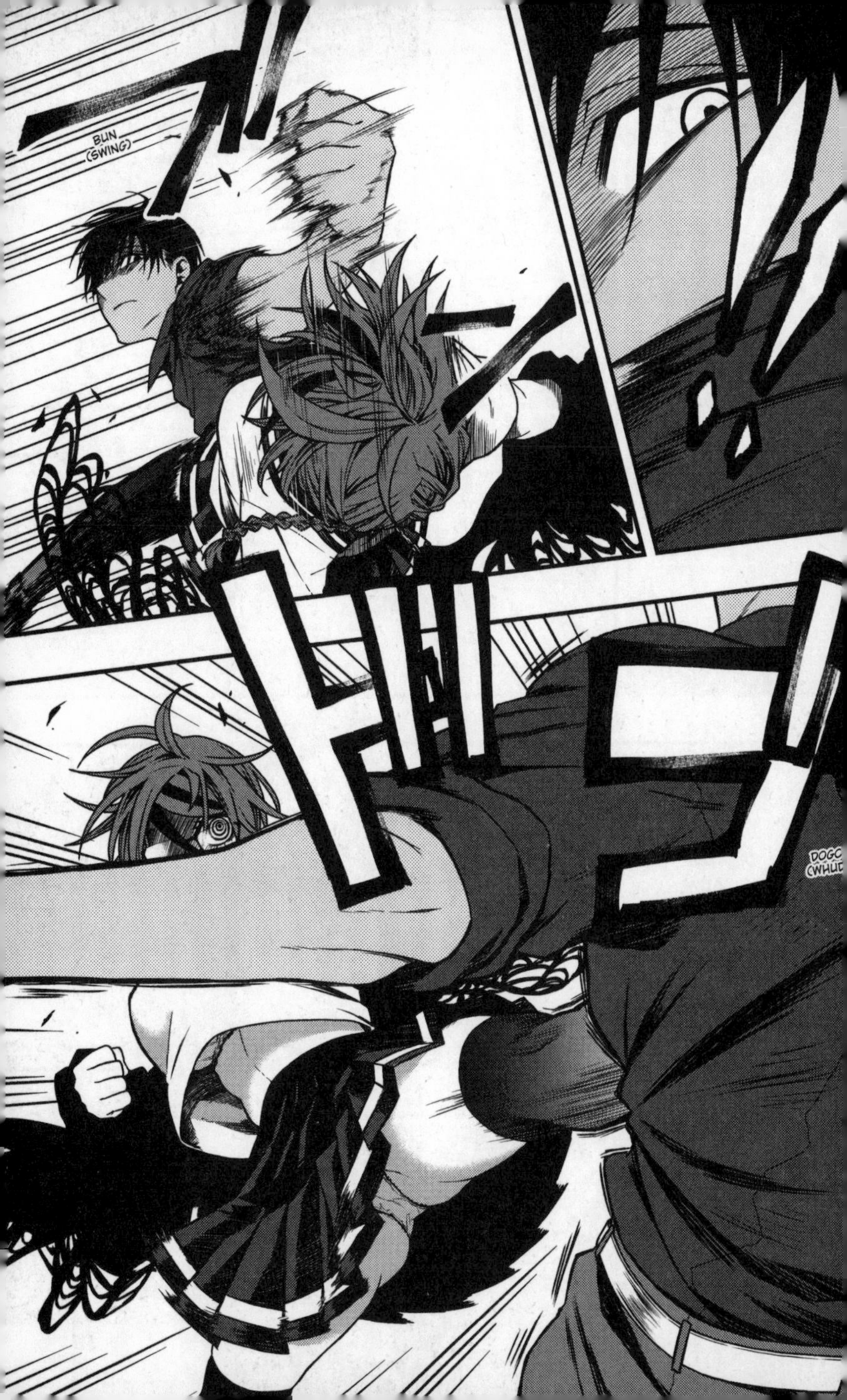
BUN (SWING)
DOGO (WHUD

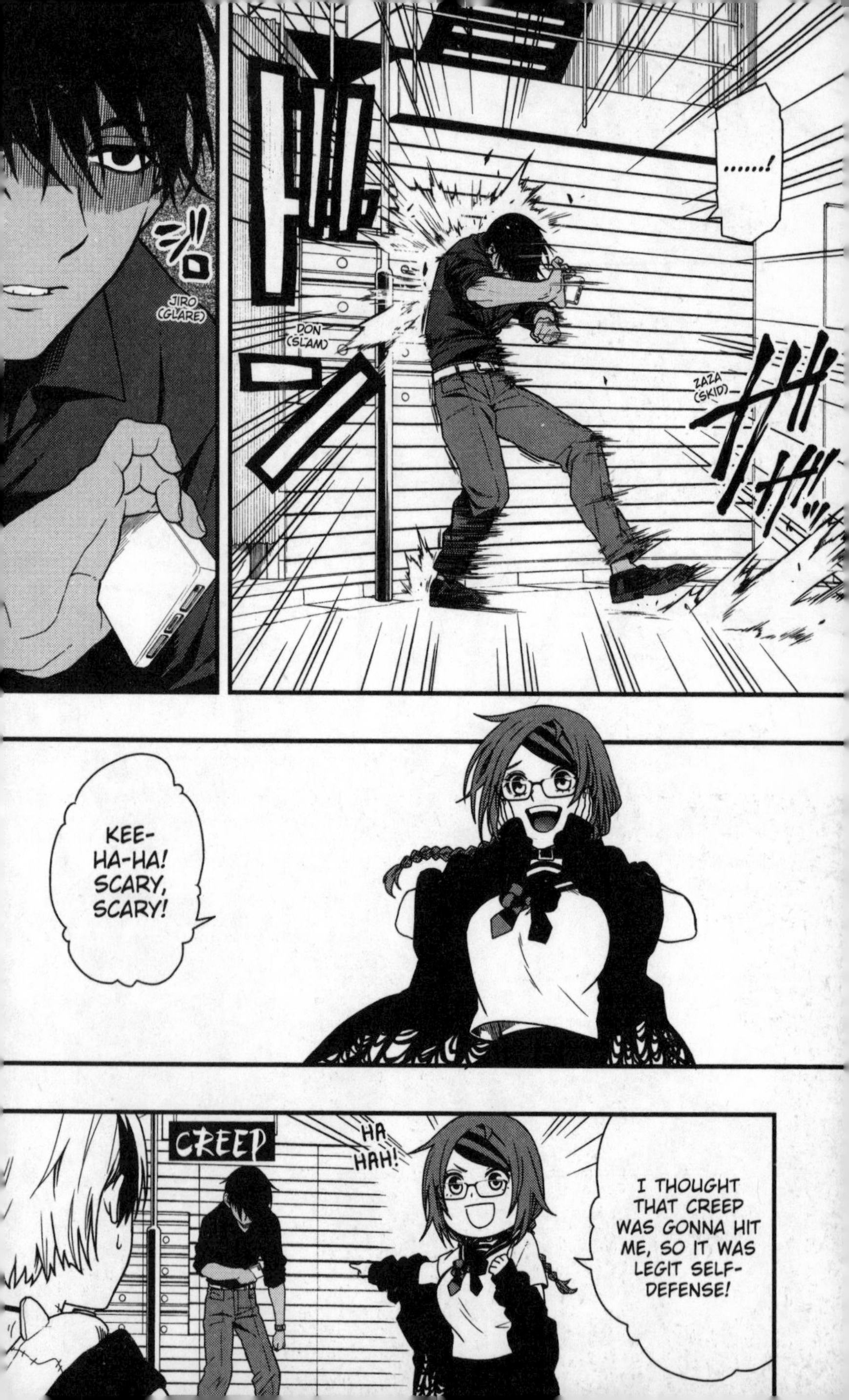
......!
ZAZA (SKID)
DON (SLAM)
JIRO (GLARE)
KEE-HA-HA! SCARY, SCARY!
I THOUGHT THAT CREEP WAS GONNA HIT ME, SO IT WAS LEGIT SELF-DEFENSE!
HA HAH!
CREEP

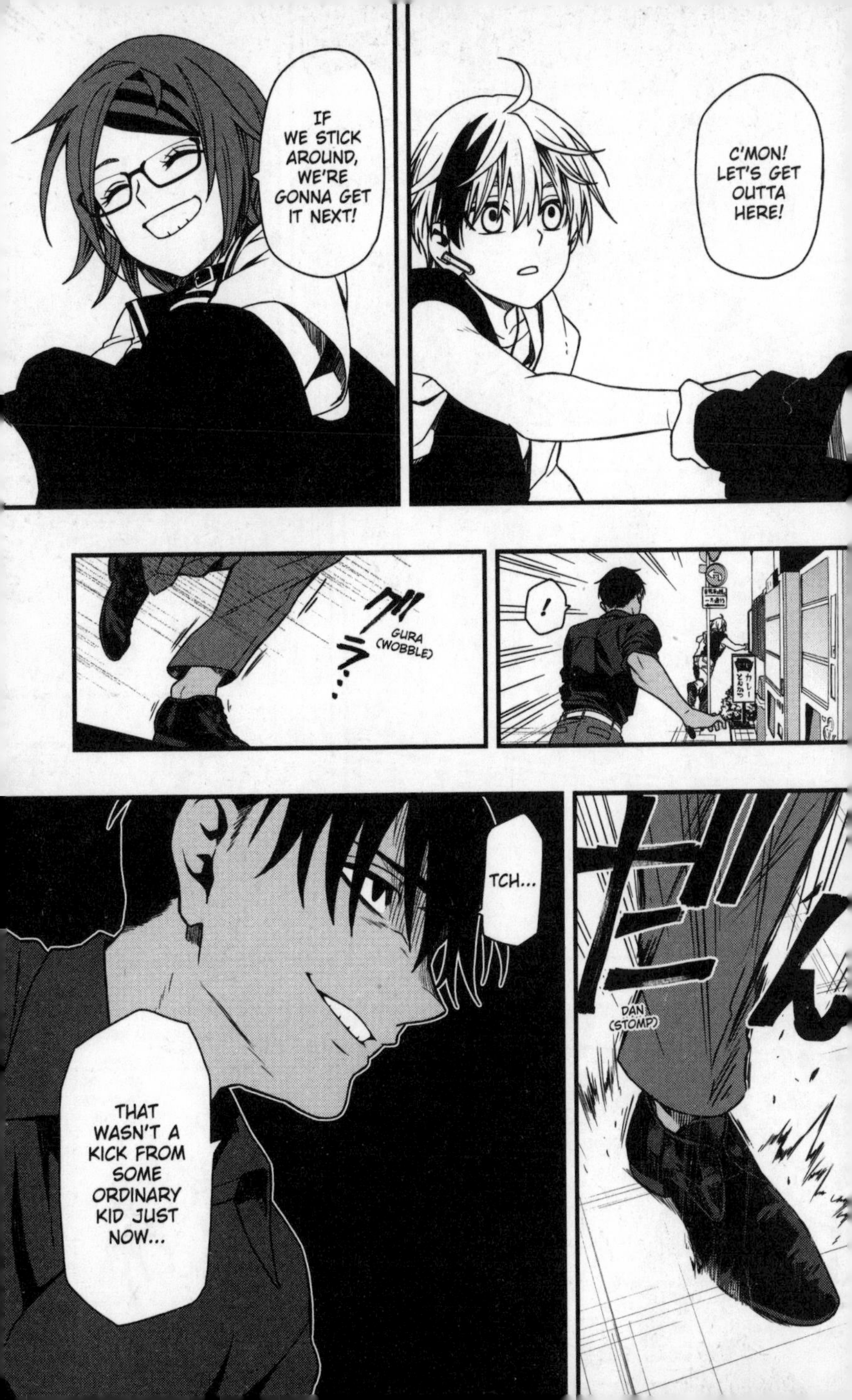
C'MON! LET'S GET OUTTA HERE!
IF WE STICK AROUND, WE'RE GONNA GET IT NEXT!
!
GURA (WOBBLE)
DAN (STOMP)
TCH...
THAT WASN'T A KICK FROM SOME ORDINARY KID JUST NOW...

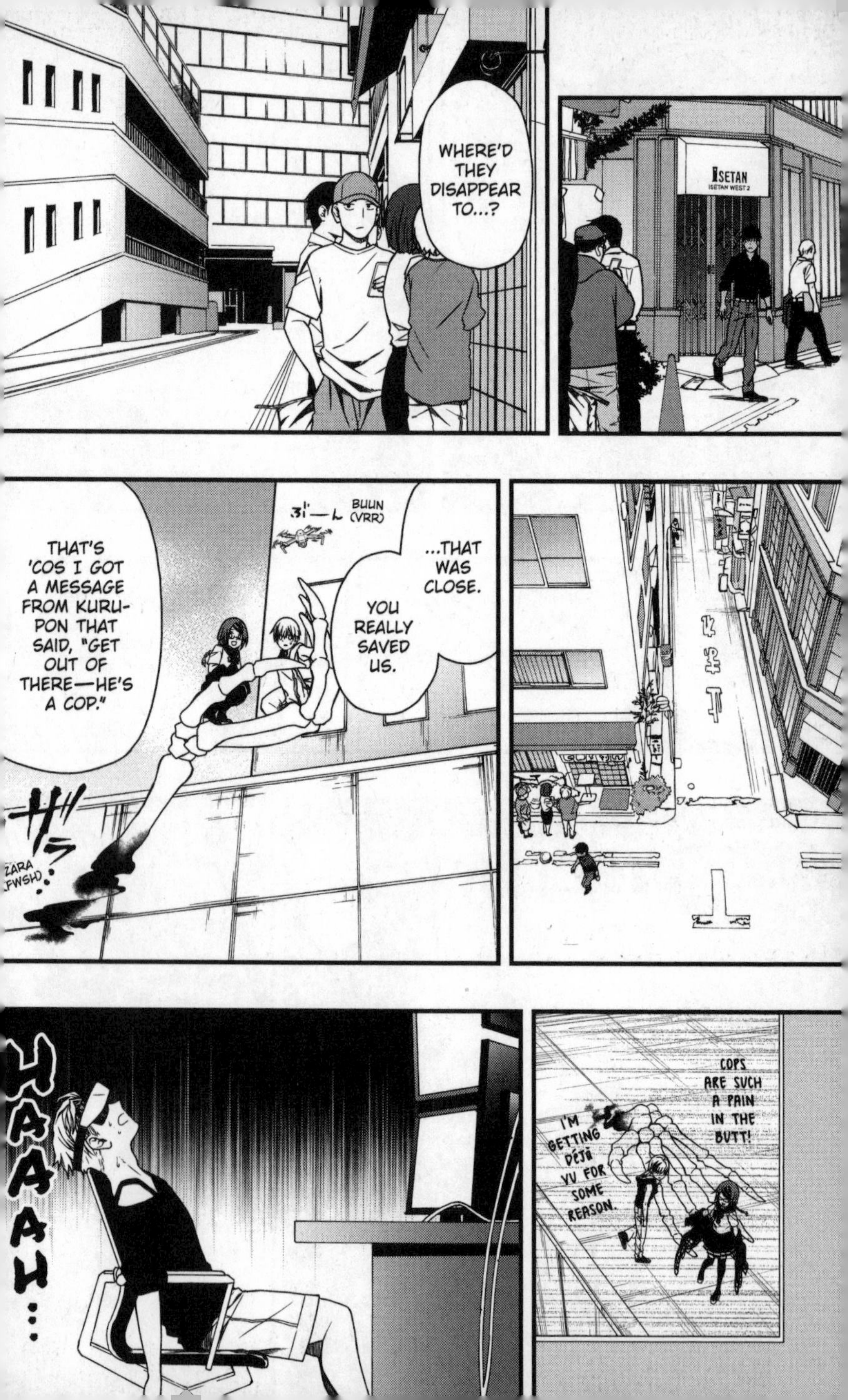
ISETAN
ISETAN WEST 2
WHERE'D THEY DISAPPEAR TO...?
BUUN (VRR)
...THAT WAS CLOSE.
YOU REALLY SAVED US.
THAT'S 'COS I GOT A MESSAGE FROM KURU-PON THAT SAID, "GET OUT OF THERE—HE'S A COP."
ZARA (FWSH)
COPS ARE SUCH A PAIN IN THE BUTT!
I'M GETTING DÉJÀ VU FOR SOME REASON.
HAAAAH...

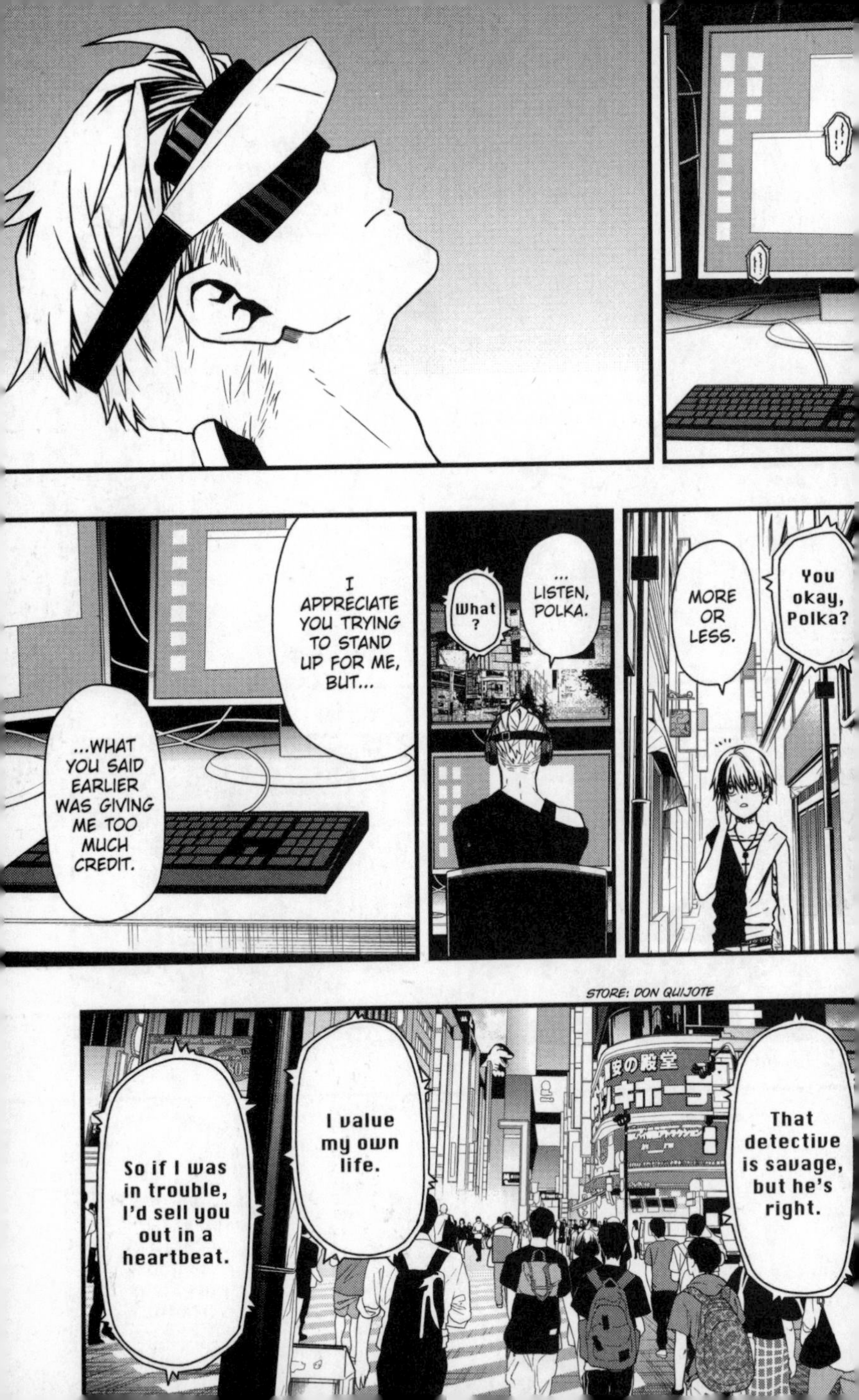
You okay, Polka?
MORE OR LESS.
...LISTEN, POLKA.
What?
I APPRECIATE YOU TRYING TO STAND UP FOR ME, BUT...
...WHAT YOU SAID EARLIER WAS GIVING ME TOO MUCH CREDIT.
STORE: DON QUIJOTE
That detective is savage, but he's right.
I value my own life.
So if I was in trouble, I'd sell you out in a heartbeat.

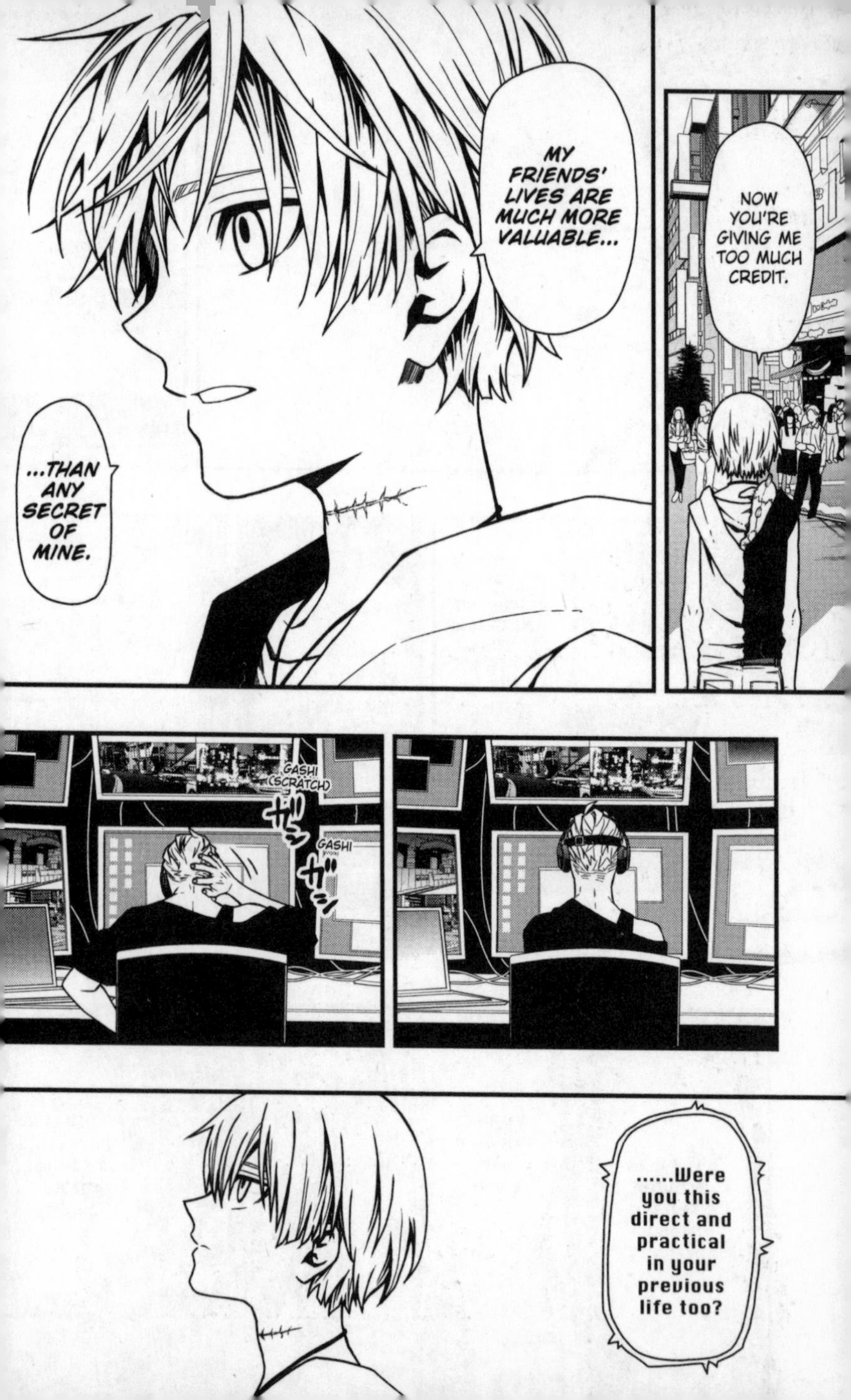
NOW YOU'RE GIVING ME TOO MUCH CREDIT.
MY FRIENDS' LIVES ARE MUCH MORE VALUABLE...
...THAN ANY SECRET OF MINE.
GASHI (SCRATCH)
GASHI
......Were you this direct and practical in your previous life too?

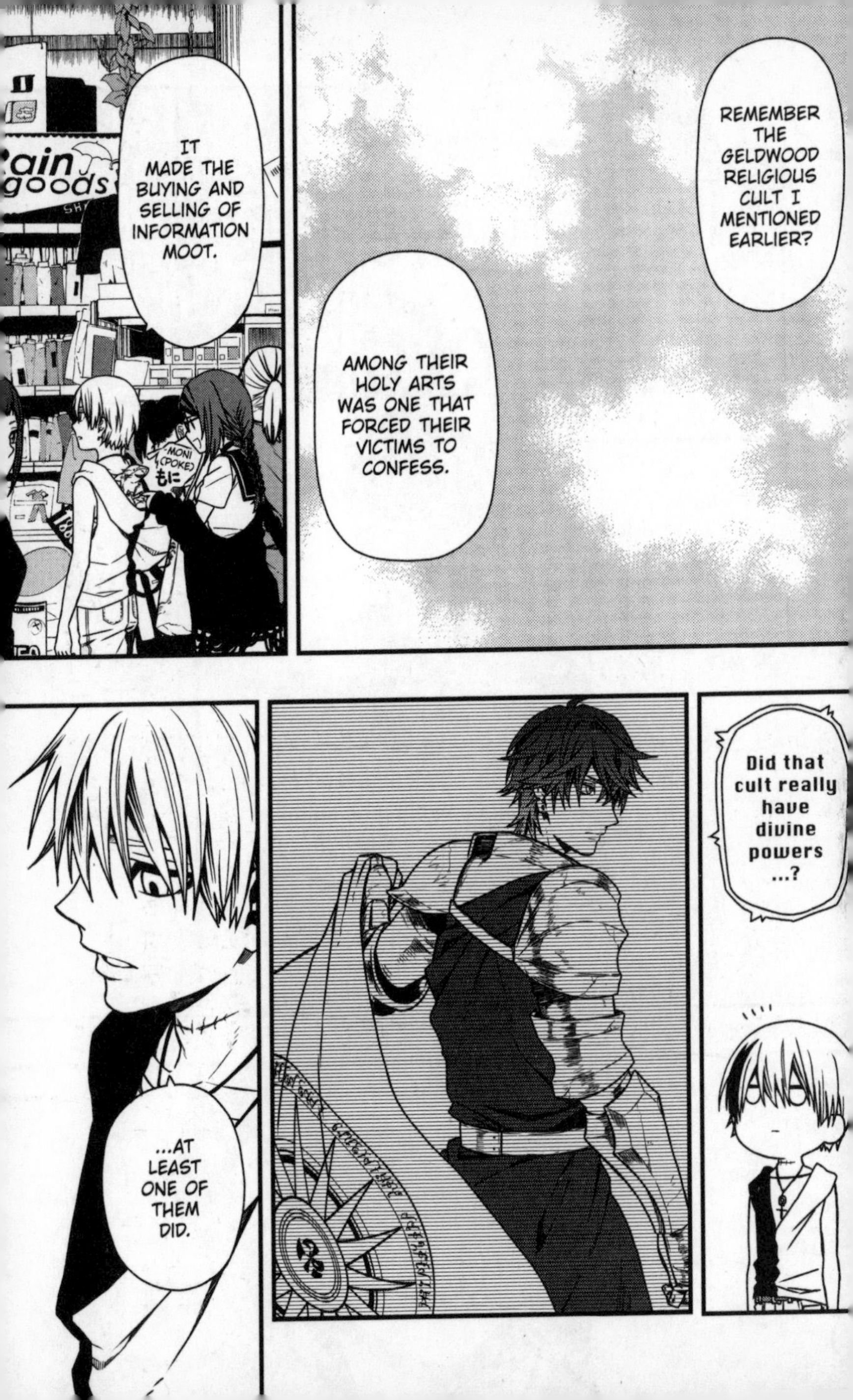
REMEMBER THE GELDWOOD RELIGIOUS CULT I MENTIONED EARLIER?
AMONG THEIR HOLY ARTS WAS ONE THAT FORCED THEIR VICTIMS TO CONFESS.
IT MADE THE BUYING AND SELLING OF INFORMATION MOOT.
rain goods
MONI (POKE) もに
Did that cult really have divine powers ...?
...AT LEAST ONE OF THEM DID.

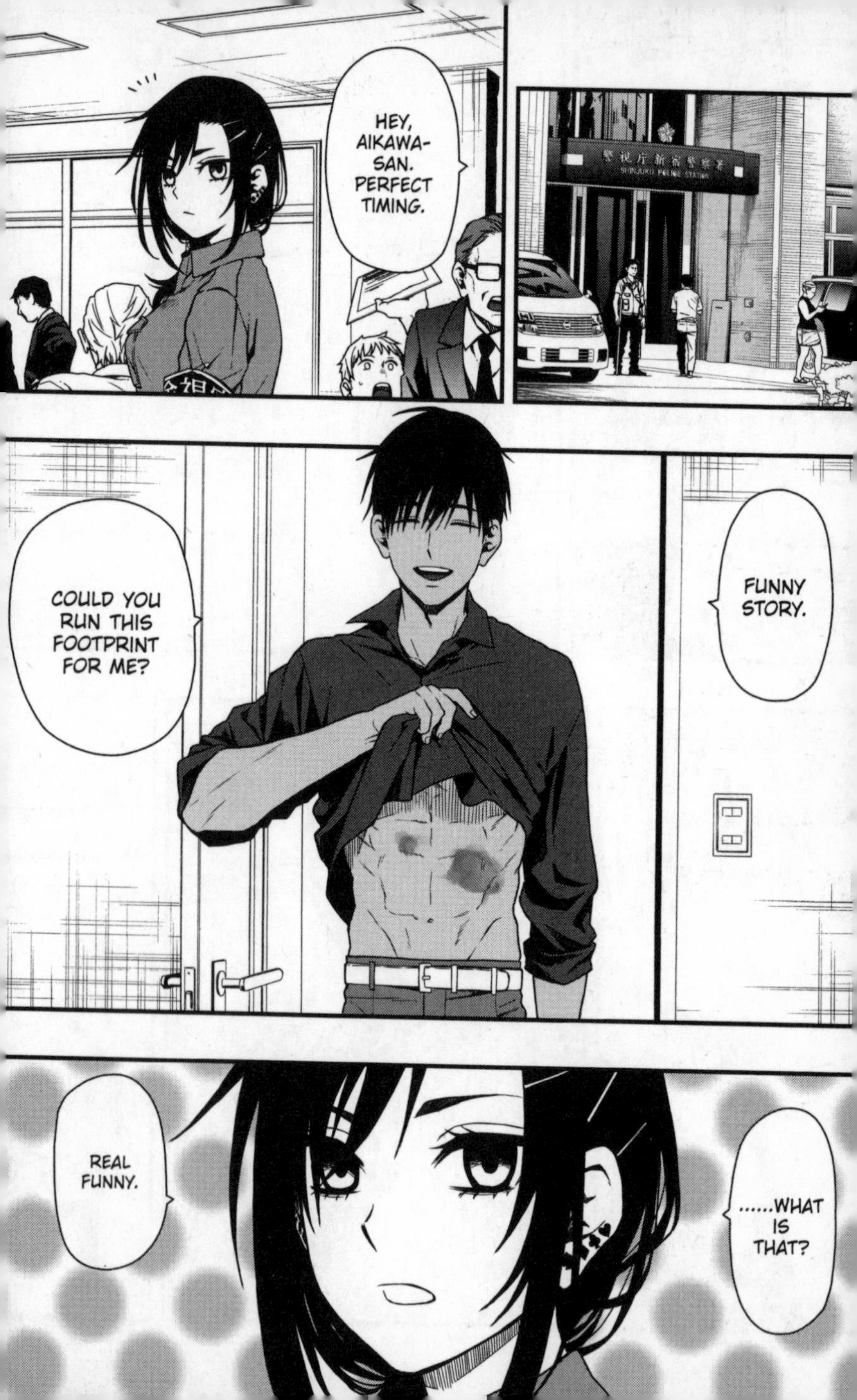
HEY, AIKAWA-SAN. PERFECT TIMING.
FUNNY STORY.
COULD YOU RUN THIS FOOTPRINT FOR ME?
......WHAT IS THAT?
REAL FUNNY.

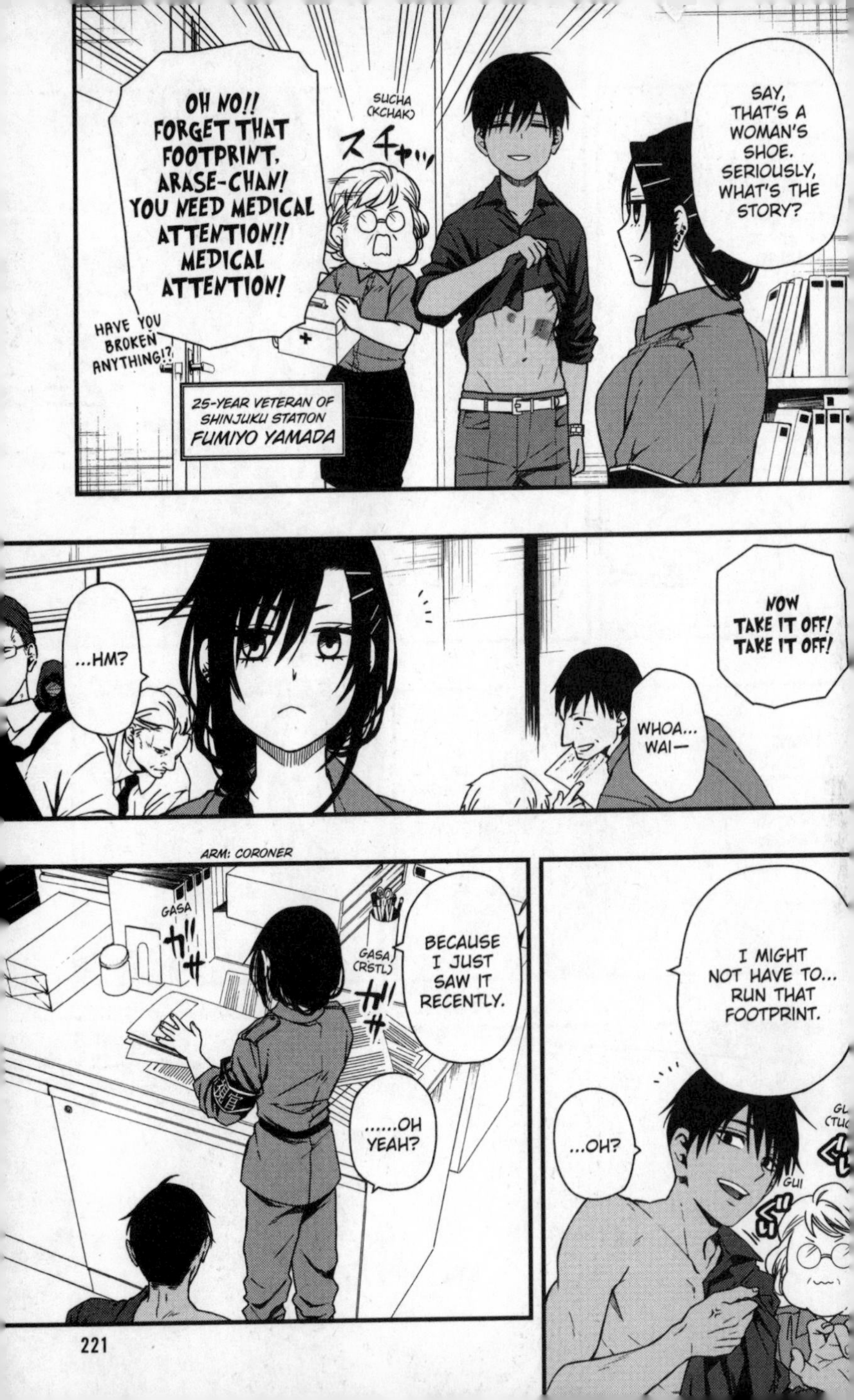
SAY, THAT'S A WOMAN'S SHOE. SERIOUSLY, WHAT'S THE STORY?
SUCHA (KCHAK)
スチャッ
OH NO!! FORGET THAT FOOTPRINT, ARASE-CHAN! YOU NEED MEDICAL ATTENTION!! MEDICAL ATTENTION!
HAVE YOU BROKEN ANYTHING!?
25-YEAR VETERAN OF SHINJUKU STATION FUMIYO YAMADA
NOW TAKE IT OFF! TAKE IT OFF!
WHOA... WAI—
...HM?
ARM: CORONER
I MIGHT NOT HAVE TO... RUN THAT FOOTPRINT.
...OH?
GUI
BECAUSE I JUST SAW IT RECENTLY.
GASA (RSTL)
GASA
......OH YEAH?

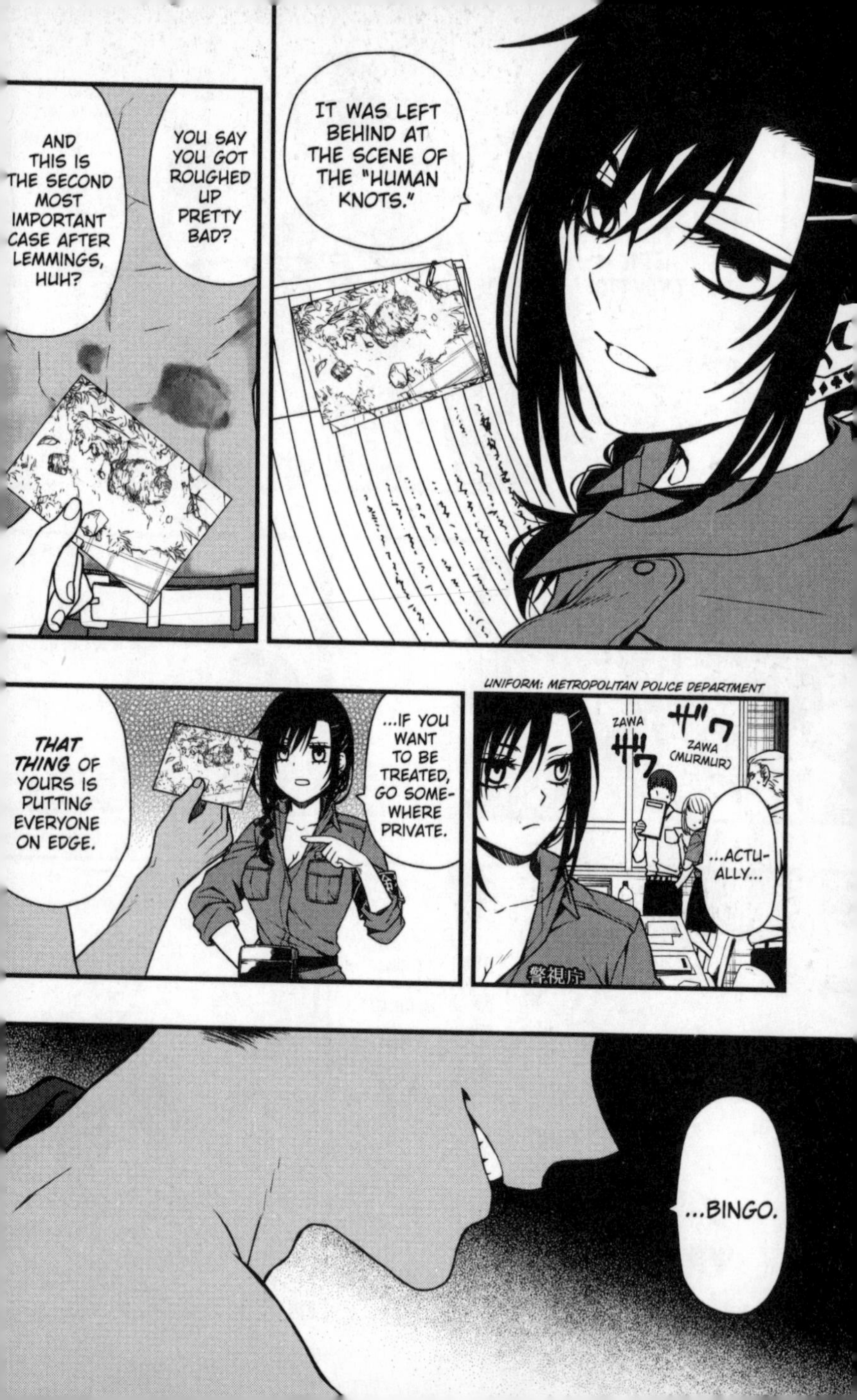
IT WAS LEFT BEHIND AT THE SCENE OF THE "HUMAN KNOTS."
YOU SAY YOU GOT ROUGHED UP PRETTY BAD?
AND THIS IS THE SECOND MOST IMPORTANT CASE AFTER LEMMINGS, HUH?
UNIFORM: METROPOLITAN POLICE DEPARTMENT
ザワ
ZAWA
ザワ
ZAWA (MURMUR)
...ACTUALLY...
警視庁
...IF YOU WANT TO BE TREATED, GO SOMEWHERE PRIVATE.
THAT THING OF YOURS IS PUTTING EVERYONE ON EDGE.
...BINGO.

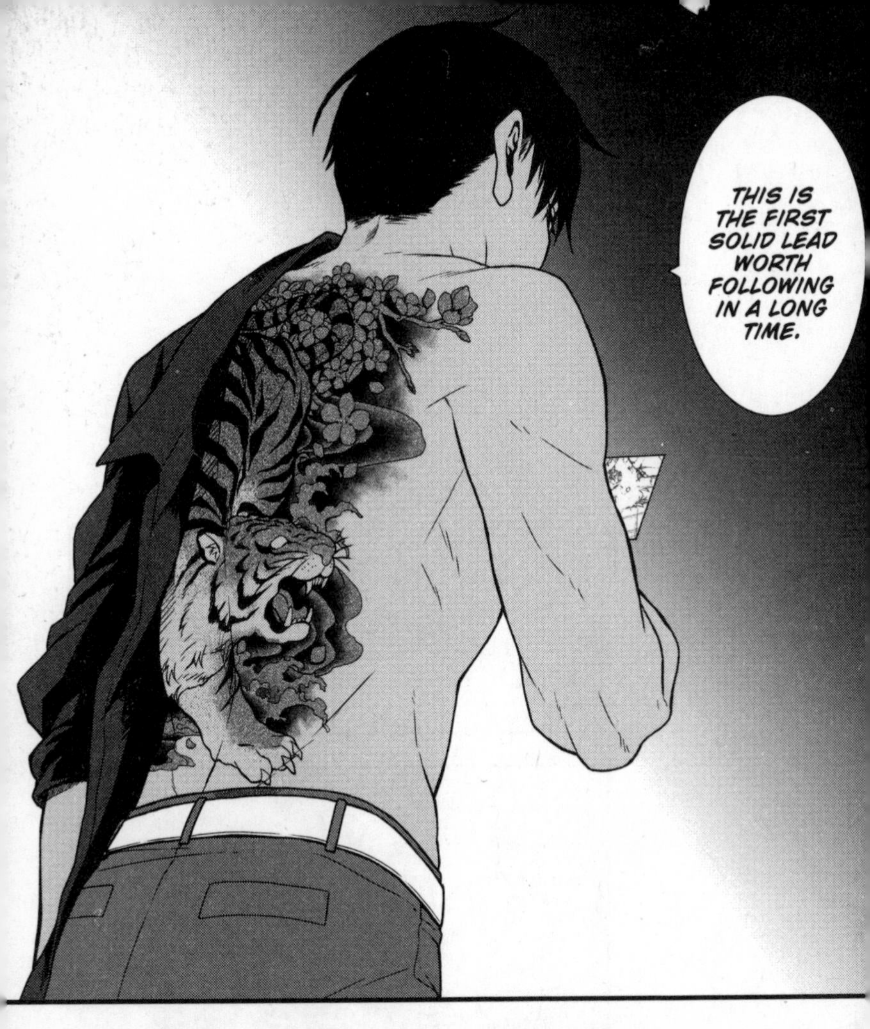
THIS IS THE FIRST SOLID LEAD WORTH FOLLOWING IN A LONG TIME.

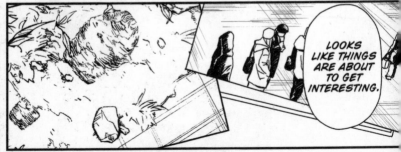

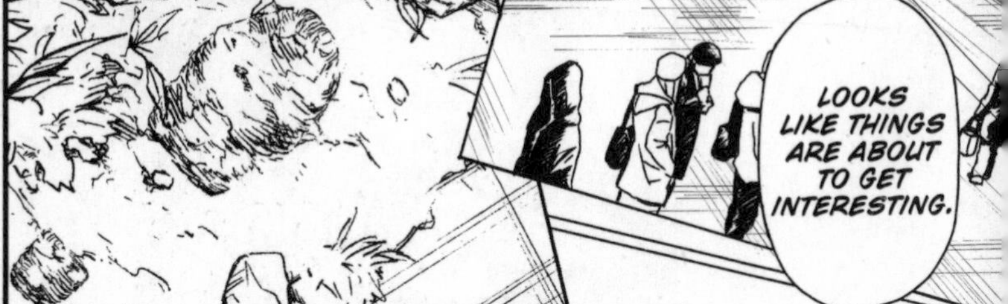
LOOKS LIKE THINGS ARE ABOUT TO GET INTERESTING.

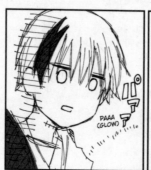

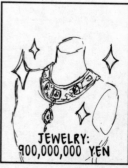

JEWELRY: 900,000,000 YEN
PAAA (GLOW)
WITH THAT MUCH MONEY, I COULD ERECT A WHOLE CASTLE MADE OF BONES!
WITH NINE HUNDRED MILLION, YOU COULD BUILD A NORMAL HOUSE.
COOL!

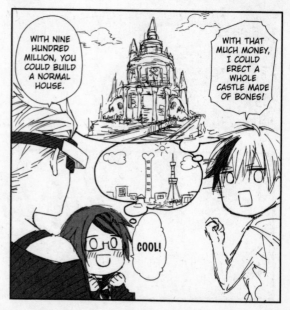

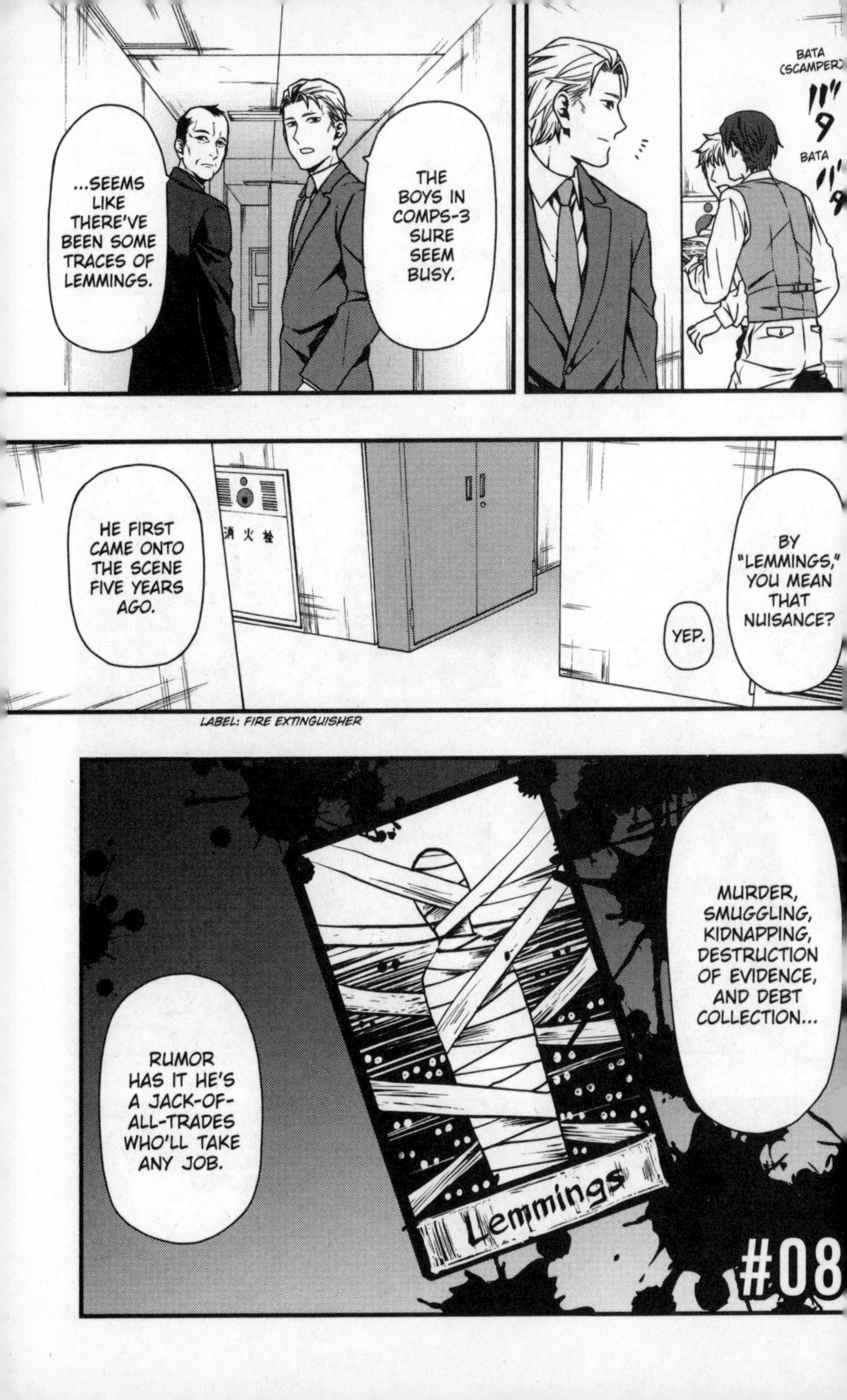
BATA (SCAMPER)
BATA
...
THE BOYS IN COMPS-3 SURE SEEM BUSY.
...SEEMS LIKE THERE'VE BEEN SOME TRACES OF LEMMINGS.
BY "LEMMINGS," YOU MEAN THAT NUISANCE?
YEP.
HE FIRST CAME ONTO THE SCENE FIVE YEARS AGO.
消火栓
LABEL: FIRE EXTINGUISHER
MURDER, SMUGGLING, KIDNAPPING, DESTRUCTION OF EVIDENCE, AND DEBT COLLECTION...
RUMOR HAS IT HE'S A JACK-OF-ALL-TRADES WHO'LL TAKE ANY JOB.
Lemmings
#08

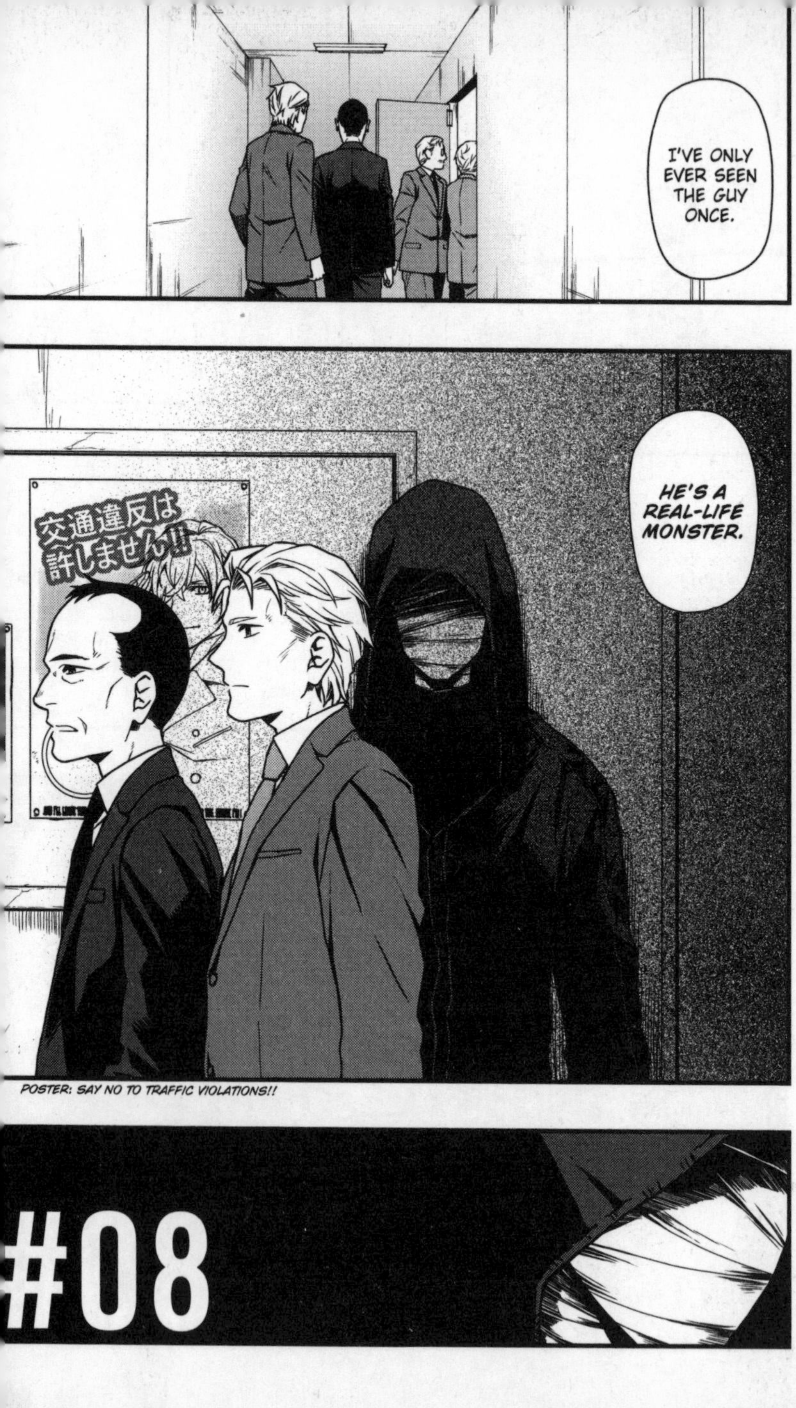
I'VE ONLY EVER SEEN THE GUY ONCE.
HE'S A REAL-LIFE MONSTER.
交通違反は許しません!!
POSTER: SAY NO TO TRAFFIC VIOLATIONS!!
#08

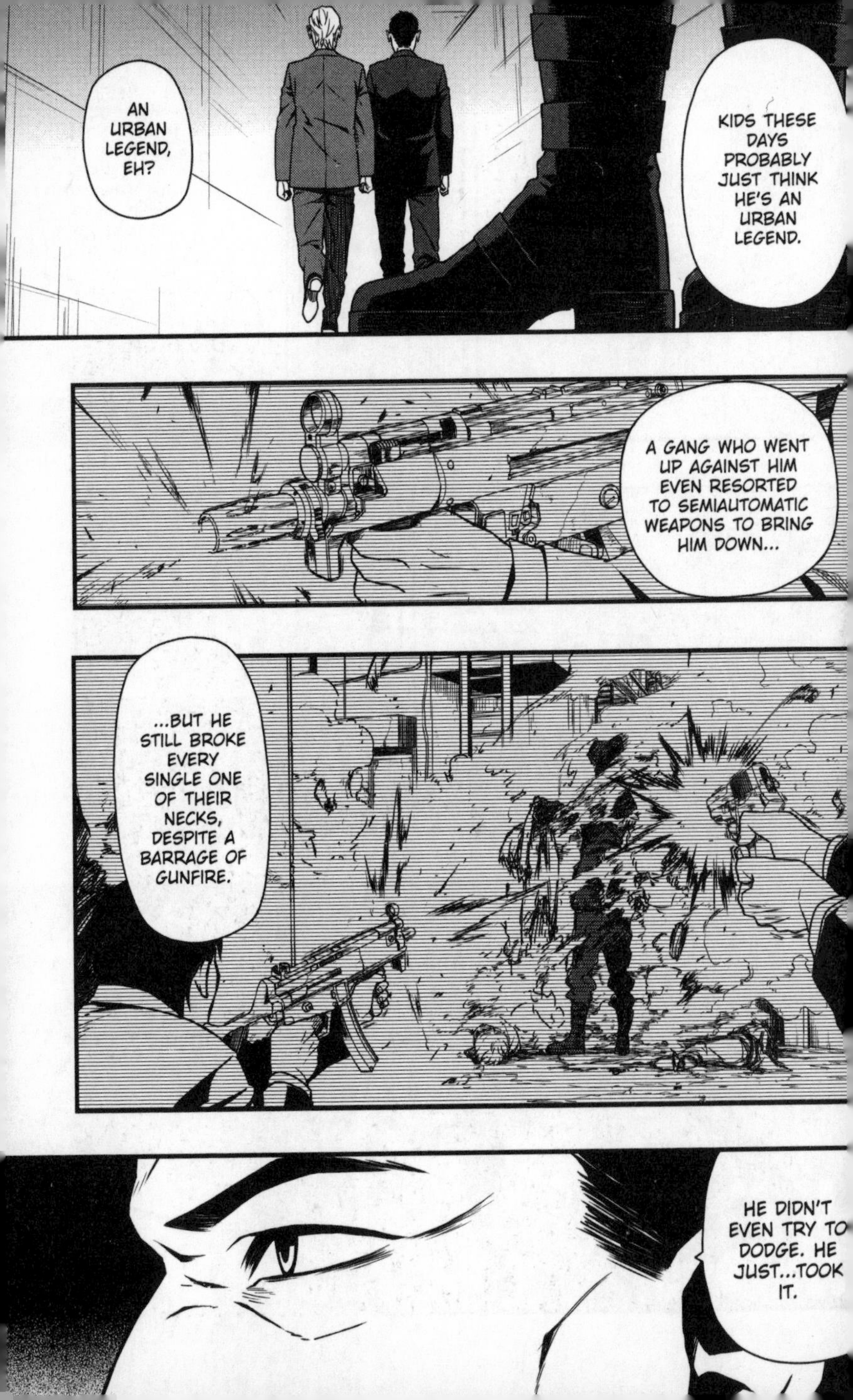
KIDS THESE DAYS PROBABLY JUST THINK HE'S AN URBAN LEGEND.
AN URBAN LEGEND, EH?
A GANG WHO WENT UP AGAINST HIM EVEN RESORTED TO SEMIAUTOMATIC WEAPONS TO BRING HIM DOWN...
...BUT HE STILL BROKE EVERY SINGLE ONE OF THEIR NECKS, DESPITE A BARRAGE OF GUNFIRE.
HE DIDN'T EVEN TRY TO DODGE. HE JUST...TOOK IT.

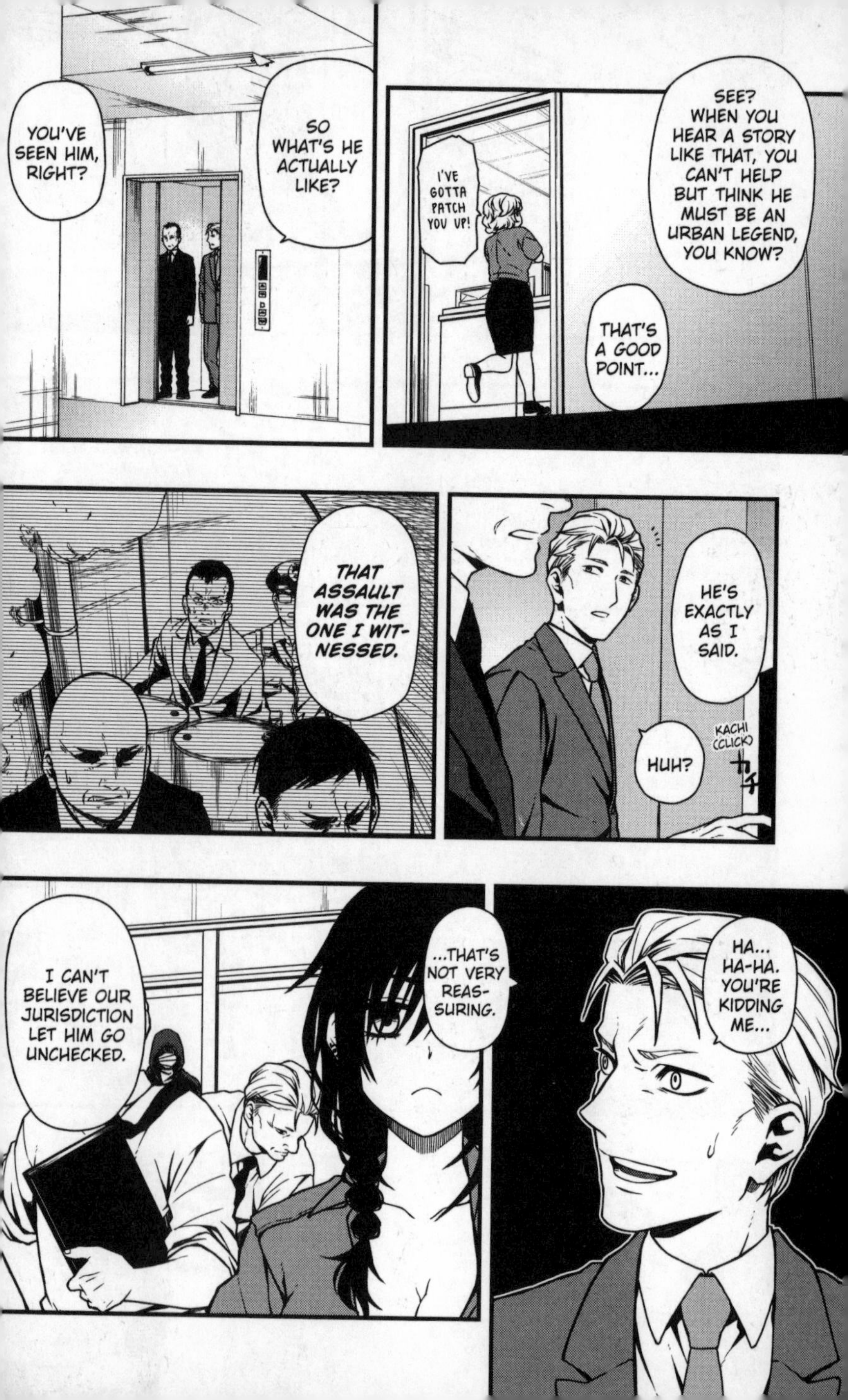
SEE? WHEN YOU HEAR A STORY LIKE THAT, YOU CAN'T HELP BUT THINK HE MUST BE AN URBAN LEGEND, YOU KNOW?
I'VE GOTTA PATCH YOU UP!
THAT'S A GOOD POINT...
SO WHAT'S HE ACTUALLY LIKE?
YOU'VE SEEN HIM, RIGHT?
HE'S EXACTLY AS I SAID.
KACHI (CLICK)
HUH?
THAT ASSAULT WAS THE ONE I WIT-NESSED.
HA... HA-HA. YOU'RE KIDDING ME...
...THAT'S NOT VERY REAS-SURING.
I CAN'T BELIEVE OUR JURISDICTION LET HIM GO UNCHECKED.

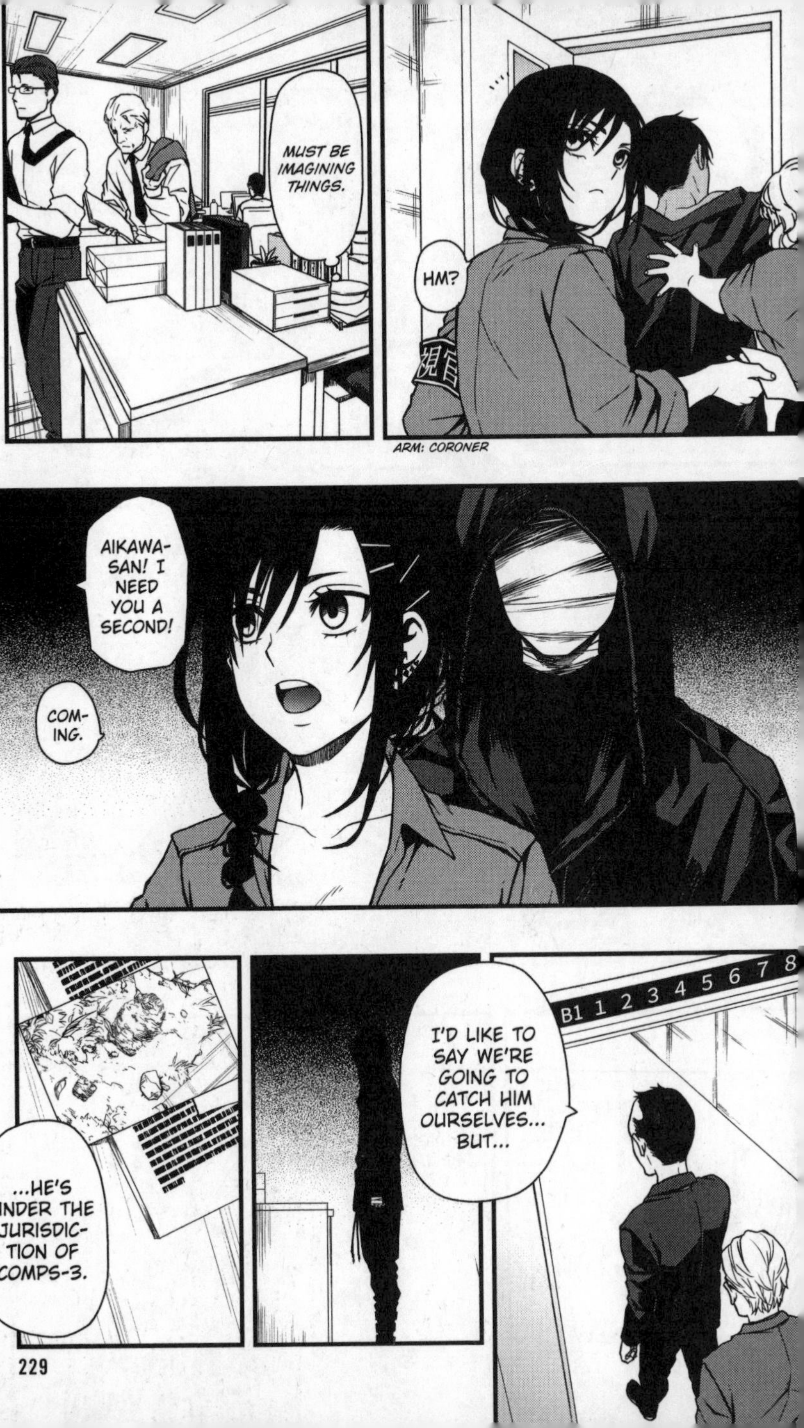
HM?
MUST BE IMAGINING THINGS.
ARM: CORONER
AIKAWA-SAN! I NEED YOU A SECOND!
COMING.
B1 1 2 3 4 5 6 7 8
I'D LIKE TO SAY WE'RE GOING TO CATCH HIM OURSELVES... BUT...
...HE'S UNDER THE JURISDICTION OF COMPS-3.

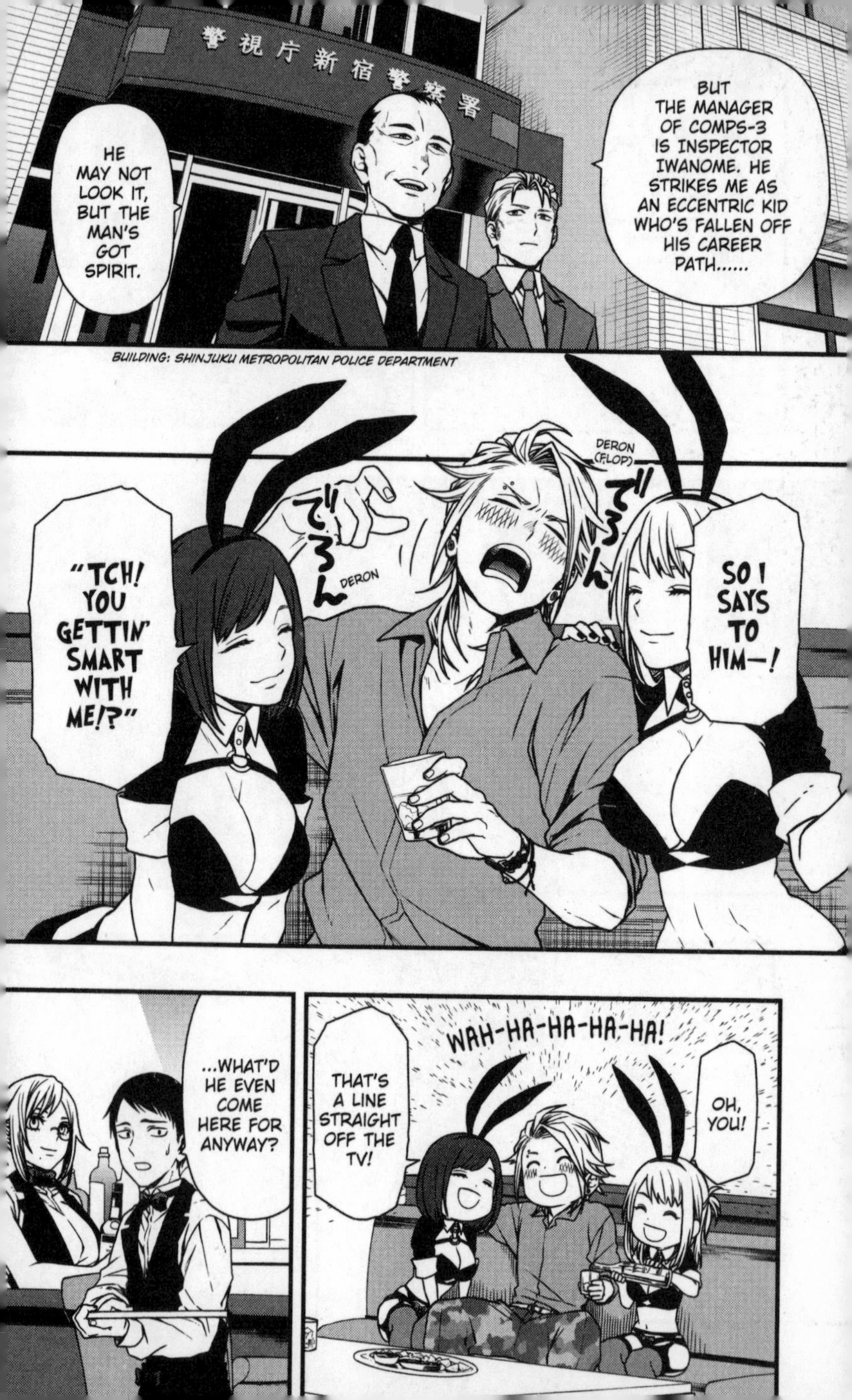
警視庁新宿警察署
BUT THE MANAGER OF COMPS-3 IS INSPECTOR IWANOME. HE STRIKES ME AS AN ECCENTRIC KID WHO'S FALLEN OFF HIS CAREER PATH......
HE MAY NOT LOOK IT, BUT THE MAN'S GOT SPIRIT.
BUILDING: SHINJUKU METROPOLITAN POLICE DEPARTMENT
でろん
DERON (FLOP)
SO I SAYS TO HIM—!
でろん
DERON
"TCH! YOU GETTIN' SMART WITH ME!?"
OH, YOU!
WAH-HA-HA-HA-HA!
THAT'S A LINE STRAIGHT OFF THE TV!
...WHAT'D HE EVEN COME HERE FOR ANYWAY?

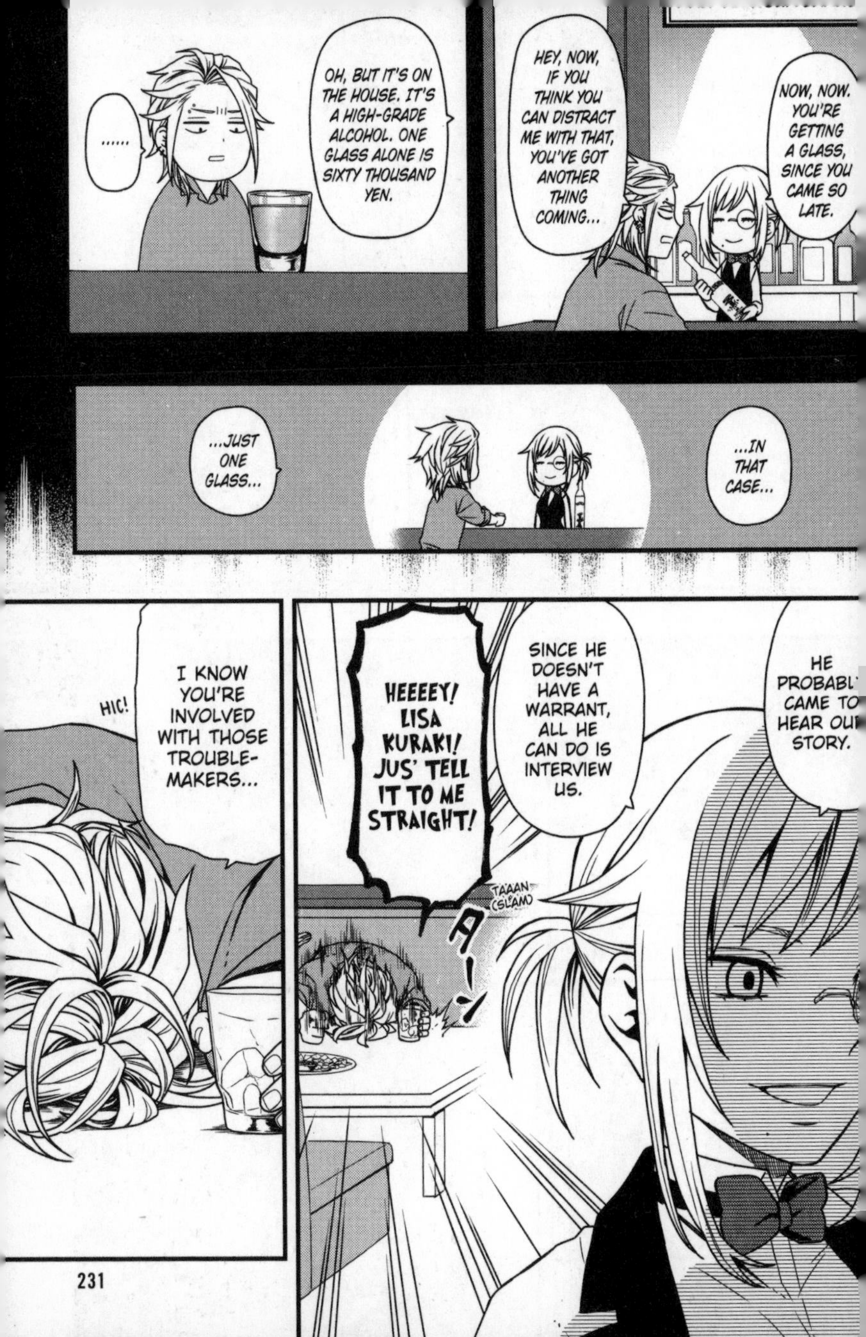
NOW, NOW. YOU'RE GETTING A GLASS, SINCE YOU CAME SO LATE.
HEY, NOW, IF YOU THINK YOU CAN DISTRACT ME WITH THAT, YOU'VE GOT ANOTHER THING COMING...
OH, BUT IT'S ON THE HOUSE. IT'S A HIGH-GRADE ALCOHOL. ONE GLASS ALONE IS SIXTY THOUSAND YEN.
......
...IN THAT CASE...
...JUST ONE GLASS...
HE PROBABL CAME TO HEAR OU STORY.
SINCE HE DOESN'T HAVE A WARRANT, ALL HE CAN DO IS INTERVIEW US.
HEEEEY! LISA KURAKI! JUS' TELL IT TO ME STRAIGHT!
TAAAN (SLAM)
I KNOW YOU'RE INVOLVED WITH THOSE TROUBLE-MAKERS...
HIC!

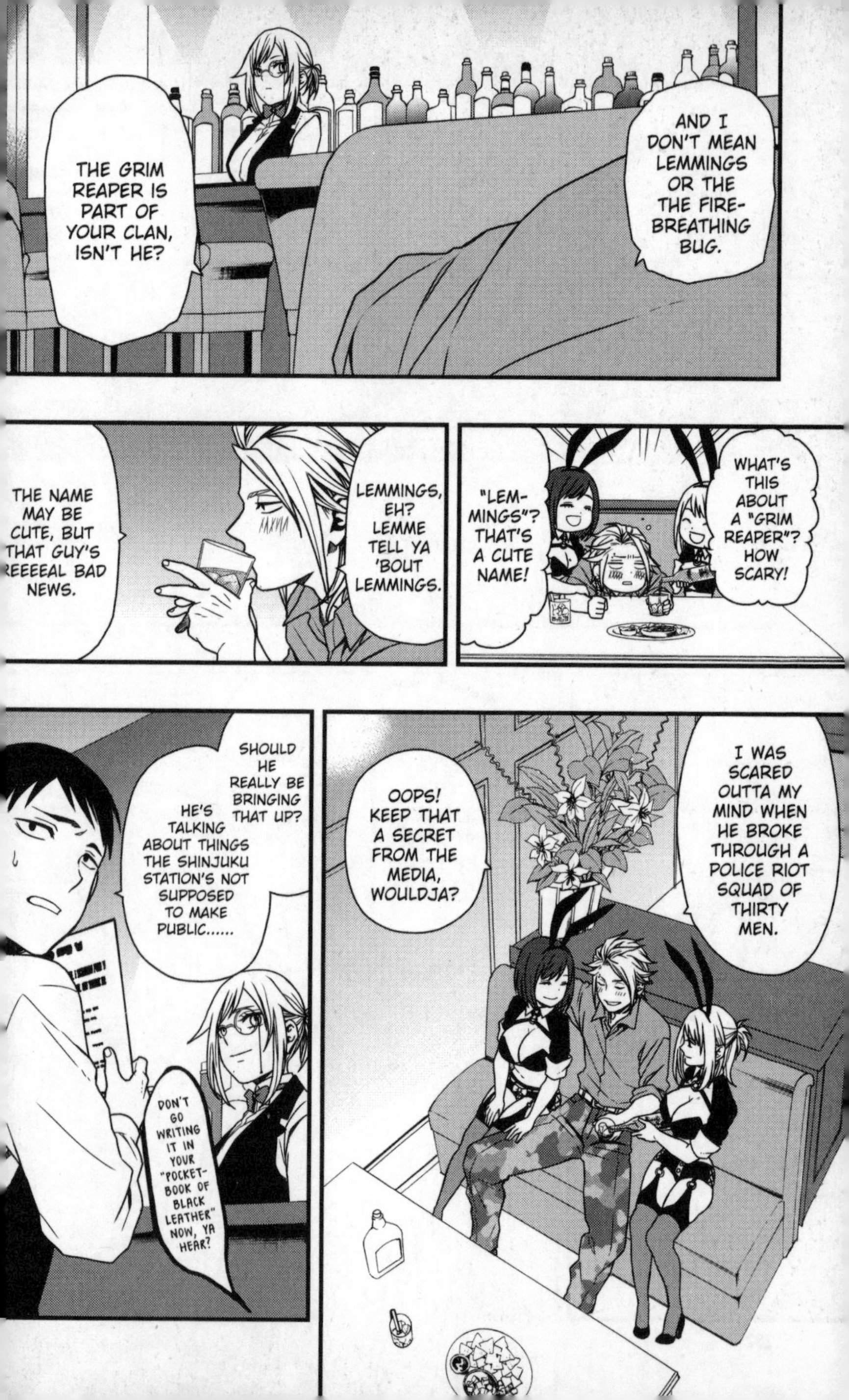

AND I DON'T MEAN LEMMINGS OR THE THE FIRE-BREATHING BUG.
THE GRIM REAPER IS PART OF YOUR CLAN, ISN'T HE?
WHAT'S THIS ABOUT A "GRIM REAPER"? HOW SCARY!
"LEM-MINGS"? THAT'S A CUTE NAME!
LEMMINGS, EH? LEMME TELL YA 'BOUT LEMMINGS.
THE NAME MAY BE CUTE, BUT THAT GUY'S REEEEAL BAD NEWS.
I WAS SCARED OUTTA MY MIND WHEN HE BROKE THROUGH A POLICE RIOT SQUAD OF THIRTY MEN.
OOPS! KEEP THAT A SECRET FROM THE MEDIA, WOULDJA?
SHOULD HE REALLY BE BRINGING THAT UP?
HE'S TALKING ABOUT THINGS THE SHINJUKU STATION'S NOT SUPPOSED TO MAKE PUBLIC......
DON'T GO WRITING IT IN YOUR "POCKET-BOOK OF BLACK LEATHER" NOW, YA HEAR?

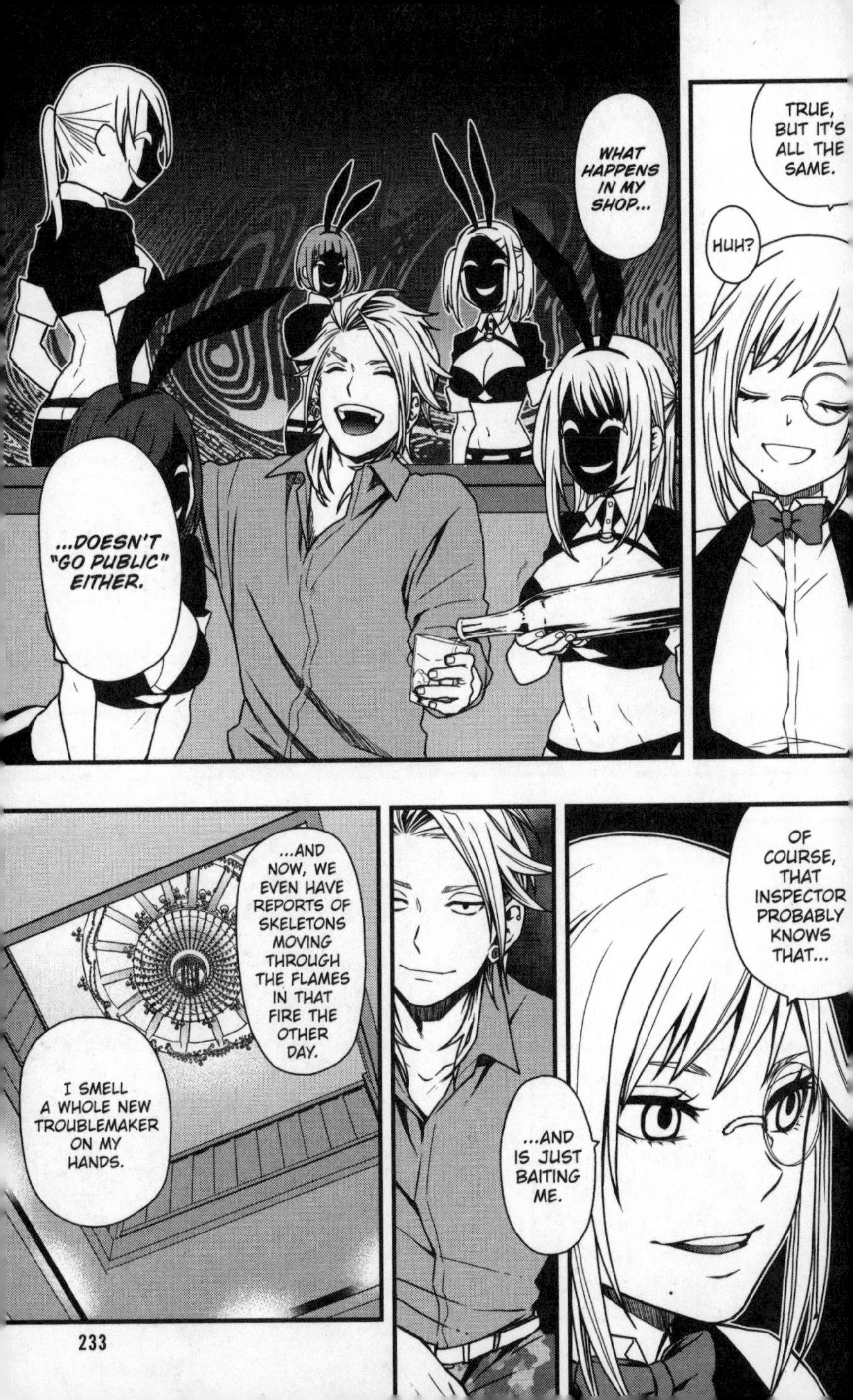
WHAT HAPPENS IN MY SHOP...
...DOESN'T "GO PUBLIC" EITHER.
HUH?
TRUE, BUT IT'S ALL THE SAME.
OF COURSE, THAT INSPECTOR PROBABLY KNOWS THAT...
...AND IS JUST BAITING ME.
...AND NOW, WE EVEN HAVE REPORTS OF SKELETONS MOVING THROUGH THE FLAMES IN THAT FIRE THE OTHER DAY.
I SMELL A WHOLE NEW TROUBLEMAKER ON MY HANDS.

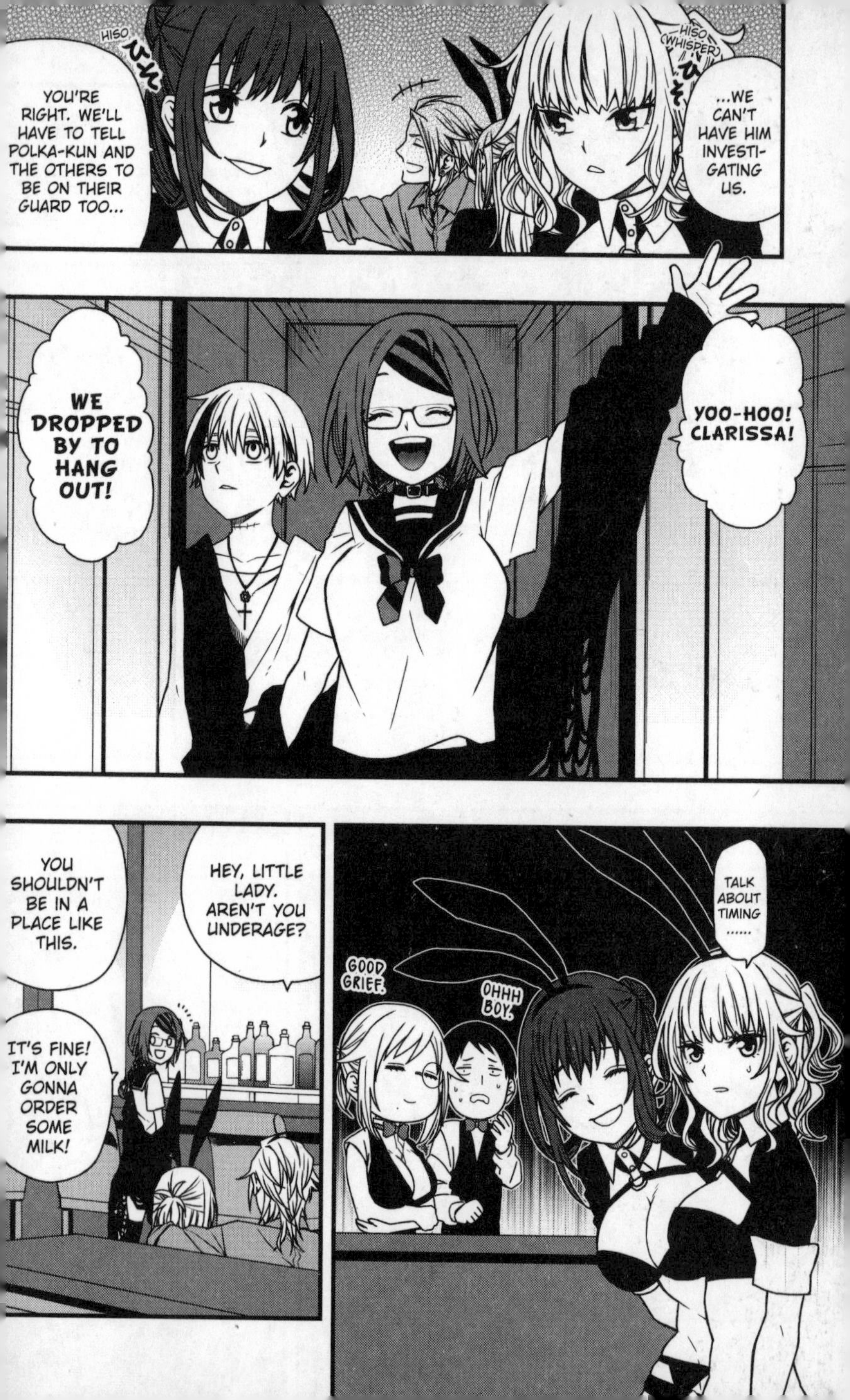
HISO (WHISPER)
...WE CAN'T HAVE HIM INVESTIGATING US.
HISO
YOU'RE RIGHT. WE'LL HAVE TO TELL POLKA-KUN AND THE OTHERS TO BE ON THEIR GUARD TOO...
YOO-HOO! CLARISSA!
WE DROPPED BY TO HANG OUT!
TALK ABOUT TIMING ......
OHHH BOY.
GOOD GRIEF.
HEY, LITTLE LADY. AREN'T YOU UNDERAGE?
YOU SHOULDN'T BE IN A PLACE LIKE THIS.
IT'S FINE! I'M ONLY GONNA ORDER SOME MILK!

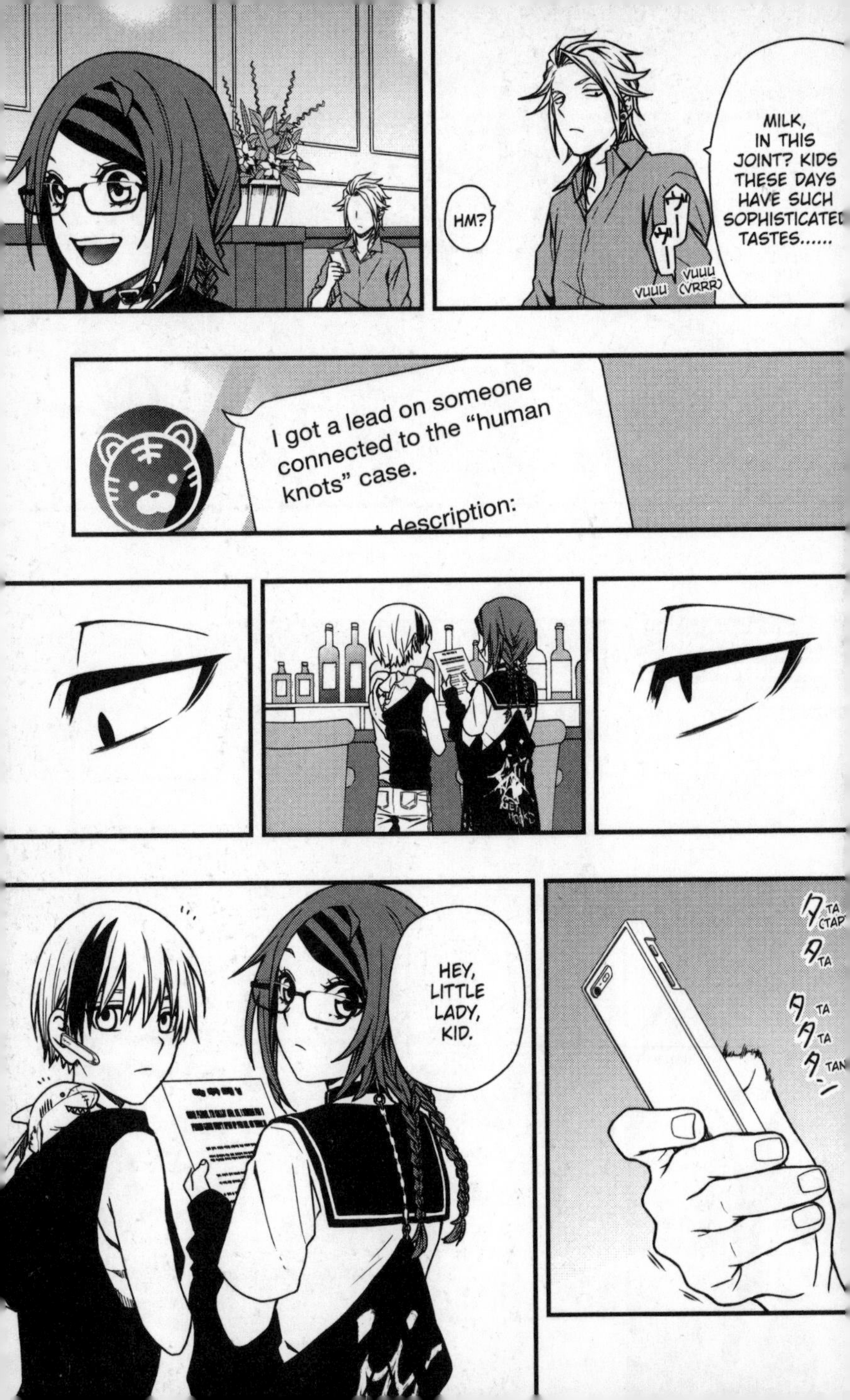
MILK, IN THIS JOINT? KIDS THESE DAYS HAVE SUCH SOPHISTICATED TASTES......
HM?
VUUU VUUU (VRRR)
I got a lead on someone connected to the "human knots" case.
description:
TA (TAP) TA TA TA TAN
HEY, LITTLE LADY, KID.

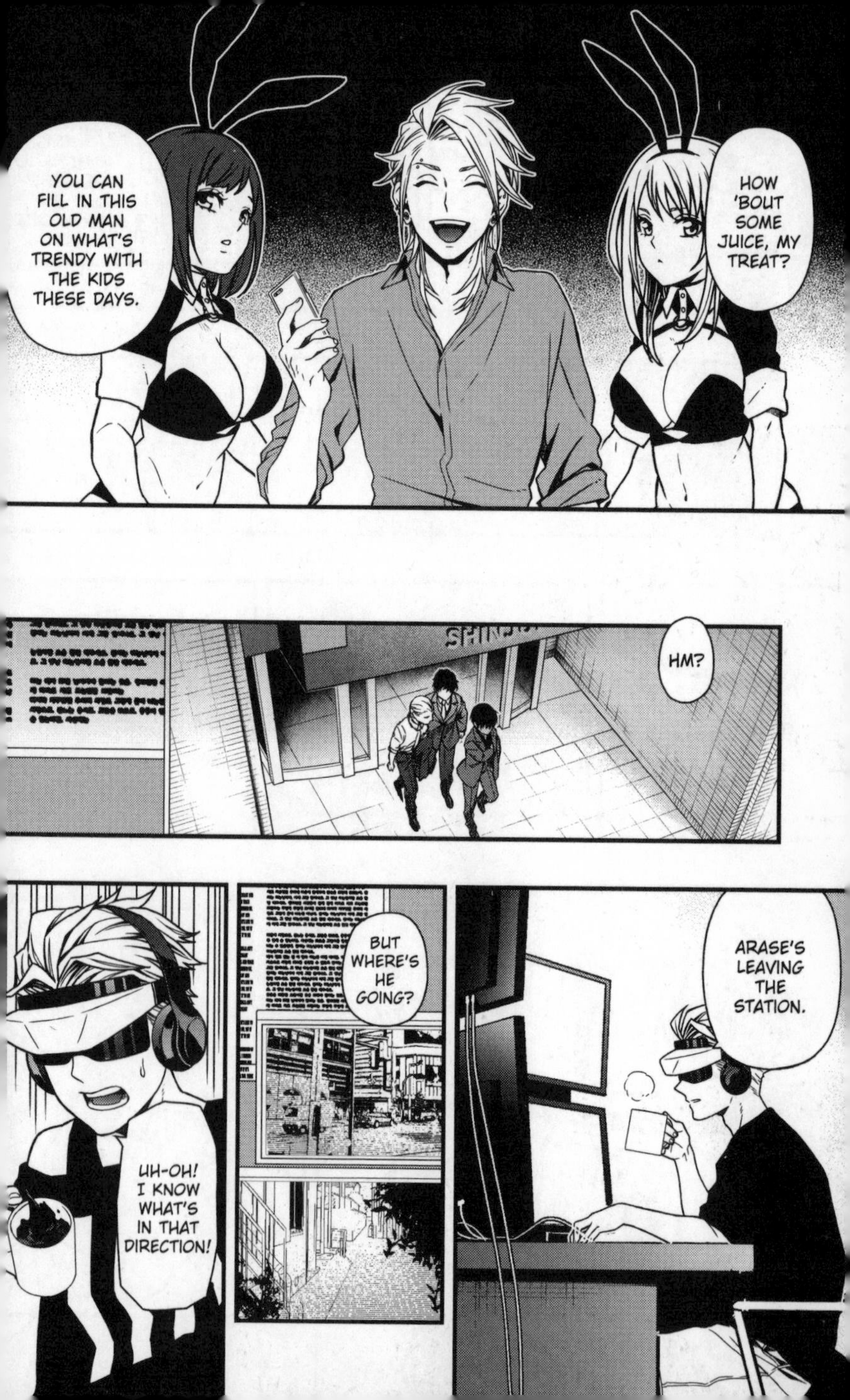
HOW 'BOUT SOME JUICE, MY TREAT?
YOU CAN FILL IN THIS OLD MAN ON WHAT'S TRENDY WITH THE KIDS THESE DAYS.
HM?
ARASE'S LEAVING THE STATION.
BUT WHERE'S HE GOING?
UH-OH! I KNOW WHAT'S IN THAT DIRECTION!

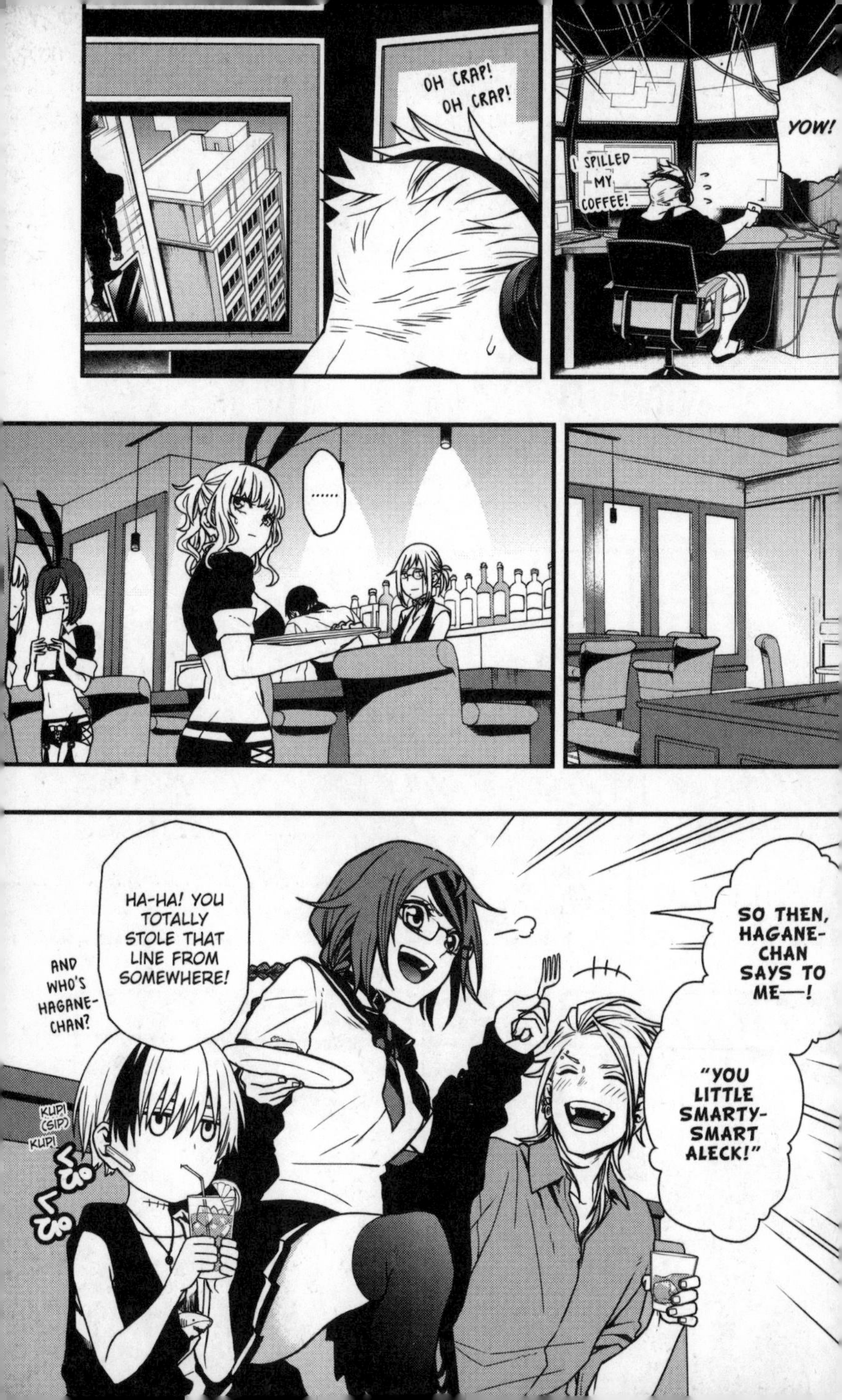
YOW!
I SPILLED MY COFFEE!
OH CRAP! OH CRAP!
......
SO THEN, HAGANE-CHAN SAYS TO ME—!
"YOU LITTLE SMARTY-SMART ALECK!"
HA-HA! YOU TOTALLY STOLE THAT LINE FROM SOMEWHERE!
AND WHO'S HAGANE-CHAN?
KUP! (SIP) KUP!

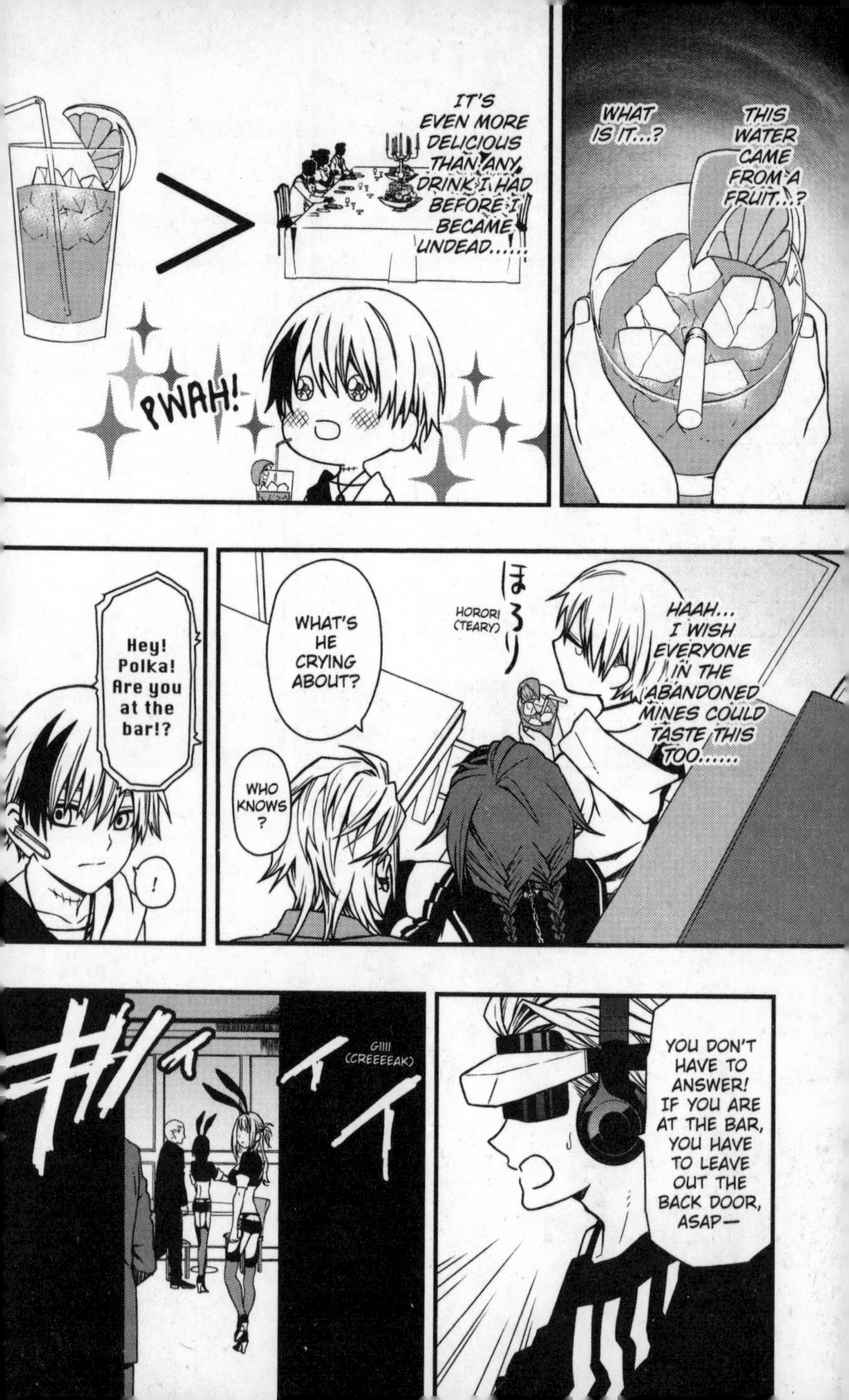
THIS WATER CAME FROM A FRUIT...?
WHAT IS IT...?
IT'S EVEN MORE DELICIOUS THAN ANY DRINK I HAD BEFORE I BECAME UNDEAD......
PWAH!
HAAH... I WISH EVERYONE IN THE ABANDONED MINES COULD TASTE THIS TOO......
ほろり
HORORI (TEARY)
WHAT'S HE CRYING ABOUT?
WHO KNOWS?
Hey! Polka! Are you at the bar!?
!
YOU DON'T HAVE TO ANSWER! IF YOU ARE AT THE BAR, YOU HAVE TO LEAVE OUT THE BACK DOOR, ASAP—
GIIII (CREEEEAK)

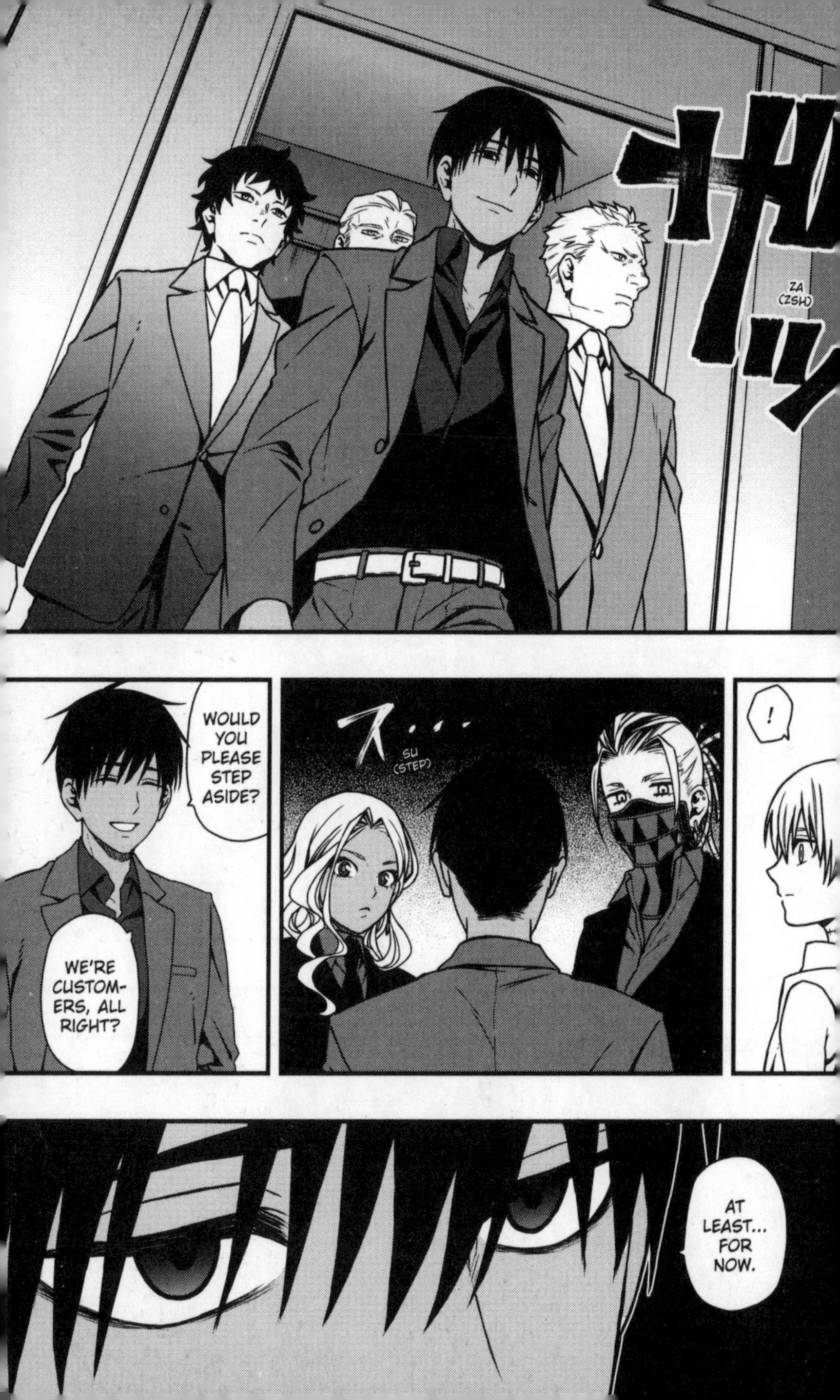
ZA (ZSH)
!
SU (STEP)
WOULD YOU PLEASE STEP ASIDE?
WE'RE CUSTOM-ERS, ALL RIGHT?
AT LEAST... FOR NOW.

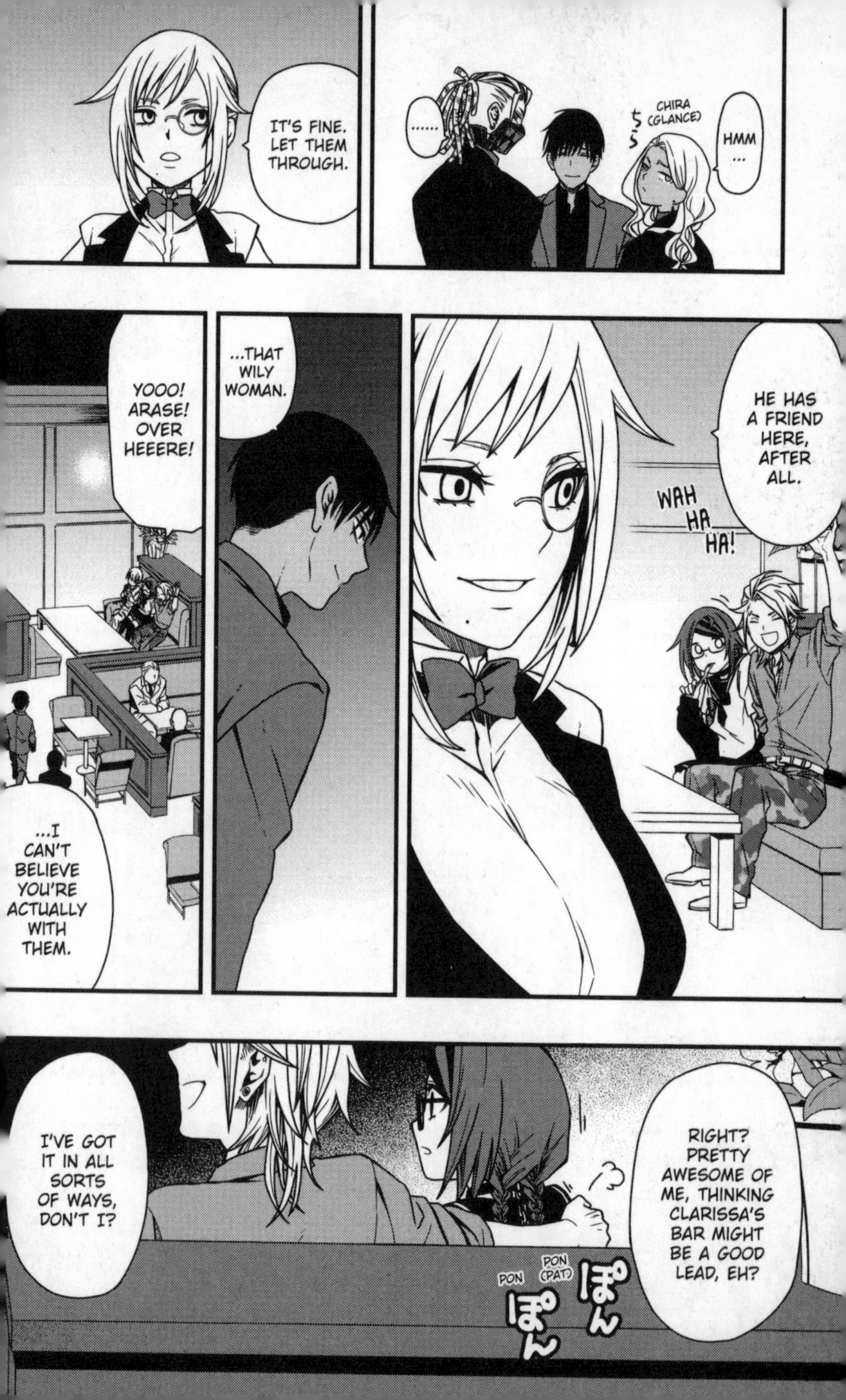
HMM...
CHIRA (GLANCE)
......
IT'S FINE. LET THEM THROUGH.
HE HAS A FRIEND HERE, AFTER ALL.
WAH HA HA!
...THAT WILY WOMAN.
YOOO! ARASE! OVER HEEERE!
...I CAN'T BELIEVE YOU'RE ACTUALLY WITH THEM.
RIGHT? PRETTY AWESOME OF ME, THINKING CLARISSA'S BAR MIGHT BE A GOOD LEAD, EH?
PON (PAT)
PON
ぽん
ぽん
I'VE GOT IT IN ALL SORTS OF WAYS, DON'T I?

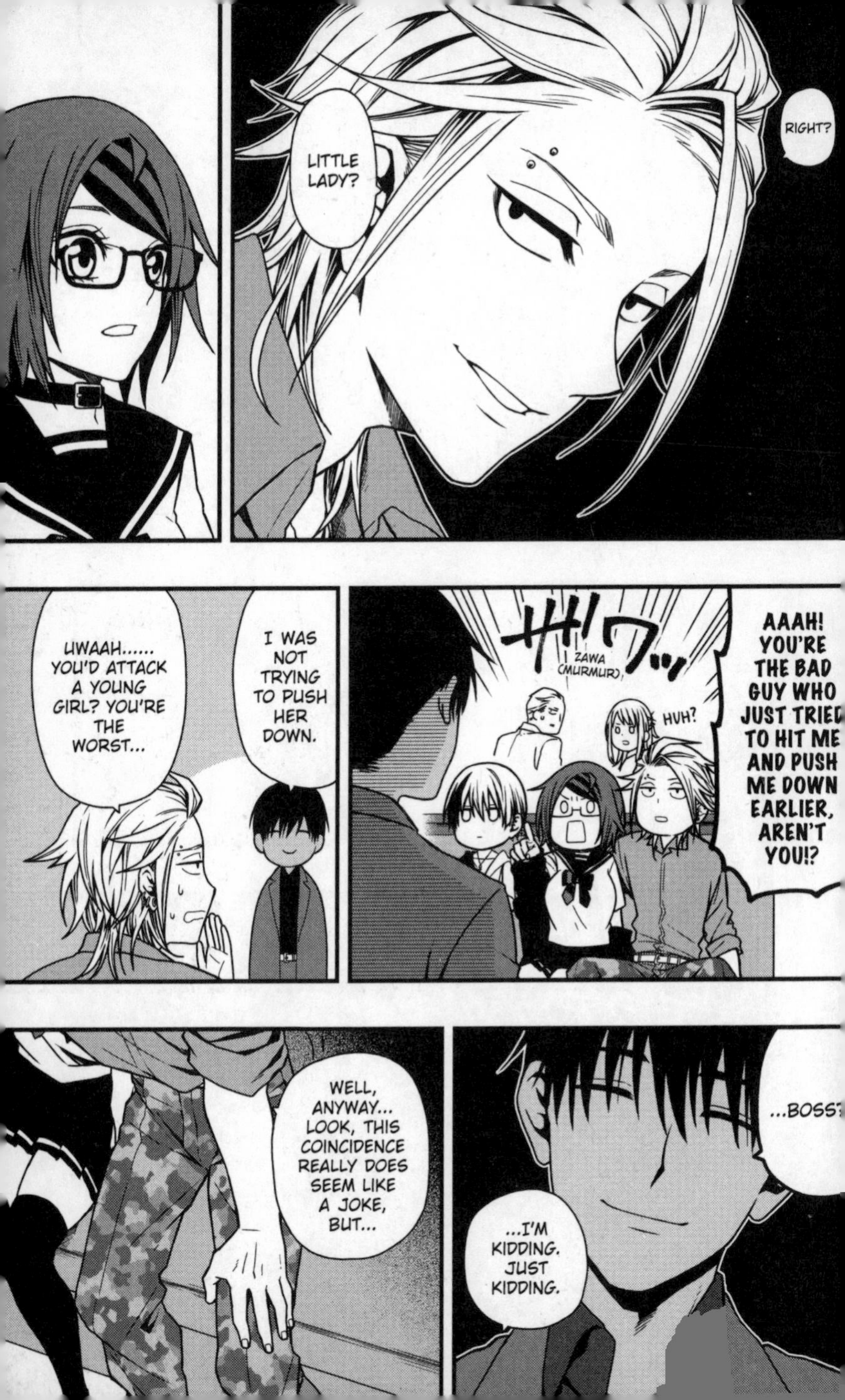
RIGHT?
LITTLE LADY?
AAAH! YOU'RE THE BAD GUY WHO JUST TRIED TO HIT ME AND PUSH ME DOWN EARLIER, AREN'T YOU!?
ZAWA (MURMUR)
HUH?
I WAS NOT TRYING TO PUSH HER DOWN.
UWAAH...... YOU'D ATTACK A YOUNG GIRL? YOU'RE THE WORST...
...BOSS?
...I'M KIDDING. JUST KIDDING.
WELL, ANYWAY... LOOK, THIS COINCIDENCE REALLY DOES SEEM LIKE A JOKE, BUT...

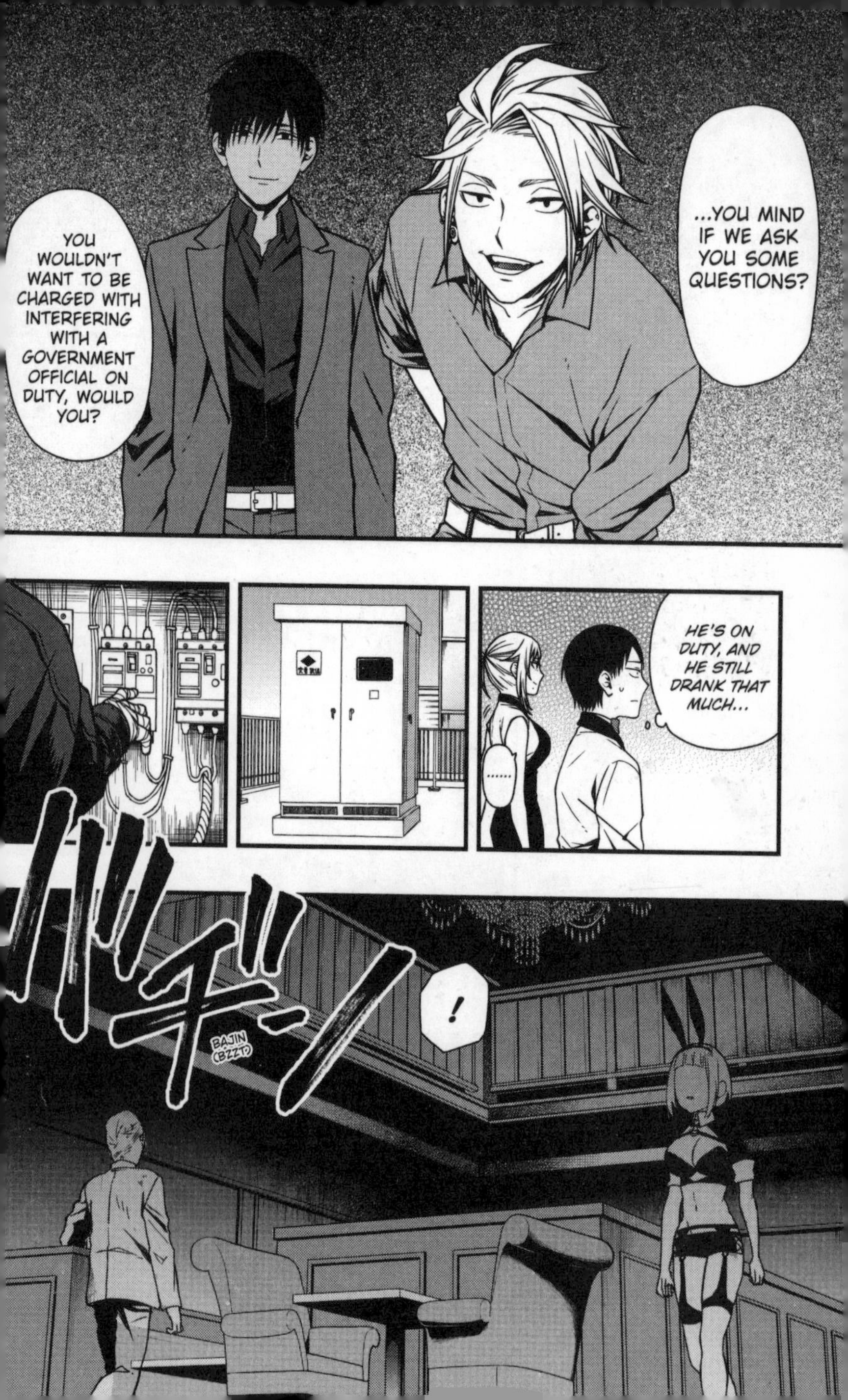

...YOU MIND IF WE ASK YOU SOME QUESTIONS?
YOU WOULDN'T WANT TO BE CHARGED WITH INTERFERING WITH A GOVERNMENT OFFICIAL ON DUTY, WOULD YOU?
HE'S ON DUTY, AND HE STILL DRANK THAT MUCH...
......
BAJIN (BZZT)
!

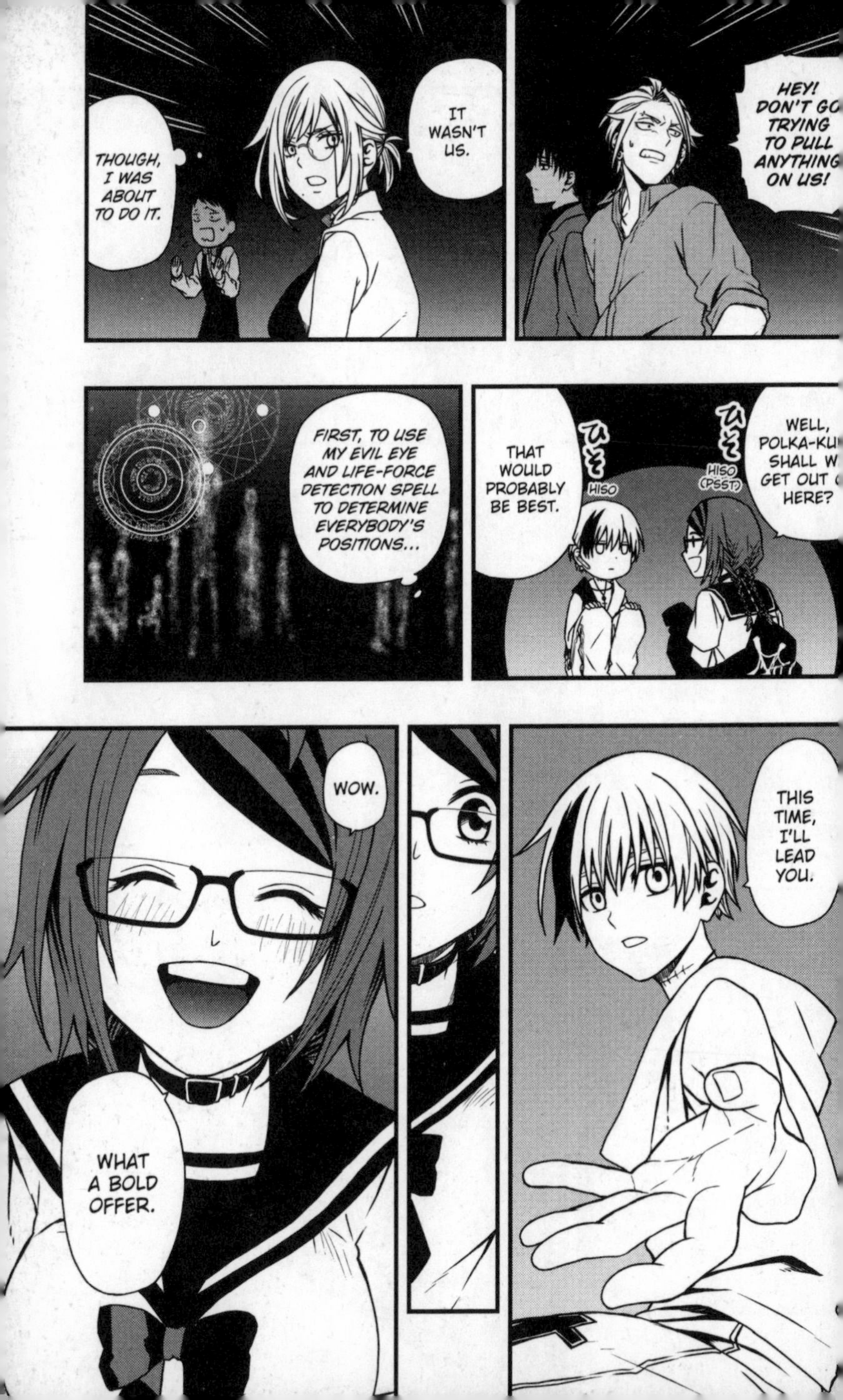
HEY! DON'T GO TRYING TO PULL ANYTHING ON US!
IT WASN'T US.
THOUGH, I WAS ABOUT TO DO IT.
WELL, POLKA-KU SHALL W GET OUT HERE?
ひそ HISO (PSST)
ひそ HISO
THAT WOULD PROBABLY BE BEST.
FIRST, TO USE MY EVIL EYE AND LIFE-FORCE DETECTION SPELL TO DETERMINE EVERYBODY'S POSITIONS...
THIS TIME, I'LL LEAD YOU.
WOW.
WHAT A BOLD OFFER.

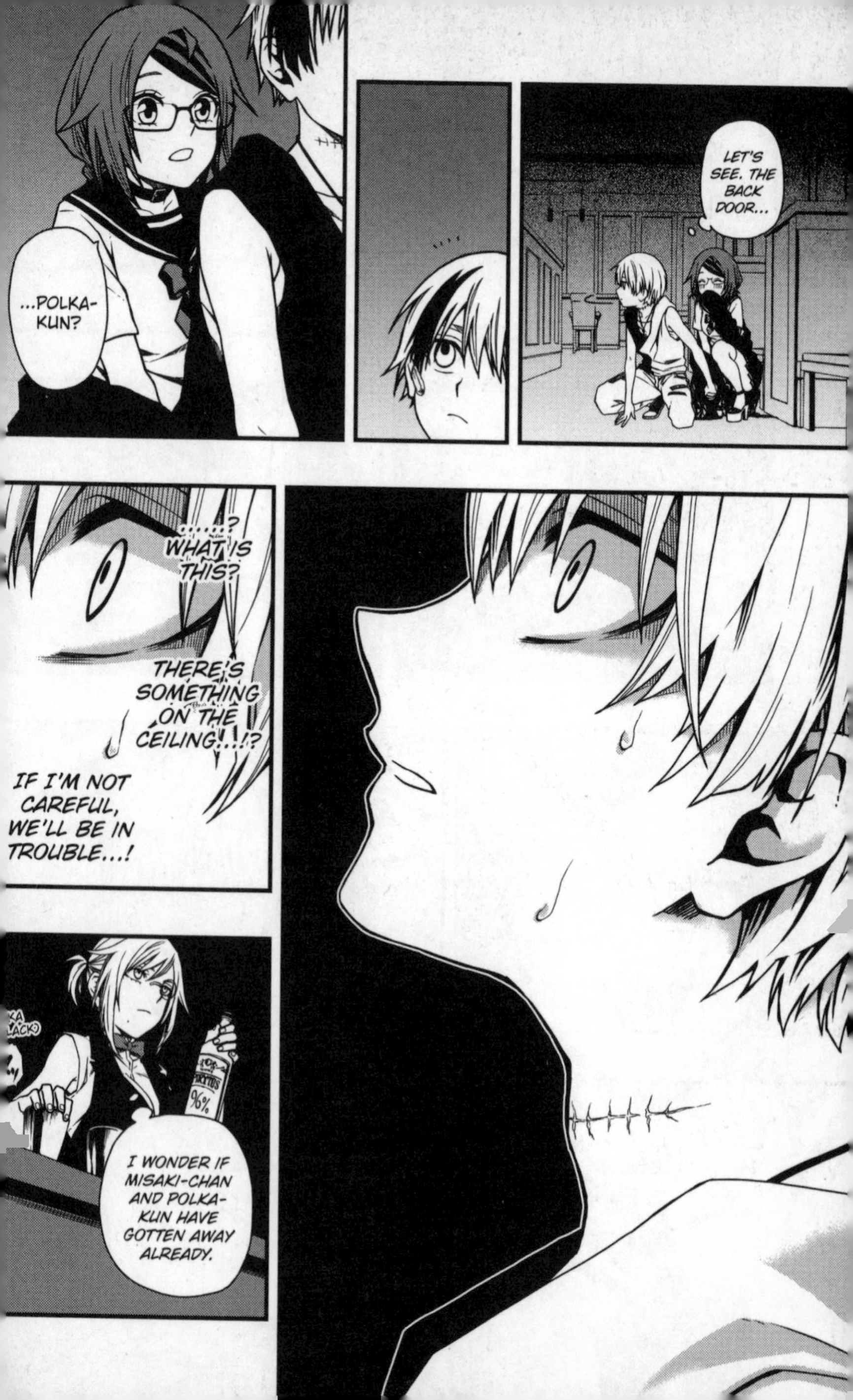
LET'S SEE. THE BACK DOOR...
...
...POLKA-KUN?
......? WHAT IS THIS?
THERE'S SOMETHING ON THE CEILING...!?
IF I'M NOT CAREFUL, WE'LL BE IN TROUBLE...!
I WONDER IF MISAKI-CHAN AND POLKA-KUN HAVE GOTTEN AWAY ALREADY.

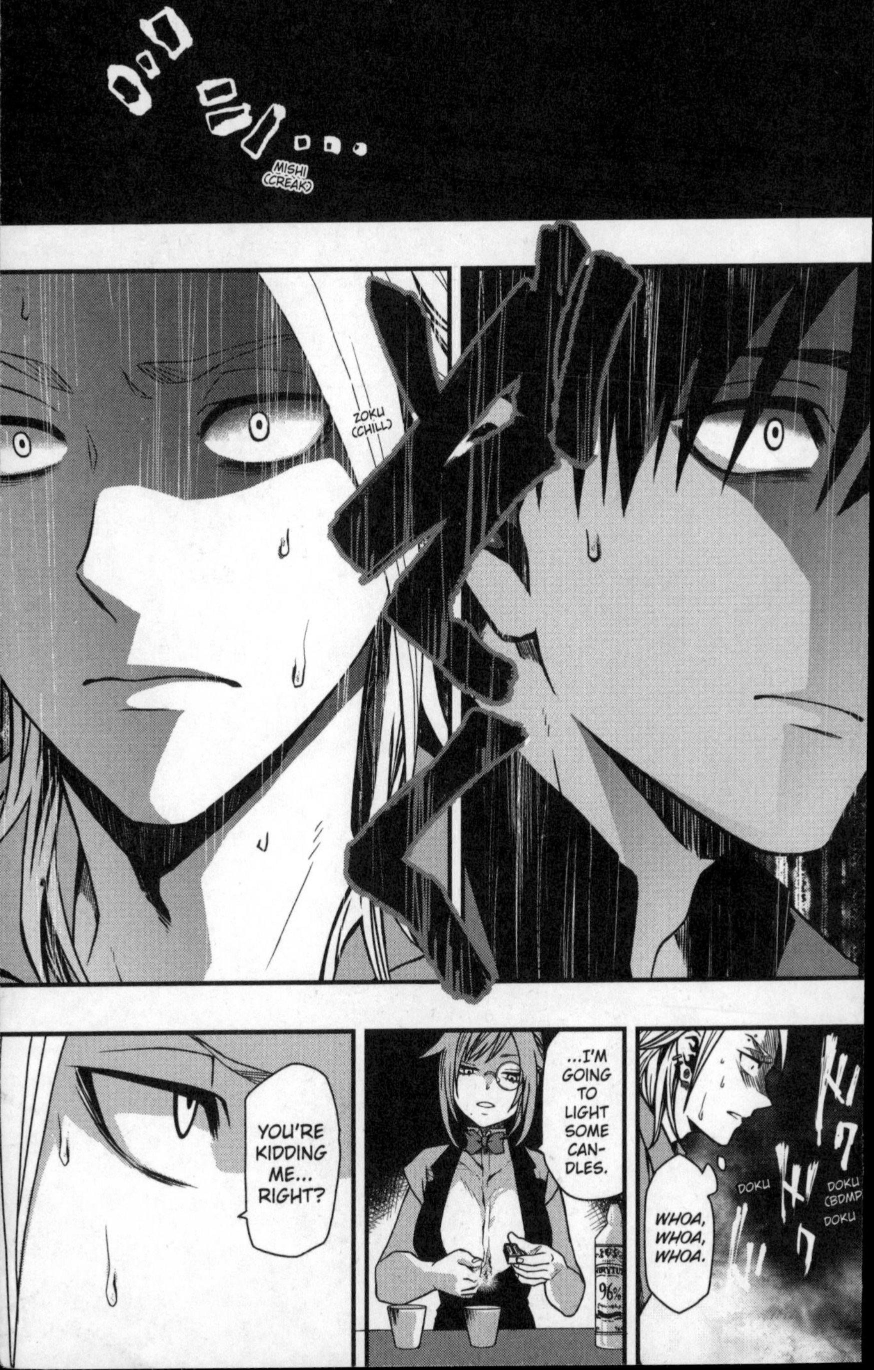
MISHI (CREAK)
ZOKU (CHILL)
DOKU DOKU (BDMP) DOKU
WHOA, WHOA, WHOA.
...I'M GOING TO LIGHT SOME CAN-DLES.
YOU'RE KIDDING ME... RIGHT?

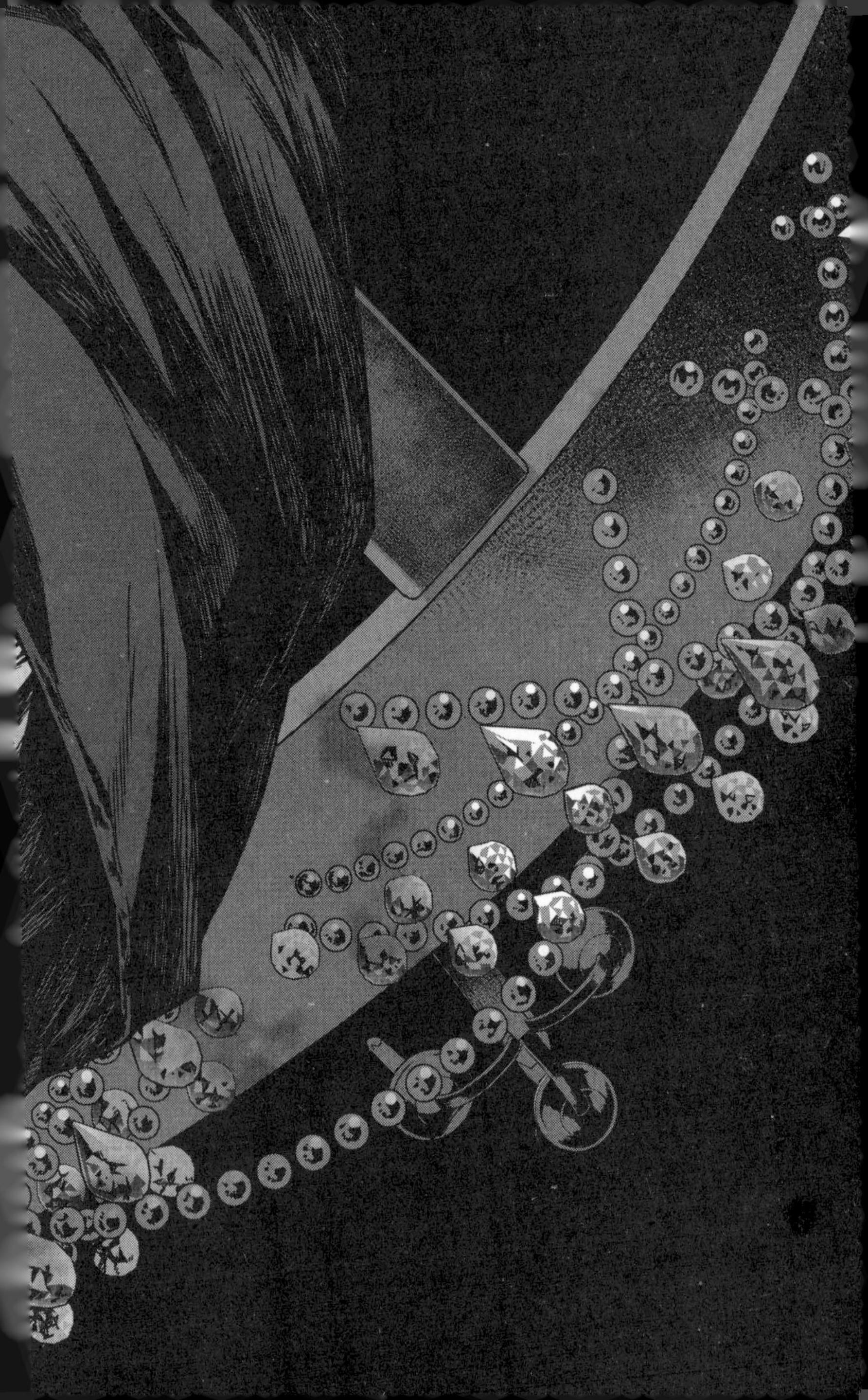

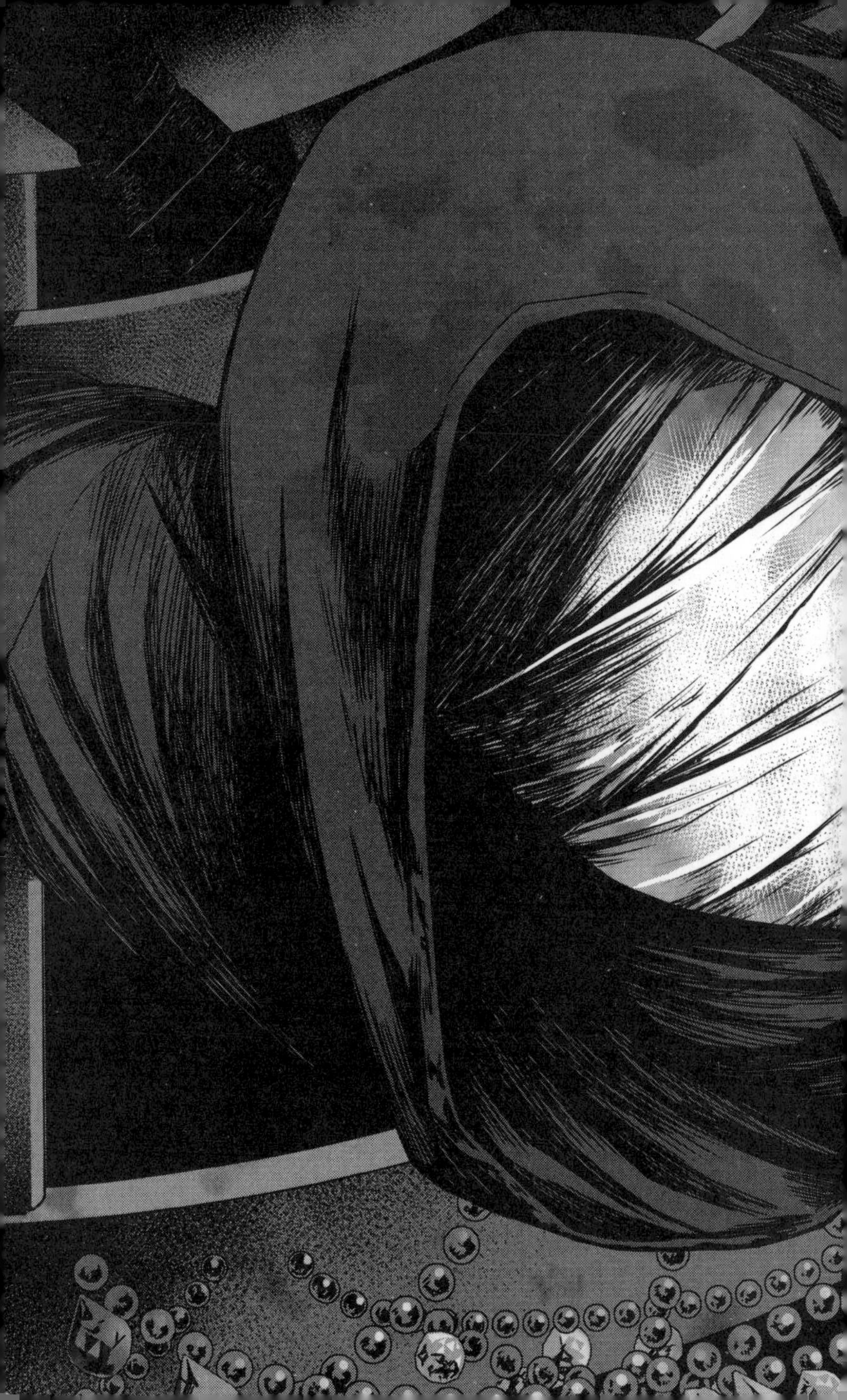

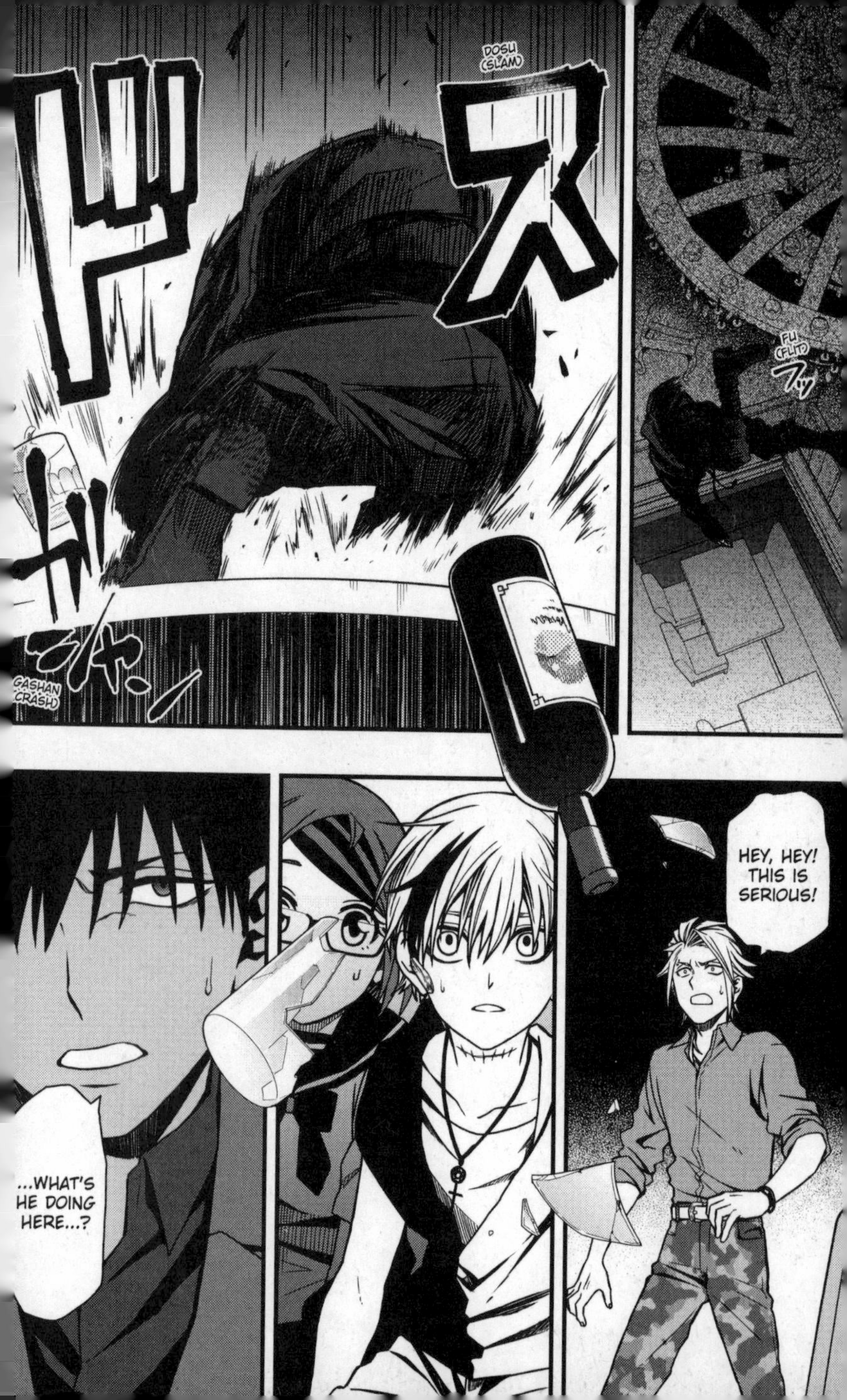
FU (FLIT)
DOSU (SLAM)
GASHAN (CRASH)
HEY, HEY! THIS IS SERIOUS!
...WHAT'S HE DOING HERE...?

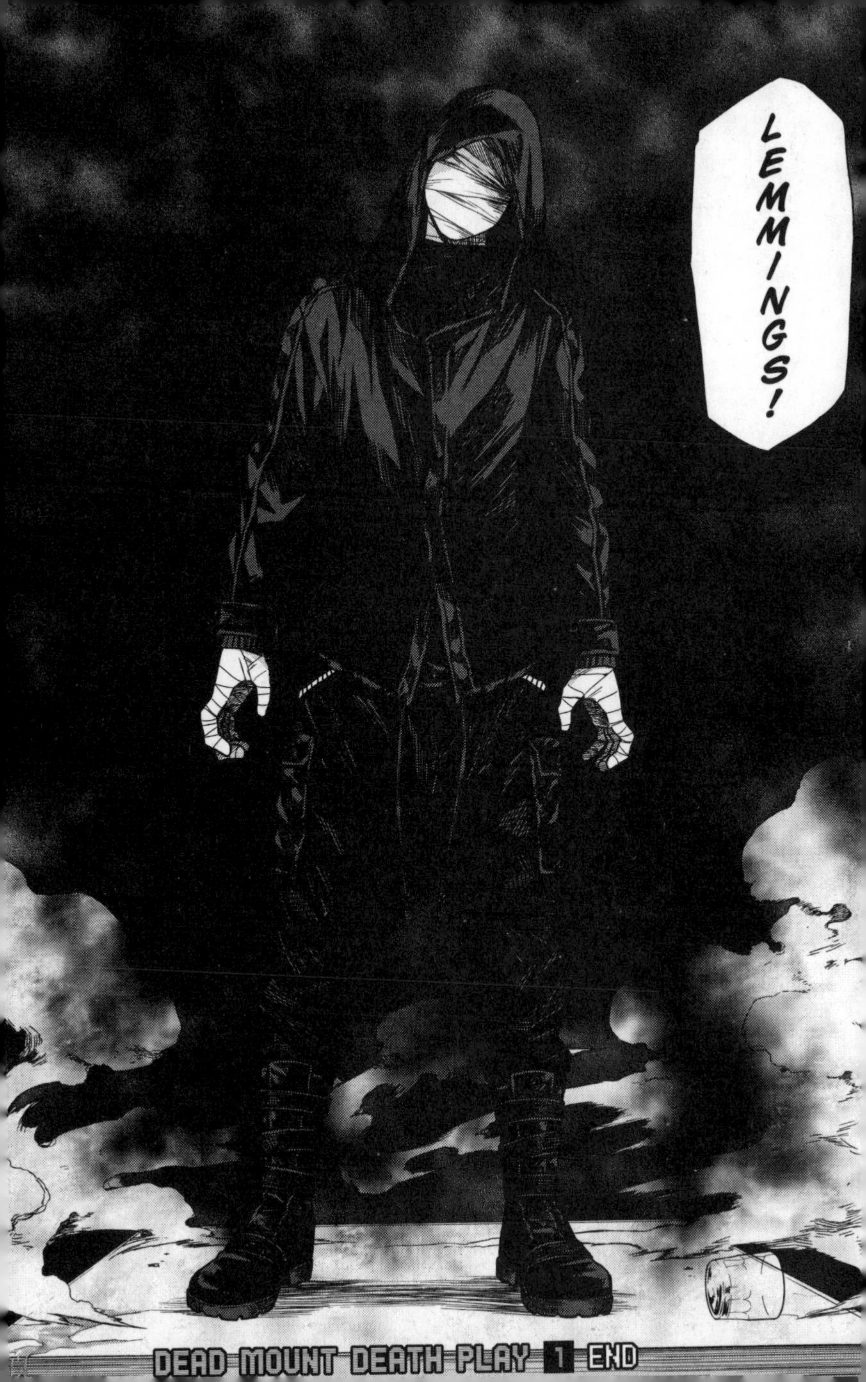
LEMMINGS!
DEAD MOUNT DEATH PLAY 1 END

BONUS MANGA

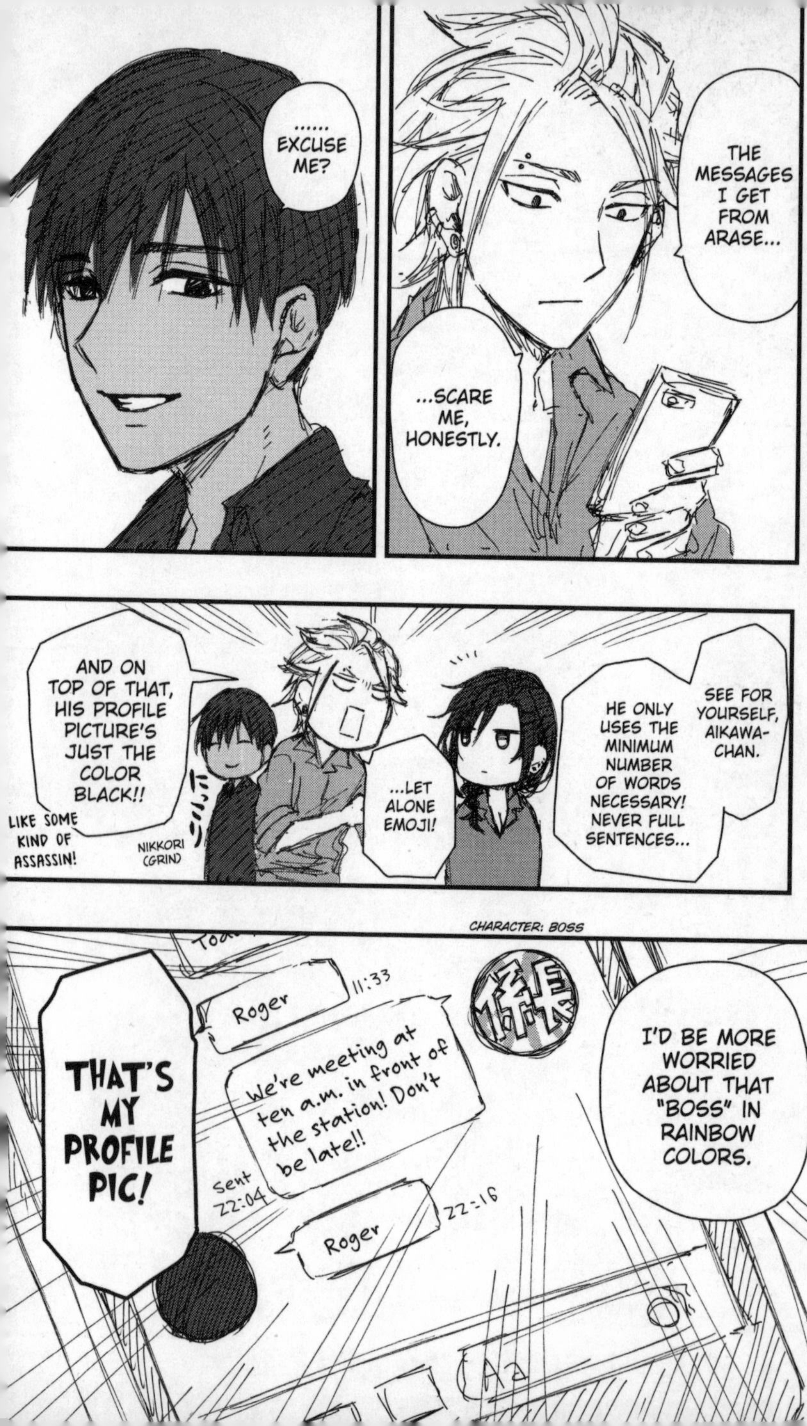
THE MESSAGES I GET FROM ARASE...
...SCARE ME, HONESTLY.
...... EXCUSE ME?
SEE FOR YOURSELF, AIKAWA-CHAN.
HE ONLY USES THE MINIMUM NUMBER OF WORDS NECESSARY! NEVER FULL SENTENCES...
...LET ALONE EMOJI!
AND ON TOP OF THAT, HIS PROFILE PICTURE'S JUST THE COLOR BLACK!!
LIKE SOME KIND OF ASSASSIN!
NIKKORI (GRIN)
CHARACTER: BOSS
I'D BE MORE WORRIED ABOUT THAT "BOSS" IN RAINBOW COLORS.
係長
Roger
11:33
We're meeting at ten a.m. in front of the station! Don't be late!!
Sent 22:04
Roger
22:16
THAT'S MY PROFILE PIC!

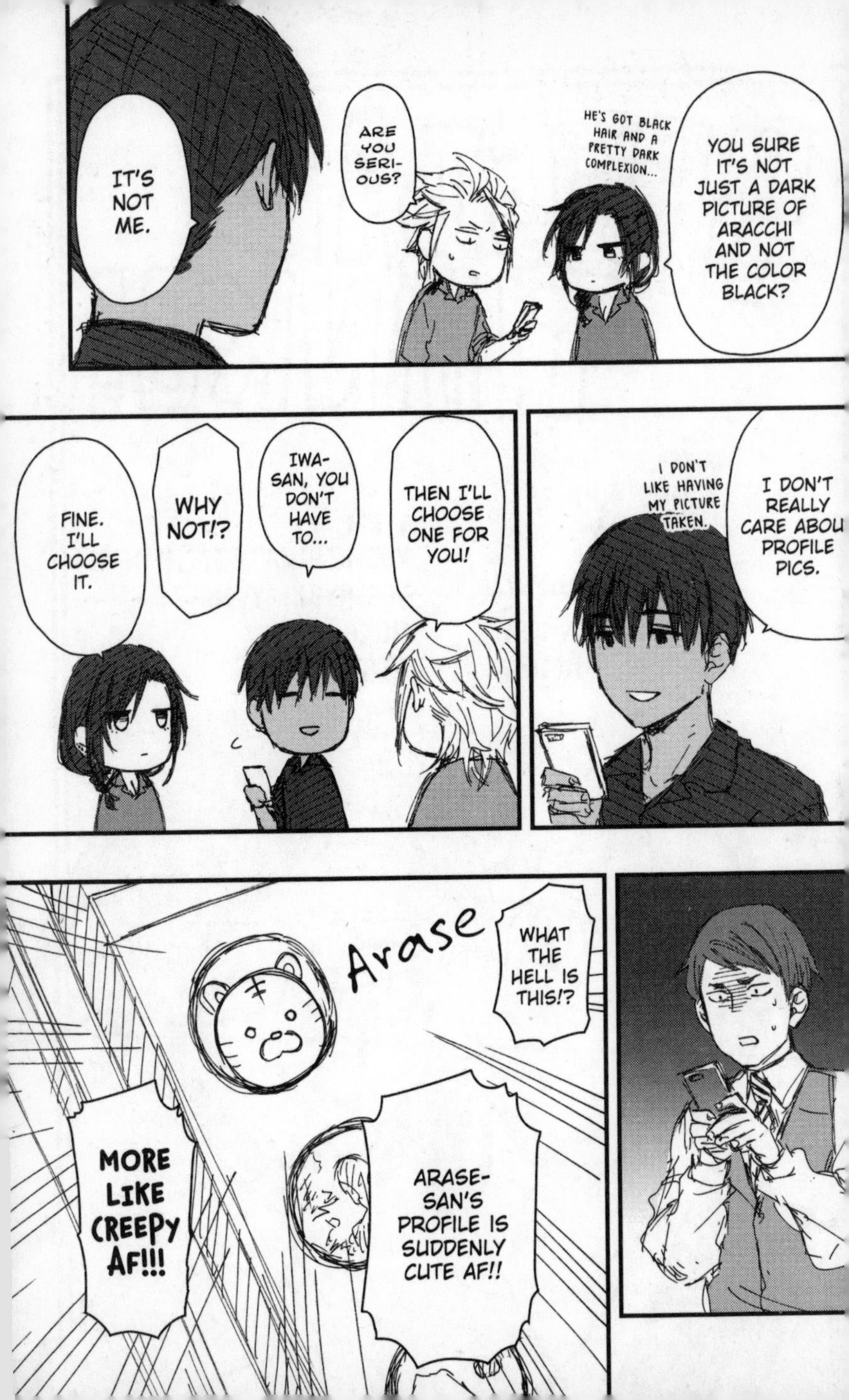
YOU SURE IT'S NOT JUST A DARK PICTURE OF ARACCHI AND NOT THE COLOR BLACK?
HE'S GOT BLACK HAIR AND A PRETTY DARK COMPLEXION...
ARE YOU SERI-OUS?
IT'S NOT ME.
I DON'T REALLY CARE ABOU PROFILE PICS.
I DON'T LIKE HAVING MY PICTURE TAKEN.
THEN I'LL CHOOSE ONE FOR YOU!
IWA-SAN, YOU DON'T HAVE TO...
WHY NOT!?
FINE. I'LL CHOOSE IT.
Arase
WHAT THE HELL IS THIS!?
ARASE-SAN'S PROFILE IS SUDDENLY CUTE AF!!
MORE LIKE CREEPY AF!!!

SPECIAL THANKS!

WRITER:
RYOHGO NARITA

EDITOR:
KAZUHIDE SHIMIZU

ENGLISH SUPERVISION:
MASAAKI SHIMIZU

STAFF:
YOSHICHIKA EGUCHI
YOSHIYUKI YUNO
NORA
OTO

Turn to the back of the book to read an exclusive bonus short story by Ryohgo Narita!

DEAD MOUNT DEATH PLAY

Episode ❶: The Calamity, Alive and Well

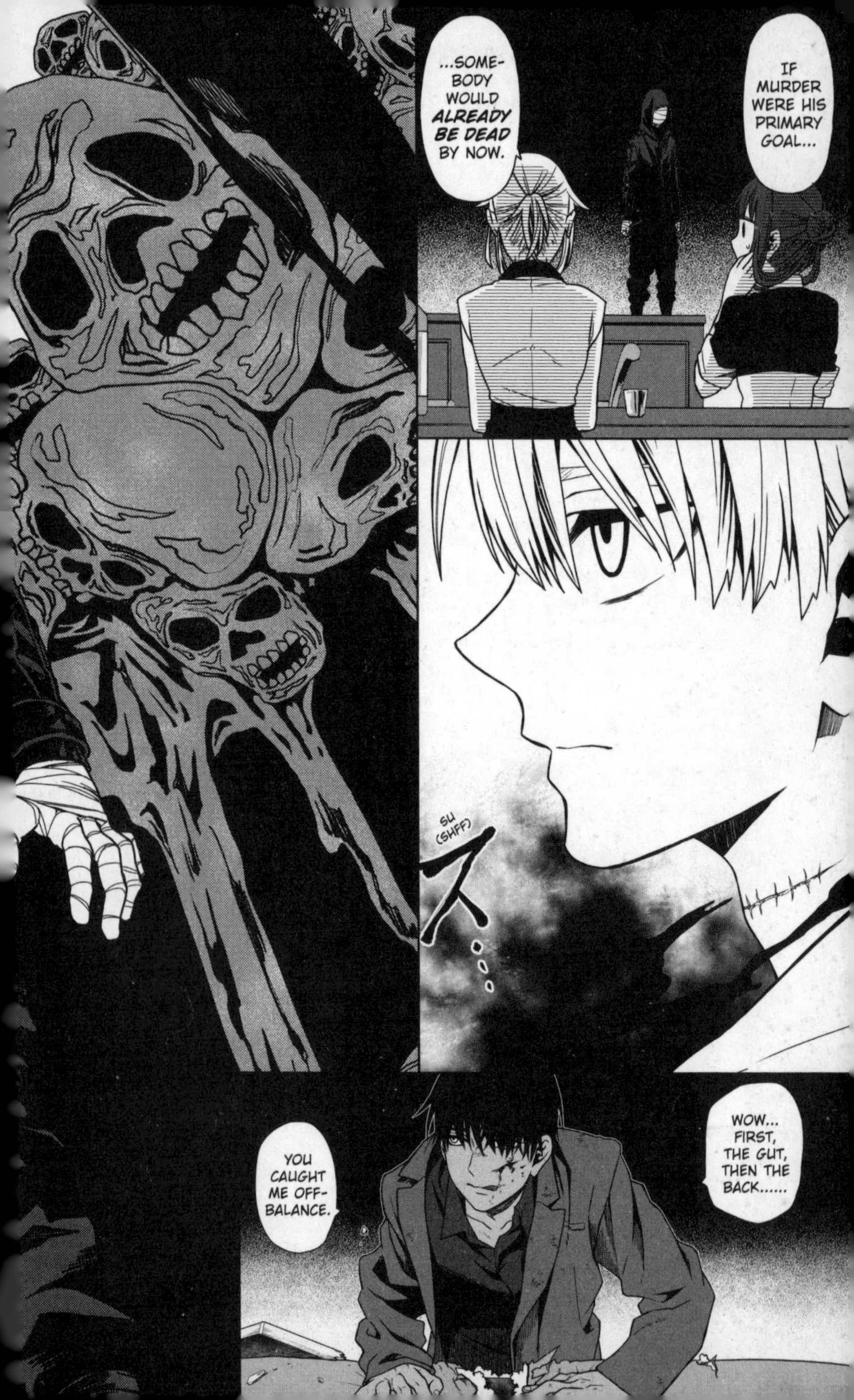
IF MURDER WERE HIS PRIMARY GOAL...
...SOME-BODY WOULD ALREADY BE DEAD BY NOW.
SU (SHFF)
WOW... FIRST, THE GUT, THEN THE BACK......
YOU CAUGHT ME OFF-BALANCE.

"Lemmings."
His very existence is a crucible of violence.

Disaster personified has arrived, but his purpose is unknown.
One thing is certain—they are in the presence of raw power.
Now we dance on the edge of death.
Shinjuku, engulfed in a frenzy, drenched with rain.
Now the true Death Play has begun.

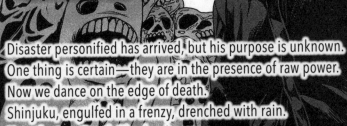

DEAD MOUNT DEATH PLAY

TO BE CONTINUED.........

DEAD MOUNT DEATH PLAY

STORY: Ryohgo Narita   ART: Shinta Fujimoto

Translation: Christine Dashiell * Lettering: Abigail Blackman

DEAD MOUNT DEATH PLAY Volume 1 © 2018 Ryohgo Narita, Shinta Fujimoto/SQUARE ENIX CO., LTD. First published in Japan in 2018 by SQUARE ENIX CO., LTD. English translation rights arranged with SQUARE ENIX CO., LTD. and Yen Press, LLC through Tuttle-Mori Agency, Inc., Tokyo.

English translation © 2018 by SQUARE ENIX CO., LTD.

Yen Press
1290 Avenue of the Americas
New York, NY 10104

Visit us at yenpress.com
facebook.com/yenpress
twitter.com/yenpress
yenpress.tumblr.com
instagram.com/yenpress

First Yen Press Edition: December 2018
The chapters in this volume were originally published as ebooks by Yen Press.

Yen Press is an imprint of Yen Press, LLC.
The Yen Press name and logo are trademarks of Yen Press, LLC.

The publisher is not responsible for websites (or their content)
that are not owned by the publisher.

Library of Congress Control Number: 2018953479

ISBNs: 978-1-9753-2925-9 (paperback)
        978-1-9753-2926-6 (ebook)

10 9 8 7 6 5 4 3 2

WOR

Printed in the United States of America

It was a land of ruin, all that remained of the giant empire said to have crumbled a hundred years prior.

No one knew the circumstances, but fearsome ghosts and monsters now roamed the landscape, and it was said to have become a cursed land that human beings could not even begin to approach.

Presently, there wasn't a single spirit near him.

In order for the Corpse God to use his final, greatest spell, he had stolen away all the magic power of the spirits that haunted Shagrua.

As a result, Shagrua had been forcibly exorcised and found himself the freest he had ever been.

I should have broken ties with the Church the moment I learned they'd been the ones who burned my village to the ground......

Maybe I hate the villagers, too.

Is there maybe a piece of me that thinks "serves you right"?

Some holy soldier I am. Or Calamity Crusher for that matter.

I'm just someone else's even greater calamity.

And with that, he started down the path.

Finally free of the hateful voices that had tormented him his entire life, Shagrua was bound for the Abandoned Peninsual, resolved to cast out the evil spirits infesting it.

He didn't know if that was atonement enough for the sins he'd committed against the Corpse God.

There was no way left to verify what the Corpse God really was—whether he was good or bad, right or wrong.

Because, at the very least...the soul of the Corpse God, who could have answered his doubts, had been completely expunged from this world.

Bearing a burden invisible even to his Evil Eye, Shagrua took the first step into his new life...

...all the while praying that the soul of the calamity known as the Corpse God was alive and well somewhere, somehow.

Corpse God has surpassed that hurdle...... That's what you are to tell people."

"I don't follow. What are you implying, Sir Shagrua?!"

"Look, you've done a lot for me, so I'll tell you and only you the truth," Shagrua murmured almost apologetically. He was fond of this priestess, so he went on to say, "I can no longer devote myself to the Geldwood faith. Not after having read the Corpse God's journal."

"......Huh?" The priestess was feeling more lost than ever.

There were mountains of books in the Corpse God's laboratory, but most of them had been blank. They should have offered no information.

"......It was written in an ink only visible to those with the Evil Eye. And not only his journal but a number of essays that expose the underbelly of the Geldwood religion. I've been spending these days researching to verify their truth. It was backbreaking work, finding the hidden vault within the research room."

"Underbelly......?"

"Yeah, the other face of the institution......of which I'm sure you're completely unaware. Please keep up the facade of not knowing, if you can."

Shagrua quietly gestured with his hand, casting a sleeping spell on the priestess while he shook his head.

"That's why I've been taken over by the Corpse God. That's the story I want you to tell them. Otherwise, by associating with me, you'd be branded by my side as an enemy of the Church."

"Sir...Sha......gru......a......"

Shagrua caught the fainting priestess's body as she fell and he propped her in a chair.

Then, he left the library and never returned.

He took with him multiple pieces of evidence proving the Geldwood order's corruption and beat to within an inch of their lives some of the higher-ups in the Church. By some mysterious magic, he was no longer the Calamity Crusher but the Corpse God in possession of Shagrua's body, pursued being high and low by the holy soldiers of the faith.

The Corpse God is alive and well. Calamity Crusher is dead.

The rumors spread across the land, and in keeping with them, the living corpse Shagrua had become headed west.

The Abandoned Peninsula.

Shagrua smiled where he sat within the library and answered, "Oh right......
I was just looking up some stuff about the Corpse God, but I can't find much
information...... What country did he hail from anyway?"

Why would he care to learn about an opponent he's already rid of? wondered the
priestess, confused. But playing the role of the supporter that she was, she
told him everything she could about the Corpse God.

"The Corpse God was a necromancer of an empire that fell over a hundred
years ago. Of the few necromancers they had, he held the second-highest
position and, of the royal necromancers, was regarded as the fourth most
capable ever. Nobody knows for sure what happened, but eventually, that
empire collapsed within the span of one short year."

"An empire...... That must be Byandy Peninsula...... I see. So it's the
'Abandoned Peninsula'......"

"Please get some rest. Look, I can already see bags forming under your
eyes...... And why do you have the look of someone possessed?"

The priestess had said that last part in jest, but upon hearing her words,
Shagrua fell silent for a time, after which he took a deep breath (as though
bracing himself for something) and slowly said, "......You're right. Let's make
that the story."

"Make that......what story?" the priestess asked suspiciously. Shagrua
continued.

"The Calamity Crusher Shagrua is dead. In the end, the Corpse God
used a teleportive magic to switch out Shagrua's soul with his own. And
the Church...... You guys had no idea when you basically welcomed in the
Corpse God who had taken over Shagrua's body. That's gonna be the story."

"What......are you saying?" The priestess felt a chill run down her back.
She wanted to believe the man to whom she was speaking was only joking
and took a pragmatic stance to counter his points. "First of all, that's
impossible. You know so yourself, Sir Shagrua. The root of one's soul......
One's personality and memories resonate with one's soul and brain.
Inorganic matter or corpses that have lost their brain function are one thing,
but to switch out one's body and soul with another while still living would
cause a rejection of the brain's 'heart' with the soul's 'heart,' and who knows
what might be the result......?"

"I know. That's why, when a necromancer dies, he can only possess a doll
or a corpse. And that corpse can either be his own or another's. But the

It was the same from the villagers who'd been burned to death, the bandits wiped out by the soldiers, and a faction of the Church's troops who'd fallen in the cross fire: They all cursed Shagrua as the "root of all evils."

The spirits of his family were not among them, probably because they had been saved.

That, or perhaps they'd been so overwhelmed by the sheer ocean of spirits that inundated him that they couldn't even retain their forms.

To blot out this chorus so full of loathing for him, Shagrua chose to fight.

When enough voices began haunting the holy soldier, the sheer volume of their jeers became indistinguishable, dissolving into static noise like the howling wind or steady rain.

Shagrua knew this respite came not because he'd been forgiven, but he still took it as a form of salvation all the same.

To escape the accusations of the begrudging spirits, Shagrua sometimes positioned himself at the forefront of a battlefield. Sometimes, he faced off against heretical cults or criminal syndicates. Sometimes, he wielded his sword against monsters such as dragons and the like said to be terrorizing the land. All this simply resulted in more voices being added to the cacophony of the dead cursing his name, though.

Before he knew it, he'd been given the title of "Calamity Crusher" and found himself revered as a hero.

Years passed.

To great acclaim, Calamity Crusher vanquished the Corpse God, who had been called the greatest plague of the past hundred years.

However...

■ ■ ■

Kingdom of Nyanild, Geldwood Church, Cathedral.

"What are you doing, Sir Shagrua? You've been holing yourself up here for days now without rest......"

It was a few days after the defeat of the Corpse God, and this was the priestess who had accompanied the hero on that mission. Hearing her voice, taking human form and, therefore, it's not a sin to kill one.

They said those who possess the Evil Eye are reincarnations of saints and fetch a handsome price when sold to religious institutions.

They said proximity to one with the Evil Eye will leave you cursed.

They said being close one with the Evil Eye brings good fortune.

They said, they said, they said...

With such a torrent of conflicting rumors, no one could distinguish fact from fiction. But with the coming of the first true Evil Eye possessor in a long time, Shagrua, the overarching consensus feared great misfortune, thus shaping the young boy's destiny.

The villagers where Shagrua's parents lived resolved to drive them out for having borne a cursed son. On the very day their exile was planned to be executed, though, when the sun was just teetering on the horizon, the boy's home was attacked by a gang of bandits, killing his entire family.

Shagrua would find out only later that the villagers had heard a rumor that "the organs of one who possesses the Evil Eye can be sold for an elixir of immortality" and leaked said information to the marauders. This was after he'd been taken on as a holy soldier by the Geldwood religion and granted salvation.

Later, not only the bandits who had slaughtered his family but the villagers who had persecuted this "Blessed Child," too, were burned to death by the Geldwood sect. A fact he learned soon after the first.

But it wasn't the members of the Church who'd told him.

In fact, they'd tried very hard to keep that knowledge from him.

However, Shagrua knew everything...

...because the spirits of the dead he saw with his Evil Eye cursed him constantly.

It's your fault we're dead.

We died because of you.

Why are you the only one allowed to live?

You should die, too.

Die. Suffer.

We want to see you squirm. Weep.

Cry your heart out. And scream.

DEAD MOUNT DEATH PLAY

Episode ❶: The Calamity, Alive and Well

by Ryohgo Narita

Manga-exclusive bonus short story

Shagrua Edith Lugrid.

This man, known throughout the land as the "Calamity Crusher," had killed numerous enemies as a holy soldier of the Geldwood religion and was, by any measure, a valiant hero.

At the age of three, it was discovered he possessed the Evil Eye that allows one to see the spirits of the dead. It's an inherent quirk said to manifest in one in every few million people.

Depending on the region and prevailing religious view, it's called "God's Protection" or "the Devil's Curse," while elsewhere—namely, countries that treat it like a psychological disorder—claim it doesn't exist.

And so, depending on the locale and governing body, opinions surrounding the Evil Eye and its possessors vary.

The land where Shagrua was born was neither particularly advanced in magic nor the sciences. Rather, it was deeply superstitious and meager in its grasp of the supernatural.

That's why they had only rumors to rely on when it came to understanding the Evil Eye.

They claimed the heart of one who possesses the Evil Eye can be used to create an elixir for immortality when boiled with certain kinds of metals and plants.

They claimed those who possess the Evil Eye are actually fairies and spirits